W9-BCD-855

Praise for *The New New Deal*

"Meticulous . . . Mr. Grunwald lays out in shocking detail how the Republican leadership decided early and wholeheartedly not to cooperate with the new president. . . . *The New New Deal* is the most interesting book that has been published about the Obama administration. Even Republicans should read it."

—*The Economist*

"Exceptional . . . The single best book on the inner workings of the Obama administration . . . In exhaustive detail, Grunwald points out how everything you think you know about the stimulus is wrong. . . . His book should be required reading for undecided voters (as well as everyone else)."

—Michael Cohen, *The Guardian*

"Masterful . . . *The New New Deal* is not only the best book about the administration, but perhaps the only one that will (and should) continue to be read long after 2016. . . . One of the two best books ever written about government."

—Mark Schmitt, *The National Memo*

"A terrific book . . . Hugely important . . . Grunwald's account explains how things work and don't work in Washington."

—Steve Brill, *Reuters*

"Michael Grunwald is one of our generation's most original and tireless journalists—a reporter who is allergic to received wisdom, a writer with an uncommon talent for illuminating hidden truths. . . . Every serious reader will see his book as a vindication of serious journalism, at a time when we need it."

—John Harris, *Politico*

"Engrossing . . . A work of serious reporting and analysis . . . *The New New Deal* will, for the most part, please supporters of the president. But its author is a journalist, not a polemicist."

—K. Anthony Appiah, *The New York Review of Books*

"The reputation of the stimulus is meticulously restored from shabby to skillful in Michael Grunwald's important new book, *The New New Deal*. His findings will come as a jolt to those who think the law 'failed.'"

—David Firestone, *The New York Times*

"In Grunwald's hands, it is a fascinating and illuminating story. He brings it to life with a style that is lively and informal, with a focus on the people involved. He does not hesitate to criticize those from across the political spectrum whom he finds to be incompetent, obstructive or self-aggrandizing (and he finds plenty of all three)."

—Colette Bancroft, *Tampa Bay Times*

"Exhaustively reported and authoritative."

—Cardiff Garcia, *The Financial Times*

"There's plenty here for everyone to get aflutter about all over again in this riveting account. Grunwald provides captivating background history on the stimulus and how it may prove to be a far greater deal than the one FDR famously launched."

—*Chicago Tribune*

"Grunwald delivered a book that taught me a great deal on a subject I thought I knew a great deal about."

—Matthew Yglesias, *Slate*

"Grunwald knows more about the stimulus than pretty much anyone else on the planet. . . . He realized the stimulus was a huge story that wasn't being told, so he started digging, interviewing more than 400 people, sitting in on Cabinet meetings, and reading original documents. What he found was very close to the inverse of conventional wisdom."

—David Roberts, *Grist*

"Grunwald is a journalist with a contrarian streak. Curious about the fog of cynicism that clung to Obama's stimulus, he dug into the data and interviewed hundreds of people. . . . The result is as entertaining a policy wonk drama as you're likely to find."

—Rick Holmes, *MetroWest Daily News*

"I recently finished Michael Grunwald's excellent book, *The New New Deal.* Grunwald is not only a crisp and engaging writer, he is a blunt one."

—Francis Wilkinson, *Bloomberg View*

"Interesting . . . A good narrative of what happened with the stimulus."

—Simon Johnson, *The Washington Post*

"Fascinating . . . Grunwald makes the case for Obama's stimulus bill more vividly and persuasively than the president ever did. . . . Grunwald peppers this Washington drama with dialogue and characters in action, which makes it a rollicking good read."

—Jamie Stiehm, *US News*

"Lo and behold, *The New New Deal* has caught on, a tribute to Grunwald's deep reporting. . . . The book offers a bracing reminder to those of us in the Washington press corps that the stimulus was not exactly our finest moment. . . . Journalism is just the first draft of history. But . . . it's a good thing we have one journalist who went back to give us a vastly improved second draft."

—Alec MacGillis, *The New Republic*

"The best book on the Obama presidency to date."

—Steve Benem, *MSNBC.com*

"*The New New Deal* will change how you look at Obama's stimulus forever. . . . The book is not only a comprehensive chronicle of what's in the bill and what it's done, it's full of revelations of how the bill was written, passed and implemented."

—Matt Zeitlin, *The Daily Beast*

"Grunwald circles the Beltway and runs through its back alleys with a savant's eye for detail and nuance. . . . A tale that reads like a book-length episode of *The West Wing* . . . Grunwald can be safely aligned with the likes of Arthur M. Schlesinger Jr., having produced a work of style, wit, pace and depth."

—James Rose, *The New Statesman*

"*The Swamp* has been a game-changer in the world of ideas. Even more so will be Grunwald's new book. While countering prevailing notions of the Obama administration, *The New New Deal* manages to be just plain fascinating reading. . . . Often brilliant, always penetrating."

—Philip Jason, *Florida Weekly*

"Assiduously researched and wonderfully written, Grunwald has given future historians the ultimate factual baseline. . . . *The New New Deal* is a gift to policy wonks and casual political observers alike."

—Jed Morey, *Long Island Press*

"Critics will not agree with everything in this book, but putting mood affiliation aside, the writing, research and conception of the work are all excellent."

—Tyler Cowen, *Marginal Revolution*

"Grunwald keeps his tone snappy and readable, while consistently grounding the political story of the Recovery Act in its real impact on everyday Americans. The result is an impressive book about the startling gap between facts and media spin."

—*Publishers Weekly*

"A cogent reality check of President Obama's Recovery Act. . . . A pointed, in-the-trenches study whose thrust will be borne out with time."

—*Kirkus Reviews*

ALSO BY MICHAEL GRUNWALD

The Swamp: The Everglades, Florida, and the Politics of Paradise

THE NEW NEW DEAL

The Hidden Story of Change in the Obama Era

MICHAEL GRUNWALD

SIMON & SCHUSTER PAPERBACKS

New York   London   Toronto   Sydney   New Delhi

Simon & Schuster Paperbacks
A Division of Simon & Schuster, Inc.
1230 Avenue of the Americas
New York, NY 10020

Copyright © 2012 by Michael Grunwald
Afterword copyright © 2013 by Michael Grunwald

All rights reserved, including the right to reproduce this book or
portions thereof in any form whatsoever. For information address
Simon & Schuster Paperbacks Subsidiary Rights Department,
1230 Avenue of the Americas, New York, NY 10020.

First Simon & Schuster trade paperback edition September 2013

SIMON & SCHUSTER PAPERBACKS and colophon are registered
trademarks of Simon & Schuster, Inc.

Credits for insert illustrations are on page 510.

For information about special discounts for bulk purchases,
please contact Simon & Schuster Special Sales at
1-866-506-1949 or business@simonandschuster.com.

The Simon & Schuster Speakers Bureau can bring authors to your live event. For
more information or to book an event contact the Simon & Schuster Speakers
Bureau at 1-866-248-3049 or visit our website at www.simonspeakers.com.

Designed by Joy O'Meara

Manufactured in the United States of America

10   9   8   7   6   5   4   3

The Library of Congress has cataloged the hardcover edition as follows:

Grunwald, Michael.
    The new New Deal : the hidden story of change in the Obama era /
by Michael Grunwald.
        p.   cm.
    Includes bibliographical references and index.
    1. United States—Politics and government—2009–   2. United States—
Economic conditions—2009–   3. United States—Economic policy—2009–
4. Obama, Barack.   I. Title.
E907.G78   2012
973.932092—dc23   2012016458

ISBN 978-1-4516-4232-2
ISBN 978-1-4516-4233-9 (pbk)
ISBN 978-1-4516-4234-6 (ebook)

To Cristina,

my stimulus

— CONTENTS —

CONTENTS

PART THREE: Change in Action

Things That Never Were

Change begins with a leap of faith—not a fairy-tale faith that tomorrow will always turn out better than today, or a rah-rah faith in the inevitable destiny of God's most favored nation, but a more practical belief that the past is not necessarily prologue, that the future doesn't have to look like the present. It's progressive in the literal sense, not the polite-way-to-say-liberal sense, a simple faith in the possibility of progress. This basic notion that there's nothing preordained about the status quo can sound corny, and it doesn't make change happen. But it makes change possible.

This is what Barack Hussein Obama meant by "the audacity of hope." And this was the wind behind his 2008 campaign, the promise of not just the change we always hear about but Change We Can Believe In, the idea that a skinny black guy with an inconvenient name and a thin résumé could ride a dream to the White House. It was easy to mock his Yes We Can hubris, his grandiose vows to transcend the pettiness of our politics and bridge the partisan divide, his messianic pledges to slow the rise of the oceans and usher in a new birth of freedom. But he inspired people. After eight exhausting years of George W. Bush—the partisan warfare, the nonexistent weapons of mass destruction, the surpluses alchemized into record deficits, the inept response to a drowned city, and finally the epic financial and economic collapse—millions of Americans were ready for a leap of faith.

What happened to that change—and that faith—is the central story of the Obama administration.

The prevailing narrative has emphasized the unfulfilled promise, the change we're still waiting for, the gap between the lofty poetry of Yes We Can and the transactional tawdriness of If We Can Round Up The Votes. The partisan divide remained un-bridged, the pettiness of our politics un-transcended. And the economy stubbornly refused to comply with Obama's rhetoric of revival, setting the tone for a narrative of disappointment: Wasn't the audacity of hope supposed to make people feel better? Hadn't he promised to "reinvent the economy to seize the future"? What happened to the strong middle class and the new American century and all those other nice things that were supposed to materialize after his historic election? "Hope and change" became a partisan punch line, the wink behind Sarah Palin's sly taunt: "How's that hopey-changey stuff working out for ya?"

In the 2010 congressional elections, Americans gave a preliminary answer, voting to change the change, smacking down Democrats, rewarding Republicans for resisting the Obama agenda. Even the president toned down the hopey-changey stuff as his approval ratings slumped, reminding supporters that he was elected to make things better over time, not to make things perfect overnight.

"We've always known that lasting change wouldn't come quickly or easily," he wrote in the strangely muted email announcing his reelection campaign. "It never does."

That's part of the story: Change is hard.

But there's more to the story: Change is happening.

It isn't happening because a politician waved a magic wand. It's happening the way change happens in American democracy, through legislation that Congress passes and a president signs and bureaucrats implement.

This is the story of Obama's most ambitious and least understood piece of legislation, the purest distillation of what he meant by change.

It aimed to repair a broken economy while reforming our approach to energy, health care, education, taxation, transportation, and more. It's starting to change our cars and our trains, the way we produce and consume electricity, the way our schools teach, our doctors practice, and our government spends our money.

It's even trying to change photosynthesis, which is as good a place as any to begin the story.

Sure, photosynthesis has been working reasonably well for 3.5 billion years, making plants grow, releasing the oxygen that sustains life on earth. But at the dawn of the Obama administration, it wasn't working well enough for the president's hard-charging energy secretary, Steven Chu, a quantum physicist who had won a Nobel Prize for trapping and cooling atoms with lasers. Chu had the toothy grin, dorky glasses, and wispy build of a tech nerd, but he had a steely side, too. He didn't accept that problems were unsolvable unless there was scientific proof.

Chu was at the vanguard of a new brigade of egghead elites—a new, ultra-confident Best and Brightest—who marched into Obama's Washington because they believed all that hopey-changey stuff. At sixty, he was a renewable energy source in his own right, exuding the boyish enthusiasm of a junior high geek dissecting his first frog. He worked eighty hours a week trying to rev up the sluggish Department of Energy, then spent his spare time doing the kinds of things geniuses do, like trying to cure cancer with nanotechnology, and using an atom interferometer to confirm a key prediction of Albert Einstein's theory of relativity. His mere presence at this perennial backwater of a bureaucracy felt surreal, as if Einstein had reported for duty as labor secretary. Most of his predecessors had been obscure politicians or businessmen, and one had been a dentist. But after three decades playing with gamma rays and quarks at Bell Labs, Stanford, and Berkeley, Chu honestly believed he could help Obama cure America's addiction to oil and help save the planet from global warming. He was a tone-deaf politician, but he quickly became Obama's most compelling green evangelist, preaching the gospel of clean energy, sharing the good news of solar power, geothermal heat pumps, and energy-saving white roofs.

He wanted biofuels in his scripture, too. Fuels derived from biomass had been hyped as the great green hope, the renewable key to a world without oil. As a farm state senator, Obama had always portrayed ethanol and other biofuels as miracle elixirs. But Chu suspected they would never outcompete fossil fuels as long as they relied on photosynthesis. It was a chemistry thing. Harvesting sunlight to grow corn or switchgrass or even algae was just an awfully circuitous strategy for producing fuel, like a journey from New York to Washington via San Francisco. More than 99 percent of the solar energy was wasted along the route. "Photosynthesis," Chu liked to complain, "is too damn inefficient."

Fortunately, a new agency called ARPA-E had just been created inside Chu's department to solve problems like photosynthesis.

The Advanced Research Projects Agency-Energy was a government incubator for high-risk, high-reward, save-the-world private energy research, the kind of place where Q from the James Bond movies would want to work. Modeled after DARPA, the legendary Pentagon agency that fathered the Internet and GPS technology, it was designed to finance out-of-the-box, early-stage experiments that probably wouldn't pan out, but just might point the way toward truly clean coal or a truly smart grid or a truly green economy if they did. Chu was ARPA-E's intellectual godfather; he had proposed the agency while serving on a National Academy of Sciences panel on U.S. competitiveness. He had handpicked its first director, his former Berkeley colleague Arunava Majumdar. And he had set its reach-for-the-stars tone, making it clear that ARPA-E wasn't about incremental improvements. The agency's mantra was: Game-changers only.

ARPA-E felt more like a high-tech start-up than a federal bureaucracy, with a foyer cluttered with intimidating textbooks on "tribology," "constructal theory," and "nanostructure physics," and walls dotted with dreamy Yes We Can messages from Martin Luther King Jr. ("We are confronted with the fierce urgency of now"), John F. Kennedy ("We need men who can dream of things that never were"), and Chu himself

("Resist the urge to accept the status quo"). It was exempt from the usual civil service rules, and it attracted an absurdly high-powered staff of brainiacs: a thermodynamics expert from Intel who had published sixty-five scientific papers, an MIT electrical engineering professor who had founded two start-ups, a clean-tech venture capitalist who also taught material science at MIT. Majumdar, a world-renowned energy expert, had run Berkeley's nanotechnology institute before Chu persuaded him to leave his tenured chair—as well as his wife, two children, and a yellow Lab—behind in California to make change in Washington. His deputy, Duke biochemistry professor Eric Toone, was also a biotech entrepreneur who had helped develop a promising glaucoma drug.

None of these men—they were all men—were in public service because they needed a job. They were the kind of dreamers President Kennedy had in mind, imagining things that never were: wind turbines shaped like jet engines, man-made substitutes for rare-earth minerals, electrical transformers the size of suitcases instead of kitchens. They saw energy as the challenge of their era, and ARPA-E as their moon mission. They were practical men who understood that even elegant laboratory advances in batteries or biofuels had to be scalable and affordable to be useful, but they were also true believers in the church of progress, confident they would reach those moons in due time.

"We chemists would say energy is a kinetic problem, not a thermodynamic problem," Toone says. "There's always a way around kinetic problems."

Toone had never studied biofuels, but he took on the photosynthesis problem. It was a real problem; just about all our energy was ultimately derived from photosynthesis, including the hydrocarbons in gasoline and other fossil fuels, even including the carbohydrates we break down when we pedal our bikes. But Toone had an epiphany after consulting with two groups of scientists who shared his inexperience in the energy field: the synthetic biology community, which manipulates cells and molecules, and the "extremophile" community, which studies microscopic organisms in exotic eco-niches like hot springs and ocean floors. Some of those organisms had evolved to absorb energy without photosynthesis, subsisting on hydrogen, ammonia, or even electric current. But none had been studied for fuel production. Toone realized that with the proper tinkering and the proper funding, it might be possible to train the kind of bacteria that eat electricity for breakfast to fuel our transportation sector someday. In October 2009, he hosted the first ever workshop on the topic, bringing together big brains from far-flung fields and encouraging them to imagine the possibilities.

"It was amazing how fast everyone went from 'This is nuts!' to 'Hmmm,'" he recalls.

Soon Toone presented his findings to the ARPA-E team. Majumdar had a knack for gouging holes in talks like this, pulverizing tenured hotshots into stammering grad students. This time he just sat in silence.

"Holy shit," he finally said in the lilt of his native Calcutta. "We're talking about an entirely new scientific discipline."

At a brainstorming session at ARPA-E's unofficial watering hole, a D.C. dive bar called the Ugly Mug, Toone came up with the new discipline's name: electrofuels. Within a few months, ARPA-E received 120 electrofuels proposals from scientists in all kinds of fields. And in April 2010, at a cabinet meeting led by Vice President Joe Biden, Chu unveiled thirteen electrofuels grants. A Boston firm planned to engineer E. coli into "a chassis for iso-octane." A University of South Carolina team would study "electroalcoholgenesis-bioelectrochemical reduction of CO_2." Biden's staff had invited me to sit in during the meeting—I'm a journalist for *Time* magazine—and as Chu explained a Harvard Medical School team's plan to create a "bacterial reverse fuel cell," I could almost see a "WTF?" thought bubble forming over the vice president's head.

Then Chu started talking a language everyone could understand; as a kid on Long Island, before his own circuitous journey from New York to Washington via San Francisco, he had been a baseball statistics nerd. "We're swinging for the fences," Chu said. "We're going to strike out a lot, but we'll hit a few grand slams." Most of ARPA-E's experiments would fail, but one successful project could kill off the internal combustion engine, or slash the cost of air-conditioning in half. Someday, electrofuels could be ten times as efficient as biofuels.

"Wow!" Biden crowed. "We're talking about research that will literally revolutionize American life!" (Biden often says "literally," or "literally, and I mean *literally*, not figuratively!" when he means "figuratively.") He then veered into a soliloquy about American ingenuity, then a shaggy-dog story about an energy-efficient lighting firm, then on to other business. But afterward, Biden was still jazzed. "Was that mind-blowing or what?" he asked, throwing his arm over my shoulder as if we were lifelong pals, when we had just been introduced moments earlier. "This is the exciting part of my job: We're building tomorrow!" We chatted for a minute about ARPA-E, and how it was a pretty striking example of the change Obama had promised during his campaign.

"That's what nobody gets about the Recovery Act," Biden said.

Yes, ARPA-E was launched by the American Recovery and Reinvestment Act, President Obama's widely ridiculed $787 billion "stimulus" package. The audacity of hope made change possible. The Recovery Act is making change happen.

President Obama signed the stimulus into law on February 17, 2009, less than a month after his inauguration, just a few months after the meltdown of the global financial system. The U.S. economy was in free-fall, and Americans were desperate for change. Obama's approval ratings were around 70 percent, Democrats had expanded their majorities in Congress, and talking heads were suggesting the Republican Party might be lurching toward extinction. Meanwhile, the rest of the world's major powers were also preparing stimulus packages to defibrillate their flat-lining economies.

Yet Obama's 1,073-page response to the worst crisis since the Great Depression swiftly became a national laughingstock—and the launching pad for the Republican revival. It was the Ur-text of the Obama administration, a microcosm of policy and politics in the Obama era. "No question about it, the stimulus was the defining moment," says former Republican senator Mel Martinez of Florida. "The Recovery Act set the tone," agrees David Axelrod, Obama's top political adviser.

Within a year, the percentage of Americans who believed the stimulus had created any jobs was lower than the percentage of Americans who believed that Elvis was alive. Resurgent Republicans mocked the law as "Porkulus," a bloated encapsulation of everything wrong with the Obama presidency. "Failed-stimulus" became a fourteen-letter GOP buzzword of choice, repeated incessantly in floor speeches, press conferences, and attack ads. Senate minority leader Mitch McConnell snarked that even Tiger Woods and John Edwards, the sex scandal stars of 2009, had better years than the failed-stimulus. A drumbeat of got-cha stories chronicled silly expenditures, like costumes for water safety mascots; silly-sounding legitimate expenditures, like a brain chemistry study of cocaine-addicted monkeys; and fictitious expenditures, like levitating trains to Disneyland or a snow-making machine in Duluth. Even Jay Leno got in a dig about communism, "or, as we call it in this country, a stimulus package."

The mockery got so intense that Democrats stopped saying "stimulus" in public. And their sidestepping got so blatant that a reporter confronted Obama about it at a news conference, asking why his aides "avoid the word 'stimulus' like the plague. Is that because the original stimulus is so deeply unpopular?"

The president wouldn't even use the word "stimulus" in his response.

The stimulus had one overriding public relations problem: The administration marketed it as a measure to prevent rampant unemployment—and then rampant unemployment happened anyway. Americans understood that Obama inherited a mess, but they didn't understand how horrible a mess, and the stimulus was touted as a job creator at a time when jobs were disappearing at record speed. A politically disastrous January 2009 report by Obama's economics team intensified this problem by warning that the jobless rate could hit 9 percent *without* the Recovery Act, while predicting it would stay below 8 percent *with* the Recovery Act, a gaffe that launched a thousand talking points after unemployment reached 10 percent *despite* the Recovery Act. These were understandable forecasting errors, based on consensus assumptions; it soon became clear that the pre-stimulus situation was much worse and disintegrating much faster than most economists realized at the time. But Republicans recognized the report as a gift that would keep on giving, and have savaged the stimulus ever since as a massive boondoggle charged to our maxed-out national credit card. Meanwhile, the left has griped that it wasn't massive enough. And the media have repeatedly dismissed it as a failure "by the administration's own standards."

The Recovery Act certainly wasn't perfect. It was the product of an imperfect legislative process, authored and implemented by imperfect human beings. It was oversold as a short-term economic fix, undersold as a long-term catalyst for change, and fumbled as a political football. It didn't create full employment. And its critics inflated the failure of a stimulus-funded solar manufacturer called Solyndra into a classic Washington pseudo-scandal.

I worked for nine years in Washington as a national reporter for *The Washington Post,* mostly writing critical stories about dysfunctional government agencies. I was familiar with the city's groupthink, the way its media narratives can harden into conventional wisdom. But I didn't live in Washington anymore, so I didn't swim in circles where suggesting that the stimulus was anything but a joke was a sign of credulity and cluelessness. And I still wrote about domestic policy, so I knew that the Recovery Act was more than the honeybee insurance, contraception subsidies, and other porky-sounding line items that got so much airtime on TV. It seemed like a big deal—actually, a collection of big deals. I didn't know if it was a good deal, but it reminded me of the New Deal, a mammoth government effort aimed at short-term Recovery and long-term Reinvestment.

I spent two years researching the stimulus, and I found that it is a new New Deal. Much of the Recovery Act's impact has been less obvious than the original New Deal's, but it's just as real.

"Bigger!"

Nostalgic liberals complain that the Recovery Act pales in comparison to the New Deal. It didn't create giant armies of new government workers in alphabet agencies like the WPA, CCC, and TVA; ARPA-E is its only new federal agency, with a staff smaller than a Major League Baseball roster. It didn't establish new entitlements like Social Security and deposit insurance, or new federal responsibilities like securities regulation and labor relations. It didn't set up workfare programs for the creative class like the Federal Theatre Project, Federal Music Project, or Federal Art Project. (Obama aides grumble that it could have used a new Federal Writers Project to churn out better pro-stimulus propaganda.) And it didn't raise taxes; it reduced taxes for the vast majority of American workers, although few of them noticed.

Obama and his aides thought a lot about the New Deal while assembling the Recovery Act, but in some ways it's an apples-to-bicycle comparison. While President Franklin D. Roosevelt forged the New Deal through a barrage of sometimes contradictory initiatives enacted and adjusted over several years, the stimulus was a single piece of legislation cobbled together and squeezed through Congress before most of Obama's appointees were even nominated. The New Deal was a journey, an era, an aura. The Recovery Act was just a bill on Capitol Hill.

But it was an astonishingly big bill. In constant dollars, it was more than 50 percent bigger than the entire New Deal, twice as big as the Louisiana Purchase and Marshall Plan combined. As multibillion-dollar line items were being erased and inserted with casual keystrokes, Obama aides who had served under President Bill Clinton occasionally paused to recall their futile push for a mere $19 billion stimulus that had seemed impossibly huge in 1993, or their vicious internal battles over a few million bucks for beloved programs that suddenly seemed too trivial to discuss. And the Recovery Act's initial estimate of $787 billion turned out to be too low; the official price tag would eventually climb to $831 billion. After a live microphone caught Biden accurately calling Obama's health reforms "a big fucking deal," I suggested to his chief of staff, Ron Klain, that the stimulus was just as big.

"Bigger!" Klain replied.

Biden's boast about the Recovery Act building tomorrow was accurate, too. It was the biggest and most transformative energy bill in U.S.

history, financing unprecedented government investments in a smarter grid; cleaner coal; energy efficiency in every imaginable form; "green-collar" job training; electric vehicles and the infrastructure to support them; advanced biofuels and the refineries to brew them; renewable power from the sun, the wind, and the heat below the earth; and factories to manufacture all that green stuff in the United States.

That's a lot of new precedents.

The stimulus was also the biggest and most transformative education reform bill since the Great Society. It was a big and transformative health care bill, too, laying the foundation for Obama's even bigger and more transformative reforms a year later. It included America's biggest foray into industrial policy since FDR, biggest expansion of antipoverty initiatives since Lyndon Johnson, biggest middle-class tax cut since Ronald Reagan, and biggest infusion of research money ever. It authorized a high-speed passenger rail network, the biggest new transportation initiative since the interstate highways, and extended our existing high-speed Internet network to underserved communities, a modern twist on the New Deal's rural electrification. It updated the New Deal–era unemployment insurance system and launched new approaches to preventing homelessness, financing infrastructure projects, and managing stormwater in eco-friendly ways. And it's blasting the money into the economy with unprecedented transparency and oversight.

"We probably did more in that one bill than the Clinton administration did in eight years," says one adviser to Clinton and Obama.

Critics often argue that while the New Deal left behind iconic monuments—the Hoover Dam, Skyline Drive, Fort Knox—the stimulus will leave a mundane legacy of sewage plants, repaved potholes, and state employees who would have been laid off without it. Even the Recovery Act's architects feared that like Winston Churchill's pudding, it lacked a theme. In reality, it's creating its own icons: zero-energy border stations, state-of-the-art battery factories, an eco-friendly Coast Guard headquarters on a Washington hillside, a one-of-a-kind "advanced synchrotron light source" in a New York lab. It's also restoring old icons: the Brooklyn Bridge and the Bay Bridge, the imperiled Everglades and the dammed-up Elwha River, Seattle's Pike Place Market and the Staten Island ferry terminal. But its main legacy, like the New Deal's, will be change.

That is also its main theme.

No, it's not the New Deal. Obama is not a classic New Deal liberal, and while he shares some of Roosevelt's traits—self-assurance bordering on egomania, a Harvard pedigree, an even keel, an allergy to ideologues—he's not the second coming of FDR. He didn't grow up rich and he didn't battle polio. He doesn't welcome the hatred of the elite and he hasn't forged a unique bond with the masses. He doesn't share Roosevelt's mistrust of credentialed experts, and he takes his campaign promises much more seriously than FDR did.

But the Recovery Act did update the New Deal for a new era. It was Obama's one shot to spend boatloads of money pursuing his vision, a major down payment on his agenda of curbing fossil fuel dependence and carbon emissions, modernizing health care and education, making the tax code more progressive and government more effective, and building a sustainable, competitive twenty-first-century economy. It's what he meant by "reinvent the economy to seize the future."

For starters, the stimulus did provide stimulus.

The Recovery Act injected an emergency shot of fiscal adrenaline into an economy that was hemorrhaging over 700,000 jobs a month. The leading independent economic forecasters—firms like Macroeconomic Advisers, Moody's Economy.com, IHS Global Insight, J.P. Morgan Chase, and Goldman Sachs, as well as the nonpartisan Congressional Budget Office—all agree that the stimulus helped stop the bleeding, averting a second depression and ending a brutal recession. The Recovery Act wasn't the only government intervention that helped stabilize the patient. The Federal Reserve's emergency support for the financial sector, Obama's unpopular rescue of the auto industry, and the even less popular Wall Street bailout that began under Bush all helped keep the economy afloat. But on the job loss graphs from the Great Recession, the low point came right before stimulus dollars started flowing. Then the situation slowly began to improve.

The Recovery Act followed the crisis response manual of the late British economist John Maynard Keynes, the godfather of fiscal stimulus. Keynes urged policymakers—including Roosevelt, who didn't listen too carefully—to "prime the pump" during downturns, to pour gobs of public money into their economies when private money was in hiding. The idea was to halt the classic death spiral where businesses facing weak demand lay off workers, which further weakens demand as laid-off workers stop spending, which leads to further layoffs and weaker demand. That's the nightmare Obama inherited after his inaugural parade. Credit was frozen, consumer confidence the lowest ever recorded. The economy was shrinking at an unheard-of 8.9 percent rate, although no one knew the numbers were that horrific at the time.

"It was obvious that the economy was going to hell," recalls Berkeley economist Christina Romer, the first chair of Obama's Council of Economic Advisers and coauthor of the infamous 8 percent unemployment report. "The question was the degree to which the economy was going to hell." Obama's team seriously underestimated that degree.

Nevertheless, the Recovery Act airlifted record amounts of Keynesian stimulus out of the Treasury to resuscitate demand: tax breaks for businesses and families to get cash circulating again; bailouts of every state to avert layoffs of teachers, police officers, and other public employees; one-time handouts to seniors, veterans, and the disabled; generous expansions of unemployment benefits, food stamps, health insurance, and other assistance for struggling families. The stimulus also put people to work directly with over 100,000 projects to upgrade roads, bridges, subways, water pipes, sewer plants, bus stations, fire stations, the Joseph R. Biden Jr. Railroad Station in Wilmington, Delaware, federal buildings, Grand Canyon National Park, trails, libraries, courthouses, the "national stream gauge network," hospitals, Ellis Island, seaports, airports, dams, locks, levees, Indian reservations, fish hatcheries, coral reefs, passport offices, military bases, veterans cemeteries, historically black colleges, particle accelerators, and much more.

Today, those independent analysts believe the Recovery Act came close to achieving its goal of saving or creating at least 3 million jobs in the short term. The concept of "saving or creating" has inspired a lot of sarcasm—Obama joked after his annual Thanksgiving pardon that he had just saved or created four turkeys—but it simply means that close to 3 million more people would have been unemployed without the Recovery Act.

Unfortunately, the housing and banking apocalypse that preceded it wiped out about eight million jobs, so it didn't come close to filling the entire hole. Unemployment soared to double digits while it was still kicking into gear. State and local governments offset much of its impact with anti-Keynesian austerity, raising taxes, slashing spending, and sucking money back out of the economy. Still, the CBO and the private forecasters concluded that at its height, the Recovery Act increased output over 2 percent, the difference between growth and contraction. It also helped balance every state budget, sparing public jobs and public services from the chopping block; many Republican governors attacked it as out-of-control spending, but all of them took its cash. It made a painful time less painful, helping millions of victims of the Great Recession keep food on their tables and roofs over their heads. And the Chicken Littles who warned that a $787 billion fiscal stimulus would lead to runaway inflation or exorbitant interest rates were wrong. Inflation remained extremely low, interest rates historically low. The stimulus didn't end America's very real pain, but then again, the New Deal didn't end the Depression. World War II ended the Depression.

Political critics have seized on that historical fact to try to discredit Obama's stimulus, ignoring the more salient facts that Roosevelt's commitment to stimulus was sporadic, the New Deal's stimulus did reduce unemployment when it was in effect, and World War II was the mother of all stimulus programs. But facts have not driven the debate. Republicans have stuck to their failed-stimulus message with impressive discipline. They've argued that government simply can't create jobs, often while attending ribbon cuttings for job-creating stimulus projects in their districts; that government shouldn't help private companies, often while writing letters seeking stimulus funds for firms in their states; and that government can only create government jobs, even though all of America's post-stimulus job growth has been in the private sector.

They've argued that Keynes was wrong about stimulus, except when it comes to high-end tax cuts, military spending, and other stimulus they like. They've portrayed the Recovery Act as larded with earmarks, when it was the first modern spending bill with no earmarks, and riddled with fraud, when investigators have been amazed by the lack of fraud.

It's been a brilliant strategy, and it planted the seeds for the Republican comeback.

"The stimulus was an Alamo moment for us, but we stuck together and made it out alive," says Republican congressman Tom Cole of Oklahoma. "Now 'stimulus' is a dirty word."

He's right. A colossal package of tax breaks and spending goodies that were almost all popular individually has become toxic collectively, as if the proper response to the crisis would have been a stiff upper lip, as if Herbert Hoover had it right the first time. Obama has struggled to explain the counterintuitive Keynesian insight that government needs to loosen its belt when families and businesses are tightening theirs. He has also struggled to make the counterintuitive political case that things would have been even lousier without the Recovery Act. It's true, but his slogan wasn't Yes We Can Keep Things From Getting Even Lousier. He didn't promise to create a somewhat-less-weak middle class. He always made it sound like the problems he inherited from Bush were kinetic problems, not thermodynamic problems.

As a kid rambling around Scranton, Pennsylvania, when Biden would break an arm or dislocate a hip, his mother would say: *Joey, it could've been worse. You could've broken both legs. You could've crushed your skull.* As the White House point man on the Recovery Act, Biden felt like he was recycling his mom's talking points, trying to persuade America to feel grateful its injuries weren't fatal. It's hard to get credit for averting a catastrophe, because once catastrophe is averted, people focus more on the pain they're feeling than the worse pain they might have felt in a hypothetical no-action case.

"One thing they never taught us in grad school was how to sell Keynesian stimulus," says Biden's former chief economist, Jared Bernstein, the other coauthor of the overoptimistic unemployment report. " 'It Would've Been Even Worse Without Us' is just a fruitless message."

In any case, the ferocious debate over the short-term Recovery has obscured the long-term Reinvestment.

ARPA-E didn't create any jobs in 2009, except for Majumdar's and his team's, and it didn't create many after that. But the stimulus was only partly about stimulus. It was also about metamorphosis. ARPA-E amounted to just 0.05 percent of the Recovery Act—a new Manhattan Project in a rounding error—and most of its breakthroughs won't produce results for years. But it's emblematic of the law's assault on the status quo. MIT professor Don Sadoway, a mad scientist in a bolo tie, has a radical vision of a liquid battery the size of a tractor-trailer that could store electricity for entire neighborhoods, so that renewable power could run our refrigerators when the sun isn't shining and the wind isn't blowing. He's got a prototype the size of a shot glass; his $7 million ARPA-E grant is helping him scale up to the size of a hockey puck and then a pizza box. Sadoway snorted when I asked how many jobs his grant had created: "If this works, I'll create a million jobs!"

Republicans have howled that many stimulus projects have little to do with short-term stimulus—and they're right. There was nothing "shovel-ready" about bullet trains designed to connect Los Angeles to San Francisco in under three hours, broadband cables designed to bring rural towns into the wired world, electronic health records designed to drag medical bureaucracy out of the leeches era, smart dishwashers designed to run when electricity is cheapest, automated factories that will manufacture electric trucks in Indiana instead of China, the first U.S. testing facility for wind turbine blades as long as football fields, or research into a new generation of "space taxis" that might replace NASA's shuttle someday. But these are the kind of long-term investments—more than one sixth of the stimulus—that Obama chief of staff Rahm Emanuel had in mind when he said "you never want a serious crisis to go to waste." The Recovery Act is also financing the world's largest wind farm in Oregon and the world's most powerful X-ray laser in California.

It's funding the largest photovoltaic solar array, largest solar thermal plant, and largest effort to install solar panels on commercial rooftops.

None of those projects was shovel-ready, either, but they were all deemed shovel-worthy.

The Recovery Act's most important long-term changes aimed to jump-start our shift to clean energy, reducing our carbon footprint, our electric bills, our vulnerability to oil shocks, and our subservience to petro-dictators while seeding green new industries. The stimulus converted Chu's cobwebbed department into the world's largest clean-tech investment fund. Overall, it pumped about $90 billion into green energy, when the United States previously spent a few billion a year.

The scale is almost unimaginable. Secretary Chu's Office of Energy Efficiency and Renewable Energy, which had a $1.2 billion budget, got a $16.4 billion infusion. New Jersey's state energy program received a 9,500 percent funding increase. The Recovery Act will also triple the smart meters in homes, quadruple the hybrids in the federal fleet, and expand electric vehicle charging stations forty-fold. It's creating an advanced battery industry almost entirely from scratch, increasing the U.S. share of global capacity from 1 percent when Obama took office to about 40 percent in 2015. Yes, Solyndra failed, but thousands of other green stimulus investments haven't.

The stimulus is also stocked with non-energy game-changers, like an initiative to sequence over 2,300 human genomes to help fight diseases like cancer and schizophrenia, when only thirty-four had been sequenced before. Or a $20 billion effort to computerize our pen-and-paper health system, which should reduce redundant tests, dangerous drug interactions, and fatal errors caused by doctors with chicken-scratch handwriting. Or the "Race to the Top" competition to promote data-driven reforms of public schools, which prompted dozens of states to revamp their education laws before they even submitted applications. Or the website recovery.gov, which lists every stimulus contract and lobbying contact, along with quarterly data detailing where all the money went.

At a time when government wasn't supposed to be able to run a one-car funeral, the Recovery Act was a real-time test of a new admin-istration's ability to spend tax dollars quickly, honestly, and effectively—and to reshape the country in the process.

"America said it wanted change," says Obama's education secretary, Arne Duncan. "Well, this is it!"

The Opening Act of the Obama Era

The stimulus had its roots in Obama's 2008 campaign agenda, which was mostly ignored while the media obsessed about his incendiary pas-tor, the ads comparing him to Paris Hilton, and other issues that had nothing to do with policy issues. It was put together during Obama's chaotic presidential transition, while the press focused on who he would choose for his cabinet, which of his nominees hadn't paid taxes, and what breed of dog he would give his daughters. It passed dur-ing his whirlwind first hundred days, when it competed for attention with his rescue plans for the auto, banking, and housing industries, his breaks with Bush on issues like torture, stem cells, and fuel efficiency, and controversies over everything from his handshake with Venezuelan strongman Hugo Chávez to the attempted sale of his Senate seat. Then its rollout was overshadowed by Obama's epic battle over health care; his push to end the war in Iraq and expand the war in Afghanistan; the rise of the Tea Party, which held its first rally ten days after he signed the Recovery Act; the weak economy; the Republican revival; and the constant dramas over Somali pirates, Iranian nukes, Supreme Court nominations, financial regulations, beer summits, birth certificates, and killings of international terrorists that add up to an eventful presidency.

Ultimately, one of the most sweeping pieces of legislation in modern history was reduced to an afterthought. In April 2011, Obama's most influential supporter asked him on national TV whether he wished he had started his presidency by focusing on the economy instead of health care. "Oprah, I've got to tell you, we did start with the economy," Obama replied with evident irritation. "Remember, the first thing we did was pass a Recovery Act." Polls have found that most Americans see the stimulus as a giveaway to bankers, confusing it with the $700 billion financial bailout that passed before Obama was elected. I interviewed several congressmen who were under the same misimpression.

This book aims to tell the story of the stimulus—how it happened, how it's changing the country, how Republicans found their voice in opposing it, and how it's been distorted by the Washington funhouse. There's never been a bill this comprehensive hustled into law this fast, and its journey after passage has been equally unique.

The stimulus is also the ultimate window into the Obama era, the opening act that foreshadows the rest of the show—the just-say-no extremism of the right, the unquenchable ingratitude of the left, the backroom deals with centrist senators, the gotcha games of the media, and the president's real achievements, as well as the limits of those achievements, and his struggles to market those achievements. Most of all, the battle over the Recovery Act made it clear that Obama's dreams of post-partisanship were doomed from the start. It was full of tax cuts and government spending that traditionally enjoyed bipartisan support, but it was greeted with virtually unanimous opposition by congressional Republicans who had secretly decided to fight Obama on just about everything.

"If he was for it," explains former Republican senator George Voinovich of Ohio, "we had to be against it."

The stimulus was also a case study in Obamaism. To left-wingers, it exposed the president as a spineless sellout, more interested in cutting deals than chasing dreams, willing and possibly eager to throw his base under the bus, desperate to compromise with Republicans who would never compromise with him. To right-wingers, it revealed Obama as a big-spending radical imposing European socialism on American free enterprise, somehow thuggish (in his I-got-the-votes partisanship and Chicago-style deal making) and wimpy (in his deference to House speaker Nancy Pelosi and other leftist congressional overlords) at the same time.

In reality, the Recovery Act provided early evidence that Obama was pretty much what he said he was: a data-oriented, left-of-center techno-crat who is above all a pragmatist, comfortable with compromise, solici-tous of experts, disinclined to sacrifice the good in pursuit of the ideal. It reflected his belief in government as a driver of change, but also his desire for better rather than bigger government. And it was the first evidence that after campaigning as a change-the-system outsider he would govern as a work-the-system insider, that despite all his flowery talk he understood that bills that don't pass Congress don't produce change.

Obama never sent a formal stimulus bill to Congress, and there's a broad perception that he punted the Recovery Act to Capitol Hill, another recurring theme in his presidency. But that's another Beltway myth. Congress helped shape it, but it was unmistakably an Obama bill. And it has been implemented in an Obama way.

Inevitably, change in the Obama era will be judged in comparison to the candidate's own rhetoric about renewing America's promise and setting aside childish things, the New Age bombast that persuaded his grassroots army of Obamaniacs that they were the change they were waiting for. He did lay it on thick. The night he won the Iowa caucus with a mere 37.6 percent of the vote, he informed his support-ers at the Des Moines Hy-Vee Hall that "years from now, you'll look back and say that this was the moment—this was the place—where America remembered what it means to hope!" There was something begging-for-comeuppance about his pose as a politician above politics, denouncing the twenty-four-hour news cycle and the ten-second sound bite, crusading against Washington's frivolity and negativity. Hadn't this guy launched his career by challenging a state senator's signatures and forcing her off the ballot? When exactly had America forgotten what it means to hope?

But even that heady night in Des Moines, Obama never suggested that he could snap his fingers and create a more perfect union. "Hope is not blind optimism," he told the ecstatic crowd. "It's not ignoring the enormity of the task ahead or the roadblocks that stand in our path. . . ." He was peddling hope, but he had been a community organizer for too long to expect change without struggle. The stimulus was a product of that audacious faith that the way things are is not necessarily the way things have to be, combined with the duller insight that things wouldn't change without sixty votes in the Senate. Reasonable people can disagree about the Recovery Act, and there ought to be great debates about its implications for government intervention in various sectors of the economy. But first, people ought to hear the real story of what was in it, how it got there, and how it's been translated into action.

This is a story about change, not just Obama. He's not the guy who's going to reinvent photosynthesis, and as he often tells crowds, change isn't just about him.

But it begins with him. It's his vision.

PART ONE

The Campaign for Change

— ONE —

A Man With a Plan

The Obama inauguration was an unforgettable spectacle, as an African American took the oath to protect and defend a nation scarred by slavery and Jim Crow. The oath itself got so muddled that Chief Justice John Roberts visited the White House the next day for a second take, to make sure the forty-fourth president's legitimacy wouldn't be questioned. (It turned out that he didn't have that power.) The weather was so frigid that Yo-Yo Ma and Yitzhak Perlman resorted to the stringed equivalent of lip-synching. But the record crowds around the Mall and around the world didn't seem to mind. When Obama was born, the marriage of his white mother, a teenager from Kansas, and his black father, a Kenyan who herded goats as a boy, would have been illegal in some of the states he'd just won. It was hard to imagine a more vivid advertisement for the American dream.

Obama's speech was memorable, too, especially the buzzkill it applied to the occasion. The media wanted to focus on race, a feel-good story that made a political event feel apolitical. Obama told a feel-bad story about national drift and economic collapse, a crisis that seemed more relevant to his first day on the job. He spoke of foreclosed homes, shuttered businesses, "a sapping of confidence across our land, a nagging fear that America's decline is inevitable." Who would want that on a commemorative plate? He concluded with a bleak image of George Washington amid the bloodstained snows of Valley Forge: "Let us brave once more the icy currents, and endure what storms may come." What a bummer.

In retrospect, though, the most important passage was not so memorable. Unlike FDR, whose nothing-to-fear-but-fear-itself inaugural was devoid of specifics, Obama outlined his immediate plans for change:

> The state of our economy calls for action: bold and swift. And we will act not only to create new jobs, but to lay a new foundation for growth. We will build the roads and bridges, the electric grids and digital lines that feed our commerce and bind us together. We will restore science to its rightful place and wield technology's wonders to raise health care's quality and lower its costs. We will harness the sun and the winds and the soil to fuel our cars and run our factories. And we will transform our schools and colleges and universities to meet the demands of a new age. All this we can do. All this we will do.

All this went unnoticed, except the swipe at Bush about restoring science.

I was live-blogging at Time.com, and my insta-response was: "This is the weak part of the speech. It's a lovely laundry list, but it's still a laundry list. Save it for the State of the Union." In fact, the State of the Union would have been too late. The Recovery Act checked off every item on the list: roads and bridges (Title XII), transmission lines (Secs. 301, 401, 1705) and broadband lines (Titles I, II), scientific research (Titles II, III, IV, VIII), electronic medical records (Title XIII), solar and wind power (over a dozen provisions), biofuel refineries (Title IV), electric cars (Sec. 1141), green manufacturing (Sec. 1302), and education reform (Sec. 14005). They were all campaign priorities, and his transition team had already made sure the stimulus would direct record funding to all of them.

Obama was not the first politician to propose any of them. In fact, except for his early opposition to the Iraq War, little about his policies had set him apart from his more experienced rivals in the Democratic primary. His agenda was largely the center-left Democratic agenda of reversing the Bush era, reviving the middle class, and investing in the future. Obama cared deeply about policy, devouring briefing papers, pressuring his staff to schedule "think time" with experts. But he wasn't a policy entrepreneur, and his campaign wasn't about new ideas. It was about his unswerving message of Change, as well as that aspirational We Can Believe In addendum, the sense that maybe this guy would follow through on the familiar ideas that never seemed to go anywhere.

And he has. On policy, he's mostly done what he said he'd do.

This is not in itself a defense of Obama. FDR broke promises as casually as he broke bread; he wouldn't be lionized today if he had kept his ill-advised promises to maintain the gold standard and balance the budget during a depression. To say that Obama's approach has been more straightforward is certainly not to say it's been more successful. But unlike FDR, he came into office with a well-defined theory of the case, and he's tried to put that theory into practice. The best way to understand the Recovery Act—and the Obama presidency—is to understand that theory of the case, both his general principles and the specifics he laid out on the trail. Perhaps this lacks a certain drama, but Obama got his No-Drama reputation for a reason.

A Reconstructed Liberal

Who is Barack Obama?

To the paranoid precincts of the right, he's a Marxist, a secret Muslim, a madrassa-schooled Kenyan who hates white people and the Pledge of Allegiance. Prominent Republicans, without endorsing these delusions, have often suggested that speculation is bound to swirl around such an international man of mystery, that Obama is "a president we know less about than any other president in history."

That's a crock. We know plenty about Barack Obama. Thanks to the daft controversy over his citizenship, we know he was born in Honolulu at 7:24 P.M. on August 4, 1961, and his life story doesn't get much murkier after that. His pet ape in Indonesia was named Tata. He used to smoke Marlboro Reds. He had enough heart to work as an organizer in a Chicago housing project for $13,000 a year, enough brain to graduate magna cum laude from Harvard Law School, enough ego to tell an adviser he "could probably do every job on the campaign better than the people I'll hire." As Biden would say, Obama's life is literally an open book.

Before he entered politics, Obama wrote a memoir called *Dreams from My Father*, a travelogue of his emotional journey to manhood. It's a raw chronicle of his inner turmoil as an out-of-place kid in Hawaii and Indonesia, a confused college student at Occidental and Columbia, and a callow community organizer trying to find himself in inner-city Chicago. But it's written in the mature voice of a law professor who clearly had found whatever he was looking for. He knew how silly he had sounded back in the day, blathering about "white folks this and white folks that," whining about the patriarchy with punk rock performance poets. His revelations about using cocaine, flirting with racial militancy, and attending socialist conferences drew attention, but his moral of the story was that he had moved on from that nonsense.

The Audacity of Hope, a political manifesto written after Obama's election to the Senate, provides a more relevant tour of his worldview as a Democrat who believes in evolution and global warming but also believes his party can be smug and dogmatic. It's partly a nonpartisan critique of Washington's win-the-news-cycle culture of conflict, partly a liberal defense of government as a force for economic security and opportunity, sprinkled with caveats about the blind spots of the left. It makes the case for a politics rooted in common ground and common decency, with pragmatism as its lodestar: "We should be guided by what works."

Aside from the wingnut screeds claiming that a Vietnam-era terrorist ghostwrote *Dreams from My Father*, or that Obama's rage was forged by the anticolonialism of the father he barely knew, most independent excavations of Obama have unearthed portraits fairly consistent with his self-portraits. They reveal a confident (some say arrogant), ambitious (some say overly so), and intelligent (everyone agrees on that) politician with an eye-in-the-storm aura of calm and a carefully calibrated mix of idealism and realism. He comes off as relentlessly, almost comically reasonable, a born conciliator who assumes that just about any difference can be bridged through rational discourse. He's clearly a calculating pol, not a crusading saint; although he navigated the cesspool of Chicago politics without getting filthy, he didn't rage against the Democratic machine. But he just as clearly emerged from his angst-ridden formative years as a levelheaded grown-up who's comfortable in his own skin.

I'd love to reveal some previously hidden Obama pathology, but my sources mostly describe the same cerebral, low-blood-pressure, somewhat aloof alpha male. They marvel at his uncanny ability to boil down a meeting to its essence. They chuckle at the authoritative way he starts sentences with, "Look," as if you'd surely agree if you just saw what he was saying. They emphasize his show-me-the-data empiricism and half-a-loaf pragmatism, but also his desire to help others.

"I worked for Ted Kennedy, the gold standard for caring about people, and Barack didn't emote the same way," says economist Daniel Tarullo, an Obama campaign adviser who is now a Federal Reserve governor. "But he was always thinking about the guy who lost his job in the Maytag factory in Newton, Iowa."

Obama has a more analytical, businesslike—some say bloodless—approach than feel-your-pain politicians like Kennedy, Biden, or Bill Clinton. He doesn't pound his fists or draw many lines in the sand. It's not his way, and he doesn't think it helps the guy from the Maytag factory. As an organizer, he helped poor people seek better government services with an unusually nonconfrontational style. At Harvard, he was elected to lead the Law Review because conservatives felt he'd treat them fairly. In the Illinois legislature, he had a liberal voting record, but was known for brokering bipartisan deals. He followed a similar path in the U.S. Senate, voting the Democratic line while working with Republicans like Richard Lugar of Indiana on nuclear nonproliferation and Tom Coburn of Oklahoma on government transparency. His MO hasn't changed much.

Obama's aides do acknowledge that there's something vaguely enig-
matic about their boss. He's so modulated, so left-brain, so unruffled.
They admire him, but they're not sure they truly know him. How did
such an alienated young man become so anchored in middle age? Did
he find peace by marrying Michelle? Did he repress his emotions to
avoid angry-black-man stereotypes?

Honestly, I have no idea. For this book, the fact that he ended up anchored seems more relevant than his mysterious journey to anchored.
And the most relevant aspects of his biography are his beliefs, which
are not so mysterious.

Obama's mother, Ann Dunham, was the warmhearted wellspring of his
social conscience, teaching him needlepoint values like empathy and
compassion. She was also a self-proclaimed "unreconstructed liberal,"
a Ted Kennedy liberal, an imagine-the-Pentagon-had-to-hold-a-bake-
sale liberal. Obama portrayed her as a naive romantic who gave money
to every beggar in Indonesia, "a soldier for New Deal, Peace Corps,
position-paper liberalism." She later became a respected anthropolo-
gist, but Obama distanced himself from the bleeding-heart ethic he associates with her. In *The Audacity of Hope*, he chided Democrats "who
still champion the old-time religion, defending every New Deal and
Great Society program from Republican encroachment." He champi-
oned a less purist liberalism, reflecting more practical influences—like
his grandmother, Madelyn Dunham, a blunt-spoken Midwesterner who
worked her way from clerk to vice president of a bank, and his step-
father, Lolo Soetoro, an Indonesian oilman who warned him that the
world is cruel and lofty ideals are luxury goods.

Obama was still a man of the left. As he explained to the uninitiated, his "views on most topics correspond more closely to the editorial
pages of the *New York Times* than those of the *Wall Street Journal*."
He embraced the New Deal ideas that Americans have a stake in each
other's success, markets sometimes fail, and government can help promote prosperity. He endorsed the New Deal concept of a safety net to
make sure Americans don't go bankrupt when they get sick or hungry

when they get old—and to promote economic risk taking the way an actual safety net promotes acrobatic risk taking. He credited FDR with laying the groundwork for the postwar growth that lifted workers into the middle class, creating consumer demand that kept the economy humming for decades. Modern Democrats, he wrote, should aim to "recast FDR's social compact to meet the needs of a new century."

In Obama's telling, New Deal liberalism simply failed to keep up with the times. In the 1960s, it came to be defined less by pocketbook issues than permissive attitudes toward the counterculture, alienating Americans who respected faith and flag. By the 1970s, liberals spoke the language of victimhood rather than community, ignoring middle-class concerns about crime, taxes, and government bloat. Ronald Reagan, with his appeal to patriotic families who played by the rules, tapped into a sense of common purpose that liberals no longer could. Their whiny attacks on kindly Ronnie as a racist meanie only made them look like "out-of-touch, tax-and-spend, blame-America-first, politically-correct elites." And they didn't appreciate the dynamism of capitalism. When factories fled overseas in pursuit of cheap labor, like the shuttered steel mills near the projects where Obama worked in Chicago, they had little to offer laid-off workers and hollowed-out communities but unemployment benefits and welfare checks. When schools failed to educate poor kids, another crisis he witnessed firsthand as an organizer, their only answer was to hike taxes and pour more money into the ratholes. As a professor at the University of Chicago, the global hub of laissez-faire economics, Obama didn't drink the neoclassical Kool-Aid, but he did grow concerned that Democrats were "more obsessed with slicing the economic pie than with growing the pie." They had become a pity party, with no vision for creating prosperity, only for redistributing it—until Bill Clinton came along.

Obama was disgusted by Clinton's shameless political posturing, especially the "frighteningly coldhearted" execution of a mentally retarded inmate before a primary. He thought the Clinton White House neglected families left behind in the global economy, trimming its policy sails to push poll-tested trivialities like school uniforms. But he credited the Man from Hope with dragging Democrats back to reality, reforming welfare, balancing the budget, and focusing on economic growth. Shortly after arriving in Washington in 2006, Obama signaled his sympathy with Clinton's "Third Way" by speaking at the launch of the Hamilton Project, a Brookings Institution policy shop founded by Wall Street bigwig Robert Rubin, the former Clinton treasury secretary and godfather of Democratic centrists. "Both sides of the political spectrum have tended to cling to outdated politics and tired ideologies instead of coalescing around what actually works," Obama said that day.

Unfortunately, Obama wrote, Clinton's biography—"the draft letter saga, the marijuana puffing, the Ivy League intellectualism, the professional wife who didn't bake cookies, and most of all the sex"— catered perfectly to Republican stereotypes of sixties liberalism. Even as the economy boomed and the rising tide lifted almost every boat, a new generation of Republican hard-liners led by House speaker Newt Gingrich raised slash-and-burn partisanship to an art form. Politics eroded into good-versus-evil, jackboots-versus-hippies warfare, "the psychodrama of the baby boom generation . . . played out on a national stage." And George W. Bush stole that stage after campaigning as "a uniter, not a divider," with a platform of "compassionate conservatism" that sounded a lot like the Third Way.

After a historically close election decided by the Supreme Court, pundits predicted that Bush would be forced to govern from the center. But soon he was slashing taxes for the rich; appointing timber, mining, and finance lobbyists to oversee their old industries; launching an unprovoked war; and generally governing as if "divider" were his job title. Republicans ditched the fiscal rectitude of the Clinton years, putting two wars, $2 trillion in tax cuts, a drug benefit for seniors, and a record earmarking binge on the charge card. Rather than ask Americans to make wartime sacrifices, Bush urged them to go shopping. His bank regulators posed with a chain saw in front of a stack of regulations. And a corruption scandal starring a sleazy Republican lobbyist named Jack Abramoff revealed the dominance of corporate interests in Bush's Washington.

Obama dropped his measured tone halfway through *The Audacity of Hope* to shred the modern GOP as a party of zealotry and magical thinking, controlled by K Street and its right-wing base, unswervingly opposed to taxes, regulation, and basic arithmetic. It was just as dedicated to redistribution as the old Democratic Party, except it redistributed wealth upward. Bush's "Ownership Society" was a euphemism for leaving families on their own, a step toward replacing the New Deal with a winner-take-all society.

Obama had an alternative vision of reconstructed liberalism. He imagined a country that embraced freewheeling capitalism, while still making sure every American could go to college, afford decent health care, and retire with dignity. It would finance forward-leaning public ventures, as Abraham Lincoln did with the transcontinental railroad and National Academy of Sciences, as FDR did with the Triborough Bridge and rural electrification, as postwar administrations of both parties did with the interstates and the Internet. Instead of squandering surpluses on pork for the connected and tax breaks for the rich, America would invest in modern schools, research, and infrastructure. Instead of ducking tough problems, it would tackle our addiction to fossil fuels and our dysfunctional health care system.

That was Obama's general case for change.

A Race Against Washington

It wasn't really a case for Obama.

It was a case for a Democratic president, but the black guy with the weird name had no reason to think he'd be that president. Hillary Clinton was the overwhelming Democratic front-runner, a star-power senator backed by her husband's political machine. When *The Audacity of Hope* was published in 2006, Obama was two years out of the Illinois statehouse, known only for his electrifying "We Are One People" speech at the 2004 Democratic convention. He had never even shown he could take a punch, gliding into the Senate after a marital abuse scandal torpedoed his main Democratic rival and a swingers club scandal torpedoed his main Republican rival.

But as Obama toured the country to flack his book and stump for Democrats, attracting mobs at every stop, he sensed he was tapping into the zeitgeist. Democrats of all stripes—liberal, conservative, urban, rural—wanted him by their side. New Hampshire's governor quipped that he was a bigger draw than the Rolling Stones. He was hot, and he doubted he would get hotter sitting around Washington for another decade, risking early-onset senatoritis while acquiring enough gravitas to satisfy the arbiters of such things. He was bored in the Senate, a change-averse, geriatric debating club with stifling procedural rules. He expected 2008 to be a change election, and he looked like change.

The case for Obama was not a substantive case for changing policies; Hillary was making a similar case with a better résumé. The case for Obama was a political case for why those policies never seemed to change. It implied that Hillary was part of the problem, that America couldn't afford another decade of Clinton wars, that the political pettiness and nastiness that exploded during the Clinton era was the fundamental obstacle to fundamental change.

Hillary's one-word explanation for the persistence of the status quo was "Republicans." Obama's was "Washington," the endless spin cycles, insult industries, and poll-driven platitudes that made tough choices and commonsense compromise impossible. As a symbol and a participant, Hillary was inextricably linked to that Washington gridlock machine, the bickering and parsing, the eternal boomer-driven relitigation of the sixties. She could never make a credible "We Are One People" speech, or bring people together to solve big problems; she had tried and failed in 1994 with her husband's health care plan. The case for Hillary was that she knew how to fight Republicans, that she was comfortable in the muck. The case for Obama was that he could move politics beyond the muck.

Obama was not a cockeyed optimist about getting the Crips and Bloods of the Beltway to call a truce. He knew a less myopic, more cordial politics might not be possible anymore:

Maybe there's no escaping our great political divide, an endless clash of armies, and any attempts to alter the rules of engagement

are futile. Or maybe the trivialization of politics has reached a point
of no return, so that most people see it as just one more diversion, a
sport, with politicians our paunch-bellied gladiators and those who
bother to pay attention just fans on the sidelines: We paint our faces
red or blue and cheer our side and boo their side, and if it takes a
late hit or a cheap shot to beat the other team, so be it, for winning
is all that matters.

Still, Obama felt like he matched the moment. He would run as an
outsider against Washington, an insurgent against a quasi-incumbent,
a start-up against a behemoth, change against business as usual. He
figured his chances were slim, but hey, sure things don't require the
audacity of hope.

In February 2007, Obama announced his candidacy outside the old
state capitol in Springfield, the site of Lincoln's "House Divided" speech.
His theme was America's divided house. "In the face of a politics that's
shut you out, that's told you to settle, that's divided us for too long, you
believe we can be one people," he told fifteen thousand shivering fans.
Obama was aligning himself not only with Lincoln, but with civility;
Springfield was also the place where he played poker with Republicans at night and legislated with Republicans during the day, the place
where "we learned to disagree without being disagreeable." Basically, he
pledged to be a uniter, this time for real.

But Obama's ideas about changing politics were always a means
to the end of changing policies. In Springfield, he listed the four main
problems he was running to solve: "a dependence on oil that threatens
our future," "a health care crisis," "schools where too many children
aren't learning," and "families struggling paycheck to paycheck despite
working as hard as they can." He argued that real solutions would be
impossible until Washington moved beyond the noise and the rage:

What's stopped us from meeting these challenges is not the absence
of sound policies and sensible plans. What's stopped us is the failure
of leadership, the smallness of our politics—the ease with which

we're distracted by the petty and trivial, our chronic avoidance of tough decisions, our preference for scoring cheap political points instead of rolling up our sleeves and building a working consensus to tackle big problems.

That was the essence of Obama's case against Hillary Clinton.

And it was wrong.

It turned out that it was possible to make progress on long-term problems even while Washington remained distracted by the petty and the trivial. The proof would be in the Recovery Act. It would produce dramatic change on energy, health care, education, and the squeeze on struggling families—the four pillars of that "new foundation for growth" he would promise in his inaugural address—without any working consensus or any pause in the scoring of cheap political points.

During the campaign, his policy proposals in those areas didn't attract much attention. But not even he imagined he'd make serious inroads on all four priorities in a single bill during his first month in office. Since he did so much of what he said he'd do, it's worth recalling exactly what he was campaigning to change.

— TWO —

The Four Pillars

Energy: The Dream of a Green Economy

In his first policy speech of the campaign, Obama paid tribute to FDR's greatest Yes We Can achievement, the transformation of the U.S. economy into a lethal arsenal of democracy after Pearl Harbor. When Roosevelt's brain trust had warned that his goals for retooling civilian factories were impossibly audacious, he had insisted "the production people can do it if they really try." And they had done it.

At the Detroit Economic Club in May 2007, Obama called for a similar miracle: the transformation of the U.S. energy sector. Once again, he warned, the future of the American experiment—and the planet— was at stake. "The country that faced down the tyranny of fascism and communism is now called to challenge the tyranny of oil," he said. "The very resource that has fueled our way of life over the last 100 years now threatens to destroy it if our generation does not act now and act boldly." Those last five words were straight out of FDR's inaugural.

Obama used his Detroit speech to call out the Big Three automakers for their overreliance on gas-guzzlers, a bit of speak-truth-to-power political theater that led the news coverage. But his deeper message was that energy was the challenge of his generation, a slow-motion existential crisis that politicians always talked about but never solved. This was the kind of problem Obama was running to fix: "It will take leadership willing to turn the page on the can't-do, won't-do, won't-even-try politics of the past, leadership willing to face down the doubters and cynics and simply say: 'We can do it if we really try.'"

Ever since 1973, when Richard Nixon vowed to end oil imports by the decade's end, every president had made we-can-do-it promises about energy independence. "I happen to believe that we can do it," said Gerald Ford. Jimmy Carter had proclaimed this crusade "the moral equivalent of war." Even George W. Bush had pledged "to move beyond a petroleum-based economy."

So far, the doubters and cynics had been right. Oil imports had more than doubled since 1973. We were shipping $1 billion overseas every day to buy crude, empowering petro-thugs, exposing our economy to the whims of OPEC and Mother Nature. When oil prices spiked, the pain we felt wasn't just at the pump; tourism suffered, petroleum products like chemicals and plastics got pricier, and our manufacturers, farmers, airlines, and shippers all faced higher costs. We were a captive superpower. Osama bin Laden recognized this addiction as our Achilles' heel, urging al Qaeda operatives to "focus your operations on oil." And we couldn't drill our way out of this mess; we were sitting on less than 3 percent of the world's oil reserves, devouring 25 percent of the world's oil.

Meanwhile, a broad scientific consensus had emerged that carbon dioxide emissions from fossil fuels were warming the planet, and that the world needed to slash emissions 80 percent by 2050 to avoid science-fiction disaster scenarios. A documentary about Al Gore's PowerPoint had just won the Academy Award, and Gore was about to win the Nobel Prize. The ten hottest years on record had all occurred in the previous twelve years; glaciers were retreating, droughts intensifying. Obviously, we couldn't drill our way out of that mess, either.

Under Bush and Dick Cheney, a pair of Texas oilmen, White House loyalty to hydrocarbons approached self-parody. Bush renounced his campaign pledge to reduce greenhouse gas emissions, and Cheney presided over a secretive energy task force dominated by Big Oil and other extraction industry interests. A former petroleum lobbyist on Bush's staff was caught editing climate reports to downplay global warming, while a hard-nosed federal watchdog named Earl Devaney unearthed proof of oil regulators having sex with oil executives, smoking pot with oil executives, and generally doing whatever oil executives asked. Congress approved new loan programs for clean-energy projects and fuel-efficient carmakers, but the administration failed to make a single loan.

So we were still hooked on oil for transportation and coal for electricity. Nearly three decades after Carter installed solar panels on the White House roof—and two decades after Reagan tore them down—solar energy produced just 0.1 percent of our power. Wind, our fastest-growing source of renewable electricity, also generated less than 1 percent of our juice. We were the world's worst energy hogs by far; the average U.S. home had over two dozen plug-in devices slurping electricity, while the average U.S. commuter spent nearly an hour a day behind the wheel burning gas. And the energy forecasts all predicted more demand, more carbon-spewing coal plants, and more oil imports from countries that hated us.

In an October speech in Portsmouth, New Hampshire, Obama unveiled his plan for a real clean-energy push. Like all his Democratic rivals, Obama proposed to cap carbon emissions and set up a market-based trading system that would reduce emissions by the necessary 80 percent by 2050. (Republican John McCain had a cap-and-trade plan, too, with a 60 percent emissions reduction.) Obama also vowed to invest $150 billion in clean energy over a decade, about five times the Bush status quo. Establishment pundits dismissed this as a brazen over-promise, "standard goody-bag politics." But the Recovery Act would get three fifths of the way there in Obama's first month.

On the trail, Obama often touted a renewable energy resource that's perfectly clean, instantly available, and almost infinitely abundant. It doesn't depend on future technological breakthroughs, and we don't need to import it. Unlike coal or petroleum, it's zero-emissions. Unlike solar or wind, it works in any weather. Unlike nuclear, it doesn't produce radioactive waste, risk a calamitous meltdown, or take a decade to build. And it's the cheapest energy resource we've got.

This magic potion is called energy efficiency. It's a boring name for a boring concept: wasting less energy—more precisely, using less energy to get our showers just as hot and our drinks just as cold. It's mostly generated by boring products like energy-saving boilers, refrigerators, air conditioners, and light bulbs. But energy wonks love it, because subtracting demand through efficiency is much less expensive, eco-destructive, and time-intensive than adding new supply through drilling or power plants. It doesn't even require us to unplug our electronic picture frames or power down our PlayStations; that's conservation, doing less with less energy. Efficiency is doing the same or more with less energy. It doesn't require behavioral change. And efficiency upgrades usually pay for themselves within a few years through lower energy costs, which is why experts always call them "low-hanging fruit." A McKinsey & Co. study found that efficiency could cut our energy demand 20 percent by 2020, which could cut our coal use in half.

To Obama, efficiency wasn't boring at all. It was "by far the cheapest, cleanest, fastest energy source." In Detroit, he proposed major increases in fuel efficiency standards, which hadn't budged since the Reagan era. (U.S. automakers had always argued that tougher rules would ruin their businesses, which they apparently preferred to do themselves.) In Portsmouth, he extended the push beyond vehicles, calling for stricter green building codes and appliance efficiency standards, pledging to phase out incandescent light bulbs. He also vowed that his administration would "weatherize" one million low-income homes per year—by upgrading furnaces, caulking windows, and adding insulation—which could save families money on their bills while reducing energy demand.

Efficiency wasn't as emotionally satisfying as "drill-baby-drill," but it appealed to Obama's Vulcan sense of logic; the cheapest fuel is the fuel we don't need to buy, and the cheapest power plant is the plant we don't need to build. Obama even called on states to revamp regulations that rewarded utilities for selling as much power and building as many plants as possible, a holy grail for hard-core efficiency geeks. In California and other states that encouraged utilities to promote efficiency instead, per-capita electricity use had been flat for three decades; in the rest of the country, it had climbed 50 percent.

Obama wanted to clean up our supply as well as reduce our demand, so he also promised to double renewable electricity during his first term. The green revolution was finally underway in Germany, Spain, and even California, which was on track to generate one third of its power from renewables by 2020. Obama thought the rest of the United States just needed a stronger push. Wind power was racing down the cost curve associated with emerging technologies, and solar, while still expensive, had similar potential to shed costs as it added scale. Obama also promised to double U.S. manufacturing of wind turbines, solar panels, and other green components during his first term, which would help create a domestic supply chain and further drive down the cost of clean power. By imposing a price on carbon pollution, cap-and-trade would help level the playing field as well.

Since our windiest plains and sunniest deserts lacked transmission lines to carry power to cities—and our antiquated electrical networks couldn't handle too much intermittent power that vanished whenever the wind died down or clouds blocked the sun—Obama also talked about modernizing the grid. It was analog in a digital world, relying on switches that still had to be switched by hand and transformers that hadn't been transformed in a century; Alexander Graham Bell would have been flabbergasted by modern telecommunications, but Thomas Edison would have recognized most of the gizmos in a modern substation. Obama wanted to build a smart grid that would self-monitor and self-heal, integrate renewables while keeping the lights on, and enable homeowners with solar roofs and even electric cars to sell power back to their utilities. He touted digital smart meters that could give us real-time feedback and control over our electricity, so we could monitor how much our individual appliances use and cost, manage them from our iPhones—no more wondering if we left the oven on—and even program them to communicate with the grid to save us energy and money automatically.

"It's safe to say this is the most a presidential candidate has ever talked about the grid," the environmental writer David Roberts gushed after one Obama riff. "Sigh. He talks so purty."

Obama's rhetoric often made enviros swoon. He pledged that all new federal buildings would be carbon-neutral by 2025, and that the United States would have one million plug-in electric vehicles by 2015. At the time, no federal buildings were carbon-neutral, and Tesla Motors hadn't delivered its first Roadster. He also bashed Bush over climate change, noting in Portsmouth that wildfires were already getting worse, polar ice caps were melting, and New Hampshire's ski industry faced shorter seasons. "Global warming is not a someday problem," he said. "It is now."

But Obama was no tree hugger. Nature wasn't something he felt in his gut, and while he rejected the GOP's drill-baby-drill mantra, he echoed its "all-of-the-above" rhetoric. He supported emissions-free nuclear power, even though it was anathema to most of the Birkenstocks-and-granola crowd; his top corporate contributor in Illinois was a nuclear utility. Representing a state that produced coal and corn, he had stumbled into alternative energy through his advocacy of "clean coal," which most environmentalists consider an oxymoron, and corn ethanol, which many scientists believe is even dirtier than gasoline. The ethanol boom has actually accelerated climate change, because rain forests and wetlands that store vast amounts of carbon have been bulldozed into agricultural land to replace the food production lost when we pump corn into our SUVs.

As a presidential candidate, Obama pledged to build five commercial-scale clean-coal facilities that would capture and store carbon—five more than America had built to date. And he continued to flack for the ethanol industry, which was displacing just 3 percent of our gasoline, while diverting nearly one fourth of our grain crops into fuel tanks, jacking up global food prices and fueling bread riots in countries like Yemen and Pakistan that really didn't need the extra instability. But he did start to talk about shutting down dirty coal plants, and he did promise to nurture the next generation of eco-friendlier "advanced biofuels" brewed from switchgrass, wood chips, and algae.

"The struggling paper mills in New Hampshire would be back in business if they could use wood to produce biofuels," he said in Portsmouth.

This was Obama's favorite argument for alternative energy investments: They would spur economic activity, not just at New Hampshire ski resorts and paper mills, but in new domestic industries on the leading edge of innovation. They were long-term investments in U.S. competitiveness, and they would repatriate cash we were sending the Chávezes of the world. Obama envisioned a future with five million "green jobs," for caulkers and electricians weatherizing homes; factory workers making energy-efficient windows and electric vehicles; scientists and engineers experimenting with better biofuels and batteries.

In the past, Americans had invented and developed green technologies like wind turbines, solar panels, lithium-ion batteries, and compact fluorescent bulbs, only to see them manufactured and used abroad. Now Germany led the world in solar panel deployment, even though it wasn't too sunny, and China led the world in solar panel production, while our share of the market had plummeted from 40 percent to 8 percent in a decade.

"The question is not *if* a renewable energy economy will thrive in the future," Obama explained. "It's *where*."

To Obama, America's energy crisis was also the ultimate example of our shortsighted politics. It reflected our neglect of yesterday's infrastructure; our grid was so outdated that a tree branch had knocked down a wire outside Cleveland and blacked out eight states. And it reflected our unwillingness to invest in tomorrow's technologies; over three decades, the Energy Department's research budget had plunged 85 percent in constant dollars, while corporate funding shriveled to the point where biotech firms like Amgen and Genentech had larger R&D budgets than the entire energy sector. Meanwhile, ExxonMobil earned

$40 billion in 2007, the largest profit ever for a U.S. firm, breaking its own record from 2006. That helped explain the lobbyist armies, political donations, and climate-denial think tanks that maintained Big Oil's stranglehold over Washington.

As a result, we had no energy policy. We hit the panic button when oil prices spiked and the snooze button when they eased. We knew what needed to be done, but we never did it. "I would not be running for president," Obama said, "if I didn't believe that this time could be different."

Health Care: Too Dysfunctional for Too Long

Health care was the second pillar of Obama's "new foundation," another recurring nightmare that politicians always chattered about but never ended. Again, he promised that this time would be different, that he'd sign legislation extending insurance to every American during his first term. Again, his plan resembled all the other Democratic plans, except it didn't include an "individual mandate" requiring everyone to buy insurance. Again, Obama suggested that the real difference was political, that only he could build the bipartisan consensus needed to drive a plan through Congress. Hillary Clinton had botched her chance in 1994.

There was one other substantive difference. While Obama echoed all the usual Democratic talking points about covering the uninsured and standing up to insurers, his health care analysis emphasized one overarching theme.

"It's just too expensive," he explained in May at the University of Iowa.

U.S. health spending had quadrupled in two decades; we were spending almost twice as much per person as any other industrialized country. Health care took up one sixth of our economy, on course for one third by 2040. Medical bills were causing half our personal bankruptcies, and insurance premiums had almost doubled on Bush's watch. Obama argued that this was the reason 45 million Americans had no coverage, so many businesses had stopped offering it, and so many families who had it were just one accident or diagnosis away from financial ruin. This was why his initial plan had no mandate, although the plan he eventually signed into law did; at the time, he doubted it would be worth the political heartburn to try to force people to buy insurance they couldn't afford. And insurance wouldn't be affordable until care was affordable.

Obama saw this crisis, like the energy crisis, as an economic as well as moral crisis, another crimp on competitiveness. "There was never a distinction in his mind between health care and the economy," recalls one of his health advisers, Harvard professor David Cutler. The skyrocketing cost of care was a disaster for individuals, driving them into debt, draining their discretionary income, dampening their entrepreneurial spirit by tethering them to jobs with benefits. It also ravaged the bottom lines of corporations; a GM car contained seven times as much health care cost as a Japanese model. And it was on track to bankrupt the Treasury. The Congressional Budget Office warned that if current trends persisted through 2050, federal spending on Medicare and Medicaid would explode from 4 percent to 12 percent of GDP. At those levels the Pentagon really would have to hold bake sales, along with every other federal agency. CBO director Peter Orszag—a Clinton White House economist who had been the first director of the Hamilton Project, and would later become Obama's first budget director—liked to say that our long-term deficit problem was a health care problem.

For all that money, we weren't buying particularly good health. Global rankings of life expectancy and infant mortality suggested that U.S. outcomes were mediocre at best. One study of preventable deaths ranked the United States last among nineteen industrialized countries. The good news was that the U.S. system was so blatantly inefficient that in some areas shrinking costs could raise quality, by reducing unnecessary tests, surgeries, specialist visits, and hospital stays.

Some of those areas required reforms of the entire system, reforms that would consume a year of Obama's presidency. But some of those areas required relatively uncontroversial investments that members of both parties had been talking about for years, investments that would get slipped into the Recovery Act.

The most obvious area was information technology. In an era of online banking, shopping, and dating, health care was our least computerized industry. The practice of medicine was a high-tech world of genomics, robotics, and artificial organs, but very few doctors used electronic medical records. David Blumenthal, another Harvard professor advising Obama, had been skeptical when his own hospital went digital; he liked his prescription pad and didn't mind scribbling X-ray requests in triplicate. But he found it helped to have instant access to medical histories and test results when he got late-night calls at home. And one day, as he discharged a patient with a prescription for the sulfa drug Bactrim, a bright red alert flashed across his screen: ALLERGIC TO SULFA.

"My career flashed before my eyes," he recalls. "I came to understand that information is the lifeblood of medicine, and health IT is destined to be its circulatory system."

By 2007, everyone seemed to understand this. All the presidential candidates in both parties were pledging to boost health IT. Several bipartisan bills were floating around Congress, and Hillary and Newt Gingrich were both hailing electronic medicine as the future of health care. But in most of the country, doctors still had to be in the same room to discuss the same file. Every minute, redundant new tests were ordered because old results weren't instantly available. Nurses and doctors wasted countless hours filling out and searching for paperwork, and atrocious penmanship still killed.

Like energy efficiency, health IT was the kind of no-brainer that appealed to Obama's hyperrational side. It seemed absurd that German doctors used laptops while American doctors used clipboards. He told his health advisers: If everyone agrees we should do this, let's do it. Bush had spent about $100 million on health IT; Obama proposed an eye-popping $50 billion over five years, and pledged that every American would have an electronic medical record by 2014. "I don't care if it's Hillary's idea," he told one adviser. "It's a good idea!"

Health experts believed better information was an even more urgent need than better information technology, which was why Obama also embraced the unglamorous cause of "comparative effectiveness research." Less than half of U.S. medical treatment was backed by solid evidence of what works; to a shocking extent, we were flying blind. To get a drug approved, pharmaceutical companies merely had to prove it worked better than a placebo, not better than any other drug or treatment. To get most medical devices approved, manufacturers just had to prove they weren't harmful.

The result was the world's least data-driven $2 trillion industry. No one knew if angioplasty or bypass surgery worked better on clogged arteries, or when blood-thinning drugs were preferable to a procedure, or which blood thinners worked best for which patients. This cluelessness had major cost and quality implications. Studies by Dartmouth researchers suggested that 30 percent of U.S. care was unnecessary, but nobody knew which 30 percent. *Consumer Reports* had compiled evidence that some generic drugs were as good or better than expensive name brands, and some hospitals had virtually eliminated line infections by enforcing simple to-do lists for nurses. But those tidbits of evidence were rare, and the efforts to spread them nationwide were paltry—especially compared to the mega-dollar marketing campaigns of drug and medical device companies.

Again, this didn't seem like a partisan issue. Gingrich coauthored an op-ed in the *New York Times* with Senator John Kerry, the 2004 Democratic presidential candidate, and Oakland A's general manager Billy Beane, the stats-head made famous by *Moneyball*, titled "How to Take American Health Care from Worst to First." The answer, they agreed, was comparative effectiveness research. "Remarkably, a doctor today can get more data on the starting third baseman on his fantasy baseball team than on the effectiveness of life-and-death medical procedures," they wrote.

This offended Obama's data-loving sensibilities, and he promised to make comparative effectiveness a priority. As he later explained, it wasn't brain surgery: "It's an attempt to say to patients, you know what, we've looked at some objective studies out here, concluding that the blue pill, which costs half as much as the red pill, is just as effective, so you might want to get the blue one. And if a provider is pushing the red one on you, then you should at least ask some important questions."

Long before he was ever accused of engineering a government takeover of medicine or pulling the plug on Grandma, Obama knew reinventing health care would be a heavy lift. Democrats had dreamed of universal coverage since the New Deal, and he expected nasty ideological fights. But some policies seemed elementary. Everyone knew the United States faced severe shortages of nurses and primary care doctors; why not offer training and scholarships for understaffed professions? It was no secret that only four cents of every medical dollar went to prevention and wellness; why not try to help more patients avoid the chronic illnesses like diabetes and heart disease that ate up 80 cents?

Politicians always included these hardy perennials in their position papers. What if someone actually did something about them?

Education: Reform for "These Kids"

The sorry state of our public schools was yet another perpetual crisis.

Politicians constantly yakked about the children—apparently, they're our future—but we still had some of the developed world's worst dropout rates. Only half our nine-year-olds could multiply or divide. Only half our teenagers understood fractions. And the cost of college tuition, like the cost of energy and health care, was soaring out of reach. Obama saw these failures, like our energy and health care failures, as affronts to the American dream as well as roadblocks to global competitiveness, morally and economically unacceptable.

Like most liberals, Obama believed public education was underfunded. As a boy in Hawaii, he received a scholarship to a posh private academy, a springboard to the elite institutions of higher learning he attended with the help of federal student loans. As an organizer in Chicago's ghetto, he saw a darker side of education, working in overcrowded schools that lacked textbooks and toilet paper, schools where computers seemed like unimaginable luxuries, schools where malnourished and illiterate children lost their innocence. And as a senator, he heard kids denounce budget cuts that ended their day at 1:30 P.M. "They wanted more school," he marveled. So as a candidate, Obama promised more money to renovate schools, expand early childhood education, and make college more affordable.

At times, though, Obama strayed from the traditional liberal script, warning that money alone would not clean up the mess.

In Chicago, Obama had seen too many undereducated kids, and too many burned-out teachers and administrators who made excuses for habitual failure. "Few of these educators sent their own children to public schools; they knew too much for that," he wrote. "But they would defend the status quo with the same skill and vigor as their white counterparts of two decades before." They spoke of "these kids," not "our kids," as in "these kids can't learn." They blamed drug-addled parents, gang-infested neighborhoods, "the system." It's tough to get Obama mad, but they managed. When he saw These Kids with absentee fathers, living with grandparents and single moms, relying on food stamps—kids, in other words, like the young Barack Obama—he wanted to make sure they got the same chance to thrive.

"It's more than an intellectual issue for him," says his pickup basketball buddy Arne Duncan, the former Chicago schools chief who became his education secretary. "It's personal. It's visceral."

Obama concluded that bold reform—paying teachers based on student performance, promoting charter schools, forcing schools to meet higher standards, demanding accountability through measurable results—was the only hope for These Kids. So even though it was blasphemy to powerful Democratic teachers unions, he supported the lofty goals of Bush's No Child Left Behind law, like putting excellent teachers in every classroom, as well as its accountability measures, like new powers to shut down failing schools. No Child was also a rare example of the bipartisan cooperation Obama admired, a compromise that Bush crafted in 2001 with Ted Kennedy and the leaders of the House education committee, conservative Republican John Boehner of Ohio and liberal Democrat George Miller of California. "Crazy me, I thought a new president deserved a chance to succeed," Miller recalls.

No Child swiftly became unpopular—partly because the Republicans never funded it, partly because parents and teachers loathed its standardized tests. During the campaign, Obama fired up Democratic crowds with swipes at Bush for "labeling a school and its students as failures one day and then abandoning them the next." But he never said No Child was a bad idea. He called it a "starting point."

He was a bit slippery about the ending point. Education reformers loved his rhetoric about accountability and charters, and his heretical suggestion that ineffective teachers should lose their jobs. They took heart in his friendship with Duncan, a hero of the movement. But they weren't sure how hard he was willing to fight the defenders of the status quo in his party. They knew that behind the scenes, he had warned the reformers on his team not to "poke the unions in the eye," and a few of his advisers were old-guard union sympathizers. His speeches tended to emphasize more-money carrots rather than get-tough policy sticks. And he seemed suspiciously optimistic about "collaboration," as if bringing together teachers, administrators, and other stakeholders could magically overcome obstacles to student achievement.

But he did talk purty. He waxed lyrical about education as the rocket of opportunity that launched the biracial son of a teenage mom to the U.S. Senate, the safeguard for America's meritocratic idea that you don't need to be born rich to get ahead: "I'm running for president to give the young sisters out there born with a gift for invention the chance to become the next Orville and Wilbur Wright; to give the young boy out there who wants to create a life-saving cure the chance to be the next Jonas Salk; to give the child out there whose imagination has been sparked by the wonders of the Internet the chance to become the next Bill Gates." Knowledge was the currency of the information age, and Obama described school reform as the only way to prepare kids for a wired economy where they'd compete with anyone with an Internet connection anywhere in the world. While two thirds of all new jobs required higher education or advanced training, our percentage of young adults with college degrees fell "somewhere between Bulgaria and Costa Rica." China was graduating four times as many engineers. We couldn't keep doing the same things—giving inept teachers life tenure, propping up dropout factories, dumbing down standards to put smiley faces on mediocrity—and expect different results.

Our schools, Obama said, "will help determine not only whether our children have the chance to fulfill their God-given potential, or whether our workers have the chance to build a better life for their families, but whether our nation will remain in the 21st century the kind of global economic leader we were in the 20th century."

That was Obama's general critique of the Bush economy: Ordinary families were losing ground, and the United States was losing its edge. Energy, health care, and education were big parts of the problem—but not the whole problem.

The Economy: "We're All in This Together"

Obama opened his first major economic speech with another FDR story. Speaking at Nasdaq headquarters in September 2007, he reminded his audience of financial executives that seventy-five years earlier, as the Depression raged, Roosevelt had called for a national "reappraisal of values" in a San Francisco campaign speech. "This vision of America would require change that went beyond replacing a failed president," Obama pointedly recalled. Just as FDR replaced Herbert Hoover's you're-on-your-own ethic with a spirit of common purpose, "the idea that we're all in this together," Obama wanted to replace Bush's Ownership Society with a renewed commitment to shared prosperity.

Again, the media focused on Obama's in-your-face challenge to Wall Street to accept stricter oversight. But again, his deeper message was his call for a new reappraisal of values. The stock market had just hit an all-time high, but wages had been flat throughout the Bush years, with income inequality reaching its highest level since the Gilded Age. The average CEO made almost as much per day as the average worker made per year, and the manufacturing sector was at its lowest employment level since 1950; Obama spoke of laid-off factory workers competing with their teenagers for minimum wage jobs at Walmart. And new data had just revealed the first monthly job losses in four years. If an upturn had failed to boost the middle class, what would a downturn do?

"We certainly do not face a test of the magnitude that Roosevelt's generation did," Obama said. "But we are tested still."

At the time, a long-simmering mess involving dodgy subprime mortgages had just boiled into the broader markets. While Federal Reserve chairman Ben Bernanke had assured Congress the subprime chaos "seems likely to be contained," and Bush was still predicting "high growth" for 2008, the United States had just entered the first stage of the worst financial implosion since the Depression.

But nobody knew that yet. When Obama visited Wall Street, his economic focus was still the long term. And his economic strategy was giving a break to the middle class, as well as low-income workers hoping to join the middle class. Bush's trickle-down approach had produced spectacular profits for oil companies and health insurers, as well as the bond traders and investment bankers in the audience at Nasdaq, but too many Americans were struggling to pay their bills.

"That pain," Obama warned, "has a way of trickling up."

It wasn't Bush's fault that U.S. corporations kept outsourcing work to countries with cheap labor and lavish government incentives, replacing workers with robots and other technologies that didn't demand pensions, and showering bonuses on CEOs who slashed payrolls. Like our dirty energy habit, broken health care system, and declining schools, those trends all predated the Bush presidency. The days when a high school dropout could land a factory job and enjoy middle-class security on a single income with the same employer for the rest of his life were long gone, and Obama never claimed he'd bring them back.

Obama's critique of Bush was not that he created these long-term challenges, but that he ignored them—and sometimes made them worse. The heart of the critique was the reverse Robin Hood effect of Bush's 2001 and 2003 tax cuts, which vaporized the surplus he inherited from Clinton to give wealthy people their money back. Bush returned more cash to the top 1 percent of taxpayers than the bottom 80 percent combined—the same top 1 percent that enjoyed almost two thirds of all U.S. income gains during his presidency. Families earning over $3 million a year received over 450 times as much as the median tax-payer, and the genetic-lottery-winning heirs of the super-rich received multimillion-dollar windfalls from the near-elimination of estate taxes. Meanwhile, the 35 million low-income workers who didn't earn enough to pay income taxes but were still on the hook for Social Security and Medicare payroll taxes, gas taxes, and other taxes received zilch. In a speech at Brookings the day after his Nasdaq talk, Obama recounted what his wealthiest campaign adviser, the billionaire investor Warren Buffett, had told him: "If there's class warfare going on in America, then my class is winning."

Bush's theory, the Republican Party's theory, saw taxes on investors and businesses as the ultimate drag on growth. But that philosophy had flunked a series of reality tests. Republicans had thundered that Clinton's modest tax hikes on high earners would tank the economy, and had crowed that Bush's tax cuts would unleash a boom. Then impressive growth throughout the Clinton years gave way to anemic growth during the Bush years. What was the point of showering all that money on "job creators," as the GOP called top-bracket taxpayers, if they weren't going to create jobs? In *The Audacity of Hope*, Obama suggested that when your drapes cost more than an average worker's yearly salary, you can afford to pay a bit more in taxes so that every child has the same opportunities. At Brookings, he proposed to end all the Bush tax cuts targeting the upper brackets, while closing tax loopholes for hedge fund managers, oil companies, and other well-wired interests.

But Obama had no intention of campaigning as a tax hiker. His mar-quee proposal was a "refundable" tax credit for 95 percent of American workers, including those 35 million workers who didn't earn enough to pay income taxes. Unless your income was in the top 5 percent, Obama would refund $500 of your payroll taxes, up to $1,000 per family. He called it the Making Work Pay credit, because it would swing the pendulum back from rewarding wealth toward rewarding work.

The Beltway was not impressed. Columnists like Ruth Marcus of the *Washington Post* dismissed Making Work Pay as an $80 billion pander, "more of the same old Democratic campaign playbook." What kind of hypocrite attacks Bush for creating deficits with unaffordable handouts to the rich, then argues for expanding those deficits with unaffordable handouts to everyone else? But Obama thought it was only fair to return some cash to the families still waiting for Bush's handouts to the investor class to trickle down. And he suspected that when those families felt insecure about their homes and jobs, when their costs and debts increased faster than their wages, the rest of America's consumer-driven economy would eventually suffer—including the investor class. Making Work Pay was a first step toward getting prosperity to trickle up again, to do a better job of growing the pie as well as sharing the pie.

"In this modern, interconnected economy," Obama said at Nasdaq, "there is no dividing line between Main Street and Wall Street."

This thinking now represented a near-consensus within the Democratic Party. In the 1990s, a battle had raged between the party's Wall Street wing of corporate-friendly, deficit-conscious centrists, led by Robert Rubin at Treasury, and its Main Street wing of union-friendly, fairness-conscious liberals, led by Robert Reich at Labor. Politically, Rubin won the "battle of the Bobs," persuading Clinton to focus on balanced budgets; Reich's pleas for public investments were largely ignored. But intellectually, after Reich retreated to Berkeley and Rubin landed at Citigroup, the Bush era's combination of fiscal irresponsibility and growing inequality created a cease-fire. By 2007, even the fierce market economist Larry Summers, Rubin's ally and successor at Treasury, had concluded that middle-class insecurity was "the defining issue of our time," warning that the widening chasm between the rich and everyone else threatened the capitalist system. A magazine profile about

"Larry Summers's Evolution" noted that he "sounds, strangely enough, a little like Bob Reich."

Sure, Summers was trying to reinvent himself as a Democratic wise man after a furor over his overly provocative remarks about women in science had forced him to resign the Harvard presidency. But he hadn't changed. The country had changed. He didn't have to be warm and cuddly to see that the economic tide was only lifting yachts. And the surpluses he and his fellow Rubinites had worked so hard to build had been frittered away—not on the Reich-style spending schemes they had spent so much time fighting, but on givebacks to the well-off and a quagmire in Iraq. In retrospect, investments in crumbling infrastructure and middle-class security no longer seemed so profligate. At least the country would have had something to show for them.

So these days, most Democrats sounded a little like Bob Reich, and Obama was no exception. Even without a surplus, he believed we needed to make strategic investments to outcompete our economic rivals. And if "strategic investments" sounded like Democratic code for "big spending," that didn't mean they weren't needed.

His investment strategy began with the first three pillars of that "new foundation for growth," lowering energy, health, and tuition costs while nurturing the clean-energy sector, computerizing the medical sector, and modernizing the education sector. But it extended wherever he thought public dollars could boost long-term output. He proposed to double spending on research, to make sure we would still lead the world in innovation. He aimed to double support for domestic manufacturing, to make sure we would still make stuff in America.

After fiascos like the levee collapses in New Orleans and a bridge collapse in Minneapolis, Obama also pledged to upgrade our infrastructure, from congested roads and runways to deteriorating dams and sewers. He was especially keen on new-economy infrastructure like broadband and high-speed rail; our global ranking for high-speed Internet access had plunged from first to fifteenth, while our intercity passenger rail remained a global joke. Obama also promised better public works, not just more public works. The Bush era's biggest infrastructure legislation, a $286 billion transportation bill called SAFETEA-LU, was a case study in bad governance, showering money on states without regard for national needs, financing new sprawl roads in sparsely populated areas while neglecting repairs to crowded urban transit systems. It was larded with a record 6,376 pet-project earmarks like the infamous Bridge to Nowhere inserted by Alaska congressman Don Young, who also named the entire bill for his wife Lu. Obama proposed to supplement the traditional asphalt-industrial complex with an independent "infrastructure bank" that would select projects by merit, a radical concept in this porky sector.

On the surface, America still seemed okay. The Dow was soaring. Unemployment was below 5 percent. But Obama saw our rickety bridges, slow trains, and obsolete grid—as well as our dropout rates, health-induced bankruptcies, and flat wages—as evidence of a country falling apart. We had done a swell job helping billionaires buy drapes, but we had neglected our common interests. We had failed to fix our national roof while the sun was shining, and now it looked like rain.

Obama was always careful to point out that government couldn't solve every problem. But he knew from his own experiences with food stamps and student loans how Uncle Sam could help bring the American dream within reach. He also knew from history how government had helped launch high-growth, high-wage industries like aerospace, semiconductors, and biotech. And as much as he admired the free market, he didn't see how it could fix our leaky pipes. He was convinced that some market failures would never be solved without government.

And the worst market failure since the Depression was coming soon.

THREE

The Collapse

Larry Summers liked to say that in economics, things take longer to happen than you think they will, and then happen faster than you thought they could.

By December 2007, bad things were starting to happen. The construction industry had stopped constructing. Lenders weren't lending. The economy had slipped into recession, although no one knew that yet; the Blue Chip forecast, the conventional wisdom of the econometrics world, still expected modest growth in the coming year. *National Review* supply-sider Larry Kudlow was still crowing that "the Bush boom is alive and well," ridiculing "the doom and gloom from the economic pessimistas. . . . These guys are going to end up with egg on their faces." But Summers, a leading pessimista, was already warning of a "perfect storm," perhaps the worst recession since the early 1980s. In a speech at Brookings, he suggested his own doom and gloom might even be overly optimistic: "History has cautioned that situations like the current one are likely to surprise on the downside for a considerable time."

In Washington, the conversation had turned to short-term stimulus, as it did whenever the economy turned sour. At the time, countercyclical Keynesian stimulus, a staple of introductory economics classes, was not overly controversial. Almost everyone seemed to agree that when the goods-and-services engine known as aggregate demand stalled, government could help get it humming again by injecting money into the economy, either by taxing less or spending more. All the major presidential candidates were assembling fiscal stimulus plans. Republican Mitt Romney proposed the most aggressive plan, $250 billion worth of tax cuts; he also criticized McCain's call for short-term spending cuts as the opposite of stimulus.

Some economists thought "monetary stimulus" from Federal Reserve interest rate cuts would be enough to reverse this particular slump. Some conservatives opposed any new spending that would make the government a bigger player in the economy. And some deficit hawks fretted about further increases in the federal debt; Keynes had prescribed fiscal expansion during emergencies, but also fiscal responsibility during non-emergencies, which hadn't happened under Bush.

Still, the general question of whether fiscal stimulus could help create jobs and revive output in the short term wasn't much of a question back then. The question was how to do it properly, a question Keynes had never fully answered.

Raising Keynes

Keynes wrote his masterpiece, *The General Theory of Employment, Interest and Money*, during the depths of the Depression. It's full of revolutionary macroeconomic concepts, like the paradox of thrift, the marginal propensity to consume, and the Keynesian multiplier. But it's mostly a book about depressions—how they happen, and how to prevent or end them. Summers thought it should have been titled *A Specific Theory of Collapsing Employment, Interest and Money.*

Before the Great Depression, most economists believed markets were automatically self-correcting. They assumed all downturns would eventually create a virtuous cycle: cheaper prices would spur consumption, cheaper money would spur investment, and lower wages would spur hiring. It was an elegant theory, but after the crash of 1929, reality didn't cooperate. President Hoover's treasury secretary, Andrew Mellon, expressed the orthodoxy of the day when he described the Depression as a useful corrective to sloth and excess that would "purge the rottenness out of the system." If you weren't a Mellon, though, the Depression was pretty rotten.

Keynes saw recessions as simple failures of demand for goods and services, not as some kind of karmic retribution for moral turpitude. And he saw how a convulsive shock like Black Tuesday could create a vicious rather than virtuous cycle: lost income led to lost confidence, which led to hoarding of cash, which led to layoffs and cutbacks that left productive workers and equipment idle, which further depressed income as well as confidence, and so on down the drain. Part of the problem was a real deterioration of purchasing power. Workers without jobs couldn't spend as much, even when prices were low, and businesses without customers couldn't invest or hire as much, even when interest rates and wages were low. The other part of the problem was psychological, what Keynes dubbed "animal spirits." Workers worried about losing their jobs and businesses worried about losing their customers would tighten their belts, too, perpetuating the paralyzing feedback loop. There's a reason economic terms like "depression," "panic," "uncertainty," and "demand" have psychological roots. Markets really can get jittery. The economy really is a confidence game.

Keynes concluded that the solution to both parts of the problem was an aggressive government effort to revive demand, an infusion of cash and confidence. Saving had always been considered a purely good thing, but Keynes saw that in a crisis what was needed was more spending. More saving would just deepen the crisis. (That's the paradox of thrift.) And when consumers and businesses were too broke or too scared to spend, government would have to be the spender of last resort. Budget deficits had always been considered a purely bad thing, but Keynes saw that when the private sector hunkered down and demand dried up, the public sector needed to send more money into the economy than it took back in taxes. Once consumers started spending again, businesses would hire more workers and make new investments, and the virtuous cycle could begin anew.

Keynes wasn't rejecting capitalism, just the laissez-faire assumption that a shattered economy could always heal itself. He wasn't recommending a new car, just a new "magneto," or ignition system, a jump-start for a stalled economic engine. And he wasn't too fussy about how that magneto was designed, as long as it got cash to flow from the government to the people. He suggested the Treasury could even "fill old bottles with bank notes, bury them at suitable depths in disused coal mines," then watch an inevitable money-mining boom create jobs and economic activity.

"It would, indeed, be more sensible to build houses and the like, but . . . the above would be better than nothing," he wrote.

But not all magnetos are created equal. Burying cash was not an alluring option. After an epic real estate bust that left entire subdivisions vacant, "building houses and the like" didn't seem so sensible, either.

So what was government to do? Traditionally, Republicans equated stimulus with tax cuts—and sure enough, the Bush White House, which would have prescribed tax cuts for a sore throat, was looking into new ones, while calling for a permanent extension of the original Bush tax cuts that were scheduled to expire in 2011. Generally, liberal Democrats preferred stimulus in the form of spending on liberal Democratic priorities—and true to form, Speaker Nancy Pelosi was pushing to cram extra cash into food stamps, public works, and renewable energy.

Summers, neither a Republican nor a liberal Democrat, did not think the question of how to stimulate the economy in the short term should be answered ideologically. He thought it should be answered correctly. At Brookings, he proposed a technocratic approach to Keynesian stimulus that has dominated the debate ever since. A stimulus package, he argued, should be *timely, targeted,* and *temporary.*

In other words, it should kick in fast enough to help cure the downturn; stimulus that isn't timely can overheat an economy that's already rebounding and unleash inflation. It should target the biggest economic bang for each buck; fortuitously, the struggling families who need it most are the families most likely to spend it quickly. (That's what Keynes meant by a high marginal propensity to consume.) Finally, stimulus should spur short-term growth without unnecessarily expanding long-term deficits, which could boost interest rates, slow down growth, and defeat the whole purpose of the exercise. Romney's $250 billion plan would have amounted to nearly 2 percent of GDP, but Summers, worried about red ink, suggested that politicians should think "two digits, not three," and let the Fed do most of the work.

The allure of fiscal stimulus from Congress was its ability to pump dollars quickly into the pockets of consumers and the coffers of businesses, as opposed to monetary stimulus from the Fed, which would pump dollars into the vaults of banks that were reluctant to lend at a time when businesses were reluctant to borrow. But fiscal stimulus had a downside, too. It would only work if a bitterly divided political system could pass timely, targeted, and temporary legislation in a hurry.

"Poorly designed fiscal stimulus," Summers wrote in a column that would be quoted frequently a year later, "can have worse side effects than the disease that is to be cured."

Stimulus, Round One

In January 2008, Hillary Clinton released her plan to juice the weakening economy. To Obama's economists, it looked like a textbook example of poorly designed stimulus. The centerpiece was $25 billion to help low-income families with heating bills, a tenfold expansion of an existing program, an administrative nightmare that made Jeffrey Liebman, yet another Harvard professor on Obama's team, wonder if Hillary had misplaced a decimal point. The money wouldn't go out until the next winter, which didn't seem timely at all. Austan Goolsbee, a thirty-eight-year-old Obama adviser from the University of Chicago who was new to presidential politics, was shocked by the economic malpractice. "A year later is not stimulus!" he kept saying.

Goolsbee, who would later advise Obama in the White House, and Liebman, who would become a deputy in his budget office, had cooked up Making Work Pay over a weekend. Now they had two days to finalize a plan for real short-term stimulus—the first dress rehearsal for the Recovery Act. "It was my only true all-nighter of the campaign," Liebman recalls. "But we knew we were going to blow Clinton's plan away. We just stuck to the basics—timely, targeted, and temporary."

The three T's were suddenly the quasi-official test of the stimulus strategies flying around Washington. And some strategies flunked.

Regardless of the merits, making the Bush tax cuts permanent would be the opposite of timely, targeted, and temporary. It wouldn't take effect until 2011; it would help well-off families with low propensities to spend; and it would explode the deficit. Permanent corporate tax cuts, a key plank of the McCain and Romney plans, also batted 0-for-3. A new Brookings stimulus analysis titled "If, When, How" rated both strategies "ineffective or counterproductive," while a Moody's Economy.com analysis of how much growth various policies would produce per dollar—the Keynesian multiplier—scored both below 50 cents. The Brookings report was written by two Clinton administration economists—Jason Furman, a Summers protégé who was running the Hamilton Project, and Doug Elmendorf, another former Summers student—but the Moody's author, Mark Zandi, was a McCain campaign adviser.

By contrast, policies benefiting lower-income families provided much more bang for the buck, because the poor can't afford to hoard. Increases in food stamps earned the highest multiplier from Moody's, adding $1.73 in output for each dollar in cost. Extending unemployment benefits, which normally expire after six months, came in second. Those strategies batted 3-for-3: The benefits would go out instantly, target families likely to spend, and fade once the economy improved. One-time tax rebates also got decent marks, but only if those 35 million low-income workers who didn't pay income tax were eligible. Many Republicans saw refundable tax cuts as glorified welfare—the *Wall Street Journal* editorial page referred to the low-income recipients as "lucky duckies"—but a new CBO report noted that making rebates nonrefundable "substantially reduces the cost-effectiveness of the stimulus."

Public works also had high bang for the buck, but economists didn't think they were timely. Under Clinton, Summers had been a savage infrastructure critic, and while the new invest-in-America Larry was more sympathetic to moving dirt and pouring concrete, the old crunch-the-numbers Larry still doubted its value as stimulus. Peter Orszag's CBO also dumped on infrastructure's glacial pace in another little-noticed aside that would resurface a year later, noting that "public works involve long start-up lags," and "even those that are 'on the shelf' generally cannot be undertaken quickly enough to provide timely stimulus."

There was one more three-T idea: aid to states. As the downturn shriveled their revenues, state balanced budget requirements were poised to force austerity measures at the worst possible time, an "anti-stimulus" that would drain more money out of the economy. Bailing out cash-strapped states could provide a jolt of anti-anti-stimulus, preventing layoffs of public employees, cuts in services for the vulnerable, and tax hikes on everyone. But the politics were awful. Why would Congress want to help states close their fiscal gaps by expanding the nation's? And why would a Democratic Congress want to help Republican governors fix their state deficits, so they could look virtuous while scolding Washington about national deficits? Senate majority leader Harry Reid of Nevada had little interest in bailing out scandal-ridden Nevada's GOP governor Jim Gibbons, whose potential challengers included Reid's son Rory, and Pelosi felt similarly disinclined to do favors for GOP governor Arnold Schwarzenegger of California.

But Obama's economists focused on the three T's. So their plan included state aid and unemployment benefits, while popular but slow infrastructure projects didn't make the cut. The centerpiece was a refundable tax rebate for almost all workers, a one-time version of Making Work Pay. Overall, the plan cost $75 billion—two digits, not three—with a trigger to go to $120 billion if the economy didn't rebound. It was somewhat bigger than Hillary's plan, but the *Times* columnist and Nobel laureate economist Paul Krugman cautioned his

liberal readers that it "tilted to the right" by including tax cuts and leaving out alternative energy: "I know that Mr. Obama's supporters hate to
hear this, but he really is less progressive than his rivals on matters of
domestic policy."

Obama explained that he loved alternative energy. It just wasn't the
fastest stimulus. "That's not going to deal with the immediate crisis," he
said. His campaign handouts were even more emphatic about three-T-
only: "The goal should be to lessen the pain that would occur from an
economy-wide slowdown, not to use economic hardship as a rationale
for enacting an ideologically driven policy agenda." Those words would
resonate a year later, too.

But in early 2008, Obama was the only candidate with a stimulus
plan that was all about stimulus. When the *Washington Post*'s Marcus
graded the campaign proposals, Obama won easily with an A-minus.
Clinton got a C-plus, McCain a D-plus.

"The moment for stimulus will be long past by Inauguration Day,"
Marcus wrote, a line that wouldn't resonate at all a year later. "But as a
way of judging how candidates balance politics and policy . . . the proposals offer a revealing report card."

The moment for stimulus had arrived. But it depended on a quick
bipartisan deal, which seemed about as likely as a quick Middle East
peace treaty.

Washington really was as polarized as the talking heads said it was.
In Congress, almost every vote was a party-line vote. House redistricting had produced reliably Democratic and Republican seats, encouraging incumbents to pander to their bases, rewarding extremism while
punishing cooperation. Members flew home every weekend and spent
their spare time fund-raising during the week, so they no longer hung
out in noncombat situations; Ray LaHood, an Illinois Republican who
would become Obama's transportation secretary, had organized bipartisan get-to-know-you retreats, but they were canceled for lack of
interest. The rise of talk radio, cable blab shows, political blogs, and
the twenty-four-hour news cycle only widened the divide, encouraging

increasingly sensational attacks in much the same way SportsCenter encourages increasingly sensational dunks. Every day was election day, and in a zero-sum game, party discipline was paramount; if the blue team said the sky was blue, the red team called a point of order.

By 2008, Bush's approval rating had collapsed, but he was staying the partisan course, starting the year by vetoing a Democratic expansion of health coverage for uninsured children even though it had some Republican support. Democrats weren't in a compromising mood, either. They had taken back Congress in 2006 with a Bush-bashing message, and it's tough to cut deals with someone you've portrayed as a heartless Neanderthal; it makes your base wonder how you could work with such a monster, and independent voters wonder if you exaggerated his monstrosity. Anyway, Speaker Pelosi, an organic-kale San Francisco liberal with a grating voice that made her sound like the nanny state come to life, was just as polarizing as the swaggering Texas cowboy in the White House. She was nails on the blackboard to Republicans, a screechy symbol of lefty extremism. Conservatives loathed her, and many of the congressional moderates who merely disliked her had been defeated in the Democratic wave.

But Pelosi, the daughter of an Italian American machine pol from blue-collar Baltimore, was much more pragmatic than her banshee-lefty reputation. Behind the scenes, she was a master vote counter and a surprisingly deft coalition builder. Her members were much more ideologically diverse than the House Republicans, so she had to keep business-friendly New Democrats and tight-fisted Blue Dog Democrats on her reservation. At times, she could be as intransigent as advertised—her no-compromise leadership helped kill Bush's plan to privatize Social Security—but she came from an urban-boss tradition of cutting deals that got things done. As shrill a partisan as she was, it wasn't her nature to sit on her hands to try to reap the political benefits of a recession on Bush's watch. She was an activist. She liked to act.

For a change, Pelosi had negotiating partners willing to negotiate. Bush's treasury secretary, former Goldman Sachs CEO Henry Paulson, was a moderate Republican who understood the art of the deal and badly wanted stimulus. And Pelosi's counterpart, House minority leader John Boehner, usually followed the administration's lead. Boehner was a conservative K Street Republican whose best friends were mostly corporate lobbyists—a self-made millionaire who got into politics because he hated taxes and government interference with his plastics company. But he was a team player, an amiable Dean Martin type who spent most of his time chain-smoking Camel Extra Lights, drinking Merlot, and playing golf. After growing up in a home with eleven siblings and one bathroom, he was comfortable with compromise. He had tried to rein in the GOP's fire-breathers while serving on Gingrich's leadership team, and he had helped forge the No Child Left Behind deal.

So there was at least a chance for cooperation, especially since stimulus wouldn't involve painful sacrifices. Politicians usually enjoy spending money and cutting taxes in election years.

On January 18, Bush visited a lawnmower factory to unveil a $150 billion stimulus plan, "a shot in the arm to keep a fundamentally strong economy healthy." Obama complained that the plan's nonrefundable tax rebates would do nothing for the working poor, but otherwise Paulson kept it relatively free of ideology; the *Post*'s Marcus gave it a B-minus. It quickly became the basis for bipartisan talks in the House's Board of Education room, the tiny hideaway where the legendary speaker Sam Rayburn used to "educate" members who crossed him.

At first, the negotiations just highlighted the gulf between the parties. Pelosi suggested all kinds of spending programs for the needy, while Boehner wanted all kinds of tax breaks for businesses. Boehner groused that the goal wasn't supposed to be redistributing income. Pelosi snapped that the goal was supposed to be preventing "*your* potential recession." One Boehner aide scribbled his partisan view of the debate in his notes: "D caucus, Tax Receivers. R conference, Taxpayers."

But it took just two days to bridge the gulf. The key moment came when Boehner offered to make the Bush rebates refundable if Pelosi dropped her spending demands. Pelosi agreed, as long as high earners wouldn't be eligible for rebates and extremely low earners would.

They soon worked out a simple deal to send checks of up to $1,200 to all low- and middle-income families, plus $300 per child. Boehner also won a tax break encouraging businesses to buy equipment. "It's almost surreal to think how rational those negotiations were," recalls Pelosi's tax aide, Arshi Siddiqui. The House overwhelmingly approved the compromise, proving bipartisanship was still possible when both sides wanted a deal.

Pelosi urged Majority Leader Reid to ram the House agreement through the Senate, to get the rebates into the mail fast. Bush had vowed to veto the spending items that Democrats wanted, and Pelosi worried that trying to resurrect them would just create gridlock. But senators, who tend to view themselves as distinguished solons, never like pressure from the House, which they tend to view as a sandbox for riffraff. Reid was one of the least pretentious senators, a former amateur boxer who grew up without running water in a small town, but he told the speaker to back off. She didn't. When Senate Democrats plumped up the House bill with the spending add-ons she had failed to extract from Boehner, Pelosi's staff secretly strategized with Senate Republicans to salvage the original deal. This mistrust among Hill Democrats would be another recurring theme. House Democrats joke that Republicans are just the opposition; the Senate is the enemy.

Reid's pumped-up stimulus received fifty-nine votes. But it needed sixty to overcome a Republican filibuster led by Minority Leader Mitch McConnell of Kentucky, yet another harbinger of events to come. Reid relented, and the Senate grudgingly passed the House bill virtually intact. On February 13, Pelosi, Boehner, Reid, and McConnell all stood behind Bush as he signed a $168 billion stimulus, the equivalent of the annual Air Force budget. Rebate checks would start going out in May.

"You know, a lot of folks in America probably were saying it's impossible for those of us in Washington to find common ground," Bush said. He then demonstrated why, interrupting the pre–Valentine's Day lovefest with a swipe at Democrats who had tried to "load up this bill with unrelated programs or unnecessary spending."

Bush's main message was that this "rough patch" would soon pass:

"So long as we pursue pro-growth policies, our economy will prosper, and it will continue to be the marvel of the world."

"Uglier and Uglier"

The rest of 2008 made that rough patch look like a golden era, as the cancer in the U.S. housing market metastasized throughout the global financial system.

The real estate bust had dire implications for trillions of dollars' worth of mortgage-backed securities, which had been sliced, diced, and used as collateral in the overnight lending markets that corporations depended on for ready cash. Now nobody knew what all that paper was worth, which triggered a run on the investment bank Bear Stearns in March. In 1929, a bank run had required an actual run to a bank, but now billions of dollars could be withdrawn with a keystroke. And global finance was so intertwined that the fall of one overleveraged behemoth could drag down the entire system; Bear Stearns had open trades and derivatives contracts with thousands of other firms. So Fed chairman Ben Bernanke, a former Princeton professor and Depression scholar, and Tim Geithner, a former Clinton Treasury official who led the New York Fed, helped J. P. Morgan Chase take over Bear Stearns and stand behind its trades, the first in a series of unprecedented interventions that upended the staid world of central banking.

Meanwhile, millions of homeowners were discovering that their primary asset was suddenly a liability. And their disposable income was being swept away by stratospheric gas prices, which topped $4 a gallon for the first time ever that summer. The turmoil on Wall Street was not yet ravaging Main Street—fortunately, Bush had failed to divert Social Security funds into the market—but retirement accounts were starting to take hits, and unemployment was starting to climb.

By the time Obama clinched the Democratic nomination, it was obvious the economy would be the dominant issue in the fall. It was not obvious this would help Obama. Even though he was running against the Bush economy and its effect on working people, many Democrats fretted about his appeal to blue-collar whites, the "beer-track" voters who preferred Clinton in the primaries. Maybe they'd gravitate toward a war hero like McCain in the general election. Even if you ignored race, Obama seemed more wine-track, an Ivy Leaguer who whined about the price of arugula at Whole Foods, a law professor caught on tape condescending to "bitter" small-town Americans who "cling" to guns and religion in hard times. It was no accident that when Biden was announced as Obama's running mate, the emphasis was less on his Washington experience or foreign policy chops than his middle-class roots, average-Joe sensibility, and daily commute on Amtrak.

But Obama's team welcomed a debate on the economy with McCain, who didn't seem to know how many houses he owned, and was basically running on the Bush agenda. McCain's campaign cochairman, former Texas senator Phil Gramm, declared America was merely in a "mental recession" ginned up by "a nation of whiners," and though he vanished from public view—McCain suggested he'd make a good ambassador to Belarus—his complaint that the media were overhyping bad economic news reflected the campaign's thinking. "It was my job to watch the data, and I kept telling the other economists advising McCain that things were unraveling," Moody's Mark Zandi recalls. "They just didn't buy it." In his stump speeches, McCain kept repeating the Bush line that "the fundamentals of the economy are strong."

Obama knew that was nuts. His economic team—now led by Jason Furman from the Hamilton Project—was telling him the fundamentals of the economy were dreck. Obama was holding regular calls with Rubin, Summers, and other Democratic heavyweights; he was talking to Paulson and Bernanke as well. No one had anything rosy to say. "We could all see this was getting uglier and uglier," adviser Dan Tarullo recalls.

In August, the jobless rate jumped to 6.1 percent, the largest monthly spike since 1981. And in September, Paulson forced the housing giants Fannie Mae and Freddie Mac into receivership, arguably the biggest economics story of the decade before it was overtaken by events. When congressional Democrats clamored for more stimulus,

Bush threatened a veto, saying the first package just needed time to work. McCain took an even harder line, promising to freeze federal spending. On September 14, nine months into the recession, a caustic *Washington Post* essay by McCain adviser Donald Luskin, headlined "Quit Doling Out That Bad-Economy Line," argued that "things today just aren't that bad," that "we're nowhere close" to a recession.

The same day Luskin was spreading his good cheer—and another century-old investment bank, Merrill Lynch, was collapsing into the arms of Bank of America—Obama held his final meeting with his political advisers in Chicago. The main topic was sharpening his economic message now that McCain had pulled even in the polls. But Obama also warned that he was getting scary intelligence from Wall Street: Another bank was on the brink, and a global panic seemed imminent. He made it clear to his hacks that he would do whatever he could to help Bush avoid a disaster; when his top strategist, David Axelrod, noted that bailouts polled terribly, Obama said he wouldn't think about that. He figured acting responsibly would be good politics, anyway. And as he told Paulson, he expected to be president. He hoped to preside over a functioning economy.

"Barack told us: 'By tomorrow, the world will probably have changed,'" recalls Anita Dunn, another strategist. "We were all like: Okaaaaay."

Lehman Brothers collapsed the next day, the largest bankruptcy in American history. Credit markets froze. Stocks tanked. Depositors began an unthinkable run on money market funds, which were supposed to be as secure as savings accounts. Hysteria erupted worldwide, with investors so desperate to park money in safe Treasury bonds that their rates of return fell below zero; people were actually paying the U.S. government to hold their money. Campaigning in Florida, McCain noted the "tremendous turmoil in our financial markets." But he couldn't resist his usual caveat: "Still, the fundamentals of our economy are strong."

Okaaaaay.

"That day marked the end of John McCain's campaign," says Biden, a longtime friend of the Arizona senator. "That poor son-of-a-gun. He was dealt a tough hand."

The next day, the Fed had to bail out AIG, a gigantic insurance company that had fallen down the wormhole selling exotic financial instruments. McCain came out against the bailout, then changed his mind the next day.

The economy was going down, and so was McCain.

At Nasdaq, Obama had tried to warn Wall Street types that carnage on Main Street could create carnage for them. But the reverse was also true. A credit meltdown could make it impossible for ordinary Americans to get home loans, car loans, or business loans. A market meltdown could eviscerate their companies, jobs, and 401(k)s. AIG showed that it could even imperil their insurance policies. The Great Depression began as a financial crisis, but it's remembered for 25 percent unemployment, black-and-white photos of impoverished families, and sagas of suffering like *The Grapes of Wrath*. As Bernanke says, when elephants fall, the grass gets trampled.

"Everyone knows that depressions suck," says Berkeley economist Christina Romer, the Depression scholar who would become Obama's first Council of Economic Advisers chair. "But when you study this stuff, you understand that depressions really, really suck."

Bernanke and Paulson decided the only way to avoid Depression 2.0 would be a mammoth Wall Street rescue. They bluntly warned leaders of both parties that unless Congress quickly backstopped the banking system, the results would make the 1930s look mild. Pelosi balked at bailing out the greed-blinded gamblers of Wall Street without helping Main Street, but Paulson warned that Main Street would be eviscerated if Washington didn't save Wall Street pronto. "Nancy, we're racing to prevent a collapse of the financial markets," he said. "This isn't the time for stimulus."

For the next two weeks, Washington was riveted by the fate of Bush's Troubled Asset Relief Program, a $700 billion bailout for the nation's largest financial institutions. Reid, McConnell, Pelosi, and Boehner all agreed to support TARP, but Boehner struggled to persuade House Republicans to back the rescue. After doing Bush's bidding for eight years, they were choosing an extremely inopportune time to rebel.

Then McCain threw the negotiations into turmoil by dragging the electoral circus to Washington, impulsively announcing he was "suspending" his campaign to help forge a deal, only to change his mind the next day after a surreal White House meeting where he wouldn't even commit to support a deal. While Obama spoke for congressional Democrats, offering constructive suggestions on a path to consensus, McCain sat sullenly at a meeting he had demanded himself. "Obama took command," says one Republican who attended. "He was the only one who seemed presidential—not the president, definitely not McCain." After McCain stunned the room by refusing to take a position, the meeting dissolved into shouting and finger-pointing; Paulson got on his knees to beg the Democrats not to blow up TARP. They didn't, but Pelosi and Reid did stage symbolic votes on new stimulus spending the next day, further poisoning the atmosphere on the Hill. They knew they couldn't pass a law, but they wanted to put Republicans on record against aid for struggling families.

On, September 29, Pelosi marched TARP to the floor, hoping the glare of the spotlight would force Republicans to support it. But her speech blaming Republicans for the crisis only solidified their opposition, as did a barrage of F-bombs from Democratic conference chair Rahm Emanuel, a force of nature from Chicago who would soon become Obama's chief of staff. "Rahm was standing in the middle of the well, frothing at the mouth, accosting people—that's one of the reasons they lost," recalls Congressman Steve LaTourette, an Ohio Republican. The vote failed, and the Dow plummeted a record 778 points.

The crash finally inspired action. The media backlash against Republicans who had whined about Pelosi's speech and Emanuel's antics—as if they had voted to sink the financial system because their feelings were hurt—also helped focus minds. On Wednesday, the Senate passed TARP, sweetened by some tax breaks for racetrack owners, arrow manufacturers, and the like. On Friday, the House reversed course and passed it as well. Obama lobbied dozens of Democrats and persuaded several to flip to yes by promising a new push for stimulus. The Wall Street rescue, he told them, was like patching a hole in a sinking boat to get it to port. When he replaced Bush, Washington would finally help Main Street, and give the boat some proper repairs.

And yes, he meant when, not if.

McCain's erratic response to the crisis, along with his embrace of a suddenly discredited philosophy, sank his candidacy. Obama helped his cause by remaining steady while the world fell apart. But if there were any doubt that 2008 was a change election, it evaporated when the world fell apart. The seventy-two-year-old Republican who had spent half his life in Congress did not look like change.

"Are we sure it's too late to hand this pile of shit to McCain and the party that created it?" Obama bantered with one of his advisers in October.

Probably, the adviser replied.

"Well," Obama cracked, "at least we're buying low."

— FOUR —

"We Were Staring into the Abyss."

Obama's campaign trip to Toledo in October 2008 is best remembered for his run-in with a bald, strapping, tax-averse plumber named Samuel J. Wurzelbacher, who got him to admit he wanted to "spread the wealth around." McCain name-checked "Joe the Plumber" nineteen times during the next debate, and Republicans still repeat the sound bite as proof of Obama's socialism. In fact, his argument for a more progressive tax code was about as socialist as school uniforms are fascist. He told Wurzelbacher he wanted to cut taxes for everyone with an income below $250,000—which included a certain plumber, before the five-minute chat catapulted him onto the conservative lecture circuit— while merely restoring Clinton-era rates on higher earners. Obama also explained that his wealth-spreading philosophy was about economic growth, not just economic justice, that in a demand-driven economy, there's no consumer demand when consumers have no money. It's the opposite of a trickle-down philosophy.

"My attitude is that if the economy's good for folks from the bottom up, it's going to be good for everybody," Obama said. "If you've got a plumbing business, you're going to be better off if you've got a whole bunch of customers who can afford to hire you. Right now everybody's so pinched that business is bad for everybody."

That's the time for stimulus, which was what Obama came to Toledo to talk about. The next day, he unveiled his "Rescue Plan for the Middle Class," an expansion of his January stimulus plan. For all the talk of socialism, its major new feature was a hiring tax credit for businesses, $3,000 for every new full-time employee. "It's a plan that begins with the word on everyone's mind. It's spelled J-O-B-S," Obama said.

The plan didn't get much attention, partly because plans make for dull copy, partly because media etiquette disguised how ambitious the plan was. Reporters described it as a $60 billion proposal, about the same size as the stimulus bills that Pelosi and Reid pushed during the TARP debate. But that's only because the press wasn't counting elements of the plan that Obama had unveiled earlier. Journalistic conventions aside, Obama was proposing to inject $175 billion into the economy, three times as much as the Democrats in Congress.

"By October," Furman says, "the world had changed."

The hole in the economy now looked like a canyon, so more stimulus would be needed to fill it. And recessions sparked by financial distress are much nastier and longer than normal downturns, so the definition of what counted as "timely" stimulus could be stretched. Obama's new plan included public works, like energy-efficient school retrofits as well as typical road and bridge repairs, even though his economic team considered infrastructure projects a leisurely way to move money. Obama even proposed some of the low-income heating aid that his economists had mocked in Hillary Clinton's stimulus proposal.

"We were no longer thinking solely about speed," Goolsbee says. "This was a totally different ball game. We were staring into the abyss: 'Whoa, is this the start of another depression? Is this something that could go on for years?'"

Consumer confidence was at a forty-year low. The Dow was still plunging, the auto industry was hemorrhaging, and Bernanke was blasting out emergency loans as if he were allergic to money. Polls suggested only 5 percent of Americans thought the country was headed in the right direction, and you had to wonder what those 5 percent were smoking. Obama was buying low, all right. In his Toledo speech, he was already trying to temper expectations about the recovery. "I won't pretend this will be easy," he said. "George Bush has dug a deep hole for us. It's going to take a while for us to dig our way out."

He just didn't realize how deep a hole, or how much digging would be required. At the time, $175 billion worth of backfilling seemed extraordinarily aggressive, more than the Pentagon spent that year on the war on terror.

"We thought we were pushing the envelope," recalls Brian Deese, Furman's deputy for economic policy. "It was amazing how fast what was considered substantial kept changing."

Once again, a Washington consensus was emerging for government action. The *Washington Post* reported that "stimulus proposals are proliferating like Halloween pumpkins," and even the conservative *Washington Times* noted widespread agreement that "the next administration should—initially, at least—open its wallet, not tighten its belt." McCain proposed emergency tax cuts, and Bernanke, who usually tiptoed around fiscal issues, urged Congress to enact a "significant" stimulus to prop up the economy. Pelosi and Reid threatened to call Congress back after the election to pass another $150 billion stimulus.

A secret team of Obama advisers was already thinking bigger.

The Shadow Transition

The Obama-Clinton fight was a bitter slog. Clintonites saw Obama as a presumptuous line cutter. Obamans saw Clinton as a poll-driven, say-anything symbol of a broken system. But once the fight was over, Obama ordered his staff to act like it was over. This wasn't just a strategy to win over the Hillary dead-enders who were calling themselves PUMAs (Party Unity My Ass) and vowing to vote for McCain. Obama needed the Clintonites. They were the Democrats with governing experience. He knew he couldn't make change happen without an executive branch that could execute.

Obama's put-the-past-in-the-past approach became a big story after the election, when he chose Hillary to be his secretary of state; tapped Congressman Emanuel, a Clinton White House adviser, to be his chief of staff; and stocked his economic team with Clinton-era veterans like Summers, Geithner, Orszag, and Furman. Quietly, though, Obama had already cast his lot with the Clinton crowd after sewing up the nomination, when he asked John Podesta, President Clinton's former chief of staff, to lead a secret "shadow transition" to prepare for an Obama administration. All nominees do at least some pre-transition planning, but Obama's was by far the most elaborate in history.

Podesta was a logical choice to lead it, a Washington insider who spent the Bush era getting ready for the next Democratic transition. He led the Center for American Progress think tank, a Democratic government-in-exile that was assembling a fifty-six-chapter blueprint advising the next administration how to handle everything from terrorist threats to the Federal Trade Commission. His own book, *The Power of Progress*, included a draft inaugural address for the next Democratic president. And he had learned what not to do by watching the Clinton transition, which bogged down after its first two directors quit to accept cabinet positions. Podesta told Obama he'd run the shadow transition and the official transition but wouldn't accept a permanent job.

Still, Obama loyalists feared that while they were working around the clock to beat McCain, Podesta would be building the architecture for a new quasi-Clinton administration. He never did much to dispel those fears. For example, he recruited President Clinton's EPA head, Carol Browner, to run an energy and environmental policy team; she later became Obama's White House energy and climate czar.

"That's when the old guard started taking over," grouses one Obama campaign aide.

The shadow transition's economic policy team was a case in point. It was a Clinton reunion, led by Bill Daley, a Clinton commerce secretary who would later become Obama's second chief of staff, and Josh Steiner, a Clinton Treasury official. It also included Jack Lew, a Clinton budget director who would be Obama's third chief of staff; Doug Elmendorf, a Clinton Treasury economist who had replaced Furman at the similarly incestuous Hamilton Project, and would soon replace Peter Orszag at the Congressional Budget Office; and Jonathan Orszag, a Clinton White House economist who was Peter's brother. Dan Tarullo, another Clinton economist, and Karen Kornbluh, another Clinton Treasury veteran, were the only representatives from Obamaworld. Robert Greenstein, the founder and longtime head of the liberal Center for Budget and Policy Priorities, was the only team member who hadn't served under Clinton. At an early meeting, Greenstein, a bearded, bespectacled budget analyst out of central casting, endured some ribbing because his PowerPoint slides weren't formatted like everyone else's.

"Guys, I wasn't in the Clinton White House!" he responded.

Podesta ordered the shadow economic team to avoid contact with the campaign, which had more pressing work that fall. (Biden didn't even want to hear about the shadow transition; he was afraid of jinxing the election.) And since secrecy was a must—publicity would make Obama look like he was already measuring the White House drapes— the team didn't do much outreach, either. Its only sounding board was an advisory committee of even more familiar Clinton-era faces: Rubin, Summers, Reich, Clinton economic adviser Laura Tyson, Lew, who doubled as an official team member and unofficial wise man, and just one outsider, Xerox CEO Anne Mulcahy.

"It definitely felt like we were getting the band back together," says one participant.

The band's modest assignment was to produce a few briefing papers to hand off to the post-election transition team, which would presumably be too busy screening job candidates to do much policy analysis. "We figured we'd do some prep work, then once Obama picked his people, they wouldn't care what we had to say," another team member recalls. But once the economy imploded, that prep work took on outsized importance. The next president would have to act with superhero speed to deal with multiple nightmares unfolding in real time. Briefing papers from Washington veterans who were already immersed in those nightmares would be extremely useful.

Lew ran the stimulus prep. Obama would inherit crises in the banking, housing, and auto sectors, but a jobs bill looked like Job One, an "early test of leadership," as Lew noted in one memo. "In addition to direct policy impact, it will be symbolic of competence to execute effectively." So Greenstein and Lew—a taller, clean-shaven version of the green-eyeshade type—tried to get a handle on the economic outlook. It felt like trying to grab a greased pig. In August, Greenstein reported that states had sliced $50 billion from their budgets to close their fiscal gaps. By October, he was warning that the states already faced $100 billion in new shortfalls. "Everything was going downhill so fast," recalls Lew, whose employer, Citigroup, was itself clinging to life. "It was so hard for our thinking to keep up with events." Lew spoke regularly with Summers, whose acerbic pessimism unnerved him.

"It really made an impression on me how Larry was getting more and more worried as he saw more and more data," Lew says.

That was the unsettling backdrop for the team's key meeting, an October 17 briefing for the advisory board in a Manhattan law office. In a logistical email, Steiner emphasized that the goal was not to relitigate the Rubin-Reich debates of the 1990s. "We are explicitly NOT making recommendations on matters such as how to prioritize between deficit reduction and investment," he wrote. "We believe that the new President, Vice President and their team will make these choices." Steiner warned that to prevent leaks, there would be no paper distributed: "With my apologies for stating what I am sure is obvious, the content of this meeting and the fact that it is occurring are both strictly confidential." He added: "This effort is independent of the Obama campaign and the materials presented should not be construed as reflecting the campaign's positions."

That was a useful disclaimer, because Lew's presentation didn't reflect the campaign's positions. Three days after Obama proposed his $175 billion stimulus plan, Lew suggested that as much as $300 billion might be needed. With credit markets seized up, consumers tapped out, businesses retrenching, and state and local governments staggering, it wasn't clear where else a jump start could come from. The Fed had already taken the obvious steps to try to jolt the economy with monetary policy, cutting interest rates almost to zero. Financially led recessions were always brutal, and this one looked like the worst since the Depression.

"People were like: Shit. That's a big number," Podesta recalls. "But it was looking cataclysmic out there. Nobody was saying: Oh, we won't need that much."

The group briefly discussed whether 2008 had anything in common with 1993, when Clinton decided to focus on deficit reduction, and the consensus was: Not much. "Every single person in that room agreed that in the long term, you had to get the deficit under control, but every single person also agreed that first there had to be a huge stimulus package," another participant recalls. Greenstein did startle the room by projecting a trillion-dollar deficit for 2009, more than twice the latest CBO forecast, and Reich worried aloud that such gigantic shortfalls would cripple Obama's long-term agenda. But nobody argued against short-term stimulus. Even the fervent deficit hawks accepted that a depression or a protracted recession would shrivel tax revenues and create more red ink than a hefty stimulus ever could.

Sure, there was always a possibility that stimulus would overheat the economy once it was in recovery, but that sounded like a fabulous problem to have. In an economy without demand, Depression-style deflation was a much bigger risk than inflation. As Summers argued, it would be much safer to err on the side of too much stimulus than not enough. If the fiscal boost overcaffeinated the economy, the Fed could always raise rates to mellow it out. The first priority, everyone agreed, should be averting a cataclysm.

A week later, a Goldman Sachs report called for anywhere from $300 billion to $500 billion worth of stimulus. A week after that, conservative Harvard economist Martin Feldstein, a top Reagan adviser, endorsed a $300 billion package in a *Washington Post* column.

In those days, it didn't take long for the unthinkable to look inevitable.

The shadow team was assigned to play the honest broker role that the National Economic Council is supposed to play at the White House, summarizing the pros and cons of various policy options. Lew's final stimulus presentation—a thirty-six-page "Confidential Discussion Draft" dated two days before election day—provided an admirably balanced overview, although it did leave clues about where the team stood. The page titled "Arguments for significant stimulus package" was so crammed with bullet points it required a smaller font, while the "Arguments for small stimulus package" page looked like it was formatted for a reader with vision problems.

Still, even in large type, Lew recognized that critics would argue the Bush stimulus and TARP had already added enough red ink. He noted that soaring deficits could conceivably spook bond markets and drive up interest rates, which could crowd out private investment. That raised a question: Should the stimulus be paid for? Democrats had adopted fiscally responsible pay-as-you-go rules after taking back Congress, and while the rules had been suspended for the Bush stimulus and TARP, Blue Dog Democrats had objected to Pelosi's stimulus plan in the fall because it didn't include offsetting spending cuts. In the short term, offsets would defeat the purpose of Keynesian stimulus; the point was to transfer public dollars into private hands. But Lew raised the possibility of offsetting short-term stimulus with longer-term austerity, or a "trigger" that would restrain spending automatically once the economy recovered. Otherwise, Congress would be tempted to decorate the package with ornamental add-ons.

"Stimulus may become a Christmas tree if it is the last chance to escape budget discipline," Lew warned.

The main problems with offsets and triggers were political: "Fast action needed and specific offsets likely to cause delay." At a time when the administration would need to avoid a protracted fight in Congress, spending cuts would be contentious, and tax hikes would be nonstarters. "It is critical to avoid controversies that would delay enactment," Lew wrote. Anyway, it seemed unfair to demand offsets for a Main Street stimulus when the Wall Street bailout hadn't been paid for. The team of Clintonites agreed that at some point there would have to be a pivot from a short-term fiscal festival to long-term fiscal discipline, but the worst economic crisis in seventy-five years didn't seem like that point.

In fact, Lew suggested that while triggers designed to roll back the stimulus if the slump ended might be unworkable, triggers designed to expand the stimulus if the slump persisted could help avert future showdowns: "avoids need for time-consuming process if additional stimulus is needed later . . . prevents need to spend political capital on multiple rounds of stimulus." The team's Clinton-era combat veterans did not assume that passing jobs bills would be easy. They remembered Republicans blocking their relatively tiny $19 billion stimulus in 1993, even after Democrats whittled it down and offered offsets. They tended to be skeptical of Obama's post-partisan dreams.

So even though unemployment benefits and food stamps were excellent stimulus, Lew warned that Republicans would criticize them as big-government welfare. State aid would be lampooned as state bailouts, and a second round of tax rebate checks would "look like more of the same when the first round did not stop the recession." A jobs bill might sound like fun, but politically, there was no perfect stimulus.

Not even the shovel-ready infrastructure projects that politicians loved so dearly.

Jack Lew first set foot in the Office of Management and Budget in 1983, to negotiate a $4.6 billion stimulus package with the Reagan administration. At the time, he was working for House speaker Tip O'Neill, the backslapping New Deal Democrat who famously believed that all politics was local. Ever the loyal staffer, Lew helped stuff the bill with money for shovel-ready local infrastructure projects that would get people to work and get O'Neill's ribbon-cutting members reelected.

When Lew returned to OMB as an associate director a decade later, the career staff remembered that money—because some of it still hadn't gone out the door.

"I got a lot of grief over those spend-out rates," Lew recalls.

Lew remained a proud Tip O'Neill liberal, just a skeptical one when it came to using infrastructure as stimulus. On this issue, he sided with the economists against the politicians. "Not clear whether plans, materials and personnel are in place to accelerate public works rapidly," his PowerPoint said. "Past experience suggests not."

But past experience had not included a financial implosion. In the postwar era, the average recession had lasted less than a year, a tight timeline for even truly shovel-ready projects. Nobody expected an average recession this time. Lew thought the prospect of a deeper, longer downturn meant projects that took two or even three years might still be timely. And that meant the stimulus package could "become a recovery package and include measures to jump-start a longer-term growth agenda." It could be a Trojan horse for Change We Can Believe In.

The shadow team recognized the pitfalls of this strategy, including "risk of package growing large and losing control," as well as "risk of driving too much spending to longer-term agenda and not providing sufficient short-term stimulus." Those were prescient concerns. It also foresaw that the rush to fund ready-to-go public works could accelerate lower-priority projects, and suggested an "absolute policy of no earmarks" to prevent Congress from larding up the package with pork. That was prescient advice.

But these battle-hardened Clintonites also had a prescient argument for using the crisis to start building Obama's new foundation: "stimulus may be only chance for quick action on longer-term growth and energy/environment agenda." Right now, Obama wore a halo of hope. Maybe his aura could survive four years of Washington slime, but just to be safe, this seemed like a good time to do the things he ran to do.

Dancing in the Streets

On election day, Christy Romer voted early. Like a giddy tourist boarding a cruise ship, she asked her husband, David—another Berkeley economist—to snap her picture outside the polling station. Then she took some rugs to the cleaners, stopped by the hardware store, and returned some clothes that didn't fit. She didn't bother to go to the office. She was too distracted to work. Romer had provided occasional advice to the Obama campaign, and would soon become a top White House adviser, but it wasn't her job prospects that had her in a tizzy. She was fired up about change.

In a field of gray eminences and dull conferences, Romer was a splash of passion and idealism. With apple cheeks and strawberry hair, a Midwestern accent and guileless smile, she gave the impression of a kindly middle-aged auntie, more likely to dispense hugs or cookies than sophisticated economic advice. She reminded everyone of Julia Child, if Julia Child had been enthusiastic about regression analysis instead of beef bourguignon. Now she was enthusiastic about Obama—not just his policies, but his interest in facts, data, experts. He seemed reality-based. And that 2004 convention speech convinced Romer he had that special something; she liked to watch it on YouTube. As a Depression scholar, she thought the United States needed a new New Deal, and she thought Obama could be a new FDR. At a time of real peril, he could help revive the American economy and restore the American spirit.

That night, the Romers had dinner guests, their Berkeley colleagues George Akerlof, a Nobel laureate, and Janet Yellen, who had chaired the CEA under Clinton and would be vice chair of the Fed under Obama. The two couples had watched the returns together in 2000, and Christy remembered the sinking feeling she had when the networks took Florida off the board, the first step toward eight years of George Bush. This time, there was no suspense. Obama was declared the winner at 8 P.M Berkeley time, and the four ecstatic Keynesian economists cheered, hugged, and drank champagne. The electorate had repudiated the Republican Party, awarding Obama more than twice as many electoral votes as McCain, expanding Democratic majorities in both houses of Congress, obliterating turnout records. The Bush era was finally over.

Soon the president-elect came on the screen, live from Grant Park: "At this defining moment, change has come to America."

But also: "This victory alone is not the change we seek. It is only the chance to make this change."

And finally: "Where we are met with cynicism, and doubt, and those who tell us we can't, we will respond with that timeless creed that sums up the spirit of a people: Yes we can!"

After her guests left, Romer was so excited she couldn't sit still. She had never felt an impulse like this before, but she needed to be part of a crowd. So she and David piled into their Honda Accord and drove into downtown Oakland. They followed the sound of honking horns and blaring music to Broadway, the troubled city's main drag. They parked a few blocks away and walked toward the fun.

Then the two MIT-trained macroeconomists began dancing in the street, just about the only white faces in an exuberant black crowd, a pair of awkward fifty-year-olds surrounded by kids a third their age. Christy just wished she had brought a flag. It felt like a good night to wave a flag.

"It was such an outpouring of joy," she later recalled. "We were all celebrating the promise of this new president who shared our values and our dreams."

The Romers drove home around 11 P.M. and did the dishes. Christy was still too jazzed to go to sleep. First, she sat at her computer and made a sign for her office door.

It said: Yes We Did.

PART TWO

Making Change

FIVE

Ready Before Day One

In private moments during his campaign, Obama liked to quote the last line of *The Candidate*, when the political newcomer played by Robert Redford, dazed after his improbable victory, wondered: "What do we do now?"

Obama's point was that he didn't intend to be that guy.

He ran for president with no executive experience beyond editing the *Harvard Law Review*, but even his detractors had to admit his own improbable campaign was a well-run operation—disciplined, cohesive, eyes-on-the-prize. And even after the Wall Street implosion, when he was joking about throwing the election to McCain, he always exuded confidence about leading the cleanup. TARP was a dry run for his presidency, and he felt more comfortable digging into policy issues than he had ever felt working rope lines. He spent so much time grilling economists that one asked him: Shouldn't you be campaigning?

Obama's first post-election move, picking the frenetic, volcanic, in-your-face Rahm Emanuel as his chief of staff, signaled an abrupt shift from the hopey-changey poetry of the campaign to the nuts-and-bolts prose of governing. Rahm—who was always known as Rahm, like a Bono or Madonna of the political world—was not a poetry guy. He was a profanity guy, a by-any-means-necessary guy, a former Clinton White

House henchman who had masterminded the Democratic takeover of
the House in 2006—and had once mailed a dead fish to a pollster who
irked him. The *New York Times* noted with dry understatement that he
was not "considered a practitioner of the 'new politics' that Mr. Obama
promised on the campaign trail to bring Republicans and Democrats
together." Uh, no. Rahm agreed with Obama about the dysfunction of
Washington—he called the city "Fucknutsville"—but he wasn't interested in trying to change the game. He was interested in winning. Two
and a half years later, during his own transition as Chicago's mayor-
elect, I asked Rahm what he had thought of Obama's lofty rhetoric
about changing Washington.

"Look, I don't really know," he said with a smirk. "I come from
Chicago."

Rahm was a different breed of Chicago pol, as confrontational and
pushy as Obama was conciliatory and cool; Obama once deadpanned
that the childhood accident that left Rahm with only half a middle fin-
ger had "rendered him practically mute." He was a perpetual motion
machine, always churning, always yapping, the opposite of No Drama.
Many Republicans saw him as a diabolical figure, and so did many liberals; he had always espoused a muscular centrism, bashing heads for
Clinton on the NAFTA free trade agreement, winning back the House
by recruiting culturally conservative Democrats. His critique of the
party—too wine-track, too goo-goo, too effete—echoed common critiques of Obama. But Obama wanted a consigliere who filled in some of
his gaps, and Rahm knew how to make stuff happen. His hiring sent a
message that Obama intended to get stuff done.

The president-elect was walking into "a giant shitstorm," as Rahm
put it, and no matter what he had said about reinventing politics, he had
to save the economy first. "You were brushing up against whatever thin
line there was between where a recession ends and a depression begins,"
Rahm says. Demand was plummeting like Wile E. Coyote clutching an
anvil. New home sales were the lowest in half a century, and foreclosures were spreading like Ebola. General Motors, America's most iconic
company, was flirting with bankruptcy. AIG needed another bailout

after losing $24 billion in the third quarter, and was on its way to blowing an incomprehensible $66 billion in the fourth quarter. To add to the warm welcome, the Dow shed another 1,000 points during Obama's first two days as president-elect, its worst tumble since the 1987 crash. The next day, the October jobs report revealed that unemployment had jumped from 6.1 percent to 6.5 percent.

"These reports don't get much worse than a loss of 240,000 jobs in a single month," the *Wall Street Journal* noted.

Oh, they would soon. Even the October report would later be revised to reflect an actual loss of 500,000 jobs.

That afternoon, Obama held his first news conference as president-elect, best remembered for his quip that he might get Sasha and Malia a "mutt like me." Mostly, though, his tone was sober, as if he had just been named CEO of a bankrupt firm: "We're facing the greatest economic challenge of our lifetime, and we're going to have to act swiftly to resolve it." He vowed that a stimulus package would be "the first thing I get done." But he also served notice that the short-term crisis wouldn't shelve his long-term agenda, that change was more urgent than ever: "We cannot afford to wait on the key priorities I identified during the campaign, including clean energy, health care, education and tax relief for middle-class families."

It was the same audacity, minus the poetry.

Another Defining Moment

FDR had to wait four months after his landslide to assume the presidency, at a time his aides feared there might be a revolution first. As Jonathan Alter chronicled in *The Defining Moment,* Hoover tried desperately throughout the interregnum to rope Roosevelt into bipartisan cooperation, but FDR steadfastly refused to co-sign any of his policies. He wanted a clean break from the past.

Obama read *The Defining Moment* during his own intense transition—the first during a freefall since FDR's, the first during wartime since Nixon's. His limbo period would only last two and a half months, but he didn't intend to repeat Roosevelt's leave-no-fingerprints, take-no-ownership gamesmanship. Obama had already embraced TARP, even though he knew he'd end up sharing blame for the bailout. The Big Three automakers loomed as another pre-inaugural morass, especially after their CEOs arrived in Washington on three private jets to beg for taxpayer aid. But Obama resisted the temptation to remain silent and let Bush own the choice between another bailout and the possible obliteration of a vital industry. Instead, Obama publicly pushed to save the automaker, further muddying his break with the past.

Bush also took a responsible approach to the transition; unlike Hoover, he ordered his administration to cooperate with his successor. But it was an awkward situation. While Obama was the center of attention, Bush was the leader of the free world. As Obama kept saying, there could only be one president at a time. And there clearly wouldn't be another stimulus as long as Bush was that president. One Bush aide recalls Pelosi pleading for a relief package, arguing that families were lining up at soup kitchens. "Madame Speaker, I wouldn't be doing my job if I didn't tell you that Republicans have a different view on stimulating the economy," the aide told her. Pelosi asked what he meant. "Most Republicans want to extend the Bush tax cuts," he explained.

"That's what got us into this mess!" Pelosi yelled.

But Obama couldn't wait to start crafting a recovery package until January 20. Rahm wanted him to *sign* a recovery package on January 20. Even though he hadn't chosen a team yet, and didn't have the federal bureaucracy at his disposal yet, the work had to start now. Campaign aides who had gone months without a decent night's sleep had to start designing complex legislation that would help define Obama's legacy. Clinton had boasted she'd be ready to govern on Day One in the White House; it was now clear that would be much too late.

"We were all so emotionally and physically exhausted," recalls Dan Pfeiffer, the transition's communications director. "You run a marathon, you feel like total zombie, and then you have to do an all-out 800-yard sprint."

Presidential transitions are usually glorified job fairs, but Obama's became a frantic policymaking exercise. The team had just a few weeks to figure out how to spend a few hundred billion dollars.

"People talk about walk-and-chew-gum moments," says Melody Barnes, Obama's top domestic policy advisor. "This was a walk and chew-gum-and-touch-your-nose-and-spin-around-and-do-a-backflip moment."

Jason Furman, who had coauthored that "If, When, How" stimulus report for Brookings in January, was assigned to run point on a stimulus plan for Obama the day after the election. If and When were no longer serious questions. Now the question was How to stop the bleeding, and How to craft a package that Congress could pass while there was still time to save the patient.

At thirty-eight, Furman understood the interplay of policy and politics as well as any graybeard economist. He was the guy who knew all the Medicaid formulas, and also the guy who knew which senators wanted to tweak them. As a teenager, he had handed out leaflets for Walter Mondale's 1984 presidential campaign in Greenwich Village; his parents, a real estate magnate and a child psychologist, were prominent Democratic activists and donors in Manhattan. Two decades later, after a stint in the Clinton White House, he had overseen economic policy for Kerry's 2004 campaign, before doing the same job for Obama. Some liberals were leery of his ties to Bob Rubin and Larry Summers, and rivals mocked him as Larry's pet. But he was infinitely more collegial than Summers, and no one doubted his candlepower. He was the kind of savant who would work a fourteen-hour day in the White House, then post a literary review on Facebook at night: "This is the best book I've read on Cleopatra in the last year. Yes, there was one other."

Furman had one week to convert Jack Lew's overview of stimulus options into preliminary recommendations for Obama. He had help from colleagues on the transition team, but there was no treasury secretary or budget director to offer guidance, no NEC or CEA head, no "principals," in Washington parlance. Questions that would help determine the fate of the economy and the Obama presidency were starting to be answered, even though Rahm was the only senior staffer in place.

The first question was the size of the stimulus. The transition team put the question to a range of economists—partly to pick their brains, partly to push them to float big numbers in the press, so Obama's big numbers wouldn't create as much sticker shock. "We were trying to expand the realm of what was possible," Furman recalls. Everyone surveyed from left to right—except for Republican Greg Mankiw, a Bush CEA chair who had been Furman's adviser at Harvard—wanted Obama to go big to fill the gap in demand. A few liberals were thinking astronomically big. At coffee with Furman, University of Texas economist Jamie Galbraith, son of the New Dealer John Kenneth Galbraith, floated $900 billion just for the first year. Nobel laureate Joseph Stiglitz, Furman's former boss at the World Bank, would soon propose $1 trillion over two years. Rahm also reached out to Paul Krugman, who thought the economy needed at least $600 billion in Year One. "You really, really don't want to lowball this," Krugman wrote on his blog.

In November, though, those numbers were still outliers. Furman's eleven-page Confidential Discussion Draft for Obama recommended a "notional package" of $335 billion, which still seemed plenty big. It was almost double Obama's campaign proposal of a few weeks earlier, and over three times the size of a stimulus bill that Senate Democrats would roll out a few weeks later. It was more than the annual budgets of the Departments of Transportation, Education, Energy, Agriculture, Justice, Interior, Labor, Housing and Urban Development, Homeland Security, and Veterans Affairs combined. At the time, 387 predominantly liberal economists—many of whom later attacked Obama for skimping on stimulus—were signing a letter urging Congress to "move quickly and decisively" to pass a stimulus bill in the $300–$400 billion range. Furman had already stretched the normal definition of "timely" from one year to two, since this wasn't a normal downturn, but he thought it would be tough to spend more than that in an effective way.

The big question was how to spend it. Unemployment benefits, food stamps, and other aid to vulnerable families would be no-brainers, acing the three-T test while providing about $50 billion to people in need. Furman's PowerPoint also included $80 billion worth of aid to states, to prevent fifty gubernatorial mini-Hoovers from undermining Obama's stimulus with drastic layoffs and other anti-stimulus.

The draft also allotted $70 billion for a one-year Making Work Pay rebate. Conventional wisdom held that the Bush stimulus checks had failed to stimulate anything. And panicky consumers were now even more likely to save extra cash or pay down debt. Even purchases of imported goods would "leak" out of the country, limiting their economic oomph. But when Furman analyzed the data, he thought the Bush rebates had a decent impact on consumer spending, before they were overwhelmed by the economic tsunami. Tax cuts were also a speedy way to get cash into circulation, with potential for bipartisan support. Anyway, as Rahm pointed out, Making Work Pay was a campaign promise. "We're checking that fucking box," he declared.

That added up to $200 billion worth of three-T stimulus. Then what? Well, it made sense to fund things that deserved funding anyway. This was Rahm's Rule: Never waste a crisis. "Look for 'win-wins'—targeted, temporary measures that lay foundation for long-term agenda," the draft said. "Stimulus as down payment on long-term goals." Obama had done lots of talking about clean energy, health care, education, and infrastructure. Now he could do lots of spending.

So Furman added $20 billion for health information technology and $25 billion to renovate schools, although he did warn that both investments could create the "appearance of throwing everything into stimulus plan." He included $30 billion for roads and bridges, which would advance Obama's infrastructure goals while building support among congressional asphalt lovers. He lifted the final $60 billion from a "Green Stimulus" memo compiled by Carol Browner's energy and environment team, proposing win-wins like home weatherization, mass transit, energy efficiency grants to state and local governments, and the smart grid.

"Suddenly, the funding we had struggled so mightily to get in small quantities was going to be available in huge quantities," recalls the green team's Dan Reicher, an assistant energy secretary under Clinton. "It was very exciting. And daunting."

The proposals had not really been vetted yet. For example, the green team's impractical plan to install a smart meter in every U.S. home would be scaled back in later drafts. The team's exorbitant initial estimate of shovel-ready transit projects, cribbed from an advocacy group, was also ratcheted down after actual transit agencies weighed in. "The whole exercise felt weird," one team member recalls. "Someone would make a single phone call, and suddenly it's, 'All righty. Put a billion dollars over there.'"

But Browner, a former Senate aide to Al Gore, had dreamed for decades about serious clean-energy investments. And Obama had said he didn't intend to wait any longer.

On November 12, the shadow economic team reconvened for the last time in Chicago, to meet with Obama and "hand off" to his new advisers. The budget guru Bob Greenstein came bearing especially bad news: State tax revenues were crashing. A few weeks earlier, he had projected $100 billion in state budget shortfalls. Before the briefing, he told Furman the gaps now exceeded $200 billion. That didn't even include local government deficits, which were also spiraling out of control. Furman was about to present his stimulus recommendations to Obama, and they already seemed out of date. After the president-elect entered the drab conference room in his transition offices, Furman asked Greenstein to repeat the chilling numbers.

"Obama was impressed—in a way he didn't want to be impressed," Greenstein recalls.

The next two hours continued in that vein, a roundup of ugh, oof, and yuck. Jack Lew had never spent time with Obama before, and while he was impressed by the president-elect's crisp sense of command, the probing tell-me-more's interspersed with brusque I-know-that's, he mostly felt sorry for him.

"It wasn't the meeting you would have chosen to start things off," Lew recalls. "There wasn't a lot of: 'Hey, don't worry, it might get better on its own.'"

Obama emphasized that while short-term calamity avoidance was his top priority, he expected action on his long-term goals. Throughout the stimulus debate, there would be a tension between speed and change, between shoveling money out the door quickly to save the economy and investing money thoughtfully to transform the country. Zipping cash to taxpayers or states or existing programs through existing formulas is always easier than trying something new. And given the spending appetites on the Hill, Furman noted, "including anything beyond clearly defined short-term spending in a stimulus plan opens the floodgates." But it's hard to shake up the status quo through existing programs, and Obama told his team he didn't want to hire unemployed workers to dig holes and fill them back in.

"The economists were giving us the advice they should have been giving us, which is the quicker you get this out, the more rapidly it gets into the bloodstream, the better it is for the economy," Biden says. "But our view was that this is also an opportunity to begin—it's a corny-sounding phrase—but literally to begin to lay the planks for a platform that can get us to the next place."

Obama also began to focus on another long-term issue: the solvency of the country. In his presentation, Greenstein forecast a deficit of $1.2 trillion, a chilling 8 percent of GDP. That would need to drop to about 3 percent to stabilize the nation's debt-to-GDP ratio; when Greenstein started to explain the concept, the president-elect cut him off, saying he understood it all too well. In his presentation, Furman did not recommend offsets or triggers for the stimulus, because it needed to pass in a hurry, but he did suggest that it should be presented in tandem with a "strategy to return to long-term fiscal discipline." Transition cochair Ted Kaufman, who had been Biden's Senate chief of staff and would soon inherit his seat, was struck by the intense concern in the room about unsustainable deficits.

"There were charts up on the wall, and it was like, 'Oh my God, where are we going?'" Kaufman recalls.

Over the next few years, Republicans would argue that Obama didn't care about deficits. Liberals would argue that Obama cared too much about deficits and not enough about stimulus, accusing his team of overlearning the balanced budget lessons of the Clinton era. But even before the team was in place, Obama cared a lot about deficits. He always assumed that once the recovery was in bloom, he'd pivot from short-term fiscal expansion to long-term fiscal sustainability. From the start, his transition team scrubbed stimulus proposals to avoid "tails," spending that would continue after the stimulus was over. Obama made a point of warning agency leaders not to try to slip their one-time windfalls into their annual budget baselines.

Still, short-run deficit reduction would have been anti-stimulus. The team agreed its first priority had to be a massive and immediate injection of deficit-expanding stimulus. Defeat or even delay would be economically disastrous, rattling fragile markets, accelerating the death spiral, and ultimately growing the deficit. As Rahm argued, it could also be politically disastrous, fueling an early narrative about the new gang that can't shoot straight. He believed in "putting points on the board," using political capital to produce victories that would build more political capital, demonstrating power by exercising power. Success would beget success, and the same was true of failure.

"We can't fuck this up," he said.

A Team of Centrists

A week later, one hundred executives converged on Washington for the *Wall Street Journal*'s CEO Council, an exclusive conference designed to tease out the business community's policy agenda. The council's number-one priority: fiscal stimulus. Republicans were already attacking Democratic stimulus desires as liberalism run amok; as Boehner put it, "more Washington spending isn't the answer." But the CEOs wanted more Washington spending, calling for a package exceeding $300 billion, featuring infrastructure, clean energy, education, and state aid. In other words, a package like the one the Obama team was preparing. In a crisis, that didn't seem like socialism to America's top capitalists.

Larry Summers, a candidate for his old job of treasury secretary, was again thinking bigger. In a panel discussion, he noted that some analysts were calling for $500–$700 billion worth of stimulus—and everyone knew that when Summers noted the opinions of others without shredding them, he was probably stating a Summers opinion he wasn't supposed to share publicly. He even suggested his timely-targeted-temporary stimulus test no longer made as much sense as it had in January, considering the utter disappearance of demand.

"I would go for speedy, substantial and sustained," he said. "I think we're going to need some impetus for the economy for two to three years."

Summers didn't get the Treasury job. Obama gave it to Tim Geithner, another Summers protégé. Geithner had been immersed in the financial crisis at the New York Fed, and while Obama had no problem with Clinton administration retreads—his anti-Hillary arguments about Change trumping Experience no longer seemed to apply—he preferred not to return them to the same positions. He wanted his team to look at least somewhat like Change. Geithner was a fresh face—an unnervingly boyish face to those who liked their treasury secretaries silver-haired—who was two weeks younger than Obama, and had bonded with him over their experiences living abroad as kids. Geithner's low-key, down-to-earth persona also meshed with Obama's no-drama ethic. Summers had, well, a different persona. It wasn't just that Larry didn't suffer fools gladly. It was that his idea of a fool could encompass almost anyone who wasn't Larry. The son of two Ivy League economists and nephew of two Nobel laureate economists, he had enrolled at MIT at sixteen and received tenure at Harvard at twenty-eight. He had always been the smartest boy in the room, and had never stopped proving it. He was a born alienator, a college debate star who was still on the lookout for stupid arguments to dismantle.

But Obama wanted Summers around. He really was as brilliant as he thought he was, even if he didn't always know as much about topics outside his areas of expertise as he thought he did. He had been ahead of the curve during this crisis, and in his last stint at Treasury he had helped resolve crises in Mexico, Russia, and Asia. The concerns about his interpersonal skills that might have carried more weight in normal times seemed less relevant on the brink of Armageddon.

"Obama felt like we were in war mode, and he needed the best people, period," transition-chief John Podesta recalls.

Obama envisioned Summers as an adviser without management portfolio, the kind of White House position that Henry Kissinger once suggested should be assigned to him on a permanent basis. But Summers insisted that if he was going to accept a staff job, he wanted to run the National Economic Council, the "honest broker" role that was expected to go to the friendlier Jack Lew. That way he'd get his own staff, and a gatekeeper status he could use to control the policymaking process. "I mean, honest broker?" says one transition official. "That's not exactly Larry." Summers was a fighter, not a referee, and he even warned Obama that making colleagues feel validated was not his forte. One economist recalls that after reviewing one of his memos during the shadow transition, Summers urged him to make one option sound less attractive, the opposite of honest brokering.

"When I heard they gave him NEC, I remember thinking: *Whoa*," the economist told me. "Strange choice."

Those were strange times. Anyway, Obama felt comfortable with technocratic elites like Summers and Geithner. He was one of them. He also felt comfortable with their brand of market-oriented centrism. It was another thing they had in common.

Obama was offering an early answer to the burning question in Washington: Would he govern from the left or the center? GOP leaders and conservative pundits were laying down markers, arguing that if Obama was really a moderate, he needed to devote some of his stimulus to tax cuts; back off his promise to undo the Bush tax cuts for the rich; ditch another pledge to pass "card-check" legislation that would make it easier to form unions; and surround himself with middle-of-the-road advisers. Rush Limbaugh and Fox News were warning their audiences that Obama would soon show his far-left colors, reinstating the Fairness Doctrine to get liberals equal airtime, cracking down on gun owners, and conceding defeat in Iraq. By choosing Summers and Geithner to lead his team, the president-elect was telling the political and financial markets that he lined up with the Rubin wing of the Democratic Party. *Washington Post* columnist David Ignatius declared Obama's fledgling administration "so centrist it almost resembles a government of national unity." Even Bush political guru Karl Rove wrote that Obama's personnel choices "provided surprisingly positive clarity."

Summers had helped deregulate the financial system in the 1990s. Geithner had spent the last year saving bankers from their own excesses. These were not granola hippies; in a populist moment, they were downright hostile to populism. Both were close Rubin allies, as was Obama's new Office of Management and Budget director, Peter Orszag, a deficit hawk who had helped Rubin launch the centrist Hamilton Project before moving to CBO. So were Jason Furman, who became a deputy to Summers, Gene Sperling, a former NEC head who agreed to help Geithner at Treasury, and Jack Lew, a former OMB director who went to work for Hillary Clinton at the State Department. As the *New York Times* reported, "a virtual Rubin constellation is taking shape." To disappointed liberals, it was only fitting that on the morning Obama announced his economic team, Bush announced that he was bailing out Rubin's Citigroup.

"Those guys were so closely associated with pro-bank policies," Joseph Stiglitz says. "You had to ask: Why would Obama want them in a crisis like this?"

To some Obama loyalists, the new team looked disappointingly like a third Clinton administration. The joke circulating among campaign staff was that Obama supporters got a president, while Hillary supporters got the jobs.

"We knew all the Rubin people would be bad optics," Podesta says. "But at a moment of crisis, Obama wasn't dwelling on that."

The main exception to all the Clinton-era recycling was the Council of Economic Advisers, the in-house White House think tank that became an outpost for "Obama people." Christy Romer, who had danced in the streets on election night, was chosen to lead it. She was a well-respected economic historian whose expertise in the Depression could not have been timelier, and Obama needed a woman on his team. But she had no experience in government or politics. "She was never going to win a bureaucratic knife fight with Larry," one transition aide says. Austan Goolsbee, the economist closest to Obama, could not understand why the Clinton crowd was vacuuming up all the top jobs, but the president-elect persuaded him to serve on the CEA as well. As a consolation prize, Goolsbee was also assigned to manage a new advisory board chaired by his mentor, Paul Volcker, the former Fed chairman famous for taming inflation, but the board never had much influence.

"When Austan got hosed, a lot of us were like: Hey! What's happening to change we can believe in?" a campaign staffer recalls.

The team's only traditional liberal was Biden's chief economist, Jared Bernstein of the union-funded Economic Policy Institute, a New Age wonk who had studied double bass at the Manhattan School of Music, then had earned degrees in social work and philosophy. He had a mellow, good-energy vibe, but he wasn't perceived as a heavyweight who could counter Summers or Geithner. Obama's labor secretary, California congresswoman Hilda Solis, was also a staunch progressive, but it was clear she wouldn't be part of the economic team.

Starting early in the transition, the Obama team seemed to go out of its way to accommodate Republican demands, signaling that it would put card-check on hold, include significant tax cuts in the stimulus, and keep the Bush tax cuts for the rich during the downturn. Obama's plans to seize guns and impose the Fairness Doctrine existed only in the fevered imagination of the right. But when it came to Main Street stimulus, Obama's team sounded a lot like traditional liberals.

"I don't know what the exact number is, but it's going to be a big number," Goolsbee declared in a TV interview. "We're out with the dithering, in with a bang."

Of course, even the CEOs at the *Wall Street Journal* conference had sounded like liberals when it came to stimulus. But Summers kept warning that the dangers were all on the side of doing too little, not too much. By the time those 387 progressive economists sent their letter urging a $300–$400 billion package, his $500–$700 billion trial balloon was already appearing in news stories as Obama's preferred policy.

"We knew this had to be big, but we didn't comprehend just how big before Larry got deeply involved," Furman says.

Christy Romer, the incoming CEA chair, felt even stronger about the need to go big. And when she was summoned to meet the president-elect for the first time in Chicago, she found out that he was on the same page.

Romer's first meeting with Obama has entered the realm of myth, but she remembers it vividly. She was waiting nervously in the Chicago transition offices to talk to him about the CEA job, finishing a last-minute comb of her hair, when she heard that familiar baritone: "Dr. Romer, so nice to meet you." The president-elect shook her hand warmly, then ushered her into another office; she was flattered he had come out to greet her, rather than send an assistant to fetch her. Obama began their chat by remarking that there wasn't much more the Fed could do to inject monetary stimulus into the economy. Romer bluntly responded that he was wrong. Even though the Fed was about to lower its key interest rate as close as it could go to zero, there were still ways it could help juice the economy.

This innocuous exchange among eggheads later sparked an odd sexism controversy, after journalist Ron Suskind wrote in his best-seller *Confidence Men* that "before exchanging hellos or even shaking hands," the president-elect tried to deliver a "zinger," saying monetary policy had "shot its wad." Suskind used this "salty, sexual language" as his Exhibit A demonstrating that "the president didn't have particularly strong women skills." But Romer is positive that Obama never said those words to her, even after exchanging hellos and shaking hands; she used them to Suskind, paraphrasing the president-elect. She says Obama was courteous and professional, and she remembers that day as one of the most thrilling of her career. She found the entire kerfuffle surreal.

What Romer remembers most about that discussion was Obama's laser focus on fiscal stimulus, and his interest in the lessons of the New Deal. Romer's academic work had emphasized how FDR's expansionary monetary policy of taking the United States off the gold standard had helped breathe life into a moribund economy. But like most scholars of the era, she also believed that FDR's expansionary fiscal policy had helped boost growth during his first term, and that his premature shift to austerity in 1937 had throttled the recovery. She saw two problems with FDR's fiscal stimulus: It was too small, and he abandoned it too quickly. "One of my early themes was that sheer size matters," Romer says. In the current crisis, even though she rejected the conventional wisdom that the Fed was out of ammunition, she thought the crisis was so grave that Congress desperately needed to act as well.

"I think we need a *very* large fiscal stimulus," she said. Obama agreed.

Romer and Obama also agreed that part of Roosevelt's genius was the way his own jaunty confidence had helped restore national confidence. Romer said it was hard to measure the effect of FDR's forceful promises to fight the Depression like a foreign invader, but they had an effect. By contrast, Hoover's passivity had left Americans feeling like no one was looking out for them, and Romer thought history was repeating itself. Where was Bush? She was glad Washington was stabilizing the banks, but who was stabilizing the rest of the economy?

Time's new cover, headlined "The New New Deal," had depicted Obama with FDR's trademark cigarette holder and pince-nez, and he was thinking a lot about the bond Roosevelt had forged with ordinary Americans through his speeches and fireside chats. Obama hoped to start a similar conversation with the public. He wouldn't tell Americans they had nothing to fear except fear itself, because that wasn't true. He lacked FDR's talent for BS. But he thought that by projecting competence and determination, by assuring the country that he was on the case and developing appropriate policies, he might be able to help soothe some anxieties.

On November 24, Obama pitched his new New Deal at his news conference to introduce his economic team, trying to project Rooseveltian resolve. "If we do not act swiftly and boldly, most experts now believe we could lose millions of jobs next year. . . . We cannot hesitate and we cannot delay." Obama refused to put a specific price tag on the stimulus, but pledged to "do what's required to jolt this economy back into shape." At the urging of Rahm, who was convinced the stimulus would need a jobs number to get traction on the Hill, he did lay out a specific goal of creating or preserving 2.5 million jobs. He also committed to use the recovery effort to attack the nation's energy, health care, education, and infrastructure problems, "to lay the groundwork for long-term sustained economic growth."

At times, Obama sounded more like a pundit than a leader, talking about the importance of restoring confidence instead of just doing it. He seemed grim, not jaunty, and he kept undercutting his message of revival with caveats about the slog ahead—partly because he didn't want to sugarcoat a nasty situation, partly because David Axelrod worried that inflating expectations now could create a backlash down the road. "I want to repeat, this will not be easy," Obama said. "There are no shortcuts or quick fixes." His exhortations about long-term investments also seemed to undercut his urgent message about short-term jobs. And the next day, Obama blurred his call for fiscal stimulus by preaching fiscal restraint. "There's no doubt that we've been living beyond our means, and we're going to have to make adjustments," he said.

Obama had a real public relations challenge. He didn't want to depress confidence. He didn't want to promote irrational exuberance, either. He needed to project forcefulness but not profligacy. Like FDR, he was about to replace an unpopular president who was leaving the economy in shambles, but unlike FDR, he would take office before Americans really felt the pain. There were no Hoovervilles, no Dust Bowl. As the Reagan speechwriter Peggy Noonan wrote in the *Wall Street Journal*, everything still looked the same: "It's as if the news is full of floods but we haven't seen it rain." Obama aides used a similar metaphor: The tidal wave was in motion, but it hadn't hit the shore.

That time lag could create major political headaches. Sure, Obama was buying low, but was he buying low enough? Summers mused that FDR was lucky; the country had already suffered through three years of depression under Hoover before he took over. Everyone understood that it was Hoover's depression.

"That's probably true," Romer earnestly replied. "But I'm so glad Obama is here. Maybe this time we won't have to suffer so long."

Two-Part Messages

The November jobs report made the October report look like a ray of sunshine. Over 500,000 jobs had evaporated, the worst monthly decline since 1974. "The economy is unraveling so fast as to defy analysis through the usual statistical methods," the *Washington Post* reported. Ordinarily sober analysts used phrases like "shockingly weak," "indescribably terrible," and "God-awful."

It was Romer's job to inform Obama the economy was in critical condition, which was not how she had imagined her first presidential briefing.

"I'm so sorry, Mr. President-Elect," she blurted out. "The numbers are just horrible."

"It's not your fault," Obama replied. "Yet."

The end of 2008 tends to be remembered as an undifferentiated blob of bad news. It's easy to forget the scary trajectory, the way bad kept getting worse. That "horrible" report of 500,000 lost jobs would later be revised to a beyond-horrible 800,000. By December, retail sales had reached their lowest ebb since 1969, wiping out chains like Circuit City, and one in ten mortgages were delinquent, a record. California governor Arnold Schwarzenegger declared a fiscal emergency. On the positive side, sort of, the global slowdown dragged crude prices 70 percent below their summertime peak. But it was hard to get excited about cheap gas when you couldn't find a job or pay your bills.

This was the kind of vicious cycle Keynes had warned about, and it bolstered the case for a Keynesian response. More Americans without jobs or health insurance meant a deeper need for jobless benefits, Medicaid, and other antipoverty aid. And a bigger hole in the economy meant a bigger stimulus would be needed to fill it. As Romer later pointed out, fiscal stimulus was not considered an exotic or ideological tool. "It is a tried and true remedy widely supported by economists across the political spectrum," she explained in a speech. "It is standard fare in both introductory textbooks and more sophisticated modern theoretical models."

At Obama's transition headquarters in downtown Washington, the stimulus plan had now grown to $580 billion. That was ten times the size of the stimulus bills Congress had voted on just two months earlier—and about as much as the United States spent on Medicare and Medicaid that year. In a four-page summary distributed in early December—with each page marked "NOT TO BE SHARED"—Summers and Furman called the plan an effort to "jolt the economy, restore America after years of neglect, and make critical 21st century investments to begin the transformation of the American economy." Rahm was already down on the word "stimulus"—overly Washington, insufficiently grand—so they called it "The American Economic Recovery Plan."

The biggest addition was the New Jobs Investment Tax Credit, the hiring incentive for businesses that Obama had proposed in Toledo. Some critics dismissed the credit as free money for firms that would have hired anyway, but even if only one or two out of ten new hires were prompted by the incentive, it would still be a fairly inexpensive way to create jobs. As for the other eight or nine hires, well, giving money to growing firms would provide stimulus, too. The main goal was to splash cash into the economy, which was why the updated recovery plan also extended the Making Work Pay tax cuts over two years. Overall, 40 percent of the new plan consisted of tax breaks, which would annoy liberals, but would also provide an easy mechanism to get money out the door. On the spending side, there was only so much pig that could be shoved through the federal python in just two years.

"With numbers that huge, it starts to be a real logistical challenge to spend money quickly and still make sure you're getting high bang-for-the-buck," explains Brian Deese, who joined the NEC staff after the transition. "Tax cuts start to look pretty attractive as part of a package."

But the new plan also jacked up spending on long-term priorities.

Geithner had told Obama that no matter what happened after the crisis was over, his main legacy would be preventing a second depression. The president-elect had replied: That's not enough. In his radio address on December 6, he announced the first five elements of his recovery program, and they sounded like his campaign agenda in new clothing: "A massive effort to make public buildings more energy efficient. . . . The single largest new investment in our infrastructure since the creation of the interstate highway system. . . . The most sweeping effort to modernize and upgrade school buildings this country has ever seen. . . . We'll renew our information superhighway. . . . We'll make sure every doctor's office and hospital in this country is using electronic medical records." Change was in the works.

At the same time, Obama wanted to hammer home his short-term message that help was on the way. In his first inaugural, FDR had proclaimed that "the nation asks for action, and action now"—a line that prompted way more applause than "fear itself"—and Obama ripped him off: "We need action, and action now."

This bifurcated approach—a short-term emergency intervention combined with a long-term foundation for growth—did not seem impossibly difficult to understand. Neither did the similarly dualistic notion of aggressive deficit spending while the economy needed stimulus, followed by fiscal restraint once the danger passed. These ideas were no more hypocritical or contradictory than Obama's proposal to raise taxes on the rich and cut taxes for everyone else. He assumed the public was capable of grasping a straightforward two-part message.

That assumption would haunt him. It turns out that one-part messages—stimulus is bad, deficits are bad, taxes are bad, government is bad—are much easier to grasp.

Obama chose his cabinet faster than any president-elect since Nixon, tapping prominent politicians (including Hillary Clinton at State and former Senate majority leader Tom Daschle at Health and Human Services), moderate Republicans (keeping Robert Gates at Defense and installing Congressman Ray LaHood at Transportation), and innovative reformers (Steven Chu at Energy, Arne Duncan at Education, and New York City housing commissioner Shaun Donovan at HUD). He also named his senior White House staff in record time.

Rahm wanted the stimulus to move just as fast. He was hot for Obama to sign a bill on inauguration day, so he could begin his presidency with an act as dramatic as FDR's bank holiday. But Phil Schiliro, a longtime congressional aide who was now Obama's legislative director, kept pointing to the calendar. What Rahm was proposing would violate every law of legislative physics. The new Congress wouldn't even arrive in Washington until the first week in January, which meant it would have two weeks to produce, debate, amend, and enact landmark legislation. "Some of the new members won't even have staff yet, and we'll be asking them to take the biggest vote of their lives," Schiliro argued. How did Rahm intend to get a bill through God knows how many committees, then the House, then the Senate, then reconcile the two versions, and then back through the House and Senate again? Maybe first someone ought to start drafting some legislative language.

"We were already doing a bridge too far," Schiliro says. "That was like ten bridges too far."

Rahm spluttered and cursed his way through a few scheduling meetings, but soon he had to admit January 20 was outlandish. Instead, the team set a deadline of Presidents' Day recess in mid-February, a slight nod toward sanity. The new plan called for Obama to build momentum first by signing two popular bills, one removing barriers to women's equal pay lawsuits, the Lilly Ledbetter Fair Pay Act, the other expanding that children's health insurance program that Bush had vetoed, known as S-CHIP. That would put some points on the board while the Recovery Act was taking shape. Rahm believed that in Fucknutsville, you're either pitching or catching. He wanted to pitch.

If the new schedule made Schiliro feel marginally better about the logistics, he still worried about the politics. Obama's first responsibility, even before he took office, would be a hideously unpopular push for Congress to approve the second $350 billion tranche of TARP. He had also pledged help for carmakers and homeowners, political land mines in their own right. Meanwhile, Congress hadn't finished last year's budget, so Obama would have to deal with a giant "omnibus" spending package, as well as a supplemental spending package to fund wars, disasters, and anything else the Hill decided to supplement—at the same time he would be preparing to unveil next year's budget. Plus the biggest stimulus ever? That was going to be a lot of spending, a lot of zeroes. To Schiliro, it felt like an Olympic dive with the highest degree of difficulty. At one early meeting, he warned: By the time we're done with all that, we'll be done spending money.

In retrospect, the stimulus has taken on an aura of inevitability, as if it were a foregone conclusion that Congress had to pass some kind of massive recovery bill. But Obama's Beltway veterans thought nothing was inevitable. They remembered President Clinton's ill-fated $19 billion stimulus. Even on a slightly more realistic legislative schedule, even during a presidential honeymoon, even in the midst of an economic bloodbath, a $580 billion package would be a heavy lift. In September, after Lehman Brothers failed, Majority Leader Reid had failed to move $56 billion through the Senate; even two centrist Democrats had voted no on enough-is-enough grounds. As Americans hunkered down, a Washington spending spree seemed totally off-key.

So Rahm kept pressing Schiliro: How much can we get?

Schiliro told him $400 billion seemed doable.

What about $600 billion?

Yeah, maybe. "Beyond that, it got shaky," Schiliro says. "I mean, even $300 billion was mind-boggling. We were talking about magnitudes of hundreds of billions of dollars more than anybody had been talking about."

Almost anybody. The economic team had settled into Obama's chaotic Washington transition offices at the corner of Sixth and E, taking over a section of the eighth floor. This team of rivals would later become notorious for its drama. In the coming months, Romer would furiously threaten to go home to Berkeley if Summers and Geithner kept huddling without her; Summers and Orszag would start holding competing budget meetings; Summers and Goolsbee would come to view each other with mutual contempt. But in those intense early days, the team was still functioning fine. Even Summers was still playing nicely in the sandbox; his detractors suspect he was behaving in hopes that Obama would name him Fed chairman when Bernanke's term expired. "He was trying really hard to control his inner Larry," one economist recalls. The key players all worked within a few feet of one another, popping their heads into each other's offices, meeting for hours on end.

At one stimulus meeting after the ugly jobs report, Romer piped up: "One of the things we ought to put on the table is that this thing is much too small. It needs to be bigger, at least $800 billion."

That was even bigger than TARP. That was about what the United States had spent so far on the wars in Afghanistan and Iraq.

To Romer's surprise, Summers immediately replied: "I agree."

"Nobody objected, so Larry took that as license to run," Romer says. "Our feeling was: We've got to hit this with everything we've got."

That feeling was the driving force behind a fifty-seven-page "Executive Summary of Economic Policy Work" that Summers wrote with input from the rest of the economic team, laying the groundwork for the first few months of the Obama administration. The December 15 memo outlined the team's thinking about the stimulus, as well as the banking, housing, auto, and budget crises. "The rule that it is better to err on the side of doing too much rather than too little should apply forcefully to the overall set of economic proposals," Summers wrote.

The memo's first and most important point was that a $600 billion stimulus would fail to push unemployment below 8 percent in two years. "This has convinced the economic team that a considerably larger package is justified," Summers wrote.

The memo did include several caveats about a larger package: It might not be politically feasible. It could conceivably unsettle the bond markets. And the bigger the stimulus got, the harder it would be to keep timely, targeted, temporary, and wise. Summers only included four options for recovery plans, from $550 billion to $890 billion, and some liberals have accused him of providing intellectual cover for inadequate stimulus, overemphasizing politics at a time he should have focused exclusively on the scary economics. It's true that Summers considered his job partly political; as he told an aide, if you're going to join the circus, sometimes you've got to dress up like a clown. But his memo doesn't read as a call for caution. The language is dry, but bureaucratic sirens are blaring on almost every page.

"Insufficient fiscal impetus," Summers wrote, "could put recovery at risk, with catastrophic consequences." It's a call for action, and action now.

SIX

The Moment

The stories Obamaworld tells about itself tend to begin in the Chicago transition offices on December 16, 2008, when the president-elect met with his economic team for the first time to discuss the horror show he was about to inherit. David Axelrod, Obama's schlumpy but savvy political guru, is a former reporter who understands the power of narrative, and he has helped spin that snowy Tuesday in the Windy City— "an unforgettable day," he reminded me two years later—into a kind of Rosebud for the Obama White House. Obama was in his analytical element, coolly leading a four-hour discussion of the unappetizing policy choices framed by the Summers memo, repeatedly coming down on the side of bold action—a perfect opening scene for his presidency's creation myth.

"Politics was in the room, but economics dominated the conversation," recalls Jared Bernstein, the house liberal of the economic team.

Politics had its moment just before the meeting, when the economists previewed their message for Axelrod: The economy was hurtling toward a depression. Axelrod knew things were bad, but there are so many degrees of bad, and even he hadn't grasped how close America was to rock-bottom bad. He said his research suggested the public had no clue whatsoever. Summers, the Washington veteran, dryly whispered to Romer, the lifelong academic: "He doesn't mean research the way we mean research."

Okay, polling. Axelrod's point was that the tidal wave hadn't yet hit the shore. There hadn't even been a real tsunami alert.

"The American people," he said, "have not had their holy-shit moment."

Stage-managing the meeting, Summers had assigned Romer to open with an overview of the emergency. With Axelrod's analysis fresh in her mind, she began with the most memorable sentence she's ever uttered, a line that Obama's aides have repeated ever since as a reminder of the mess dumped in his lap:

"Mr. President-Elect," she said, "this is your holy-shit moment."

"It's Like, Boom!"

Romer had searing memories of the recession of the early 1980s, the worst of the postwar era, the downturn triggered when Paul Volcker's Fed jacked up interest rates to curb inflation. She was at grad school at MIT when her father told her he had been "sacked" from a Philadelphia chemical plant—but don't worry, he had set aside money for her upcoming wedding. Her mother soon found out her teaching job was in jeopardy, too. But once inflation subsided and the Fed started lowering rates, consumption and investment came roaring back. By the time Romer returned from her honeymoon, her mom's contract had been renewed. Her dad soon found a new job.

The gist of Romer's Chicago presentation was that this wasn't her father's recession. With what Obama later described as "a chilling set of charts and graphs," she showed that the situation was threatening to make 1982 look like the good old days. And this downturn had been triggered by a financial meltdown, not high interest rates, so it couldn't be reversed by lower interest rates. The only comparable collapse had ushered in the Depression, the era Romer knew best.

Romer's cheery demeanor made her awful news sound somewhat

less awful—"like swallowing a pill in applesauce," Axelrod says—but she laid out two potentially catastrophic scenarios. The death spiral could spin out of control, shredding the banking system and starting a depression, or we could muddle our way through a Japan-style lost decade, an era of prolonged stagnation. She explained why depressions really, really suck—the wasted human capital, the lost tax revenue, the immeasurable suffering—but she also warned that the slow-bleed Japanese route could end up almost as badly as 25 percent unemployment.

Fortunately, economists had learned a lot about avoiding catastrophes. They knew from the errors of the Depression that tax hikes, spending cuts, or tighter money would make the crisis worse. And they were confident that fiscal stimulus could make things better, filling the "output gap" between actual production and the economy's potential production at full capacity. But the current gap was almost unfathomable, over $2 trillion over the next two years. Romer's advice was to attack it with overwhelming force. Government wouldn't be able to plug the entire hole, even with Keynesian multipliers magnifying the impact of every dollar, but she argued for the biggest stimulus in history, somewhere between $800 billion and $1.2 trillion worth of jet fuel, an unheard-of 5 percent to 8 percent of GDP over two years. In FDR's most aggressive year, the New Deal's stimulus only amounted to about 1.5 percent of GDP.

Rahm looked like he was about to pass a kidney stone.

"We were all thinking: 'Oh, my God,'" Goolsbee recalls.

It later became clear that Romer's ugly analysis, while based on the most current data, was way too rosy. The Federal Bureau of Economic Analysis had just pegged growth for the third quarter at −0.5 percent; it would later revise that to −4.0 percent, an unprecedented adjustment. Still, Romer recognized that the economy was in free fall, even though she had no idea how far it had already fallen.

Orszag, a nerdy-chic budget hawk with an independent streak—he wore cowboy boots even though he grew up in an academic family in the Boston suburbs—was about to assume responsibility for the biggest deficit in history. So he would have preferred to start smaller, closer to $600 billion. Geithner, who was so worried about the banks that he thought Obama would need to launch a second TARP, also seemed uneasy about the incoming tide of red ink. He thought the financial rescue would be the real key to recovery; he'd later tell Romer there was more stimulus in TARP than in the stimulus. Romer would shoot back that there was more financial rescue in the stimulus than in the financial rescue; she thought the key to Wall Street stability would be restoring the health of its Main Street customers.

Anyway, no one voiced strenuous objections to Romer's numbers.

"Yeah, there was sticker shock. It's like, boom! But nobody was saying, whoa, whoa, no, no, it can't be $800 billion," Biden told me. "Everybody kind of forgets: We had just lost a couple trillion dollars. It wasn't like it got picked up here and moved over there. It was lost! Lost! We all knew this was absolutely critical."

Summers hadn't mentioned Romer's $1.2 trillion figure in his fifty-seven-page memo, which later prompted widespread criticism that he had tried to shrink the stimulus by surreptitiously limiting the policy menu. It also came out that Romer had suggested in one draft that it would require $1.8 trillion to fill the output gap, which Summers had declared "non-planetary"—a Larry-ism for unrealistic—triggering more accusations that Summers had withheld information from Obama. But that was a bum rap. His final memo mentioned that several outside economists—including Stiglitz, Reich, and former McCain adviser Ken Rogoff—supported at least $1 trillion. The memo also made it clear that even an $850 billion stimulus would close "just under half the output gap," insufficient to "return the unemployment rate to its normal pre-recession level." As one White House economist told me, whatever you think of the president, he knows how to multiply by two.

The memo went through fourteen drafts, and the entire economic team signed off on the final product. Romer had no issue with the deletion of her $1.8 trillion figure, which was less a proposal than an illustration of the scope of the problem. The fiscal stimulus package didn't need to plug the entire output gap; monetary policy could help, as could emergency aid for banks, car companies, and distressed homeowners.

"Even I knew $1.8 trillion was non-planetary," Romer says. She did think her $1.2 trillion figure should have been in the memo, but it was never a major topic of discussion, and she did mention it to the president-elect. In any case, she didn't feel like Summers was undermining or censoring her; she felt like Summers was on her side, a fellow maximalist, similarly worried about undershooting rather than overshooting. Orszag, more of a minimalist, later complained to colleagues that Summers had orchestrated the entire Chicago meeting to advance his "make-it-big" agenda.

"I kept saying: Look, guys, there's no danger of doing too much. It's like worrying about how much weight I should lose," says the bulky Summers. "There's no danger that I'm going to become anorexic." Larry was the pill without the applesauce.

The Summers memo did include a caveat that "an excessive recovery package could spook markets or the public and be counterproductive." And it did warn that in the world of stimulus, higher quantity tends to produce lower quality: "While the most effective stimulus is government investment, it is difficult to identify feasible spending projects on the scale that is needed to stabilize the macroeconomy." But the main reason he kept the $1.2 trillion option out of his memo was that it didn't seem like a real option. Rahm had told him there was no way Congress would go over $1 trillion. Pelosi didn't even want to go past $600 billion. Maybe the B-word had lost some of its power, but the T-word could still drop jaws on Capitol Hill, especially after the blowback over TARP, which was already generating stories about bailed-out firms wasting taxpayer dollars on junkets. A trillion was a psychological Rubicon. "It just wasn't going to happen," says Phil Schiliro, Obama's legislative chief. "Nothing I had seen in my time in Washington led me to believe that was a workable proposition."

Failure would be unthinkable—the Obama team didn't want a reprise of the market crash that followed the House vote against TARP—and delay could be almost as damaging. But getting a bill done quickly would be impossible if congressional eyes were popping out of sockets. "If we tried for a trillion, we'd chew up four or five months, the economy would fall off a cliff, we'd end up with nothing, and we'd have to start all over again," Schiliro says. He thought $800 billion was a huge reach, but it was at least imaginable.

Most of Obama's advisers also assumed that if more stimulus was needed in the future, they could always go back to the Hill and get it. Congress loved jobs bills, especially in election years. Surely by 2010, there would be plenty of appetite for additional tax cuts and spending goodies if Americans were still struggling. On the other hand, if the stimulus somehow turned out to be too large or too late, there would be no plausible way to roll it back to prevent inflation. "It is easier to add down the road to insufficient fiscal stimulus than to subtract from excessive fiscal stimulus," Summers had written. Adding was always easier than subtracting in Washington—especially when it came to tax cuts, since the vast majority of Republican legislators had signed no-new-taxes pledges.

"It seemed blindingly obvious at the time: Who would want to run for reelection without a jobs bill?" Furman recalls. "It was a perfectly reasonable judgment."

It wasn't a universal judgment. Some liberals questioned whether Obama would get a second bite at the apple if the stimulus turned out to be insufficient. House Appropriations chairman David Obey, a prickly New Deal Democrat who kept a picture of FDR above his desk, warned Obama's economists that the Blue Dogs in his caucus would never agree to multiple deficit spending bills: "You damn well better know how much you need to get this job done, and you damn well better err on the high side, because you won't be able to come back for a second kick at the can!" After a meeting with Jared Bernstein—who privately admitted to his union pals that the Obama proposal wasn't big enough to restore full employment—the AFL-CIO's chief economist warned in an internal memo: "There does not appear to be a Plan B. . . . An inadequate fiscal effort following a heavily contested congressional battle will leave economic policymakers with very few alternatives." Paul Krugman also predicted that if the initial stimulus failed to fix the problem economically, the whole concept of stimulus would be discredited politically.

"In retrospect, that was prescient," says Summers, who does not make this kind of admission often. "At the time, I didn't agree. That was a mistake."

In any case, the political team was unanimous that a one with twelve zeroes would freak out the Hill and gum up the machinery. This was the dominant view among Democratic leaders, although again, not a unanimous view. When Rahm told Obey he feared the shock value of the word "trillion," Obey replied that shock value was exactly what was needed. "It will help people understand this is a damn serious problem," he said. The solution, he said, needs to be just as damn big.

On December 16, Obama decided his administration's stimulus goal should be in the 800s, which seemed plenty damn big—just big enough, his economic experts said, to avert an epic disaster, yet conceivably small enough, his political experts said, to avoid paralyzing sticker shock.

"The economic team wanted 899.99," one economist recalls. "The political team wanted 800.01. Either way, we were going where nobody had gone before."

Obama's advisers made one more miscalculation about size: They assumed that whatever number they suggested to Congress would grow once lawmakers inflated the package. I made the same assumption in a *Time* article titled "How to Spend a Trillion Dollars," arguing that Obama "doesn't need to beg Congress to spend; that's like begging Cookie Monster to eat." Democrats were eager to plus up their favorite programs, and Republicans had exhibited few qualms about deficit spending when they ran the show. Capitol Hill did not seem burdened by an excess of fiscal restraint.

So Obama's team agreed to propose a stimulus between $675 and $775 billion to Congress, while emphasizing the higher end of the scale.

"We figured Congress would take all our stuff and add its own stuff," Furman says. Another reasonable judgment that turned out to be wrong.

To Obama's liberal critics, December 16 was less Rosebud than original sin, the first step down a road of inadequate half measures. But it sure didn't feel that way at the time. Obama had approved a package well over four times the size of his campaign proposal from just two months earlier. "People were talking $50 billion, maybe $150 billion, and then suddenly it's $800 billion," recalls his former press secretary, Robert Gibbs. It's true that a few progressive voices were calling for even more, but very few. Obama's political team was worried that hardly anyone outside the transition offices seemed to grasp the depth of the crisis— not the public, not congressional leaders, not even most of the left.

"You've got the unions calling for $300 billion, and a week later, you're saying: Fuck! That's not half what we need!" recalls Jim Messina, Rahm's similarly unexpurgated deputy.

Rahm kept pushing the economists to push outside groups to push for more stimulus, so Obama wouldn't look like the only big spender in town. If you need it, he said, then build the case for it. Ron Klain, who had been Vice President Gore's chief of staff and was now Biden's— the rule against Clinton retreads returning to the same job was not absolute—recalls plenty of discussion about how to get Congress to pass more stimulus, and how to get the country ready for more stimulus. He doesn't recall any discussion about settling for less.

"The idea that everyone knew this would be too small and we just punked out, it's ridiculous," Klain says. "We felt like we were in the deep end of the pool."

Klain was another behind-the-scenes Washington veteran; he had staffed the Clarence Thomas hearings in the Senate for Biden and the recount battle in Florida for Gore. Now his political antennae sensed danger. Obama was blaming the meltdown on Wall Street leveraging money it didn't have and homeowners taking out mortgages they couldn't afford—so his solution was for government to spend $800 billion worth of borrowed cash? Klain accepted the gospel of Keynesian economics, but he wasn't looking forward to preaching it in a time of retrenchment.

"This is going to be a hard thing to message," Klain told Summers.

Summers shrugged. The politics might seem complicated, but the economics did not. As odd as it sounds, financial crises caused by too much borrowing, too much confidence, and too much spending are solved by more borrowing, more confidence, and more spending.

"We have to do what we have to do," Summers said.

Thinking Big

The sour news on December 16 did not end with Romer. Geithner reported that the financial system was in virtual lockdown, and nobody knew how many banks were genuinely solvent. Goolsbee said housing futures were plunging, putting millions more homeowners at risk of foreclosure. Meanwhile, the U.S. auto industry was almost broke; mass liquidations and the collapse of the supply chain seemed imminent. "Then to cheer everybody up," Axelrod says, "Orszag talked about the budget implications."

Great, one aide thought. We just spent two years campaigning to inherit the economy of Brazil.

Afterward, Goolsbee told Obama: "That must have been the worst briefing any president-elect ever had." The president-elect replied that it wasn't even his worst briefing of the week. But when he discussed it in a speech a year later—he called it "unforgettable," too—he recalled wondering if he could request a recount.

Obama's main message to his team was to think big, think bold, think out of the box. This was no time for smallball. "The sentiment was: Don't feel constrained. Don't build a tight corral around your thinking," Bernstein recalls. Obama wanted iconic programs that would create a legacy of change, an updated version of the New Deal. And he urged his advisers to channel FDR's spirit of experimentation.

They did come up with a few unconventional ideas. Romer, worried that public works would just create jobs for burly men, suggested a new brigade of teacher's aides. Summers, eager to ignite consumer spending, proposed free-money debit cards that would expire by a certain date. Furman, thinking along similar lines, floated a sales tax holiday. The economists all supported a Cash for Clunkers program that would offer drivers incentives to junk their gas-guzzlers and buy more fuel-efficient vehicles. They also discussed intensive New Deal–style labor projects, like nationwide efforts to repair water infrastructure or refurbish parks.

Most of these out-of-the-box ideas ran into objections that revealed why they hadn't been in the box in the first place. Summers argued that it made no sense to thrust new teacher's aides into schools that were facing epic budget cuts; why not just give the schools more money so they wouldn't have to lay off as many teachers in the first place? The political team thought the debit card and sales tax holiday proposals sounded gimmicky, too evocative of Bush telling Americans to go shopping. The debit cards also seemed likely to make news once they started stimulating the strip club and head shop industries. Summers actually put Cash for Clunkers to an informal vote; while the economists loved it, the policy types thought it was an overly expensive way to reduce fuel consumption, and the political types thought paying people to buy cars sounded cheesy. The nays had it.

New Deal–style public works did make sense at a time when infrastructure needed repair and construction workers needed jobs, but pouring disproportionate amounts of money into one single-purpose marquee program did not. Advocates had identified $10 billion in shovel-ready water and sewer projects, but it wasn't clear how throwing any more than that into waterworks would get any more shovels into the ground. And the National Park Service had less than $1 billion in ready-to-go projects. Logistically, there was only so much money that could be squeezed through these channels. There was also a diminishing returns problem; if you had to go further down the agencies' lists of projects, you'd fund less ready and less worthy public works. It was fun to kick around grandiose goals, like renovating every school in America. But some schools didn't need to be renovated. Others weren't ready to be renovated. Putting too many eggs in a school renovation basket would just shortchange better public works that could provide better stimulus.

Obama kept pressing: Where's our Skyline Drive? Where's our

Hoover Dam? But times had changed since the New Deal. The construction of the Hoover Dam had employed five thousand men with shovels, and hadn't required environmental studies to get shovel-ready. Now a comparable project might require a few hundred workers with bulldozers, after the years it would take to get permits. And even five thousand jobs would replace less than 1 percent of the losses from November 2008 alone.

Some liberals were clamoring for massive government hiring programs like FDR's beloved Civilian Conservation Corps, which had employed three million young men to plant trees, build parks, and otherwise transform the American landscape. History has bathed the CCC in a romantic glow, but it's hard to imagine a modern government herding unemployed urban youths into militarized rural work camps—often called "concentration camps," before the term took on a darker connotation—for less than a dollar a day. When FDR took office, there were no unemployment benefits or federal safety net to ease hard times; modern job seekers were at least marginally less desperate. And standing up a modern bureaucracy takes time.

In general, Obama's economists were less interested in replicating the iconic programs of the New Deal than producing timely, targeted, and temporary stimulus. They recognized that delaying some spending until 2010 and even 2011 could be a feature, not a bug, avoiding an abrupt contraction when the stimulus ran out. But they believed short-term need-to-do's should trump long-term nice-to-do's.

"The farther you were from being an economist, the more you were into the transformational and inspirational stuff," Orszag recalls.

Obama was no economist. He wanted a moon mission, a program that would convey a sense of historic significance while producing tangible results. "We were searching for something big and aspirational but also substantively beneficial," Biden says. Obama thought the smart grid could be that something, a twenty-first-century version of the interstates or the Internet, this time connecting Americans with digital meters (the smart part) and high-voltage wires (the grid part). "We said:

'God, wouldn't it be wonderful?'" Biden recalls. "'Why don't we invest $100 billion?'"

During a break to celebrate Orszag's fortieth birthday, Obama found out it was also Carol Browner's fifty-third. He didn't have another cake, so he told his new energy and climate czar she could have a smart grid.

"Let's just go build it!" he declared.

Browner shared Obama's enthusiasm about the smart grid. She was eager to see new transmission wires carry the wind of the Dakotas to the people of Chicago. But just go build it? Um . . . no. She explained that the feds didn't need to build wires. Utilities could do that, and had money to do that. The holdup was that siting high-voltage wires had become a maze of red tape, requiring approval from hundreds of zoning boards and other regulators, not to mention entire states that would derive no benefits from the lines slicing through their borders. This was not a problem that could be solved in a stimulus time frame.

"I'm sorry, sir," Browner said. "We wouldn't be able to spend the money."

Obama would not drop the issue. "Let me worry about the politics," he said. "There's got to be more we can do." Biden piled on, telling Browner to stop dwelling on problems and start talking about solutions—as if that would make the problems go away. At one point, Obama and Biden suggested they could personally persuade state and local officials to drop their not-in-my-backyard concerns.

Orszag tried to imagine the president of the United States calling hundreds of mayors to beg for right-of-ways through their towns.

"There was this sense of frustration. Here's the first African American president, the economy has fallen off a cliff, history is calling, and really? I can't just do a smart grid?" Orszag recalls. "He really wanted a moon shot, and these seemed like such mundane reasons not to go big. But Carol said no, this is reality."

Ultimately, Browner was right. The grid was not the interstate highway system. It didn't make sense for government to try to take it over. And a smart grid will require much more than meters and wires: It's a complex merger of modern information technology that distributes 1's and 0's with aging infrastructure that distributes electrons. It's going to be a lot harder to build than Skyline Drive.

But Obama was right, too. His people could do more to accelerate the modernization of the grid—and by harping on the issue, he made sure they did. Some of their ideas would die on the Hill, like a plan to pay states to accelerate transmission projects, and an elaborate scheme to subsidize oversized lines. But some of their ideas would end up in the Recovery Act, like matching grants for smart grid projects, and new transmission lines for federal power agencies.

"It's not sexy stuff, but it's how you start changing the energy world," Browner says.

When Obama's aides recall December 16, they often marvel how little political considerations intruded on the technocratic discussion, for better and for worse. The political team attended along with the policy wonks—in Rahm-speak, Tammany Hall as well as the Aspen Institute—but Obama made it clear he believed that if he got the policy right, the politics would take care of itself. Obama often bristled when aides offered political analysis during policy debates, and it felt especially un-cool during a crisis. Axelrod compares the atmosphere to a MASH unit; the focus was triage. "When people start throwing around phrases like 'Great Depression,' it changes the nature of the discussion," he says. "It's not a political discussion. It's a national emergency discussion. When the house is on fire, you put out the fire." Politics was in the room, but it rarely got much traction.

For example, Rahm thought state aid was political insanity. When Obama had visited the National Governors Association in Philadelphia in early December, conservative Republicans like Mark Sanford of South Carolina, Haley Barbour of Mississippi, and Rick Perry of Texas had insisted they didn't even want federal cash. Why help them balance their budgets without pain, so they'd look like heroes when they ran against Obama in 2012? Now Illinois governor Rod Blagojevich had been arrested for trying to sell Obama's Senate seat. Why bail out these jokers? In the post-TARP anti-bailout climate, even Democratic governors were reluctant to admit they needed aid. In Philadelphia, only Ted Strickland of Ohio had dared to ask Obama publicly to help states avoid drastic cuts in health care and education. "I said, would any governors express a similar view?" Strickland recalls. "It was pretty quiet."

The problem was, state budgets really were in flames, whether the governors admitted it or not. The budget guru Bob Greenstein would soon ratchet up his estimate of state shortfalls yet again, this time to over $350 billion, a 350 percent spike in six dizzying weeks. California's bonds carried a higher risk premium than Mexico's. Thirty governors were already balancing budgets with Hoover-style austerity; in Nevada, Jim Gibbons was trying to slash the state workforce, cut funding for textbooks in half, and eliminate vision care for uninsured children. Ultimately, Obama approved his economic team's proposal to seek a stunning $200 billion in state aid, putting substance before politics.

Still, some of Obama's substance-first policies now seem politically daft. The most damaging was his decision to dribble out the Making Work Pay tax cuts through reduced federal withholding, instead of sending out fat rebate checks that would let people know he had cut their taxes. In the end, most Americans would get an extra $16 per week slipped into their paychecks, but polls would find that fewer than 10 percent of them were aware of the largest middle-class tax cut in a generation.

Incredibly, that was the point. Studies in "behavioral economics" have shown that we're more likely to save money when it arrives in a big chunk. When we receive the same windfall without noticing it, we're more likely to spend it without thinking. So Summers and the rest of the economic team argued for leaking out the tax cuts without fanfare, to mainline more cash into the economic bloodstream. Or as Rahm later described the strategy: "The geniuses on the economic team wanted the money dripped out so nobody fricking saw it."

Behavioral economics had become trendy in the wake of best-sellers like *Freakonomics, Animal Spirits,* and *Nudge.* And its central challenge to laissez-faire theories—its recognition that real-world human beings are not as economically rational and free markets are not as perfectly efficient as neoclassical models assumed—seemed especially potent after the financial implosion. Most of Obama's economists had done some behavioral work, and Summers had once begun a paper with the ultimate takedown of rational-actor assumptions: "There are idiots. Look around." Really, using science to produce change was the essence of Obamaism. The president-elect had read *Nudge*—coauthored by his friend Cass Sunstein, who would oversee regulation at his OMB—and designing tax cuts not to be noticed was a classic policy nudge to encourage desirable behavior, in this case, spending.

Politically, though, when you give people a tax cut, you want them to notice it and appreciate it and remember it. This felt like sending flowers to a romantic interest without signing the note. Rahm argued that "we're denying ourselves an Ed McMahon moment," the grateful squeal of Publishers Clearinghouse pleasure that would greet an envelope arriving from Obama. As Axelrod puts it, "our political imperatives conflicted with our responsibility to get this economy moving again."

Obama decided the economic imperatives came first.

"The *economists* thought it was important to do it *their* way," Rahm told me. "The president correctly sided with them on policy grounds." His rolling eyes and gritted teeth did not suggest a deep belief that Obama had in fact decided correctly.

But Obama's aides weren't even sure the political imperatives were clear-cut. The Bush stimulus rebates had been a political dud; replicating them felt dumb as well as false to the Obama brand. Also, Democrats had criticized Bush for spending tens of millions of dollars on letters announcing his rebates, so a publicity campaign calling attention to Obama's rebates might look hypocritical. Deputy budget director Rob Nabors, who had been Obey's staff director on House Appropriations, remembered how Democrats had ridiculed "Bush's PR money."

Months later, when Republicans were blasting Obama as a tax hiker even as Americans were receiving his tax cuts, Nabors mused to colleagues: Maybe we should've included our own PR money.

"The political theory was if you do the right thing, and you get results, that's good politics," Klain reminisced later. "There was an ethos that policy came first, and in this case the politics seemed like a close call." Then he winced.

"In retrospect, it just seems stupid."

Hindsight always provides an unobstructed view. But even at the time, Klain thought the entire discussion felt "a little Alice in Wonderland-ish." That night, he called his fellow Clinton White House alumnus Gene Sperling, and said he had just attended the strangest meeting of his career.

"In the Clinton years, we had a surplus, and we'd have knock-down drag-out battles over $20 million for an education program," he later recalled. "Now Peter's saying we've got a trillion-dollar deficit, and the president is berating the policy people for saying they're not spending enough money!" Klain is an ardent defender of the Recovery Act's substance, but he thinks December 16 should have raised a red flag about the politics. "If we thought it was odd that we were struggling to find ways to spend more money, it probably shouldn't have surprised us that the American people would find it odd, too," he says.

Axelrod never expected the stimulus itself to be so unpopular. But December 16 was a holy-shit moment for him, too. After the meeting, he told Obama he already knew three things about the next two years: Our poll numbers aren't going to stay this high for long. All of us geniuses are going to start looking like idiots. And we're going to have a brutal midterm election.

"We didn't create this problem, but we'll be held accountable for it," Axelrod told the president-elect.

The Art of the Impossible

If politics is the art of the possible, Schiliro felt like he was about to explore a new realm. Six weeks to get $800 billion seemed insane. And Obama had decreed that the stimulus would have no congressional earmarks, which had always been used as catnip to build support for controversial bills, giving lawmakers something they could brag about bringing home. Passing something this unimaginably big this unimaginably fast through a pork-free process, Schiliro thought, would be like driving a convertible through a car wash without getting wet.

"Things that would normally take a month had to get done in two days," he says.

There wasn't a minute to waste. After the Chicago meeting finally broke up, Obama's advisers rode the El to the airport, and began devising strategy in the back of a crowded train. Schiliro, Furman, and Nabors discussed what they would say the next morning when they briefed Congress about the stimulus. Geithner, Summers, and Romer huddled nearby.

"No one else on the train has any idea who these clowns are, and they're plotting economic policy," Nabors recalls. "I'm like, 'The treasury secretary just called me over to the corner of an El to figure out what should be in the Recovery Act.' That's when I knew this was a pretty remarkable thing we were trying to do."

As it prepared to defy the laws of legislative gravity, the Obama team could at least draw on a wealth of congressional experience. The president-elect may have campaigned as an outsider, but he stocked his administration with Capitol Hill insiders.

Of course, Obama and Biden both came from the Senate, and while Obama had barely located the bathrooms before launching his presidential campaign, Biden had spent thirty-six years in the institution. (Obama once joked with him: "Look, you were a senator. I was never a senator.") Clinton, Daschle, and Interior Secretary Ken Salazar were also former senators, while Emanuel, Solis, and LaHood came directly from the House. Orszag, surprisingly political for a numbers geek, had been the congressional budget watchdog. Obama's White House staff was also teeming with former legislative aides, including Carol Browner; Ron Klain; Rob Nabors; senior adviser Pete Rouse, known as "the 101st senator" when he worked for Daschle; Domestic Policy Council head Melody Barnes, a longtime Ted Kennedy aide; and Jim Messina, who was like a son to Senate Finance chairman Max Baucus of Montana.

Schiliro's boss of twenty-five years, Henry Waxman of California, had just taken over the House Energy and Commerce Committee. Obama's people would not have to introduce themselves to the key players on Capitol Hill.

Obama could also take heart in the new balance of power there. Pelosi and Reid were both strong allies; Reid had privately encouraged him to take on Hillary, and Pelosi had been secretly pleased when he did. Now Democrats had gained twenty-one seats for a commanding 257–178 advantage in the House, where the hyper-partisan, majority-rules culture would assure Pelosi tremendous power to move legislation. "They didn't even have to ask us to turn the lights on," says Republican congressman Mike Rogers of Michigan. Democrats had also picked up seven seats in the Senate for a 58–41 lead, with comedian Al Franken hoping to claim an eighth in a Minnesota recount. The Senate had a less majoritarian ethic, and Reid remained short of the sixty votes he needed to block united Republican filibusters. But every vote counted, and Reid wanted all the allies he could get.

That included independent senator Joe Lieberman of Connecticut, the 2004 Democratic vice presidential nominee who had quit the party in 2006 and stumped for McCain in 2008. Liberals ached to see him punished for questioning Obama's patriotism—not to mention showing up on Fox News every few minutes to whack the Democratic Party—and Reid did ask if he would give up his Homeland Security Committee chairmanship. Lieberman refused, and threatened to caucus with the Republicans if he were stripped of his gavel. At Obama's request, Senate Democrats voted to let Lieberman remain chairman. So he stayed on their side of the aisle and pledged to help out when he could, which would start to pay dividends quickly.

"What made that happen was the president saying he didn't want any recriminations," Lieberman says. "A different kind of person would have been vindictive."

Obama was the kind of person who liked to reach out. And the United States isn't a parliamentary democracy, where the head of state puts forth an agenda, his party dutifully passes it, and the nation judges its results. Even with numbers on his side, he had no intention of trying to shove a detailed stimulus plan down the throats of Democratic leaders. Bill Clinton had tried that with Hillarycare—"the stone tablets approach," Axelrod calls it—and it hadn't ended well. Bush's strongarming of the Republican Congress hadn't ended any better, producing policy fiascoes and a Democratic political revival. Obama told his transition aides he wanted them to listen as well as talk.

"For reporters, either the president is dictating to Congress or Congress is dictating to the president," Schiliro says. "He felt very strongly that he wanted a different model."

Obama felt no need to control every subsection of the stimulus, and he figured his old colleagues would act faster if they felt a sense of ownership. Even if he had wanted to write the Recovery Act, his transition team didn't have the manpower to do it. Rahm was also leery of making formal requests that would make Obama look weak if Congress rejected them.

So Schiliro settled on an 80-20 strategy: If the stimulus included at least 80 percent of what Obama wanted, Congress could fill the other 20 percent with its own priorities. There wasn't time to haggle over every dollar, and Obama wanted lawmakers on his side. It would be impossible to make change without them.

"We don't want to come in as conquering heroes," Schiliro told the team.

Rob Nabors had spent eight years at David Obey's side, and was still technically on Obey's payroll. A few weeks earlier, he had staffed Obey on a House stimulus bill. But now he was an Obama aide, briefing his old boss on Obama's stimulus bill, reading a list of line items while Obey grunted and grumbled.

"He kept throwing things back in my face that we had worked on together," Nabors recalls. "Just Obey being Obey."

Nabors and Obey were like a May-December odd couple—the baby-faced, affable, thirty-seven-year-old African American staffer and the professor-bearded, irascible, seventy-year-old Wisconsin congressman.

Obey was a throwback to the high-handed, hard-drinking Democratic "old bulls" who once dominated Congress, smart and cantankerous, a no-filter, equal-opportunity denigrator who had spent four decades on Capitol Hill. Nabors was a mild-mannered, self-effacing number cruncher who listened more than he spoke, but projected an aura of quiet authority when he did speak. He was the son of an Army general, and as Obey often said, Nabors didn't take any crap.

Nevertheless, Obey was giving him some.

"You know, this would be much easier if you gave me that piece of paper," Obey snapped.

"I'm not giving you my piece of paper," Nabors parried. "This is official transition paper." Nabors had noticed Obey peeking at legislative language of his own; apparently, he had started work on a draft without waiting for Obama.

"You can look at your own piece of paper," Nabors said with a grin.

Nabors, Furman, and Schiliro now had a plan to pitch, even though it existed only as a spreadsheet on Nabors's laptop, and they needed to unite Hill Democrats around that plan in a hurry. Obama wanted a bipartisan bill with bipartisan ideas, and his aides planned to reach out to Republicans once there was a basic consensus among Democrats. But with such a compressed schedule, they didn't think they had time for the interminable back-and-forth of a standard legislative process. Their mission was to get Democrats to embrace Obama's plan and write it into a bill.

Yet they did not want to present it as a definitive plan. In a marathon series of briefings for Democratic staffers, they described their work as ideas, suggestions, the start of a process. They said things like: "The president-elect suggests that $25 billion would be a good number for school modernization." Or: "The president-elect thinks $6.5 billion for neighborhood stabilization would help address foreclosures." They avoided words like "ask" or "request." They did not hand out any paper.

This cagey approach helped fuel the myth that Obama punted the Recovery Act to Congress. He never submitted a formal draft, and many Hill Democrats grew frustrated with his team's refusal to nail down exactly what he wanted and what he needed in the bill. Some saw his nonplan plan as a page out of the Bush playbook, a passive-aggressive effort to direct policy without leaving fingerprints.

"In the olden days, which weren't that long ago, presidents used to send up proposals," says one senior House aide. "They used to say, 'I want this, this, and this, and this is the language I want.' You don't own it until you put it on paper."

As one Senate staffer puts it, most legislators are like kids: They say they want freedom, but deep down they crave guidance. So Democrats who had spent years demanding respect from the White House quickly decided that Obama's team was too deferential. "People were like: Just tell us what the hell you want!" recalls Tom Perriello, a Virginia Democrat who had just been elected to the House.

But Obama's plan was real, even if Congress never saw it on paper, and it immediately became the foundation for the Recovery Act. His team's briefings, while strictly verbal, laid out general goals as well as specific funding ranges for specific programs. On December 19, for instance, Nabors and Furman held a marathon session of back-to-back meetings in the Capitol basement with rotating groups of staffers, laying out Obama's vision—uh, suggested vision—for the six major spending areas: energy, education, health care, infrastructure, protecting the vulnerable, and "other." The plan—whether or not they called it a plan—got a friendly reception.

As the team reported in a four-page memo the next day: "Overall, congressional staff appeared accepting of most of our numbers." On energy, there was "general support for most of the elements and packaging." On health care, transition aides had already been speaking with the Hill, and "work is reasonably far advanced on a package looking a lot like what we have proposed." On the vulnerable, "they are largely taking our proposals and refining them." On taxes, "House and Senate staff largely view their role as drafting the Obama tax proposals and refining the details."

The team's suggestion of a $675–$775 billion overall price tag did draw a few gasps. "The first look we'd get was, 'That's crazy, there's no way,'" Schiliro recalls. The team hinted strongly that the final number ought to be even higher, suggesting that markets might react badly to anything below $800 billion. By the end of the day, Democrats "appeared willing to do whatever number we thought was appropriate," the memo said. They also accepted Obama's general principles for what should go into the stimulus: items that would create jobs, avoid permanent tails, spend out reasonably quickly, and advance sound policies. The three-T test would be the main test, although there might be a few deviations for the core of Obama's agenda.

"We have communicated our willingness to work within these parameters as closely as possible and urge all offices to do the same," Reid's chief of staff wrote to Senate Democrats. When it came to the broad strokes, most Democrats seemed willing to follow their new leader.

"We didn't have the lawyers or the staff to do the drafting, but everyone knew this was our bill," Nabors says. "There wasn't that much disagreement."

A Moving Vehicle

Democrats on the Hill didn't love everything in Obama's plan.

For starters, $200 billion worth of aid to states sounded like a truckload of political spinach. Partisanship aside, why would members of Congress want to write checks that would make them look like bigger spenders and their governors look like better stewards? State aid was especially unappealing to Democrats from states with conservative Republican governors who were unlikely to use their windfalls to preserve services for the poor or save the jobs of state employees. They had slashed taxes irresponsibly when they were flush; why help them avoid the consequences now that they were broke?

"A lot of us were saying: Don't give the governors slush funds!" recalls Congressman Xavier Becerra of California, the vice chair of the Democratic caucus.

Hill Democrats weren't interested in giving Obama slush funds, either. The transition team wanted large pots of money with minimal strings attached, so the administration could steer the cash where it could create the most jobs and drive the most reform. But steering cash is what legislators do. Letting presidents make spending decisions was not the kind of change Congress tended to believe in.

"We came in saying, look, we want some flexibility, we want to fundamentally transform education, we want better transportation projects," Nabors says. "They felt like flexibility had been abused under Bush. They wanted constraints."

The one clear nonstarter in Obama's plan was an infrastructure bank, which he had proposed during the campaign to promote merit-based funding for public works. Most lawmakers preferred the existing system of pork-based funding. The seventy-four-year-old chairman of the House Transportation and Infrastructure Committee, Jim Oberstar, had bragged about snagging fifty-seven "high-priority projects" for his rural Minnesota district in the bloated SAFETEA-LU bill, including a bridge for snowmobiles in Onamia, population 878, and a $3 million road to ease the notorious congestion between County Road 565 in Hoyt Lakes and the intersection of Highways 21 and 70 in Babbitt. Oberstar had first joined the committee as an aide in 1963. He wasn't about to surrender its power now that he had the gavel.

Democrats were willing, though not eager, to accept Obama's demand for an earmark-free stimulus. They saw how it could be awkward to let 535 lawmakers lard up a bill with pet projects during a crisis. But they still expected to plus up their pet programs, proposing over a hundred different line items for infrastructure alone. Committee chairmen all saw pressing needs in their jurisdictions. When would there be a better time to buy the Coast Guard a new polar icebreaker, or install the next generation of airline security, or prepare for a flu pandemic? Wouldn't House Agriculture chairman Collin Peterson of Minnesota know if the Farm Service Agency needed new computers? Arkansas senator Blanche Lincoln wanted emergency aid for catfish farmers suffering from high feed costs; didn't catfish farmers need stimulus, too?

"The biggest issue is less the reaction to our topline numbers and

major components but the very large number of miscellaneous requests," the Obama team's memo said.

Many of these requests were worthy, and perfectly defensible as
stimulus. New border stations and child care centers on military bases
could inject money into the economy just as effectively as new highways. Workers hired for nuclear waste cleanups and wildfire management would be just as likely as construction workers to spend their
paychecks at local grocery stores. In fact, because of the diminishing
returns problem, sprinkling stimulus money through multiple funding streams would have an even greater impact on aggregate demand
than pouring it all into a few simple buckets. And realistically, who was
going to tell House majority whip James Clyburn of South Carolina, the
top-ranking African American in Congress, that he couldn't reserve
$15 million—2 cents out of every $1,000 in the Recovery Act—for job-
creating historic preservation projects at black colleges?

It just seemed messy. Rahm worried that all these "cats and dogs,"
as the Obama team described random congressional desires, would
make the Recovery Act look like spending on steroids—money here,
money there, money everywhere. Summers huffed and puffed about
"the Democratic moment," the danger of using the stimulus to reward
every Democratic constituency, scratch every Democratic itch, and revive every long-neglected Democratic program. This was what Jack Lew
and the shadow team had warned about, the risk of losing control of
the stimulus and letting Congress turn it into a grab bag.

The chum of a must pass mega-bill was already creating a feeding
frenzy, as lobbyists for shoe companies, telecoms, zoos, student lenders, ethanol refiners, and anyone else who could afford their retainers
scrambled to rebrand their client wish lists as stimulus proposals. The
tourism industry wanted a loan to promote the United States as a destination. The maritime industry highlighted the deplorable condition of
seaports, while the airline industry spotlighted the deplorable condition
of airports. The concrete lobby pushed for longer-term infrastructure
projects that tend to be more transformative, and use more concrete,
while the asphalt lobby pushed for shorter-term road repairs that tend

to be more stimulative, and use more asphalt. The U.S. Conference of Mayors identified $180 billion worth of locally approved projects that could go into a stimulus, including a $350,000 fitness center in New Mexico, a $1.5 million water slide in Florida, and a $4.8 million polar bear exhibit in Rhode Island.

One less inspiring legacy of the New Deal was the word "boondog-gle," a reference to leather knickknacks made by unemployed Americans in federally funded arts-and-crafts classes. Obama hadn't run for president to build water slides, and he repeatedly warned his staff that modern boondoggles would discredit the stimulus, his fledgling administration, and government activism in general.

"I know it's Christmas," Biden said after a December 23 meeting with the economic team. "But President-Elect Obama and I are absolutely determined that this economic recovery package will not become a Christmas tree."

This was also important for legislative reasons. Obama needed at least two Republican votes to break a filibuster in the Senate, and he wanted more to set a post-partisan tone. A Democratic Christmas tree would alienate potential aisle crossers. Obama also had to make sure Blue Dogs in the House and centrist Democrats in the Senate didn't jump ship; they were already sounding alarms about runaway spending. Indiana senator Evan Bayh had voted against his party's modest stimulus package in the fall, and he went on Fox to warn that Democrats were already misinterpreting their electoral wave, assuming voters wanted Washington to start squirting cash in all directions.

"My concern was that if you let Congress draft this, it becomes a laundry list of long-deferred desires," Bayh recalls. "The old adage in Congress is that you get your stuff attached to any vehicle that's moving. This was moving!"

Obama's political aides figured that once they had their Democratic ducks in a row for the Recovery Act, some Republicans would be likely to follow. GOP leaders had called for tax cuts and infrastructure; Obama's blueprint had plenty of both. And once Democrats agreed on a basic vessel, it could always be tweaked to lure more Republicans on board. Why would an unpopular minority want to block a popular new president's jobs bill during an existential crisis? Who would want to vote against unemployment benefits, highways, and middle-class tax cuts? Democrats had just put aside partisanship to help Bush pass a Wall Street bailout two months before the last election; why wouldn't Republicans help Obama pass something for Main Street twenty-two months before the next election?

To which some Democrats replied: Because they're Republicans! Rahm's former colleagues in the ultra-polarized House were especially dismissive of Obama's post-partisan promises; Barney Frank of Massachusetts quipped that they were giving him post-partisan depression. "You're not going to get anything from the Republicans," Frank told Rahm. "Everything's a holy war for them." Why would partisans who had just spent months attacking Obama as an America-hating socialist want to help him pass his tyrannical left-wing agenda? Their only likely rewards would be primary challenges from the right in 2010.

There were already signs that after nearly derailing TARP, House Republicans planned to embrace their inner obstructionists. They were closing ranks against a bailout for GM and Chrysler, even after Vice President Cheney warned they might cement the GOP's reputation as the party of Hoover. And most Republican appropriators—usually considered the likeliest targets for bipartisan cooperation on spending bills—boycotted Chairman Obey's first stimulus hearing. The old saying that there were three parties in Washington—Democrats, Republicans, and appropriators—no longer seemed to apply.

Rahm understood the radicalization of the GOP and the cutthroat culture of the House as well as anyone, but he figured that if business groups like the U.S. Chamber of Commerce could be persuaded to endorse the Recovery Act, Republicans would follow. He suspected they wouldn't want to oppose a jobs bill. Their eagerness to get home for Presidents Day recess—"the smell of jet fuel at National Airport," as Rahm put it—would help, too. "Start those airplane engines, they'll fucking figure out a way to get to yes really quickly," he explains.

Obama seemed even more likely to pick up Republican votes among his recent colleagues in the Senate, where "bipartisan alliance" was not yet a complete oxymoron. Senators didn't face reelection every two years, and running statewide tended to encourage moderation. Schiliro was spreading the word that the stimulus could attract as many as eighty votes in the Senate. "There was an assumption that in a time of national emergency you could get bipartisan support," Axelrod says.

The Obama team made plenty of faulty assumptions—underestimating the scale of the downturn, overestimating their ability to go back for more stimulus, expecting the initial stimulus to expand on the Hill—but that was the faultiest.

SEVEN

The Party of No

Republicans were talking about change, too.

How could they not? They had just followed George W. Bush into political oblivion. After preaching small government, balanced budgets, and economic growth while producing bigger government, exploding deficits, and economic collapse, they had gotten pasted for the second straight election. And the electorate was getting less white, less rural, less evangelical—in short, less demographically Republican. Just a few years earlier, books like *One Party Country* and *Building Red America* had heralded Karl Rove's plan for a permanent Republican majority. Now publishers were rushing out titles like *The Strange Death of Republican America* and *40 More Years: How the Democrats Will Rule the Next Generation*. If the GOP brand were dog food, one retiring congressman warned, it would get pulled off the shelves.

"We were in disarray," recalls Congressman Pete Sessions of Texas, who had just taken over the House Republican campaign committee. "People were comparing us to cockroaches, saying we weren't even relevant. We had to change the mind-set."

Beltway conventional wisdom held that chastened Republicans would be forced to cooperate with a popular new president during a national emergency. But Congressman Eric Cantor of Virginia, the new minority whip, thought chastened Republicans should start acting like Republicans. Cantor, an ambitious forty-five-year-old conservative who was the only Jewish Republican in Congress, summoned his whip staff to his condo building that December to plot strategy for the coming year. In a word, the strategy was: Fight. The liberal media might want Republicans to roll over and give Obama a honeymoon, but the base didn't. Why have an opposition party if it wasn't going to oppose?

"We're not here to cut deals and get crumbs and stay in the minority for another 40 years," said Cantor, a Richmond lawyer with a genteel Southern accent and sunken cheeks. Cantor dripped with disdain for get-along Washington Republicans who happily supported Democratic bills as long as they extracted a bit of pork for themselves. "We're not rolling over," he said. "We're going to fight these guys. We're down, but things are going to change."

Cantor's chief of staff, Rob Collins, had invited two pollsters to address the group, and no policy experts. That's because he recognized that House Republicans were now communicators, not legislators. They didn't have the numbers to stop Pelosi from steamrolling Obama's agenda through the House. They needed better PR strategies, not better policies. "They're just going to ram right over us anyway," Collins explained. When House Republicans had the numbers, they had done the same thing. Now their battle was in the arena of public opinion.

To win that battle, Cantor believed, the whip team had to keep Republicans united, so Obama wouldn't be able to brag about bipartisan support for his agenda. That would require picking fights carefully, focusing on stark conflicts that could define their party and the president. There was no point in whipping Republicans against a children's health bill like S-CHIP—and maybe hurting them back home with voters who liked the sound of children's health—now that Obama was sure to sign it into law. Whips didn't have much power to enforce unity anyway, especially minority whips. They had few carrots and fewer sticks. They could only build team spirit, so Republicans would voluntarily stick together on more fundamental legislation—not to block it, but to send a message about its flaws.

The challenge would be developing a consistent message of No without looking like a reflexively anti-Obama Party of No. The whip team agreed that at first the targets should be Pelosi and "Washington Democrats" rather than Obama. The president-elect was riding a wave of goodwill, while Pelosi remained unpopular, especially among the independent voters who had abandoned Republicans in November. There was little upside to whacking "Saint Barack" now, and little downside to attacking ancient Democratic power brokers like Ways and Means chairman Charlie Rangel, a nineteen-term Harlem liberal with a raspy voice, slicked-back hair, and an ongoing ethics investigation. Cantor also insisted that Republicans needed to offer solutions—not with the delusion that they'd be implemented, but to give members something to say yes to while voting no on the Obama agenda. He'd begin by recruiting thirty-three colleagues, nearly one fifth of the conference, to an Economic Recovery Working Group that would draft a GOP alternative to the stimulus. Its details would matter less than its existence.

But the main theme of the meeting was that the fetal position was for losers. Cantor and his deputy, Kevin McCarthy, represented a new generation of GOP leaders who looked like Wall Street traders and projected the same lean-and-hungry vibe; along with Paul Ryan, the budget wonk of the caucus, they were known as "The Young Guns." They weren't interested in playing footsie with Democrats, and they didn't intend to spend decades out of power. "That was the relentless focus: We're going to do everything we can to take this thing back," Collins recalls.

The Purpose of the Minority

In early January, the House Republican leadership team held a retreat at an Annapolis inn. Pete Sessions, the new campaign chair, opened his presentation with the political equivalent of an existential question:

"If the Purpose of the Majority is to Govern . . . What is Our Purpose?"

Not to govern, that was for sure. His next slide provided the answer: "The Purpose of the Minority is to become the Majority."

The team's goal would not be promoting Republican policies, or stopping Democratic policies, or even making Democratic bills less offensive to Republicans. Its goal would be taking the gavel back from Speaker Pelosi.

"That is the entire Conference's Mission," Sessions wrote.

House Republicans were now an insurgency—an "entrepreneurial insurgency," Minority Leader Boehner declared—and Sessions thought they could learn from the disruptive tactics of the Taliban. The key to success in this asymmetrical warfare, he argued, was to "change the mindset of the Conference to one of 'offense,'" to take the fight to the enemy. The Democratic landslides of 2006 and 2008, while decimating the Republican conference, had created a target-rich environment for Republican artillery. There were now eighty-three Democrats representing districts Bush won in 2004, and Obama-Pelosi liberalism was unlikely to help any of them politically. Michigan's Mike Rogers, a brash former FBI agent who had been tapped to play bad cop for Sessions on the campaign committee, says that PowerPoint served as a wake-up call, a reminder that Democratic control of Washington could be the Republican ticket back to power.

"You just got pounded. It's the lowest of the lows," Rogers says. "And then you look at the numbers, it's not as bad as you thought. All those guys winning in red seats, they're going to vote with Obama and his agenda, and I don't think the people who sent them here really want that. Hey, here's how we can come back."

Two consecutive drubbings, while shrinking the Republican conference, had also dragged it even further right. Staunch conservatives from safe districts had survived, while the herd of moderates from competitive districts had been culled, including the entire House GOP delegation from New England. The Republican Study Committee, once a marginal outpost for hard-line conservatives, now included a solid majority of the conference, including Cantor, Sessions, and Mike Pence of Indiana, a former RSC head who was now conference chairman.

Boehner had an occasional history of bipartisan behavior, cutting the No Child Left Behind deal with Senator Kennedy and Congressman George Miller in 2001, but that was "in a universe far, far away," as Miller puts it. Even if Boehner had wanted to reach out to Obama, he had to guard his right flank against Cantor, whose interest in his job was poorly concealed. So Boehner was already mocking the idea that spending could ease the recession, berating Democrats to "start listening to the American people" as if Election Day had never happened.

Some establishment Republicans feared the party was slipping into a suicidal feedback loop, doubling down on an anti-government, anti-immigrant, anti-science, anti-gay agenda that could command excellent ratings for Rush Limbaugh, but not a national majority. As the GOP downsized to its Fox News base, it would be tempted to pursue even harder-line policies, which could lead to further losses and an even harder-line caucus, surrendering the center to Obama. After Republicans got whipped in 2006, party stalwarts like the House campaign chairman, Tom Cole, a rock-ribbed conservative from a rock-ribbed Oklahoma district, had argued for a less dogmatic message. Cole had been a political consultant before running for office—House Republicans had hoped he could be their Rahm—and he had warned that the country was center-right, not right-wing. But after history repeated itself in 2008, Cole lost his post to the more dogmatically conservative Sessions.

The new leaders who gathered in Annapolis had a new mantra: Our mistake was abandoning our principles, not following our principles. They saw John McCain as a typical Republican In Name Only who had sought electoral salvation in ideological equivocation—and look what happened to him. They even revised their opinions of George W. Bush, who in retrospect seemed less a conservative hero, more a big-spending apostate. And they viewed the homogeneity of their conference as an advantage. For the outside game, it could help them reclaim their brand as the party of limited government, firing up their base, and reminding the rest of the country what they stood for. For the inside game, it would be easier to unify a purer conservative team against Obama and Pelosi. They would have fewer "problem children," as they privately described the conference's moderates and iconoclasts.

This was the main theme of the retreat, the need for unity. Boehner kept channeling Ben Franklin: If we don't hang together, we'll hang separately. And the only principles capable of uniting Republicans were traditional Republican principles.

"That's when you saw the seeds of: 'We're going to earn back our majority,'" says Collins, the Cantor aide. "Those were the kind of words we were going to use. We had to convey to the American people and our base: Sorry, we kind of screwed up the last few years. Got it. Message received. New team. Turn the page."

Around that time, Chairman Obey met with the top Republican appropriator, Jerry Lewis, to explain what Democrats had in mind for the stimulus. "David says: Jerry, this is what we're going to do—now take notes," Lewis says. "That way he could say he consulted me." The last time they had chatted, they had discussed a $300 billion bill. Now Obey said it would be $800 billion.

"I said, for God's sakes, David, you've shifted gears," Lewis recalls.

Obey remembers something else Lewis said, after Obey asked whether Republicans had anything they wanted in the stimulus. "Jerry's response was: 'I'm sorry, but leadership tells us we can't play,'" Obey recalls. "Exact quote: 'We can't play.' What they said right from the get-go was: It doesn't matter what the hell you do, we ain't gonna help you. We're going to stand on the sidelines and bitch."

Lewis blames Obey for the committee's turn toward extreme partisanship. He says the chairman short-circuited regular order, cooking up a bill with Pelosi and jamming it through the House. He says Obey never made a genuine effort to reach out, and even ordered his committee staff to stop talking to Republicans. "That's not a negotiation," he said on the House floor. "That's a travesty, a mockery, a sham."

But Lewis doesn't deny that GOP leaders made a decision not to play. "The leadership decided there was no play to be had," he says. "Obey was all-controlling. He can be very obnoxious and arrogant. Our people were turned off very early."

Boehner also telegraphed the Republican leadership's unwillingness to play at an odd meeting in Pelosi's office. The minority leader and the speaker had a cordial relationship, generally limited to discussing House logistics. They rarely bothered to debate policy; the southwest Ohio conservative and the San Francisco liberal knew they inhabited different ideological planets. But this time, Pelosi tried to persuade Boehner to work with Democrats on the stimulus, making an impassioned case that spending programs had higher Keynesian multipliers than tax cuts. Boehner didn't believe in Keynesian theories any more than he believed in global warming or the tooth fairy.

"Boehner was like: 'Okay, let me get this straight, we're going to take a dollar and turn it into $1.75?'" one of his aides recalls.

Pelosi's staffers recall the meeting a bit differently, although the upshot was the same. "Nancy said: We need to do something on jobs. And Boehner said: Why would we want to help you on that?" a senior Pelosi aide recalls. "You saw the beginning of their strategy right there: They didn't want their fingerprints on anything. And then if the economy didn't turn, they'd win."

Democrats weren't interested in bipartisanship out of altruism; they wanted Republican fingerprints on the Recovery Act for similarly political reasons. As Tom Cole, now a deputy whip, wrote in his diary on January 7: "Dems are worried about a unified GOP opposition—not because they will not prevail but because they want joint responsibility." In any case, House Republican leaders had already decided not to give it to them. They wanted the Democrats solely responsible for the economy.

"It was apparent very early that this wasn't going to be bipartisan," Cole told me. "We wanted the talking point: 'The only thing bipartisan was the opposition.'"

"We Should Stand Up"

Senate Republicans had endured an even rougher November than their House counterparts, and they felt even gloomier as they met for their own retreat in early January at the Library of Congress. McCain, who had endured the roughest November, lectured his colleagues that

Republicans could not win national elections if they kept alienating women and Hispanics. "We might find ourselves in the minority for generations," groaned Utah senator Bob Bennett. Five of the forty-one surviving Republican senators would announce their retirements within a month.

"We were discouraged, dispirited, and divided. Some of us were worried whether the party would survive," Bennett recalls. "The one guy who recognized that it need not be so was Mitch McConnell."

The owlish, studiously bland Senate minority leader was the unlikeliest of motivational speakers. With his droning monotone and dour demeanor, McConnell was human Ambien. He was a strategy guy, cynical and clinical, a relentless repeater of messages, a master of arcane Senate rules, an inside player best known for his dogged efforts to thwart campaign finance reform in the 1990s. He had dubbed himself the Abominable No-Man, and his office walls were still cluttered with cartoons lampooning him as a defender of corruption. McConnell was a determined fighter who had overcome childhood polio, rehabbing at FDR's Warm Springs spa, but he was nobody's idea of an inspirational leader.

At the retreat, McConnell reminded the Republican senators that there were still enough of them to block the Democratic agenda—as long as they all marched in lockstep. In the library's historic Members Room, amid oak-paneled walls, Italian marble mantels, and ornate mosaics, McConnell cautioned his own members to stay calm, stay true to their principles, and stay united. Politically, they had nothing to gain from me-too-ism. As always, he stuck to his talking points:

"We got shellacked, but don't forget we still represent half the population."

"Even though we lost, we still have an obligation to represent those ideas."

"It's important to keep an eye on regaining the majority."

"Most importantly, Republicans need to stick together as a team."

McConnell had invited pollsters, too. Their data suggested the election was about Bush fatigue, Iraq fatigue, and the Wall Street debacle;

they saw no evidence of a pro-Democrat or pro-government wave. Americans were still much more likely to call themselves conservatives than liberals. And after TARP, the all-important independent voters were deeply concerned about the historically Republican issues of spending and debt. Sure, the Bush era had featured a Republican orgy of spending and debt; the CBO had just *tripled* its deficit projection to a staggering $1.2 trillion. McConnell's own vote for the bank bailout had turned an easy reelection campaign into an unpleasantly tight race. But with deficits and debt at an all-time high, and Obama preparing to expand them, McConnell saw an opportunity for a revival if Republicans could rediscover fiscal conservatism. We don't have to change who we are, he said. We're the party that cares about spending and debt.

"We're the last line of defense," he said.

McConnell did not advocate immediate Obama bashing, even though conservative activists were clamoring for war, and he also emphasized the importance of offering solutions, to avoid looking like a Party of No. But his message was that No was a perfectly acceptable position: "When Democrats propose something we oppose, we should stand up and express our opposition."

"People were pretty demoralized, and there were two totally opposite thoughts on how to approach the situation," a McConnell aide recalls. "One was, 'we don't like the president, we ought to pop him early.' The other was, 'he's really popular, we should work with him, because that's what people want us to do.' The boss's take was: Neither." McConnell realized that it would be much easier to fight Obama if Republicans first made a public show of wanting to work with him.

The minority leader understood the power of partisanship as well as anyone in Washington. He knew that few Americans have the time or inclination to follow the nitty-gritty details of policy debates, so issues tend to filter down to the public as either "bipartisan," shorthand for a reasonable consensus approach, or "controversial," shorthand for the usual political bickering. McConnell wasn't sure he could stop Obama's agenda, but he was determined to keep it controversial.

"He wanted everyone to hold the fort," recalls former Republican senator George Voinovich of Ohio. "All he cared about was making sure Obama could never have a clean victory."

McConnell recognized that Obama's promises of bipartisanship gave his dwindling minority real leverage. Whenever Republicans decided not to cooperate, Obama would be the one breaking his promises. And since Democrats controlled Washington, Obama would be held responsible for whatever happened there. As long as Republicans refused to follow his lead, Americans would see partisan food fights and conclude that Obama had failed to produce change.

"We thought—correctly, I think—that the only way the American people would know a great debate was going on was if the measures were not bipartisan," McConnell explained later in one of his periodic outbreaks of candor. "When you hang the 'bipartisan' tag on something, the perception is that differences have been worked out."

Maybe Obama had rewritten the rules of electoral politics, but the rules of Washington politics still applied. The dream of hope and change was about to enter the world of cloture votes and motions to recommit. That was McConnell's world.

The stimulus was exactly the kind of legislation that McConnell wanted Republicans to oppose en masse, to create a narrative of conflict while letting the Democrats own massive increases in spending and debt. The goal was to portray it as a trillion-dollar spending bill at a time of trillion-dollar deficits, rather than an economic recovery bill at a time of economic crisis. Even before the bill was unveiled, he was raising public alarms about a partisan rush to fund "mob museums." (A Las Vegas museum devoted to organized crime was on the Conference of Mayors list of eleven thousand local stimulus requests.) After Obama upped his Recovery Act jobs estimate to three million, and pledged that at least 80 percent would be in the private sector, McConnell slyly questioned why America needed 600,000 new government jobs. Obama was talking about rescuing the existing jobs of teachers, cops, and other public employees, but that kind of saved-or-created nuance tended to get lost.

McConnell knew that after TARP, Republicans wouldn't have to attack every provision of the stimulus; they just had to convey that Congress was up to its old tricks. There was no way a bill this gigantic could slip through the sausage-making process without picking up dubious provisions; the mob museum, which was never in the bill, was just a placeholder for big-government bloat. "If the president wants to spend more money, let's debate money," McConnell told his members. Judd Gregg of New Hampshire, the top Republican budgeteer, suggested attacking Democrats as the party of trillion-dollar bills.

Still, McConnell knew it would be tough to maintain a united front. The Senate is less of a top-down institution than the House, and his caucus was more ideologically diverse than Boehner's. Gregg himself had just published an op-ed in the *Wall Street Journal* endorsing several of Obama's spending proposals for the Recovery Act, including roads, bridges, mass transit, and health IT. "It is fairly obvious that serious deficit spending is needed immediately," Gregg had written, directly undercutting McConnell's message. And Gregg was one of those New England fiscal hawks inevitably described as "flinty," because "cheap" was considered impolite; plenty of his colleagues enjoyed deficit spending far more than he did.

"We were really worried that everyone would just say, 'Let's cut a deal,' and the president would get this big bipartisan accomplishment with eighty votes," says one McConnell aide.

The caucus trusted McConnell. His wooden delivery and matter-of-fact approach actually enhanced his credibility as a messenger of hope. But realistically, even his staff thought Republicans would be roadkill for the foreseeable future.

"We didn't leave the room like in *Braveheart,* pounding our chests," says Derek Kan, a young budget analyst on McConnell's staff. "Things didn't look good for the next two years."

"He'd Tell You to Go to Hell!"

On January 5, the president-elect, just back from a Hawaii vacation, sat down with congressional leaders, just back from winter recess. They met in the Capitol's historic LBJ Room, another opulent space with frescoed ceilings and an elaborate crystal chandelier, a lovely setting for a ceremonial exchange of bipartisan platitudes. Obama said the freefall was an American problem, not a Democratic or Republican problem. He promised a balanced stimulus package with serious tax cuts, and urged everyone to put aside partisan differences. "There are times to score political points," he said. "This is not one of those times."

McConnell and Boehner dutifully agreed that these were perilous times, that something needed to be done, that tax cuts were fine things indeed. They did stress the importance of letting Republicans shape the bill, and Cantor had a strained exchange with the president-elect about posting stimulus contracts on the Internet. But the only congressional leader who directly confronted Obama was Jim Clyburn, the House Democratic whip, who delivered a pointed lecture about the racism of the New Deal. He said he'd heard a lot lately about FDR, but he preferred Harry Truman. When he thought of the New Deal, he thought of "Whites Only" signs at CCC camps.

"It was a raw deal for the communities I represent," Clyburn said. "Whatever you do in this recovery package, it better be fair to those communities."

Welcome back to Washington, Mr. President-Elect.

Will Rogers famously said he didn't belong to an organized political party; he was a Democrat. Decades later, Democrats still had a habit of giving Democratic presidents a hard time. They say it's because they're more diverse than Republicans, more small-d democratic, less inclined to play follow-the-leader. They don't have a Limbaugh or Fox News to galvanize message discipline among their base. "Look, we don't always smile and agree with each other," Clyburn says. "We're Democrats!"

Whatever the reason, Democratic leaders wasted no time sending the message that while they supported Obama's agenda, they did not intend to bow down to his White House. Biden was about to become the presiding officer of his beloved Senate, but Reid announced that he was no longer welcome at Democratic caucus meetings. "I do not work for Barack Obama," Reid told reporters. Pelosi owed her gavel to Rahm, but sternly warned him not to meddle in House matters or even backchannel with his former colleagues without notifying her.

This muscle flexing extended to substance, not just process. While Republicans were preparing a united front against the Recovery Act, Democrats were already squabbling about the details.

Chairman Obey was not one of the Democrats griping about bailouts for governors. He knew state aid was terrible politics, but it was still his top Recovery Act priority; it didn't make sense to inject stimulus if states were just going to counteract it. So when Jason Furman and Obama's top domestic policy advisers, Melody Barnes and Heather Higginbottom, suggested $200 billion in state fiscal relief, Obey readily agreed. When they suggested half the money should flow through Medicaid to prevent states from cutting health care for the poor, Obey agreed again. Then they suggested sending the other half through an education fund that would require governors to adopt sweeping school reforms in order to qualify for the cash.

What? Obey definitely did not agree.

He blasted the fund as an "absolutely horrendous mistake" that could sink the bill. He predicted Republicans would trash it as "more social engineering from Washington," while Democrats in thrall to teachers unions would be just as hostile: "I cannot think of an operation that will do more to discredit this entire package."

This blowback was not a surprise. Furman, Barnes, and Higginbottom had proposed the fund in a post-Christmas memo to Rahm. "May be hard to enact without significant consensus reached among congressional stakeholders," they noted. "Some will say the President-Elect is using an economic crisis to jam a controversial reform agenda." They recognized "the political imperative to develop a package that would actually pass Congress at a time when bailout fatigue is setting in." Unity would be nice, but their party didn't work like that.

So one evening, deputy budget director Rob Nabors and his colleagues went to Obey's office to try to work out a deal with his old boss and some Senate Democrats; he let himself in with his old key. The members of Congress wanted to convert most of Obama's school reform fund into a more flexible "stabilization fund" that states could use to patch holes in their budgets. Obey and Senator Tom Harkin of Iowa then hashed out a plan to distribute about $25 billion through existing programs for high-poverty schools and special education. They agreed to chip in $1 billion for Obama's reforms.

That's when Nabors finally spoke up. "We can't go along with that," he said.

Obey was livid, pounding his fist on the table. This was supposed to be a stimulus, not a backdoor effort to reinvent schools. He was trying to prevent brutal education cuts; he didn't have time for trust-us-on-the-details reforms. "If you guys want to reform the hell out of the education system, do it when people aren't drowning," he snapped. And Nabors was Obey's guy. How often had they fought together to steer education money to poor and disabled children?

"If my staff director was still here, he'd tell you to go to hell!" Obey bellowed.

Obey grabbed his coat to storm out of his office.

"Wait a minute, Mr. Chairman," pleaded Phil Schiliro, Obama's legislative director. "Let us check in."

Obey, who enjoyed his gin-and-tonics, grumbled that if he wasn't going to leave, he was going to have a drink. He poured one from his private stash.

After calling Emanuel and Arne Duncan, Nabors calmly outlined a deal: Obey could have his business-as-usual money, but Obama needed $15 billion for reform. The meeting broke up around midnight on a friendlier note, but this wouldn't be the final skirmish. Not even the president could dictate terms to a crotchety old bull like David Obey.

"We all saw *Schoolhouse Rock*," says one Obama aide. "We knew how a bill becomes a law."

Obama delivered his first formal speech of the transition on January 8 at George Mason University, making an urgent case for what he now called his American Recovery and Reinvestment Plan. The speech was a cross between the professorial and inspirational Obama, explaining what he wanted to do and how it would change the world:

> We cannot depend on government alone to create jobs or long-term growth. But at this particular moment, only government can provide the short-term boost necessary to lift us from a recession this deep and severe. Only government can break the vicious cycles that are crippling our economy, where a lack of spending leads to lost jobs, which leads to even less spending. . . . This is not just another public works program. It is a plan that recognizes both the paradox and the promise of this moment—the fact that there are millions of Americans trying to find work, even as all around the country there is so much work to be done.

It was a compelling defense of Keynesian economics, but hardly anyone noticed. Obama wanted to start a conversation with the public, but in a conflict-addicted party and a conflict-driven media climate, he couldn't even control his own end of the conversation.

That's because shortly after he finished speaking in suburban Virginia, Summers and Axelrod met with Senate Democrats in the Capitol. Axelrod shared his latest polling, noting that two thirds of the public had confidence in Obama. But powerful Democrats like Budget chairman Kent Conrad of North Dakota and Finance chairman Max Baucus as well as reliable liberals like Harkin spent most of the meeting picking apart Obama's plans for $300 billion worth of tax cuts. They were all dismissive of his tax credit for firms that hire new workers, ridiculing the idea that a $3,000 check would motivate businesses to add employees when demand for their products was evaporating. Several senators were also skeptical of Making Work Pay. "Twenty bucks a week—how much of a lift is that going to give?" Conrad asked. Liberals were particularly concerned about Obama's proposed tax breaks for businesses, like a "carryback" provision that would allow firms with large losses to claim refunds for taxes paid over the previous five years, a windfall for the big banks and home builders that had helped shred the economy. Harkin understood why Republicans were pushing carryback, but why was Obama?

"To me it looks a little bit like trickle-down," he said.

This was normal Democratic kvetching, not a vicious family feud. Summers told the senators: "Message received, loud and clear." Obama had asked for ideas; he didn't expect U.S. senators to behave like potted plants. And the transition team took their criticisms seriously. Even Furman and Treasury's Gene Sperling, the hiring credit's strongest advocates, agreed they ought to drop it after its hostile reception on the Hill. Sperling was such a fan of the credit that he had been teased at his wedding for peddling different versions to different presidential candidates, but it wasn't worth a dispute that could delay the stimulus. "We had to let it go," Sperling says. The Obama team also worked with the Senate to draft new tax credits for green manufacturing and college tuition.

Of course, the media did not emphasize this collaboration when the whiff of conflict was in the air. The day after Obama's call to arms on the Recovery Act, the headlines were all about friendly fire: "Senate Allies Fault Obama on Stimulus." "Democrats Make Clear They Will Guard Turf." "Democratic Congress Shows Signs It Will Not Bow to Obama."

Obama's own party was doing McConnell's work for him, slapping the stimulus with a "controversial" label. Every critical Democratic quote gave McConnell ammunition to use with colleagues tempted to burnish their bipartisan credentials by endorsing Barack Almighty's first big initiative. "If you're a Republican, you can't be to the left of these Democrats who are saying there's a bunch of crap in there," a McConnell aide explained. "If they're not embracing it fully, there's no reason on God's green earth you should."

House Democrats weren't embracing it fully, either. In early December, for example, Chairman Oberstar had proposed $45 billion worth of infrastructure for the Recovery Act. But when Obama's proposal landed in the same ballpark, Oberstar upped his request to $85 billion. He saw infrastructure as the backbone of American prosperity, promoting long-term growth by making the U.S. economy more efficient, providing short-term jobs for U.S. workers with calluses on their hands, stoking demand for U.S. products like the iron ore mined in his district. He couldn't stand watching China build better railways and Brazil build better ports. And when Summers visited House Democrats, the day after his tussle on the Senate side, Oberstar objected to his uncontroversial point that public works take a long time. "You're wrong!" Oberstar cried. "You don't understand how this works." As Oberstar droned on about the intricacies of transportation projects—bidding processes, the difference between outlays and obligations, his summer job during college puddling concrete—Summers looked like he was back at a Harvard faculty meeting, trying not to roll his eyes while getting chastised by some wrinkly professor of medieval literature.

Democratic leaders did not want the circular firing squad to get out of hand. They really did support Obama's agenda, and they knew their political fates were tied to his. At the next Senate caucus meeting, Reid reminded his members there was "a new sheriff in town." They could criticize Obama's plans, but they should call Rahm or Schiliro before going public. At the next House caucus meeting, when Oberstar started carping again, asking why Obama wanted so many tax cuts when public works create more jobs, Pelosi unceremoniously cut him off.

"The only reason we're talking about stimulus is that Barack Obama won the election," she declared. "He promised tax cuts, so that's going to be in the package."

But the sniping continued. As Obama raced to pass the Recovery Act and stave off a depression, Democrats complained that it was too big and too small, too rigidly partisan and too accommodating to the GOP, too focused on short-term stimulus and too focused on long-term transformation. It wouldn't pour enough concrete; it wouldn't

do enough about housing; it ought to be paired with deficit reduction. Obey, incapable of staying on anyone's message, publicly mocked
Obama as "the crown prince."

Republicans accepted every gripe as a political gift.

And they were about to receive an even better gift.

Nobody Reads Footnotes

The day after Obama's little-noticed speech, the December employment
report brought more nauseating news. Another 700,000 jobs had disap-
peared, the equivalent of Detroit's entire population getting laid off for
the holidays. The way things were going in the auto industry, that didn't
sound so far-fetched. At a stimulus hearing, the former McCain adviser
Mark Zandi warned that the economy was "shutting down."

The next day, the transition released happier news: the Romer-
Bernstein report. It was a preliminary analysis of the Recovery Act's potential jobs impact, the first macroeconomic evidence that the stimulus
could help jolt the economy out of cardiac arrest. It was also the most
politically damaging document of Obama's first term—and the term
wouldn't start for another ten days.

Romer-Bernstein actually originated with Rahm. He was happy to
stuff campaign priorities like solar panels and school reforms into the
stimulus, but when it came to selling it, he preferred a simpler message:
Jobs. He liked to say jobs would be Obama's number-one priority—and
number-two, and number-three. Now that he had a jobs number for the
Recovery Act, he wanted an official report to enhance the credibility
of that three million figure on the Hill. In essence, he wanted a talking
point to help sell the stimulus. The report would end up providing the
most enduring talking point of the Obama era.

"Rahm decided he needed to attach a jobs number to sell this thing,"
snipes one Obama aide. "I thought that was the most damaging thing
we could've done. It was 1990s thinking."

Summers assigned the work to Romer, who did most of the big-picture analysis, and Bernstein, who focused on the specific impact on women and other demographic groups. They spent the bulk of their time crunching numbers and evaluating multipliers to try to nail down how much the stimulus would increase employment compared to the no-action baseline, the "delta" between what would happen with and without the Recovery Act. They spent less time assessing that no-action baseline, the economy's expected trajectory without stimulus. Romer mostly followed forecasts from the Fed and two private firms. If anything, Romer says, their report's no-action baseline was somewhat more negative than the Blue Chip consensus forecast, the usual starting point for White House calculations.

It wasn't nearly negative enough. Page 4 of the report included a chart that has dogged Obama ever since. It predicted that without the Recovery Act, unemployment would peak at about 9 percent, but with the Recovery Act, unemployment would remain below 8 percent, and would fall to 7 percent by the end of 2010.

Most analysts believe Romer and Bernstein came close to the delta, their prediction of how much the stimulus would improve the economy. They just overestimated the baseline, the economy's starting point. They worried at the time that they were being too optimistic; Bernstein had been quoted saying: "We'll be lucky if the unemployment rate is below double digits by the end of next year." But they figured their forecast would lack credibility if they strayed much further from the Blue Chip. They would have sounded like Chicken Littles.

"The fact remains that 8 percent was a conservative forecast at the time," Bernstein says. "In hindsight, obviously, we just should've focused on the delta."

Their report—just thirteen pages, barely half of that text—was cluttered with caveats: "It should be understood that all the estimates presented in this memo are subject to significant margins of error." And later: "The uncertainty is surely higher than normal now because the current recession is unusual both in its fundamental causes and its severity." Unfortunately, nobody remembers caveats.

Romer-Bernstein even included a humdinger of a footnote about the baseline: "Some private forecasters anticipate unemployment rates as high as 11% in the absence of action." Unfortunately, nobody reads footnotes.

Before releasing the report, Romer shared it with the economic team, as well as some academic peers. Summers and Furman advised her not to put her name on it before she was confirmed, but she says her husband was the only reader who raised concerns about including the unemployment prediction. He reminded her that a fellow economist who had muffed an employment forecast based on an overly optimistic baseline once told them ruefully that forecasters should stick to predicting changes in unemployment, not levels of unemployment.

"Oh, for heaven's sakes," Romer replied. "If unemployment goes to 10 percent, we'll have much bigger problems than this."

Romer and Bernstein both say that no one else flagged anything amiss with their report. "Rahm loved it," Bernstein recalls. "He said: Do more stuff like that!" The political team did exchange emails about the potential damage from the report's suggestion that men would get more stimulus jobs than women, but no one seemed worried about putting the optimistic unemployment forecast in writing.

Republicans did not even make a fuss when the report was first released. But two weeks later, McConnell aide Derek Kan, who had a very un-Washington habit of actually reading reports, mentioned the 8 percent forecast in an email to Don Stewart, McConnell's communications director. Stewart immediately raced over to Kan's desk. "Are you telling me they're predicting the unemployment rate?" he asked.

Looks like it, Kan said.

"Oh my God!" Stewart shouted. Economists all seemed to think the situation would be even worse in a year. Now Obama was promising instant relief? Stewart quickly started blasting the 8 percent figure out to reporters, and he never stopped.

"If I were doing this over again, I'd be more politically astute," Romer says. "But those were our best estimates at the time. We weren't trying to puff up confidence or do the reverse. We were trying to do an honest forecast."

It was honest. It just wasn't accurate. Several days after Romer-Bernstein hit the streets, the private forecasters at Macroeconomic Advisers downgraded their economic outlook. They told Romer they had collected hideous new data from Japan and Europe. The entire global economy was now gasping for air.

"That was my first inkling that, oh God, our forecast might be quite wrong," Romer says. "It's even worse than we thought."

— EIGHT —

"Wow. We Can Actually Do It."

The big-ticket items in the Recovery Act—state aid, middle-class tax cuts, extended unemployment benefits—would not even make it halfway to Obama's goal of $800 billion. That left a lot of room for Change We Can Believe In. For the transition team, it was an exhausting but exhilarating time, a chance to chart a new path for the country while trying to stop it from collapsing. Obama's wonks thought both goals were achievable, even if they weren't always perfectly aligned.

One of the enduring criticisms of the stimulus has been that Obama exploited an emergency to do things he wanted to do anyway. It's true. He thought they were good things to do. He had just spent a long campaign explaining why he wanted to do them. And he had said throughout his transition that he expected the Recovery Act to create a footprint for future growth as well as an instant spark. Did his critics expect him to fill out the $800 billion with things he didn't want to do? When did they want him to start keeping his promises and pursuing his vision?

"Administrations go fast. You don't have that much time to change things," says Brookings official Bruce Katz, a Clinton administration housing aide who led the Obama transition's review team for HUD. "The narrative coming from the top was: 'Let's make sure we take advantage of this disruptive moment.'"

Investments in Obama's long-range agenda wouldn't always inject the swiftest short-term stimulus. But the economy clearly needed support for an extended period, so just about any investments would provide some stimulus. And in some cases, Obama's priorities would be excellent stimulus. For example, aid to poor families with high propensities to spend would provide high bang-for-the-buck, while advancing Obama's spread-the-wealth agenda. So the transition team secured hefty increases in safety net programs like food stamps, child care, rental assistance, and the Earned Income Tax Credit for low-income workers. It also subsidized the COBRA premiums that help laid-off workers keep their health insurance. Obama even gave seniors, veterans, and people with disabilities a one-time $250 check, because—well, why not? Economically and morally, it beat giving tax breaks to billionaires. It would drop more cash into circulation, helping people who needed help while nudging the inequality dial in a fairer direction.

Similarly, as long as Obama was creating jobs for construction workers, it made sense to have them advance his education agenda by modernizing schools, or his research agenda by renovating labs at science agencies like the National Institute of Standards and Technology, or his health agenda by building new community medical clinics that would expand access to low-cost care. Upgrading decrepit electrical substations, Amtrak trains, and public housing would promote his priorities, too. He didn't want to pour more money into weapons systems, but building wounded-warrior complexes and child-care centers at military bases would be solid stimulus. He didn't want to boost agricultural subsidies either, but paying farmers to restore flood-prone land to its natural state, while only mediocre stimulus, would at least create wetlands and reduce crop insurance payouts. And as long as he was spending more, why not keep his promises to spend more on things like early childhood education, preventive medicine, and the Americorps national service program? These were all opportunistic ways to use dollars to drive incremental change—and nursery school teachers, physician's assistants, and even community organizers needed jobs, too.

But the Obama team was also looking for openings to drive more lasting change. Summers was concerned that the desire to exploit "the Democratic moment" could overshadow the need for timely stimulus, but he thought this was an ideal time to invest in research and critical infrastructure that could build long term prosperity. Borrowing was cheap, and there was only so much money that could be spent both quickly and effectively. A wind farm that was approved now and created jobs for a U.S. turbine manufacturer later in the year but didn't begin construction until 2010 would still help fill the output gap.

"No matter how you structured it, you couldn't get too much out the door in 2009," Orszag says. "It was okay if some of it wasn't so fast. You couldn't let the perfect be the enemy of the good."

Anyway, this was, in fact, a Democratic moment. Republicans had already exploited their moment. Obama thought he had been hired to do better.

"He wanted to break through the conventional wisdom right away and do some big things that people had never been able to get done," press secretary Robert Gibbs told me. Then his voice trailed off. "Arrgh. Washington. It's not used to doing big things."

The Entire Food Chain

Of all his exploitations of the Democratic moment, the biggest was Obama's effort to launch America's transition to a low-carbon economy.

Clean-energy investments were win-win-win-wins: reducing our thug-empowering oil dependence, our planet-broiling emissions, and our wallet-straining exposure to oil shocks, while replacing the unsustainable housing jobs of the bubble years with the green jobs of the future. A permanent transition to clean energy would still require government to impose costs on dirty energy; as Summers put it, stimulus would be one blade of the scissors, cap-and-trade the other. Still, the Recovery Act would be a hell of a start.

"You talk about this stuff all your life, then suddenly, it's: Wow. We can actually do it. Like, now," marvels Obama energy adviser Heather Zichal.

The stimulus allowed Obama to make inroads on all his energy promises at once, to start transforming the entire food chain—reducing energy use through efficiency; shifting from fossil energy toward renewables; accommodating those renewables with a smarter grid; financing cutting-edge green research; and building a manufacturing base for a green economy. "We didn't want to put our thumb on the scale for any one sector or one technology," Carol Browner explains. "We wanted to do *everything*." Any proposal that could reduce fossil fuel dependence on the electricity side or the transportation side while at least passing the laugh test when it came to the three T's and job creation was fair game. And Rahm's Rule was in full effect. When a former Clinton budget aide on the transition reviewed the green team's initial proposals, his reaction was: You're not spending enough.

"That was probably the first time in history an OMB guy said that to anyone," says Joe Aldy, the environmental economist for the green team and later the White House.

Even clean-energy advocates were flabbergasted by the magnitude of the money. State energy offices that had expected a total of $50 million in 2009 would get $3.1 billion. The stimulus would pour another $3.2 billion into energy-efficiency grants for cities and towns, most of which didn't even have energy offices yet, and $4.5 billion into smart grid programs that had never received a dime. It would also include $3.4 billion for clean coal, more than Bush had managed to spend in eight years of devotion to the extraction industries, and $5 billion for low-income home weatherization, almost as much as the program had spent in over three decades.

Now it was Obama's turn to produce numbers that seemed to have the decimal point in the wrong place. For example, in 2007, Congress had authorized a $100 million grant program to finance advanced battery factories for electric vehicles, but had yet to provide any funding. The Recovery Act flooded the zone with $2 billion. "It was such an extraordinary time," says the green team's David Sandalow, a Michigan native and the author of *Freedom from Oil.* "It was like, okay, let's see if we can create a new American manufacturing industry that can make a real difference in the Midwestern economy. And yeah, it turned out that we could."

Obama aides joked about *Brewster's Millions,* the movie where Richard Pryor's character rushes to spend a vast inheritance in a month. Congressional staffers began quoting the late senator Everett Dirksen's famous line: A billion here, a billion there, pretty soon you're talking about real money. Still, they accepted almost all of Obama's proposals, and added some of their own.

"Some people think we were just trying to spend as much as possible. Well, they're right!" recalls one transition aide. "You'd find this great program that needed $1 billion. Then someone would ask: Can you do it for $10 billion?"

Obama's energy experts and the Hill's veteran energy staffers didn't have much time to plan how to reinvent a multitrillion-dollar slice of the economy. But they had been thinking about this stuff for years. They had reams of reports about cost curves and supply chains at their fingertips. They were ready for their Democratic moment.

It's often forgotten that in early 2009, green energy was not just a tiny industrial sector. It was a tiny dying industrial sector. Renewable electricity projects were financed with tax credits, and after the financial meltdown, investors didn't need tax credits, because they had lost so much money they didn't have tax liabilities. The credit crunch had ravaged project finance in general, but funding for wind farms and solar installations in particular had totally dried up, and U.S. manufacturers of wind turbines and solar panels were rapidly shutting down.

"Renewables were dead in the water," recalls Denise Bode, a former natural gas lobbyist who had just taken over the American Wind Energy Association.

The Recovery Act's solution, forged over several meetings between Obama's aides and Democratic congressional staffers, was to replace the tax credits with equivalent cash grants. "Monetizing" the credits was not, perhaps, the most exciting public policy, but it was exactly what wind, solar, and geothermal developers needed to resurrect their industries. Joe Aldy was assigned to inform the clean-energy advocates, and he still remembers their tense faces when he arrived a bit late.

"Once I explained what we were doing, you could just see the daggers turn to joy," he says. "Those guys were really desperate."

Unfortunately for literary purposes, that's about as dramatic as the energy discussions got. Again, the Obama team pushed for flexibility, while congressional Democrats preferred specifics. And the Hill's energy staff did question some of Obama's more audacious requests. Were there really $2 billion worth of shovel-ready battery factories? How did he expect to ramp up weatherization more than 1,000 percent in a stimulus time frame? How on earth would state energy offices handle even bigger windfalls when governors were slashing their administrative budgets?

"We said, 'Hey!'" recalls one Senate aide. "There's no capacity out there!"

In general, though, the discussions were collegial, wonky, earnest efforts to achieve Obama's goals. A fly on the wall would have gotten extremely bored, unless the fly had an abiding interest in diesel retrofits or smart grid network protocols or EISA Title V Subtitle E. Nothing sexy happened, except the wardrobe malfunction that Zichal suffered while getting out of a cab on her way to a January session on the Hill. (It forced her to wear her overcoat for two hours in a sweltering basement meeting room.) Some participants graciously gave me binders full of spreadsheets, notes, legislative text, and other documents from these meetings, and I hope I don't sound ungrateful when I say that Hollywood is unlikely to option the rights.

The drama was in the substance, the promise of change. Behind all those dry spreadsheets lurked a new approach to powering and fueling America.

"For eight years, unless you mined coal or drilled oil, you couldn't get the time of day," says Chris Miller, Harry Reid's energy staffer. "And suddenly there we were, planning a low-carbon future."

Obama set the agenda, but Congress added several of its own twists. For instance, Majority Leader Reid, who envisioned Nevada as the Saudi Arabia of geothermal power, secured $400 million for advanced geothermal technologies, twenty times the program's 2008 budget. Hill Democrats not only adopted Obama's ambitious energy efficiency pro posals for retrofitting government buildings, schools, and homes, they added programs to retrofit factories and hospitals. Overall, the Recovery Act would include over $25 billion for efficiency, far more than the most optimistic advocates had requested.

"We're used to asking for pennies," says Kateri Callahan, head of the Alliance to Save Energy. "And then: Whoa! The numbers kept going up and up and up."

Even the congressional fine print could be transformative. For example, Reid stuck $80 million into the Recovery Act for regional transmission planning, an unprecedented effort to address some of the siting problems that Carol Browner had explained to Obama in Chicago. House Energy chairman Henry Waxman of California also attached some eyes-glaze-over policy strings to the state energy grants that could significantly reduce U.S. electricity use. Before governors could get their money, they would have to sign a pledge to enact strict green building codes, and to pursue regulations giving utilities incentives to help customers save energy—that holy grail of efficiency that Obama discussed during the campaign. House energy staffer John Jimison hashed out the arcane provision at a late night negotiating session, then read it aloud to colleagues. Total silence. "Sheer poetry," he joked.

The Hill was also responsible for the most controversial program in the stimulus, although it wasn't controversial at the time. Reid and Senate Energy chairman Jeff Bingaman of New Mexico pushed to extend the Energy Department's loan guarantee program to a broader swath of clean-tech projects, even though the Bush administration had failed to back a single loan in four years. The program had bipartisan support; in fact, Bush's political appointees scrambled to try to complete their first loan before leaving office, until the department's career staff concluded in early January that the application—for a California solar start-up called Solyndra—wasn't quite ready. "The apparent haste in recommending the project meant that certain credit procedures were not adhered to," the staff wrote. Some market economists—including one Lawrence H. Summers—thought governments were lousy lenders, but banks had fled the clean energy space, and the beauty of loans was that a few billion dollars in federal exposure could leverage tens of billions of dollars in eco-friendly private sector activity. "That was the best bang for the buck you could get," Bingaman says. Everyone understood that some loans would go bust, but economists Aldy and Jeff Liebman figured they'd be happy even if half the loans failed, if the other half helped change the energy game.

That was the whole point of investing in efficiency and renewables instead of hiring workers to dig holes and fill them in: The fossil fuel game was unsustainable. The stimulus was stuffed with potential game-changers—ARPA-E's research, the first commercial refineries for post-corn biofuels, fast charging stations for electric vehicles, clean-tech manufacturing, green job training, and more. The goal was to help clean-energy businesses reach critical mass, so they could cut their costs enough to compete with dirty energy. "You always say you just need a push," Browner kept telling them. "This is your push."

The Recovery Act was not just the biggest clean-energy bill ever. It was the biggest energy bill ever.

"By leaps and bounds," Browner says.

"I Seen My Opportunities"

Obama's advisers still resist the notion that the stimulus was a Trojan horse for the president's agenda. After all, the bulk of the bill was basic stimulus. The transition team cast a wide net for ideas that could satisfy the three-T test and create jobs quickly, vetting thousands of line items that had little to do with his larger vision. The Census Bureau needed to hire extra door knockers? "Hire" was a good word, and there was little danger they would stay beyond the 2010 decennial. The Commerce Department was running out of coupons to help Americans convert their analog televisions to digital? Extra coupons might sound like a goofy use of stimulus dollars, but they would stimulate purchases of converter boxes by families who would otherwise lose their signals. Banks had stopped lending to small businesses? Waiving Small Business Admin istration fees and increasing the federal guarantee for new loans could thaw a frozen credit market. The Labor Department could ramp up a summer jobs program for young people? "Jobs" was a great word.

The transition team also rejected dozens of ideas that would have promoted the Obama agenda, usually because of skepticism of their timeliness or suspicion about their budgetary tails. Browner's green team wanted to convert the Postal Service fleet to electric vehicles, but concluded it wouldn't create jobs quickly enough. Operating subsidies for local transit agencies could have helped avert damaging fare in creases, but Obama's aides had a feeling the subsidies would never dis appear. One transition official compared the anti-tail ethic to a sign he saw at the Grand Canyon, warning tourists not to feed the squirrels. "It said: You won't be here in the winter, but the squirrels will, and they're still going to expect to get fed," the official recalls. Obama did not want the Recovery Act to create entitled squirrels.

But yes, Obama's team was looking for line items that could help transform the country. Most of them flew under the radar.

For example, the U.S. unemployment insurance system was an an tiquated vestige of the New Deal, designed for a workforce of male breadwinners. It served only about a third of jobless workers, and they had to wait three months to qualify for benefits, a legacy of the pre computer age when labor data was much tougher to track. So Furman and Bernstein worked with House Democrats like New York's Charlie Rangel and Jim McDermott of Washington to modernize and expand the system, providing $7 billion in incentives for states to eliminate the time lags and loosen their eligibility rules. Governors would be re warded for extending benefits to part-time workers, as well as workers who quit jobs to care for a family member, follow a spouse who had to relocate, or escape domestic violence. These reforms wouldn't attract much attention, but they would extend the New Deal safety net to new cohorts of deserving workers while providing an automatic Keynesian stabilizer in times of high unemployment.

"My view of legislation is, you should always have ideas ready," says McDermott, who first proposed the reforms in 2002. "Like George Washington Plunkitt said: I seen my opportunities and I took 'em."

That would be a good slogan for the whole Recovery Act—not in Plunkitt's original Tammany Hall graft sense, but in the Rahm's Rule sense of taking advantage of the Democratic moment. A few more examples of the seeds it planted for change:

Build America Bonds. The municipal bond market was another casualty of the financial crisis. Muni bonds were fueled by tax exemptions, and investors had just as little appetite for exemptions as they had for clean-energy tax credits. So Rangel's staff devised new bonds that replaced the exemption with a direct subsidy, hoping to lower rates enough to attract investors and jump-start public works. These Build America Bonds would be exponentially more popular than anyone expected, financing thousands of local infrastructure projects that put Americans to work in all fifty states.

Homelessness Prevention. The longer homeless people remain on the streets, the harder it is for them to repair their lives, and the more they end up costing society. In 2008, a pilot program had shown that modest interventions to help Americans on the brink of homelessness—helping out with utility bills, security deposits, moving expenses, or rent—could help keep a roof over their heads while slashing shelter costs, prison costs, and medical costs for taxpayers. The Recovery Act approved a sixty-fold funding increase to take the program national.

"For $1.5 billion, you get a systemic reform that changes the way we deal with the problem," says Shaun Donovan, Obama's HUD secretary.

Green Infrastructure. America's long-neglected waterworks were typical of the hidden infrastructure crisis that Obama had vowed to tackle, wasting billions of gallons of clean water and releasing billions of gallons of raw sewage every year. The Recovery Act provided over

$6 billion in new investments, a significant though not transformative effort to upgrade leaky pipes and inadequate treatment plants.

What was potentially transformative was a new rule reserving 20 percent of the cash for "green infrastructure" like permeable pavement, green roofs, rain barrels, and wetland restoration projects, an unprecedented investment in eco-friendlier water management. The idea was to keep stormwater out of overwhelmed sewers instead of building new capacity, to reduce demand for treatment instead of increasing supply, to make urban jungles function more like natural forests.

In Philadelphia, for example, an aging stormwater system was dumping raw sewage into local waterways after heavy rains, and engineers had proposed a $9 billion outflow tunnel underneath the Delaware River to stop the overflows. Instead, Mayor Michael Nutter launched a stimulus-funded campaign to capture runoff from one-third of his city's impervious surfaces. He's not a tie-dyed tree hugger—although he does enjoy converting parking lots into parks—but he didn't feel like burying $9 billion 150 feet underground. Greening his infrastructure instead could save $7 billion.

"It's revolutionary, but it's really a no-brainer," he says. "We help the environment, and we don't have to waste all that money tearing up the city."

Electronic Medicine. Obama saw computerization as a crucial foundation for health care reform, a way to cut extraneous costs, reduce fatal errors, and start collecting the data needed to rationalize a chaotic system. But after announcing he wanted the Recovery Act to spend $20 billion to get every American an electronic medical record within five years, he left most of the details to Congress. And while there was strong support for health IT on the Hill, a slew of competing bills had stalled over disagreements over how to protect patient privacy, how to get doctors and hospitals to go digital, and how to get computer systems to talk to each other.

The Recovery Act forced the major players into a deal. For example, Congressman Pete Stark of California had to drop his idea of mandating adoption of the Veterans Administration's computer system, which would have squelched innovation and forced early adopters to "rip and replace" competing systems. But Stark successfully argued that to qualify for financial incentives, physicians should have to prove they're "meaningful users" of digital systems, not just purchasers, to make sure they're e-prescribing, getting lab reports online, and reaping the benefits of the new technology. The negotiators eventually agreed on carrots and sticks that provide up to $48,400 for doctors and $11 million for hospitals that put electronic medicine into action, while slowly reducing Medicare payments for those that don't. Patients will have to give consent before their data can be transferred electronically, but won't have to reiterate their consent before every transfer.

As short-term stimulus, health IT didn't pass the laugh test. Most of the money wouldn't begin to go out the door until 2011. But even Summers thought it was exactly the kind of investment that government should make, helping to overcome private disincentives to build a network that would have huge public benefits once it reached critical mass. Summers had spent one of the most traumatic hours of his life waiting helplessly in a hospital after a lab technician misread a handwritten record—it said "Simmons," not "Summers"—and thought his blood counts were crashing. So he understood in his gut how crazy it was that the average 7-Eleven used more information technology than the average doctor's office.

Anyway, Obama figured he was entitled to a few exceptions to the three-T rules. Health IT was a bipartisan cause, and a campaign promise, too.

Comparative Effectiveness. Bush's prescription drug bill had included a token effort to expand comparative effectiveness research, but only authorized $15 million a year, when a single study comparing the performance of antipsychotic drugs had cost $67 million. During the campaign, Obama promised to finance a real effort to figure out which medical treatments work best in which situations. The Recovery Act would pour in $1.1 billion, by far the most aggressive effort ever to transform a system driven by habit and assumption into a system driven by data and evidence.

Rahm's brother Zeke Emanuel, a noted oncologist and bioethicist who would become Orszag's health adviser, happened to be one of America's leading advocates of comparative research. He still remembers his first visit to a cancer ward as a medical student, when the white coats ordered a transfusion for a teenager with Hodgkin's disease because her platelets were below 20,000. Zeke asked: Why 20,000? Because that's what we do here, one doc replied. "It drives me fucking nuts—the ignorance is overwhelming," says Zeke, who shares Rahm's linguistic proclivities. (So does their brother Ari, a Hollywood super-agent who was the model for the potty-mouthed Ari Gold on HBO's *Entourage*.) A billion dollars was 0.05 percent of our annual health care expenditures, but it could go a long way toward shifting that's-what-we-do-here to that's-what-works.

Lobbyists for drug and device makers, eager to protect the veil of ignorance around their products, pressured Congress to water down the comparative effectiveness language, warning it would lead to "cookbook medicine" and medical rationing. And after Republican health care propagandist Betsy McCaughey wrote a column portraying the combination of comparative effectiveness and health IT as a plot to let federal bureaucrats track clinical decisions electronically and punish doctors who prescribe costly treatments, Rush Limbaugh began trashing the provisions as the first step toward government-controlled medicine. (McCaughey would later dub Zeke Emanuel "Dr. Death.") Nervous lawmakers eventually added language clarifying that they didn't intend the money to be used to drive payment decisions, as if the goal was to produce purely academic research.

"There was a real fear about the government saying: We know what's best, that drug's too expensive, you can't have it," says Tony Coelho, a former Democratic congressional leader who is head of the Partnership to Improve Patient Care, an advocacy group funded by drug and device companies. "We never said: Don't do the research. We said: Don't use it to make decisions for patients and doctors."

But advocates were confident the $1.1 billion worth of new information wouldn't just sit on the shelf. With better information, patients and doctors could make better decisions for themselves.

"It's going to be a tremendous driver of change," Zeke says. "It's going to provide a tsunami of data."

High-Speed Rail. Zeke was staying at Rahm's house in Chicago over the holidays when a fax arrived listing the transition team's stimulus priorities. Zeke knew he shouldn't snoop, but he snooped. He was thrilled to see his own priorities, electronic medicine and comparative research, in line for serious cash. But when Rahm got home from the gym, Zeke confronted him: "Where the fuck is high-speed rail?"

The predictable response would have been a family-unfriendly version of: Why are you reading my faxes? Why is an oncologist lecturing me about infrastructure? But Rahm agreed with his nosy brother.

America's freight rail was the envy of the world, but our intercity passenger rail wasn't even the envy of the Third World. While 220-mile-per-hour bullet trains were zipping around Europe and Asia, most U.S. trains still trudged along at speeds first achieved in the 1830s. Rahm and "Amtrak Joe" Biden had pushed high-speed rail early in the transition, but the economic team had objected that it would be too slow to spend out and too costly relative to its benefits to travelers. Now Rahm decided to resurrect it, and ordered the transition team to assemble a plan. "I got a call at 7 A.M. on a Sunday: Help! We need high-speed rail!" recalls Mort Downey, the head of the transition's transportation group.

High-speed rail wouldn't be timely, either. But it could advance Obama's vision in multiple ways, easing road and air congestion, reducing fuel consumption, and jump-starting a domestic train-making industry. Spain, a country the size of Texas, was pouring $200 billion into a high-speed network. China was building more high-speed track than the rest of the world combined. Nations like Brazil, Turkey, and Russia were getting into the game, too.

"Tell me, how are we going to have an efficient twenty-first-century transportation system without high-speed rail?" Biden kept asking.

Broadband. America's sagging global ranking in high-speed Internet access—behind Korea, Japan, and even Lithuania—was another Obama hobbyhorse. Universal broadband access was not just a top priority; it was also vital for so many of Obama's other priorities that relied on information technology, like the smart grid, electronic medicine, cutting-edge research, and twenty-first-century schools. But when he announced the Recovery Act would help the United States catch up to its competitors on the information superhighway, his technology advisers were caught by surprise. It was hard to imagine a more complex legal and technical issue with higher financial stakes, raising thorny questions about natural monopolies, wireless spectrum, network neutrality, and the inalienable right of all Americans to download stupid cat videos. It would pit cable companies against telecoms against satellite operators; broadband providers against content providers; big against small; urban against rural.

"And we didn't have a plan," recalls Blair Levin, who oversaw broadband issues for the transition.

Levin held a series of meetings with various telecom players, who all seemed to agree that the stimulus should help them a lot and their competitors not at all. He then helped float a plan to expand rural wireless, but some of his colleagues doubted the moderate speeds would justify the massive investment. The transition team also looked into preserving a slice of the spectrum for public safety agencies, but half a dozen Capitol Hill committees started battling over who would control it. And even though health IT and high-speed rail had gotten a pass, Obama's economists insisted that broadband stimulus should actually provide stimulus.

Ultimately, the transition team settled on a multibillion-dollar competitive grant program that would let providers apply for subsidies to extend service to underserved areas, an effort to connect Americans to the Internet the way FDR's rural electrification program had connected Americans to the grid. There would also be money for the FCC to complete a long awaited national broadband map, which would document in granular detail the state of American high-speed access.

"Ideally, you'd do the map first, and then a plan based on the map, and then you'd spend the broadband money based on the plan," Levin says. "But we couldn't wait until 2013."

Race to the Top. After David Obey's tantrum over school reform, Phil Schiliro and David Axelrod were hesitant to pick that fight in the Recovery Act. But Rahm and Obama's policy advisers wanted to press forward anyway. The president-elect agreed, and the vague plan that had sent Obey into a tizzy soon became a bold competitive grant program called Race to the Top. States would be judged according to their plans to adopt rigorous standards; build data systems to measure student improvement and teacher effectiveness; recruit and retain top teachers and principals; promote innovation; and turn around their worst schools. The winners would get big checks. The losers would get nothing. Axelrod was not looking forward to the political fallout of saying no to governors while alienating unions, but Obama insisted he wanted to prioritize kids over adults. The status quo wasn't working for kids.

Obey still resisted, dismissing Race to the Top as "walking-around money" for Secretary Duncan, trying to divert its funding into traditional programs for low-income schools. "You don't know what the hell you're talking about!" Rahm shouted at him. "This isn't your bill, you prick! This is the president's bill—and this is his priority!"

In his inaugural address, just before that laundry list of commitments he would honor through the Recovery Act, Obama declared a new era of seriousness in Washington. "We come to proclaim an end to the petty grievances and false promises, the recriminations and worn-out dogmas that for far too long have strangled our politics," he said. "We remain a young nation, but in the words of Scripture, the time has come to set aside childish things."

That was one more false promise right there. Washington would remain a political Toys "R" Us during the Obama era, a superstore for childish things.

Another critique of the stimulus has been that it perpetuated the old Washington politics that Obama had pledged to change, tarnishing hope and change out of the gate. There's some truth to that, too. The brawls over the Recovery Act made it instantly clear that petty grievances and worn-out dogmas were still strangling American politics. And with jobs vanishing at a heart-stopping pace, the bill was rushed through the chaotic legislative process that existed, not the pristine legislative process that reformers wanted. Rahm recalls negotiating that line item for waterworks from $1 billion to $9 billion during a ride to Capitol Hill: "We ended up at $6 billion—but still!" Congressman McDermott says the Recovery Act reminded him of the adage that a camel is a horse put together by committee.

"It was helter-skelter, everyone running into the room and saying: 'You've got to put this into the bill!'" McDermott recalls.

But the Recovery Act would make inroads toward a different kind of Washington change that Obama promised in his inaugural: "Those of us who manage the public's dollars will be held to account, to spend wisely, reform bad habits, and do our business in the light of day."

For starters, at Obama's insistence, the stimulus would be the first spending bill without legislative earmarks in decades. There was one fairly egregious quasi-earmark inserted by Senate majority whip Dick Durbin, a $1 billion clean-coal grant that was clearly designed to revive "FutureGen," an Illinois carbon-capture project that had gotten so expensive that even the coal-friendly Bush administration had pulled the plug before construction. A few other almost-earmarks would inspire a barrage of gotcha journalism—$50 million for restoration of the San Francisco Bay watershed, $25 million for Smithsonian renovations— but they paled in comparison to the six-thousand-plus pet projects in the last highway bill. Journalists tortured the definition of "earmark" beyond recognition to try to cast doubt on Obama's claims; a short list compiled by ProPublica included an amendment to boost transit funding, because the sponsors hailed from states with transit systems. That's quite different from the earmark for that snowmobile bridge in Onamia, Minnesota.

Obama also made sure the stimulus included the most stringent transparency and accountability measures in history, creating a new independent oversight board, empowering existing watchdogs (and giving them $250 million in extra funding) to provide unprecedented scrutiny, and letting the public follow the money online. Even though wasteful projects are no worse than worthy projects when it comes to providing stimulus—safeguards that make it harder to spend money badly make it harder to spend money quickly—Obama was determined to avoid screwups or scandals that could tarnish the entire enterprise. Politicians always rail about waste and fraud—plus "abuse," whatever that is—but Obama warned his staff that he was serious.

"There was such a tight focus on trying to demonstrate that government could work," recalls Seth Harris, who oversaw the transition's Labor Department review team and later oversaw the department's stimulus programs as deputy secretary. "It's so far from the caricature."

There was also a quiet bureaucratic revolution embedded in the stimulus, through programs like Race to the Top and the broadband grants, an effort to harness the power of competition to award tax dollars to the worthiest applicants. That may not sound radical, but usually the federal government spreads cash around the country like peanut butter, making sure every state gets its share through quality-agnostic, check-the-box formula programs. That's a fast way to move money, and a safe way to avoid scandal, because it strips subjectivity out of the process. If your project meets the eligibility criteria, you get your money. The only problem with this entitlement mentality is that your project might not serve any national purpose.

"Fill out the forms in triplicate, do your air quality models, show you're in archaeological compliance—congratulations! We'll give you a grant," says Roy Kienitz, Obama's undersecretary of transportation for policy. "We don't ask if your project makes any sense."

The Obama team used the Recovery Act to create dozens of results-oriented competitive programs, for everything from lead paint removal to health care job training to fire station renovations. Money for battery factories, the smart grid, and ARPA-E was distributed competitively as well. And while Obama's plan for a merit-based infrastructure bank was dead on arrival on the Hill, a Senate staffer named Peter Rogoff—soon to become Obama's transit administrator—drew up a merit-based grant competition for innovative transportation projects called TIGER. These programs were arguably riskier and more vulnerable to shenanigans than automatic formulas, and much easier to second-guess. But they were much likelier to produce good projects.

All in all, the Recovery Act would devote about $150 billion to long term change. (That doesn't include basic public works or the Making Work Pay tax cuts, which were part of Obama's long-range agenda, but only incremental steps toward better infrastructure and a fairer tax code.) Most of it would be swept into law with little debate. This was not because Democrats limited debate, although the legislative process was extremely rushed. It was definitely not because Republicans embraced the Obama agenda, although there was a history of bipartisan support for renewable energy, the smart grid, electric vehicles, health IT, school reform, and other Recovery Act innovations.

No, the Republicans simply preferred to debate other things.

— NINE —

Shirts and Skins

Republican leaders didn't want to talk about clean energy or education reform. They definitely didn't want a public fight over Obama's middle-class tax cuts. As Congress took up the American Recovery and Reinvestment Act, they wanted to debate cats and dogs. The day after Obama's inauguration, House GOP leaders held a news conference to denounce the emerging bill as a grab bag of boondoggles and bailouts, a typical Washington assault on taxpayer wallets. It had no formal earmarks, the usual definition of pork, but they portrayed it as a pork platter for the ages.

Their Exhibit A was a $200 million line item for revitalizing the National Mall. The bulk of the money was to repair collapsing seawalls and prevent the Jefferson Memorial from sinking into the Tidal Basin, but in Republican talking points this provision would henceforth be known as "Sod on the Mall." Boehner also seized on a measure expanding family planning services for low-income women. "How can you spend millions on contraceptives?" he asked. "How does that stimulate the economy?" On the Senate side, Derek Kan, the budget aide with the reading habit, compiled lists of dubious-sounding provisions for McConnell, including the census ("Failed Census Bailout") and digital TV coupons ("DTV Transition Bailout"), as well as Amtrak upgrades ("Failed Passenger Rail

Bailout") and fuel-efficient cars for the federal fleet ("More Auto Bailout"). Republicans also had fun with a $50 million increase for the National Endowment for the Arts, a modest throwback to the New Deal's subsidized murals and music. Eric Cantor claimed that it would direct $300,000 to a Miami sculpture garden, which simply wasn't true.

Truth wasn't the point. Republicans ginned up all kinds of press about projects to build Frisbee parks, skateboard parks, and corporate jet hangars that were on the Conference of Mayors list, just because they conceivably *could* receive funding. When Congress added language specifically banning the use of stimulus funds for casinos, aquariums, zoos, golf courses, or swimming pools, Republicans just asked: What about mob museums? What about water slides? What about the Sunset View Dog Park in Chula Vista, California?

"We were in full kill-the-bill, let's-make-everything-famous mode," Kan says.

The Republican spinners understood that Americans would form their impressions of the stimulus long before fact checkers sorted the myths from reality. So they rebranded a previously uncontroversial disaster aid program for livestock as "honeybee insurance." They accused Democrats of trying to spend $248 million on "government furniture," a wild distortion of an ongoing project to build a new Department of Homeland Security headquarters. The Drudge Report had a field day with similarly bogus charges that Pelosi stuffed $30 million into the stimulus to save an endangered mouse. "In fact, there's no money in the bill for mice," PolitiFact's truth squadders concluded. Republicans kept harping on the mouse anyway.

The point was to paint the Recovery Act as a potpourri of silliness masquerading as stimulus, forcing Democrats to defend dozens of hilltops at once. In reality, National Mall repairs would be just as stimulative as road repairs, and arts grants could save jobs that were vanishing at symphonies and theater companies just as surely as state aid could save jobs that were vanishing at schools and police departments. Upgrading the federal fleet's efficiency would be textbook stimulus, pumping cash into the ailing auto industry quickly while reducing government vehicle purchases and fuel costs down the road. The CBO concluded that the family planning money would also increase short-term spending while decreasing long-term spending, by reducing pregnancies and postnatal care.

There were certainly some questionable items, like $198 million in payments to Filipino veterans of World War II. Senate appropriations chairman Daniel Inouye inserted them to honor a promise made by FDR, but sending money to old men in Manila wouldn't provide much stimulus for Milwaukee. Still, none of the outrages on Kan's lists were indefensible. Some were easily mockable, like "rehabilitation of all-terrain vehicle trails" or "removal of small-to-medium-sized fish passage barriers." Others were unremarkable, like "alteration of bridges" and "military construction." Quite a few were more complex than they seemed, like a $246 million tax break for the film industry. It sounded like a crass giveaway to the Hollywood elite, but it merely aimed to reverse a crass takeaway by a Republican lawmaker, who had excluded the industry from a Bush tax break as a punishment for hiring a Democrat as its chief lobbyist. Kan also thought "hybrid vehicles for the military" sounded goofy—"That'll really scare Al Qaeda," he wrote—but the Pentagon was desperate for energy-saving solutions. Fuel was one of its top costs, and convoys to fetch fuel were getting soldiers killed in Iraq.

In any case, most of the contentious items amounted to a tiny slice of the stimulus; the arts money, for instance, was less than 0.01 percent of the package. All together, though, they sounded like a smorgasbord. And Democrats made them sound worse by dismissing them as "a trifle," in Durbin's words. "Let me say this to all the chattering class that focuses on those little, tiny, yes, porky amendments: the American people really don't care," said New York senator Chuck Schumer. Fox News replayed that quote for days.

"The Republicans played such a cynical game," Obey says. "This was not Democrats saying, 'Oh, goody, goody, we get a chance to spend money.' We were desperate to find programs that would spend out fast and actually put people to work." But Obey became a convenient poster child for goody-goody liberalism, especially when he declared the stimulus ought to be even bigger. "I got scalped: Good God, it's not enough, he wants to spend a trillion!" Obey says. The conservative *Washington Times* even trumpeted an "exclusive" suggesting Obey had steered cash in nefarious directions: "Stimulus Has Plum for Lawmaker's Son." The "plum" was funding for national parks; Obey's son was a lobbyist for a parks advocacy group.

It helped that Republicans had access to the ideological network that Hillary Clinton famously dubbed the "vast right-wing conspiracy," which was almost as effective as paranoid left-wingers imagined. A private listserv served as the stimulus wing of the VRWC, injecting Republican talking points into the media bloodstream. Kan and a few other Hill aides would post information about government supercomputers, abandoned mine cleanups, and other stimulus flotsam and jetsam to a Google Groups file, so they could be launched into the conservative blogosphere by writers like Michelle Malkin, think tanks like the Heritage Foundation and Cato Institute, and activist groups like the National Taxpayers Union and the Club for Growth. Soon they would become fodder for Drudge, Fox celebrities like Glenn Beck and Sean Hannity, and the Limbaugh brigade of talk-radio hippie-bashers.

"The idea was to create an echo chamber about the wastefulness," Kan says.

The echoes quickly ricocheted into the mainstream media. For example, just before Obama's inauguration, GOP leaders cherry-picked a preliminary Congressional Budget Office analysis to claim that only 7 percent of the stimulus would go out the door that fiscal year. The liberal group ThinkProgress chronicled eighty-one mentions of the "report"—which wasn't even a report—on TV news during Obama's first few days in office, even though it was mostly meaningless. The CBO had limited its analysis to discretionary spending, ignoring faster-acting tax cuts, unemployment benefits, and state aid. And the fiscal year ending in eight months was an arbitrary milestone; Orszag pledged that 75 percent of the entire stimulus would go out within eighteen months, a more relevant time frame, and the CBO confirmed that in an actual report. But the too-slow-for-stimulus meme was already established. The Associated Press ran an "analysis" headlined "Stimulus Bill That's Not All Stimulating."

"First impressions tend to be lasting," says former senator Evan Bayh. "What the Republicans knew, and our people didn't believe, was that the public is highly skeptical that government spending works."

ThinkProgress later documented that cable networks interviewed Republican lawmakers twice as often as their more numerous Democratic counterparts during the stimulus debate. (GOP leaders gleefully circulated the analysis as proof that "Republicans have owned the airwaves.") And while Republicans pushed a consistent message about Washington-as-usual waste, Democrats and progressive activists tended to focus on their own quibbles with the Recovery Act. For example, environmentalists attacked a provision authorizing an additional $50 billion worth of loans for new nuclear reactors—even though the Bush administration hadn't made any loans with its existing authority, and the economics of nuclear construction were imploding. They had a point, but the Recovery Act was becoming toxic without surrogates to defend it. Even Obama kept talking about the importance of trimming the fat out of the bill, and one Blue Dog, Jim Cooper of Tennessee, let slip that White House officials had encouraged him to add to the drumbeat about unnecessary spending.

"They know it's a messy bill, and they want a clean bill," Cooper said.

The problem is, it's not easy to sell a bill while calling it a mess.

Obama was genuinely surprised by the intensity of the attacks and wall-to-wall coverage of the attacks. He hadn't expected a lovefest, but he hadn't expected an economic emergency to trigger a national debate over honeybees and fish ladders. His new White House just wasn't ready to respond to the onslaught. There were perfectly valid rationales for Mall repairs and contraceptives, but they weren't the ground Obama would have chosen to defend.

"Suddenly, you're in charge of the country," says Dan Pfeiffer, Obama's deputy communications director at the time. "The phone starts ringing, and you don't know where the bathroom is, and oh, by the way, the banking system might crash anyday now, and the market might drop 3,000 points if the Recovery Act doesn't pass. You're not having the strategic discussions you'd have if there was time to think."

The good news for Obama was that the Republicans usually focused their fire either on the general size and composition of the Recovery Act, or on the random additions at its margins. They mostly ignored the transformative stuff that would advance his agenda. "It was unintentional misdirection," says Jason Furman, the White House economist who helped design the stimulus. "They were so obsessed with condoms and grass on the Mall, they didn't notice the biggest unemployment insurance reforms in history." And after a call from Obama, Pelosi reluctantly agreed to take family planning and the Mall out of the bill to blunt the partisan attacks. She refused to remove the arts funding—she had received a call from Robert Redford, too—but the top two Republican targets were out of the bill.

"All of a sudden, the logic of the Republican argument fell apart," Furman says.

But the Republican argument was never about logic. It was about creating the impression of a mess. Republican leaders argued that the Recovery Act was too slow to be stimulus, but also that it needed more infrastructure projects, which would make it slower. They argued that it would expand the deficit, but also that it needed permanent tax cuts, which would expand the deficit even more.

"They were always falling off both sides of the same horse," Obey grouses.

Republican leaders didn't view Obama's concessions as signs they could work with him. They viewed his concessions as signs they could beat him. After condoms and sod were removed from the legislation, they moved on to new targets, like programs to prevent sexually transmitted diseases and help smokers quit. When Obama got those items removed as well, Republicans found new things to complain about. Sometimes they continued to complain about condoms and sod.

"A Fight We Could Win"

The same day the House Republican leaders held their news conference, Eric Cantor met with his whip team to share a poll he had commissioned. Some of the results were unnerving: Americans overwhelmingly approved of Obama, 71–14, as well as his recovery plan, 64–19. But they still disliked Pelosi. And their responses to the poll's leading (and often misleading) questions designed to test-drive potential Republican messages suggested public support for the stimulus was unusually soft.

When asked which would be better for the economy, increasing spending and running trillion-dollar deficits or reducing spending to cut deficits, Americans chose austerity over stimulus, 63–28. By a similar margin, they thought cutting taxes was a better way to create jobs than, as the poll phrased the alternative, "increasing federal government spending for government programs." And after hearing the stimulus cost $250,000 per job, most respondents agreed it was "seriously flawed." Dollars-per-job was a misleading test of the Recovery Act; the dollars would not just finance jobs, but subway cars, solar arrays, food stamps, and whatever recipients of the tax cuts used them to buy. But political messaging is not about fairness. The whip team used its eighteen-page poll summary to assure wavering Republicans that opposing Saint Barack's economic recovery bill wouldn't be political suicide, because Americans were still suspicious of big government.

"It showed members this was a fight we could win," recalls Cantor chief of staff Rob Collins. "We'd take them through it: 'Look at the numbers. America hasn't changed. This is scary for people!'"

The poll also suggested strong support for small business tax cuts, while 71 percent said Obama's plan to "give refund checks to people who don't pay federal income taxes" was unfair. Of course, the poll didn't mention that those people pay gas taxes, payroll taxes, and other federal taxes. But this was what Republicans wanted to hear: Voters wanted business-friendly tax cuts, not liberal borrowing and spending.

Cantor's whip staffers still expected some Republican problem children to cave and vote with Obama. But they were increasingly confident they could turn the stimulus into an us-against-them moment, a chance for Republicans to stand up against *government* spending on fuel-efficient *government* cars and energy-efficient *government* buildings and aid to state *governments*.

"The message was simple: It's not where the voters are, and it's not Republican," says Tom Cole, the former House Republican campaign chair who was now a deputy whip.

In his fourth day in the White House, Obama hosted congressional leaders from both parties in the Roosevelt Room to talk stimulus. After the president repeated his mantra that he welcomed everyone's ideas— he often said he had "no pride of authorship"—Cantor asked if he could hand out a one-page list of his working group's ideas. Meetings tend to focus on someone's piece of paper, and House Republicans figured it might as well be theirs.

We're not going to have a markup, Obama said, but go ahead.

The president looked over the handout, which included several tax cuts he already supported, including the carryback credit for businesses with big losses. "I don't see anything too crazy," Obama said. But he pointed out that the Recovery Act already included significant tax cuts. And when Cantor and his colleagues argued that the refundable Making Work Pay tax cuts for families who paid no income taxes were more about income redistribution than job creation, Obama held firm.

"On some of these issues, we're going to have ideological differences," Obama said. "Elections have consequences. And Eric, I won."

He said it in a lighthearted way. "We took it in jest," Cantor recalls. But "I won" became a rallying cry for Republicans, "a real shirts-and-skins moment," as one GOP aide put it. When Cantor later described the scene in print, he claimed Obama's message was: It's my way or the highway. Deal with it.

"The 'post-partisan' president sure had a big partisan streak," Cantor wrote.

•   •   •

At the time, House Republicans avoided attacking Obama publicly.

Oh, they didn't dare criticize Limbaugh for declaring he wanted Obama to fail; their base would have crucified them. (One Republican congressman who said Limbaugh should "back off" set off such a firestorm he had to apologize the next day for his "stupid comments.") But GOP leaders pointedly contrasted the president's soothing words with the actions of "Washington Democrats." They praised Obama's commitment to timely, targeted, and temporary stimulus, sighing that they were so sorry that Pelosi, Obey, and Rangel had defied him by loading up the Recovery Act with pent-up liberal demands. They quoted his rhetoric about bipartisanship, accusing House Democrats of undermining him by writing the bill without Republican input. The speaker provided the perfect talking point for these gripes during her first press conference of the Obama era.

"Yes, we wrote the bill," she said. "Yes, we won the election."

Both Obey, who wrote the spending section, and Rangel, who wrote the tax section, say Republicans declined their invitations to participate. But the result was a partisan process. There were only a few legislative hearings and markups, and most Republican amendments were defeated on party-line votes. The Energy and Commerce Committee did approve six minor GOP amendments, but three vanished before the bill hit the floor. Even Majority Leader Steny Hoyer of Maryland, the most conservative Democrat on the leadership team, thought inviting Republicans to help shape a recovery bill would be like recruiting pyromaniacs to work for the fire department.

"I am hard put to take the advice of people whose policies have put us deeply in debt and led to the weakest economy since the 1930s," Hoyer told reporters.

After a month of all-Democratic planning, Furman and Rob Nabors did hold courtesy briefings for Republican leadership staff, where they talked about conservative economists who favored a big stimulus, and suggested the Recovery Act was bipartisan in spirit because it was heavy on tax cuts. "I remember thinking: You guys are insane," one senior Republican Senate aide recalls. The Republicans made it clear they wanted a lot more tax cuts—and real tax cuts, not welfare handouts wearing refundable tax cut masks.

"There's nothing we could do that you'd be happy with," Furman complained.

Understandably, Republicans rejected the idea that a bill without serious bipartisan input could be bipartisan simply because Obama decided it had bipartisan ideas. "Democrats operated under the assumption that they got to choose what bipartisanship means," Cantor says. "There was no willingness to work together."

It's a fair point. But Furman had a point, too. Republican leaders did not really want to work together. They were about to make that abundantly clear.

Getting to Zero

Boehner opened the weekly House GOP conference meeting on January 27 with an announcement: Obama would make his first presidential visit to the Capitol around noon, to meet exclusively with Republicans about the Recovery Act.

"We're looking forward to the President's visit," Boehner said.

The niceties ended there, as Boehner changed the subject to the $815 billion stimulus bill that House Democrats had just unveiled. "The bill Congressional Dems have written is not focused on jobs or tax relief. It's focused on slow and wasteful Washington spending," he told his members. Boehner said it would spend too much, too late, on too many Democratic goodies. He wanted to see members trashing it on cable, on YouTube, on the House floor. "It's another run-of-the-mill, undisciplined, cumbersome, wasteful Washington spending bill," he repeated.

"I hope everyone here will join me in voting NO."

Cantor's whip staff had been planning a "walk-back" strategy where they would start leaking that fifty Republicans might vote yes, then that they were down to thirty problem children, then that they might lose twenty or so. The idea was to convey momentum. "You want the members to feel like: Oh, the herd is moving, I've got to move with the herd," Rob Collins explains. That way, even if a dozen Republicans defected, it would look like Obama failed to meet expectations.

But when he addressed the conference, Cantor adopted a different strategy. "We're not going to lose *any* Republicans," he declared. His staff was stunned.

"We're like, uhhhhh, we have to recalibrate," Collins recalls.

Afterward, Cantor's aides asked if he was sure he wanted to go that far on a limb. Zero was a low number. Centrists and big-spending appropriators from Obama-friendly districts would be sorely tempted to break ranks. "We had people who were really being Nervous Nellies," Collins says. Take Anh Cao, a Vietnamese American who had just won a fluke election in a heavily African American New Orleans district after the Democratic incumbent was caught with cash bribes in his freezer. Why would Cao want to use his first big vote to defy a president his constituents revered? If Cantor promised unanimity and failed to deliver, his team warned, the press would have the story it craved: Republicans divided, dysfunction junction, still clueless after two straight spankings.

But Cantor said yes, he meant zero. He was afraid that if the Democrats managed to pick off two or three Republicans, they'd be able to slap a "bipartisan" label on the bill. And he figured leaders ought to lead.

"We can get there," Cantor said. "If we don't get there, we can try like hell to get there."

Shortly before 11 A.M., the AP reported that Boehner and Cantor had urged Republicans to oppose the stimulus. Press secretary Gibbs handed Obama a copy of the story in the Oval Office, just before he left for the Hill to make his case. Here we were, making this real effort to go talk to them as a group," Gibbs says. "You know, we still thought this was on the level." Axelrod says that after the president left, White House aides were buzzing about the insult. And they didn't even know that Cantor had vowed to whip a unanimous vote.

"It was stunning that we'd set this up and before hearing from the president, they'd say they were going to oppose this," Axelrod says. "Our feeling was, we were dealing with a potential disaster of epic proportions that demanded cooperation. If anything was a signal of what the next two years would be like, it was that."

Republicans point out that the House bill was scheduled for a vote the next day; did the West Wing expect them not to have a position? "It's not so much a rebuke against Obama," one leadership aide says. "It's recognizing the sky is blue." But if Obama's aides thought the fix was in, they were right. Congressman Mike Castle, a moderate Republican from Delaware, says his leadership and most of his colleagues were always determined to fight Obama no matter what he did.

"The caucus had decided we weren't going to give Obama a bipartisan victory on this," Castle says.

Obama's hour-long visit with the House Republicans was cordial enough. Some of them asked for his autograph. Many were impressed with his command of policy details. He got a cheer when he said he was running late to a meeting with Senate Republicans—and they could wait. But he didn't win any converts. There was an ideological divide in that conference room, and an undercurrent of hostility. Republicans didn't need to hear the professor-in-chief lecture them about change. They didn't like his insinuations that they didn't know what was in the bill, and they resented his suggestion that they ought to be happy with his tax cuts, as if he knew what they wanted better than they did. Some of them were annoyed that he mentioned his legacy, which seemed a tad presumptuous after a week in office.

"When Bush talked about his legacy in his seventh year, people started ripping on him," recalls Representative Mike Rogers, the former FBI agent.

The basic problem was that House Republicans didn't want a new New Deal. Most of them didn't think much of the old New Deal. During the Q-and-A, eighty-two-year-old Roscoe Bartlett of Maryland told Obama he was six when FDR took office, old enough to see that government couldn't spend its way to prosperity.

"I don't remember that Roosevelt's spending had anything to do with bringing us out of the Depression," Bartlett said.

At the time, the must-read book in Republican circles was *The For-*

gotten Man, a revisionist history of the Depression by the conservative columnist Amity Shlaes. "That book caught fire," one House leadership aide recalls. GOP leaders like Boehner as well as right-leaning pundits like George Will were flogging its argument that FDR, the New Deal, and fiscal stimulus actually made the Depression worse. But Shlaes relied on a slew of skewed statistics and selective anecdotes to make that case; her employment data, for instance, left out work-relief jobs at New Deal agencies. Most economists agree that some New Deal initiatives unrelated to fiscal stimulus were unhelpful, and the Depression didn't end until World War II took fiscal stimulus to new extremes. But as Obama told the House Republicans, there is voluminous evidence that in FDR's first term, deficit spending helped slash 25 percent unemployment almost in half. Then in 1937, after FDR's shift toward austerity, the recovery stalled and unemployment spiked. The New Dealers, Obama suggested, didn't spend enough.

Republicans weren't buying what he was selling.

"Mr. President, I don't think there's any precedent in history that says this will work," Bartlett said. The conference burst into applause.

The Republicans were just as irate about process as they were about substance. Before Obama left, conference chairman Mike Pence asked him to remember three things. First, House Republicans would pray for him. Second, he was welcome back anytime. The third message was less pleasant.

"Several times, you talked about 'the bill that was negotiated in the House,'" Pence said. "There was no bill that was negotiated in the House, because Democrats didn't negotiate with us." Once again, the Republicans cheered.

Rahm Emanuel was Obama's fixer, doing deals, putting out fires, offering his two unexpurgated cents on strategy, policy, and anything else that had occurred to him within the last second or two. He was basically, as it said on a nameplate in his office—which, he liked to point out, was bigger than Biden's office—the Undersecretary of Go Fuck Yourself. He set the frantic pace for Obama's first two years in the

White House. He always seemed to have a million contradictory ideas in his head, and that head often seemed like it was about to explode.

While Obama was visiting the Republicans, Rahm was in Hoyer's office meeting with Blue Dog Democrats, who were almost as critical of the House bill. They didn't like Obey, who called them "bed wetters," and they believed in fiscal discipline, although some of them seemed to forget that when it came to weapons systems, farm subsidies, and other goodies. In any case, they were tired of waiving pay-as-you-go rules to pass deficit-busting bills. In Congress, Rahm had shared their policy concerns about drunken-sailor spending and their political concerns about out-of-touch liberalism; he had persuaded many of them to run in the first place. Now Baron Hill of Indiana, one of his recruits, told him the Blue Dogs wouldn't vote for Obey's money pot without some changes, and without a firm presidential commitment to rein in the deficit once the crisis passed.

"You motherfuckers!" Rahm screamed. "You mean to tell me you're going to vote down the very first piece of legislation the president puts forward?"

"Rahm, I'm sympathetic," Hill replied. "I'm just the messenger here."

Rahm eventually persuaded most of the Blue Dogs to back off the ledge, assuring them Obama cared about budget discipline as much as they did. He had already agreed to kill the money for contraception and the Mall. Rahm also promised that Orszag would write a letter pledging the White House's commitment to pay-as-you-go.

"The Recovery Act wouldn't have happened without Rahm," Orszag says. "He was pure energy, banging heads, freaking out. Just a force of nature."

That same night, Rahm hosted some Rust Belt House Republicans in his spacious new office, which was still full of unpacked boxes. Rahm was an avid practitioner of pre-post-partisanship, but he had cultivated good relations with this group of moderates as a congressman, working together on Midwest issues like Great Lakes restoration, meeting for Tuesday lunches at the Monocle restaurant on the Hill. Now Rahm told his Monocle pals that Obama wasn't just lip-synching bipartisanship.

They told him the House bill was a strange way to show it. The final text had just been released yesterday, with the vote scheduled for tomorrow. Members had submitted over two hundred amendments, and Pelosi was only allowing votes on eleven. It felt like a typical spending bill fast-tracked under the pretense of stimulus, freezing Republicans and even rank-and-file Democrats out of the process.

These were the kind of Republicans who wouldn't be automatically opposed to stimulus. Their industrial districts were being crushed, and they weren't violently antagonistic to federal spending. "Everybody at home wanted something done," says Steve LaTourette of Ohio. A businessman in his Cleveland district had walked up to him and said: "If you don't think we need stimulus, you're a jackass." But LaTourette wanted to see more infrastructure in the bill. Others wanted more tax cuts. At the same time, the Republicans were all unnerved by an $815 billion price tag so soon after TARP.

Eventually, Rahm stopped bathing his guests in four-letter words long enough to get to the point: Were Republicans going to support this or what?

Probably a few, they mumbled.

Anyone here?

Uh . . . no.

Rahm figured it was still early in the game. These guys could vote no on the initial House bill, then switch to yes on the final bill after it was worked out with the Senate. But so far, the scoreboard didn't look the way he had hoped.

"The Dogs Just Didn't Like the Food"

Cantor's whip team wasn't sure it could persuade the entire conference to march in lockstep. "You had a popular president, a financial meltdown, people talking about whether there was going to be a Republican Party," recalls Patrick McHenry of North Carolina, another deputy whip. "I thought half the Republicans might vote for the stimulus." But the whip count cleaned up quickly, with only five problem children the day before the vote. Louisiana's Anh Cao was the only "Lean Yes."

What brought the Republicans together were the Democrats. Obama's "I won" and Pelosi's "we wrote the bill" helped rally the troops. Some Republicans thought their best whip was Obey, whose smarter than-thou bombast helped persuade members to be against anything he was for. The actual content of the bill was a unifying force, too. The whip team portrayed it as Democratic overreach and an undemocratic outrage, the kind of hodgepodge no Republican could support.

"It was larded up with every Democratic policy wish since they lost the House in 1994," McHenry says. "It was so big and atrocious, we couldn't be for it."

For example, many Republicans were willing to extend unemployment benefits. But the Recovery Act seemed to plus up every antipoverty program under the sun: food stamps, food banks, Head Start, Early Head Start, public housing, plus a new "emergency fund" for families on welfare. Not to mention $87 billion to help states keep people on Medicaid. It sounded like a Liberals Greatest Hits album.

"What Republican was going to vote for all that?" Tom Cole asks. "It's not virtue if you're not tempted."

The Democrats had beaten most of the Republicans who might have been tempted. And Cantor included LaTourette and several other moderates on his working group, keeping them inside the partisan tent. But the whip team was still worried about centrists like John McHugh of New York, who later became Obama's army secretary; Peter King of New York, who had carried water for public employee unions pushing for state aid; and Fred Upton of Michigan, who had delighted environmentalists by leading the fight to phase out incandescent light bulbs. The whips applied pressure, but mostly they supplied information, sending out memos reminding the conference that the NEA recently spent $190,000 on "various artistic endeavors in San Francisco," that the STD prevention program had once advertised HIV testing at a transgender beauty contest in, yes, San Francisco. Castle was planning to run for Biden's Senate seat in blue-state Delaware, and he found his party's knee-jerk opposition to Obama unnerving; he had said the stimulus should be about $800 billion. But he never came close to voting yes.

"It felt like an ordinary appropriations bill," he told me. "I mean, school construction, I couldn't vote for that in a stimulus. And handing states all that money, it seemed like a government takeover kind of thing."

Castle has intellectual-looking glasses and a quiet decency that make him seem thoughtful, but he couldn't explain why repairing schools wouldn't create jobs, or how preventing layoffs of state workers would produce a government takeover of anything. In fact, he complained that the aid to states only saved time-limited jobs, as if he would have preferred a more permanent expansion of government. When I tried to explore these contradictions, he backtracked: "I don't know. It was just too much to swallow." He simply had a bad feeling about the stimulus, solidified by Republican groupthink and Democratic high-handedness.

"The dogs just didn't like the food," Cole says. "And once you get down to just a few dogs still sniffing around the food, they start thinking: 'How come none of the other dogs are eating the food? Maybe it's poisoned.'"

Cao was sniffing the hardest. Obama had vacuumed up 75 percent of the vote in his district, and Cao didn't think much of his constituents' ability to judge his positions on the merits. "I was in a very difficult position," he said later. "I represent an African American district; all of them wanted to support a black president. Obviously, they wouldn't know whether or not these bills are good for them." But Cao didn't want to alienate his new Republican colleagues by breaking ranks, either; Boehner had written a memo titled "The Future Is Cao." Cantor and his whip team called Cao constantly, while arranging additional lobbying calls from McCain (who had a fund-raiser in common with Cao) and Newt Gingrich (who had, bizarrely, offered to help Cao with African American outreach after his victory). Cao, who had joined the Transportation and Infrastructure Committee, became convinced the bill was too heavy on social services and too light on public works.

"Traditionally, when you look at federal programs that create jobs, it's road construction, infrastructure rebuilding," Cao says. "The bulk of the stimulus went into Medicaid, unemployment benefits. It was essentially a massive spending bill."

In fact, state aid and unemployment benefits were solid stimulus, too. But quite a few Republicans wanted more infrastructure spending, especially the thirty Republicans on Transportation and Infrastructure. They saw nothing partisan about filling potholes, cutting ribbons, and posing with oversized cardboard checks. "You know the one thing that brings Democrats and Republicans together?" Rahm says. "Concrete!"

As the House vote approached, that created a dilemma for Republican leaders.

Cantor and Mike Pence were both part of the conservative Republican Study Committee as well as the leadership team. But as one aide put it, Pence rolled out of bed thinking about being a conservative, while Cantor woke up thinking about being a leader. Infrastructure reflected the difference. In leadership meetings, Cantor argued that the Republican stimulus alternative should go big on public works, so Cao, La-Tourette, and other GOP concrete lovers would feel comfortable voting against the Democratic bill. His aides were afraid that if Democrats added a lot of extra infrastructure, dozens of Republicans might support the stimulus. Pence pushed back: Aren't we supposed to be against government spending?

"You can't say spending does nothing for economic growth and then on the other hand, let's put it all in highways," one conservative leadership aide recalls.

Why not? Many Republicans liked highways, and John Mica of Florida, the ranking Republican on the transportation committee, kept complaining that only 8 percent of the House bill went to infrastructure. He wasn't counting cyber infrastructure like broadband, health IT, and the smart grid, or even veterans hospitals, park roads, and other traditional infrastructure that didn't flow through his committee. But Mica wanted more. He claimed that every $1 billion invested in infrastructure "creates or sustains" thirty thousand jobs, the kind of Keynesian argument the GOP ridiculed when Democrats made it.

Cantor wasn't making Keynesian arguments. He just didn't think the centrists would join the crusade against the stimulus unless they could vote for something that moved dirt. "I have no memory of hearing principled arguments," says one conservative House aide. "It was all just retail politics. 'Well, this is a state we could win in the future.' Not the kind of arguments that sat well with ideology-based thinkers." Pence, the most ardent ideology-based thinker in the leadership, kept insisting the GOP should not try to out–New Deal the Democrats.

Ultimately, the leaders decided to fall off both sides of the horse. The official $478 billion Republican alternative consisted entirely of tax cuts and an extension of unemployment benefits. But the GOP also crafted a second $715 billion substitute that included far more traditional infrastructure than the supposedly lavish Democratic bill. That way, moderates like Cao and Castle who couldn't back the right-wing alternative could vote yes on something other than the actual bill.

Republicans never bothered to explain how $715 billion could be good public policy while $815 billion was freedom-crushing socialism. In the minority, they didn't have to.

Getting Their Mojo Back

"I am tempted to ask the chair: What year is this?" It was 2009— January 28, to be exact—and Obey was on the House floor, fending off a Republican effort to slash spending before the final stimulus vote. "Yeah, I didn't think it was 1933," Obey said. "You know, they don't look like Herbert Hoover, but there are an awful lot of people in this chamber who think like Herbert Hoover."

Grumpy and weary, his voice hoarse from weeks of stimulus defense, Obey ranted about the Republican "mosquitoes" who had turned a historic debate into a trivial spat over sod and condoms that weren't even in the bill. Yes, the arts money was still there, but Obey, who played harmonica in a bluegrass band, was not about to apologize for saving arts jobs; the Baltimore Opera Company had just gone bankrupt, and Florida was slashing its cultural funding in half. His larger point was that the economy was losing over 100,000 jobs a week. The blizzard of rhetoric about imaginary earmarks for polar bear exhibits couldn't obscure the need for a government rescue.

"The rubber band has finally snapped," Obey said. "The markets are in chaos, people are panicked, and we've got to do something to stabilize the situation. Sooner or later, we have to recognize this is not Herbert Hoover time."

Most of the Republicans who spoke on the floor agreed something needed to be done—just not this. They quoted Summers about poorly designed stimulus, Orszag about the slow pace of public works, Romer about the power of tax cuts. They called state aid an "unfunded mandate"—when most of it was unmandated funds. They warned that the Recovery Act could siphon money to the left-wing community activists at ACORN, the latest Fox News bugaboo. They claimed that the "emergency fund" for the down-and-out would reverse welfare reform, even though Ron Haskins, the former Republican congressional aide who wrote the 1996 welfare reform bill, says it did no such thing. "I was extremely worried that Democrats would try to undermine welfare reform, but they didn't," Haskins says.

No matter. The Republicans attacked the stimulus as "one of the worst abuses of power in the history of Congress," "the most colossal mistake in the history of Congress," "a steamroll of socialism being forced down the throats of the American people," a blob of climate change research and digital TV converters.

Republicans then introduced their tax cut alternative, claiming it would create twice as many jobs at half the cost of the House bill. Democrats noted that the Republican record of economic forecasting and fiscal stewardship did not inspire confidence in that claim. And Obey noted that after all the Republican rhetoric about infrastructure, the alternative had not one dime for transportation: "Those jobs go blooey." Ditto for the grid, broadband, and health IT: "Those jobs go blooey."

Predictably, the House rejected the $478 billion alternative, with only two Blue Dog Democrats voting yes and nine moderate Republicans voting no. Without skipping a beat, the Republicans introduced their $715 billion substitute, which doubled Democratic spending on highways and quintupled spending on the water projects of the scandal-plagued Army Corps of Engineers. It failed, too, with thirteen Blue Dogs voting yes and thirty-one conservative Republicans voting no.

So more than three fourths of the GOP conference voted for a plan with no infrastructure as well as a plan with extra infrastructure. Really, the only thing the plans had in common was that they weren't the Democratic plan. "The Republicans were never burdened by principle," says John Dingell of Michigan, who had served in the House since 1955. "I've never seen it this partisan and nasty. You almost saw the country collapse, but they didn't give a damn about anything but power."

In the end, every single House Republican voted against the Democratic bill, along with eleven Democrats. It still passed easily, but as Cantor had hoped, the only thing bipartisan about the vote was the opposition.

"They just wanted us to do this ourselves, so they could beat the living hell out of us afterwards," Dingell says.

Some White House aides still thought some Republicans would end up voting for the bill on final passage, to avoid accusations of doing nothing as the economy unraveled.

"It's an old playbook," Obey said on the floor. "It's exactly what they did to FDR on Social Security. When they couldn't beat it, they joined the parade. . . . They went along so people wouldn't know they tried to kill it in the first place."

Other Democrats wondered: Which part of zero didn't Obey understand? Any Republican who voted for Porkulus would be begging for a primary challenger.

"The Republicans had a concerted strategy to oppose everything. They were betting on the failure of the economy," says Chris Van Hollen of Maryland, the head of the House Democratic campaign committee. "If that wasn't totally obvious before the zero vote, it should have been obvious after it."

• • •

House Republicans had voted against tax cuts for 95 percent of the country; unemployment benefits for laid-off workers; Head Start for kids and Meals on Wheels for seniors. They had rejected aid to save the jobs of teachers, cops, firefighters, janitors, and school nurses. They had marched in lockstep against special education, levees, and highways, wind and solar farms, cancer research, crime victims, border security, and high-speed Internet. They had tried to stop Democrats from sending $250 checks to senior citizens and disabled veterans.

"Washington insiders and media pundits thought it was insane to oppose so popular a president on a bill that spread so much money around," Cantor wrote later.

In a memo the next day titled "The Republican Problem," Pelosi's office suggested the GOP was committing electoral suicide, voting against jobs in their own communities during a jobs crisis. "The House Republican leadership put its members in another politically untenable position yesterday," the memo said. Van Hollen predicted that in 2010, Republicans would pay for rejecting the stimulus. A coalition of liberal groups and unions immediately ran ads pummeling Republicans for opposing Obama's plan, a move that Cantor unironically declared would "undermine our nation's desire for bipartisanship."

The GOP's doom-and-gloom rhetoric and unified opposition reminded Pelosi of the war over Clinton's 1993 budget, which then Minority Leader Newt Gingrich had predicted would "kill jobs and lead to a recession, and . . . actually increase the deficit." The budget passed without a single Republican vote, and actually helped usher in an era of vibrant growth and record surpluses. Now once again, Democrats were trying to clean up a Republican mess without Republican help.

"There's a pattern here," her memo said.

Pelosi wasn't the only politician thinking about 1993. The next day, Gingrich addressed a House Republican retreat at a posh resort in the Virginia mountains, and said the stand against the stimulus brought back the same memory. What he remembered about the Clinton budget's aftermath was not the spectacular failure of his economic predictions, but the Republican political revival that culminated in his rise to power the next year. Now he made a more accurate prediction: Boehner would become speaker "at a speed that will shock the Democrats."

The Republicans were not behaving like a team that had just gotten pasted. They felt like insurgents who had just pulled off their first ambush. Boehner replayed the C-SPAN video of the vote, prompting a standing ovation. "I know all of you are pumped about the vote the other day," Cantor said. "We'll have more to come!" Pence showed a clip from *Patton* of the general rallying his troops against their Nazi enemy: "We're going to kick the hell out of him all the time and we're going to go through him like crap through a goose!"

That night, Cantor had his whip team sign a celebratory bottle of red wine, not to be uncorked until Republicans took back the House.

"I was very confident the country was heading in the wrong direction," Cantor told me. "I thought if we stayed the course, we could earn back the majority."

There was one discordant note when Boehner suggested that the stimulus was so egregious it had practically whipped itself, prompting Cantor to pull him aside and tell him not to rewrite history. "We had to send a little message: 'Uh, we worked our asses off for that vote,'" says one Cantor aide. "Holy cow! We just had two million people show up in D.C. saying: 'Yes, We Can!' The pollsters were saying America had shifted underneath us. The president was wildly popular, even with Republicans. Don't sit there and say it was an easy victory."

Otherwise, the mood was buoyant. The Republicans had said no to Obama, and it felt good. In a later roundtable discussion, the Young Guns Cantor, Kevin McCarthy, and Paul Ryan, all agreed that the stimulus woke up the Republicans and launched their comeback.

"It became a very defining moment for this conference," Cantor said.

"Very much so," Ryan chimed in.

"I think that's when we got our mojo back," McCarthy agreed.

The new leader of the free world seemed a bit mojo-deficient. His honeymoon was over before it had started, and he was already losing control of the stimulus narrative. "Republicans—short on new ideas, low on votes, and deeply unpopular in the polls—have been winning the media war over the president's central initiative," the liberal *Washington Post* columnist E. J. Dionne wrote. A *Politico* news story drew the same conclusion: "Obama Losing the Stimulus Message War."

Obama was sending mixed stimulus messages: It's my bill, but I don't like everything Congress is doing with it, and this flawed legislation needs to pass right away. He was peddling a short-term rescue but also long-term change, an immediate fiscal fiesta but an eventual shift to fiscal responsibility. He was trying not to oversell the crisis, because his economic team feared that talking down the economy could depress confidence and deepen the slump, but he didn't want to undersell it, either, because his legislative team wanted Congress to feel a sense of urgency.

Republicans had a much simpler narrative: No.

It was resonating. In the week after the House vote, support for the stimulus sank from 52 percent to 38 percent. Polls showed that the closer respondents were following the debate, the less likely they were to support the stimulus.

To try to seize control of the narrative, Obama's team summoned the anchors from all five major news networks to the Oval Office for one-on-one interviews. This would be the president's best chance to pitch the stimulus directly, to get his conversation with the public back on track. "We really wanted to drive the message, to compete against all the myths," Phil Schiliro recalls. But the morning of the sit-downs, Tom Daschle withdrew from consideration for health secretary because of unpaid taxes, so Obama's sit-downs with Katie Couric, Anderson Cooper, and the rest of the media elite focused almost entirely on the botched nomination. "That was a key moment," Schiliro says. "He didn't get to rebut all the false information out there."

Instead, the big news from the interviews, replayed for days, was Obama's assessment of the Daschle snafu: "I screwed up."

Obama couldn't afford to screw up the Recovery Act. The economic carnage was worsening by the day. January was the worst month yet, with 800,000 more job losses, including mass layoffs at iconic firms like Microsoft, Boeing, Home Depot, and Starbucks. It felt like an economic 9/11, without the bipartisan determination to fight back. Somehow, he had to find sixty senators willing to follow him into battle.

In his diary, the Republican consultant-turned-congressman Tom Cole speculated that the president was already saying to himself: "And I asked for this job?"

"Obama is finding that controlling his party's large majorities is tough—and reining in the GOP is tougher," Cole wrote. "As he knows, he will own the economy at some point. Once he does, we will clobber him in the midterms."

TEN

From Zero to Sixty

Bipartisanship can become a habit, which is one reason the Obama team wanted the new Congress to start with two motherhood-and-apple-pie bills that already had some Republican support. The Lilly Ledbetter gender equity legislation followed the script perfectly, and Obama got to host a bipartisan signing ceremony in the East Room. The S-CHIP children's health expansion turned out to be trickier.

In the last Congress, Senate Finance chairman Max Baucus of Montana and ranking member Chuck Grassley of Iowa had cut a deal to cover four million more kids, but Bush had scuttled it. Now Baucus, a moderate Democrat from a ranching family, and Grassley, a conservative Republican from a farming family, wanted Obama to make it law. Baucus and Grassley were more than "my good friend from Iowa" friends; their mutual admiration bordered on old-man bromance. "We're family," Grassley says. Their alliance looked like a starting point for the kind of deals that could attract eighty votes in the Senate, maybe even for comprehensive health reform.

But their relatively modest deal on children's health soon ran into trouble. The problem was that the deal had excluded noncitizens, to make it palatable to more Republicans. Now Democrats had larger margins in Congress, and no longer needed a two thirds majority to override Bush's veto. So the Obama team insisted on covering legal immigrants. To Grassley and other Republicans, this was a defining moment, proving Obama's rhetoric about cooperation was just rhetoric.

"Once they controlled everything, they shoved us off to the side," Grassley says. "They decided to go partisan. It's not how you treat a partner."

Obama aides found this pique ludicrous. Why should the president throw immigrant children under the bus to preserve someone else's obsolete deal? "We had just won a landslide, and this was offensive to our values," one official says. "It's one thing to compromise if you need the votes, but we didn't." The idea that Obama should offend pro-immigrant groups that had supported his election in order to help his political adversaries avoid a political quandary seemed delusional. From Rahm's perspective, a bill that helped children while putting more Republicans on record against helping children was practically ideal. Obama cared more about bipartisanship than Rahm did, but not for its own sake, and certainly not at the expense of sick kids.

"These are kids! They're here legally! Sorry, that busts the deal," says Congressman Becerra, himself a child of working-class Mexican immigrants.

Still, Grassley felt burned. He and several GOP allies had gone out on a limb against Bush, only to see it sawed off by his supposedly postpartisan successor.

"It was a real tactical error," says one congressional aide. "It let Mitch McConnell go to Grassley and say: 'See? You can make a deal with Max, but the president is just going to fuck you.'"

Obama did get his bipartisan victory. The day after he signed the Ledbetter bill, the Senate approved the new S-CHIP by a comfortable margin, even without Grassley's vote. But it left a partisan taste in some Republican mouths.

"We got screwed," Grassley says. "It got things off to a terrible start."

Reaching Out

Some White House officials truly believed the stimulus could attract eighty votes in the Senate. The White House official who knew the Senate best was not one of them. Vice President Biden would lead the administration's outreach to his former colleagues, and he had close friends in the institution of every ideological stripe. But he says that even before the GOP posted its zero in the House, he never thought he could pick off more than a few Republicans in the Senate.

"Never for one single instant," he told me.

Biden says that during the transition, he was warned not to expect any cooperation on major votes. "I spoke to seven different Republican senators who said: 'Joe, I'm not going to be able to help you on anything,'" he recalls. His informants said McConnell had demanded unified resistance. "The way it was characterized to me was: 'For the next two years, we can't let you succeed in anything. That's our ticket to coming back,'" Biden says. The vice president says he hasn't even told Obama who his sources were, but Bob Bennett of Utah and Arlen Specter of Pennsylvania both confirmed they had conversations with Biden along those lines.

"So I promise you—and the president agreed with me—I never thought we were going to get Republican support," Biden says.

One Obama aide says he received a similar warning from a Republican Senate staffer he was seeing at the time. He remembers asking her one morning in bed: How do we get a stimulus deal? She replied: Baby, there's no deal.

"This is how we get whole," she said with a laugh. "We're going to do to you what you did to us in 2006."

Pillow talk aside, writing off the Senate minority was not an option. Even if all fifty-eight Democrats lined up behind the stimulus—by no means a sure bet—Biden still needed at least two Republicans to break a filibuster. And he soon realized he'd need three, because no Republican wanted to be the sixtieth vote for an Obama victory. So he had to figure out who was truly persuadable.

The vice president never thought Grassley was likely to bolt, even before his fit over S-CHIP. He saw Grassley as someone who might walk up to the edge of cooperation with a Democratic president, but would never jump. Sure enough, Grassley would become a strident critic of the stimulus, and would later scuttle bipartisan health reform negotiations after stringing the White House along for months. Biden also discounted the usual speculation about his old friend John McCain, the Beltway-celebrated maverick. Even though Obama had hosted a dinner to honor McCain's record of bipartisanship the night before the inauguration, Biden could tell he was too bitter to help the rival who crushed his dreams. In fact, during the stimulus debate, McCain would clamor for partisan unity behind the scenes, amusing GOP colleagues who had never considered him much of a team player.

"Look, it's tough, man," says Biden, who had watched defeated presidential candidates like Hubert Humphrey and John Kerry return to the Senate, and had endured two unsuccessful campaigns himself. "It's a hard thing to be that close."

Republicans who had deviated from right-wing orthodoxy in the past and were up for reelection in 2010—including McCain, Grassley, Specter, Bennett, and Lisa Murkowski of Alaska—also had to worry about primaries. Specter had barely survived a right-wing challenge in 2004, and he told Biden that supporting the stimulus would guarantee him another brutal primary. "Joe thought I could still keep the seat," Specter says. "But I told him: It's not your seat. It's my seat." Even Bennett, a Mormon bishop who had been part of the Republican leadership, told Biden he expected a challenge from the right. The vice president thought he was joking.

"I couldn't believe the Bishop would be viewed as too liberal," Biden says. "Who would've thunk it?"

So Biden targeted the Republicans he thought he had a shot at peeling away: Specter and Maine's Susan Collins and Olympia Snowe, the remaining moderates, plus George Voinovich of Ohio and Mel

Martinez of Florida, who were preparing to retire and were somewhat less anti-government than their brethren. He also stayed in touch with his pal Bennett and Obama's pal Richard Lugar of Indiana; they opposed the stimulus from the start, but Biden considered them patriots, and thought they might be willing to help rescue the economy in a pinch.

Biden, the son of a car salesman, is a deal maker at heart, renowned on Capitol Hill for his relentless pitches. He tracked Collins down over the holidays in her hometown of Caribou, Maine; the patchy cell phone service in the north country kept cutting off their chat, but Biden kept calling back. And he basically became Specter's stalker. "Joe says he called me fourteen times," Specter says. "That sounds about right." Biden told his targets that the nation would plunge into depression without stimulus, that Obama deserved a chance to lead, that the country needed their help. He schmoozed them, flattered them, and repeatedly asked them: Whaddya want? Specter, who had just beaten cancer for the second time, wanted research money for the National Institutes of Health. Voinovich, a former Cleveland mayor and Ohio governor, wanted more infrastructure.

"Biden said: Look, man, we really need this to be bipartisan," Martinez recalls. "I could've negotiated a pretty good deal for Cape Canaveral. I could've saved the Everglades!"

To Biden's dismay, his targets were all echoing the complaints of their party leaders about the Recovery Act: too much money, too much spending, too much stuff that didn't seem like stimulus, too much of a wish list for back-in-power liberals.

"If you put a six-year-old kid on a diet for a month, then put him in a bakery and say: 'Okay, do what you want,' that's what this was like," Martinez says.

Reid had a dozen Republicans on his own target list. And he had received at least one stimulus request from every senator in both parties. But as the Senate prepared to start debate in early February, he was getting the same negative feedback from across the aisle. "He turned over every stone," a senior aide recalls. "He didn't have commitments from anybody." Feeling desperate, he called three veteran conservative Republicans into his office—Grassley, Thad Cochran of Mississippi, and Mike Enzi of Wyoming—and urged them to support the bill for the good of the country.

"He was basically pleading for our votes," Grassley says. "He said: 'You all know something needs to be done. The Democrats did TARP for Bush. You've got to look past the substance.'"

When his appeal to patriotism didn't fly, Reid tried an appeal to heartstrings. Ted Kennedy was home battling brain cancer, and Reid told the Republicans he didn't want to call him back to work to break a filibuster.

"He said if you can't vote with us, we're going to have to bring Kennedy to the floor, and it really could kill him," Grassley says. "We looked at each other like: Huh?"

If you can't support the bill, Reid asked, could one of you at least vote on Kennedy's behalf to spare him the trip? There was a long history of senators "pairing votes" as a courtesy in times like this, but not this time. Reid made a similar request to Kennedy's best friend in the Senate, Orrin Hatch of Utah, to no avail.

"They all said: 'Sorry, we have to be voting no on this,'" the Reid aide recalls. "These are people who profess to care about the man and the institution and all that. But he's on his deathbed, and they wouldn't pair their votes."

McConnell didn't bother to make emotional appeals to his members. He made political appeals. He spoke a lot about 1984, the year of "Morning in America," when a vibrant economic recovery carried Reagan to reelection. What people tended to forget was that the same recovery carried congressional Democrats to reelection. The only Republican to defeat an incumbent senator that year was the young Mitch McConnell.

His point was that Republicans ought to stand tough against Obama's plan, because they wouldn't pay a price if it succeeded, and they'd reap the benefits if it didn't. An aide described his pitch: "If this thing works and the economy is booming and everybody is happy, your vote against the stimulus won't be held against you. In good times, people get reelected." On the other hand, if the economy wasn't booming by 2010, Republicans could return from the wilderness.

"He was already looking two years ahead," the aide says.

In the meantime, McConnell tried to build support for a filibuster. There were limits to his obstructionism; he talked Tom Coburn out of deploying a procedural trick called a "clay pigeon" that could have tied the Senate into knots. Reid had promised an open process, and McConnell thought abusing it would just create a media storm over the Party of No. "It would've fed the Democrat narrative very well," an aide says. But McConnell didn't consider the filibuster an abuse, at least not when he was in the minority. In fact, he was the senator most responsible for transforming an extreme measure reserved for *Mr. Smith Goes to Washington* situations into a routine procedural weapon. The Founding Fathers never envisioned a sixty-vote threshold, but they did envision the Senate as a check on tyrannical majorities, the proverbial saucer to cool the passions of the House. McConnell believed the filibuster honored that conservative spirit, requiring change to proceed by consensus.

So McConnell focused on making sure no consensus materialized. Reid made his job easier by promising unlimited amendments on the stimulus, giving Republicans unlimited opportunities to vote for things other than the stimulus. They tried to craft an official alternative, but quickly decided there was no point trying to unite forty-one senators around a single plan. What mattered was staying united against the Obama plan. "We just said: Forget it. We don't need to do this," recalls one Senate GOP aide. "We'll let the Democrats sink themselves." Instead, McConnell encouraged them to propose whatever alternatives, additions, and subtractions struck their fancy, with no pressure to vote one way or the other on anything but the overall bill. He didn't care what they said yes to, as long as they ended at no when it counted. When Lisa Murkowski approached his staffers with a slew of energy amendments, including one to boost Alaska's oil and gas revenues, their reaction was, Great, we're with you all the way—and you'll oppose the stimulus, right?

"We were very much of the theory of let a thousand flowers bloom," says one senior aide. "We weren't trying Soviet-style top-down management. Where we were going to exert our muscle was rallying the caucus against the Democrat proposal."

McConnell pushed his staff to find ammunition he could use to fire at the stimulus. One morning, he was surprised to see Derek Kan, his bookworm budget analyst, wearing glasses in the office for the first time. "I had my contacts in for ten straight hours last night," Kan explained. "I was reading the bill."

"I'm glad somebody's reading the bill," McConnell mused.

Kan read everything. After a new CBO analysis concluded the Senate bill would indeed meet Obama's goal of getting 75 percent of the money out the door in eighteen months, he alerted the conference to some fine print: Less than half the discretionary spending would go out in eighteen months, and the total cost with interest would exceed $1.2 trillion. That number didn't mean much—who calculates the price of a home by adding up decades of mortgage payments?—but it reinforced the message of bloat. Kan also highlighted a sloppy Democratic report that tried to pinpoint how many jobs various programs would create; State Department cyber-security upgrades penciled out to $1.35 million per job. Meanwhile, McConnell's communications team blasted out every Democratic criticism of the stimulus—not just from centrists like Ben Nelson of Nebraska, but from liberals like Roland Burris, Obama's successor in Illinois.

"No one wants to be to the left of Roland Burris," as a senior Republican aide says.

For the most part, the Senate stimulus bill looked a lot like the House version that hadn't attracted a single Republican. The only major difference was the addition of a $70 billion "AMT patch," an annual must-pass ritual that exempts over twenty million upper-middle-class families from the Alternative Minimum Tax. The AMT fix would provide virtually no stimulus, but Baucus included it as a favor to his buddy Grassley, even though Grassley and his party were trashing the rest of the bill.

The Senate bill also included somewhat more generous tax relief for businesses. For example, Baucus expanded a tax break for firms that restructured their debts, an urgent priority for Las Vegas casinos, the private equity behemoth the Carlyle Group, and the Chamber of Commerce. The Senate bill adopted several of the business community's top priorities, and Democrats put heavy pressure on the Chamber and other Republican-leaning business groups to endorse it. Depressions, they pointed out, are bad for business. During one call, when a National Association of Manufacturers lobbyist said his group might have to remain neutral, a congressional aide exploded: "This is bullshit! Don't you ever come here telling us to support business if you can't support this!" He threatened that business groups would lose all credibility with the Democrats who controlled Washington if they parroted the Republican line when the economy was at stake. This wasn't some environmental regulation that was irritating some manufacturer in Toledo. "This is the whole fucking enchilada!" the aide said. "This is whether we wake up in the morning with 20 percent unemployment!"

In the end, despite equally heavy pressure from their Republican allies, the Chamber and the manufacturers did endorse the stimulus. The Chamber did not label it a "key vote"—which meant Republican lawmakers could vote no without getting dinged on their annual pro-business report cards—but even the grudging nod from corporate America helped blunt charges of woolly-headed liberalism.

"A lot of Republicans said: I can't believe you're getting behind this," says Chamber lobbyist Bruce Josten. "But when you sit where I sit, you don't want a complete imbalance of supply and demand."

On the other hand, the extra tax breaks that helped win the Chamber's support inflated the cost of the Senate bill to $885 billion, providing even more ammo for McConnell. He told his members: This is bigger than TARP, and politically, it could be just as toxic. Let the Democrats be the party of Monopoly money. And don't buy the postpartisan hype. Look what Obama did to us on S-CHIP.

"McConnell wanted to hold the line," Martinez recalls. "He kept saying: 'This is a partisan bill. Don't give it a bipartisan imprint. Obama's going to have to eat the results of this thing.'"

Obama believed he was going to extraordinary lengths to reach out to Republicans, and getting nothing in return. They demanded tax cuts; he gave them tax cuts. They complained about sod on the Mall, condoms, herpes prevention, and "smoking cessation"; he killed all those Democratic cats and dogs. Obama showed unprecedented deference by visiting the Republicans on their turf in his first week; they signaled he was wasting his time before he even got into his motorcade.

Still, the president felt like he had to keep reaching out. If he couldn't find a few Republican senators to work with, the Recovery Act—and the rest of his legislative agenda—would be doomed. Anyway, Obama was by nature a conciliator, even when his enemies were vowing to kick the hell out of him and run through him like crap through a goose. As an organizer, he had been trained to seek common ground and bipartisanship was part of his brand. Maybe Republican leaders would pay a price for rejecting his overtures.

"It's like diplomacy with the Iranians," explains one senior aide. "It's important to extend your hand, even if you know they probably won't shake it. You want the world to see you extending your hand."

Obama also needed to make it clearer that Republican congressional leaders were not the only Republicans in America. Four moderate GOP governors—Schwarzenegger of California, Charlie Crist of Florida, Jodi Rell of Connecticut, and Jim Douglas of Vermont—had already endorsed the Recovery Act. Even the fiscally conservative Jon Huntsman Jr. of Utah was praising it as "the kind of stimulus that we could benefit from." Plenty of Republican mayors, county executives, and ordinary citizens wanted stimulus, too. Obama strategist Anita Dunn wrote an email warning that the White House could not afford to let "bipartisanship" get defined in the media as whatever Eric Cantor wanted. "We made a huge mistake early on when we let Washington Republicans set the narrative," Dunn says.

The president tried to unbake that cake. On February 1, he hosted several rank-and-file Republicans at his Super Bowl party, handing out oatmeal cookies, gently teasing Senator Specter for wearing a tie. The next day, he talked up the stimulus with Governor Douglas, who provided a perfect image of bipartisan cooperation when he helped Obama move a couch after their Oval Office photo op. The day after that, Obama announced stunning bipartisan news: New Hampshire's senator Judd Gregg—a bona fide conservative—would be joining his cabinet as commerce secretary.

Gregg had voted against Lilly Ledbetter and S-CHIP, and had trashed the Democrats as a party of trillion dollar price tags. But he had been impressed by Obama and his economic team during TARP, and thought he had the potential to be a transformative president. Reid recommended Gregg for the job, Rahm got excited about the concept, and before he really thought about it, Gregg was at the White House saluting his future boss. "You've outlined an extraordinarily bold and aggressive, effective and comprehensive plan for how we can get this country moving," Gregg told Obama as the cameras rolled.

McConnell tried to talk Gregg out of jumping ship, and so did less partisan colleagues. Mel Martinez, who had led HUD under Bush, reminded Gregg that cabinet secretaries don't get to pursue their own agenda. Kent Conrad, Gregg's closest Democratic friend in the Senate, also hinted that the fit might not be great, although he didn't say so directly. "Judd was so enthusiastic, I didn't want to be a skunk at the picnic," Conrad says. Obama transition head John Podesta was even more skeptical.

"He doesn't believe the things we believe," Podesta told Rahm.

"If he takes the job, he'll believe," Rahm replied.

Gregg announced that he would recuse himself from votes on the stimulus, which struck some White House aides as oddly ungrateful. "Nobody was under the illusion that he would be a Barack Obama Democrat," Gibbs says. "But you kind of expect your commerce secretary to support your recovery plan. Some of us were like: 'Huh. That's weird. Maybe this isn't such a great idea.'" Still, the upside for Obama was obvious. A conservative Republican was on record describing Obama's supposedly scattershot plans as "extraordinarily bold and aggressive, effective and comprehensive." *Politico* declared that Gregg's mere presence would "make it harder for his fellow Republicans to demonize Obama and refuse to give the new president the running room he needs to put together his economic recovery plan."

Oh, really?

Some congressional Democrats suspected the Republicans would find it easy to refuse to give Obama running room, even if he put Limbaugh on his cabinet. Their question was when the president would wake up and notice this. His first two weeks in the big chair suggested he had no clue what he was up against. Barney Frank's quips about post-partisan depression already seemed to be coming true.

"We had watched the Republicans move further and further and further to the right," Frank says. "I thought the president was seriously overestimating their willingness to be reasonable."

Obama seemed to think he could float above the fray, distancing himself from the bickering on the Hill. Democrats wanted him to rejoin his team, take some damn pride of authorship, and start fighting for his own legislation, before Republican nihilists drove the country into a depression and blamed it on him. They understood why he had to make bipartisan gestures, but even Pelosi was irritated by his swipes at the House bill, as if he had nothing to do with its contents. She privately told Obama to stop throwing her under the bus. Democrats thought he was helping Republicans steer the debate toward the slices of the bill that sounded questionable, while failing to promote the bulk of the bill that was unobjectionable. And outreach to the opposition wasn't supposed to be a full-time job. Democrats joked that the best way to get face time with the president was to join the Republican Party.

"We got it. He wanted to be *inclusive*," Xavier Becerra told me in a tone that made "inclusive" sound like a hallucinogen. "But this is a tough playground, and you learn the hierarchy fast. The other guys were kicking sand in his face."

Obama couldn't afford to alienate his allies on the Hill. So when he visited the House Democratic retreat in Williamsburg that week, he temporarily shed his Mr. Nice Guy persona, unloading on the Recovery Act's nitpicking Republican critics and their assumption that tax cuts for the rich were the answer to every question. "If you're headed for a cliff, you've got to change direction," he said. He mocked their complaints that the stimulus was a spending bill: "What do you think a stimulus is? It's spending! That's the whole point." He marveled at the gall of Republicans who doubled the national debt, dropped a trillion-dollar deficit in his lap, and then accused him of fiscal irresponsibility for trying to fix the economy they wrecked. He was back in campaign mode, right down to his rallying cry. "Fired up?" he asked.

"Ready to go!" the lawmakers shouted.

Republicans, with straight faces, immediately attacked Obama for promoting partisan divisions. Pence, just a few days after rallying his colleagues with the *Patton* clip about attacking Nazis, told reporters he was disappointed the president had "resorted to tough political rhetoric." Gingrich, the father of modern Republican scorched-earth tactics, criticized Obama for reducing himself to a "partisan leader."

Pot, kettle, whatever. The White House was learning the hard way that it was tough to send a bipartisan message in a partisan town. Obama was getting clobbered when he reached out and clobbered when he fought back. "We didn't realize yet that the Republican game was: Take your money and give you nothing," Gibbs says.

Somehow, they needed to find a few Republicans willing to give them something.

The Gang

Senator Jim DeMint, a conservative firebrand from South Carolina, began his floor speech on the stimulus with kind words for the new commander-in-chief. Well, six kind words. "I like President Obama very much," he said. He then showed his affection by calling the Recovery

Act "the worst piece of economic legislation Congress has considered in 100 years," a "trillion-dollar socialist experiment," a European-style assault on freedom that would "strap a big rocket on the back of our economy and launch it all the way to Brussels."

"This bill is not a stimulus," DeMint declared. "It is a mugging! It is a fraud!"

DeMint was presenting his stimulus alternative, "The American Option," as opposed to Obama's presumably un-American option. It was not the official Republican alternative, because there wasn't one, and if there had been, DeMint—who considered McConnell an unprincipled squish—wouldn't have been picked to present it. DeMint's aides candidly describe the American Option as a kind of right-wing fantasy, a $3 trillion alternative to what they saw as a left-wing fantasy. It had no spending whatsoever. Instead, it made the Bush tax cuts permanent, slashed personal and corporate tax rates, repealed the Alternative Minimum Tax, and almost eliminated estate taxes.

The American Option got almost no attention, because it had no chance in a Democratic Senate. It was a hair-of-the-dog solution, doubling down on Bush with even bigger permanent tax cuts for the rich. What was striking was that only four Republicans opposed it: Collins, Snowe, Specter, and Voinovich. After all their rhetoric about deficits, the other Republicans voted to launch the deficit into the stratosphere. After all their focus on the three-T test, they supported a plan that clearly flunked. After all their demands for infrastructure, they voted for a plan without any.

The DeMint amendment showed that the meltdown of 2008 had not changed the Republican approach to economics. But it did suggest that at least four senators might be open to another approach.

Reid kept his word about an open process. On the Senate floor, Republicans not only offered amendments, they passed amendments. Johnny Isakson of Georgia, a former real estate agent, won approval for a $15,000 tax credit for home purchases. Sam Brownback of Kansas helped insert new tax incentives for car purchases. Kit Bond of Missouri got low-income housing developers a new tax credit.

What all those additions had in common, aside from bipartisan support, were price tags that made the stimulus grow. As the Senate bill shot past $930 billion, Christy Romer was thrilled. "I was doing a little dance: Wow, we're going to hit a trillion!" she recalls. This was what Obama's aides had anticipated, Congress taking their stuff and adding its own stuff. The House had reserved only $300 million for high-speed rail, but Rahm and Biden pressured Senate leaders to think much bigger, reminding them that Las Vegas (in Reid's state), Chicago (in Durbin's), New York (in Chuck Schumer's), and Seattle (in Patty Murray's) could all use faster trains.

"At one point, we were close to $40 billion, $50 billion," Rahm says. "Everyone in the leadership was for it, because they could see a future for themselves in it."

But to the moderate Republicans whose votes were needed to pass a bill—and several moderate Democrats as well—bigger was not better. If a deal was going to happen, the stimulus was going to have to shrink. That's why the Senate floor action was largely a sideshow. Starting on Wednesday, February 4, the real action was on the third floor of a building appropriately named for Everett Dirksen of a billion-here-a-billion-there fame. In a committee hearing room, at least a dozen Democrats and half a dozen Republicans—Biden's five targets plus Murkowski of Alaska—tried to hammer out a compromise to slice over $100 billion out of the stimulus. Dirksen would have agreed: That was real money.

The consensus in the room was that the final package should be below $800 billion, and should have a much tighter focus on jobs. Nobody had an economic theory to justify $800 billion, but it was the minimum Obama had said was needed to avoid a calamity, and more just sounded like too much.

"We thought a number in the 700s would be more palatable," Specter explains. "You know, a trillion seems scary. Even $900 billion, it looks so big."

Disgusted liberals still fume that Specter and his fellow Republican moderates—"President Collins and President Snowe"—dictated the size of the stimulus. There's some truth to that. Obama needed their votes, and they wouldn't accept more than $800 billion. But many of the

Democrats in the room felt just as strongly about an $800 billion cap. Obama needed the votes of Ben Nelson, Evan Bayh, Claire McCaskill of Missouri, Mary Landrieu of Louisiana, Mark Begich of Alaska, and other centrists in his party as badly as he needed President Specter's.

"The overall number was getting way too big to manage," says Begich, who had just been elected and did not want to give a reckless first impression. "The goal was to get a lid on it. We said, under 800, no more, we cannot go above that."

The group's leaders, Collins and Nelson, were veterans of the bipartisan Gang of 14 that had cut a deal to avoid filibusters of judicial nominations in 2005. Their new gang of 18 or so was less formal, and some members dropped out quickly. Kent Conrad, the leading Democratic deficit hawk, wanted a more focused bill, but he thought the gang's obsession with a smaller bill that would create a smaller deficit was economically ignorant. "I left. I thought they were going the wrong direction," Conrad says. Joe Lieberman agreed; despite his well-earned reputation for wandering off the Democratic reservation, he thought the Recovery Act was terrific. He only remained in the gang because Reid had asked him to stay close to Collins, his friend and partner on the Homeland Security Committee.

"Personally, I didn't think the numbers were too high at all," Lieberman says.

On the other side, Mel Martinez thought the stimulus ought to be sliced in half, stripped of its social spending, and rewritten entirely. When it became clear the gang merely planned to trim the existing bill, he withdrew from the negotiations. Murkowski soon followed him out the door, leaving the four Republicans who had opposed the DeMint amendment as the only potential stimulus supporters.

"People were asking: Mel, what can we give you to sign on? I'm saying: You can't give me anything," Martinez says.

In general, the remaining gang members favored more infrastructure and less state aid, even though state aid would save jobs much faster than infrastructure would create jobs. The most contentious discussions centered on education, where the Republicans wanted huge cuts. Nelson, a conservative Democrat who looked like an overgrown garden gnome, was also worried that temporary expansions of Pell Grants and special education funding would become permanent. Collins and Voinovich were particularly adamant that the federal government didn't belong in the school construction business at all.

"When I was a governor, I spent a couple billion dollars rebuilding schools," Voinovich said. "Why the hell should the feds do it?"

Otherwise, the group tried to chip away one item at a time. Begich, the former mayor of Anchorage, argued that grants to help cities hire cops wouldn't spend out as quickly as advertised. "Ain't no way in hell," he said. Begich also sparred with Lieberman over the Homeland Security headquarters, and with Blanche Lincoln over her catfish farms. "We hate fish farming in Alaska," he joked. Most of the gang wanted to get rid of certain cats and dogs, like the State Department cyber-security and the Coast Guard icebreaker. Other items were more contentious, like child care subsidies and a historic preservation fund.

The Washington press corps showered the gang members with the ecstatic praise it always lavishes on politicians who declare a pox on both houses. Center-left *Washington Post* columnist Dana Milbank described them as the Senate's workhorses, in contrast to the partisan showhorses who "prefer drama to lawmaking." Center-right *New York Times* columnist David Brooks wrote that the fate of the Obama presidency would depend on whether he embraced the gang's moderation or his party's orthodoxy, whether he joined a broad bipartisan coalition or merely picked off a few Republican votes.

But by the time the Brooks column ran on Friday, his beloved gang wasn't a very broad bipartisan coalition. Voinovich dropped out after a hard sell from party leaders, leaving just the three Republican moderates willing to deal. There wouldn't be any difference between embracing the gang and picking off a few votes.

"The Republicans were dropping off, one by one," Specter says. "The leadership was putting a lot of pressure on us to say no. I mean, a LOT of pressure."

The Brooks column reflected the up-is-down media narrative about the stimulus, completely mischaracterizing the bill, the president who supposedly had little to do with the bill, and the bipartisan statesmen who were supposedly fixing the bill. For example, Brooks criticized the Recovery Act for shoveling money into education programs and infrastructure projects without reforms, while hailing the gang as the true reformers. In fact, the Senate bill included a mind-boggling $15 billion for the Race to the Top school reforms—and a draft proposal that Nelson and Collins circulated among the gang eliminated every dime. The bill also included $5.5 billion for the innovative TIGER infrastructure grants—and the Nelson-Collins plan eliminated them as well.

The gang members didn't seem to have a theory of the case, other than a desire to split the difference between the two parties, distance themselves from Speaker Pelosi, and bask in the centrist glow of Beltway pundits.

"It was all driven by Washington stupidity—not what the economy needed, just this arbitrary number of 800," Rahm says. "If you were at 801, you were unreasonable. If you were at 799, you were a very thoughtful person."

The moderates called themselves "the jobs crew" and claimed they were on the prowl for fake stimulus, but their main target was state aid that aced the three-T test. They wanted to gut school construction but add highway construction. They wanted to erase science grants but boost environmental compliance grants. They proposed to slash prenatal screening, child nutrition, immunizations, and aid to crime victims, while adding spending for redeveloping contaminated brownfields that were rarely shovel-ready.

"There was, in my view, no rhyme or reason," one Reid aide says. "But you can't argue. You're not going to have an Economics 101 debate with Senator Nelson."

That's because Reid needed Nelson's vote. He'd been herding squirrels in the Senate long enough to see where this was going. In public, Reid kept insisting he wouldn't let the gang hold the president of the United States hostage. In reality, he knew the ringleaders could demand any ransom they wanted. While the gang was deliberating, Obama invited Specter, Collins, and Snowe—plus Nelson, the most troublesome Democrat—to the Oval Office for one-on-one powwows.

He needed them, and they knew it.

Specter had only two ransom demands. First, the stimulus had to cost less than $800 billion, because—well, because. That was the hard limit for the three remaining Republicans, and for quite a few Democrats. Second, Specter wanted $10 billion in the bill for NIH, because medical research was underfunded.

"Are you fucking *kidding* me?"

Rahm seemed to think $10 billion sounded high.

"What the *fuck* does a vote cost around here?"

"Snarlin' Arlen" was a stubborn coot, a former prosecutor who lacked the backslapping social graces of his fellow politicians. This isn't a negotiation, he said. This is my bottom line. No, I won't take $8 billion. No, there's nothing to discuss.

"How the *fuck* am I supposed to keep this under $800 billion if I have to give every senator $10 billion?" Rahm screamed.

The Recovery Act was a complex bill, and the negotiations to get it through the Senate were complex, too. There were a lot of moving parts, and the different players had different priorities. But as they started cutting the deal in Reid's office that Friday, February 6, the bottom line was pretty simple. The Democrats wanted a stimulus, and they couldn't get one without Specter, Collins, and Snowe.

Lieberman was in the room to support Collins—she joked that she needed a Jewish lawyer—and he watched Specter's shakedown with a mix of amusement and admiration. Rahm had all the logic on his side, but Specter had all the power.

"Everyone's saying: 'Come on, Arlen. Get real.' But he wouldn't budge," Lieberman says. "He negotiated the most noble quid pro quo I've ever seen. It wasn't like he was asking for some water project. It was NIH!"

The Republican trio clearly had all the leverage; Reid privately called them "the king and two queens." And along with Nelson, they maximized their leverage by agreeing that unless all four of them were satisfied, none of them would support the stimulus. That was the Democratic nightmare scenario: Republicans would get to say the only thing bipartisan about the Recovery Act was the opposition, Obama would look impotent, and the economy would crater. Rahm didn't like the idea of negotiating at gunpoint, and he really didn't like the idea of a few preening senators telling the leader of the free world what to put in his recovery plan. But unless somebody could figure out how to get Al Franken seated, Rahm didn't see a route to 60 votes that didn't involve serious ass-kissing followed by serious capitulation.

"You're confronted with what was possible versus what was ideal, with the prospect of inaction completely unthinkable," David Axelrod says. "So yeah, the house was burning, and we had to haggle with a handful of senators over the cost of the hose."

Reid knew the time for posturing was over. It was time to pay the kidnappers and free the hostage.

"Harry basically said: How do we get your vote?" recalls Senator Byron Dorgan of North Dakota, a member of Reid's leadership team who attended the talks. "It was just: What are you willing to support? We had to get to yes."

By late evening, the group had hashed out $110 billion in cuts, about half in education, with a final goal of slimming the package to $780 billion. Collins insisted on deleting the entire $16 billion for school construction, a presidential priority. Lieberman tried to broker some middle ground, but Collins wouldn't budge. "Look, she wasn't going for it," Lieberman says. "So what could we do?" Collins also declared pandemic flu preparations a nonstarter, but Lieberman persuaded her to shift that $870 million to community health clinics rather than kill it outright.

"I hope they have that on my list of good deeds when I get to the gates of heaven," he says.

The deal also whacked over $40 billion in state education aid, $8 billion for energy efficiency retrofits of federal buildings, and $6 billion in preventive health programs. Rahm managed to save Race to the Top, but its funding was cut in half. There were also significant cuts to food stamps, Head Start, health care for laid-off workers, and other antipoverty spending. High-speed rail was whittled to $2 billion—more than the House bill, but a long trip from $40–$50 billion.

"We've trimmed the fat, fried the bacon, and milked the sacred cows," Nelson crowed on the Senate floor.

Dorgan and Durbin, the New Deal liberals in the room, didn't see what was so fatty about food stamps and preventive care. They thought slimming the stimulus would just lop off jobs and hurt people in need. But they didn't have three votes in their pockets, so they had to accept whatever the swing senators would accept. They consoled themselves with the thought that $780 billion was still massive.

"Yeah, I would have liked it even more massive. But there simply wasn't room for anything bigger," Dorgan says.

Even after the deal was done, Rahm had a last minute freak-out: Are we sure Specter is on board? "He went radio silent," Rahm recalls. He called Obama: We can't find Specter! He called Biden: Can you find Specter? "I went to sleep not sure where he was, physically or on the vote," Rahm recalls. But at six the next morning, he checked his Black-Berry and found a note from the vice president: Specter was okay. At that morning's intelligence briefing, Rahm and Biden exchanged gleeful high fives, as the national security team wondered what exactly in the intel had gotten them so excited.

The Senate passed the slimmed-down bill, 61–37, with still-Senator Gregg abstaining and not-yet-Senator Franken cooling his heels in Minnesota. Pale and weakened, Ted Kennedy had to be flown in for the vote on a government plane, because no Republicans would risk the wrath of the right by voting his proxy. At least Obama could finally point to a bipartisan deal, with support from the Chamber of Commerce as well as the AFL-CIO, the National Governors Association as well as the U.S. Conference of Mayors, not to mention advocates for seniors and kids, the poor and the environment, technology and manufacturing.

Nevertheless, Washington Republicans continued to dismiss the stimulus as partisan giveaway to Democratic interest groups. On the

Sunday political shows, where he would remain a near-permanent fix-
ture, John McCain scoffed that Obama would need more than three
Republicans on his side to prove he was serious about bipartisanship.
Evidently, governors, mayors, and cabinet members didn't count.

"That's not bipartisanship," McCain declared with the definitive air
of an official arbiter. "That's just picking off a couple of Republican
senators."

"I am *so* happy bipartisanship is important to the Republicans again!"
Pelosi sneered. "For eight years, they didn't seem to care about reaching across the aisle. But now it's 'Boo, hoo, what about us?' After they
treated us like sewer rats for eight years, we were worried that bipartisanship didn't matter to them."

Okay, that wasn't really Pelosi. It was a *Saturday Night Live* actress
playing Pelosi in all her crazy-eyed, ultra-partisan glory, bragging about
how she didn't pander to Republicans, chastising Reid for agreeing to
cut education spending in the stimulus. "Let's try to remember something," the fake Pelosi said. *"We won!"*

The real Pelosi's reaction to the Senate deal was not that different.
She said the Senate's cuts would "do violence to what we are trying to
do for the future." And she fumed about Washington's obsession with
bipartisanship, the Beltway habit of judging legislation according to
how many Republicans supported it rather than what was in it. The real
Pelosi understood why Reid made concessions, but the House and Senate still had to reconcile their versions of the stimulus, and she did not
feel bound by the demands of Presidents Specter, Collins, and Snowe.

"She was pissed," says one senior Pelosi aide. "Look: She's a whip
at heart. She understands realpolitik, and she knows the Senate needs
sixty votes. But she didn't want the House taken for granted."

In *The Audacity of Hope*, Obama had written about the pathologies
of modern Washington: politics as an endless war between potbellied
gladiators from the red and blue teams, split-the-difference centrists
who assume they're in the right as long as they're in the center, Repub-

licans who don't traffic in facts and can't take yes for an answer. It still seemed surreal from his new vantage point.

The economy had shed nearly four million jobs, half of them in the last three months, yet he was stuck in a head-of-a-pin debate about how many Republicans it took to make a bipartisan deal bipartisan. Congress was on the verge of passing a sweeping bill to bandage a bleeding economy, cut taxes for working families, help victims of the slump, and attack intractable social problems, and the cable chatter was about "ACORN-eligible block grants" (McConnell's creative rebranding of community development assistance to cities) and aid to small shipyards. Meanwhile, purity-test progressives were whining about the most progressive piece of social and economic legislation in decades. And Republicans who had praised his call for $300 billion in tax cuts were bashing a bill with over $300 billion in tax cuts.

At his first press conference, Obama mused that he probably should have pretended he didn't want tax cuts, then let Republicans take credit for adding them.

"I get the sense that there's some ideological blockage there that needs to be cleared up," Obama said. "But I am the eternal optimist. I think that over time people respond to civility and rational argument."

— ELEVEN —

Done Deal

The Senate passed its version of the stimulus on Tuesday, February 10. Now House and Senate leaders had to negotiate a deal in time for both chambers to pass a final version by Friday. There was no longer time for polite suggestions and hints. That night, Rahm delivered a White House list of funding directives to Pelosi and Reid, who immediately instructed staff to convert them into legislative language. The critics who mock Obama for punting the stimulus to Congress have never seen this list, which designated specific dollar amounts for over 150 specific programs. It looks an awful lot like the final bill.

The one shocker on the list was high-speed rail. With school construction in danger, Rahm believed the stimulus badly needed a new marquee project. Initiatives like the smart grid and education reform would be transformative, but virtually invisible. High-speed rail would put men in hard hats to work on a visionary mission that Americans could see and appreciate. Obama loved the idea, and while his economists didn't, Rahm told them a massive investment in fast trains would persuade moderate House Republicans to support the stimulus.

"They're horny for high-speed rail!" he said.

Normally, high-speed rail would have ended up somewhere between the House mark of $300 million and the Senate's proposal of $2 billion. But the White House list pegged it for $10 billion.

"Whoa, where did this come from?" one Senate staffer asked.

It came from a four-letter word that starts with R and rhymes with bomb.

"This is the way it's going to be," Reid told the staff. "Just get it done."

"And It Wasn't My Money!"

The delivery of the White House list kicked off twenty-four hours of chaotic shuttle diplomacy. Rahm and Peter Orszag—who was thrown into the talks because of his strong relationships with the Senate moderates as well as his budget chops—met Tuesday night with Democratic leaders in the speaker's office to discuss tweaks. After the meeting broke up around 11:30 P.M., staffers worked all night drafting, before their bosses started negotiating again in the morning.

Aside from the abrupt expansion of high-speed rail, the talks were about subtraction. The Congressional Budget Office had priced the Senate bill at $838 billion, even after the cuts demanded by the moderates; the House version was $819 billion without the Alternative Minimum Tax patch. So there would have to be further shrinkage to keep the moderates on board. "We were backed down by Specter and the twin princesses of Maine," Obey grouses.

The obvious place to start cutting was the AMT fix. Initially, the White House hadn't objected to its inclusion in the stimulus, even though it wasn't really stimulus. Everyone knew Congress would get around to passing it sooner or later, and many Democrats—including Pelosi—were happy to deal with it now, to avoid a messy fight over how to pay for it later. But once the overall size of the package was capped, $70 billion for the AMT meant $70 billion less stimulus, a stiff price to pay to help Congress with its housekeeping. Obama's economists were clamoring to get rid of it, but the Senate moderates said no, the AMT had to stay, even though averting a tax hike no one expected wouldn't create jobs. Snowe was particularly insistent; she had promised her friend Chuck Grassley she would protect the patch.

"She wants to make Grassley happy, even though he's not voting for the bill," Rahm says. "It was the weirdest $70 billion I ever spent, and it wasn't my money!"

Rahm was tired of sucking up to Republicans and getting nothing in return, which is why his next target was the carryback tax credit for banks, builders, and other businesses with severe losses. Boehner had told Rahm it was the GOP's top stimulus priority, so initially Rahm had lobbied hard to get skeptical Democrats to include a $15 billion carryback, hoping it would entice Republicans to support the overall bill. "The way Rahm was screaming, you would've thought it was the thing he cared about most in the world," one staffer recalls. But his here-kitty-kitty strategy hadn't attracted GOP votes, so now Rahm lobbied just as hard to kill the carryback. The final deal limited the credit to small businesses, which slashed its cost below $1 billion. Rahm warned his Monocle pal Steve LaTourette that the disappearing carryback should be a lesson to Republicans about the consequences of intransigence.

"He basically said: 'Fuck Boehner, it's coming out,'" LaTourette recalls. "'We're not putting anything in for you if you guys aren't going to help us.'"

Senator Isakson's tax credit for homebuyers was another juicy target, partly because the CBO priced it at an astronomical $35 billion, partly because a program that would pay you $15,000 to buy your brother's house seemed sketchy, partly because Isakson voted against the stimulus, too. "I don't understand the Senate," Rahm kept saying. "If you get your stuff in the bill, don't you have to vote for the bill?" No? Well, then screw Senator Isakson. The final deal only included an $8,000 credit limited to first-time homebuyers, cutting its cost over 80 percent.

But Rahm thought the White House needed to put some skin in the game, too. After insisting that the Making Work Pay tax credit was non-negotiable, he now agreed to scale it back from $1,000 to $800 per year per family, trimming over $20 billion from the price tag to try to get the deal done. The White House also reluctantly accepted only $5 billion for education reform, which had been in line for $15 billion a week earlier. At the last minute, even high-speed rail got trimmed to $8 billion.

"We had to show we were willing to shave our goodies, too," one aide says.

"Nancy, this ain't gonna work."

Jim Clyburn was not a happy camper. Democrats had just won a historic election, and now they had to shave their goodies and weaken their bill to make sure Republicans didn't filibuster in the Senate? Clyburn wanted to see them actually filibuster, Mr. Smith–style. Let them haul in cots and explain to the public why they were so eager to block a recovery bill. But Pelosi said no, this is no time to play chicken. So the House plan to revamp the Farm Service Agency computers that seemed to freeze every harvest season was cut 79 percent to appease three Republicans from nonagricultural states. The House plan to aid struggling cities was cut 67 percent, because God forbid some money might go to ACORN. Senator Collins even killed a House provision that would have protected government whistle-blowers from retaliation if they raised alarms about waste or fraud. Clyburn decided it was time to draw a line in the sand, and he drew it at rural broadband.

Clyburn's beef wasn't even about how much money to spend, but which bureaucracy would spend it. The House had split its broadband cash between Commerce and Agriculture, while the Senate had given it all to Commerce. The White House sided with the Senate for policy reasons; Obama's advisers wanted to promote "middle-mile" projects that could extend high-speed Internet to institutions like schools and hospitals, while Agriculture tended to favor "last-mile" projects serving individual homes at more modest speeds. And an independent watchdog had concluded that Agriculture's program was an ineffectual mess. But Clyburn was sure his rural constituents would never get wired if Commerce got all the money. (An Agriculture Department lobbyist was making that very case to lawmakers behind the new president's back.) While Pelosi was negotiating with Obama, Clyburn insisted he'd oppose the stimulus if Agriculture didn't get its share. She threw up her hands and handed Clyburn her cell phone.

"Mr. President," Clyburn repeated, "this ain't gonna work."

In the end, Clyburn managed to steer about a third of the Recovery Act's $7.2 billion in broadband grants to Agriculture. "Oh, Obama got it," Clyburn says with a laugh.

At the time, many House Democrats felt like they were getting rolled on just about everything else. "It always felt like an unequal partnership," Becerra says. "The president would say: You've got to jump, because otherwise the Senate will filibuster. And the House would say: How high?" Actually, House Democrats scored several victories over the Senate. For example, they secured $15 billion to expand the child tax credit, providing extra help to thirteen million low-income children. They killed the Senate's risky plan for new nuclear loans, and most of its tax incentives for car buyers. Pelosi, who liked to say her top three priorities were science, science, and science, also protected the House's line items for labs and basic research.

"Nancy said: Maybe we'll have to compromise somewhere else, but we're not compromising on science," says Bart Gordon of Tennessee, the House Science Committee chairman.

But the most intense negotiations were about education, where the House really was getting rolled. "Oh, that was way beyond frustration," Charlie Rangel says. "Whichever senator wants to be wooed, we're just supposed to accept it." Obey was scrambling to restore some of the Senate cuts, but that required trims to other items lawmakers liked: veterans hospitals, public housing repairs, construction at the Centers for Disease Control. Meanwhile, Rahm and Orszag seemed to be competing for a job as Susan Collins's personal valet.

"I was getting vilified in the House," Rahm recalls. "How could I be so disloyal? How could I be locked in a room with three Republican senators?"

Pelosi didn't mind Rahm talking to the Republicans; she minded him caving to their threats. She had a hard time believing that anyone would vote against a jobs bill just because it included money to fix schools, and she repeatedly screamed at Rahm and Phil Schiliro to drive a harder bargain. I asked Rahm if it was true that Pelosi was yelling at him daily. "Hourly," he replied.

"There was a lot of frustration about the Senate Republicans driving the train," says one Pelosi aide. "She wanted to see the administration pushing back."

Rahm did try to steer $10 billion back into school construction, but the moderates said no. Orszag proposed limiting the money to repairs of existing schools. Still no. Could states at least use their general education aid to fix schools? That was at least something to talk about. But it raised other arcane questions: How much of the aid would be eligible? Would governors control the money? During one technical dispute over how some language would affect Maine's school construction agency, Orszag begged Collins to give ground.

"Please," he said. "Do this for me."

Collins just laughed.

"That's funny," she said. "You still want people to like you."

The final spat on the Senate side did not pit the moderates against the leadership, but Specter against Ben Nelson, who wanted to tweak the Recovery Act's formula for distributing Medicaid funds to get rural states extra cash. Specter said: No way. Orszag did some calculations in his head, and informed Rahm that Nelson was hijacking the entire stimulus over $25 million. Rahm pulled Nelson aside and told him: Don't fuck this up. We'll get you $25 million some other way. This wouldn't be the last time Nelson held up major legislation to extort some extra swag for Nebraska; his "Cornhusker Kickback" would become the most notorious provision in Obama's health care bill.

It was perhaps fitting that on Wednesday afternoon, after Reid announced that the House and the Senate had reached a final agreement that would spend less money and create more jobs, Pelosi denied that the deal was done, and angry House Democrats blew off a public meeting with their Senate counterparts. By evening, the two sides had finalized a $787 billion deal, but House Democrats were still carping. Reid understood their frustration with the Senate's get-to-sixty culture, and the way it turned random backbenchers into power brokers. But this wasn't his first game of Senate poker, and he knew Collins and her fellow moderates held all the cards.

"They give me three aces, Susan pulls out a full house," said Reid, who got his start in politics on the Nevada Gaming Commission. "No matter what I was dealt, she had a better hand."

Progressives like Becerra wanted to call the Republican bluff. He didn't think this was the time to establish a precedent that Republicans could water down the Obama agenda whenever they wanted. When were Democrats ever going to have a better hand than they had when the president was at 70 percent, the Republican brand was radioactive, and the economy was teetering on the brink?

"My argument was: The public just hired us to produce," Becerra says. "If we don't produce, nobody's going to care that the stimulus morphed into something less stimulative because we needed a few Republican votes. They're going to remember that they gave us the reins."

For Obama, it was time to escape the Washington bubble.

Somehow, the narrative had shifted from economic suffering and change to horse-trading and catfish subsidies. So while Rahm was haggling on the Hill, Obama took his first road trips, to try to remind Americans what the fight was about. His first stop was the recreational vehicle capital of Elkhart, Indiana, a hard-scrabble industrial town with the nation's fastest-growing unemployment rate. He then visited the seaside foreclosure mecca of Fort Myers, Florida, where Governor Crist hugged him, warmly endorsed the Recovery Act, and reinforced his bipartisan message. But even back in campaign mode, the White House struggled to get its point across. The Elkhart trip was overshadowed by Obama's first press conference. The Fort Myers trip was overshadowed by Treasury Secretary Geithner's speech outlining his plans to address the real estate bust—and by the market's brutal reaction to his inability to articulate those plans.

Obama's third trip of the week, to the bellwether city of Peoria, Illinois, was another messaging mess. The president visited a Caterpillar plant that had just announced mass layoffs, and declared the heavy-equipment company would start hiring again once Congress passed the stimulus. But after the event, the company's CEO told reporters he might let even more workers go regardless of the stimulus. That did not play well in Peoria or anywhere else. "You had the story that whole day: The president said this, Cat said that," recalls Aaron Schock, the area's Republican congressman. In his speech, Obama called out the twenty-seven-year-old Schock, who had hitched a ride to the event on Air Force One, and urged him to follow the bipartisan example of his predecessor from Peoria, Transportation Secretary Ray LaHood. But afterward, Schock told reporters that not a single Caterpillar employee had asked him to support the stimulus—and that he still intended to vote no, because it didn't include enough infrastructure spending that would put Caterpillar's earthmovers to work.

As if Caterpillar and Schock weren't doing enough to drown out Obama's message of jobs and bipartisanship, news broke while he was on the factory floor that Senator Gregg was withdrawing from consideration for Commerce. Gregg let it be known that the main reason for his bait-and-switch was his discomfort with the stimulus he had called "extraordinarily bold and aggressive, effective and comprehensive." Gregg publicly apologized for changing his mind, but his sudden withdrawal made it sound like the Recovery Act must be egregiously partisan to provoke such an act of conscience.

When I spoke to Gregg two years later, he called the stimulus a "monstrosity," and seemed to forget he had ever praised it. "It was fundamentally flawed from the beginning," he told me. "A serious package would have been mostly infrastructure: schools, research, transportation, things that add physical value to the economy. I mean, health IT? A bunch of hospitals wanted money. Basically, the stimulus was walking-around money for appropriators."

So why on earth did he pursue an administration job?

"I guess I got caught up in the euphoria of the moment."

In fact, Gregg's *Wall Street Journal* op-ed in January specifically called for stimulus investments in "integrated IT in public industries like health care," describing them as twenty-first-century infrastructure. Schools? Republicans were blocking additional investments, not Obama. Research? The Recovery Act included the largest funding increase in history. Transportation? Again, the stimulus had plenty of it, and again, Republicans blocked efforts to add more of it.

No, Gregg's about-face was less about the substance of the stimulus than his own identity as a Republican. He was under intense pressure from McConnell and other party leaders not to give Obamaworld a bipartisan imprimatur. Even former First Lady Barbara Bush called to tell him to come to his senses. Once Gregg agreed to flip-flop, he swiftly began denouncing the "Obama Spend-o-rama." He even wrote a bill to ban the use of stimulus funds on signs identifying stimulus projects. "Those signs cost $2,000 apiece!" he says. "That money could have stimulated the economy. It's pure self-promotion. It's Chicago politics." In fact, sign makers are part of the economy, signs routinely inform taxpayers how their money is spent, and Gregg had never expressed concern about self-promotion when he was earmarking $500,000 for the "Judd Gregg Meteorology Institute." But once Gregg—or "Secretary Gregg," as he was derisively known at the White House—decided to stick with the red team, he fully embraced the party line that the blue team was run by thuggish radicals.

"I suspect this was an eye-opener for them, too," Gregg admits. "From that point on, there was no bipartisanship."

"I Couldn't Believe How Much They Got"

Not enough bipartisanship. Not enough presidential leadership.

Not enough infrastructure. Not enough tax cuts.

Not enough stimulus.

As Congress prepared for its final vote on the Recovery Act— on Friday the 13th—the national debate focused almost entirely on what it lacked. "Mr. Obama's victory feels more than a bit like defeat," Paul Krugman wrote. Nobody seemed to be dwelling on what the stimulus had.

With so many big numbers being thrown around, it was easy to forget how impressive $787 billion actually was. It was about the size of the annual economic output of Florida or the Netherlands. It was bigger than the military budget or the nonmilitary discretionary budget. Since it included the nonstimulative $70 billion AMT patch, plus a few long-range projects like high-speed rail and health IT, the immediate fiscal jolt was shaping up as a bit less than $700 billion. But it was still the boldest countercyclical push in U.S. history, far more aggressive as a percentage of GDP than the New Deal's ever was. It dwarfed the stimulus packages passed by most of our economic rivals, with the glaring exception of China, which had announced plans to pour $586 billion into an economy one third the size of ours.

"Look, more stimulus would've been better," says Jared Bernstein, the most liberal economist in the White House. "But Paul Krugman in his wildest dreams couldn't have offset an $8 trillion loss in housing wealth, and trillions more in output. No conceivable stimulus could have offset the Great Recession."

Anyway, the White House didn't have the votes for more stimulus, not one more dollar. Krugman didn't have to get his column passed by a supermajority.

"Give me a break," Biden says. "I've been doing this my whole career. I'm going to say something outrageous: I don't know anybody who counts votes better than me in the Senate. And you tell me you could've gotten better, you could've gotten $900 billion or $1 trillion? I mean, come on. I love the left saying, well, we could've gotten more. Okay, you go get it. You tell me how to get the sixty votes."

Some liberal activists say Obama could have gotten a better deal if he had campaigned for it, harnessing the grassroots energy that had gotten him elected instead of playing inside baseball. Adam Green, who founded the Progressive Change Campaign Committee that January, thought he should have barnstormed across Maine and Pennsylvania to pressure Collins, Snowe, and Specter to back off, rather than settling for a smaller stimulus that would give stimulus a bad name. "That was a defining moment," Green says. "It sent the message right from the start that he could be rolled."

Obama has scoffed at this "notion that somehow I could have gone and made the case around the country for a far bigger stimulus," as if suddenly the automatons of the Senate would have done his bidding. He was the president, not the king. And he didn't just need the votes of Collins, Snowe, and Specter to pass the stimulus; he also needed Ben Nelson and the other centrist red-state Democrats who weren't willing to spend a penny more than $800 billion. Should he have flown to Alaska to put pressure on Senator Begich, too? Time was a bit of an issue, with the country plunging into a depression.

"If folks think we could have gotten Ben Nelson, Arlen Specter, and Susan Collins to vote for additional stimulus, I would just suggest you weren't in the meetings," Obama later said. "We didn't have the luxury to say to the Senate, our way or the highway."

With so much attention focused on Obama's concessions, it was just as easy to forget how much of what he wanted he was getting. Rahm estimated that the figure was 90 percent, well over Schiliro's original 80–20 threshold. For example, the Recovery Act included about $300 billion worth of tax cuts—the number Obama initially proposed—almost entirely for the middle class and the working poor. It also authorized $140 billion in new safety net spending, the largest one-time expansion ever. And even after the haircut from the moderates, the stimulus still provided an unprecedented $165 billion in fiscal aid to help states avoid layoffs and cuts—about half of it through Medicaid, most of the rest through education funding. That wasn't enough to fill all the state budget gaps that Bob Greenstein's think tank had identified, but it was over 80 percent of what Obama requested, and way more than most progressives expected.

"I couldn't believe how much they got compared to what I thought was possible," Greenstein says.

It is an article of faith in Washington that the Recovery Act was light on infrastructure, but it was the most ambitious new commitment to public works since Dwight Eisenhower's administration. It poured nearly $50 billion into transportation; according to Congressman Mica's formula, that alone would "create or sustain" about 1.5 million jobs.

And while progressives complained that over half of that funding would go to highways—"Stimulus for Planes, Trains, but Mostly Automobiles," blared a Center for Public Integrity headline—the percentage for mass transit was over twice as high as it had been in the last transportation bill. The stimulus launched a slew of other infrastructure investments as well, including $13 billion for water and sewer projects, $11 billion for grid upgrades, and $7 billion for new broadband. According to Senator Gregg's definition, the $40 billion allotted to research and health IT should count as infrastructure, too. There was another $20 billion or so in the stimulus for energy efficiency retrofits and other construction projects at military bases, border stations, public housing, and other government buildings. And that was on top of the Recovery Act's unprecedented investments in geothermal technologies, advanced biorefineries, electric vehicles, green-collar job training, and the rest of the clean-energy food chain.

That didn't leave much room for cats and dogs. Yes, the money for artists and catfish farmers survived in the final package, along with the census and digital TV coupons. Senator Inouye also jammed in the payments to Filipino veterans. But most of the Recovery Act's extras were relatively uncontroversial. There were about $4 billion in grants to law enforcement agencies, with specific carve-outs for fighting violence against women, Internet crimes against children, drugs in rural towns, and guns along the Mexican border. There was $16 billion for expanding Pell tuition grants, $6 billion for nuclear waste cleanups, $1 billion for preventive medicine. Then there was education reform—$4.35 billion for Race to the Top, plus $650 million for Investing in Innovation, another groundbreaking grant competition designed to scale up reform models with proven records of success, and $3.5 billion for School Improvement Grants, which would finance radical transformations of America's worst performing schools. Those programs were controversial, but with liberals and unions, not with Obama's usual critics.

Obama and his centrist economists also blocked several populist add-ons. For example, Obama's friend Dick Durbin wanted to include a popular "cramdown" proposal to let bankruptcy judges modify underwater mortgages, which would give at-risk homeowners much more leverage in their dealings with banks. The Obama team kept it out of the bill. The Recovery Act did deliver one slap at Wall Street, restricting salaries and bonuses for firms receiving TARP funds. But Geithner persuaded Senate Banking chairman Christopher Dodd to add language clarifying that bonuses approved before the stimulus could not be rescinded. Ultimately, the limits would go virtually unnoticed, while the exception to the limits would create a firestorm.

Basically, though, the stimulus was what Obama said it would be. It didn't launch a nationwide school construction binge, and it had less money for education reform than he had hoped. It had the AMT patch instead of a hiring tax credit, and it didn't have an infrastructure bank. Otherwise, it almost precisely followed the framework Obama gave Congress during his transition, providing the down payment on his long-term agenda that he promised during his inaugural address. In Peoria, he predicted it would unleash "a new wave of innovation and construction all across America."

"We'll put people to work building wind turbines and solar panels and fuel-efficient cars," Obama said. "We'll computerize our health care system to save billions of dollars and countless lives; lay down broadband lines to connect rural schools and businesses so they can compete with their counterparts anywhere in the world; rebuild crumbling roads and bridges; repair dangerous dams and levees so we don't face another Katrina. Think about all the work out there to be done!"

The only remaining suspense was whether House Republicans would remain united. Anh Cao told reporters he was leaning toward supporting the stimulus, and Emanuel and LaHood were pitching rail-friendly moderates like John Mica, Fred Upton, and Mike Castle on the wonders of fast trains. They still thought a dozen Republicans might vote yes. "I didn't think the die was cast," LaHood says. He wasn't hearing many substantive complaints about the stimulus; his old colleagues mostly seemed annoyed with Pelosi's influence over the process.

Cantor and his whip team worked the vote hard. He spent most of his time on the floor lobbying Upton, at one point leading him through that eighteen-page polling presentation. His deputy, Kevin McCarthy, hovered near Cao. The White House also helped Cantor out with a head-scratching political blunder, compiling a list of the Recovery Act's predicted job creation numbers for all 435 congressional districts—with Cao's dead last. He says that list persuaded him to vote no, and the rest of his Republican colleagues joined him. At one point, Boehner theatrically dropped the 1,073-page bill on the House floor, where it landed with a symbolic thud. This time, the Republicans were joined in opposition by only six Blue Dog Democrats, plus one liberal, Peter DeFazio of Oregon, who switched to no because he thought the final deal had too many tax cuts and not enough infrastructure.

"You think about the New Deal: It built things," DeFazio says. "For us, it's going to be: What did you do in the war, Grandpa? Oh, I got a few tax cuts."

The Senate vote, while less suspenseful, was one of the longest congressional votes in history. Since Kennedy was too ill to attend, Reid had to hold the roll call open for five hours so that Ohio Democrat Sherrod Brown could fly back from his mother's funeral on a government plane to record the sixtieth vote. He then immediately flew back to Ohio for the memorial service Saturday morning. This time, Reid didn't even bother to ask Republicans if they would pair Brown's vote to spare him from crisscrossing the country during his time of grief. They clearly didn't intend to do Democrats any favors.

"A lot of Republicans thought the stimulus was necessary," Specter says. "They just wanted it to pass without their fingerprints. It was all so partisan. You had the sentiment: 'We're going to break Obama.'"

Voters wanted action, and Democrats predicted that Republicans would be punished for their stimulus obstruction. In New Orleans, Cao almost instantly faced a movement to recall him from Congress. Robert Menendez of New Jersey, the head of the Senate Democratic campaign fund, gloated that obstructionist Republicans were racing over an electoral cliff. "They are in essence betting against the president and against an economic recovery," he said. "At the end of the day, acting to turn this economy around is going to look a lot better than just being naysayers."

That was yet another wrong assumption.

• • •

"**N**amasté. Namasté? Nah-Mah-STAY."

It's a Sanskrit greeting of peace and respect, usually associated with yoga types, not usually with Joe Biden. But the vice president was preparing to introduce Blake Jones, the CEO of Namasté Solar, and he wanted to get the pronunciation right. "If I say it wrong, you can call me Bidden!" he told Jones.

It was Tuesday, February 17, and Obama was about to sign the Recovery Act into law—not in Washington, the scene of all the squabbling, but 1,700 miles away at the Denver Museum of Science, where Namasté had installed the solar panels on the roof. In its three years in business, Namasté had grown from three to fifty-five employees, but in the last few months, it had announced a hiring freeze, slashed its budget, cut work for subcontractors, slashed its budget again, and started planning its first layoffs. Now, thanks to the stimulus, Jones was looking to hire again. Solar installations, he told Biden, were "wrench-ready."

Biden believed in stories, not statistics; he thought the public was hearing too much about 3 million theoretical jobs and not enough about Namasté—which, true to form, he pronounced Nah-MAH-stay in his introduction. Jones began his speech by taking Biden up on his offer: "Thank you, Vice President Bidden," he deadpanned. But then he told Namasté's story, the tale of an employee-owned company that converts sunshine into energy, money, a stronger nation, and a healthier planet. Because of the stimulus, Jones said, Namasté expected 40 percent growth through 2010.

"Our pessimistic outlook has been injected with new hope and optimism," he said. "We're hoping thousands of carpenters, plumbers, electricians, roofers, sales people, marketing people and executives laid off by building industries will join us in the solar industry. Green jobs aren't just good for those of us who have them. They're good for everyone."

When it was his turn to speak, Obama did not dwell on the compromises behind the Recovery Act. He hailed it as "the most sweeping economic recovery package in our history," with "the largest investment in education in our history," "the most meaningful steps in years towards modernizing our health care system," "the most progressive tax cuts in our history," and "the biggest increase in basic research in the long history of America's noble endeavor to better understand our world."

Some White House economists hoped the president would point out that a bigger stimulus would have been even better for the economy, to start laying the groundwork to ask for more if the need should arise. And Axelrod was always nervous about overinflating expectations. But Rahm was a triumphalist. He wanted everyone to see the president celebrating his victory, because winners tend to keep winning. Obama took Rahm's side of that debate. He preferred bragging about what he had done to griping about what he hadn't been able to do.

"We have begun the essential work of keeping the American dream alive in our time," Obama said. "Today does not mark the end of our economic problems. But it does mark the beginning of the end."

After his expansive description of his new New Deal, the president pivoted. The Recovery Act, he said, was only the first step to a vibrant economy. The financial system still needed to be stabilized and reformed. The auto industry needed to be salvaged. So did the housing market, starting with a $50 billion plan he'd announce the next day. His message was: Onward. Critics of the stimulus would continue to pound it, but Obama didn't intend to spend the rest of his presidency defending it. He had work to do. He assumed that if he did that work well, the politics would take care of itself.

"If I had my druthers, I would've loved to make the case for the Recovery Act over a longer period of time, and run campaigns around each element of it," Axelrod says. "I would've loved to promote the more popular parts of it like the tax cuts in a more traditional way. But time was of the essence. We just didn't have that luxury."

Blake Jones got to show Obama and Biden around the rooftop that day, and he was struck by the contrast between the two pols. Biden looked him in the eye and made him feel at home, spinning yarns, cursing up a storm. Obama was all business: What are the best policies for promoting solar? How should they be structured?

"I tried cracking a joke, and the president didn't laugh," Jones recalls. "He was working. He had twenty minutes, and he was going to make the best use of every one. He was purpose-driven. I was thinking: Is he on like this all the time?"

Lessons Learned

Rahm's backroom dealmaking wouldn't have looked good on C-SPAN, but Obama knew the Recovery Act wouldn't have happened without it. When Rahm called to congratulate him, the president said: "Look, man, you did all the work."

"Don't worry, you'll get all the glory," Rahm replied. "And I know who's gonna get the blame."

Rahm was an operator, and he had been hired to operate; Washington backrooms were his natural habitat. His tactics—however unsightly, however jarring after Obama's rhetoric about a new kind of politics—had gotten the stimulus through the swamp, while allowing the president to stay out of the muck.

"Come on, man, he was pure! It was his chief of staff who was the whore," Rahm cackles.

Still, Obama had lost his first message battle. That may have been inevitable; as the president later said, any stimulus bill was going to be "easy to caricature as a big-spending liberal agenda." And the inside game of passing legislation is inherently messier than the outside game of campaigning; it's always tough to stay on message in a game with 535 other players. But some aides thought the White House's immersion in congressional sausage making had taken an unnecessarily heavy public relations toll, making the president look too much like a Washington politician and not enough like an inspirational leader. The Obama campaign had prized itself on discipline, on ignoring the news cycle and taking the long view. Rahm didn't work that way.

"The message suffered, because we were all over the place," one senior official says. "Rahm must have cut fourteen thousand deals. You can't win messaging like that."

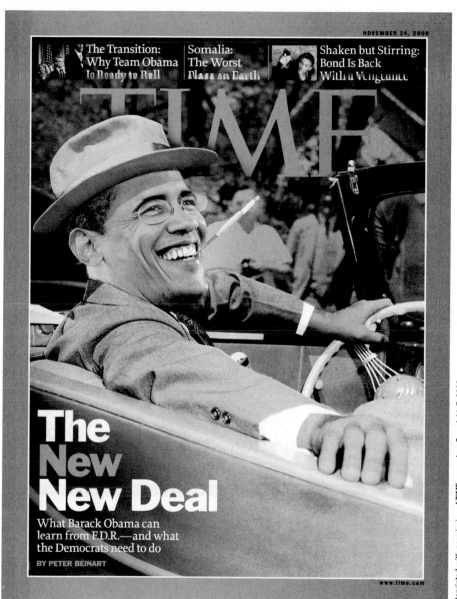

The Transition: Why Team Obama Is Ready to Roll

Somalia: The Worst Place on Earth

Shaken but Stirring: Bond Is Back With a Vengeance

TIME

The New New Deal

What Barack Obama can learn from F.D.R.—and what the Democrats need to do

BY PETER BEINART

www.time.com

Reprinted with permission of TIME magazine. Copyright © 2003.

1   President Obama faced the greatest economic challenge since Franklin D. Roosevelt took office in March 1933 during the Depression, and the comparisons began shortly after his election.

(*Above*) President Obama put Vice President Biden in charge of the Recovery Act, and relied on him for unfiltered advice about the stimulus and everything else. "He wanted me to be the bastard at the family picnic," Biden says.

(*At right*) Chief of Staff Rahm Emanuel reads a story about the White House's struggles with messaging. Some Obama aides thought Rahm's frantic horse-trading had tarnished the president's theme of change. "Come on, man, he was pure!" Rahm says. "It was his chief of staff who was the whore."

4

President Obama's cabinet was responsible for putting the Recovery Act into action. The White House considered (*from left*) Education Secretary Arne Duncan, Energy Secretary Steven Chu, and Housing and Urban Development Secretary Shaun Donovan to be its leading reformers.

5

Transportation Secretary Ray LaHood, a former Republican congressman from Illinois, runs interference for President Obama before a meeting with House Republicans. LaHood's loyalty to the president was not a surprise, but his enthusiastic embrace of reform was.

President Obama's economic team was not a well-oiled machine, but it helped prevent a second depression. The team met in the Roosevelt Room on February 6, 2009. In the left foreground, Treasury counselor Gene Sperling talks numbers with Office of Management and Budget director Peter Orszag, while Treasury Secretary Tim Geithner makes a point to National Economic Council director Larry Summers. In the background, OMB deputy Jeff Liebman chats with NEC deputy Jason Furman.

The president walks in the Rose Garden with senior adviser Valerie Jarrett (*far left*), Vice President Biden's chief economist Jared Bernstein (*holding coffee*), Peter Orszag (*holding a diet Coke*), Council of Economic Advisers chair Christina Romer, and Jason Furman.

8

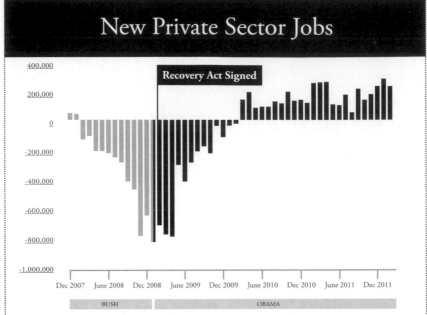

New Private Sector Jobs

Monthly Change   Source: Bureau of Labor Statistics

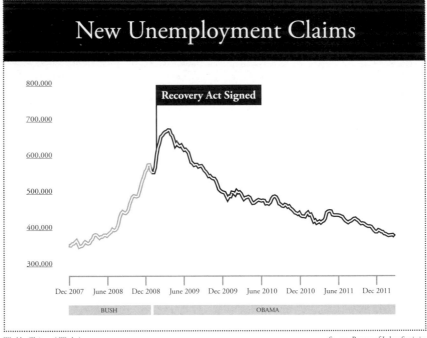

New Unemployment Claims

Weekly Claims, 4-Week Average   Source: Bureau of Labor Statistics

After shedding over 800,000 jobs in January 2009, the economy slowly started to improve after the Recovery Act began to inject stimulus into the economy. Private forecasters and the nonpartisan Congressional Budget Office would later conclude that the stimulus helped avoid another depression and end a brutal recession.

Blake Jones, the CEO of Namasté Solar, talks to Vice President Joe Biden and President Barack Obama on the roof of the Denver Museum of Science on February 17, 2009, minutes before the president signed the American Recovery and Reinvestment Act into law. Jones tried cracking a joke, but Obama didn't laugh; he wanted to talk solar policy. "He had twenty minutes, and he was going to make the best use of every one," Jones later recalled. "He was purpose-driven. I was thinking: Is he on like this all the time?"

What Was in the Recovery Act

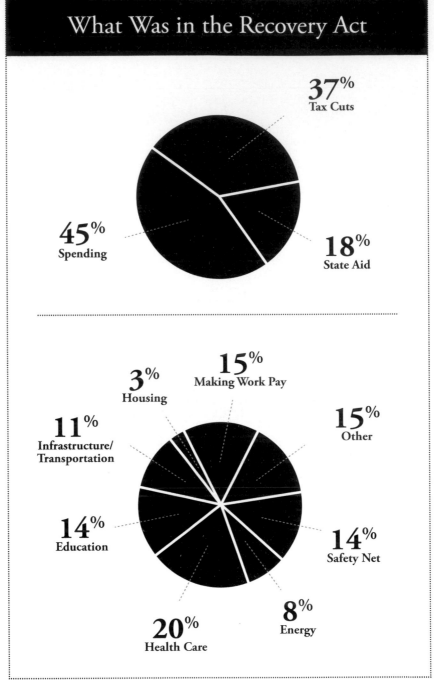

37%
Tax Cuts

45%
Spending

18%
State Aid

3%
Housing

15%
Making Work Pay

11%
Infrastructure/
Transportation

15%
Other

14%
Education

14%
Safety Net

20%
Health Care

8%
Energy

Source: Recovery Act Conference Report, Congressional Budget Office, Joint Committee on Taxation and Agency Data

Most of the Recovery Act was tax cuts, emergency fiscal relief to help states avoid layoffs and massive cuts in services, and aid to unemployed workers and other victims of the Great Recession.

(*At left*) Governors were not required to post signs identifying stimulus projects, and the cluttered Recovery Act logo didn't do much to drive the message, either. But the projects made a real difference. (*Below*) For example, the Recovery Act included $6 billion for cleaning up the radioactive legacy of America's nuclear program. Here a shuttered reactor's exhaust stacks are demolished at the Savannah River Site in South Carolina, the largest stimulus project.

There was often friction between the White House and congressional Democrats, but they agreed on almost all of their policy goals and accomplished a lot together. (*Above*) Obama listens to House Speaker Nancy Pelosi, while Vice President Biden holds the lapel of House Democratic Whip Jim Clyburn. (*Below*) Obama listens to Senate Majority Leader Harry Reid before an event in Nevada.

(*Above*) Even if House Minority Leader John Boehner (*left*) had been interested in working with Obama, he had to guard his right flank against House Republican Whip Eric Cantor. (*Below*) Senate Minority Leader Mitch McConnell wanted to prevent Obama from claiming bipartisan victories; he publicly acknowledged that his top priority was making Obama a one-term president.

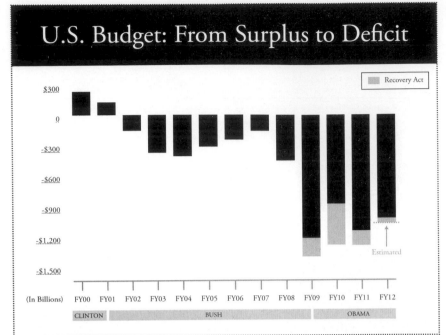

U.S. Budget: From Surplus to Deficit

Source: Congressional Budget Office

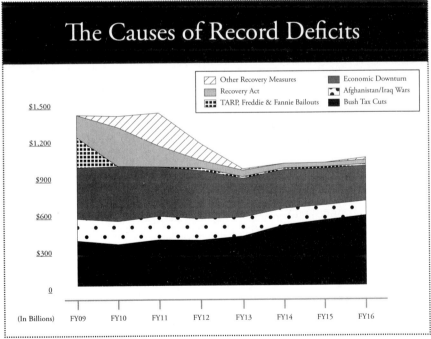

The Causes of Record Deficits

Source: Center on Budget and Policy Priorities

The top chart shows how President Bush converted President Clinton's surpluses into record deficits. The second chart shows that the deficit was mostly created by the Bush tax cuts, the Great Recession, and the wars in Iraq and Afghanistan. The stimulus did add to the deficit for a few years, but its impact on our current fiscal situation is negligible.

President Obama speaks at Solyndra, alongside a robot holding one of the company's innovative solar panels. Solyndra was once the toast of Silicon Valley, raising a billion dollars from elite investors and a half-billion-dollar stimulus loan. It became a Republican attack line after it went bankrupt in September 2011, but the Obama administration always knew that some of the Recovery Act's $90 billion worth of clean-energy investments would fail. Overall, the solar industry has expanded sixfold since 2008, and U.S. renewable power has doubled.

The New Deal dammed dozens of U.S. rivers. Obama's new New Deal included the largest dam removal in U.S. history, restoring salmon runs on the Elwha River in western Washington.

The Recovery Act also jump-started New York City's Second Avenue subway project, which had been on the drawing board for decades.

(*Above*) A General Motors manager delivers the first Chevy Volt battery from its new plant in Brownstown, Michigan. The Recovery Act included $2 billion to create an advanced battery manufacturing industry almost from scratch, financing 30 domestic factories. (*Below*) A Navy Riverine Command Boat tests algae-derived biofuel produced by the stimulus-funded company Solazyme. The Recovery Act dragged the advanced biofuels industry out of the lab, financing the country's first commercial bio-refineries.

Vice President Biden gives President Obama some support.

Rahm thought the real communications error was putting too many eggs in the bipartisanship basket, and some of his colleagues agreed. The president let Republicans control the narrative, because he didn't want to get into a partisan brawl, but when the partisan brawl happened anyway, Republican obstructionism only seemed to prove that he had failed to change Washington. Most of the Clintonites on Obama's staff had been skeptical of post-partisanship all along, and the Recovery Act seemed to confirm their suspicions.

"From the beginning, a lot of the Clinton types were like: Okay, Barack, awesome speeches, now it's grown-up time," says one Obama loyalist. "After that House vote, they got to say, I told you so, Republicans are never gonna play."

Biden says that when Obama entered the White House, he was neither as naive about bipartisanship as liberals claim, nor as disinterested in bipartisanship as Republicans claim. "He was in between," Biden says. He extended his hand to GOP leaders, but was always deeply skeptical that any hand would be extended back.

"If it had been, he would've grabbed it," Biden says. "Did he believe anything would happen? Highly unlikely. Was he hoping maybe something would change? Look, there was a faint hope that when our Republican colleagues realized how bad things were for the country, they would have said: 'Okay, let's go. Grab my hand.'"

In any case, the White House concluded after the stimulus that Republican leaders had no interest in hand grabbing. Obama would keep reaching out publicly, but as Obama told a group of liberal columnists: I'm an eternal optimist, but I'm not a sap. Another eighteen months would pass before his next private conversation with McConnell. After the 2010 midterm elections, his aides would realize they didn't even have a phone number for Boehner. If Obama was going to continue to advance his agenda, it clearly wasn't going to happen by consensus. It was going to require scratching out sixty votes.

"It was a real wake-up call," Ron Klain says. "When Republicans can't support tax cuts and infrastructure they've always supported in the past, that's a pretty strong sign they're not going to support anything with Obama's name on it."

For the White House, the main political lesson of the Recovery Act was the importance of getting to sixty. Obama would have to draw an inside straight on every major piece of legislation, and that had powerful political implications. When push came to shove, the Obama team figured it would always be able to roll House Democrats, but it needed to keep moderate Republican and Democratic senators on his side. In fact, when liberal groups began attacking Democrats in the gang of 18 for obstructing Obama's agenda, Jim Messina, Rahm's deputy, yelled at them to stop.

"I said: You've got a mandate. The president needs to call Ben Nelson into his office and say: Stop messing around!" says Bob Borosage, director of the Campaign for America's Future. "Messina said: Back off. We know how to handle this."

A related stimulus lesson was the importance of congressional relations in general. *Schoolhouse Rock*'s bill-to-law rules still applied, and Rahm and Schiliro did not want to alienate the Democratic leaders who would be needed to move Obama's agenda on health care reform, cap-and-trade, and Wall Street reform. Obama's first major dilemma after the Recovery Act was whether to sign a porky $410 billion omnibus budget that Congress had failed to complete in 2008. It was larded with over eight thousand earmarks, and Axelrod warned that embracing it would further muddy the message of change. The legislative team argued that it would send a chilling message if Obama rewarded Reid and Pelosi for their loyalty on the stimulus by humiliating them with a veto on the omnibus. The president agreed it wasn't worth picking a fight; he'd pledge to reduce earmarks on future bills, but would accept this last pork platter as leftover business from the Bush era.

"Later, the president regretted signing that," says one aide. "It just looked weak. And it didn't feel right."

For Republicans, the main political lesson of the Recovery Act was the upside of resistance to Obama. For the first time in ages, their base was fired up. And independent voters seemed to be responding to the politics of austerity.

"Once we voted no, we started hearing cheers, and we were like,

'Hey, this is great! Life just got better!'" Tom Cole says. "We didn't have a convincing message yet. We were just against Obama. But we stood up, and we didn't get overrun."

The stimulus did not make it inevitable that Republicans would accuse Obama of bowing down to the Saudi king, trying to indoctrinate children by giving a back-to-school speech, demeaning the presidency by filling out a March Madness bracket, or disrespecting Christmas by putting his dog on a holiday card. Obama probably didn't expect Republican congressman Joe Wilson of South Carolina to scream "You lie!" in the middle of a presidential address, or his corpulent colleague James Sensenbrenner of Wisconsin to suggest that Michelle had a "large posterior." But by the end of Obama's first month in office, it was already clear the next forty-seven would be dominated by partisan warfare. A week after lampooning Pelosi, *Saturday Night Live* opened with a skit of Boehner, McConnell, and other Republicans debating whether to try to impeach Obama.

"My gut tells me it's too soon," the fake Boehner said. "Maybe in April."

On the campaign trail, Obama had promised to bridge the partisan divide and reform the ways of Washington. To the cynics who claimed it would be impossible to change the Beltway's political culture, he had said: We don't have a choice. As long as politicians insisted on slagging each other instead of working together, as long as Washington remained obsessed with evanescent nonsense instead of things that matter to ordinary families, America wouldn't even be able to start solving festering problems like its addiction to fossil fuels, its broken health care system, its shameful public schools, and the decline of its middle class. Substantive change, he argued, would be impossible without political change. Transactional politics could not produce transformational results.

It was a powerful argument. But then the economy imploded, and Obama inherited a crisis. He needed to pass something audacious in a hurry, and he simply didn't see any way to change Washington overnight. It seemed impossible. Instead, he pursued what he had said was impossible but now seemed at least conceivable: substantive change without political change.

The Obama campaign had been all about defying conventional wisdom, thinking out of the box, changing the rules of the game. As a candidate, Obama had accepted the nomination in an open-air stadium, taken an overseas trip, and done all sorts of things candidates weren't supposed to do. Two years later, I asked Axelrod why the president didn't try to re-create that defiant spirit in the White House.

"The campaign was conducted in America, not in Washington," he told me. "We were operating in a different arena, and we were able to overcome some of the traditional thinking and some traditional obstacles. But Capitol Hill is a different arena. The ability to change the dynamic up there was a lot more difficult."

It's a fair point. The Republicans were plotting to destroy Obama even before he took office. As the PowerPoint said, "The purpose of the minority is to become the majority." And the Recovery Act proved that transactional politics could produce transformational results, that substantive change without political change was possible. It was just extremely hard. It required unpleasant compromises. It looked messy. But in four weeks, Obama had already made tremendous progress on his agenda for energy, health care, education, and the economy. He hadn't forged a post-partisan consensus or reinvented the legislative process, but he cared more about changing the country than changing Washington.

The Obama fans who expected the mess of the last eight years to vanish the second he stepped into the White House were bound to be disappointed. The Recovery Act was never designed to restore full employment; by the time it passed, the economy had already shed more jobs than it was designed to save or create. "We knew that single act wasn't a horse that could pull the whole sleigh," Biden says. And the mess was far worse than anyone realized at the time. At the time the stimulus passed, the official GDP estimate for the fourth quarter of 2008 was −3.8 percent. That was disastrous, but a couple weeks later, it would be revised to an unthinkable −6.2 percent. And it would eventually be rerevised to −8.9 percent. That's Great Depression territory.

Passing the Recovery Act was a big step toward change, but the stimulus wasn't going to spend itself. Change takes work, and the real work was just beginning.

PART THREE

Change in Action

TWELVE

Ready or Not

Before the final vote, Vice President Biden also took a road trip—literally!—to pitch the Recovery Act on Route 34 outside Carlisle, Pennsylvania. There he toured one of the state's six thousand structurally deficient bridges, an eighty-year-old span that seemed to be groaning for stimulus. A jagged crack like something out of a Road Runner cartoon sliced across the roadway. Biden poked his shoe through a badly rusting steel girder. "This is actually missing rivets," he marveled.

Governor Ed Rendell, an infrastructure evangelist who cochaired the group Building America's Future, then delivered his standard sermon about the power of public works. He explained that bridge repairs and other hard-hat projects were the key to reviving the middle class, supporting construction jobs that can't be outsourced and manufacturing jobs at U.S. steel and concrete firms. And no matter what the killjoy economists said about speed, this was a perfect example of a shovel-ready project. The plans and contracts were all set—just add cash.

"The point you're making is, if the stimulus passes, you'd be able to get jackhammers out here," Biden said for the camera.

This raggedy bridge over Conodoguinet Creek—Rendell dubbed it the Biden Bridge—offered a simple yet powerful argument for the Recovery Act. Pennsylvanians obviously needed work, and here was work that obviously needed to be done. After the president signed the stimulus, Ron Klain called to find out when Biden could return for the groundbreaking, so Americans could see that work getting under way.

Eventually, a Rendell press guy got back to him: We're thinking June.

"JUNE?" Klain was flabbergasted. "This was the number one project on your list!"

Apparently, school buses depended on the Biden Bridge to reach a local neighborhood, so the town didn't want it shut down until summer vacation. Biden had to wait four months for the ribbon cutting. By then the story was less about the thirty jobs the project was creating than the hundreds of thousands of jobs that were still disappearing.

"From the town's perspective, it made perfect sense," Klain says. "From our perspective, it was a disaster. We had told everyone this would happen *fast*."

Obama aides sometimes joke about the three big lies: The check is in the mail, I'll respect you in the morning, and my project is shovel-ready. "Shovel-ready," the president later mused, "was not as shovel-ready as we expected." Unfortunately, the killjoy economists had been right. Infrastructure work was tough to get started, even a routine bridge repair that seemed to have all its jackhammers in a row.

"People had this vision that the day the law was signed, we'd have tens of thousands of guys out there building projects," Klain says. "It doesn't work like that."

The Biden Bridge delay was an early warning that the Recovery Act's strict spending deadlines—the entire $27 billion for highways had to be committed to projects within a year—would require unheard-of bureaucratic speed. And if the stimulus couldn't even start repairs on the 182-foot Biden Bridge right away, it certainly wouldn't have time to build a twenty-first-century version of the Brooklyn Bridge—although it would help repaint and repave the nineteenth-century version of the Brooklyn Bridge. The bulk of its transportation dollars would go toward relatively quick and easy upgrades that wouldn't captivate the public imagination, but would provide real public benefits: resurfacing pitted roads, bridges, and runways; buying new buses and trains; replacing old railroad ties; installing cable barriers to prevent drivers from plowing across highway medians.

The innovative TIGER grants had looser deadlines, so they would promote more transformative projects, like new streetcar lines in Dallas, Tucson, Cincinnati, New Orleans, and Salt Lake City; light-rail expansions in Charlotte and Los Angeles; and new networks of bicycle and pedestrian trails in Philadelphia, Indianapolis, and the Bay Area. They funded green-themed improvements throughout a low-income Kansas City neighborhood; an "electric vehicle corridor" of fast-charging stations along I-5 in Oregon; and New Urbanist projects to revitalize streetscapes in the Everytowns of Peoria and Dubuque. In the New York metropolitan area alone, the Recovery Act has jump-started three long-stalled transit megaprojects—an expansion of Penn Station, a Second Avenue subway, and a new commuter rail route from Long Island to the East Side of Manhattan. It also would have jump-started an equally massive rail tunnel from New Jersey to the West Side of Manhattan if New Jersey governor Chris Christie hadn't killed the project.

But the main emphasis would be repairs. In its first year, the stimulus financed over 22,000 miles of road improvements, and only 230 miles of new roads. This fix-it-first mentality, whatever it lacked in inspiration, pushed money into the economy faster than grandiose new Skyline Drives ever could. It made fiscal and environmental sense, too. Repairs reduce swollen maintenance backlogs and future budget deficits, while new projects increase backlogs and deficits. And the new rural roads that many state highway departments yearned to build would have worsened sprawl and deepened our oil addiction.

Still, the Biden Bridge hiccup was a daunting reminder that the Recovery Act would be the mother of all management challenges. Here was a no-brainer fix-it-first project, totally shovel-ready, and it was already making the administration look silly.

When Biden thought about it, the entire Recovery Act had the potential to make the administration look silly. It would fund over 100,000 projects through 275 separate programs at 28 federal agencies, with endless opportunities for headaches and glitches. Tax dollars could get wasted on saunas, picnic tables, makework jobs for the nephews of county commissioners. Spending deadlines could be missed, or overwhelmed agencies could make stupid mistakes to avoid missing them. There could be political scandals, financial scandals, corruption scandals. Had anyone ever doled out $787 billion without some of it getting stolen or squandered?

Biden realized that someone in the White House would have to ride herd on the stimulus to make sure the money was spent fast and spent well. It would have to be an energetic senior official with the president's ear, someone who could haul in a cabinet secretary for a come-to-Jesus meeting if a problem festered. It would have to be a people person, an arm-twister as well as a cheerleader, someone who could wheedle and coax Democratic and Republican governors and mayors to pump money into the economy in a hurry. At his weekly lunch with Obama on February 20, Biden handed the president a memo outlining how that official could run point for the entire stimulus adventure.

Obama scanned the memo, then flipped it back across the table. Biden was in many ways his polar opposite, an exuberant, unfiltered Irish pol from Scranton, fire to his ice, id to his superego, insider to his outsider. Two decades older than the president, Biden sometimes evoked that blowhard uncle who makes the family cringe at holiday dinners; when they had been rivals during the Democratic primary, he had said Obama wasn't ready for the White House, and was only generating buzz because he was "the first mainstream African American who is articulate and bright and clean and a nice-looking guy." The tensions in their shotgun marriage surfaced publicly the day after the inauguration, when Biden teased Justice Roberts for flubbing the oath, and Obama shot him a stop-it glance that could have frozen lava. But Obama respected Biden's Washington experience and man-of-the-people horse sense, if not his message discipline. And there was only one senior official who fit the memo's description.

"Great," the president said. "Do it."

Biden told Obama before joining the ticket that he wasn't looking to build Cheney-style independent fiefdoms. He just wanted to be a valued adviser, invited to every big meeting, included in every big decision. Obama agreed, and they ended up spending several hours together almost every day. But Biden also said he'd be happy to take on a few discrete tasks with definite "sell-by" dates. Overseeing the U.S. withdrawal from Iraq would be one. Overseeing the Recovery Act would be another.

"Honest to God, I had no intention of doing this," Biden told me, with somewhat less than his usual honesty to God. "But it was all about credibility. People don't think government can deliver."

Joseph Robinette Biden Jr. was determined to prove those people wrong.

"Nobody Messes with Joe"

"The first principle of politics, the foundational principle, I learned in the 1950's in my grandpop's kitchen." Thus begins *Promises to Keep*, Biden's 365-page stream of consciousness masquerading as an autobiography. And then he's off, stopping at the Handy Dandy to get caps for his cap gun, checking out the live monkey at Mr. Thompson's market, reenacting the latest Tarzan movie with Charlie, Larry, and Tommy, and so on for a few thousand words until he gets to grandpop's principle. Except it's two principles, one about equality, one about honesty. And then he's off again, a few thousand more words about his heroes, his passion for the Senate, his tumultuous career, the horror of September 11, until suddenly he remembers grandpop's real principle: "*Get up! The art of living is simply getting up after you've been knocked down.*"

Joe Biden is an American original.

He was a stutterer as a kid, teased as Joe Impedimenta and Buh-Buh-Biden, but he tirelessly practiced his elocution—*Get up!*—and is now a veritable tornado of verbiage. His first wife and baby daughter were killed in a car crash after his first Senate election. He was forced out of the 1988 presidential race over a plagiarism scandal, and nearly died of a brain aneurysm a few months later. But he's always gotten up. He's still an enthusiastic backslapper with a "hey man" for everyone, constantly respinning his favorite yarns, quoting his Scranton relatives, giving his solemn word as a Biden.

Sure, he can be a gasbag; during one of Biden's Senate soliloquies, Obama handed an aide a note that read: "Shoot. Me. Now." Sure, Biden's mouth often outruns his brain. He had just aired his off-message concerns about the stimulus: "If we do everything right, there's still a 30 percent chance we're going to get it wrong." But that was Joe being Joe. Muammar Gaddafi once asked him why the United States still classified Libya as a terrorist nation, and he replied: "Because you're a terrorist!" As an aide says, you never have to wonder what Biden thinks, because he just said it. He's the least mysterious politician in Washington. And while Beltway types often caricature him as a buffoon, he's smart in a nonacademic way, with an acute understanding of human needs. Some of the best-and-brightest Ivy Leaguers filling up the West Wing rolled their eyes at his simplistic comments—okay, okay, we'll explain what this means for an ordinary middle-class family—but he had some insights that they lacked.

By the time Biden moved into his office—which, while indeed slightly smaller than Rahm's, had priceless portraits of former vice presidents John Adams and Thomas Jefferson on the walls—he no longer doubted Obama's readiness. In private, Biden could still mock the president's people skills, chilliness, and inability to curse properly. When talking about policies, he often said the president "gets it," a condescending Bidenism for "agrees with me." But he also talked up his boss in genuinely awestruck tones: a steel backbone, a brain bigger than his skull, a heart in the right place, a guy who gets the facts and makes the call and never looks back. After watching Obama's crisp decision making during the transition, he told Klain: They got the order of this ticket right. Obama warmed up to Biden, too. He was a straight shooter, giving the blunt advice presidents often have trouble finding. "He wanted me to be the bastard at the family picnic, which, politely, I am," Biden says. He had Beltway knowledge that Obama lacked, and he embraced the personal-contact side of politics that Obama found tiresome; his Energizer Bunny salesmanship had come in handy during the stimulus debate. A week after signing it, Obama announced that Sheriff Joe would be his enforcer, holding mayors, governors, and cabinet members accountable for every buck.

"Because nobody messes with Joe," Obama said with a smile.

Over the next two years, Biden would convene twenty-two cabinet meetings on the Recovery Act, more than the president would convene on all topics, and visit fifty-six stimulus projects. He'd host fifty-seven conference calls with governors and mayors, and spend countless hours checking in, buttering up and banging heads to keep the cash flowing. He'd speak about the stimulus with every governor except Sarah Palin, who abruptly resigned to pursue a career in punditry and reality TV before he had a chance. He'd also block 260 Recovery Act projects that didn't pass his smell test, from recreational bike paths to skateboard parks to a $120,000 Army Corps of Engineers plan to print brochures advertising a lake cleanup in Syracuse.

"We said, 'Hey, man, put it on a website,'" Biden says. "Stupid little thing, but it saved that dollar amount."

Another time, Republican Pat Roberts complained on the Senate floor about a Kansas highway that was about to be resurfaced with stimulus money, just in time for heavy trucks working on a nearby stimulus-funded environmental cleanup to rip up the road again. Biden says he immediately picked up the phone and told the Transportation Department to rearrange the schedule: "Hey, man, don't pave that road before the project is finished with the heavy trucks. Flip it!" The next day, Roberts sheepishly returned to the floor. "The White House moved in an expeditious fashion," he admitted. "Quite frankly, I didn't expect they could move that fast."

Biden heard that a lot about the Recovery Act, and he developed a stock response: "Look, I'm in charge of it, man. My rear end is on the line." If the Recovery Act perpetuated business as usual, he often warned, Americans would never trust government again. So he promised state and local officials that any stimulus-related question would be answered within twenty-four hours, stunning his own staff as well as the officials. "If you have any problems getting an answer, just call me," he told them. "People used to call me all the time. I miss it!" He demanded monthly updates on major projects, even though the law only required them quarterly; he told the cabinet that anyone who had a problem with that could take it up with Obama.

Biden often stressed that the push for accountability was coming from his boss. Obama frequently grilled him about the Recovery Act, especially about waste and fraud. At an introductory meeting in Washington for stimulus coordinators from every state, there was a gasp when Obama barged into the room unannounced, as if Santa Claus had arrived during a reading of "The Night Before Christmas."

"All of you are on the front lines of what is probably the most important task we have in this country," he said. He gave a stirring pep talk, but he also warned that his administration wouldn't stand for misspent money. Keynes might not have cared if stimulus cash got into the economy in a messy or crooked way, but in the words of Biden's devoutly Keynesian chief economist, Jared Bernstein: "I'm loath to be critical of the master, but that's not how we rolled." Scandals wouldn't just be bad politics; they could stop the stimulus in its tracks, which would be disastrous economics.

"If someone can prove we wasted a billion dollars, it's gone, man!" Biden told his staff. "Gone!"

Biden and Obama sent a zero-tolerance message from the top. But human nature being what it is, they also wanted a tough cop walking the stimulus beat.

Earl Devaney was ready to retire to Florida. He had spent forty years in law enforcement—as a local officer, Secret Service agent, and finally inspector general for the Interior Department, where he had exposed the sex-and-drugs scandal among Bush's oil regulators and broken open the Jack Abramoff lobbying scandal. When Biden summoned him to chat about running the new Recovery Accountability and Transparency

Board, he practiced saying no to the vice president in the mirror. But once he arrived, Biden immediately ushered him into the Oval Office. "I hadn't practiced saying no to the president," Devaney says with a rueful laugh. "Hey, I'm Secret Service."

A few minutes later, Obama was introducing Devaney to the nation as the new independent stimulus watchdog. Golf in the sunshine would have to wait.

"I hadn't even mentioned anything to my wife," Devaney recalls. "Someone told her: 'Hey, your husband's on TV.' Whew. Mother's Day was expensive that year."

Devaney has the gift of gab, but as Biden says, he is one hard-ass dude, a hulking former college lineman and a junkyard-dog investigator. On his first day on the job, Biden told him: Earl, I know we're at arm's length now, but I'd like to ask a favor. If you see anything going wrong, please tell me so I can announce it.

"That's a novel idea," Devaney said. "But sorry, we can't." And he didn't.

The next day, Devaney had a request for Biden. The White House had put together the initial version of recovery.gov, the official stimulus website, and had just handed it over to Devaney to run independently. But on the home page, the lead video was Obama hailing the importance of transparency and accountability, which didn't send a very independent message.

"Mr. Vice President, the video's got to go," Devaney said. And it did.

Now Devaney had to set up new systems to follow all the money, an unglamorous task he compared to building a ship while it was leaving the port. His so-called RAT board had five months to create a centralized reporting system from scratch, to track what tens of thousands of stimulus contractors were doing with their money. The board also had to scramble to upgrade recovery.gov, so that citizens could look up every grant, loan, and contract online. Meanwhile, in a nondescript office building near the White House, Devaney set up a state-of-the-art command center that felt like a mini–Mission Control, where investigators from the worlds of finance and intelligence as well as law enforcement could use advanced software tools to prevent and detect fraud. When I visited, they were tracking a day care operator who had been flagged electronically after receiving a grant to help crime victims. Database checks suggested she was more likely to create crime victims; she had been disqualified from federal contracting in the past, and her corporate documents revealed links to all kinds of sketchy enterprises.

"This is a completely new way of doing oversight," Devaney told me. "The old way was: Whoops! The money's missing. I wonder who took it. Now it's: Hey, there's a risky situation. Let's stop the fraud before it happens."

According to Devaney and other watchdogs, Recovery Act fraud has been virtually nonexistent. Devaney thinks there were just too many eyeballs on the stimulus money; any minimally intelligent criminal would go after different money. Outside experts had warned that 5 percent of the stimulus could be stolen, but by the time Devaney finally got to retire at the end of 2011, the RAT board had documented only $7.2 million in losses, about 0.001 percent.

"It's been a giant surprise," Devaney says. "We don't get involved in politics, but whether you're a Democrat, Republican, communist, whatever, you've got to appreciate that the serious fraud just hasn't happened."

People don't appreciate that, because fraud that doesn't happen gets about as much media coverage as planes that land safely.

Biden was glad to have a bulldog of a cop patrolling the stimulus. But as he told Ed DeSeve, a Clinton-era management official who had come to his office for a job interview, what he really needed was a crackerjack CEO running it. The fireplace in Biden's office was roaring, and DeSeve—another big-boned guy who used to match up with the legendary linebacker Chuck ("Concrete Charlie") Bednarik in pickup hoops games "about forty years and forty pounds ago"—was sweating through his wool suit. He figured, what the heck, maybe this will be a short interview.

"With all due respect, sir, I don't think you need a CEO," DeSeve said. "You need a coordinator."

The cabinet was stocked with CEOs. America's statehouses had fifty CEOs. Biden didn't need someone to tell them what to do. He needed someone to keep them on the same page, hold them accountable for results, and help them troubleshoot problems. DeSeve was a student of management, and he thought the Recovery Act, like the war on terror or a hurricane response, required a network, not a command-and-control hierarchy. He didn't think the job called for a team manager; he envisioned it more like a league commissioner.

DeSeve got the job. He also got a closet of an office with a view of scaffolding, which sent a penny-pinching message to visiting politicians and corporate titans. He got a team that never exceeded eight people. But he didn't need fancy trappings or a big staff; all he needed was the authority to help the trains run on time. He was given three titles to reflect the high-level support for his mission, as a top aide to Obama, Biden, and Orszag. He attended Rahm's staff meeting every morning, and ran daily conference calls with every agency. The message from the top was simple: This is a big deal. Don't blow it.

The White House's main concern was the spending deadlines. Dollars parked in the Treasury would not stimulate the economy, and busted deadlines would create failed-stimulus political feeding frenzies. So DeSeve's list of his top priorities on his office wall started with "Get The Money Out" and "Get The Money Under Contract." Often, that would be relatively easy. Making Work Pay, food stamps, and most of the other tax cuts and safety net benefits would start going out the door almost automatically. Aid to states was mostly a matter of tweaking formulas and cutting checks; the first Medicaid dollars went out on Day Eight. New funding for existing programs to help local police forces hire new officers or Americorps take on new volunteers didn't worry DeSeve, either. The feds would just pour money into the top.

But getting transformative programs like health IT and Race to the Top up and running would be a brutal challenge. An obscure Commerce Department agency with a $19 million budget was supposed to distribute $4.5 billion in broadband grants. A small safety agency inside the Transportation Department would run the $8 billion high-speed rail initiative. The sclerotic Energy Department would be responsible for a mind-boggling 144 stimulus programs. As the Biden Bridge illustrated, traditional infrastructure projects would be a struggle, too. And when Obama launched the Recovery Act in mid-February, he hardly had any appointees in place to deal with all these problems. Only two of his fifteen cabinet departments had deputy secretaries in place, and three didn't even have confirmed secretaries.

The bureaucratic blocking and tackling that got the money moving was not the stuff of epic poetry. Peter Orszag's sixty-two-page single-spaced implementation memo, which was sent to every agency the day after the bill signing, was not gripping literature. But a week later, HUD secretary Shaun Donovan announced that his notoriously troubled agency had obligated 75 percent of its stimulus funds to local housing agencies. "That was a jaw-dropper," Donovan says. The Recovery Act required the similarly calcified Labor Department to rule within fifteen days on all appeals by laid-off workers denied COBRA health subsidies—and the department didn't even have an appeals process in place. "It seemed like Mission: Impossible," says deputy labor secretary Seth Harris. The department would receive over 25,000 appeals, and would adjudicate 99.8 percent of them within fifteen days.

Harris likes to tell the story of 13(c), a preexisting rule that requires his department to sign off on all transit grants, usually after a few months of haggling between transit officials and their unions over labor issues. But the Recovery Act had use-it-or-lose-it rules, so its $8.4 billion in transit grants needed speedy approvals. "I was waking up in the middle of the night screaming: 13(c)!" Harris says. "The vice president was pounding on the table saying: Get the money out! The grants were going to get delayed, and it was all going to be our fault." But after intense outreach by the department—calls, meetings, "webinars"—most stakeholders agreed to skip their usual 13(c) confrontations. The grants all went out on time. "It's probably not the most exciting story," Harris says. "But this could have been a gigantic barrier to success."

Every agency had to report on every stimulus program every week, so DeSeve could see in real time when programs lagged behind schedule. One chronic problem was the Environmental Protection Agency's water and sewer projects, and after DeSeve's chats with agency officials failed to solve it, Biden called in EPA administrator Lisa Jackson for a come-to-Jesus chat. After she explained the contracting bottlenecks, Biden called some of the laggards around the country and threatened to take their money back. "To tell the truth, I wasn't sure I had the authority to take the money back," Biden recalls with a grin. The deadline for getting those EPA projects under contract was the Recovery Act's one-year anniversary, and DeSeve says the last contract was signed just a few minutes before midnight.

Two months later, at the same cabinet meeting where Secretary Chu explained his swing-for-the-fences theory of clean-energy research, I watched Biden badger the cabinet about another upcoming deadline as if he were a junior high teacher. He warned that if any agency couldn't hit its targets, he wanted a written explanation. "I know I'm harping on this," he said. "But guess what, folks? We're going to be held accountable. And we have No. Margin. For. Error."

Biden then put Secretary LaHood on the spot, asking why transportation spending was behind schedule. Like the kid in the back row who hadn't done the reading, LaHood started stammering about bad winter weather, then quickly realized that wasn't the right answer, especially now that it was springtime. "No excuse. We need to hold everyone's feet to the fire," he said. "We've got to tell these governors to get the contracts out."

The vice president's face lit up. Just give me some names, he said. I'll call from Air Force Two tonight. "It's the new slogan!" he said. "You don't say no to Joe!"

Ultimately, the Obama administration would meet every one of its stimulus funding deadlines, athough a few did go down to the wire.

"As the Duke of Wellington said, it was a near-run thing," DeSeve says. "But we hit every mark."

Needless to say, the deadlines that weren't missed got about as much coverage as water mains that don't break.

Rogers' Billions

The Recovery Act essentially required the Energy Department to transform itself into a venture capital and project finance operation, which felt like requiring Homer Simpson to transform himself into an Olympic decathlete. The lumbering bureaucracy that had struggled to distribute a few billion dollars in annual clean-energy grants—and had failed to distribute a single clean-energy loan in four years—would now have eighteen months to hand out $37 billion in grants, and even more in loans. This was by far the Recovery Act's scariest management challenge. For its three decades in existence, the department's main task had been overseeing nuclear materials. Now it was suddenly the largest clean-tech fund in history.

"We had to change the mentality, or this was going to be a huge bust," Secretary Chu says.

Chu was Obama's only political appointee in place at the department, and he was about as apolitical as political appointees get. During the first week of the Recovery Act, he toured an energy-efficiency project with Biden, and made the mistake of contradicting the vice president in public. "He won a Nobel Prize," Biden snapped. "I got elected seven times." But while Chu was a newcomer to Washington and the political world, he had spent most of his career around Silicon Valley and the business world. And as the department began to evolve into a government version of Sand Hill Road, Chu's senior staff took on a Bay Area influence, including assistant secretary Cathy Zoi, a clean-tech businesswoman who had run Al Gore's climate nonprofit; ARPA-E director Arun Majumdar, Chu's nanoengineering pal from Berkeley; Sanjay Wagle, a green venture capitalist who had helped run CleanTech for Obama; and Steve Spinner, a Silicon Valley entrepreneur and Obama fund-raiser. The emphasis was private sector expertise: The Chevron executive in charge of biofuels took over the department's biofuels program, and an executive with almost four decades of experience in the utility industry took over the department's fossil energy program.

Chu's most important recruit was his stimulus czar, Matt Rogers, the San Francisco–based founder of McKinsey & Co.'s clean-energy consultancy. Rogers wasn't wild about the government-as-venture-capitalist analogy—government wouldn't get to share the profits or meddle with management, and couldn't accept a 90 percent failure rate—but he'd bring private sector rigor and impatience to the Energy Department as it built an investment portfolio. His wife, a judge, would remain in the Bay Area with their three kids, so Rogers took the job on the condition that he would leave Washington on September 30, 2010, the department's deadline for committing its stimulus dollars.

To prepare, he read a report chronicling the department's history of dysfunction, and highlighting specific Recovery Act risks.

"I don't think I slept for three days," Rogers says. "Oh, my God. It was remarkable to see the sheer number of ways things could go badly."

Rogers now had had to figure out how to set up those 144 programs to produce results. For example, Congress had provided $2 billion for competitive grants to create an advanced battery industry, but hadn't provided much guidance beyond that. Before the department could solicit bids, it had to decide what to solicit. Should it just finance new battery factories, or should it also promote U.S. manufacturing of anodes, cathodes, separators, and other components? Rogers concluded the new industry wouldn't be sustainable without a domestic supply chain. What about next-generation technologies? Rogers decided no, only ready-to-build, ready-to-compete factories; to qualify for grants, companies would have to show they had lined up real orders from real customers. The recipients would also have to match their grants with private funds, a test of their competitiveness; the Massachusetts-based battery manufacturer A123 Systems raised its $250 million cost-share through the largest clean-tech IPO of 2009.

This was, after all, a stimulus program, and Rogers wasn't interested in funding the factories of the future if they didn't have credible short-term business plans.

"It was risky enough to try to create a domestic industry out of thin air," Rogers says. "We couldn't just build on spec."

Clearly, creating a new industry constituted "industrial policy," a toxic phrase in U.S. politics. And a government department selecting companies for grants reeked of "picking winners and losers," another red flag. But Chu recruited over 4,500 outside experts to peer-review Energy's grant applications, to make sure decisions were made according to merit. Anyway, as Rogers liked to say, the department wasn't really picking winners and losers. It was picking the game: clean energy. So it wouldn't just support one advanced battery maker; it would support thirty promising firms in the battery space, all with unique technological and entrepreneurial approaches. And it wouldn't assume that advanced batteries and electric vehicles were the only path to green transportation; it would also support a variety of advanced biofuels, and several strategies to promote more fuel-efficient combustion of fossil fuels, like better engines, lightweight materials, and vehicles powered by natural gas. Meanwhile, ARPA-E would finance blue-sky research into cheaper and more powerful batteries, cheaper and more sustainable biofuels, and other paths away from petroleum.

Then the market would sort out the winners and losers.

"We rejected the model where you put all your money on one horse. But we're also rejecting the model where you give everybody money and let a thousand flowers bloom," Rogers says. "Those are both I-hope-we-get-lucky models." Instead, the department focused on technologies that seemed to be on the cusp of a breakthrough, and let the various companies in its portfolio fight amongst themselves.

"This isn't like Japan, Incorporated, picking Nissan," Biden says.

As Obama often says, the free market is the most efficient economic engine ever invented, and even his advisers were skeptical about some federal investments in private enterprise. Summers groused that projects that made sense usually didn't need government help, while projects that needed government help usually didn't make sense. But the credit crunch had changed some of those calculations, making it virtually impossible to finance green projects. And the sweeping arguments Republicans were making against any government interference in the economy sounded like a combination of libertarian purism and political opportunism. As Bernstein argued, "we're already so much more than a little bit pregnant." The U.S. government had provided seed capital for the transcontinental railroad, the Internet, and most of our high-tech industries. It still distorted private economic decisions through a panoply of subsidies and tax breaks for everything from homeownership to cotton farming. One could argue that the best way to promote clean energy would be to tax dirty energy, but Congress wasn't doing that, and global warming wouldn't wait for cloture.

It was true that government investments could introduce market inefficiencies, even when experienced capitalists oversaw the process. But the global financial meltdown was a reminder that the private sector wasn't perfectly efficient, either. And CEOs tend to underinvest in long-term innovation that doesn't move quarterly numbers.

"We know some of these firms will fail. That's capitalism," Bernstein told me. "But we're saying: Clean energy is important to our environmental and economic future. We're going to make sure there's a path for good clean-energy firms to succeed."

These ideological questions wouldn't even matter unless Rogers could solve the logistical challenge of getting a dysfunctional department with enough employees to fill the Rose Bowl to move at stimulus speed. Rogers knew that a fivefold increase in its nonnuclear budget would be a challenge, but what really worried him were deadlines that would require spending about four times faster than usual. So he started "morning tag-ups," daily meetings where the civil servants overseeing every stimulus program had to explain what they planned to achieve today, what they had achieved yesterday, and if they hadn't met their goals, what went wrong. Best practices were shared, problems addressed. Everyone's work was on display; the mantra was Accountability Every Day. "When you shock rats in a maze at random intervals with random intensity, they curl into a ball. It's called 'learned helplessness,' and it's what happens in a bureaucracy," says one colleague. "But if you make the shocks predictable, they learn how to deal. Matt empowered the rats, so they could find the cheese." Of course, bureaucrats are not rodents. Some of them fit the lazy and sullen stereotypes, but many of them were knowledgeable and dedicated public servants who were thrilled to be part of a mission that felt important, and would work extra hours for no extra pay when stimulus deadlines loomed.

Still, when Rogers scoped out his battlefield, he saw land mines everywhere. He had to set up grant competitions for advanced biofuel refineries that only seemed semi-ready to deploy, and clean-coal plants that didn't seem ready at all. ARPA-E only had three employees when it made its first request for proposals, which attracted such an overwhelming response that it crashed the government's online application system—3,700 abstracts for just 37 grants.

And speaking of the Duke of Wellington, energy efficiency looked like a potential Waterloo; in Obamaworld, the more common description was a three-syllable word starting with "cluster." The stimulus was plowing a gulp-inducing $11.3 billion into three programs—low-income home weatherization and grants to state and local governments—that had puttered along with a few hundred million per year. You didn't have to watch Fox News to worry whether hundreds of ragtag ACORN-style community agencies were equipped to handle tenfold weatherization funding increases. Or how tiny state energy offices would handle even larger increases; New Hampshire's funding spiked from under $300,000 to over $25 million. Most of the 2,300 cities and towns in line for the local grants didn't even have energy offices. And the red tape surrounding these programs was like something out of an Ionesco play. Routine green-building retrofits would require approvals from historic preservation boards. Eco-friendly co-generation projects to convert waste heat into electricity would require time-consuming environmental impact analyses. And nobody was sure how the Recovery Act's "Buy American" rules would apply to insulation or programmable thermostats. What if the buttons on the thermostat were made in China?

These programs went way beyond *Brewster's Millions*; Rogers's staff made a portrait of him floating in money captioned: "Rogers' Billions." The Department of Energy would have to shovel over $1 billion out the door every week to deliver on its Recovery Act commitments, and the White House was watching. "We will need to demonstrate the ability to deliver large early wins," Rogers wrote in his action plan.

Chu and Rogers saw three obvious opportunities for early wins that could move money in a hurry: science projects at national labs, nuclear waste cleanups, and those clean-energy loans that the Bush administration had failed to deliver.

Basic science was an easy call—not only because it was Chu's passion, or because he had run a national lab, but because Energy's science office already had thick notebooks full of beaker-ready plans for its $1.6 billion in stimulus grants. It was mostly gee-whiz stuff involving "radio frequency niobium cavities" and "femto-second X-rays" that even Rogers found mystifying, but some of the projects had benefits that didn't require a Ph.D. to comprehend. One $62 million investment is connecting the national labs via the world's fastest Internet network; its download speed is over ten thousand times faster than an iPhone's, a godsend for researchers using supercomputers to study climate models and high-energy physics. And just as the World Wide Web began with researchers who wanted to share data, this network should expand beyond nerd-world as well. In 2009, the commercial market for ultra-high-speed equipment did not exist; now the U.S. manufacturers who landed the stimulus work are building similar networks on Wall Street and in South Korea.

"We wanted to make the market," says Steve Cotter, a national lab official who oversees the network. "This could pioneer the next era of Internet innovation."

The stimulus also included over $6 billion for cleaning up nuclear waste, the equivalent of two normal years of funding. As the media pointed out at the time, Energy's cleanup program had a sordid history of delays and overruns. But its contractors were already in place, and Rogers thought better management could produce better results. Ultimately, the Recovery Act work would come in on time and under budget. It would also make an unprecedented dent in the Cold War's radioactive legacy, shrinking the nation's contaminated footprint by more than two thirds after years where it barely budged. At the Hanford nuclear reservation in Washington State, workers would demolish seventy-five buildings and reduce the footprint by 385 square miles, slashing surveillance and maintenance costs while minimizing the threat to the Columbia River. The department also completed seven smaller cleanups—as in, all done, the land is clean, no need to come back.

"The program hadn't finished a cleanup in *years*," Rogers says. "Finishing just wasn't part of its lexicon. We wanted to prove this stuff doesn't have to last forever."

The third plank of Energy's quick-victory strategy was the clean-energy loans that had languished under Bush. The Obama team was eager to send a message that the days of inaction were over. "I asked the loan office: What's the soonest we could get a loan guarantee out the door?" Chu told me before the program became controversial. "They said: A year, maybe a year and a half. I said no, that won't work. How about we shoot for a couple weeks?" Of the 143 companies that had sought loan guarantees in the last four years, there was only one whose application was almost ready for prime time. So Chu and Rogers instructed the loan office to focus on Solyndra.

Solyndra has become Republican shorthand for ineptitude, cronyism, and the failure of green industrial policy. But in early 2009, it was the toast of Silicon Valley, a hot start-up with a potentially game-changing product it was already starting to sell. It had raised $1 billion from elite investors like the Walton family of Walmart fame, Oklahoma oil magnate George Kaiser, and British mogul Richard Branson, whose Virgin Green Fund selected Solyndra from a pool of 117 solar firms. It was not some hackish Democratic operation. Kaiser was an Obama fund-raiser, but the Waltons were Republican donors. The Bush administration had embraced Solyndra, and had tried to speed up its $585 million loan application for a state-of-the-art solar panel manufacturing facility in Fremont, California. The civil servants on the department's credit committee objected to the rush job, and refused to approve the loan before Bush left office, but suggested they would sign off once a few concerns were addressed. "The project appears to have merit," they wrote. Bush's political appointees had been so encouraging to Solyndra founder and CEO Chris Gronet that they apologized when the loan was delayed.

"I find the response completely unacceptable," Gronet emailed a department official in January. "An apology is not enough."

Solyndra's slogan, "The New Shape of Solar," was more than marketing hyperbole; its technology was truly revolutionary. Most solar panels look like tinted windows. Solyndra's looked like horizontal ladders for lizards. Most panels harvest sunlight with silicon wafers. Solyndra's relied on a metal mixture called CIGS etched onto elongated glass cylinders. Solyndra's panels were more expensive than traditional panels, but they were easy to install, which drove down their overall cost; they clicked together like Legos, so they didn't require elaborate mounting devices, or even tools. The company was burning through cash, and its financials evoked the old joke about losing money on every sale but making it up in volume. But its executives believed a more efficient factory and new economies of scale would slice their production costs, at a time when sky-high silicon prices were brutalizing their competitors.

The Obama team knew solar manufacturing was a risky business, but the point of the loan program was to help firms like Solyndra cross the so-called Valley of Death for innovative technologies with major start-up and scale-up costs. Some loans would go bust, but Congress had reserved enough money to cover plenty of Solyndra-sized failures. And Solyndra felt like a classic American story of innovation, founded by a Silicon Valley scientist from the semiconductor industry, improving technology originally developed by a national lab, aiming to reinvigorate a U.S.-born manufacturing industry that had fled overseas. Its loan would create 6,000 construction jobs, more than the Hoover Dam, and 1,800 permanent jobs. It would rally an additional $200 million in private capital off the sidelines, and finance a high-tech factory that could produce enough solar panels to replace a medium-sized coal plant every year.

The Recovery Act made the loan program less onerous; if you think of the loans as mortgages, it paid for the mortgage insurance. But the

Obama administration made the terms of the Solyndra loan more oner-ous, requiring the company to raise more capital—in the mortgage analogy, a larger down payment. OMB, traditionally skeptical of gov-ernment loans, raised some concern about the state of the solar market, but Rogers figured the extra capital requirements would be a good test for Solyndra. It would have to persuade private investors that the new factory made sense before it could get the government loan. In March, the credit committee decided its concerns had been addressed, and ap-proved a conditional loan commitment. It felt like an early win.

Republicans later subpoenaed nearly 200,000 pages of administra-tion documents about Solyndra, and they did reveal some internal debate over the loan. An Energy Department loan officer was irritated when Chu prematurely told reporters the deal was almost done: "This nonsense has got to stop." During a technical dispute over cash flow models, an OMB analyst presciently suggested that Solyndra could run out of money in 2011. And just a week before Biden was scheduled to announce the final loan, an OMB official requested more time to analyze whether a recent slump in silicon prices could affect Solyndra's market position. In retrospect, that would have been a good idea.

But these debates were mostly about how to "score" the loan's risk of default to determine how much money to set aside in reserves, not whether to make the loan in the first place. OMB did nudge the score upward to reflect a 20 percent chance of failure—risky, but nowhere near as risky as the 50 percent rating for a $5.9 billion loan to help Ford build factories for fuel-efficient cars, a loan that's looking fine.

In any case, there was no evidence of any improper political influ-ence in any of the emails, inside or outside the administration, and officials testified under oath that there wasn't any. There clearly was logistical pressure in the last two weeks, when the White House wanted to make sure the loan was finalized in time for Biden's announcement. Steve Spinner, the Chu adviser who had bundled money in Silicon Val-ley for Obama, said in an email that the White House was "breathing down my neck." This later became grist for the scandal mill, because Spinner's wife was a partner in Solyndra's law firm, and he had recused himself from decisions about the firm's loan. But the decision to grant Solyndra a loan had been made months earlier, before Spinner joined the department.

It did turn out to be a bad decision. And it was not an entirely unforseeable bad decision. "When I heard they got the first loan, I thought: 'Oh, no! Noooooooo!'" a department official told me in 2010, a year before Solyndra went bust. But busted loans are a part of project finance. In any case, Rogers says he never felt an iota of White House pressure to approve Solyndra's application.

"It wasn't a hard call," Rogers says. "We were trying to drive change, right?"

The day the February jobs report came out, Obama traveled to Columbus, Ohio, to show what change looked like. It was graduation day at the cash-strapped city's police academy, and the president shared the stage with twenty-five happy recruits wearing white shirts and caps with black ties and pants. A few weeks earlier, they had all received layoff notices, but thanks to a $1.25 million stimulus grant, they were being sworn in to protect and serve. It wasn't clear if their jobs had been saved or created, but it was clear they wouldn't have had their jobs without the Recovery Act.

In his speech, Obama invited stimulus skeptics to visit Ohio and talk to teachers who were still educating kids, nurses who were still caring for the sick, firefighters who were still keeping their towns safe.

"I ask them to meet the 25 men and women who will soon be protecting the streets of Columbus because we passed this plan," he said. "I look into their eyes and I see their badges, and I know we did the right thing."

It was a nice day for the cadets, but their reprieve seemed insignificant compared to the news that 650,000 more jobs had vanished, spiking the unemployment rate to 8.1 percent. Two weeks into the stimulus, the White House forecast that joblessness would peak at 8 percent was already wrong. And while it made no sense to blame Obama for the 1.5 million jobs already lost "on his watch," his aides knew they'd end up on his political ledger. If Obama had been inaugurated in March, like FDR, Americans might have gotten a better sense that the economy he inherited was not just troubled but mangled.

"For the country's sake, thank God he didn't have to wait," Obama strategist Anita Dunn says. "But politically, it would've been nice to have the January and February numbers accrued to the last guy."

During the Great Depression, America had its holy-shit moment well before FDR took office; during the Great Recession, it happened with Obama already in the chair. It was hard to sell a message of a better tomorrow when today was so much worse than yesterday. The president's cross-country trip to highlight twenty-five Americans who hadn't lost their jobs seemed pitiful when 650,000 others had. And it didn't fit the prevailing bad-news narrative. Axelrod liked to quote Walter Cronkite's line about the media: "We don't report the cats that don't run away." After her home state of California approved a massive anti-stimulus of spending cuts and tax increases, Romer tried to explain that without the Recovery Act, the cuts would have been much bigger, and the state might have defaulted. "It certainly doesn't feel like we've accomplished anything, but we have," she said. That was true, but as Barney Frank liked to say, no one ever got reelected with a bumper sticker that said: "It would've been worse without me." The same rule applies to: "It certainly doesn't feel like we've accomplished anything, but we have."

This was the counterfactual problem that would haunt the Obama presidency, the impossible task of persuading people to be glad their broken arm wasn't a crushed skull. People rarely ask: Compared to what? This problem came with what Rahm called "the gift bag," the overseas quagmires, crushing deficits, and economic freefall that Bush bequeathed to his successor. Like the stimulus itself, Obama's post-stimulus to-do list was heavy on catastrophe mitigation: a long-term budget plan to rein in unsustainable deficits someday; a housing plan to contain the foreclosure epidemic somewhat; "stress tests" to try to stabilize the reeling financial sector; a radical restructuring of the auto industry to try to limit job losses to a few hundred thousand rather than a couple million. It was hard to get credit for disaster prevention, and it didn't sound much like hope and change, but it beat disaster.

At one point, Axelrod mused to Obama that he wondered what it would be like to govern in good times. The president just laughed.

"Are you kidding?" he said. "In good times, we never would've gotten the job."

THIRTEEN

Tea Leaves

The opposition response to a presidential speech is always a tough gig—no pomp and circumstance, no cheering crowd, hostage-video atmospherics—but Louisiana governor Bobby Jindal's response to President Obama's first address to Congress was particularly lame. Jindal was a rising conservative star, a Rhodes Scholar who was America's youngest governor, but he sounded like he was reading a bedtime story to a nation of toddlers. The blogosphere instantly dubbed him Kenneth the Page, for the wide-eyed hillbilly dork on the sitcom *30 Rock*.

As Jindal became a punch line, so did his nitpicking about the Recovery Act, which seemed tone-deaf after the new president had urged Republicans and Democrats to work in harmony to fix the economy. Jindal seemed especially amazed that the stimulus included "$140 million for something called 'volcano monitoring,'" as if monitoring volcanos was some kind of exotic fetish. Jindal overstated its funding by 1,000 percent, but he clearly thought the phrase was comedy gold.

"Instead of monitoring volcanoes," he chirped, "Congress should be monitoring the eruption of spending in Washington!"

If it sounded silly for the governor of post-Katrina Louisiana to suggest that preventing disasters was self-evidently wasteful, it sounded even sillier a month later when Mount Redoubt erupted in Alaska, spewing plumes of ash ten miles above Anchorage. Sure enough, volcano monitoring had helped alert people and planes to stay out of harm's way—and stimulus-funded GPS systems that will measure ground tremors at Mount Redoubt and other volcanoes should make forecasts even better in the future.

The Kenneth the Page debacle just highlighted the Republican Party's difficulties navigating the line between skepticism about government and hostility to basic services. Similarly, a swine flu outbreak served as a reminder that Senator Collins had stripped pandemic flu money out of the stimulus, and a terrorist's failed attempt to blow up a flight to Detroit evoked memories of Republicans ridiculing a Recovery Act provision to upgrade explosives detection at airport checkpoints. Who was supposed to finance volcano monitoring and other disaster prevention efforts if not government? And if those weren't government responsibilities, were there any government responsibilities?

"We can't be the antigovernment party," Senator Snowe told me that spring. "That's not what people want."

"A Very Narrow Party of Angry People"

Mount Redoubt did feel like a hint from the universe that the Republican Party was blowing itself up.

Minority parties often look inept in the penalty box, but the GOP was starting to look like a new Donner party. In the words of one critic, it had become "a very narrow party of angry people," "gasping for air," consumed by "gratuitous partisanship"—and that critic was Utah's Republican governor, Jon Huntsman. Party chairman Michael Steele confessed there's "absolutely no reason, none, to trust our word or our actions." McCain's campaign manager said the party was extinct on the West Coast, nearly extinct in the Northeast, and endangered in the Mountain West and Southwest. It remained strong in the South, but while Texas governor Rick Perry's speculation about secession resonated with the party's base of older white conservatives, it was not a national outreach strategy.

"We're excluding the young, minorities, environmentalists, pro-choice—the list goes on," Snowe said. "Ideological purity is not the ticket to the promised land."

But Republican politicians couldn't afford to ignore the Republican base, which was growing in influence as the party was shrinking in size. So they were catering even more to the base's biases, trashing the New Deal, denying climate science, doubling down on supply-side economics. Washington Republicans also overcame their initial reluctance to attack a president with approval ratings in the mid-60s, denouncing him as a big-spending radical, a smooth-talking con artist, an affirmative action mediocrity who'd be lost without a TelePrompTer. Boehner accused him of launching "a new American socialist experiment." To the base, Obama was a threat to American values.

That base now had a name: the Tea Party. Two days after Obama signed the stimulus, a CNBC commentator named Rick Santelli unleashed an antigovernment rant on the floor of the Chicago Mercantile Exchange, attacking Obama's plan to help homeowners as Cuban-style statism, calling for a Chicago Tea Party. The historical reference seemed off; the original Boston Tea Party was a protest against an unelected leader who raised taxes, while Obama was an elected leader who had just cut taxes. But Santelli's diatribe went viral. At a time of economic pain and anxiety, it tapped into widespread resentment of Obama and big government, deep-seated suspicions that the deserving were being looted to reward society's moochers.

"The real nerve struck seems to be the pent-up emotions felt by millions of Americans regarding spending TRILLIONS of dollars to fix the housing market, the banks, and the economy," Santelli wrote later. "SPECIFICALLY WHO WILL PAY . . . WHO WILL BENEFIT . . . and above all the government's role in all of this."

Washington-based conservative groups sprang into action, organizing the first Tea Party rallies in forty cities a week later. A movement was born. And it got a boost with the news that bailed-out AIG executives would get to keep $165 million in bonuses after producing the worst results in capitalist history—in part because of Senator Dodd's late stimulus addition preventing the feds from rescinding perks retroactively. The rest of the Recovery Act was directed at Main Street, and even Dodd's provision was mostly about limiting pay at TARP-funded firms. But the bonus furor helped critics caricature the stimulus as another Wall Street bailout. For casual observers of politics, the $700 billion giveaway to banks and $787 billion package of tax cuts and investments for ordinary Americans all started to blur together.

The Tea Parties made for great TV—the mad-as-hell suburbanites in colonial hats; the fiery rhetoric about Marxism and Obama's birth certificate; the wacky signs depicting the president with the Joker's makeup or a Hitler mustache. But embracing the spectacle did not seem like great politics for Republican politicians, who would risk looking like extremists and having to play defense every time an overcaffeinated protester said something racist or dumb. Anyway, the organizing principle behind the Tea Party was resistance to spending and debt, and Hoover-style austerity during a vicious recession seemed like self-immolating politics. The Recovery Act's debt-expanding components—middle-class tax cuts, roads, research, schools—were extremely popular. Taking the other side didn't sound like a path to regaining swing voters.

Yet Boehner called for a national spending freeze, and Republican governors Jindal, Perry, Barbour, Palin, and Mark Sanford of South Carolina vowed to turn down stimulus dollars headed for their states. Sanford, a former congressman who had been one of the most committed deficit hawks in the Gingrich revolution, bragged to me about the unpopularity of his austerity policies. "Nobody likes Dr. Doom," he chortled. Like a modern-day Andrew Mellon, he argued that the nation needed to purge the rottenness from its system, even if that meant enduring even deeper pain. For too long, he said, the GOP had been a party of pastry chefs, urging Americans to eat all the dessert they wanted.

"We need to become a party of country doctors, telling people that this medicine won't taste good at all, but you need it," Sanford said.

Not all Republicans adopted the politics of castor oil. Governor Schwarzenegger offered to take any money his colleagues didn't want. Governor Huntsman said the stimulus should've been even larger. And scores of Republicans who had opposed and denounced the stimulus took credit for stimulus funds in press releases and public events, or wrote letters seeking stimulus funds for colleges, broadband providers, military bases, and clean-energy projects in their states. "All that matters is the politics," Schwarzenegger told me. "They attack and attack, isn't this terrible, and then when it's time for the photo op, they say: Fantastic!"

The staunch conservative Mike Pence asked LaHood to approve a TIGER grant for a "Cultural Trail" of bike and pedestrian pathways in Muncie, Indiana, while Republican budget hero Paul Ryan urged Labor Secretary Hilda Solis to fund a green jobs training program in Wisconsin. Fire-breathing Tea Party Republicans like Michele Bachmann of Minnesota and Joe "You Lie!" Wilson of South Carolina made multiple requests to multiple agencies. Senate minority leader Mitch McConnell wrote at least five letters pushing transportation projects, House minority whip Eric Cantor lobbied for a high-speed rail line to his hometown of Richmond, and Congressman Pete Sessions made at least nine pitches for Recovery Act funds that would "create jobs [and] stimulate the economy." Even Boehner said the bill would fund "shovel-ready projects that will create much-needed jobs."

"Oh, the hypocrisy is unbelievable," Congressman Rangel told me. "They cuss Obama, cuss the stimulus, and then they come with their scissors to the ribbon cuttings to brag about bringing jobs to the community. I'm sorry, but I wouldn't be able to do it if I was raising hell on the floor." Then he stopped and grinned. "Maybe I'd send a staffer."

The House Democratic campaign committee's "Hypocrisy Hall of Fame," featuring 128 "cash-and-trash" Republicans who chased stimulus money after opposing the stimulus, was a bit unfair. Politicians weren't necessarily hypocritical to say nasty things about the Recovery Act and then seek their fair share of its bounty for their constituents once it passed, although it did take chutzpah for Governor Jindal to pass along stimulus money to a Louisiana community by presenting an oversized check with his own name at the top. In any case, Republican leaders believed that the stimulus would work out for them in the end, that it would force Obama to take ownership of the soaring deficit and collapsing economy he had inherited from Bush.

"We lost that legislative battle, but we won the argument," Pence told a conservative conference. "Welcome to the beginning of the comeback."

That hypothesis would be tested on March 31 in upstate New York, in a special election for the state's 20th Congressional District.

Six weeks before the vote, Republican Jim Tedisco, a veteran Albany power broker who was the state assembly's minority leader, held a 21-point lead over Democrat Scott Murphy, a young entrepreneur who had never run for office. The district had a Republican tilt, and Tedisco, who had represented the area since Murphy was in junior high, had a huge advantage in cash and name recognition. But once the Recovery Act passed, the race instantly became a referendum on the stimulus.

The Democratic businessman quickly endorsed the bill, calling it "far from perfect" but essential for reviving demand. By contrast, the Republican career politician did not endorse the bill. Or oppose the bill. Instead, Tedisco smothered reporters in word salad, refusing to engage in hypotheticals, criticizing the bill's length, praising its infrastructure, attacking its pork. As one headline observed: "Asked About Stimulus, Tedisco Talks a Lot."

Tedisco was torn. Some of his advisers warned that opposing tax cuts for his constituents and road repairs for his district would be electoral suicide. But Washington Republicans suggested they would stop bankrolling his campaign if he sided with Obama. "They were saying: 'You don't want to go against us,'" recalls Tedisco aide Dan Bazile. "Was it an overt threat? No, more like: Do your part, and we'll keep helping you raise money." Pete Sessions, the House Republican campaign chair, acknowledges pressuring Tedisco to toe the party line.

"I told him he had to be against the bill," Sessions says. "The base hated it."

Republicans ran ads tying Murphy to the "pork-laden federal stimulus," while Murphy hammered Tedisco for refusing to stand up for jobs.

When Tedisco finally announced he would've voted no, unions immediately aired ads of an ostrich with its head in the sand: "Doesn't Jim Tedisco notice that our economy is in trouble?"

In Washington, there was bipartisan agreement that the results would be a bellwether. "Tedisco's victory will be a repudiation of the spending spree," GOP chairman Steele proclaimed. But Murphy eked out a 726-vote upset. "He proved you could run on the Recovery Act and win," says Chris Van Hollen, the House Democratic campaign chair.

Really, it was hard to tell whether voters had punished Tedisco for opposing the stimulus or dithering about the stimulus. His waffling helped reframe the race as a choice between an energetic entrepreneur and a finger-in-the-wind politician. Republican operatives thought Tedisco would have won easily if he had started bashing the bill sooner. And he did get some traction late in the race by attacking Murphy over AIG, making the Recovery Act sound like a $787 billion excuse to protect fat Wall Street bonuses.

But Tedisco believes that if he'd opposed the bill earlier, his margin of defeat would've been larger. The more Murphy talked about the Recovery Act, the more voters seemed to like him.

"It was heads you win, tails I lose," Tedisco says. "The bill was $1 trillion, it had a multitude of infrastructure projects, and every elected official in every village and town was saying: 'I have a bridge I want built.'"

In the Senate cloakroom, after Arlen Specter secured his $10 billion windfall for NIH's medical research and endorsed the stimulus, one of his Republican colleagues said: Arlen, I'm proud of you.

"Then why don't you vote with me?" the grouchy Pennsylvanian asked.

That will get me a primary, the senator replied.

"You know I'm getting a primary," Specter snapped.

He sure was. The free-market Club for Growth was the scourge of Republican moderates, bankrolling right-wing primary challenges around the country to enforce supply-side orthodoxy in Washington. And club president Pat Toomey, a former banker and Pennsylvania congressman, had himself almost unseated Specter in 2004, despite Specter's support from Bush and the party establishment. Now the club was denouncing Specter's stimulus vote as "the ultimate act of treason," and Toomey wanted a rematch. In the past, Republicans had overlooked Specter's apostasies, like his support for abortion rights and his refusal to convict Clinton. (In typical Lone Ranger fashion, he also refused to acquit, insisting on voting "Not Proven.") But now after twenty-nine years as a Republican senator, he had a 29 percent approval rating among Republican voters. They didn't care what he had done for NIH—only what he had done for BHO.

Biden and Specter had been Amtrak buddies for nearly three decades; before getting off in Wilmington, Biden had often teased Specter about switching parties. He and Rendell applied more friendly pressure at a public meeting in Philadelphia shortly after the stimulus vote, condemning the abuse Specter was taking from Republicans, suggesting another party's voters might be more appreciative of his stand for jobs and medical research. "You could make life easier for yourself by taking that registration card of yours and making that little change from R to D," Rendell suggested.

When Specter started to protest, Biden interrupted: "Don't make your decision now!"

He made his decision in late April. "I now find my political philosophy more in line with Democrats than Republicans," he announced. "It has become clear to me that the stimulus vote caused a schism which makes our differences irreconcilable."

Republican operatives declared good riddance, scoffing that Specter was only defecting to try to save his political skin. They were right. He knew he'd have no chance in a Tea Party–dominated primary. "I won by the skin of my teeth in 2004, and 200,000 moderate Republicans had left the party," he told me. But his switch was still a huge setback for the GOP. A Republican primary would have put constant pressure on Specter to prove his anti-Obama credentials; instead, facing a Democratic primary, Specter became a reliable vote for Obama. And Specter represented the fifty-ninth Democratic vote in the Senate; once Al Franken was finally seated in July, Obama would have a filibuster-proof majority. Anyway, regardless of the balance of power, Specter's departure sent a powerful message that the modern Republican Party was no place for middle-of-the-road politicians.

"There aren't any Republican moderates left in the Senate," Specter says. "Even Snowe and Collins can't vote as moderates. They wouldn't get reelected."

Quite a few Republicans were convinced the GOP would be better off without wobblers like Specter tarnishing its brand. DeMint said he'd rather have thirty Republican senators who believed in limited government than sixty who believed in nothing. "I don't want us to have power until we have principles," he told me at a Tea Party rally at the South Carolina capitol. Governor Sanford argued that Chick-fil-A would never let its franchisees cook their chicken however they wanted; why should the Republican Party let its politicians promote big government?

"We're essentially franchisees, and right now nobody has any clue what we're really about," he said. "You can't wear the jersey and play for the other team!"

But it's hard to put together a center-right coalition when you've said good riddance to the center. The popular Governor Huntsman, feeling out of step in a narrow party of angry people, accepted Obama's offer to be ambassador to China. The genial Governor Crist was just as popular, but when he ran for Senate, a young conservative named Marco Rubio refused to step aside, bashing Crist for supporting the stimulus. "That was the moment I realized what was at stake," Rubio told me. Rubio started the race 40 points behind, but the hard-right activists who dominate Republican primaries adored him. I watched him charm a sun-weathered group of party faithful on the Treasure Coast; they loathed Obama, loathed Crist for aiding, abetting, and even hugging Obama, and devoured every morsel of Rubio's red meat. "I'm not here to tell you Barack Obama is Fidel Castro," he said. "But the imperialism of this government is very real!" Crist would soon quit the GOP to run as an independent. Like Specter, he didn't want to make his case before a Tea Party jury.

Even some across-the-board conservatives in the Republican establishment started to worry that enforced purity could relegate them to permanent minority status. It might feel righteous to purge the Specters of the party, but it would also help Obama pass his agenda without any Republican votes. Ronald Reagan had preached a big tent, and his former political director, Governor Barbour, wished DeMint and Sanford understood that not all of America was as conservative as South Carolina.

"Chick-fil-A can get fabulously wealthy with a 20 percent market share," Barbour said. "In our business, you need 50 percent plus one."

It was easy to rail against government spending in theory. But when it came to actual government spending on math teachers and traffic lights, even South Carolina turned out to be less hostile than advertised.

Republican governors talked a big game about turning down Obama's freedom-crushing stimulus money. And a few did reject a few million dollars, mostly the strings-attached cash for expanded unemployment insurance that Democrats slipped into the Recovery Act while Republicans were railing about condoms. In the end, though, almost all of the governors accepted almost all the state aid. Rick Perry not only took the cash, he tried to use some of it to renovate his governor's mansion. (Granted, it had been firebombed.) Sarah Palin did turn down the state energy grants that required governors to pledge to promote green building codes and utility regulations, but after she quit, her Republican successor quickly signed the pledge. When Senator Jon Kyl of Arizona slammed the stimulus on a talk show, Rahm ordered several cabinet secretaries to write letters to his state's Republican governor, Jan Brewer, asking which stimulus funds she didn't want. She wanted all of them.

Sanford was the only governor who really tried to put less money where his mouth was, turning down $700 million in state aid designed to prevent layoffs of teachers and other public employees. He argued that the one-time windfall—and its "maintenance of effort" rules prohibiting education cuts—would prevent South Carolina from making the tough decisions necessary to live within its means. The first rule when you're in a hole, he said, is stop digging.

When it came to fiscal conservatism, Sanford was the real deal, "Tea Party before Tea Party was cool." A former financial analyst and real estate investor, he had distributed bumper stickers during his 1994 run for Congress that said DEFICIT with a *Ghostbusters*-style slash through it, and his standard-issue stump speech had been an apocalyptic chronicle of great civilizations undone by debt. Unlike many of his fellow Republican revolutionaries in the Gingrich army, he had kept faith with the conservative principles in the "Contract With America," voting against popular spending programs, keeping his pledge to serve only three terms. He had dedicated his political career to the proposition that there was no free lunch. He believed in a right-wing Rahm's Rule; this crisis was an opportunity to make the painful cuts that politicians habitually avoid "when times are good and people are fat, dumb and happy."

Sanford only wanted to turn down 8 percent of his state's stimulus cash, less than 2 percent of his state's budget. But the backlash was ferocious. Protesters built a tent city called "Sanfordville" in a Columbia park. Business-funded scare ads predicted horrific consequences if Sanford got his way. At a hearing of the state Senate finance committee, I watched legislators line up to denounce Sanford as a heartless Scrooge intent on "budgetary Armageddon," warning that without the extra cash South Carolina would have to fire teachers and firefighters, shutter programs for autistic and disabled kids, jack up tuition at state colleges, fling open the doors to state prisons, and dismantle the safety net when it was needed most.

And those weren't Democratic legislators.

"The governor has one of the most radical philosophies I've ever seen," said the seventy-eight-year-old Republican committee chairman, Hugh Leatherman. "I'm a conservative, but I've got compassion for the poor, the blind, the mentally ill. Sanford wants chaos. Absolute chaos! He's destroying this state, and the Republican Party, too."

The consensus in the Republican-dominated legislature was that when the feds offer money, you take it. "Most of us are Ronald Reagan Republicans, Strom Thurmond Republicans," said Senate majority leader Harvey Peeler. "Republicans control everything around here. It would be nice if we could accomplish something."

When I sat down with Sanford, the venom didn't seem to bother him much. Wearing jeans and a denim shirt, he lounged on his office couch like he was home watching a game. "I sleep like a baby," he said. South Carolina had the nation's third-highest jobless rate, and he knew the extra money from Obama could avert short-term suffering. But he wasn't interested in postponing the day of reckoning. If generational theft through deficit spending was the only way to avoid a depression, he said, then we might as well have our depression now. If America wanted to avoid the fate of overleveraged empires like Rome and Spain, it needed to stop relying on fiscal child abuse.

"I get it: I'm supposed to be *proactive*," Sanford said. "But we're at an incredible tipping point. The principles that made this country great are being eviscerated." America had too much credit card debt, too much housing debt, too much government debt; the deleveraging had to start now. "I know, more spending is supposed to lead to recovery, and then we'll be able to pay back all our debts," Sanford said. "Everything's going to be beautiful. That's a hope, not a plan."

Sanford wasn't surprised he was taking flak from fellow Republicans. He thought fiscal conservatism should be to the GOP brand what tasty chicken is to Chick-fil-A, but he had watched his party binge on spending and debt for years. He regularly clashed with the fraudulent Republican franchisees in his legislature, and once brought live piglets to the Capitol to protest their pork. They reminded him of his former Washington colleagues whose anti-spending fervor cooled once they got a chance to do some spending themselves. He was pleased to see Republican congressional leaders rediscovering the old-time religion of No, but it seemed mighty convenient that their passion for limited government only reignited once they lost control of the federal purse strings.

"They were on the opposite side just a few months ago when they had the keys to power," Sanford said.

Ultimately, Sanford didn't even have the power to turn down the

free money. Jim Clyburn, the Democratic whip who represented Columbia, had anticipated a situation like this during Obama's transition,
when Sanford and his fellow Southern Republicans began trashing the
stimulus preemptively. Clyburn saw racial politics at work. "Let's just
say they were states' rights governors," he told me. So he inserted language into the Recovery Act allowing state legislatures to accept stimulus money that governors refused, and the Republican legislature in
South Carolina did just that.

So economically, Sanford's stand had little impact. And politically, it
seemed to highlight the limited appeal of antigovernment absolutism.
Even South Carolina Republicans sounded like ACORN when their
own handouts were at risk. I remember thinking that Sanford could be
Obama's opponent in 2012—a handsome, principled, non-rage-aholic
spokesman for the Tea Party philosophy—but that the philosophy
would never attract 50 percent plus one.

I didn't expect that two months after we met, Sanford's political
career would implode. After telling his staff he was going hiking on the
Appalachian Trail, he vanished for a few days, prompting a Where's
Waldo?-style frenzy in South Carolina. After his return, he admitted
at a weepy press conference that he had gone to visit his mistress in
Buenos Aires. His local paper published his love emails about "magnificent gentle kisses" and worse.

When we spoke again two years later, Sanford said the ruckus over
the stimulus bothered him more than he let on, and hinted it may have
influenced his erratic behavior. "There's a remarkable loneliness when
you push against the current," he said. "It was the loneliest I've been in my
life. It doesn't justify my actions. But it was an unbelievably lonely time."

Muddling the Message

Obama's first hundred days were a whirlwind of activity.

"I think even our critics would agree that at the very least, we've
been busy," he said April 14 at Georgetown University.

The Recovery Act was the centerpiece of his crusade for change, but he also loosened Bush's restrictions on stem cell research; began winding down Iraq and ramping up Afghanistan; kept his promises to boost fuel efficiency rules for vehicles and energy efficiency standards for appliances; banned torture; imposed strict White House ethics rules; passed S-CHIP and Lilly Ledbetter; fired the General Motors CEO, setting the stage for his overhaul of the auto industry; approved the plan to help homeowners that got Santelli so irate; and conducted "stress tests" that would stabilize the financial industry without nationalizing banks. And in case anyone thought he was ready to take up smallball, he passed a budget blueprint signaling his desire to enact universal health care and cap-and-trade in his first year.

So yes, he'd been busy. This was serious stuff, a barrage of government activism at a time when many Americans had lost faith in the institution. Not every move worked out. His executive order closing Guantánamo did not, in fact, close Guantánamo. His plan to prevent foreclosures was much less aggressive than advocates had hoped or Santelli had feared. But beyond the Tea Party fringe that considered Obama an anti-American usurper, most Americans still thought he was trying to make the best of a tough situation.

"The obsession with race, the slurs about celebrity politics, the doubts about preparedness all seem dated now," *Politico* concluded in its hundred-day overview. "This is a presidency at light-speed that looks and feels remarkably mature."

The challenge would be converting all that light-speed activity into a coherent message. At Georgetown, Obama made his most comprehensive case for his economic program, expanding his inaugural theme of "The New Foundation." He borrowed his central image from the Sermon on the Mount, comparing the old economy's reliance on maxed-out credit cards and sketchy subprime mortgages to the proverbial house built on sand. He vowed to create a sturdy post-bubble economy built on a rock, "a new foundation that will move us from an era of borrow-and-spend to one where we save and invest." The New Foundation consisted of his four pillars of prosperity from the

campaign—economic reform, health reform, energy reform, and education reform—plus long-term deficit reduction. And deficit reduction
would depend mainly on health reform, since the skyrocketing cost of
care was the reason Medicaid and Medicare were driving long-term
shortfalls. The Recovery Act, Obama said, began that foundation—
through Race to the Top and a dramatic expansion of early childhood
education, to prepare kids to compete in a global economy; unprecedented spending on renewables and efficiency, to create clean energy
and green jobs; and the largest investments ever in preventive care and
electronic health records, to save money and lives.

His presidency, in other words, would be about revamping the economy for the long term. Anita Dunn, who took over the rudderless
White House communications team shortly before the speech, thought
this made more sense as an overarching theme than jobs-jobs-jobs.
Why pretend long-term investments like health IT and high-speed rail
were about short-term jobs when they weren't?

"The New Foundation should've been the message of the first two
years," Dunn says. "I actually thought about setting up a website and
trying to brand it."

The phrase appeared in fifteen Obama speeches over the next
month, and the New York Times ran a story suggesting it was being
groomed as Obama's unofficial slogan, his answer to the New Deal.
But it soon faded away, overshadowed by the furor over autos, the war
over health care, and the Tea Party jihad against spending. At a dinner
Obama hosted for presidential historians, Doris Kearns Goodwin said it
sounded like a woman's girdle. "It wasn't translating in that chaotic environment," says Dan Pfeiffer, Dunn's deputy. "We weren't as disciplined
as we should have been about repeating it."

Instead, the main White House message was: Jobs.

Which were disappearing fast.

March and April were as ghastly as February: over 1.2 million more
jobs lost, with unemployment shooting up to 8.9 percent. Analysts were
happier about May: only 345,000 jobs lost, although unemployment

soared to 9.4 percent. Yes, the economy was still shrinking and jobs were still vanishing—but not as quickly. And jobs are always a lagging economic indicator. Consumer confidence was creeping back.

"The recession has entered a new phase, pulling away from an economic abyss into a period of steep but orderly decline," the *Washington Post* reported.

Hooray! A steep but *orderly* decline!

Well, it beat the abyss.

Inside the White House, nagging fears that at any minute a bank collapse or foreign crisis or market hiccup could plunge the economy back into Lehman-style chaos did subside. But it was hard to get too excited after a month when enough Americans to fill seven Yankee Stadiums had received pink slips. Candidate Obama had not promised "steep but orderly decline," and 9.4 percent unemployment would've been tough to explain even if his economists hadn't predicted the stimulus would keep the rate below 8 percent. Lagging indicator or not, the jobless rate was a PR nightmare, and public support for the president's handling of the economy started to droop. The White House was still talking about saving or creating 3 or even 4 million jobs with the stimulus, but over 6 million had been lost since the start of the recession. Republicans now had a stock response to anything Obama said or did: Where are the jobs? Boehner released a YouTube video of a bloodhound named Ellie Mae searching for stimulus jobs around the country. "She hasn't found any yet, and neither have the American people," Boehner said.

"By any objective standard, this has been a failure," McConnell sniped.

By any objective standard, this was baloney. As Romer pointed out, if your doctor gives you an antibiotic for strep throat, and then your fever spikes anyway, it doesn't mean that antibiotics are useless. It means you were probably even sicker than you thought—and it's a good thing you started the antibiotics when you did.

"Fiscal stimulus is a well-tested antibiotic, not some new-fangled gene therapy," she said in a speech. "The economic theory of how tax cuts and increases in government spending can help counteract a recession is almost as widely accepted as any in economics—practically up there with supply and demand."

Absolutely right. Impeccable logic. On the other hand: nine-point-four percent! Even some White House officials thought they were overplaying a losing stimulus hand.

"It's fucking irrelevant to be talking about how many jobs you're creating when the economy is shedding so many more," one Obama adviser grumbles.

On June 8, Jared Bernstein learned this the hard way during his Recovery Act update for the White House press corps, a half hour of vultures feasting on roadkill. Bernstein suggested the stimulus had already saved or created 150,000 jobs, but it was too early for him to specify how many saved and how many created, or catalogue what kind of jobs, or provide any supporting data other than the original Romer-Bernstein forecast—the forecast that had wildly underestimated the jobless rate. And 150,000 jobs sounded anemic when forty times that many had vanished.

"With hindsight, what we did was throw raw meat to wild dogs—and then ask them politely to step back while we explain," Bernstein recalls.

After Robert Gibbs finally intervened to stop the feeding frenzy, reminding the media the stimulus wasn't designed to fix the economy overnight, he endured a half hour pummeling of his own. "Do you think there's a danger here of a credibility deficit developing on the issue of the economy?" one reporter asked. As McConnell aide Don Stewart watched Bernstein stammering about "confidence intervals," Gibbs spinning about "the best available data that we had," and the press piling on about "saved or created," he kept thinking: We're winning.

"The press smelled blood, and ate 'em alive," Stewart chortles.

Some Obama aides saw this as the inevitable result of a flawed messaging strategy, a shortsighted focus on jobs—saved, created, green, direct, indirect, whatever. Jobs bills are expected to add jobs, and the best Obama could hope for while Americans were forming their opinions of the Recovery Act would be to lose jobs at a slower rate. "We set ourselves up for surefire failure," one aide says. In private, Biden also argued the message was too jobs-centric, too much about "numbering jobs" at a time when the numbers were unavoidably dismal. He didn't expect the White House to get much credit for averting a depression once the depression was averted.

"The inclination is: 'See? You were wrong. There wasn't a depression,'" Biden says. He suggests that while Obama's young Ivy Leaguers might have expected gratitude for their Keynesian heroics, "I have some sense of human nature."

Other Obama aides and allies thought his message should have been even more jobs-centric. Rahm liked to joke that Obama's big mistake was passing the Recovery Act too quickly; if he had dragged it out, there might have been a depression, but at least the country would have seen him focused on the economy. Oprah wasn't the only American who forgot that he tackled the economy first, before the political conversation shifted to health care. When times were this tough, talking about anything but jobs-jobs-jobs made the president look detached.

In June, Obama's shift in focus contributed to an underappreciated blunder, his decision to scuttle a $450 billion, six-year transportation bill that could have helped revive the construction industry. Transportation Committee chairman Jim Oberstar had waited his entire career for this moment, and he had bipartisan support for his blueprint. It would have financed some of the more ambitious long-term projects that were bypassed during the stimulus because they weren't shovel-ready. But hours before Oberstar's press conference to unveil the bill, Secretary LaHood informed him the White House wouldn't support it. "Poor Jim," says his Republican counterpart, John Mica. "I've never seen him that mad." Obama's political team didn't think the president had enough time or political bandwidth to deal with another huge spending bill while health care was heating up, especially since Oberstar hoped to raise gas taxes. The White House had a rare opportunity to work out a compromise; congressmen love concrete, and the six-year funding stream would have given contractors more confidence to make permanent hires. But after reading a memo about Oberstar's plan, Obama wrote "No"—and underlined it. Oberstar went on the warpath, seething that White House economists who had never held a shovel in their delicate hands couldn't understand the anxieties of unemployed workers, or even the frustrations of commuters stuck in traffic.

"I suggest that those highfalutin economists get out of their chauffeured limousines and get on the street and drive like the rest of America," he complained.

That summer, as health care bogged down and the Tea Party caught fire, the prairie populist Byron Dorgan of North Dakota visited the Oval Office to beg Obama to focus full-time on the economy.

"If I had been elected president," Senator Dorgan said, "I'd want people to know one thing and one thing only: That I was spending every waking moment focused on putting people back to work and getting the economy moving again." Obama reminded Dorgan he had promised to reform health care during the campaign. "Yes, and then the bottom fell out," Dorgan said. "We're sitting in a much deeper hole, and you're still trying to reach just as high."

The White House did schedule frequent events about jobs. For example, when Boehner scoffed on Fox News that in Ohio, not one Recovery Act infrastructure contract had been awarded, Biden promptly visited his district to show that over fifty transportation projects were under way in the Buckeye State. Obama then used his weekly address to chide critics who "are already judging the effort a failure although they have yet to offer a plausible alternative." But at times it felt like he doth protest too much. If he was so focused on the economy, why was it so weak? If he cared so much about jobs, why were they disappearing? And whenever he made the elephant-in-the-room observation that Bush had gifted him a calamity, critics tsk-tsked about his un-presidential finger-pointing.

"I know voters in Ohio, just like voters in my state, are beginning to understand this economy is owned by Barack Obama," Eric Cantor said the day of Biden's visit.

House Republicans were amazed by how often the White House

took their bait, elevating attacks that would have been ignored without a presidential response. On July 14, in the battered auto town of Warren, Michigan, Obama veered off his text to swallow Cantor's bait hook, line, and sinker. "I love these folks who helped get us into this mess and then suddenly say, 'Well, this is Obama's economy,'" he said. "That's fine: Give it to me. My job is to solve problems, not to stand on the sidelines and carp and gripe."

Back in Washington, Republicans could not believe their good luck. Obama was *already* taking ownership of the Bush economy?

"I remember when he did it," says one Cantor aide. "We were like: Heyyyyyy!"

Better Economics, Worse Politics

Actually, the stimulus was working.

Bernstein didn't have the evidence to prove it yet when he ventured into that hostile briefing room, but the Recovery Act's medicine was already stabilizing the patient. After plunging another 6.4 percent in the first quarter, GDP only dipped 1.0 percent in the second quarter, the second-biggest improvement in twenty-five years. The second-quarter jobs numbers, while still grim, were the biggest improvement in almost thirty years. Economists later calculated that the Great Recession ended in June 2009, "just when the Recovery Act was providing its maximum benefit to the economy," notes Mark Zandi, the former McCain adviser from Moody's. Google searches for "economic depression," which had spiked over the last year, were returning to normal levels.

The Recovery Act didn't end the recession by itself. TARP stopped the financial meltdown, and Obama's stress tests helped restore confidence in the banking system. His auto rescue provided vital anti-anti-stimulus by bringing GM and Chrysler back from the dead, preventing the collapse of the industrial Midwest. The White House also goosed demand for cars by reviving its Cash for Clunkers idea, ginning up 700,000 purchases in two months; the program's initial funding ran out in a week, so Congress raided $2 billion from the Recovery Act's clean-energy loans to keep it going. And Bernanke helped save the global economy with his aggressive improvisations, loaning trillions of dollars to hedge funds, investment banks, manufacturers, and other borrowers who had never dreamed of receiving Fed cash.

But the data told a powerful story of how the Recovery Act was pulling the economy out of the ditch. State and local government spending that had plummeted for months increased 3.6 percent in the second quarter, after the aid to states helped governors cancel layoffs and cuts. The states that got the most aid lost the fewest jobs, and outside government, the sectors with the biggest improvements were the sectors targeted by the stimulus. Globally, countries that enacted larger stimulus packages had better economic results than countries with more modest ones.

"If you study the data and look at the timeline, there's no question the Recovery Act saved us from something much, much worse," Zandi says.

Unfortunately for Obama, the American people were not studying the data or looking at the timeline. The economy was getting better. His poll numbers were getting worse. His policies were working. His politics weren't. And his opponents, whatever they lacked in credibility, had an unmuddled message: Big government is bad.

"What can you sell when you do not have the White House, the House or the Senate?" a Republican National Committee staffer wrote in an internal strategy document. "Save the country from trending towards Socialism!"

Maybe Obama had inherited a mess, but it was his mess now.

For example, his overhaul of the auto industry would become a stunning success, minimizing taxpayer losses, avoiding the erasure of countless jobs, and restoring the Big Three to profitability. But at the time, the intervention was a political drag. Republicans accused Obama of engineering a Soviet-style assault on free enterprise, bailing out his union pals, and creating a doomed Government Motors. While he got little credit for the meltdown that didn't happen, he was savaged for the inevitable layoffs at the restructured firms, and the downsizing of politically connected car dealers.

"It's a classic avoided problem," says Ron Bloom, an investment banker and union adviser who cochaired Obama's auto task force. "We were preventing a disaster that would have had multigenerational impacts. But the reaction was: Why are you cutting jobs?"

Health reform and cap-and-trade—Obamacare and cap-and-tax, to Republicans—further inflamed the Tea Party. Obama's health bill was modeled on Governor Romney's reforms in Massachusetts, and cap-and-trade was a market-based energy policy the McCain-Palin ticket had supported. But the grassroots right came to see them as evidence of Obama's insatiable desire to dismantle capitalism. Even beyond the Tea Party, polls suggested that Americans were skittish about government rearranging two of the nation's largest private industries during tough times. The Republican drumbeat about fictitious "death panels" and "$3,000 energy taxes" did not soothe their anxieties.

Obama let Democrats in Congress take the lead on both issues, and they didn't do him any political favors. Senator Baucus tried desperately to negotiate a health care deal with his pal Grassley, resisting Rahm's pressure to end the futile talks until Grassley publicly accused the president of trying to "pull the plug on Grandma." It was, Axelrod says, "like waiting for Godot." At the White House, Obama asked Grassley point-blank whether he would support the bill if Democrats gave him everything he wanted; Grassley said no, unless ten other Republicans agreed to vote with him. In other words: No. In fairness to Baucus, he felt he had to go to extremes to show good faith toward the Republicans, because the same centrist Democrats who had helped keep the stimulus under $800 billion did not want to support partisan health reforms.

Meanwhile, still irked by the way the Senate had rolled the House on the Recovery Act, Pelosi rammed through a cap-and-trade bill that had no chance in the Senate, despite Rahm's pleas to wait until there was a real chance of getting something done. Many Democrats were furious about taking a hard vote for no apparent reason. And the handful of Republicans who voted yes were furiously denounced as traitors by their base, which would make them think twice about crossing the aisle in the future. Americans for Tax Reform founder Grover Norquist, Washington's most influential antigovernment activist, says Republican lawmakers learned during that Tea Party summer that their core constituency did not want them to work together with a Euro-socialist president. The base wanted knife fighters, not "collaborators."

"You could make a list of guys who thought their job was to cut the best deal that they could," Norquist says. "Then they'd go home and find out their voters wouldn't be pleased. They'd be pissed."

The Recovery Act remained at the heart of the case against Obama as a spread-the-wealth big-government radical. Inside the conservative echo chamber, Porkulus was all about dubious-sounding projects like a $3.4 million "Turtle Tunnel" designed to prevent wildlife from getting squashed on a Florida highway, along with made-up scandals like a $1.19 million purchase of two pounds of ham. (It was really 760,000 pounds of ham in two-pound packages, a cost-effective way to get food to the hungry, but the Drudge Report led with it anyway.) A former health care CEO named Rick Scott, whose firm had engineered the largest Medicare fraud in history, bankrolled ads claiming an "innocent-sounding board" created by the Recovery Act to oversee comparative effectiveness investments was "the first step in government control over your health care choices." For the Tea Party, the stimulus was the ultimate symbol of Obama's reckless deficit spending, even though he had inherited the record deficit. The rallies were full of signs like "Stimulus: The Audacity of Dopes" and "Hey, Barack, Go Stimulate Yourself!"

By the summer's end, independent analysts like Macroeconomic Advisers, Goldman Sachs, and Moody's all agreed the stimulus had added at least 2 percent to GDP. And the administration had fulfilled all of its pledges for the Recovery Act's first two hundred days: saving 135,000 education jobs, funding 200,000 summer youth jobs, starting work on 2,200 highways, 500 military facilities, and 100 national parks. In the soft economy, bids were routinely coming in under budget; the FAA was using its savings to fund another 60 airport projects. Things were in motion. A Buffalo veterans hospital was building a state-of-the-art hospice wing. Families in the Tar Creek mining region of northwest

Oklahoma, where the lead-poisoned creek dyed turtles orange and lead-poisoned children struggled in school, were relocated through a stimulus-funded Superfund project. And the paychecks of 120 million working Americans earning less than $200,000 were a bit fatter.

But these short-term benefits didn't register with the public, not when the jobs numbers were still negative. And the long-term benefits at the heart of Obamaism weren't visible yet. One poll found that 45 percent of Americans wanted to cancel the stimulus and return its unspent funds to the Treasury; only 36 percent wanted it to continue. Biden wrote a *New York Times* op-ed titled "What You Might Not Know About the Recovery," bemoaning how the stimulus "remains misunderstood by many and misconstrued by others." In politics, when you're explaining, you're losing. In a speech at Brookings, Biden tried to remind his audience just how awful things had been when Obama was sworn in, how every day "there was a new revelation to be added to the economic parade of horribles." He recounted the headlines from February: "Automakers Bankruptcy Looms." "Credit Freeze Leaves Thousands of Student Borrowers Stuck in Default." "Governments Brace for Hard Times." "Newly Poor Swell Lines of Food Banks."

"It's hard to remember, even though it's only been eight months," Biden said.

Inside the White House, Ron Klain pushed for Obama to attend stimulus events to help revive the Recovery Act's popularity. (Other aides wanted to keep Obama away from stimulus events to protect his own popularity.) One day, Rahm felt an urge to put the president in front of workers in hard hats; the best excuse the Transportation Department could come up with was a celebration of its two thousandth stimulus project. An initial plan to bring the president to the Baltimore airport raised logistical problems, so the event ended up in a department briefing room, a dispiriting place to discuss a lane widening in Kalamazoo. When the event was over, Obama told his staff: "This is bullshit."

"Everything about it was wrong—nothing exciting, nothing real, nothing visual," one White House official says. "And of course the press just said: Nyah, nyah, unemployment is still going up."

Around the same time, Rahm persuaded the president to hold an even sillier pseudo-event in the Cabinet Room to broadcast his concern about wasteful spending. Rahm dubbed it "Project *Dave*," after the cinematic pseudo-president who secretly invites his accountant to the White House to slice fat out of the budget. So Obama announced that to restore public confidence in government's ability to spend wisely, he was challenging his cabinet to report back to him with . . . $100 million in cuts.

Huh? After spending $787 billion-with-a-b on a stimulus, then unveiling a $3.6 trillion-with-a-t budget plan, Obama was proposing $100 million-with-an-m in rollbacks? That was supposed to restore confidence in government?

The ultimate visual representation of the muddled message could be seen at stimulus projects around the country: the Recovery Act logo. Designed by a hipster Chicago ad agency, it was supposed to evoke a retro New Deal feel. And its bottom half was supposed to represent long-term investments: a plant for green energy initiatives, gears for infrastructure projects, and a tiny red cross for health care investments. But it just looked cluttered. I never even noticed the cross, much less connected it to health care, until I Googled an explanation of the logo.

"We just couldn't get our story straight on the Recovery Act," says one senior White House official. "We had no message. And every time there was a bad story in the paper, we'd all turn into kids at a soccer game, everybody chasing the ball."

By the end of the Tea Party summer, Obama's approval ratings had fallen almost as sharply as the Recovery Act's. He was down in the low 50s, mere mortal territory. The partisan divide that preceded his presidency was firmly back in place.

Congressional Democrats were starting to worry about the ominous trajectory of public opinion. At a White House tribute to country music, the Blue Dog Baron Hill told the president: The stimulus was great, but you're not doing enough to sell it.

"I know exactly what you're saying," Obama replied. "And you're exactly right."

FOURTEEN

Change Is Hard

The first time Rahm Emanuel summoned Energy Department stimulus czar Matt Rogers to his office, he wanted to know what was happening with the smart grid. More specifically, he wanted to know: Why the fuck wasn't anything happening with the smart grid? The Recovery Act had included a $4.5 billion grant program. So? Hello?

Rogers explained that there had been some delays in designing the new grant competition, and then some disputes with OMB bean counters about those designs. What he didn't bother to explain was: Change is hard. Transforming America's antiquated grid—and America's fossil-fueled economy—wouldn't happen overnight.

Rogers's mission statement for the Recovery Act was: "Money Out Quickly—To Good, Enduring Projects—With Unprecedented Transparency—Making a Down Payment on the Energy & Environmental Future of the Country." But there was real tension between the first part of that mission and the rest of that mission. In the fall of 2009, the Government Accountability Office found that most of the stimulus was spending out ahead of schedule. But the long-term investments designed to change the country were a lot trickier to get out quickly than business-as-usual investments.

Rahm wanted long-term change, too. Rahm's Rule, after all, was his rule. And he knew his boss was obsessed with that frigging grid. But that was all the more reason to produce some quick results. Why couldn't Rogers just buy Americans $4.5 billion worth of digital smart meters? It would be easy. It would give the public something visible. And it would help fulfill Obama's promise of forty million meters, so Rahm wouldn't have to worry about the frigging grid anymore.

Rogers was hoping to avoid another fusillade of F-bombs, but he pushed back. Handing out smart meters before starting work on the rest of the smart grid—sensors, routers, automated substations, "synchrophasors"—would be like handing out iPhones before there was a 3G network. Smart meters could be an amazing tool, helping consumers track their electricity use and reduce their electricity bills. They could make meter readers obsolete, and help utilities pinpoint problems automatically instead of deploying battalions of trucks to troubleshoot entire neighborhoods. But they'd be virtually useless if the rest of the grid was still dumb. They needed to be part of a digital ecosystem with smart substations and smart transmission lines, where information would flow along with electrons. Synchrophasors might sound like *Star Trek* wackiness, but these dishwasher-sized metal boxes could monitor and control high-voltage wires hundreds of miles away, providing reams of data every 1/30 of a second, limiting costly outages and wasteful leakage. Anyway, it made sense to let utilities devise solutions for their own networks, rather than dictate from Washington. Maybe they'd have good ideas. Maybe those ideas would spread.

Rahm grudgingly agreed to a comprehensive approach, though he wasn't thrilled about paying for doodads nobody would see. But he did demand a faster timetable. And he had one additional demand.

"I *never* want to hear you say the word 'synchrophasor' in public," Rahm said. "Nobody will know what the fuck you're talking about."

"What a Nightmare"

The second time Rogers was summoned to Rahm's office—and the third, and the fourth—the topic was low-income home weatherization. The Recovery Act created all kinds of bureaucratic headaches, but weatherization was a bureaucratic aneurysm. There's no better example of the bumps on the road to change.

American homes waste ungodly amounts of energy, and studies suggest that modest efficiencies—sealing ducts; adding insulation; upgrading furnaces, air conditioners, and windows—could save homeowners $40 billion a year. This was the kind of policy no-brainer that Obama loved. At an event at a Home Depot in Virginia, he declared that contrary to popular belief, insulation was sexy: "Here's what's sexy about it: Saving money!" Saving energy, slashing emissions, and employing an army of workers with caulk guns sounded alluring, too. Obama had vowed to weatherize one million homes a year during the campaign, and had steered $5 billion into Energy's $200 million weatherization program through the stimulus. The goal was not only to "green the ghetto"—a phrase coined by White House green jobs adviser Van Jones, a charismatic urban activist and author of *The Green Collar Economy*—but to train a weatherization workforce, spur demand for green products, and eventually create a national culture where tuning up homes would be as routine as tuning up cars.

"The idea was, if you put in a chunk of change, you can stand up a new sector," says Jones, who had founded an advocacy group called Green For All that had called for a Green New Deal. "And damn! That was a serious chunk of change."

It was a nice idea, although Jones wouldn't get to see it through; he was forced to resign after Glenn Beck used his pre-White House activism to make him a poster child for White House radicalism. And by summer's end, many states had yet to weatherize a single home. At the rate the money was moving, it would have taken a century to do a million.

To put it mildly, Rahm wasn't pleased. How hard could it be to seal a drafty window or insulate an attic? What the—oh, you get the idea.

"What a nightmare," Rogers recalls. "That program had issues."

Early on, the White House wanted to see the Energy Department's plan for weatherizing one million homes a year.

We're not going to do one million homes a year, Rogers said. We're not going to do one million homes, period.

Say what? The president had promised one million homes a year. Recovery Act coordinator Ed DeSeve told Rogers: This isn't optional.

Rogers was a can-do guy, but he was also a numbers guy. He had enough funding to do 600,000 retrofits over three years. "We're not trying to be cute," he told DeSeve. "The arithmetic is the arithmetic."

That was just the first snafu. Soon a bigger one threatened to turn even the 600,000-home goal into a pipe dream. Weatherization had always been exempt from the Hoover-era Davis-Bacon law, which required federal projects to pay the "prevailing wage" for similar jobs in the local area. But in the fine print of the Recovery Act, union-friendly congressional Democrats extended Davis-Bacon to weatherization, even though the Labor Department had never set prevailing wages for weatherization jobs. So hundreds of local nonprofits that should have been hiring to handle the surge of new cash were waiting for instructions, unwilling to risk fines for underpaying employees or misfiling reports. Davis-Bacon would delay the program six months and make it a national symbol of stimulus sluggishness.

The issue itself was mind-numbingly dull. Rogers didn't care all that much whether caulkers were paid as "laborers," "carpenters," or "construction workers." He just wanted guidance, so the local agencies could start hiring and start caulking. But after months of haggling— and heavy union lobbying—the Labor Department decided to create an entirely new job classification for weatherization, which required an entirely new wage survey of every U.S. county. Secretaries Chu and Solis signed a joint letter encouraging the agencies to start hiring anyway, suggesting they could estimate prevailing wages under existing classifications. But the agencies were flummoxed. At one point, Rogers and assistant energy secretary Cathy Zoi surfed the Labor Department's website to try to figure out an appropriate wage for Chicago. They were flummoxed, too.

"And I think we're reasonably intelligent people," Rogers says.

"They didn't even have a search function," Zoi scoffs.

Labor did rush to compile the new wage rates in just a few months. But then it ruled that the new rates couldn't apply to more ambitious building retrofits funded through state and local energy efficiency grants. Those projects would have to determine wages on a case-by-case basis. Labor even decided that consumers who used stimulus incentives for efficiency upgrades in their own homes should pay prevailing wages, a ruling so nutty that Chu called Solis from India to get it reversed.

But the damage was done. The Government Accountability Office, the department's inspector general, and the media all savaged the weatherization program's slow pace. In 2009, it only finished 30,252 homes. California, which was supposed to do 2,500 a month, completed 12.

The Energy Department couldn't put all the blame on Davis-Bacon, not when its own bureaucratic follies evoked Dilbert cartoons. Its Office of Weatherization and Intergovernmental Programs, which oversaw $6.3 billion worth of state and local grants as well as the low-income retrofits, was known as "The Turkey Farm" for the quality of its staff. Since it's almost impossible to fire non-performing civil servants, Bush's Energy Department officials had stockpiled their stiffs in the weatherization division, hoping to get rid of the deadwood en masse by killing the program or shifting it to another department. And the Obama team struggled to bring in new blood to handle all the new money—described in one agency PowerPoint as "Massive Funding: BBBBBBBBIL-LIONS!"—in part because a bureaucrat in Golden, Colorado, nearing retirement, wasn't signing off on new hires. Her boss in Washington had fallen off a roof hanging Christmas lights—shades of *The Office*—so the process slowed to a near halt. And the civil servant overseeing the division in Washington, an enthusiastic advocate for weatherization, was not the kind of headbanger who could battle the bureaucracy and end the inertia. When the numbers failed to improve, Zoi and Rogers shifted him to an outreach role.

The Turkey Farm needed a leader who could ruffle a few feathers.

Claire Broido Johnson was another best-and-brightest wunderkind you wouldn't expect to find in middle management at a federal agency. She majored in environmental science and public policy at Harvard—she helped create the major—and later graduated from Harvard Business School. After stints structuring energy deals for major banks and corporations—including ill-fated Enron, as her detractors often noted—she helped found SunEdison, which used an innovative financing model to become the nation's largest solar provider. She wasn't much of a diplomat, but she had the brains, private sector instincts, and bull-in-a-china-shop mentality the department needed to get its creaky weatherization office up to stimulus speed.

"She was like a hurricane hitting the building," says one civil servant.

Johnson's mission was simple: Get the money out. So she set metrics and goals for every weatherization agency and state energy office, forced program officers to call them weekly to monitor their progress, and distributed national rankings of spend-out rates to encourage interstate competition. She launched initiatives with military-style code names like Operation GreenLight, Operation QuickDraw, and Operation FastTrack to streamline grant procedures and pressure spending slowpokes. When it became clear that local governments applying for grants were struggling to navigate federal red tape—the department's procurement requirements for energy-efficient furnaces and radioactive nuclear materials were not that different—Johnson moved dozens of her top performers (the "SWAT team") into a makeshift call center in the department's basement (the "dungeon"), where they spent weeks leading small-town mayors and big-city energy officials through the process.

"I was spending my own money at Costco to bribe them with cookies and candy and lunches," Johnson says.

The cookies were nice, but Johnson was a tough one. She had no patience for stupid rules or stupid people. Her focus was getting the money out, and she expected that to be everyone else's focus. "Her mantra was: Spend!" says one of her internal critics. "Claire, I broke my arm. Fuck it! Spend!" When her underlings wanted to forge an interagency partnership that seemed worthy but wouldn't have helped get the money out, she shot it down with a caustic email: "I really don't understand why we're spending time on this." Many state and local officials resented the department's harassment over spend-out rates, and its bias toward quick and proven efficiency upgrades like LED streetlights and traffic lights. New Hampshire set up several unusual initiatives—a revolving loan program for green businesses, rebates for wood pellet heating systems to replace fuel oil—and found itself on the receiving end of frequent federal nasty-grams.

"The word that comes to mind is 'eviscerate.' We had our guts pulled out through our noses," says Laura Richardson, the state energy office's stimulus coordinator. "All they cared about was: Get the money out."

Johnson set the brutal tone, but she was responding to pressure from Rogers, who was responding to Chu, who was responding to the White House. Maybe her bulldog style might have been hailed as "hard-charging" if she had been an older man, rather than a petite blonde in her mid-thirties. But she was not hailed at the Turkey Farm. Early on, when she asked all of the division's staffers what they were accountable for, two responded: "You can't make me accountable for anything." One employee buried his nose in a newspaper whenever she approached. When she chastised another lifer for napping on the job, he filed a union grievance.

Increasingly frustrated, Johnson launched a secret "Operation Cupcake" to try to fire the worst laggards, but she never stood a chance against the cupcakes. They knew that political appointees come and go, but civil servants are forever. They called themselves "WeBe's," as in: We be here, you be gone.

They were right. Johnson's enemies leaked internal emails to the inspector general that revealed she had violated federal procedures to fast-track the hiring of a deputy. "The HR process is just too slow," she had written. "I need competent bodies now who can help." No one claimed Johnson was motivated by anything other than her desire to get flailing programs on track, and the investigative report acknowledged that the Recovery Act created extraordinary pressure to hire fast. But it still ended Johnson's career at the department.

"I'll never work for the federal government again," she says.

It's an unfortunate bureaucratic saga, except for the uplifting coda: Johnson and the Turkey Farm got the job done. On her watch, the weatherization program's "run rate" increased from 30,000 homes a year to 30,000 homes a month. The program ultimately surpassed its goal of 600,000 homes three months early. Despite audits that found sporadic cases of shoddy work, a national study estimated that the retrofits saved the average homeowner over $400 a year. They also provided jobs for fifteen thousand workers. Republicans continued to seize on mini-scandals, like an audit identifying substandard work on fifteen Chicago homes, and pseudo-scandals, like a grant to a legitimate inner-city weatherization nonprofit with the unfortunate name of the African Heritage Dancers and Drummers of Washington. But a follow-up by the GAO found the program's start-up problems were largely solved.

"It's a heartwarming story," Cathy Zoi says.

Zoi recalls reminding Governor Rendell during the program's dismal first year that Pennsylvania's quota was 1,500 homes a month. "How many did we do last month?" he asked. Sixty-seven, she replied. She had a similar what's-the-holdup chat with Governor Schwarzenegger in his famous smoking tent outside the California statehouse. "We'll fix the prah-blems," he promised. Governor Perry didn't even return Zoi's calls, but his weatherization director assured her not to worry about politics; Texas would make the program work. And eventually they all came through.

Of course, the press was no longer interested in weatherization now that its prah-blems had been fixed. It was just another cat that hadn't run away.

Obama's Moon Mission

The economy remained weak throughout 2009, but not the clean-energy economy. Clean-tech became the leading U.S. venture capital sector for the first time, eclipsing biotech and infotech. The wind industry, which had anticipated a 50 percent decline in new generation before the Recovery Act converted its useless tax credits into cash grants, instead had its best year ever. It added enough new turbines to power over one million homes, the equivalent of twenty coal plants. Solar had its best year ever, too, with forecasts for even better years ahead.

"Before the Recovery Act, we were shutting down our U.S. projects and reallocating our capital around the globe," says Don Furman, senior vice president of the Spanish-owned wind developer Iberdrola Renewables. "The day it was signed, our chairman turned on a dime and put $6 billion back into the U.S."

The more America relied on renewable energy, the more it would need a smart grid. But the growing pains of the Recovery Act's grid program, while less public than its weatherization delays, were in some ways even worse. The smart grid wasn't just slow stimulus. Initially, it was anti-stimulus.

Everyone agreed that America's outdated grid needed an overhaul. Its managers constantly scrambled to maintain a balance between generation and consumption, like those old switchboard operators who manually connected every phone call. When demand spiked, they often had to fire up inefficient fossil-fuel "peaking plants" to prevent rolling blackouts. Yet outages still cost Americans as much as $150 billion a year. And the analog grid was a major obstacle to a world of renewable energy and electric transportation. A digital grid could make it much easier to shift juice where it's needed when the wind stops blowing or clouds hide the sun. It could also help utilities smooth out demand to reduce peak loads without bringing new plants online. And it could give consumers more information and control, so they could save energy and money, and sell extra power from solar panels on their roof and electric cars in their garage back to the grid.

Before the Recovery Act, almost every U.S. utility was at least starting to plan for a smart grid, and a few were already installing their first smart meters and other digital equipment. But while the passage of the stimulus accelerated the planning, because utilities had to think about their needs before applying for grants, it initially slowed down the installation, because utilities didn't want to splurge on upgrades if there was a chance the feds would help pay for them. So until Obama announced the winners in October, grid investment froze, which was not the kind of response the stimulus was supposed to stimulate. "It was frustrating. The utilities put everything on pause," says Raj Vaswani, chief technology officer for Silver Spring Networks, a Silicon Valley smart grid firm. And after Obama's announcement, the awards were delayed again because utilities objected to paying taxes on them.

"It was one holdup after another," Rogers says.

Once the grants were exempted from taxes, the first order of business for most of the winners was installing smart meters, just as Rahm had hoped. The stimulus will increase the U.S. totals from 8 million to 26 million. But inconveniently, the main up-front benefit of digital meters is their ability to replace human meter readers. The Phoenix-area utility Salt River Project's new meters helped it complete over one million service orders remotely in the first year, saving 82,000 hours of labor, the equivalent of slashing forty jobs.

Smart meters weren't the political hit that Rahm had hoped, either. Across the nation, ratepayer advocates and consumer groups like AARP have fought rate increases to help pay for them. In Northern California, a stimulus-funded push to install millions of meters sparked a particularly intense backlash, mainly because a heat wave made customers think the new devices had jacked up their bills, partly because of unfounded health fears about radiation, but partly because by themselves smart meters don't do much for consumers. I found this out when my own analog meter in Miami Beach was replaced with a Silver Spring digital model through a $200 million stimulus grant to my utility, Florida Power & Light. Now my family can check online to see how much power we use and when we use it. But so what? We can't tell how much energy our various appliances are wasting, and we can't save money yet by running the dishwasher at different times of day.

"It's like giving people Ferraris, without giving them the keys," says Jon Wellinghoff, Obama's top energy regulator.

It's ironic, since what Rahm liked about smart meters was their visibility, but so far their benefits have been largely invisible. The utility savings on meter readers and home visits should eventually translate into lower rates; for example, in addition to its reduced labor costs, Salt River saved 44,000 gallons of gas from avoided "truck rolls." And digital meters will help utilities do a better job keeping the lights on. But as a political matter, customers don't notice when their meter alerts the grid to a potential problem they didn't know they had.

"The holy grail in outage management is to avoid the outage in the first place," says Elster Solutions CEO Mark Munday, whose firm provides smart meters to Salt River. "There's so much you can do without even engaging the customer."

That's true of the entire grid. The better it works, the less we notice it. In that sense, Obama's moon mission is another things-would've-been-worse-without-us achievement. Another example: Millions of fans watched Stanford defeat Virginia Tech in the 2011 Orange Bowl, but none of them knew that an aging transformer almost overloaded while feeding power to the stadium, triggering voltage alerts that gave new meaning to the term "red zone." The problem was detected by Florida Power & Light's new smart grid equipment, which quickly diverted the electricity to healthier transformers, avoiding a midgame blackout. The utility used to inspect its transformers annually; its new sensors and other smart machines now monitor them every second. "It's like having an EKG or a blood pressure machine strapped to you twenty-four hours a day," says Bob Triana, the operations manager for the stimulus-funded Energy Smart Florida project.

And yes, the synchrophasor revolution is quietly under way. The Recovery Act is financing a 500 percent increase in "phasor measurement units" that are producing rivers of real-time data, giving grid managers visibility over the entire high-voltage transmission system for the first time, dramatically reducing the chances of another wayward tree branch downing a power line and blacking out eight states. Industry researchers believe the new gadgetry will eventually reduce electricity losses over transmission wires by 20 percent, saving enough energy to power two million homes.

"It's incredibly cool, and it's a very inexpensive way to prevent the next New York City blackout," Rogers says. "But it's pretty hard to explain."

It certainly isn't as easy to explain as the New Deal's grid upgrades, which extended electricity to families that never had it. But the Recovery Act's grid money may be jump-starting America's next trillion-dollar industry.

I got a glimpse of how my smart meter Ferrari might run with keys at FPL's home automation lab in Miami. Two screens displayed competing "home energy controllers"—from Cisco and General Electric—with dashboards for tracking and adjusting the electricity use of every appliance in a home. They weren't fancy, but they provided actionable intelligence a family could use to save energy. "We're still in a 1.0 world," lab manager Patrick Agnew explained. "We haven't gotten from the lab to the living room. So customers haven't seen what a smart grid could be."

The grid is physical infrastructure, but the smart grid is a tech play, using megabytes of data to move megawatts of electricity. As a business opportunity, "we think it can be way bigger than the Internet," says Cisco's top smart grid executive, Laura Ipsen. It will require lots of the kind of hardware that Cisco built for telecommunications networks, and lots of sophisticated software to help utilities manage an avalanche of data. It will also inspire applications that haven't been dreamed up yet. No one knows what the eBay or Wikipedia of the grid will look like—or the pets.com of the grid. But it's no coincidence that Silicon Valley giants like Cisco and Oracle have moved into the hardware space, while start-ups are racing to develop software and apps. Since the Recovery Act passed, the mega-players have created scores of alliances to offer utilities one-stop "networked solutions," just as they once did for telecoms.

"This feels a lot like the early days of the Internet," says Tropos Networks CEO Tom Ayers, a Silicon Valley entrepreneur whose wi-fi firm has expanded into the grid. "Because of the stimulus, we've moved beyond the early adopters. Around here, we talk a lot about 'crossing the chasm.' This market is crossing the chasm."

Silver Spring is the kind of cutting-edge green business that Obama has in mind when he talks about the post-bubble economy. Founded in 2003 by software engineers who realized no one was building networks for the grid, it has raised $300 million and deployed ten million advanced meters worldwide. The smart grid now reminds the bearded, ponytailed Vaswani of the Internet circa 1994; just as the browsers of that era foreshadowed online banking and video on demand, today's smart meters are harbingers of smart refrigerators that can adjust their temperatures according to price signals sent by utilities—I saw a prototype in FPL's lab—and software that alerts you when an appliance needs to be fixed.

"I try not to use the word 'explode' when I talk about the electric grid, but that's what's happening," Vaswani says. "There was a lot of talking, then a lot of thinking, and the Recovery Act pushed this over the edge into doing."

Gotcha!

"It's hard to amaze me," said Glenn Beck, who actually professes to be amazed all the time, "but this is one of the more amazing stories about what our country and our government has turned into." Beck loved stimulus stories—the nonexistent subsidies to ACORN, the porn he imagined the NEA must be funding, a bogus report of a $1.4 million door at a military base—and this was a stimulus story about green energy, another one of his go-to targets. But it was really a story about the corruption of the Obama administration, his favorite source of amazement. His guest was fellow Fox personality John Stossel, who told the saga of Serious Materials, another Silicon Valley firm that manu-factured energy-efficient windows. Stossel announced that Serious had been mentioned in a speech by Obama, which was true, and visited by Biden, also true, before receiving "a special tax credit that goes to no other window company," which wasn't true at all.

"We found that the head of the weatherization department of the Department of Energy is sleeping with the vice president of policy for the company!" Stossel said.

"John, the arrogance of these people astounds me," Beck said.

Yes, Cathy Zoi was sleeping with a Serious executive. They were married. But Zoi hadn't started yet at Energy when Obama and Biden were citing her husband's firm as an eco-friendly innovator. And Seri-ous never got special treatment from Zoi or anyone else, just a green manufacturing tax credit that other window makers received as well. A geologist by training, Zoi had led a clean-tech fund in Australia and had developed the Energy Star program for energy-efficient appliances in George H. W. Bush's administration. But to Beck and Stossel, she was just a Gore lackey who had run his Alliance for Climate Protection and was now scamming taxpayers in the name of eco-nonsense. "She said she's going to recuse herself from anything having to do with this com-pany, but basically she would have to recuse herself from her whole job," Stossel said. "Her whole job is weatherization!" More lies: Zoi oversaw all of Energy's efficiency and renewables programs, and anyway, Serious windows were too expensive for the home weatherization program.

But in Beck's antigovernment universe, wisps of smoke were always evidence of a raging fire. To Beck's delight, Zoi left government to run a clean-energy fund for the left-wing financier George Soros. And speak-ing of dynamic women hounded out of public service, Claire Broido Johnson is now an executive at Serious Materials, where she's launched a new program to finance energy efficiency retrofits at Fortune 500 companies.

Buried under Beck's rants, there was a legitimate debate about the

federal role in promoting efficiency. "Do you think maybe the government has gotten too big when we have someone we pay in tax dollars
in charge of weather stripping?" he asked. It was a fair question, despite
the unfair description of Zoi's job. The Obama administration argued
that weatherization, in addition to saving money for families less fortunate than Beck, promoted our national, environmental, and economic
security by reducing our energy consumption and carbon footprint
while providing stimulus and creating jobs. But Beck—and the Republican leadership—rarely addressed this kind of argument on the merits.
Instead, they created a caricature of the stimulus as a political con, a
payoff to ACORN, a sleazy collection of sweetheart deals. Yeah, right,
"weatherization." Obviously, some lefties must be sleeping together.

The Republican case against the Recovery Act—beyond the overriding
fact that the recovery didn't feel like a recovery—still consisted mostly
of cats and dogs. The lead inquisitors were Senators Tom Coburn and
John McCain, whose reports crammed with allegedly wasteful stimulus
projects gave the right its anti-stimulus talking points.

Many of the projects they singled out were badly distorted, like
a $54 million grant for a Napa Valley wine train, which was actually
a flood control project for the entire valley, or a $10 million grant to
renovate "an abandoned train station that hasn't been used in 30 years,"
when in fact its ridership had almost doubled in five years. Other
projects sounded truly wasteful, like a $25,000 arts grant for an anti-
imperialist puppet show. Quite a few of the projects had already been
canceled by the administration, like a guardrail for a dried-out Oklahoma lakebed. But the facts didn't matter much. The point was that
government can't do anything right, and Obama is tossing around your
hard-earned money like a degenerate gambler.

To Coburn and McCain, the green-energy revolution was nothing
more than a costly joke on taxpayers. In one report, their number-
one boondoggle was a $5 million grant to retrofit an "almost empty"
Tennessee mall to run on geothermal power; it was almost empty because it was being redeveloped. The top ten also included a $787,250

smart grid pilot program on Martha's Vineyard, because Coburn and McCain apparently thought "smart appliances" that utilities could adjust remotely—"Big Brother–style"—sounded creepy. In fact, most utilities already use "demand response" for commercial customers like Walmart, paying them for the right to tweak thermostats a few degrees or dim lights a bit during peak demand. It's voluntary, it's unobtrusive, and it's the future of the grid, saving customers money, helping utilities meet peak loads without building new power plants, and fueling a multibillion-dollar industry devoted entirely to demand response. Meanwhile, GE is taking advantage of the same tax credits that helped Serious Materials in order to manufacture smart washers and dryers in Senator McConnell's hometown of Louisville, creating over eight hundred green jobs.

But that's a complex story about change. The Republicans made the Recovery Act into a simple story about the fleecing of America, about small-business loans for martini bars and taxpayer-funded studies of malt liquor consumption, the Icelandic environment in the Viking Age, and the division of labor in ant colonies.

Medical research may be the best example of the gap between the substance and perception of the Recovery Act. Senator Specter's insistence on the $10 billion windfall for NIH is already financing breakthroughs, especially in the futuristic field of genomics and personalized medicine. Stimulus-funded studies have already pinpointed genetic variations linked to Alzheimer's disease, a rare birth defect called Kabuki syndrome, and a range of childhood brain disorders. The Recovery Act has also produced new advances in hip replacements, new proof that brains of different ethnicities are made of the same genetic building blocks, and new treatments of epilepsy, ovarian cancer, and lung cancer. It has accelerated the Cancer Genome Atlas, so that scientists will have a comprehensive catalogue of mutations associated with the twenty most common cancers by 2014. And NIH director Francis Collins, the former leader of the Human Genome Project, says the stimulus is producing technological advances that are swiftly driving down the costs of genomic research, so that standard patient records could soon include a full genetic portrait.

"This could be a tipping point for personalized medicine," Collins says. "The stimulus really created space for the out-of-the-box research that doesn't get support when budgets are tight. You'll hear about some game-changers."

So far, Americans have heard about research like a $144,541 Wake Forest University primate study of cocaine's effect on a brain chemical called glutamate. Or as McCain and Coburn described the research: "Monkeys Get High for Science." Collins says the study could provide vital insight into the science of addiction, and it's not the kind of experiment that can be conducted on humans. He also points out that research can provide just as much stimulus as tax cuts; NIH's Recovery dollars would create or save fifty thousand jobs. But coked-up monkeys sound funny—and so do studies of "hook-up behavior" by drunken co-eds, the effect of methamphetamines on the sex drives of rats, and a $221,355 investigation into why young men don't like to wear condoms. Whenever White House officials heard those stories, they stifled curses about their new Democratic friend Arlen Specter.

"If you took all the negative clips about the Recovery Act, the biggest pile would be the NIH studies, the teen sex habits and cocaine monkeys," Ron Klain says. "And Republicans say: See? It's classic government waste. Well, Specter was the sixtieth flipping vote! Without cocaine monkeys, there's no tax cuts and no roads."

Of course, the monkeys would have languished in Republican press releases and right-wing blogs if the media hadn't found them irresistible. When it came to the stimulus, the national press was almost all-gotcha-all-the-time, missing the forest for the $564,635 grant to help undergraduates study Costa Rica's trees.

There is only one congressional district in North Dakota, but according to the first batch of Recovery Act data posted on recovery.gov in October 2009, the stimulus sent $2 million to its 99th district. South Carolina's 7th district was credited with $27 million, even though it was eliminated in 1930. And most of Montana's stimulus jobs were supposedly created in its "00" district.

"Exclusive: Jobs 'Saved or Created' in Congressional Districts That

Don't Exist," ABC News reported. Gotcha! The $6.4 billion the stimulus purportedly distributed to "phantom districts" became a huge national story.

In fact, no money was distributed to phantom districts. There were just some clerical glitches in the 131,000 reports that stimulus recipients had filed that fall, and the independent Recovery Accountability and Transparency Board had posted them to the new website without vetting their accuracy. The mistakes were soon corrected, but the uproar continued. Welcome to the age of federal transparency.

"To read some coverage, one might conclude that a scandal worthy of Sherlock Holmes had befallen the Recovery program," the stimulus watchdog Earl Devaney wrote. "Not really—just critics hyperventilating."

The Recovery Act's unprecedented transparency was yet another reflection of Obama's vision of change, backing up his good-government rhetoric about sunlight being the best disinfectant. As a senator, Obama had teamed up with Senator Coburn himself on a "Google for Government" bill that created the first searchable website for federal spending. After his election as president, he insisted the stimulus should go even further to help Americans track every dime online.

This noble effort handed Coburn and other critics a convenient sledgehammer to bash the Recovery Act. As Glenn Beck put it: "Now you can go right online and see how they're peeing your money away!" Congressman Wilson, just two months after his "You lie!" outburst, declared the phantom districts were evidence that "the government website charged with reporting waste, fraud, and abuse is its very own worst offender." The comedian Stephen Colbert, in character as a right-wing blowhard, fulminated that the stimulus was creating jobs for "leprechaun polishers" and "Yeti podiatrists." Even Democratic allies like David Obey blasted the Obama administration, which didn't manage the website and didn't control Devaney. "The administration owes itself, the Congress and every American a commitment to work night and day to correct the ludicrous mistakes," Obey fulminated.

It was just one more example of no good stimulus deed going unpunished. "Everybody says oh, transparency, that's good government, that's a good thing," Biden says. "Hell, transparency is costly. Every wart, you see."

The press had a field day with the jobs data in those 131,000 initial reports, even in districts that existed. It seemed like every investigative reporter in America was exposing saved jobs that hadn't really been in danger, created jobs that weren't really stimulus jobs, raises being counted as jobs, and jobs claims that made no sense. When the administration intervened to scrub a dozen blatantly unrealistic recipient reports from the website—one community college's $27,000 stimulus grant supposedly saved 14,500 jobs—Republicans again cried foul. "Now we learn that OMB is playing an active role in trying to filter information," howled Congressman Darrell Issa, the ranking member of the House oversight committee. How dare Obama remove all that erroneous data before he could be properly ridiculed for failing to remove it? When Devaney and other independent watchdogs testified that there was nothing nefarious about the problems, that recipients were just as likely to understate the jobs they were creating or saving, the media just spun that as more evidence of miscues. "Undercounting Concerns Stimulus Investigators," USA Today reported.

Recipients were obviously confused about how to report a saved or created job, and Devaney was confused, too. So the administration simplified the definition for the next round of reporting to include any job directly funded by the stimulus. After that, the data problems dissipated. In the first round, Devaney's "Wall of Shame" exposed over four thousand recipients who failed to file timely reports. Over the next two years, those numbers declined over 90 percent.

But again, the PR damage was done. Macroeconomists believed the stimulus had already saved or created one million jobs, but the coverage revolved around phantom jobs in phantom districts. It was no coincidence that a poll during the controversy found 62 percent of the public thought the Recovery Act had hurt the economy or made no difference.

The tone was set the day Obama signed the Recovery Act, when OMB went live with a rudimentary version of recovery.gov that it had created in just four weeks. The Associated Press story announcing this experiment in government openness was headlined, "Promises, Promises: Web Site Likely to Fall Short." Why? Because Obama had said Americans would be able to track money spent in their community—and on the first day, recovery.gov only offered state-by-state estimates for stimulus spending and job creation, without breaking it down locally.

That's because no one had any clue how much money any particular community would get from the earmark-free bill. The AP conceded this: "The problem facing the administration is that it's impossible to put decisions on the website that have not yet been made." The 2.0 version of recovery.gov would break down contracts by Zip Code, with GIS mapping to show visually where money was being spent. Transparency advocates say the Recovery Act's sunlight efforts, while imperfect, are by far the best ever. "It's a sea change," says OMB Watch director Gary Bass. *Governing* magazine concluded "the stimulus has done more to promote transparency at almost all levels of government than any piece of legislation in recent memory."

On Day One, though, the AP was already writing its obituary for Obama's promise of greater openness. From the start, the narrative was: What a mess.

My favorite example of this narrative was a *USA Today* story from May 2009, as the stimulus was starting to accelerate. Despite the Biden Bridge stumble, Pennsylvania transportation officials told the paper they expected a "record building program" that summer. But when it came to the Recovery Act, every silver lining had a cloud. The headline was: "Traffic Set to Slow as Stimulus Gears Up."

This was not isolated nitpicking. Three weeks later, the same reporter, Brad Heath, had a new scoop: "Stimulus Projects Bypass Hard-Hit States." Gotcha! But he only analyzed 0.5 percent of the Recovery Act, an absurdly tiny sample. His primary example of a victimized state was Michigan, even though he acknowledged that its officials were "generally satisfied with the pace of federal aid." He didn't mention that the

Energy Department had just announced its advanced battery grants, and five of the six largest factories would be built in Michigan.

In September, Heath was at it again: "Pace of New Stimulus Spending Slows." Gotcha! But as he conceded, that was only because the feds had finished cutting multibillion-dollar fiscal relief checks to the states. In reality, the pace of new projects was, as he had already reported, gearing up. Later that fall, Heath tweaked the Recovery Act for sending too large a share of its highway dollars to rural America: "Stimulus Takes Detour Around Ailing Metropolitan Areas." This was a more plausible critique, but it would have been more compelling if Heath hadn't published another gotcha making the opposite case three months later: "Metro Areas Get Chunk of Rural Stimulus Aid."

Maybe it's unfair to single out Heath, who wasn't the only aggressive investigative reporter trying to dig up dirt on the Recovery Act. I've been a grouchy journalist for two decades; I'm familiar with the ethic that if you don't have anything nice to say, put it in the paper. Reporters are supposed to follow the money, hold public officials accountable, and shine a light on failure; investigations that don't uncover wrongdoing don't make Page One or win prizes. But something about the stimulus seemed to turn reporters into runaway prosecutors, desperate to pin something on their target. Another example from my overflowing gotcha file: A month after a ProPublica article claimed the weatherization program was too focused on cold regions, a *New York Times* article suggested it was too focused on warm regions. "The nation spends twice as much on heating as on cooling," the *Times* declared. Yes, and the program was spending twice as much in regions that relied more on heating—neither too hot, nor too cold, but just right.

When programs like weatherization had early problems, the media pounced; when the problems got fixed, the media were nowhere to be seen. For example, Wall Street firms initially charged high fees for underwriting Build America Bonds, prompting a slew of stories portraying the program as a backdoor bailout. But underwriters often charge high fees for new products; the fees gradually came down to the level of regular municipal bonds. And Build America Bonds were far more successful than even the White House had hoped, financing over $180 billion worth of school renovations, road improvements, and other local infrastructure projects, from a seismic retrofit of the Bay Bridge to a widening of the New Jersey Turnpike to a new performing arts center in Alliance, Nebraska. They were like a Recovery Act tucked inside the Recovery Act. But the media weren't interested in that story.

They were more interested in digging up dirt—and when they couldn't find dirt, they trafficked in innuendo about "potential conflicts" that "raised questions." My beloved alma mater, the *Washington Post,* was a serial offender, publishing reams of articles implying that the Recovery Act's green investments were somehow sketchy. One story tarred CleanTech for Obama cofounder Sanjay Wagle—a green true believer who had worked at a venture capital firm before advising Rogers at the Energy Department—because his former firm had invested in a few stimulus-funded companies. There are thousands of stimulus-funded companies, and most venture capital firms invested in a few of them. Wagle was dinged because his former firm had stakes in Tesla and BrightSource, which both received hefty loans. But he had nothing to do with those funding decisions, or with the loan program in general. Wagle made a real financial sacrifice to enter public service, cutting his salary in half, cashing out his holdings at pennies on the dollar to avoid conflicts of interest, only to get smeared for all his hard work.

Local reporters often wrote positively about stimulus spending (a nuclear cleanup, a sewer plant) they saw in their communities, and issue-oriented reporters often wrote thoughtfully about stimulus programs (Race to the Top, high-speed rail) related to their issues. Business reporters wrote about the stimulus as a straightforward economic phenomenon; more of it boosts growth, less of it creates slack. But when national reporters focused on "the stimulus," their coverage was overwhelmingly negative. White House officials understood that their recovery bill wasn't likely to get much positive coverage when the recovery was so weak. Still, the one-sided groupthink drove them crazy. "The journalism was amazingly lazy," Pfeiffer complains. "It's easy to look at a super-long list, find something that adds up to one one-hundredth of

1 percent of the money, and make it sound silly." Unemployment was higher than the Romer-Bernstein report predicted, so everything about the stimulus was by definition a failure?

Yes, pretty much. The public debate over the stimulus was over, and the stimulus had lost. Even Democrats had stopped trying to defend it. Under the radar, though, it was just starting to drive change.

The Race

As a boy in Chicago, Arne Duncan spent countless hours at his mom's after-school program for inner-city kids. He wrote his Harvard thesis about the dreams of the urban underclass. He believed that every child could learn, that poverty wasn't destiny, that tough standards and great teachers and evidence-based innnovation could turn around hellish schools. Some of the things he believed sounded corny, but his pickup hoops buddy in the White House believed them, too. Race to the Top would give them a chance to back up their beliefs with $4.35 billion.

Secretary Duncan wouldn't get to pick the Race's winners—the judges would be independent—but he would get to write the rules of the competition, to make sure the states that pursued the reforms he favored would receive extra points. He wanted to be prescriptive, because he wanted to drive lasting change, not just help states extend school hours and restore music classes until the stimulus ran out. He believed that by the time the Race was over, it would shake up education.

That belief turned out to be inaccurate. The Race shook up education before it even started.

For example, Duncan believed in metrics as strongly as he believed in anything. He knew test scores couldn't tell the whole story about a student, her teacher, or her school, but they told a story nonetheless. So he wanted the Race to encourage states not only to collect data but to use it—to intervene with struggling students and underperforming schools, even to decide how much to pay teachers. His advisers asked: What about states with firewalls? Duncan had no idea what they meant. They explained that states like California and New York—both Democratic states with powerful teachers unions—had prohibited linking test scores to teacher pay. "Are you joking?" Duncan asked. "That's unacceptable." He couldn't force states to change laws, but he decreed that states would be ineligible for the Race if they didn't get rid of their firewalls. So they all got rid of their firewalls. States like Delaware and Illinois—again, Democratic states with strong unions—passed laws *requiring* the use of test scores in teacher evaluations. In Illinois, the reforms passed with only one dissenting vote in the entire legislature.

"When I was there, I couldn't have gotten a unanimous vote that it was August!" Duncan marvels.

Before the first Race grant was awarded, forty states adopted Duncan-friendly education reforms to ensure their eligibility or improve their chances of winning. They removed or loosened caps on charter schools. They expanded testing regimes. They made it easier to fire bad teachers and reward good ones. And a bipartisan coalition of forty-five states began collaborating on uniform K–12 curriculum standards to prepare students for college and careers, shattering an age-old tradition of local control.

"That was the third rail in education. You couldn't even talk about it," Duncan says. A former pro basketball player in Australia, Duncan attributes the shift in the zeitgeist to the power of competition. "There's been more reform in the last year than we've seen in decades, and we haven't spent a dime yet," he told me early in 2010.

The mere existence of the School Improvement Grants to finance radical reforms at failing schools was also driving change. In Central Falls, Rhode Island, the teachers union refused to endorse a turnaround plan for a troubled high school that included longer hours. So the school board fired the school's entire faculty, and Obama voiced his support. "If a school continues to fail its students year after year, then there's got to be a sense of accountability," he said.

Investing in Innovation, the initiative for scaling up proven reforms—reading programs, teacher ratings, successful approaches to gifted or delayed students—was also starting to shake up the status quo.

James Shelton, the assistant secretary overseeing the grants, was a former Gates Foundation executive, a tall, energetic, charismatic African-American who reminded me of a younger version of the president. He explained his vision in the data-driven language of venture philanthropy, diagramming "Paths to Innovation" on his office whiteboard. But he also spoke the language of inspiration; he had an "Imagine the Possibilities" poster on the wall near his whiteboard.

"We're creating a pipeline of innovation in education, and that's never existed in history," Shelton said. "There's just incredible demand for new ways of doing business." Investing in Innovation would receive over 1,000 applications for just 49 grants.

These programs were already transforming the national conversation about schools, swinging many Democratics over to the side of reform, inspiring high-profile debates about and within teachers unions, drawing praise from Republicans like Schwarzenegger, former Florida governor Jeb Bush, and Indiana governor Mitch Daniels. But it failed to transform the national conversation about the stimulus, which retained its reputation as a partisan Democratic hack job.

If Secretary Duncan was the kind of cosmopolitan forty-something Harvard wonk you'd expect to find in the Obama cabinet, Ray LaHood seemed out of place, a lumbering sixty-something Republican pol from Peoria who looked like Abe Vigoda in *The Godfather*, a former civics teacher who had worked his way through junior college and Bradley University. He was not a transportation expert, unless bringing highway pork home to his district counted as expertise. He only got the job because he was the closest Republican friend of Rahm Emanuel, who originally wanted to make him agriculture secretary. Transportation reformers were horrified, dismissing LaHood as "an unbelievably disastrous pick," "status quo we can believe in," "same.gov." But he became a passionate Obama loyalist, calling out stimulus critics in his own party, defending the Recovery Act as if it were his own child. "No earmarks, no boondoggles, no sweetheart deals," he told me.

In his office, LaHood has a photo of himself walking in front of the president, running interference on an outreach mission to his former House Republican colleagues. "Great downfield blocking!" Obama scribbled. One former colleague jokes that if LaHood had been at Jonestown, he would've been the first one dead. But LaHood has been more than a stand-up guy. He has been almost as energetic a reformer as Duncan. At a department known for mindlessly shoveling money to states to pour concrete, he became a vocal advocate for sustainability and "livability," transit-oriented development and smart growth. The bicycling community embraced him as a hero; Lance Armstrong sang his praises on Twitter. LaHood even got to create his own race to the top, courtesy of the Recovery Act.

That was the TIGER program, which LaHood and his staff designed to reward nontraditional projects with the highest economic and environmental benefits—and to start changing the culture of the department. "The beauty of TIGER was you didn't have to go through the rigmarole of the bureaucracy," LaHood says. "It's just about solving problems." LaHood brought together volunteers from all the department's silos into "TIGER teams" to judge the competition, empowering bureaucrats to think seriously about national needs instead of just making sure projects had submitted their minority hiring plans and traffic studies.

"We're creating a new normal, where we reward excellence, where substance trumps process," undersecretary for policy Roy Kienitz told me. "The culture of TIGER is infecting our entire world."

Nationally, the demand for the new approach was overwhelming; TIGER received $38 worth of applications for every $1 in grants. And the competition produced some real surprises. For example, the three largest first-round grants ended up going to freight rail projects, which hadn't received federal aid in years. The TIGER teams realized that the public benefits of, say, elevating overpasses to allow the double-stacking of cargo would be huge, reducing shipping costs, energy use, and highway congestion by shifting freight away from long-haul trucks. And since the projects had obvious private benefits as well, railroads matched the grants almost dollar for dollar. "It just hadn't fit into any boxes before TIGER," says federal railroad administrator Joe Szabo.

LaHood also emerged as the leading evangelist for Obama's high-speed rail initiative. And just as Duncan used the Race to promote education reform before the grants even went out, LaHood used the lure of high-speed money to promote transportation reform. The best example was in Florida, where even Republican congressmen who voted against the stimulus signed a letter urging LaHood to approve a bullet train between Tampa and Orlando, predicting it would "provide significant economic and environmental benefits to the state, as well as a showcase for the potential of high speed rail in the United States."

In many ways, Florida looked like an ideal high-speed launching pad. It's flat, which meant low construction costs. It's densely populated. It's a tourist mecca, attracting millions of foreigners who ride fast trains at home. The initial leg between Tampa and Orlando included a stop at Disney World, making the economics much more attractive. And for quirky historical reasons, it was the nation's shovel-readiest project. Jeb Bush had shut down a statewide high-speed rail initiative when he was governor, but at the time a rail-obsessed Tampa civic leader named Ed Turanchik—known as Choo Choo—had been leading an effort to attract the 2012 Olympics to the area. He persuaded Bush the bid would be doomed without a Tampa–Orlando train, so planning for that line was allowed to continue. By the time the Recovery Act passed, the route from downtown Tampa to the Orlando airport along the Interstate 4 median had almost all its land and permits in place. The real prize would be extending the line to Miami, connecting Disney to South Beach, competing with seventy-seven daily flights between south and central Florida. But Tampa–Orlando was Obama's best chance for an early win.

There was just one problem. High-speed rail works when it's connected to public transit, not when you have to drive to the station on one end and hail a cab at the other. But Florida's Republican legislature had blocked a new Orlando-area commuter rail system, and shredded funding for an existing Miami-area line. So in October, LaHood flew to Orlando and delivered a blunt message to the region's civic leaders: "Get your act together." If Florida didn't get serious about commuter rail, he warned, it wouldn't get high-speed rail. This was another oversubscribed program, with $7 in applications for every $1 in grants, so LaHood could afford to be selective.

LaHood had provided similar ultimatums to New York, Georgia, and Texas, to no avail. But Florida's traditionally loony-tunes political system responded. Governor Crist called a special session, and the legislature overwhelmingly reversed itself on commuter rail, and even created a fund for high-speed rail.

"Las Vegas oddsmakers would've given a billion to one," Turanchik told me. "This project has united Republicans and Democrats, labor and business. It's giving people hope."

It seemed like the next stop would be change.

FIFTEEN

Gas Versus Brakes

Remember when Christy Romer told her husband that if the jobless rate hit 10 percent, the White House would have bigger problems than her wrong 8 percent prediction?

She wasn't wrong about that.

Unemployment hit double digits in October 2009, and Obama's approval ratings slipped below 50 percent for the first time. Democrats promptly suffered humiliating losses in governor's races in Virginia and New Jersey. The economy was growing, corporate profits were rebounding, and the long-term outlook was improving. But as the New Dealer Harry Hopkins once said, people don't eat in the long run. They eat every day. With 27 million workers now unemployed or underemployed, the Republican drumbeat continued: Where are the jobs? Democrats were asking, too. And at the White House, Romer was pushing for more stimulus that could create more jobs.

Romer, the Great Depression historian, had been thinking a lot about the New Deal, especially direct government jobs programs like the WPA. She loved pointing out that the Roosevelt administration had managed to hire over four million Americans in the winter of 1934. Obama hadn't proposed any federal hiring programs in the Recovery Act, because temporarily growing the government seemed like a logistical and political nightmare. But the stimulus did include a $1.3 billion welfare-to-work experiment that helped states subsidize 260,000 private sector jobs, an impressive $5,000 per job. That was a drop in an immense bucket, but it illustrated the possibilities. At one point, Romer started calling the Agriculture Department and other agencies just to see how many new employees they could put to work in 2010 if funding were available.

"They'd say, 'Oh, we could hire a lot, maybe even 20,000!'" Romer says. "That's a long way from four million."

Jared Bernstein, the economic team's most ardent Keynesian, was thinking along similar lines. Despite all the vitriol about Obama's big-government liberalism, the U.S. public sector was shrinking. The Recovery Act's aid to states limited the shrinkage, but governors and mayors were still slashing services and jobs to balance their budgets, and states now faced yet another $200 billion shortfall. That fall, Bernstein pitched Biden chief of staff Ron Klain on three ways to boost government employment: More direct aid to save more public employee jobs. New grants to help cities hire extra staff for menial tasks like cleaning up blighted neighborhoods and digitizing public records. And extended deployments for temporary census workers to create a National Inventory of Structures.

A national inventory of what?

"You're kidding, right?" Klain interrupted.

Nope. For $1 billion, 750,000 temporary census workers could stay on payroll for two extra months to create a "geo-coded" database of every structure in America. This could be used for "improved statistics on economic development and land use," as a "resource for local planning departments to identify issues and opportunities," as a "source of aggregate data . . ."

"What are you trying to do to us?" Klain groaned.

Alas, people counters would not be converted into structure counters.

"I think we could sell a plan to build buildings," Klain said. "We cannot sell a plan to *count* buildings." In fact, Obama's political team wasn't too keen on trying to build buildings, either.

"There wasn't a lot of appetite for a new WPA," Bernstein says.

After the Recovery Act passed, the White House's primary focus quickly shifted to health care. But in Washington, the stimulus debate never really ended. The question of whether to push for more fiscal stimulus or pivot to deficit reduction—more gas or more brake—would be the central question of Obama's first term.

Obama's economic team basically agreed that in a slack economy, the ideal approach would be more short-term stimulus, along with a credible commitment to medium-term deficit reduction—gas now, brake later. But with the nation in a sour mood and the Recovery Act perceived as a failure, Obama's political team didn't see any way to push a second stimulus package through Congress, much less a New Deal–style government jobs program. Even within the increasingly fractious economic team, there was intense debate about the relative merits of gas and brake, and how aggressively to press the pedals. Romer and Bernstein wanted to keep jamming the accelerator to boost growth and jobs. They did not want to repeat FDR's error of 1937, when his premature embrace of deficit reduction derailed a promising recovery. Larry Summers also advocated short-term stimulus, although he was often dismissive of actual stimulus proposals. Peter Orszag and Tim Geithner, while not necessarily opposed to short-term gas, emphasized the importance of tapping the medium-term brakes, to slow the growth of the deficit and send a fiscally responsible message to the markets. Orszag often suggested that commitments to rein in red ink down the road could themselves provide stimulus, by boosting the confidence of businesses and bondholders.

Meanwhile, Republican leaders were calling for immediate and massive spending cuts, which they claimed would create jobs by . . . well, the mechanism was never clear. Economically, it was hard to see how slamming the brakes would make the car go faster. As Governor Sanford had acknowledged, the country-doctor approach of strict austerity, whatever its long-term merits, was a prescription for short-term pain. But politically, the notion that government should skimp in hard times, just as families and businesses do, had real emotional appeal. Refusing to spend money the country didn't have sounded appealing in theory, even if in practice it would mean sucking cash out of the economy, cutting aid to desperate families, and rolling back long-awaited infrastructure projects.

This debate had been brewing since the transition, and Obama could see both sides. He cared about jobs and he cared about deficits. His emphasis shifted over time, and helped determine the arc of his presidency.

"It's Not Where the Electorate Is"

It can't be said often enough: President Bush inherited a budget in the black, and bequeathed Obama a record-obliterating tide of red ink. In 2001, the projected ten-year surplus had been $5.6 trillion, enough to fund seven Recovery Acts and still balance the budget. In 2009, Bush's gift bag included a ten-year deficit of $8 trillion. Eliminating the entire U.S. military wouldn't have closed that gap.

Of course, the gift bag also included a dizzying economic nosedive. This not only created the jobs crisis, it was the main driver—even more than Bush's tax cuts, wars, and all-around fiscal recklessness—of short-term deficits, because unemployed workers and unprofitable firms pay fewer taxes and receive more government aid. So for Obama, tackling the jobs crisis was not only much more urgent than tackling the deficit, it was the best way to start tackling the deficit. By avoiding a depression, the stimulus would keep the fiscal outlook merely unsustainable rather than unsalvageable. "When the economy was falling off the cliff, the Keynesian imperatives overshadowed everything," Bernstein says.

But Obama always expected to pivot to fiscal discipline once the recovery was in gear. Temperamentally, he was more of a brakes guy than a gas guy, more comfortable in the role of dad taking away the credit card than teenager binging at the mall. He seemed defensive about the stimulus, often noting that he never planned to start his presidency with a spending spree, complaining it reinforced the Republican narrative that he was a typical liberal Democrat. Deficit reduction better

suited his self-image as a centrist, a maker of hard choices, a cleaner of
Bush-era messes; he joked about his "inner Blue Dog." He had promised
"a new era of responsibility," which became the title of his budget plan.
He had pledged to rein in the out-of-control medical costs that imperiled America's long-term solvency, which was the main reason he risked
his presidency on health reform. And his pollsters were picking up the
same independent voter anger about spending and debt that Republicans were trying to exploit. Obama's political advisers, while opposed
to his plunge into the health care swamp, were keen for him to convey
concern about deficits in other ways. That's what led to the *Dave* fiasco.

Obama had also stocked his economic team with deficit-conscious
Bob Rubin disciples, who pressed him to do more than just convey
concern. Geithner and Orszag started preaching the gospel of the pivot
early in the transition, warning that exploding deficits could rattle markets and depress confidence; Orszag was also the leading advocate of
health reforms that could "bend the cost curve." Summers was on the
gas side of the gas-brakes debate, but his fifty-seven-page memo before
the December meeting in Chicago—which included input from the rest
of the team, but had his name on top—still urged Obama to start scaling back his campaign promises to prepare for a fiscally constrained future. And conveying concern was important, too. The Clinton veterans
all agreed that Obama needed to let the world know he was more than
a big spender. Sure enough, the president hosted a "fiscal responsibility
summit" a week after signing the stimulus, and vowed to slice the deficit in half by the end of his first term.

"The Clinton people were obsessed with deficit reduction from the
start," says one senior Obama aide. "They had that Rubinesque worldview."

Since it quickly became clear that the hole in demand was much
deeper than the Romer-Bernstein report suggested, some step-
on-the-gas advocates—including Romer and Bernstein—began pushing for more stimulus as early as that spring. Productive workers and
equipment were idle; federal borrowing costs were negligible; why
not put more money and more people to work? Orszag and Geithner

pushed back: Why not give the Recovery Act a chance to work? "At first, everyone said: This is going to get worse before it gets better, and we'll have to ride it out like a bad fever," says one Orszag aide. "Then when it started to get worse, there was this mad scramble to find something else to do. Wait! We knew this was coming! Why are we going nuts?" Even some officials on the gas side of the debate thought that politically, calling for a second stimulus so quickly would sound like an admission of failure, a validation of Republican attacks. They figured that once the Recovery Act started generating jobs and visible progress, there would be more appetite for more stimulus on Capitol Hill.

"The theory was, once we could show a demonstrable climb, people would see the train was moving, and then we could shovel more coal in the engine," Klain says.

The brake advocates also kept raising the specter that bond markets would go haywire if the president didn't assure them he wasn't a rabid spendaholic. The Clinton veterans all recalled how focusing on deficits over investments had helped keep interest rates low and bond markets happy during the 1990s. Secretary Geithner often seemed to suggest that unless Obama pledged to reduce deficits to precisely 3 percent of GDP, investors would suddenly lose faith in the dollar. After staring into the abyss of the financial crisis for a year, Geithner wanted to avoid another disaster at any cost; a second stimulus that might shave a point off the unemployment rate didn't seem worth even a small additional risk of potential chaos. Of course, fretting about market stability and tail risks was part of the treasury secretary's job description, but Orszag made similar arguments, and even Summers sometimes echoed them.

"I understand that there's a treasury secretary," Romer complained during one of these discussions. "I'm tired of having three."

Obama's more gas-inclined advisers sometimes felt like they were battling an invisible austerity scold named Bond Market, who sounded like an irrational worrywart. The actual bond market seemed perfectly calm about the actual deficit. The actual bond market wasn't clamoring for austerity that could nip the recovery in the bud.

"Tim was always warning that the bond markets were about to freak out and punish us," one White House adviser says. "Really? If we commit to 4 percent of GDP instead of 3 percent in ten years, everything goes to hell? But he's the treasury secretary. If he says we've got to do x and y to calm the markets, what are we supposed to say?"

What Romer tried to say was: High unemployment is a disaster, too. At the annual economic symposium in Jackson Hole in August 2009, Romer was appalled by the aura of triumphalism, as if policymakers could rest easy now that they had saved the banks and averted a worst-case scenario. Businesses weren't hiring, and long-term joblessness was surging. There were real people behind all that data, and workers who stay out of the labor force for extended periods tend to suffer for the rest of their careers. Every point the government could cut off the unemployment rate would relieve untold human suffering. Romer kept reminding the Clintonites on the team: This isn't 1993. It made sense to do fiscal contraction when unemployment was 7 percent and falling, but it's 10 percent and rising. At one White House meeting, when Geithner described stimulus as a sugar rush, Romer shot back that it was a necessary antibiotic for a sick patient, not some junk food lollipop for a child.

"We're not done!" she kept telling Obama.

Sometimes, these big-brained economists just seemed to be talking past each other. Orszag was close to Senator Kent Conrad and other budget-conscious centrists, and he kept insisting the Hill had no appetite whatsoever for an aggressive second stimulus. During one White House debate, he also argued that since Congress would never pass anything close to what was needed to plug the output gap, there was no point pushing an inadequate half-measure that would barely make a dent in the problem if it did pass. He now says he wasn't arguing that $100 billion in extra stimulus wouldn't help; he just thought a "naked" stimulus proposal that wasn't coupled with deficit reduction would be doomed. But Romer thought he was arguing that since Congress wouldn't plug the entire gap, there was no point trying to plug any of it, which seemed ridiculous. Why not reduce as much pain as possible? At one point, she thought the president was parroting Orszag's half-measure argument, and she blurted out: "That is oh, so wrong."

Obama raised an eyebrow. "Not just wrong, but oh, so wrong?"

In his early White House speeches, Obama had tried to explain counterintuitive Keynesian concepts like the need for public spending when private spending dried up. But he hadn't persuaded the public, and he had mostly stopped trying. He reminded his economic team that he was a pretty good communicator, and his stimulus message hadn't gotten through at all. He was learning, as presidents usually do, that the bully pulpit doesn't come with magical powers to change minds. The professor-in-chief wasn't inclined to deliver more edifying macroeconomic lectures that would drag down his popularity and decrease his chances of getting the rest of his agenda through Congress.

"Look, I get the Keynesian thing," he said. "But it's not where the electorate is."

It wasn't where Congress was, either. Moderate Democrats did not want to take another big-spending vote, especially if anything that could be attacked as "stimulus" was involved. "Nobody on the Hill would go near it, because the politics were so bad," Pfeiffer recalls. The problem boiled down to three words: Enough is enough. Romer found the situation intensely frustrating. Eighteen months earlier, the vague prospect of 6.5 percent unemployment had seemed so terrifying that President Bush, Speaker Pelosi, and Leader Boehner had worked together to jam stimulus through Congress. Now the nation yearned for the halcyon days of 6.5 percent, Democrats controlled Washington, and a second stimulus wasn't even worth discussing?

"There just wasn't any appetite," Gibbs says. "It wasn't like we had a meeting and said: Hey, should we do more? It was just: No. We'd have conversations, but they'd last ten seconds. Can we get it done? No. End of conversation."

Romer still tried to advocate for more stimulus at every opportunity, eventually prompting Obama into a rare flash of temper during a meeting that fall. "Enough!" the president shouted. "It's not going to happen!"

Substantively, the Recovery Act seemed to be doing exactly what it was supposed to do. "The accumulation of hard data and real-life experience has allowed dispassionate analysts to reach a consensus that the stimulus package, messy as it is, is working," the *New York Times* reported. But politically, "stimulus" was a dirty word. Even Democrats who wanted a second stimulus were joining the chorus trashing the first: not big enough, not focused enough, not creating enough jobs. The criticisms recalled the old joke about the bad restaurant whose portions were too small.

Biden finally called House majority leader Steny Hoyer to suggest that "it's working; we need more of it" would be a much smarter message than "it's failing; we need more of it."

"Joe was right," Hoyer says. "The Recovery Act was having a real effect. But it was hard to be too upbeat with 10 percent unemployment."

Obama's economic team had earned its reputation for dysfunction.

Everyone tussled with Summers, who no longer seemed to be controlling his inner Larry now that Obama had reappointed Chairman Bernanke to his dream job. Egregiously miscast as an honest broker, he was a jealous turf warrior, whining about breaches in protocol, limiting access to the president, insisting on first-among-equals status. At times he seemed almost pathologically argumentative, and his meetings often devolved into academic cage fights that made consensus even less likely. Orszag was even less popular among his colleagues, who resented his glowing geek-chic press attention, and thought his I'm-just-the-budget-guy pose masked a self-aggrandizing infighter. There was some Schadenfreude in the West Wing when tabloid gossips discovered that Orszag's ex-girlfriend had his "secret love child" just before he got engaged to another woman. "It was all so high school," says one administration economist. "I could never understand why these people were at each other's throats." Orszag later told me he never felt like himself inside the White House: "When everyone else in the sandbox is throwing mud, you start to say: Okay, this is how it's gonna be? Bring it on!" The team's incessant bickering and on-the-other-hand one-upmanship seemed to irritate Obama, whose absentee father, for whatever it's worth, had been an economist, too.

Often, the psychodrama was irrelevant background noise. Romer once stormed out of the White House after she felt Summers and

Geithner were marginalizing her, but Rahm immediately called to promise that it wouldn't happen again. When Summers froze Austan Goolsbee out of a key meeting on the auto bailout, Obama summoned him to the Oval Office to make sure his case against rescuing Chrysler got a fair hearing. No harm, insignificant fouls. But economists on both sides of the gas-brakes divide believe the team's dysfunction delayed the White House response to the soft economy during the miserable fall of 2009. The Summers style was to debate new ideas to death—one of his mantras was the Hippocratic oath to do no harm—which created a bias toward inaction. "The process just broke down completely," says one team member. "People say process doesn't matter, but jeez. We weren't that far apart on substance." Today, everyone on the team says they supported more short-term stimulus coupled with belt-tightening in the out years. But at the time, they couldn't get on the same page.

"Most of the time, we managed to work incredibly well together despite some tiffs," Romer says. "The squabbling that fall was a little more troublesome."

For example, when the team searched for new stimulus measures that could pass the timely-targeted-temporary test as well as the political realism test, it kept coming back to the business tax credit for new hires that Obama had proposed in Toledo during the campaign. Romer and her staff worked overtime to build a case for it. Geithner supported it, in part because two of his top aides, Gene Sperling and Alan Krueger, were in love with it. Orszag was fine with it, too. This time, the holdout was Summers. Even though he believed the economy needed more gas to reach "escape velocity," and his trusted deputy, Jason Furman, was another avid fan of the credit, the born contrarian kept offering objections: Firms were unlikely to hire as long as demand remained slack. Rahm didn't think Congress would go for anything but new infrastructure. CEOs were saying the tax credit wouldn't affect their hiring decisions.

Krueger conducted a quick survey of human resources managers, who suggested the credit would in fact promote hiring. But the debate never seemed to get anywhere.

"We can't keep going around in circles here," the president chastised the team.

What finally broke the logjam was double-digit unemployment. With speculation starting to build about a jobless recovery, the White House scheduled a jobs summit, which meant it would need to announce some jobs initiatives. At the summit, Obama made a pragmatic case for moderate gas now, moderate brake later. "It's not going to be possible for us to have a huge second stimulus, because, frankly, we just don't have the money," he said. But he warned that pivoting too hard toward deficit reduction could trigger a double-dip recession: "If we move too abruptly in that direction . . . then we're going to be in a negative spiral." He even used the car analogy, suggesting that he would love to "press the accelerator in terms of jobs growth," but that the tricky part would be knowing "when to apply the brakes in the out years."

In a speech a few days later at (where else?) Brookings, Obama made his pitch for more gas, outlining several tax cuts and spending ideas, including the hiring credit. He also suggested expanding several Recovery Act provisions: capital gains relief for small businesses, tax breaks for green manufacturers, infrastructure projects, and "Cash for Caulkers" tax credits for consumers who weatherized homes. It added up to nearly $200 billion in new stimulus, although no one in the White House dared call it that publicly.

But Obama's political team wanted him to use the State of the Union address to pivot to themes of spending restraint. There was some debate among the advisers whether voters truly cared about the deficit, or just said they cared as a way of expressing frustration about the economy. Either way, they figured Obama ought to show he cared, too. One internal memo warned that America's excitement about change had given way to a "resurgence of jaundice" about Washington. All the public could see was big spending, partisan squabbling, and rising unemployment.

Meanwhile, even though the jobless rate—that infernal lagging indicator—was still rising, Obama and his economic advisers were growing more confident that their medicine was working. The November jobs report was the best yet, with a loss of only eleven thousand jobs, down 98 percent from Obama's first month in office. Losing jobs at a dramatically slower rate is not the same thing as putting people back to work, but the trajectory felt promising. Romer hand-delivered the report to the president, and he gave her multiple hugs. "A thrilling moment," Romer recalls. Privately, Geithner was telling Obama the economy had turned the corner for good. "The deficit hawks thought we were on a path out of the woods," says one White House economist. "And in his heart, I think the president was a deficit hawk." Ultimately, the entire economic team signed off on a modest pivot toward austerity in the State of the Union. Even Summers, still a pessimista, figured the president signaling a desire to brake might actually provide political cover for Congress to provide a bit more gas.

In his speech, Obama proposed a three-year discretionary spending freeze that would start in 2011, which would be almost insignificant to the macroeconomy but sounded austere. He also announced he was creating a bipartisan deficit commission by executive order, which would anchor the political debate around budget cutting. (Congress had tried to create the commission through legislation, but McCain and other Republican cosponsors had scuttled it once Obama endorsed it.) The president even echoed the anti-Keynesian rhetoric commonly heard at Republican press events and Tea Party rallies: "Families across the country are tightening their belts and making tough decisions. The federal government should do the same."

The left was furious about his call for fiscal retrenchment, and wasn't appeased by his push for fiscal stimulus. "That was a ruinous moment," says Bob Borosage, a participant in the White House's weekly "Common Purpose" meetings with liberal activists. "Right there, he conceded the argument on the economy." Needless to say, his call for belt-tightening didn't satisfy conservatives, either. But Obama's aides figured the sulky reactions had more to do with suffering in the land than anything he said.

"At the end of the day, unemployment was 10 percent," Pfeiffer says.

"It doesn't matter if you're Bill Clinton or Ronald Reagan or Andrew Jackson, there's no message that's going to make you popular."

It was an odd moment. Polls suggested that Americans wanted stimulus—more road repaving and education funding and unemployment benefits—but they didn't want "stimulus." At the same time, they wanted "deficit reduction," but they didn't want the actual spending cuts or tax increases that could reduce the deficit. And while economic performance was improving, public approval of Obama's economic performance kept declining. Obama fatigue even spread to liberal Massachusetts. After Senator Kennedy died, an unknown Republican named Scott Brown won his seat, undoing the filibuster-proof Democratic majority and threatening to upend health care reform just before the finish line. The House and Senate had both passed reform bills, but it was unclear how they'd get a final version to Obama's desk.

Brown's victory didn't bode well for more stimulus, either. When he was asked about the economy, he declared the first stimulus had failed to create a single job.

In late January, the president visited the Chesapeake Machine Company in Baltimore to pitch his plan for a $33 billion hiring tax credit. After a tour through the noisy belly of the industrial beast, wearing blue protective glasses that looked like wraparound shades, Obama seemed energized by all the sawing and shearing and grinding of heavy equipment being made in America.

"It's nice to see a functioning, well-oiled machine," he bantered. "That's a nice change of pace from what we see in Washington."

Even with undivided government, the legislative process had little in common with an efficient assembly line, except for the grinding and noise. By 2010, it was clear that no matter what happened in the labor market, getting new stimulus through Congress—even business tax breaks that Republicans traditionally supported—would be far tougher than the Obama team had imagined in 2008. If the Recovery Act was the first hint, the battles over health care, cap-and-trade, and the deficit commission left no doubt: If the president was fer it,

Republicans would be agin it, even if they were fer it in the past. And Brown's victory meant Obama would again need at least some Republican support in the Senate. That would further limit his options for jobs bills.

Even Senate Democrats were divided about stimulus. For months, while Max Baucus was slow-walking his health care negotiations, Byron Dorgan had been a man on fire, telling his colleagues the same thing he told Obama: We've got to lead on jobs. In the fall, he and Dick Durbin led a series of brainstorming sessions, trying to unify the caucus around a Democratic jobs agenda. But at the final meeting in January, Baucus of all people showed up to propose a more bipartisan approach. "He basically threw his crowbar into the transmission," Dorgan says. Soon the caucus had two competing plans. Baucus and other centrists thought the Dorgan plan, heavy on spending, had no hope of sixty votes. Dorgan and other populists thought the Baucus plan, heavy on business tax cuts, was straight out of the trickle-down Republican playbook. Eventually, Majority leader Reid rejected both. He decided the only stimulus measures that could actually pass were a short unemployment insurance extension and an almost unrecognizable version of Obama's hiring credit, watered down and slimmed down to $13 billion.

For the White House, it was a letdown. But it was better than nothing.

Obama's critics on the left often claim he crippled his presidency by pushing too small a stimulus in early 2009, then failing to follow up with more stimulus in 2010. As one liberal economist puts it, the Recovery Act was Obama's version of Bush's "Mission Accomplished" moment in Iraq—and he didn't even follow up with a surge. But there weren't sixty votes for an economic surge. And the Republican minority was close to breaking the Senate filibuster record it set in the last congressional session, so legislation that didn't have sixty votes wasn't going to make it to Obama's desk.

In fact, one untold story of the 111th Congress is how much stimulus Obama did manage to wring out of that poorly oiled machine. "We never stopped planning and plotting and pushing for jobs bills," Bernstein says. In a hostile political climate, the president ended up supplementing the Recovery Act with about $200 billion in additional fiscal pop before the 2010 elections. So the left got its trillion-dollar stimulus after all.

It wasn't an easy lift. For example, Republicans filibustered a state aid bill designed to prevent more teacher layoffs, but a shrunken $23 billion version finally squeaked through the Senate when Snowe and Collins agreed to vote yes. It also took months to finagle two Republican votes for a $42 billion bill to cut taxes and expand credit for small businesses. Voinovich, the decisive vote on the small business bill, could not believe his party was marching in lockstep against "job creators," even though the bill—like the hiring credit and the state aid—was fully offset over 10 years.

"I said: What could be more Republican than that? But McConnell was furious with me," Voinovich says. "Come on. My good Republicans are dying on the vine, the banks are cutting off their credit, and you're telling me I can't do this for them? Oh, I didn't like that. Instead of doing what was right, partisan politics always came first."

Senate Republicans even fought Obama's efforts to extend unemployment benefits for victims of the Great Recession. In late 2009, GOP senators used procedural shenanigans to hold up an extension for a month—and then voted for it unanimously. "You can only categorize that as malicious mischief," Axelrod says. By mid-2010, even though unemployment was still 9.5 percent, with five times as many job applicants as openings, the Republican strategy had shifted from delay to all-out obstruction; Snowe and Collins were the only GOP senators to support another extension of unemployment benefits without offsetting cuts, which had never been required for emergency relief. Ben Nelson, the most conservative Democrat, had turned against unemployment insurance as well, so when Robert Byrd died in June, the Democrats could no longer break a filibuster. Two million laid-off workers had their benefits lapse before Byrd's replacement was appointed.

The Republican Party's newfound concern about deficits did not end its push for deficit-exploding tax cuts with no offsets. And it did not translate into a single vote for Obamacare, which the CBO projected would cut the deficit by $1 trillion over two decades. In fact, at the same time Republicans were slamming the president's leftist plot to create a government health plan, which Obamacare isn't, they were bashing his heartless cuts to Medicare, which actually is a government health plan. While some Republican positions were consistent with a desire to put the brakes on the deficit, they were all consistent with a desire to put the brakes on the president. The GOP had become the Groucho Marx character in *Horse Feathers*:

> *"Your proposition may be good,*
> *But let's have one thing understood,*
> *Whatever it is, I'm against it.*
> *And even when you've changed it or condensed it,*
> *I'm against it!"*

Rage on the Right, Whining on the Left

Bob Bennett was a loyal soldier in McConnell's army of No. The Utah senator voted against the stimulus, against the omnibus, against Obamacare. Bennett had been just as loyal a soldier in President Bush's army of Yes.

But to the Tea Party, that was no longer a point in Bennett's favor. The Republican base now mocked him as "Bailout Bob," the turncoat who voted for TARP. And while he was a solid conservative partisan, he wasn't an angry conservative partisan. He was pals with Biden, and described Obama as "misguided" rather than "socialist." He didn't seem to realize the Constitution was under assault. One leading Utah Republican told him: Bob, we want to see *passion*. At the state Republican convention, he tried to explain to the mad-as-hell grass roots that TARP had prevented a catastrophe, that the banks were paying back the money with interest.

"It was just: 'You betrayed us! You voted with Bush!'" Bennett says.

"I remember being at Republican conventions where people would say: 'Stand firm with Bush!' So I did, and now you hate me?"

The convention didn't even give Bennett a chance to defend his seat in a primary, selecting two Tea Party activists to run instead. Bennett says his friend Mitt Romney commiserated with him about the ingratitude of the Tea Party, telling a presumably apocryphal story about getting bitten by a ferret he had tried to rescue from a dishwasher.

"Mitt said the Tea Party people are like that ferret in the dishwasher," Bennett says. "They're so frightened and angry, they'll even bite Bob Bennett, who's trying to get the country out of this mess."

For Republican officeholders, insufficient anti-Obama fervor was now politically fatal. Centrists like Specter and Crist had no shot of winning rage-a-thon Republican primaries, and even establishment conservatives like Bennett were in danger of being "scozzafavaed," a new verb describing what happened to Republicans who ran afoul of the Tea Party. It was coined after a November 2009 special election in upstate New York, where the moderate Republican congressman, John McHugh, had committed partisan treason by accepting a job as Obama's army secretary. To try to hold his seat, local GOP power brokers handpicked another centrist named Dede Scozzafava, who had supported the Recovery Act. The Tea Party revolted, and rallied Republicans behind a third-party right-winger instead. Scozzafava eventually dropped out and endorsed her Democratic opponent, who ended up winning the race.

Establishment Republicans fretted that if their most electable candidates kept getting scozzafavaed, they'd lose a historic chance to exploit Obama fatigue in 2010. Congressman Mike Castle, a beloved figure in Delaware and a strong favorite to move up to the Senate, got scozzafavaed by a loopy far-right activist named Christine O'Donnell, best known for dabbling in witchcraft as a teen and crusading against masturbation as an adult. Castle had first realized he might face a rough primary during the Tea Party summer, when he was raucously booed at a town hall meeting for saying Obama was a U.S. citizen. "I voted against the stimulus and health care, but I guess I wasn't adamant enough," he says. Tea Party Republicans also won Senate primaries over less dogmatic candidates in Colorado, Connecticut, Kentucky, Nevada, and Alaska, where Senator Murkowski had to launch an independent write-in campaign after getting scozzafavaed.

The most obvious results of this intraparty cannibalism were the nominations of extremist Republicans like O'Donnell in otherwise winnable races, and the drift of scozzafavaed Republicans (including Scozzafava herself, who ended up in Democratic governor Andrew Cuomo's administration) across the aisle. Republican leaders who had portrayed Obama as a radical threat to American values were reaping what they sowed, as their base demanded maximum ferocity in the war it had been told was being waged for the nation's soul. Even McConnell's preferred candidate for Senate in Kentucky, an establishment conservative named Trey Grayson, got scozzafavaed by Tea Party firebrand Rand Paul, the son of the libertarian icon Ron Paul. And in Florida, Rick Scott, the disgraced health care executive who had founded an advocacy group to fight Obamacare and comparative effectiveness research, rode a Tea Party wave of Obama hatred to upset a Republican insider for the GOP gubernatorial nomination.

The threat of Tea Party retribution also had a real impact on policy, giving congressional Republicans who might have been cooperation-curious an even stronger incentive to double down on obstruction. For example, Scott Brown's election provided a clear opening for Republicans to cut a favorable deal with the shell-shocked White House on scaled-back health reforms; instead, they stuck to their strategy of no-no-no, and Democrats with no option of settling for half a loaf eventually used parliamentary legerdemain to get the whole loaf to the president's desk. Politically, Obamacare would be an albatross for Democrats in 2010, partly because of the side deals—the "Cornhusker Kickback" for Senator Nelson, a nonaggression pact with the drug industry—the White House cut to get to sixty. But substantively, if Republicans had been a bit nicer to Specter, or offered Obama some modest reforms as a face-saving compromise, they could have stopped a big liberal victory.

Republican leaders decided before Obama even took office that their main goal, the "purpose of the minority," would be regaining power. And unpopular Democratic laws like the stimulus and health reform would help them achieve that goal; for example, Chairman Obey, under fire for writing the Recovery Act, suddenly decided to retire after twenty-one terms in the House. But those unpopular laws were also achieving age-old Democratic policy goals. So who was really winning? Republicans took pride in their political successes as an insurgent minority, and the backlash against Obama was helping them motivate voters, recruit candidates, and raise money. But he was also enjoying one of the most productive legislative sessions since the New Deal.

"They got what they wanted," says Josh Holmes, a senior McConnell aide. "That's to our dismay."

President Obama liked to remind the Clinton veterans on his staff: *We're not here to do school uniforms.* Maybe he had botched some of his politics—he admitted that after Scott Brown's election—but his policies were making change. Clinton and every other postwar Democratic president had dreamed of universal health care; Obama's reforms would get it done, while cracking down on insurance abuses and starting to bend the cost curve. Obama had also put two progressive women on the Supreme Court, signed a Credit Card Bill of Rights to crack down on surprise fees and retroactive rate hikes, pushed through long-sought reforms of the predatory student loan business, and saved the U.S. auto industry. Not to mention the change he was driving through the Recovery Act's investments in energy, education, health IT, infrastructure, and a fairer tax code. Or the end of the war in Iraq.

Yet the left was unhappy. While the right was trashing Obama as a new Che Guevara, congenitally disillusioned liberals were trashing him as a wimp and a sellout.

Sometimes liberal activists and bloggers had genuine ideological disagreements with Obama's less liberal policies, like his escalation of the war in Afghanistan, his refusal to nationalize banks, or his empty rhetoric about helping homeowners. But often they merely seemed to resent Obama's insistence on playing the hand he was dealt. Why didn't he fight harder for immigration reform, for cap-and-trade, for card-check for unions? The same reason he didn't fight harder for a larger stimulus in 2009, or an aggressive second stimulus in 2010: He didn't have the votes. Sure, Obama had increased clean-energy funding ten-fold and ushered in a new era of energy efficiency, but a column on the eco-website *Grist* still declared: "Environmentalists Need a New President." Sure, Obama's historic health reforms would cover 32 million uninsured Americans, but the disillusionment addicts on the left were upset he hadn't insisted on a government-run "public option." Again, there weren't sixty votes in the Senate for a public option, and that wouldn't have changed if Obama had lobbied harder or talked purtier.

Obama often tweaked these "griping and groaning Democrats" who seemed to think presidents were endowed with superpowers. "Gosh, we haven't yet brought about world peace," he mock-whined at a fund-raiser. "I thought that was going to happen quicker!"

Liberal activists often complained that the Obama team was nastier to them than to Republicans, and there they had a point. Gibbs publicly mocked the "professional left." Rahm showed up at a Common Purpose meeting to denounce a liberal group's decision to run ads attacking Blue Dog Democrats as "fucking retarded." At one closed-door House caucus meeting, the usually conciliatory president called out Peter DeFazio, the one liberal who had voted against the Recovery Act: "Don't think we're not keeping score, brother." Whining from the left seemed to irritate him more than abuse from the right, the way a rebellious teenage son causes more angst than a crazy old neighbor.

One of the more thoughtful liberal critiques of Obama—echoed by some White House aides—was that he ought to fight some losing battles, to highlight Republican obstructionism and fire up his base. In Washington, this is called "getting caught trying." But Rahm believed that losing begat losing, and didn't want Obama associating himself with liberal crusades just to get caught trying. The president didn't want to spend time or political capital picking unnecessary fights with Republicans. It would alienate centrists in both parties whose votes he still needed for Wall Street reform and other legislative priorities, and it just wasn't his style. Anyway, staying above the fray had political benefits for Obama. Even in the intensely polarized climate, he was still way more popular than his fellow Democrats, especially with independent voters. He figured he'd keep focusing on making progress, whether progressives liked it or not.

— SIXTEEN —

Green New World

Higher-Speed Rail

Let me ask you a question," Vice President Biden said. It was the day after the 2010 State of the Union, and he was warming up a crowd at the University of Tampa. "How can we, the leading nation in the world, be in a position where China, Spain, France, and name-all-the-other-countries have rail systems far superior to ours?"

Amtrak Joe and his boss were in town to announce the Recovery Act's $8 billion in high-speed rail grants, including $1.25 billion for that Tampa-to-Orlando route that had miraculously united Florida's politicians. These investments wouldn't provide much short-term stimulus; the bulk of them wouldn't be spent until 2011. And they wouldn't get America anywhere close to name-all-the-other-countries; China was spending forty times as much on its high-speed network. But for a car-crazed nation that spent more on highways in a year than it had spent on intercity passenger rail in four decades, this was real change. It was a down payment on Obama's goal of creating fuel-efficient alternatives to long drives and short flights—and on Biden's prediction that Obama would lead "the most train-friendly administration ever."

As a Chicago resident, Obama probably took more trains in an average month than Bush took in his life. Rahm Emanuel, the godfather of high-speed rail, was another Chicago guy, as was Obama's federal railroad administrator, Joe Szabo. To Republican critics, this explained a lot; they saw high-speed rail as cosmopolitan elitism, a Euro-socialist assault on the freedom of the open road. But while the high-speed program did represent an investment in a metropolitan future, an implicit vote for Chicago over Crawford, there were plenty of culturally and politically neutral reasons to like trains. You didn't have to watch the road, stew in traffic, or pull over to eat, stretch your legs, or buy gas. You didn't have to risk arrest or accident by drinking or texting. As Obama pointed out in Tampa, you didn't have to take off your shoes at security.

Anyway, bullet trains felt like the future.

"I mean, those things are *fast*," Obama said. "They are *smooth*."

The Tampa–Orlando line would be eighty-four miles, short for a high-speed line, with a top speed of 168 miles per hour, slow compared to the wow machines whipping around Europe and Asia. But it would be a showcase, a project that, if not exactly shovel-ready, was at least plan-ready, unlike any other U.S. bullet train. It could be the proof of concept for high-speed rail in America, producing images of sleek trains shooting past bumper-to-bumper congestion on I-4. It was expected to be profitable, thanks to the Disney stop, and while it wouldn't be completed until 2015 at the earliest, it was the only bullet train that Obama would have any chance to ride as president.

"You all have a date!" Obama told the crowd. "When that thing is all set up, we'll come down here and check it out."

I rode a train from Miami to Orlando that March. I had a comfortable seat with Shaq-worthy legroom. I avoided the schlep of the airport and the maniacs on the highways. I did some work, ate a passable spinach lasagna, and watched *Funny People* on my laptop; it wasn't Amtrak's fault the people weren't funny. At one point, we stopped in the middle of an old-Florida ranch, beside a majestic oak dripping with Spanish moss, and I thought: There's no better way to see America.

Unfortunately, for the next half hour, I remained beside that majestic oak. Door to door, the journey took ten hours for a trip I usually drive in four. My seat cost only $36, but taxis to and from the stations cost twice that. It was a stark reminder why America's passenger rail system was a laughingstock, and why Obama was pushing an upgrade.

His high-speed rail program awarded $3.5 billion to Florida and California to start building dedicated lines for snazzy new bullet trains. It spread the other $4.5 billion around thirty-one states to repair bridges, straighten tracks, and otherwise upgrade existing Amtrak lines that would still go much slower than bullets but would more consistently go faster than oaks. Once again, the administration was sending a two-part message—somewhat faster trains soon, super-fast trains later. The program's official (and more accurate) name was High-Speed and Intercity Passenger Rail. For all the rhetoric about catching Spain with a fleet of ooh-and-aah bullet trains, it was really "higher-speed rail."

The morning after my slow-speed rail experience, I joined three hundred business types at a conference of the year-old U.S. High Speed Rail Association, one of those Washington lobbying outfits that spontaneously generate whenever multibillion-dollar initiatives are born. At a Hilton alongside the future location of a high-speed station, vendors hoping to cash in on the Tampa–Orlando line displayed slick models of German, Spanish, Korean, and Japanese super-trains, as well as video of a French train traveling a record 357 mph. Thirty foreign manufacturers had already pledged to build U.S. factories if they landed contracts, and the national market was so lucrative that everyone wanted a foot in the door in Florida. A marketing rep for one European firm was bragging to me about its expansion plans when she spied the head of Florida's rail program across the room, broke off our chat in mid-sentence, and raced off to introduce herself. When I asked one lobbyist what he was doing there, he grinned and rubbed his thumb against two fingers.

If greed was the conference's main theme—a promising sign, I thought—then grumbling was the subtheme. USHSR leaders were all about bullet trains; few of the firms that paid their pricey membership and conference fees were interested in improving Amtrak's hundred-year-old tunnels, eighty-year-old electrical systems, and sixty-

year-old trains. So their initial excitement about Obama's high-speed
program had given way to gripes about his investment choices: Why
throw money at old Amtrak lines that bleed cash and share track with
slow-moving freight, instead of focusing exclusively on game-changing
new 200 mph bullets? How on earth did Ohio's 3-C Corridor linking Cleveland, Columbus, and Cincinnati at a pitiful average speed of
39 mph and a top speed of 79 mph—first achieved in Andrew Jackson's
administration—qualify as "high-speed"?

One of the sharpest critics at the Hilton was Orlando congressman John Mica, the ranking Republican on the House transportation
committee. Mica was an enthusiastic infrastructure advocate who had
led the chorus of complaints about the stimulus being light on public
works; he had always been an enthusiastic advocate of high-speed rail
as well. But now he wasn't even enthusiastic about the bullet train in his
backyard. It would have five rapid-fire stops, and none would link up
with Orlando's new commuter line, prompting talk of a sixth. "You can't
have real high-speed rail if you're stopping all the time," Mica told me.
"I should be as happy as a hog eating trash. But we need a real success,
and this is pretty marginal." Mica said the only high-speed grant worthy
of the name went to California, to start building a route that would connect Los Angeles to San Francisco in less than three hours. But the land
had yet to be purchased, the route wasn't set, and the estimated cost
was ballooning in a state that was already broke. "California is the only
hope—if they don't totally screw it up," Mica groused.

Mica was even harsher on the Amtrak upgrades, calling them "slow-
speed trains to nowhere," perpetuating a "Soviet-style monopoly" that
lost money on every ticket it sold outside the Northeast Corridor. If
Obama was so desperate to improve Amtrak, Mica asked, why not
focus on that profitable stretch in the Northeast, where Biden's beloved
Acela trains already reached 150 mph but averaged only half that? In
Acela's first decade, rail had displaced air as the dominant mode between New York and Washington, but the majority of U.S. flight delays
were still at congested New York airports. Imagine how many more
travelers would switch if Acela ever reached its potential.

"We need to pick routes that make sense," Mica said. "If we pick dogs, we'll end up scratching fleas."

Later that week, in LaHood's office overlooking the Washington Nationals ballpark, I recounted what his former Republican colleague had said. LaHood's eyes narrowed. His face turned fuchsia. "It's just a stunning about-face!" he shouted. "It's schizophrenic! We did everything John asked!" It was Mica who invited him to Orlando to deliver his stern message about commuter rail, and later thanked him for saving high-speed rail in Florida. LaHood was starting to feel like the only Republican allowed to say nice things in public about anything Obama supported.

No, Tampa–Orlando was not a classic bullet route, but it would knit together two boomtowns quickly and cheaply, showing the country what trains could do. And the extension to Miami was perfect for high-speed rail; my ten-hour slog would be sliced to two hours. Sure, the dense Northeast Corridor was train heaven, but eliminating its urban bottlenecks would require huge investments to produce modest reductions in trip times. Anyway, none of the name-all-the-other-countries relied exclusively on state-of-the-art bullet trains. Why should we?

LaHood's larger point was that Tampa–Orlando would be just one link in a more balanced, more sustainable, less dangerous transportation network. Population was growing and fuel prices were rising, while road and airport capacity was dwindling. "We can't just keep building more highways that turn into parking lots," he said. Making rail a viable option outside the Northeast would require better trains, not just bullet trains.

The way to go fast, railroaders say, is to stop going slow.

My train to Orlando took so long because of that half hour beside the oak, plus several longer stretches at jogger speeds. Almost all of Amtrak's tracks are owned by freight lines, and they're riddled with time-sucking choke points, like sharp curves and grade crossings that require slow speeds for safety, or long single-track stretches that force trains to wait next to oak trees for oncoming traffic to pass. In Chicago,

I visited one of America's worst blockages, an old-fashioned "diamond" in the Englewood neighborhood that pits seventy-eight commuter trains against sixty Amtrak and freight trains every day. It's like an intersection in the middle of an interstate. I arrived well after rush hour, but I still saw gridlock; one Norfolk Southern train hauling grain, lumber, and steel across the country was delayed at least forty minutes. Amtrak trains from Detroit routinely wait even longer.

That's why the high-speed grants included $133 million for an overpass that will replace the diamond and ease the chronic Amtrak delays. The Englewood Flyover will also save suburbanites over twenty minutes a day on their commutes, and start untangling the spaghetti bowl of convoluted tracks that carry one fourth of the nation's freight through Greater Chicago. Throughout the area, I saw similar workaday projects that would add capacity and subtract choke points: sidings to allow faster trains to pass laggards, grade separations to avoid conflicts with cars, advanced signal systems with automated crossovers to replace hand-thrown switches. The goal is to make Chicago the hub of a truly competitive Midwestern rail network—not by building new bullet-only lines from scratch, but by gradually improving the existing network.

"It's not sexy," says Szabo, a fifth-generation railroader who once worked as a switchman on the Illinois Central and a conductor on Chicago's commuter rail. "But if you take out enough pinch points, you're going to make trains more attractive."

For example, over $1 billion worth of Recovery Act upgrades will slice over an hour off travel times between Chicago and St. Louis. The work will only increase the top speed to 110 mph, half as fast as the California bullet plan. But it will make the Amtrak option faster than driving, which should make it more attractive, so that Amtrak can run more frequent trains, which will make it even more attractive. One reason the Northeast Corridor is so popular is the convenience of knowing the trains run every hour. Similarly, a new bridge to eliminate a single-track snarl between St. Louis and Kansas City should dramatically improve on-time performance, converting a train people don't take unless they have to into a train people might take because they want to.

Ever since Amtrak was chartered in 1971 to take over the money-losing passenger lines of freight railroads, it's been the ugly duckling of the transportation world, starved of funding for maintenance, neglected by presidents of both parties, notorious for dreadful service. The Recovery Act was a first step toward respectability.

"There's been a total focus on aviation and highways in this country. It's nuts!" says Amtrak CEO Joe Boardman, another Republican. "Now we can start to build a railroad that works."

At the same time, projects like the Englewood Flyover and that bridge in Missouri will help freight railroads, which move our stuff around the country less expensively and more fuel-efficiently than long-haul trucks, and maintain their tracks on their own dime. This is another untold story of the stimulus, its unprecedented aid for freight upgrades that will unclog the arteries of our commerce—including a $100 million TIGER grant for further untangling of Chicago's spaghetti bowl. Shifting cargo from gas-guzzling trucks to trains that can move a ton of freight 457 miles per gallon is one of the most powerful ways to reduce oil dependence and promote economic competitiveness.

But that's not how high-speed rail was marketed. By the spring of 2010, Obama had overhyped high-speed, underplayed intercity, and barely mentioned freight. The bullet train projects that got all the love didn't have shovels in the ground, while the incremental improvements that were under way didn't seem to justify his lofty rhetoric. The administration had spread the cash around multiple states to try to build broad support for future investments; instead, it created multiple targets for political attacks.

"We're giving birth," Szabo told me. "That can be messy and painful."

High-speed rail was the Recovery Act's most extreme example of a long-term project—not only because of its start-up lags, but because it would require a sustained national commitment to achieve its objectives. Tampa–Orlando made sense as the first leg of Tampa–Orlando–Miami, but as a stand-alone project it was basically an expensive commuter line and glorified Disney shuttle. California's $2.25 billion grant, the largest in the country, was only enough to finance a start-up track to nowhere in the Central Valley, from the small farm town of Corcoran to the unincorporated burg of Borden; it would require tens of billions more to get anywhere near Los Angeles or San Francisco. And as a one-off investment, $400 million for Ohio's 3-C service would be a laughable waste; at go-kart speeds, it would never draw drivers off the highway. It was defensible only as a first step toward competitive speeds, as a link in a real regional network, as a hedge against oil shocks that could make long drives expensive and short flights extinct.

In other words, the legacy of the stimulus investments in high-speed rail would depend on what happened after the stimulus. Congress did approve another $2.5 billion in 2010, but at that rate catching name-all-the-other-countries could take over a century.

Still, as Szabo pointed out, you've got to start somewhere. He liked to show a photo of some smiling men in suits surrounded by desolate Kansas flatlands. Behind them is a sign celebrating the first eight-mile stretch of the interstate highway system.

"It didn't get built all at once," LaHood says. "People had a vision."

Driving Change

It was hard to imagine a more vivid argument against our addiction to oil than the fiery explosion on BP's Deepwater Horizon in April 2010. It killed eleven men on the rig, and it spilled five million barrels of crude into the Gulf of Mexico, ravaging the coastal economy and filling the airwaves with pitiful images of blackened pelicans. It felt like a teachable moment about the hidden costs of fossil fuels; all that oil amounted to less than one third of what Americans used in an average day. But Obama had stopped talking about climate change in public; it polled badly, and cap-and-trade was dead. And in a culture that holds presidents responsible for everything that happens "on their watch," the spill didn't make Obama look prescient. It made him look impotent. Why couldn't he stop the gusher? Why wasn't he hauling anyone to jail? Even Malia asked him: "Did you plug the hole yet, Daddy?" So the BP spill, like the Massey coal disaster in West Virginia before it, or the Fukushima nuclear meltdown in Japan after it, did not create much of a groundswell for renewable energy. It just forced the president to spend three months talking about something other than jobs.

Behind the scenes, though, Obama was doing more than any previous president to wean the nation off oil. Promoting high-speed rail and freight rail that would take cars and trucks off the road was just one strategy. He also jacked up fuel efficiency standards for cars and trucks, which should eliminate one sixth of U.S. oil imports by 2025. And he went all-in on electric cars and trucks, starting with the stimulus. It provided $7,500 rebates for early adopters, funded a forty-fold increase in the number of charging stations, and created an advanced battery industry from scratch. It was no coincidence that the first mass-produced plug-ins, the Chevy Volt and Nissan Leaf—"Obamobiles," to skeptics— hit the streets "on his watch."

The battery effort was one of the most ambitious stimulus programs, positioning the United States as a major player in a twenty-first-century manufacturing industry almost overnight, repatriating lithium-ion technologies that were invented in America but had followed the consumer electronics business to Asia. Before the Recovery Act, the U.S. had a chicken-and-egg problem: Nobody wanted to build or buy electric cars because the batteries were too weak and expensive, and nobody wanted to try to make better and cheaper batteries because nobody wanted to build or buy electric cars. But now thirty stimulus-funded factories are creating a supply chain that could support half a million plug-ins by 2015. Battery packs aren't easy to import—the Volt's weighs more than a washer-dryer—so if plug-ins are going to be made in America, batteries probably have to be as well. And if plug-ins are going to be popular in America, batteries have to get much cheaper; they're the main reason the first-generation Volt retails for luxury-car prices without luxury-car features. So the Recovery Act also aimed to cut battery costs 70 percent by 2015, while improving their power and extending their range.

A123 Systems, the firm that raised its stimulus matching funds by going public, was founded in Massachusetts by MIT geeks who named it for a techno-measurement used to calculate forces at nano dimensions. Its initial research into the "nanophosphate powder" that gives its batteries extra kick was financed by an Energy Department grant. But it still built its first five factories in Asia, partly because of cheaper labor and land, mostly because that's where the supply chain and know-how were. Thanks to the Recovery Act, A123 built its next two factories in Michigan. Four of its suppliers also won stimulus grants to build U.S. plants. So did one of its customers, Navistar, which retrofitted a shuttered RV factory in Indiana to make electric trucks for companies like FedEx. Another customer, Fisker Automotive, snagged a federal loan to make electric cars in a shuttered GM plant in Delaware.

"Without government, there's no way we would've done this in the U.S.," A123 chief technology officer Bart Riley told me. "But now you're going to see the industry reach critical mass here."

A123 built its first U.S. production line in Livonia, Michigan, in a former Technicolor plant that once made VHS tapes; at the opening, Obama hailed the birth of a new industry providing good-paying green jobs. But the first thing I noticed on a tour of the cavernous factory— and I often noticed this in stimulus-funded plants—was how few people were working there. Robotic arms, conveyor belts, and stacking machines were doing the heavy labor. "We're automating the hell out of this stuff," explained my tour guide, Jason Forcier, the head of A123's automotive division. I saw a few welders, and some employees monitoring the machines; robots haven't yet learned to engineer or maintain or repair themselves. But battery production is high-tech, capital-intensive work. It's not like T-shirt production, where the United States can't compete with lower-wage countries. It means fewer jobs, but it also means the jobs might not migrate overseas.

"We know we're going to get undercut on repetitive-labor jobs," Biden says. "The answer is to move to the next thing."

MIT professor Yet-Ming Chiang, the Taiwanese-born material scientist who developed the nanophosphate powder that is A123's special sauce, believes America's special sauce is our what's-next culture of creativity and experimentation. He started messing around with chemistry sets in his bedroom after coming to America as a boy, and he doubts he would have become such an unconventional thinker within the structure of an Asian education. His latest venture, another alphanumeric firm called 24M, emerged from a brainstorming session about the smart grid at A123; it has spun off to create an unorthodox "flow battery" that could store renewable energy on a game-changing scale.

If we want that kind of innovation in America, Chiang says, we need to make things in America, so that those brainstorming sessions keep happening in America. When high-tech factories flee the country, high-tech people follow.

"This is what we're good at," he says. "We can't just be a service economy."

A123's stimulus grant did create a thousand jobs in Michigan, mostly for laid-off autoworkers, but the company still could fail. In late 2011 it announced 350 layoffs of its own after Fisker had problems with its Karma sports car. Its stock has tanked. Overall, though, Michigan expects its new battery industry—which received nearly half the Recovery Act's battery grants—to employ 63,000 people in a decade. Those aren't WPA numbers, but they're a lot more than zero; the entire U.S. steel industry only employs about 60,000 workers. That helps explain why the battery program, like the auto bailout, now has bipartisan support in Michigan. "It helped save this state," says Jack Kirksey, the Republican mayor of Livonia. "Things were looking like: Last one to leave Michigan please turn out the lights." At the ribbon cutting for a new battery plant in Holland, Michigan, Obama archly noted that some stimulus opponents—he was talking about Republican congressman Pete Hoekstra—had shown up despite making "the political decision that it would be better to obstruct than to lend a hand." He had a point, but politicians like ribbon cuttings, and they like major employers; batteries are now Michigan's fastest-growing industry.

"All our competitors are setting up shop here, and so are our suppliers," says Forcier, whose father and two grandfathers worked at GM. "It's all coming together."

Some analysts predicted the battery push would be a flop reminiscent of President Carter's botched bet on synthetic fuels, producing a glut that would outstrip demand for electric cars. Fossil fuels, while terrible for our security and our environment, are highly efficient for transportation; the Leaf can go less than eighty miles on a charge, while the Volt has even less battery stamina, although it has a backup gas tank to combat "range anxiety." Even Steve Rattner, the private equity investor who oversaw the auto rescue for Obama, blasted the battery program in his book *Overhaul*, predicting weak returns on investment.

"Green jobs may be the fad of the moment, but in supporting them we need to forgo irrational exuberance," Rattner warned.

Sure enough, Ener1, the owner of one stimulus-funded Indiana battery factory, would follow its best customer, the Norwegian electric carmaker Think, into bankruptcy in early 2012. On a visit to the plant, Biden had proclaimed that firms like Ener1 would "reshape the way Americans drive, the way Americans consume, the way Americans power their lives." Privately, though, he had been underwhelmed by the Think. "It looked like a Yugo, a midget car," recalls one aide. "It looked like a car you put in the back of another car." Biden asked his team: "Who the fuck names their car 'Think'?"

But creative destruction is part of capitalism, far preferable to the government propping up troubled companies forever. As Obama told the CEO of A123: We're just getting you started. You've got to make this sustainable. Stimulus-funded failures naturally attracted far more attention than the routine failures of businesses that receive run-of-the-mill subsidies and tax breaks ever do. They invariably prompted accusations of Democratic "crony capitalism," even though Indiana Republicans like Governor Mitch Daniels and Senator Richard Lugar were avid supporters of Ener1. But if battery investments had been completely risk-free, they would have been made long before the Recovery Act.

Some pioneers always get scalped.

"Are some of these companies going to fail? Duh! Of course!" says Ron Bloom, Obama's former manufacturing czar. "It's no different than Pell Grants. Some of those students getting government assistance are going to end up drunks on the corner. But overall, society gains enormously from investments in education, so we make the grants. What's your alternative? Give up? Let China make everything?"

Bloom's views were not a majority opinion inside the White House. Obama's economists—except Jared Bernstein—were skeptical of his efforts to single out manufacturing for government support. Larry Summers had a revealing email exchange with a Solyndra investor who said the federal loan to the solar firm, while nice for him, seemed "haphazard," an indication that "the government is just not well equipped to decide which companies should get the money and how much." Summers replied: "I relate well to your view that gov is a crappy vc and if u were closer to it you'd feel more strongly."

But Obama took a broader view of "return on investment" than a profit-minded private equity firm would. As Biden says, it would be a shame to trade our dependence on foreign oil for dependence on foreign batteries. Even Summers told the Solyndra investor that "there are all kinds of externalities to renewable investments," suggesting that lower emissions were the kind of public goods that private investors undervalue. And whatever valid concerns economists had about industrial policy, they hadn't convinced our competitors; China's stimulus poured hundreds of billions into its green industries. I kept hearing the same mantra from clean-energy executives and industrial-state politicians: We're not competing with companies. We're competing with countries.

"We're in a war for jobs, and we can't just forfeit," former Michigan governor Jennifer Granholm says. "Yeah, we're doing some industrial policy. Good! It's about time! Because China *really* does industrial policy."

The Recovery Act didn't provide cradle-to-grave corporate welfare. It offered a one-time injection to create a domestic battery industry, which was a prerequisite for a domestic electric vehicle industry, which may become a prerequisite for a domestic car industry. Automakers ended up selling about twenty thousand electric vehicles in the United States in 2011, about twenty thousand more than they would have sold without Obama's help. Some industry analysts still doubt electric vehicles can compete on their own, and their association with Obama, who has pledged to buy a Volt when he leaves office, has turned them into culture-war fodder. "You can't put a gun rack in a Volt," Newt Gingrich snarled, inaccurately, while campaigning in Oklahoma. The industry also endured a blitz of awful publicity when a Volt battery (assembled at a stimulus-financed factory in Brownstown, Michigan, with cells from the plant Obama visited in Holland, Michigan) caught fire three weeks after it was destroyed in a crash test. Chevy made fixes to protect drivers who might be tempted to remain in a destroyed Volt for three weeks after totaling it, and regulators pronounced the car safe. But the Volt fire seemed to create a teachable moment in a way that the BP spill never did, and right-wing critics have declared Obamobiles dead.

They're not dead, though. Lithium-ion batteries still aren't as good or as cheap as they need to be for mass-market appeal, but every major automaker is now developing plug-ins for the U.S. market. Even pessimistic analysts believe sales will double in 2012.

And even if they don't, the Recovery Act didn't just bet on batteries. It bet on alternatives to fossil fuels. The gyrating robots I saw at the A123 factory in Livonia were part of that story, but so were the cookies and ice cream I ate in the San Francisco offices of a biotech company—really, a twenty-first-century oil company—called Solazyme.

Solazyme makes oil in much the same way that nature made oil, with microalgae. The difference is that nature's algae evolved over billions of years, while Solazyme's are genetically engineered in a lab. And while nature's production process unfolded over millennia deep underground, Solazyme's takes a few days in a stainless steel fermenter that could be used to make beer. The company's patented microbes work in the dark—remember how Secretary Chu warned that photosynthesis was inefficient?—converting sugar, grasses, and almost any other cellulosic material into renewable alternatives to petroleum. Solazyme is making the exact same molecules we use in fuels, but from plant-based carbohydrates instead of fossil-based hydrocarbons.

"We're leveraging evolution," says CEO Jonathan Wolfson. "We take what the planet is good at making, plant sugars, and turn it into what the planet needs, oils."

Solazyme feels less like an oil company than a Silicon Valley start-up launched in a garage—which, in fact, it once was. And Wolfson, a forty-year-old dreamer who once spent a year volunteering on a Navajo reservation, seems less like an oilman than a software entrepreneur—which, in fact, he once was. But Solazyme is already converting carbo-hydrates into designer biofuels. The Navy and United Airlines already have flown jets powered by Solazyme's genetically tailored bugs. This isn't pie-in-the-sky someday stuff.

"It's just a question of scaling up, so we can drive down our costs," Wolfson says. "Then we can change the world."

The Recovery Act is spending over $1 billion to move the renew-able fuel industry beyond corn ethanol, scaling up advanced biofuels that won't accelerate the destruction of rain forests or compete with the food supply. "The entire industry was shutting down in 2008, because nobody could get financing," Rogers says. "Now the U.S. has a chance to lead." The stimulus is financing America's first three commercial-scale cellulosic biorefineries in Iowa, Kansas, and Mississippi, as well as eighteen smaller projects that will test a variety of feedstocks, fuels, and chemical processes; Solazyme won $22 million for a Peoria plant that will produce over half a million gallons of jet fuel every year. Without federal aid, it's doubtful that any of these companies could have crossed their Valleys of Death. The technical and market risks were too high, the factories they needed to build too costly, and the lead times to prof-itable fuel sales way too long.

Even with a boost from Uncle Sam, it won't be easy to compete with Big Oil in such an incomprehensibly gigantic industrial sector. If all the Recovery Act projects exceed their targets, they could conceiv-ably produce 140 million annual gallons of fuel; Americans use 140 *billion* annual gallons. And unlike ExxonMobil, BP, and other energy incumbents, advanced biofuel firms don't have tens of billions of dollars sitting around to finance the massive refineries they'll need to generate economies of scale.

Which brings me to those desserts I ate at Solazyme. I started with algae-derived chocolate ice cream that had one third the fat and one tenth the cholesterol of regular chocolate ice cream. It tasted like chocolate ice cream. I also tried an algal chocolate chip cookie, which was even tastier than the Mrs. Smith's version I ate for purely comparative purposes. It turns out that high-end food oils sell for $20 to $50 a gallon, as opposed to $4 a gallon for jet fuel, and Solazyme's microbes can make them, too. So the company has forged a potentially lucrative partnership with the European food giant Roquette to produce ingredients and nutritional supplements. It's also working with corporate partners like Unilever and Dow on algal substitutes for soaps, plastics, and chemicals that usually require petroleum-based oils. And Solazyme's Algenist brand of cosmetics has been a hit with consumers on QVC and in Sephora stores.

It just so happens that high-end skin creams can fetch over $5,000 a gallon. Those cosmetics revenues helped Solazyme go public in 2011, raising cash for its gradual advance toward the multitrillion-dollar fuel market. Obviously, the Energy Department didn't anticipate that Solazyme would be selling anti-aging creams to baby boomers when it helped the company cross the Valley of Death with taxpayer dollars. But it did anticipate that savvy firms in areas where technologies were at "inflection points" would find ways to produce breakthroughs—not every company, but some of them.

"We don't know which of these approaches will work," Rogers says. "We don't care."

Vultures were circling as the Swiss petrochemical giant INEOS broke ground for another biorefinery at a former grapefruit juice plant in Vero Beach. Not metaphorical vultures—actual turkey vultures, trolling for food at a landfill behind the construction site. "Those vultures are circling above a dying way of life," declared Paul Bryan, the former Chevron executive running the Energy Department's biomass program.

Thanks to a $50 million stimulus grant, the newfangled refinery will convert organic waste into eight million annual gallons of cellulosic ethanol, as well as electricity that will power its operations and send a couple megawatts to the grid. So instead of taking their loads to the landfill, trucks can just bring it to the plant to create renewable fuel and power. It's a bummer for the buzzards, but that's part of the point.

After searching the globe for a waste-to-fuel biochemistry break-through, INEOS executives had found it in a musty University of Arkansas lab, where an ornery professor named James Gaddy had spent years developing ethanol-producing bacteria he found in the chicken manure so abundant in that part of the world. At first, Gaddy refused to relinquish control of his super-bugs—he wanted INEOS to build him a control room in Fayetteville to oversee its refineries—but he finally agreed to let the chemical conglomerate handle the chemical plants in exchange for royalties for an evangelical charity. "I care about saving the earth through Jesus," the seventy-eight-year-old Gaddy told me. "I'm glad this will help the environment, but that's secondary. And I'm not interested in wealth."

Well, INEOS is. It's betting that in a carbon-constrained economy, communities will pay good money to reduce their waste streams while producing green power and fuel. The Florida biorefinery will be able to convert just about any feedstock, and if it performs as expected, they plan to replicate it around the world.

"We want to do millions of barrels, not just millions of gallons," said INEOS executive Peter Williams. "This will be the template for the future."

Or maybe it won't. There are visionaries like Gaddy and Wolfson and Chiang behind many of the Energy Department's five thousand stimulus projects, and not all of them will pan out. Range Fuels, a venture-backed cellulosic ethanol firm that had attracted $150 million worth of grants and loan guarantees from the Bush administration, went bust just a couple weeks before the Vero groundbreaking. The press took no interest in the story, which was comforting to Obama administration officials who worried about the response to the Recovery Act's inevitable failures. But it was still disturbing to see a company once hailed as a template for the future shut its doors before producing a single gallon of fuel.

"You never know with new technologies," Bryan told me. "If they weren't risky, they wouldn't need our help. But if we don't take risks, we'll just have the status quo."

Green Power

Greener cars and better trains would reduce demand for fossil fuels, but transportation accounted for less than one third of America's energy use. The rest came from "stationary sources"—homes, offices, power plants, factories—and the coal that powered many of them was even dirtier than oil. So while Obama pushed to reduce fuel use and promote renewable fuels, he was also pushing to reduce electricity use and promote renewable power.

The low-hanging fruit of efficiency came first. Just as he did with fuel economy standards for cars and trucks, Obama tightened efficiency standards for light bulbs, furnaces, refrigerators, dishwashers, air conditioners, and other electrical devices. Those energy savings can add up; one mandate requiring cold-drink vending machines to reduce their own juice consumption will reduce electricity demand enough to power 1.4 million homes. The Recovery Act's arcane language requiring governors to pledge to promote efficiency-friendly utility rules and greener building codes—the pledge Sarah Palin refused to sign— also drove quiet regulatory shifts. In two years, the number of states with California-style rules encouraging utilities to help customers save power increased from six to fifteen. The number of states with residential building codes that met strict international standards soared from one (if Washington, D.C., counts as a state) to twenty-three. Those boring bureaucratic tweaks will avert the need for scores of coal plants.

Building efficiently in the first place is easier than retrofitting buildings after they start heating and cooling the outdoors, but America is so spectacularly inefficient that retrofits are also, as Chu says, not just low-hanging fruit but fruit lying on the ground. Our power plants alone waste enough energy to electrify Japan. And the main barrier to upgrades, even upgrades that pay for themselves within a few years, is our reluctance to front the cash, especially in tough economic times. So the Recovery Act fronted it for us, financing thousands of retrofits of federal buildings, data centers, border stations, public housing projects, colleges, military bases, city halls, fire stations, and more. The low-income home weatherization program got most of the attention, because it got off to such a slow start, but the stimulus also funded $150 million worth of industrial efficiency initiatives matched by over $600 million in private funds, including co-generation projects that will recycle waste heat into electricity at America's largest medical center in Houston and America's largest steel plant in Indiana. A $450 million competitive grant program will weatherize entire neighborhoods in cities like Phoenix and Philadelphia, just as cable companies wire entire neighborhoods at once.

"We're making retrofits the norm," Cathy Zoi says. "Every project is on-the-ground evidence that this isn't airy-fairy stuff from *The Jetsons.* It's here and it's now."

The Recovery Act has already transformed the General Services Administration, the federal government's unglamorous real estate arm, into "the green proving ground for the building industry," in the words of former GSA building commissioner Bob Peck. The agency got $5.5 billion to improve federal energy efficiency, four times its annual construction budget. "NASA had its moon shot. This is ours," Peck told me. GSA is converting an abandoned munitions factory in St. Louis into green Social Services offices. It's installing solar panels on dozens of federal rooftops, including an Indianapolis federal building that will serve as a "solar lab" measuring the performance of competing brands. It's renovating a century-old courthouse in Grand Junction, Colorado, into the first "net-zero" building on the National Historic Register, which means it will generate as much energy as it uses. Peck told me the federal government is such a huge purchaser that it's moving markets, driving demand for geothermal heat pumps, LED lighting, and eco-certified contractors.

"We're seeing a tipping point in the industry," Peck said. "Before long there won't be 'green architects' or 'green contractors.' Everyone's going to be green."

The GSA later became a symbol of the follies of big government, after its inspector general exposed its lavish spending on clowns, psychics, and other lunacy on a Las Vegas junket. Peck and other top officials were fired. But the cynics who say Washington never changes ought to see what GSA is doing to the physical city, starting with its own World War I–era headquarters, which had wires duct-taped to its ceilings and antique air-conditioning units in its windows when I first visited. Now it's installing state-of-the-art heating, cooling, and electrical systems, with motion sensors, sun-tracking window shades, and other green features that could cut the agency's energy bills in half. And as Peck pointed out, going green isn't just about high-tech bling. The remodeled headquarters will also accommodate thousands more GSA employees, saving the agency over $20 million a year on leases for spillover office space. (That would fund two dozen over-the-top Sin City conferences.) The result will be greener in the same way dense cities are greener than sprawling exurbs. When I visited, Peck had moved four staffers into his eight-hundred-square-foot McMansion of an office.

"Who needs all that territory?" he asked. "We're not Neanderthals anymore."

Meanwhile, at the St. Elizabeths Hospital campus in southeast Washington—best known as the home of mental patients from Ezra Pound to John Hinckley, and as a stately red-brick backdrop in the film *A Few Good Men*—GSA has launched the largest federal construction project since the Pentagon was built, the new Homeland Security complex that Republicans perversely attacked as "government furniture" during the stimulus debate. It will convert dozens of abandoned nineteenth-century hospital buildings into energy-efficient offices; GSA has set up shop in the former morgue. I watched workers pouring concrete for a 1.2-million-square-foot Coast Guard headquarters, which will cascade down a hillside overlooking the marble edifices of federal Washington. It will feature one of America's largest green roofs, and is expected to attain LEED (Leadership in Energy and Environmental Design) Gold eco-status. In fact, starting with the Recovery Act, every GSA project will aim for at least LEED Silver.

"We've changed everything we do," says Kevin Kampschroer, head of

GSA's Office of Federal High-Performance Green Buildings. "And we'll never go back to the old way."

In early 2009, the U.S. "base case" energy forecast expected that it would take more than two decades for wind power to grow from twenty-five to forty gigawatts. It took less than two years. Solar power was growing even faster, with photovoltaic installations doubling in 2010. By year's end, the wind and solar industries employed nearly 200,000 Americans, more than the coal industry. It was quite a recovery from a near-death experience.

"What the stimulus did for renewables, I want a stronger word than 'transform,'" says Ed Fenster, CEO of San Francisco–based Sunrun. In 2009, Sunrun helped 400 homeowners go solar; in 2010, its numbers soared to 5,400. "Solar was failing, and now it's the fastest-growing industry in America," he says.

The Recovery Act also jolted green energy manufacturing. In 2006, the United States imported 75 percent of the content of its wind turbines, which was inconvenient and costly; they have thousands of parts, and can weigh as much as jumbo jets. By 2010, only 40 percent of the typical turbine was imported, thanks to dozens of stimulus-funded factories, many producing gear boxes and other high-value components that had never been made in America. The stimulus sparked a similar boom in solar manufacturing, to the point that the United States became a net exporter of solar products. Its tax credits also helped finance factories for energy-efficient window makers like Serious Materials, smart appliance manufacturers like General Electric, and LED lighting ventures like Cree, which Obama and Biden both hailed as a firm of the future in visits to its North Carolina headquarters.

Again, the Energy Department did not dictate the winners and losers of the clean-electricity game. It financed a bit of everything, including advanced geothermal and more efficient hydropower as well as wind and solar. Within solar, it funded just about every conceivable approach to harnessing energy from the sun, rooftop approaches as well as utility-scale projects. Within the rooftop realm, it funded cadmium-telluride thin-film modules from First Solar and Abound Solar and silicon panels from SunPower and Suniva as well as Solyndra's lizard ladders. For utilities, it financed several different types of concentrated solar projects, vast arrays of lenses or mirrors that focus sunlight on a single power generator as well as vast arrays of photovoltaic panels that convert sunlight into electricity directly.

"They're helping to scale up all kinds of technologies," says Bright-Source CEO John Woolard, whose Oakland firm is installing hundreds of thousands of mirrors in the Mojave Desert for the world's largest solar thermal plant. "Then we'll all battle it out."

It's not a fair fight. Fossil fuels enjoy all kinds of subsidies and tax breaks—more than renewables—and don't have to pay for their carbon pollution. The shale boom has ratcheted down natural gas prices. But even on a non–level playing field, the Recovery Act helped clean power get more competitive. Wind gradually approached coal and natural gas. Solar prices, while still higher, fell by half in two years. Companies like BrightSource were signing long-term deals to deliver power to utilities at market rates, while firms like Sunrun and Silicon Valley–based SolarCity were offering no-money-down solar leasing deals for home-owners as well as companies like Walmart; rooftop solar was no longer a luxury limited to families who could afford to plunk down $30,000 up front. In California, homebuilders began providing it as a standard feature in new subdivisions.

"Solar has a massive stigma as being expensive, but it's not true anymore," says SolarCity's South Africa–born CEO Lyndon Rive, another former infotech entrepreneur whose cousin Elon Musk, the Ironman-inspiring founder of PayPal and Tesla, chairs his board. "We can already offer you a deal to buy future electricity for less than you're paying now, and our costs are coming down every day."

It was no accident that green energy ventures like SolarCity, Sunrun, BrightSource, and Tesla—as well as SunPower, Serious, Solazyme, and yes, Solyndra—were so often rooted in the Bay Area. (Or that Chu and so many of his top aides were rooted in the Bay Area.) California had America's strictest mandates for energy efficiency and renewable power. It was about to implement a cap on carbon. And the pioneering mega-state that gave us microchips, iPhones, Google searches, and the Hollywood vision of success was still America's most powerful engine of innovation.

Clean-tech was the next California gold rush, as software and chip industry veterans adapted their skills to the digital grid and solar technology. Risk takers like Rive—who came to California for an underwater hockey tournament, got swept up in the Internet boom, and stayed to launch an IT start-up—were trying to reinvent the energy landscape, with help from legendary Silicon Valley venture capitalists like John Doerr and Vinod Khosla. SunPower chief technology officer Tom Dinwoodie took me to the roof of the historic "daylight factory" overlooking San Francisco Bay, where Ford built Model As before World War II, where the real Rosie the Riveter built jeeps and tanks during the war, and where SunPower now assembles the world's most efficient silicon panels. He showed off the sleek solar array on the roof, then pointed across the bay at a collection of hulking tanks that Chevron uses to store fossil fuels.

"Someday," Dinwoodie said, "we'll turn those tanks into hot tubs."

Dinwoodie was basically expressing the California creed, which was not all that different from the audacity of hope. There was a lot of Californification in the Recovery Act, and the entire Obama agenda.

The right tends to caricature California as a hotbed of hippie-lefty vegan politics, the land of Daily Kos and the Sierra Club, yoga and medical marijuana, "Hollywood values" and "San Francisco values." After the subprime collapse, when state government was paying employees with IOUs and headlines were ridiculing "California's Wipeout Economy," conservatives blamed government activism and a hostile business climate. But that hostile business climate had somehow nurtured Google, Apple, Facebook, Twitter, Disney, Cisco, Intel, eBay, and countless other futuristic companies that shape how we live. Even in the throes of the recession, California's wipeout economy was attracting more venture capital than the rest of the nation combined. And government activism helped explain why. Public support for the University of California, federal energy labs, and the military-aerospace-industrial complex had helped fuel the infotech and biotech booms, and now eco-friendly energy policies were promoting the clean-tech boom. The Recovery Act would export a taste of California to the rest of the country.

When I watched the Tea Party candidate Marco Rubio trash the stimulus in Florida, he riffed about how at that very moment someone in a garage was probably inventing a battery the size of a wineglass that would power a whole building—with no help from the government. But Yet-Ming Chiang had invented the pixie dust for A123's early batteries with help from a six-figure Energy Department grant. Now Chiang was trying to invent the kind of battery Rubio had in mind through 24M, with a seven-figure ARPA-E grant to help him. A123 was working on a separate ARPA-E project to recycle used car batteries for the grid.

Rubio was peddling a libertarian fantasy of technological innovation. ARPA-E was promoting the real thing.

The Game-Changers

The batteries of today are much better than the batteries of yesterday, but they can't compete with the incredible power of gasoline. Envia Systems, another Silicon Valley start-up, is developing the batteries of tomorrow. Chief technology officer Sujeet Kumar showed me around the small lab where Envia is developing "nano-coated silicon-carbon composite anodes" and "high-capacity manganese-rich layered composite cathodes." There was a dishwasher-sized vat where chemicals are mixed, a furnace where they're cooked into black powders, a room full of multicolored wires where they're subjected to intense thermal testing. It was typical lab stuff, except for the results: Test batteries stocked with Envia's nano-glop are producing world-record energy densities of 400 watt-hours per kilogram. That's three times as good as the first-generation Volt, a major step toward all-electric vehicles that go three hundred miles on one charge. The frustrating lead times of automobile production will keep this breakthrough off the streets until at least 2015, but it could shave over $5,000 off the price of a Volt.

"We'll make electric vehicles profitable without subsidies," Kumar says.

Kumar is a nerdy scientist and a proud capitalist, an Indian immigrant who says he came to America "because of free enterprise." When Silicon Valley was all about pets.com and flooz.com, he patiently worked on nano-materials for batteries that nobody wanted; now, he says, "it's my time." But Kumar is the first to admit that Envia, which was founded in 2007 in the Palo Alto public library, would be nowhere without the federal government. Its underlying technology was licensed from an Energy Department lab. When it was struggling to raise seed money, ARPA-E awarded it a $5 million grant. Envia was then able to produce results that helped it raise $17 million in private capital—and its lead investor is General Motors, which owes its existence to the feds.

"Clean-tech is capital-intensive and slow. It isn't software," Kumar says. "The risky technologies really need government support, or the innovation won't happen."

When Summers called government a "crappy vc," he was really objecting to its project finance work; he's a big supporter of ARPA-E, which is more like a traditional early-stage venture capital firm. Even Mitt Romney has said he supports federal research "through programs such as ARPA-E." And Envia is just one of the agency's early success stories. In its first two years of high-risk, high-reward science experiments, eleven of its grant winners went on to raise nearly $200 million in private financing.

Investors poured $27 million into FloDesign, which is developing next-generation wind turbines shaped like jet engines. Chiang's 24M attracted an additional $10 million for its flow batteries. Another MIT-generated venture, 1366 Technologies—this one wonk-named for the number of watts of solar energy that hit each square meter of the earth's atmosphere—raised $33 million for a manufacturing process that could slash the cost of silicon solar cells. Instead of sawing paper-thin silicon wafers out of ingots—an expensive, energy-intensive process that wastes half the material as dust—1366 plucks the wafers directly from molten silicon.

Majumdar calls 1366 the agency's first grand slam, a game-changer for solar power. "It's amazing to see this stuff pan out so quickly," he says.

I've never felt dumber than I felt following Secretary Chu around the ARPA-E Innovation Summit, already known as the Woodstock for energy geeks, watching him grill scientists and engineers on the technical intricacies of their out-of-the-box research into carbon capture, power conversion, and the like. In my semidefense, he made some of the scientist and engineers feel dumb, too. One of his first stops was a showcase for a super-efficient "wave disk engine," which would replace pistons with shock waves that blast hot gas into rotors that . . . oh, I lost track. "Where are the thermo-efficiencies?" Chu asked. It wasn't the kind of question that cabinet secretaries usually ask. "If the shock wave goes turbulent, does it clear before the next detonation?" The team of Michigan State techies shot each other nervous glances.

"Errr . . . we don't know," one of them stammered.

This was Chu's favorite part of his job. He was a true science junkie; after the oil spill, he studied diagrams of the well and calculated flow rate equations as if he had been detailed to the containment team. Chu also believed that this was the most vital part of his job, that the United States faced a Sputnik moment, that the brainiacs at the ARPA-E summit represented the best hope for another American century. China was installing more wind farms, high-speed rail lines, and high-voltage transmission wires than the United States. Thanks to a Recovery Act upgrade, the Energy Department's "Jaguar" supercomputer had become the world's fastest in 2009, but a Chinese model had taken over the top spot in 2010. "We're in a technological race," Chu told me later. "Our advantage is in that room."

ARPA-E aimed to steer all that brainpower into "white space," the gaps in human knowledge where breakthroughs could reshuffle the energy landscape. Its first question was never: "Will it work?" It was: "Would it matter?" For example, air-conditioning hadn't improved much in a century; it depended on an inefficient vapor compression process that clumped together dehumidification and cooling. Under the guid-ance of Ravi Prasher, another nano-genius who had overseen Intel's ther-mal technologies, the agency's BEETIT program—a strained acronym for Building Energy Efficiency Through Innovative Thermodevices—was seeding all kinds of alternative approaches, from "magnetic refrigera-tion" to "thermo-elastic cooling" to "ventilation enthalpy recovery."

Similarly, Envia's batteries of tomorrow will approach the theoreti-cal limits of lithium-ion technology, but they still won't match gasoline, which is why ARPA-E is also financing the batteries of the day after tomorrow. Led by Dave Danielson, a gung-ho clean-tech venture capi-talist, the BEEST program (Batteries for Electrical Energy Storage in Transportation) has invested in magnesium-ion, lithium-sulfur, and other speculative battery chemistries. Polyplus CEO Steve Visco, a for-mer chemist at a national lab, is working on "lithium-air," which could be ten times as powerful as lithium-ion. The problem is that lithium-air is highly reactive, and batteries aren't supposed to explode; Visco showed me video of a lithium cube dropping into water and instantly vanishing. But then he showed me footage of a lithium cube encased in a Polyplus ceramic membrane dropping into water, and nothing hap-pening. "That's our magic right there," he said. "If we can get the dura-bility right, we'll beat gasoline."

All of ARPA-E's programs are chasing far-out dreams. GRIDS is investing in far-flung technologies that could store renewable energy on a massive scale; as Majumdar puts it, the current grid is constrained in much the same way a human being without a bladder would be con-strained. AGILE is promoting more efficient transistors, inductors, ca-pacitors, and other unseen building blocks of the grid. Cree, the lighting firm that Obama and Biden visited, won a grant to develop transistors that could cut electricity losses in half, while shrinking transformers from the weight of an elephant to the weight of Kate Moss. The goal is to replace ancient substations that occupy entire city blocks with tiny high-tech basement vaults that use one tenth the power and suffer far fewer outages.

Electrofuels, the discipline invented by ARPA-E to overcome the inefficiencies of photosynthesis, was its most radical program, and the only one without an acronym. Deputy director Eric Toone, the biochemist who devised the concept, was amazed by the audacity of the proposals, many from renowned scientists who had never done energy work. "The intersection of really smart and really creative is a really exciting place," he says. But he wasn't sure any of their schemes to reengineer microbes would actually produce fuels. For years, genetic research funding had focused on human disease; the molecular biology of these organisms was still a complete mystery. "We didn't know if we had the tools to manipulate them," Toone says. "We had this great story, but we had no idea if any of this stuff was going to work."

We do now. In his introductory speech at the ARPA-E summit, Majumdar spoke of the dream of electrofuels, a word that wasn't even in the dictionary yet, a dream barely one year old. And then he stunned the crowd. "If you think this is in the future, if you think this is science fiction, think again," he said. He held up a vial of electrofuel engineered by a team at North Carolina State in collaboration with a Colorado biotech start-up called OPX; at energy.gov, there's video of that fuel powering a jet engine. Majumdar then held up another vial of electrofuel, this one brewed by a team at MIT.

Toone says he's been astonished by the success of the electrofuel projects, and OPX has raised $36 million in follow-up financing. But the energy world is all about scale. A vial can prove a concept, but it's a long way from refueling our way of life.

"Now we know it works," Toone says. "We just don't know if it matters."

— SEVENTEEN —

Political Recovery

Behind the numbers, beyond the shouting, the Recovery Act was about middle-class everymen like Duane Bartley, a bearded Paul Bunyan type from a small mountain town in Colorado, a husband and father and electrical engineer who suddenly found himself unemployed and bankrupt in 2009. Bartley is a hard worker, a gentle giant who likes tinkering with engines with his dad and fixing appliances for neighbors in need. But the Great Recession didn't just purge rottenness from the system. Bartley's wife's veterinary business failed, because her clients couldn't afford pet care, and then the battery company where Bartley was working failed, because consumers couldn't afford much of anything. He blasted out hundreds of résumés; not only didn't he get a job, he didn't get a single response. He didn't even send out Christmas cards, because he couldn't think of anything cheery to say.

But in April 2010, Bartley landed a quality-control job with UQM Technologies, which was tripling its workforce after winning a stimulus grant to build motors for electric vehicles. Three weeks later, Bartley was introducing Biden at a Recovery Act event at UQM's new factory, wearing one of those crazy-loud ties that guys who never wear ties wear, explaining how happy he was to give his teenage daughter some security.

"We'll be putting stamps on our Christmas cards this weekend," Bartley said.

Bartley, as the newspaper cliché goes, was not alone.

In the spring of 2010, recipients reported that Recovery Act grants directly funded nearly 700,000 jobs. And that reporting only applied to a third of the stimulus; it didn't capture the impact of tax relief or aid to the vulnerable, much less the indirect impact of new hires like Bartley spending their paychecks. Overall, the White House estimated the Recovery Act had already increased employment by at least 2.5 million jobs, only slightly higher than estimates from independent forecasters.

But Biden had been around politics awhile, and he didn't think people responded to numbers. He thought people responded to people, to testimonies like Duane Bartley's.

"That story can be told time and again, all over the country," the vice president told the crowd. "Our job is to have Duane's story repeated and repeated and repeated."

To Biden, it was a story about resilience, about America getting back in the fight. It was also a story about the Recovery Act's investments in innovation, about the public sector helping the private sector manufacture the green products that will—"literally!"—drive progress in the twenty-first century. At UQM, Duane Bartley was troubleshooting motors for the all-electric buses that another U.S. company called Proterra was building in another stimulus-funded factory in South Carolina. The Recovery Act was also helping transit agencies in Los Angeles, San Antonio, and Tallahassee buy Proterra's new buses. Biden thought that if Americans could see this new ecosystem taking shape, the politics of stimulus would improve.

That was the basic idea behind the "Recovery Summer" of 2010, the West Wing's last-ditch effort to revive the Recovery Act's reputation.

Obama sometimes humble-bragged about the "perverse pride" his administration took in putting policy first and letting the political chips fall where they may. He wanted his White House to behave more like the Aspen Institute than Tammany Hall, and the Recovery Act reflected that. The two biggest high-speed rail grants went to states with Republican governors. The biggest stimulus project was a nuclear cleanup in South Carolina, where Governor Sanford was savaging the stimulus. The competitive programs often attracted intense political pressure, but a slew of independent audits of the Recovery Act failed to uncover the administration putting its political thumbs on any policy scales.

The White House, however, was not the Aspen Institute. Politics may not have dominated the conversation, but it was in the room. As the midterm elections approached, Rahm and other political aides often called Biden and his team with political questions: Do we have anything Blanche Lincoln can announce in Arkansas? The White House arranged frequent events in Nevada for Harry Reid, who was fighting for his political life against another Tea Partier. And there was a strong desire to deodorize the general stench around the Recovery Act, which, as Obama half-joked to his cabinet, was "the only thing less popular than I am," even though its individual items still polled well. That suggested a political failure, and Biden was eager to correct it.

By the Recovery Summer, more than half the stimulus had been spent, and it seemed to be winding down. But as Ron Klain told Democrats on the Hill, only the under-the-radar elements—tax cuts, state aid, food stamps—were winding down. The visible, marketable stuff was ramping up. That summer, there would be six times as many highway projects under construction as the last summer, eight times as many park projects, twenty times as many water projects.

Finally, the shovels were ready. It would be nice to get some credit for them.

Congressional Democrats were less eager for their constituents to see the Recovery Act in action.

They thought Obama had done a horrible job selling the stimulus early on, letting Republicans dictate the narrative, getting bogged down in health care instead of pounding a jobs message. But by 2010, most Democrats had stopped clamoring for presidential backup on the stimulus. They no longer wanted to discuss the stimulus. The narrative of failure was set, and an election year when the major issues were sky-high unemployment and sky-high deficits seemed like a strange time to try to rewrite it. They were more concerned with salvaging their own jobs than the Recovery Act's reputation. "It got to be so toxic," says one House leadership aide. "It didn't make any sense to talk about its benefits."

Hill Democrats were already frosted at Obama on multiple fronts—his scuttling of the transportation bill; his handling of the health bill, cap-and-trade, and the seemingly endless war in Afghanistan; his failure to ask them for advice, invite them to events, and otherwise make them feel special; and his habit of denouncing "Congress" rather than "Republicans." Anyway, the stimulus debate felt like a ball game that had been out of reach since the first quarter. One poll found only 6 percent of Americans believed it had created any jobs. That was less than the percentage of Americans who believed Elvis was alive or the moon landing was faked.

Some Democrats, not content to ignore the Recovery Act, began attacking it. Chuck Schumer, the camera-loving New Yorker in charge of messaging for Senate Democrats, began howling that 80 percent of the stimulus grants for wind projects had gone to foreign manufacturers. "The point of the stimulus was to create jobs in the United States, not in China," Schumer said. In fact, those foreign manufacturers were creating jobs in the United States, no matter whose name was on the corporate polo shirts. The Recovery Act not only saved the U.S. wind industry, it nearly tripled the domestic content of U.S. wind farms, and only three of America's 33,000 turbines were made in China. But for Republicans, the jingoism from Schumer—who usually knew which way the political winds were blowing—was pass-the-popcorn proof that the debate was over.

"It's one thing if Republicans say the stimulus is wasteful," gloats one senior GOP Senate aide. "It's another thing if Chuck Schumer says it."

For the White House, the political calculus of the Recovery Summer was simple: The stimulus was creating jobs, so people ought to hear about it. Duane Bartley was as real as the moon landing. The Recovery Act would probably remain unpopular as long as times remained tough, but if Obama showed what he was doing to turn things around, voters would remember once things turned around. It reminded Biden of the crime bill from the 1990s; crime wasn't going to drop right away, but you had to be there every time a new cop was sworn in, so that when crime did drop people would give you credit.

"We've got a story to tell. Let's tell it!" Biden argued.

At the end of May, Obama visited a factory under construction in Silicon Valley to tell one of those stories, a tale of the Recovery Act unleashing the next generation of California ingenuity. In retrospect, he should've left that particular story untold.

"It was here where weary but hopeful travelers came with pickaxes in search of a fortune," Obama said that day. "It was here that tinkerers and engineers turned a sleepy valley into a center of innovation and industry. And it's here that companies like Solyndra are leading the way toward a brighter and more prosperous future . . ."

(Not Glossy)

The White House went to amusing lengths to stage-manage Obama's visit to Solyndra. "Can you confirm that his greeters will be wearing their normal everyday work clothes and safety gear?" the advance team emailed. "We want to make sure we have the construction worker feel." Yes, confirmed, along with the twenty-foot-by-thirty-foot American flag, coffee and donuts for the press, and a robotic arm that would display a solar panel onstage during the president's speech. Also, the team wanted a solid backdrop behind Obama: "Preferably not white. Something darker and matte (not glossy)."

Republicans claimed that the reams of Solyndra-related documents the administration later turned over to investigators exposed the true nature of the Obama White House, a Tammany Hall masquerading as an Aspen Institute. And it's true that the email trail revealed White House aides obsessing about the political appearances of his visit to Solyndra. Not only did they choreograph that "construction worker feel," they fretted the president might be embracing a corporate loser. With hindsight, the internal debates make for painful reading.

Solyndra had bled over $400 million in two years, and its auditor had just cited "substantial doubt about its ability to continue as a going concern." So when it was announced that Obama would stop by Solyndra in a week, one OMB official sniped: "Hope doesn't default before then." The clean-tech venture capitalist Steve Westly, a California politician and Obama fund-raiser, warned White House senior adviser Valerie Jarrett that Silicon Valley had grave doubts about Solyndra.

"I just want to help protect the president from anything that could result in negative or unfair press," Westly wrote. "If it's too late to change/postpone the meeting, the president should be careful about unrealistic/optimistic forecasts that could haunt him in the next 18 months if Solyndra hits the wall, files for bankruptcy, etc."

Westly's email was immediately forwarded to Matt Rogers, who said the "going concern" language was standard for a fast-growing company preparing an IPO. Still, he saw three real problems for Solyndra. Silicon prices were plunging, which meant its high costs could be a crippling disadvantage. Europe was on the brink of another crisis, which was weakening demand in its top export market. And the company was "counting on an energy bill to pass" to build U.S. demand, which was like counting on *Zookeeper* to win an Academy Award. On the other hand, Solyndra's sales were rising, and the stimulus-funded factory that would help it cut costs was on schedule to open that fall.

"Sounds like there are some risk factors here—but that's true of any innovative company that POTUS would visit," Klain told Jarrett. "It looks OK to me, but if you feel otherwise, let me know." Jarrett said she was comfortable if Klain was comfortable. He assured her that Solyndra's situation was common for high-tech start-ups.

"The reality is that if POTUS visited 10 such places over the next 10 months, probably a few will be belly-up by election day 2012—but that to me is the reality of saying that we want to help promote cutting-edge, new-economy industries," Klain wrote.

"I agree," Jarrett replied. "There is an inherent risk in highlighting a single company before they have a track record."

Klain responded: "Or even after they have one : -)"

Republicans have exploited this paper trail to accuse the White House of "playing politics." Newt Gingrich called Solyndra "a half-billion-dollar photo op."

It's true. Politics were played. Photos were taken. Is it news that presidential events are political? Perhaps Obama's advance team went overboard micromanaging the Solyndra CEO's sartorial choices—"I know he might think about wearing a suit, but I advise against it if at all possible"—and it was a sad day for the Republic when White House officials began using emoticons in their emails. But there's nothing scandalous about trying to present policies in a positive light. Actual scandals involve actual policies. If anything, the White House didn't think enough about the politics of Obama's visit. "Going concern" letters are common, but Solyndra was burning cash like MC Hammer; there was no need to send the president to the riskiest stimulus project in California.

Sure enough, a month into Recovery Summer, Solyndra had to cancel its IPO, triggering another round of bad-news stories. It also replaced CEO Chris Gronet, the scientist who founded the firm and invented its technology, with veteran Intel executive Brian Harrison, a burly, buzz-cut former minor-league power pitcher who had manufacturing experience and an imposing presence. As Harrison described it to me later, Solyndra was the corporate equivalent of a science geek who hadn't grown up. It was still obsessed with perfecting its technology long after it should have shifted into making and selling mode. Its research team was still far bigger than its marketing team, as if revenue was an afterthought. And its strategy was ludicrous. It was trying to appeal to the entire solar market, as if its technology were so incredibly cool that everyone would pay more for it, instead of focusing on the flat commercial rooftops where it had a genuine advantage.

"This is a very bad situation," Harrison told his new employees. "You don't need an MBA to figure out that this has to change, or we're in big trouble."

Maybe the Energy Department should have foreseen these problems. But there's no evidence that "crony capitalism" had anything to do with the original decision to approve the Solyndra loan, or any other loan for that matter. Rogers did tell me he once encountered White House pressure, when a uranium enrichment company called USEC was pursuing a loan for a nuclear fuel plant in Ohio, but even that tale illustrates the limits of political interference in Obamaworld. The president had promised to support the plant during his campaign, so after Rogers rejected the loan, he was summoned to explain his decision to Jarrett—in the Situation Room, of all places. (It looks exciting in the movies, with all those video screens and blinking lights, but the West Wing is so overcrowded that it's sometimes used as an ordinary conference room.) Rogers explained his skepticism about USEC, a former government enterprise. For one thing, it would still be short of the cash it needed to complete the plant even if the loan went through, a neon red flag in project finance. Deals are supposed to cover the cigars for the closing dinner—in other words, everything.

"You realize the president made a campaign promise?" Jarrett asked.

Yes, Rogers did.

"Well, if you're sure, you're sure," Jarrett said. "But you better be sure."

Rogers was sure, and the White House let him make the call.

Nevertheless, Boehner and McConnell have slammed the White House over USEC, not for pushing a flimsy loan that could have cost taxpayers $2 billion, but for *rejecting* the flimsy loan. Both Republican leaders usually attack the administration for picking winners and losers, but USEC operates in Ohio and Kentucky. McConnell also urged Chu to approve a loan for an electric vehicle plant in his home state. "I hope you will realize the importance of such job creation to Kentucky," he wrote.

Politics aside, there were real tensions baked into the loan program, and it became a source of intense debate inside the administration.

The Energy Department was supposed to finance projects safe enough that taxpayers would get repaid, yet risky enough that banks wouldn't finance them without federal help. So the budget monitors at OMB often delayed loans for months, demanding endless due diligence to make sure borrowers wouldn't default. "It was a root canal every time," an Energy Department official complains. And once OMB was finally satisfied a loan was safe, Treasury officials often asked: Then why does the government need to back it?

"You're basically searching for Goldilocks projects—not too safe, not too risky, just right," Klain says. "It's a lot trickier than just giving people cash."

Personalities inflamed the tensions. The head of the loan program, Jonathan Silver, was a brash Wall Street financier who was wearing a pink tie, monogrammed shirt, and bull-and-bear cuff links when I met him. He frequently antagonized the White House by demanding more autonomy to build his portfolio as he pleased, opening interagency meetings with long gripes about bureaucratic interference. On the other side of the debate, Summers was even less of a shrinking violet, and a harsh skeptic of government loans. He and Geithner intervened behind the scenes to kill a loan for Bloom Energy, the heavily hyped fuel cell company backed by the financier and Obama donor John Doerr. "Why the hell do they need our help?" Summers asked. Despite the loan program's strong support in the clean-tech world, it was the only Recovery Act initiative scaled back after passage. Its $6 billion in reserves for bad loans shrank to $2.5 billion after it was raided to fund Cash for Clunkers in 2009 and the teachers jobs bill in 2010. Doerr and Al Gore both called to protest, but the White House held firm.

That $2.5 billion in reserves was still enough to finance nearly $40 billion worth of the most ambitious clean-energy projects in history, including a half dozen of the world's largest solar plants and two of the nation's first large-scale cellulosic ethanol plants. The Shepherds Flat wind farm in Oregon will also be the largest in the world, featuring 338 American-made General Electric wind turbines, generating enough green power to replace two coal plants. The first-of-its-kind Project Amp will install solar panels on over 750 commercial rooftops across twenty-eight states, producing a nuclear reactor's worth of green electricity. Silver built the loan office into the world's largest project finance team, hiring scores of Wall Street veterans laid off during the financial crisis, and that team invested more in green energy than the next ten largest American funds combined. It backed all kinds of loans the private sector wouldn't otherwise provide, for companies like Solyndra with innovative technologies, as well as projects like Shepherds Flat with relatively mature technologies but unprecedented scale.

"Every bank wants to finance the second project," Silver said. "We're the bank that finances the first project."

Summers just didn't think the government belonged in the banking business. He was particularly galled by the $1.9 billion Shepherds Flat project, which would provide investors an expected 30 percent return on equity. "Larry didn't get it, or didn't want to get it," one official says. "I wanted to grab him and say: You ignorant fuck! We *want* people to make money in clean energy!" Summers tried to kill the entire loan program, pushing to shift its funding into the renewable energy grants that Schumer was attacking in the press. They were creating more jobs at a faster pace than the loan guarantees, while requiring recipients to put more skin in the game.

Silver understood why his program was an inviting target. Companies were always complaining to Congress when they didn't get loans, or didn't get loans quickly enough, or their competitors got loans. The political system didn't handle failure well, and failure was inevitable, because all banks make bad bets. It was a complex program, maybe too complex. But Silver was convinced that it was moving the country toward a low-carbon economy, carrying green technologies through the Valley of Death so that the private sector would finance them in the future.

"I'll stipulate there's a better way to do this: Put a price on carbon," Silver told me. By making pollution expensive, a carbon price set through cap-and-trade or a tax on emissions would offset dirty energy's market advantage. "But let me ask a question: Ya got one?" Silver continued. "No? Then this is the way to get clean energy to scale."

Silver was so unpopular in the West Wing that Chu was warned not to bring him to the Oval Office meeting to decide the fate of his program. But Obama decided not to kill it.

"We're not going to relitigate this," Obama said.

Recovery Bummer

Obama kicked off Recovery Summer with another trip to Columbus, to celebrate the 10,000th Recovery Act road project with more construction workers in hard hats. The stimulus, he said, was doing exactly what it was intended to do. "As my friend Joe Biden would say, this is a big"—he replaced the expletive with a smile—"deal." He pointed out that the last time he visited Columbus, for the police graduation, the economy was shedding 700,000 jobs a month and shrinking at a Depression-level pace. Now it was adding jobs and growing.

Still, unemployment was a gruesome 9.9 percent. So it was a muted celebration.

"I'm under no illusion that we're where we need to be," the president said.

The Recovery Summer was pure politics, a transparent effort to sell the stimulus in an election year. Obama spent a grand total of fifty-eight minutes in Ohio, just long enough to speak and pose for pictures. But the problem with Recovery Summer was not that it reeked of politics; stimulus critics played politics, too. The problem with Recovery Summer was that it reeked of terrible politics, because as LaHood said in Columbus, "the economy is still lousy."

And then, inconveniently, it got worse.

The recovery stalled during Recovery Summer. Home sales hit an all-time low after the homebuyer tax credits from the stimulus expired that spring. Job growth slowed to a crawl, and economists began to fear a double-dip recession.

"We went out there just as the bad news was mounting," Klain says.

The main problem was a debt crisis in Greece that was dragging down global growth. Meanwhile, states were slashing their budgets again, and Republicans were blocking Obama's push for more fiscal relief. And the Fed, after its whatever-it-takes exertions to save the financial sector, was curiously passive about the moribund labor market. At their monthly lunches, Christy Romer prodded Bernanke: "You need to do more monetary stimulus." But Bernanke didn't want to unless he absolutely had to. As he reminded Romer, there were other ways to jolt the economy: "You need to do more fiscal stimulus!"

Eventually, Congress approved a bit more fiscal stimulus, the Fed approved a bit more monetary stimulus, and modest job growth resumed that fall. But not before Recovery Summer crashed and burned. People saw more Recovery Act projects, but they didn't see more recovery. "If you look at what we said, we were right. The construction numbers went way up," Klain says. "But we still got lampooned. The narrative was: Biden predicted recovery, and look what happened."

Between the gushing oil and the wilting recovery, Obama had a rough summer, too. He was mocked for golfing on tony Martha's Vineyard while the economy tanked. "He created 70,000 new jobs this month," Jay Leno said. "Too bad they're all vacation planners for his family." The White House put out word that he was pressing his economic team for bold new jobs ideas—he led a conference call from the Vineyard—but the sudden burst of activity just looked lame: *Now* he wanted ideas? Once the media decided he was drowning, every drip of bad news reinforced the narrative, especially after he defended the so-called Ground Zero mosque in Manhattan; during the spat, one poll found nearly half of Republican voters thought he was Muslim. As his approval ratings dipped into the low 40s, some Democrats began running ads bragging that they had stood up to the president. Even the artist behind the Obama campaign's iconic "Hope" poster told reporters he was losing hope.

Republicans had a field day with Recovery Summer. "How was YOUR summer?" asked one GOP ad. "The Recovery Starts November 2." Democrats had once crowed that the stimulus would be political gold; now almost half the Republican campaign ads attacked it, while Minnesota's Jim Oberstar was the only congressional Democrat to tout it. The House Republican committee borrowed Schumer's wind farm rhetoric to produce absurd scare ads featuring red flags, menacing-sounding gongs, and Asian calligraphy fonts, accusing stimulus-supporting Democrats of outsourcing jobs to China. One ad ended with a cartoon image of Cultural Revolution–style upraised fists: "He's created massive debt here, while he created renewable energy jobs *over there*. Baron Hill: For Indiana, or China?"

In Wisconsin, Republican Scott Walker made high-speed rail the centerpiece of his campaign for governor, vowing to send back the state's $810 million award for a Milwaukee-to-Madison line. It was a perfect wedge issue for 2010: anti-Obama, antigovernment, anti-Madison's citified professors and bureaucrats. At notrain.com, Walker posted video of Obama celebrating the stimulus, splicing in his own mockery. "Change isn't easy," the president said in one clip. "But stopping runaway government spending is," Walker replied. John Kasich, the Republican candidate in Ohio, also pledged to kill the slow-speed 3-C line, and the Tea Partier Rick Scott, running in Florida, suggested he wasn't a fan of the Tampa–Orlando bullet train.

Obama did find time that summer to sign the Dodd-Frank financial reforms, the most comprehensive rewrite of Wall Street regulations since the Depression. That was another big deal, ensuring stricter regulation of derivatives, hedge funds, and insurance companies like AIG, as well as a consumer financial protection agency that could rein in predatory mortgage lenders and credit card companies. Again, Republicans opposed the bill en masse, with only three GOP senators willing to support tougher financial rules after a financial meltdown. And again, the left accused Obama of selling out in his search for sixty votes, failing to crack down hard enough on too-big-to-fail banks or reinstate Depression-era financial laws.

"The president argues that this has been the biggest moment of progressive reform since the Great Society. And it's true. But that's a pretty low bar," says the liberal activist Bob Borosage. "It's been a tragically flawed moment. Great for the banks, not so great for the middle class."

In a testy interview with the lefty comic Jon Stewart, Obama ridiculed his base's ingratitude: "We didn't get 100 percent of what we wanted, we got 90 percent, so let's focus on the 10 percent we didn't get." He felt like he had put out a raging fire, and his allies were yelling at him for hosing down their furniture. He mused that maybe his slogan should have been: Yes We Can, But It's Not Going to Happen Overnight.

The root of Obama's political problems was not a deep mystery. "You don't have to be a savvy political analyst to say that if unemployment is 9.5 percent, the party in power is going to have some problems, regardless of how much progress we've made and how much worse it would be if the other side had been in charge," he said. It's a simplistic explanation, but the economy often is destiny for presidential popularity. That's why Axelrod had warned Obama in December 2008 that the midterms already looked bleak.

But voters also had a skewed view of what Obama had done, which suggested a failure to communicate. For example, by a 52–19 margin, the electorate thought he had raised middle-class taxes, when in fact he had cut middle-class taxes. After the Recovery Summer, the president told the *New York Times* he might have been overconfident that good policy would translate into good politics.

"I think anybody who's occupied this office has to remember that success is determined by an intersection of policy and politics, and that you can't be neglecting of marketing and PR and public opinion," he said. I later asked Axelrod whether he thought the White House had failed to make the case for the stimulus before Recovery Summer.

"Do people fully understand what the Recovery Act is and what it has meant? The answer is no, and I'd be obtuse to say we did everything we possibly could or everything well," he said. Axelrod has a perpetually beleaguered, hangdog look, and at that moment he seemed even more mopey than usual. "I'll ponder that for a long time," he said.

Recovery Summer felt like one migraine after another.

Early in the summer, for example, a controversy erupted over the Recovery Act's financial incentives for "meaningful users" of health IT.

The administration had proposed shockingly stringent rules defining what doctors and hospitals would have to do to qualify as "meaningful users," and not even tech-savvy health IT pioneers like Kaiser Permanente and the Mayo Clinic thought they could meet the twenty-five rigid criteria. "The goal was to stretch the providers, not break them," says David Blumenthal, the head of Obama's health IT office. "There was a pretty clear consensus that we went too far." Even Blumenthal's former boss at Partners Health Care was quoted in the *Times* blasting the White House's "unrealistic expectations" and "unachievable timelines."

The administration did not want a war with the medical industry at a time when the Tea Party was on a rampage against Obamacare. And while some officials—most vociferously Zeke Emanuel—were pushing for the strictest possible rules to lay the strongest foundation for health reform, Blumenthal thought it was more important to encourage widespread adoption of electronic medicine. So in July, the White House softened the rules. Doctors would only have to e-prescribe 40 percent of the time, instead of 75 percent. They would only have to use one form of "clinical decision support"—like a program that warns about potentially dangerous drug interactions—instead of five. And they could qualify for incentives even if they didn't meet all twenty-five criteria.

"You can ask people to run so fast that they collapse in fatigue, but that's not how you change the system," Blumenthal says. "We tried to be practical. Now you're going to see just about every hospital and medical group moving towards meaningful use."

Race to the Top also became a political flashpoint, after New Jersey barely missed a grant, in part because its application was docked several points for including incorrect budget information. Republican governor Chris Christie claimed his education officials had tried to submit the correct information during an interview in Washington, but federal reviewers had refused to accept it. "That's the stuff that drives people nuts about government," Christie told the press.

The budget error was not the main problem with New Jersey's application. The state lost more points because it lacked buy-in from its teachers unions, which was Christie's fault; his education commissioner, Bret Schundler, had worked out a deal with the unions, but the governor had scuttled it. Still, Christie's allegations were about as close as the Recovery Act had come to a legitimate scandal.

Except the allegations were bogus. A videotape of the interview proved that Christie's aides never tried to correct their error. Christie, forced to find a new scapegoat, fired Schundler.

"Thank God we taped it," Education Secretary Arne Duncan says.

Duncan kept the Race clean, sometimes at the expense of his agenda. The conflict-of-interest rules for the reviewers basically disqualified anyone who had run schools or advocated reform, and the emphasis on "buy-in" gave unions inordinate power over state applications. When pro-reform states like Colorado and Louisiana failed to win grants, Duncan had to resist the temptation to meddle.

"If you play it straight, things usually work out in the end," he says.

FutureGen, the billion-dollar clean-coal project killed by Bush and then revived as a quasi-earmark by Senator Durbin, became yet another political headache.

The plan called for an "integrated gasification combined cycle" plant in Mattoon, Illinois, which would capture carbon dioxide from the plant's waste stream and pump it into rock formations underground. But the Energy Department team soon realized that Bush's aides had been right: FutureGen cost way too much. Chu pored over the blueprints to slice out gold plating, but the project just didn't pencil out. It had been conceived in 2005 as a model for the world, the first carbon-capture-and-sequestration plant at commercial scale. But it no longer felt like the future. The Recovery Act's clean-coal grants were financing several plants with similar technology, similar scale, and much lower costs. And its developers said they might need $1 billion more. It was starting to look like NeverGen, and Matt Rogers wanted a Plan B.

Jim Markowsky, a longtime utility executive who led the department's fossil energy program, had an idea. Reducing emissions at America's six hundred existing coal plants was a much more urgent priority than building cleaner new plants, but the stimulus hadn't done much to address it. What if FutureGen could be reinvented as a retrofit, pioneering an "oxy-combustion" technology that would produce carbon dioxide directly, skipping the expensive carbon-capture process? Chu persuaded Durbin that FutureGen 2.0 could keep the project alive—still in Illinois, although not in Mattoon—and Rahm grudgingly approved the new plan after grilling the Energy team. "That was one of the longest hours of my professional life," Rogers says. At least it was until Rogers visited Tim Johnson, the Republican congressman representing Mattoon, who screamed that Rogers was corrupt and incompetent, unleashing a bug-eyed tirade that made Rogers think he was mentally ill. After throwing Rogers out of his office, Johnson publicly demanded an investigation, producing more bad stimulus headlines.

It's not certain that FutureGen 2.0 will ever get built. Low-emissions coal plants are tough to justify without a price on carbon; to the marketplace, they're just high-cost coal plants. A stimulus-funded carbon-capture project in West Virginia has already been scrapped. But whatever happens to FutureGen 2.0, there was nothing corrupt about trying to transform an out-of-control boondoggle into a potential game-changer that could make the U.S. coal industry viable in a carbon-constrained economy, and rewrite the future of coal-dependent nations like China and India.

"We've got a chance to make clean coal competitive by 2020," Markowsky says. "Without the Recovery Act, we'd have no chance."

The Recovery Summer was a political dud, but the Recovery Act was still on track. On September 17, Ed DeSeve opened another cabinet meeting with an upbeat update: The stimulus had met all its deadlines, hit all its jobs targets, and avoided humiliating screwups. "I've never seen this many GAO reports with this little news in them," DeSeve said. "Knock wood!" He noted the latest Republican horror story was that Northwestern University might have used stimulus funds to hire a lifeguard—not exactly Teapot Dome 2. OMB controller Danny Werfel, who oversaw federal finances, said the budget office was baffled by the Recovery Act's low incidence of fraud.

"We're trying to figure out what we're doing right here, so we can bottle it," he said.

Biden burst in a few minutes later, straight from a meeting with the Kuwaiti prime minister, bubbling with hyperbole. "The Recovery Act has been the most successful government program in history!" he announced. "This is a big deal, man!" Even without the expletive, he clearly believed what he was saying.

Biden did have a larger point beyond self-congratulation: Obama had pledged to spend 70 percent of the stimulus by the end of the fiscal year, which meant a total of $550.9 billion had to be out the door within two weeks. "Not 549.6. Not 550.3. We have to meet the president's goal, and I'm going to be a royal pain in the neck until we do it," Biden said, banging his fist on the table. "I'm not screwing around here. I don't care if you need to work twenty hours a day. Get it done! No ifs, ands, or buts. Get it done!"

Biden's staff let me sit in again, and as I watched him gab, it was hard to believe he ever had a speech impediment. But he was clearly worried about the optics of failure: "If we miss the goal by a nickel, the headline is that we missed the goal—and frankly, we don't have the PR firepower to overcome that." He was also worried what would happen to unspent stimulus funds after the election. He expected Democrats to hold Congress, but Republicans would clearly gain seats. "If you think we're pushing rope now, it's just going to get harder. I still have great relationships with Republican senators, and they tell me: *We're coming for your money, Joe,*" he said in a horror-movie singsong. The GOP was already blocking an extension of that New Deal–style subsidized wage initiative, even though it was widely considered a welfare-to-work success story. Even Governor Barbour had praised it as a model program, but it was about to disappear, because congressional Republicans were determined to stamp out anything associated with the stimulus.

"If we don't get the money out, it will go away," Biden said. "And if I'm wrong about the House and Senate, we will enter a know-nothing period in American politics."

Biden reminded the cabinet that Obama had inherited a $2 trillion hole in the economy, probably much bigger, yet the folks who dug it were whining that he hadn't filled it yet. And the public thought the stimulus was a waste. "We've already got Democrats starting to buck, because it's so hard to explain," Biden said with a sigh.

Soon he was on another roll, recycling his riff about his mom telling him to be glad his broken arm wasn't worse, reminding the cabinet that when your neighbor loses his job it's a recession and when you lose your job it's a depression, telling another shaggy-dog story about renovating his Senate office. It was all variations on a theme: The Recovery Act was proving that government could work, even though America hated it.

"You know, my mother always used to say: Joey, virtue is its own reward," the vice president said. "I'd think: Like hell it is!"

That fall, Obama hit the road with a modest new jobs plan that his bickering economic and political advisers had managed to agree on. It featured a $50 billion boost for transportation projects—"roads, rails, and runways"—along with several tax cuts. The package looked, walked, and quacked a lot like stimulus, although no one in the White House dared call it that in public. Democrats didn't use the S-word anymore.

Republicans did. Eric Cantor dismissed the plan as "yet another government stimulus," while the Republican National Committee dubbed it "stimulus déjà vu." In 2009, Republicans had blasted the Recovery Act as thin on infrastructure, holding a news conference in front of a giant road sign covered in red tape to demand more shovel-ready projects. But in 2010, their party line was that government was incapable of creating jobs, except through tax cuts. Of course, they opposed Obama's tax cuts, too; at this point, they would have marched in lockstep against apple pie if Obama were serving it.

Then again, the Obama plan wasn't designed to attract Republican support. It was a campaign document designed to highlight Republican extremism, to remind voters that the president wanted to do stuff and his opponents didn't, to frame the midterms as a referendum on anti-government absolutism. In fact, the White House did not include the stimulus idea that had the most Republican support, a temporary Social

Security payroll tax reduction, because if Obama had made it his own it would have lost its Republican support. "We decided to keep it in our back pocket," Jason Furman recalls.

House Republicans would soon unveil their own campaign document, the "Pledge to America," a vow to make the Bush tax cuts permanent, slash more taxes for "job creators," repeal Obamacare, cut unspecified spending, and cancel unspent stimulus funds. They were casting the election as a referendum on Obama. The president was casting the election as a choice between the future against the past, the sensible team that was getting the car out of the ditch against the radical team that drove the car into the ditch, fixers against whiners.

"We got our mops and our brooms out, we're cleaning stuff out, and they're sitting around saying: 'Hold the broom better. That's not how you mop,'" Obama said at a fund-raiser. "Don't tell me how to mop. Pick up a mop!"

He had a point. The Pledge to America really was a throwback to the Bush era. And Republicans really were standing on the sidelines and refusing to help mop up the mess; McConnell publicly declared that his top priority was making Obama a one-term president. But America didn't like the way the Democrats were mopping, and few of them were willing to defend their mopping on the merits.

Election day, as Obama put it, was a "shellacking." House Republicans gained a whopping sixty-three seats, achieving their goal of taking back Speaker Pelosi's gavel, allowing Cantor and his whip team to uncork that wine they had saved for their return to the majority. Senate Republicans also picked up six seats, but Tea Partiers lost winnable races in Delaware, Connecticut, Colorado, and Nevada, so Reid kept his job and his majority.

"The Republicans had Obama to thank for the House, and the Democrats had the Tea Party to thank for the Senate," says ex-senator Bennett, an early Tea Party victim.

Still, plenty of Tea Party Republicans were headed to Washington, including newly elected senators Marco Rubio in Florida, Rand Paul in Kentucky, and Pat Toomey in Pennsylvania. And Democrats of every stripe were heading home: Blue Dogs like Baron Hill and Blanche Lincoln, old bulls like Jim Oberstar, and young reformers like Scott Murphy, the businessman who rode the stimulus to victory in upstate New York, and Tom Perriello, a Virginia freshman who was targeted by the first GOP stimulus ad the day Obama signed the bill. Veterans like Obey, Byron Dorgan, and Chris Dodd retired rather than face the headwinds, while Arlen Specter lost his first Democratic primary. Governor Strickland, a big Recovery Act booster, was ousted by John Kasich in Ohio, one of twenty-nine Republicans to take over governor's offices. Scott Walker and Rick Scott won in Wisconsin and Florida, too, putting the future of high-speed rail in doubt. The only Republican incumbent to lose was Anh Cao, whose black Democratic district predictably returned to a black Democrat.

"The Democratic Party has become the party of pure *logos*, and the Republicans are the party of pure *mythos*," says Perriello, using the terms for reason and imagination from ancient Greek philosophy— which, come to think of it, probably proves his point. "We think we can just tell people something once, and the facts will tell the story. They understand that you have to repeat your message over and over again: socialism, socialism, socialism. Factually, it's ridiculous. But it works."

The wave election produced the usual recriminations, with centrist Democrats blaming Obama's liberalism, liberal Democrats blaming Obama's centrism, and everyone agreeing that the gifted wordsmith who had unspooled such a poetic narrative about his candidacy had failed to tell a coherent story about his presidency. He had stepped on his economic message by flitting around from issue to issue, tarnished his aura of change by cutting backroom deals, and allowed his agenda to be defined by the calculus of sixty votes in the Senate. He needed to be more populist in a populist moment, more combative at a time of all-out political warfare. He had failed to make a forceful case for climate action. He had undermined the case for Keynesian economics, and even echoed the Republican fantasy that spending cuts were an appropriate economic antidote to hard times. He had failed to change the nasty, vapid, ultra-partisan culture of Washington.

There is some truth to all these critiques. But it was never clear how better messaging or a sharper focus on jobs or a more (or less) confrontational attitude toward Republicans would have produced better political results in a battered economy. The academic literature on presidential persuasion suggests that the bully pulpit is vastly overrated. That's especially true in such a polarized political climate; Obama could have devoted more time to explaining, say, Keynesian economics, but that only would have made a large swath of the country hate it more. Even if he changed it or condensed it, they'd be against it.

In any case, politicians are supposed to try to win elections so that they can govern, not the reverse. And Obama had been pretty busy governing during his first two years. Perhaps his message had suffered, but he had gotten an awful lot done.

And his first two years weren't quite over yet.

— EIGHTEEN —

Not Quite Done

The Second Stimulus

At the White House, change was already in motion.

Peter Orszag, tired of infighting, quit during Recovery Summer. Christy Romer, still enamored of Obama but increasingly frustrated with Washington, returned to Berkeley in the fall. Larry Summers, having fulfilled his prophecy that making colleagues feel validated would not be his forte, was about to go back to Harvard, leaving Tim Geithner the only principal from the original economic team. David Axelrod, the guardian of Obama's message, would soon depart for the reelection campaign; Robert Gibbs, Obama's spokesman, was on his way out, too. And Rahm Emanuel, the screaming, schmoozing, fuck-you-ing force that made the White House go, had left the building to run for mayor of Chicago. The West Wing felt oddly quiet as it mourned the shellacking.

The president wasn't much of a mourner. The day after the election, he surprised his morose staff with a list of big things he expected to achieve during the lame-duck congressional session. It would be the last chance for Democrats to move legislation before Republicans seized the House, so he wanted to repeal the "Don't Ask Don't Tell" policy that barred gays and lesbians from serving openly in the military, and pass the DREAM Act to grant residency to illegal immigrants who came to America as kids. He also wanted the Senate to ratify his New START nuclear arms reduction treaty with Russia. And with the jobless rate hovering near double digits, he hoped to extend unemployment benefits and other Recovery Act programs that were about to expire, injecting more of the S-word into the slack economy. His staff thought his to-do list was borderline delusional.

Before he did anything else, Obama would have to deal with the Bush tax cuts. They were scheduled to expire on December 31, the final party favor in the Bush gift bag. And McConnell was vowing to paralyze the Senate until they were all extended.

As a candidate, Obama had promised to repeal the Bush tax cuts that solely benefited the top income brackets. But as president, he had repeatedly kicked that can down the road. Economically, tax hikes are anti-stimulus, although less so when skewed toward the rich. And politically, many Democrats were terrified to discuss tax hikes during a recession—or any other time. Ideally, the White House would have preferred to extend Bush's middle-class tax cuts, which were popular and decent stimulus, while repealing the high-end tax cuts, which were unpopular and weak stimulus. But vulnerable Democrats simply didn't want to discuss the issue before the midterms. The attack ads about tax-and-spend liberals would have written themselves.

After the election, Obama had to stop kicking the can and decide what to do. Republicans were holding the middle-class tax cuts hostage to try to force him to extend the upper-income tax cuts, and their leverage would only increase once Boehner became speaker. So the president had only two real options. He could let all the Bush tax cuts expire, which would violate his pledge not to raise middle-class taxes, and possibly trigger a double-dip recession. Or he could cut a deal to continue Bush's regressive policies, and see what he could get in return. The left itched for a new fight over tax cuts for Richie Rich, but Obama was happy to have that fight in 2012. He had just gotten annihilated in his last fight; he was eager to remind independent voters that he was a reasonable man. And with the Recovery Act starting to peter out and the recovery sputtering, he hoped to give the engine more gas.

To broker the deal, Obama turned to his most experienced Washington hand, his only adviser who had a working relationship with McConnell: the vice president. Biden was still a Senate man at heart—he called it "the greatest institution man has ever created"—and he was still the son of a salesman. He and McConnell didn't agree on much, but they were both rational politicians, and Biden sensed there was a deal to be had. The basic framework would have to be Obama accepting two more years of the Bush tax cuts, a political victory for Republicans, and McConnell agreeing to extend unemployment benefits and a host of tax cuts for the poor and the middle class, a substantive victory for Democrats. McConnell agreed with the general thrust, but Republicans were viscerally opposed to extending anything in the Recovery Act. They still saw "refundable" tax cuts for the working poor as glorified welfare for lucky duckies. And if Obama was submitting a wish list, then Republicans wanted a huge reduction in estate taxes for the heirs of multimillionaires.

Obama and his aides found these priorities offensive, but they figured it was more important to help ordinary people than to stop Republicans from helping rich people. Unemployment was way too high to walk away from a significant stimulus deal out of pique over goodies for the wealthy. Biden finally told McConnell: We'll do your stuff, but you have to do our stuff, including the "refundables."

As staffers hashed out the details, the main sticking point was the allergic Republican reaction to the Recovery Act. GOP aides even objected to extending bipartisan technical fixes that had been tacked onto the stimulus as a matter of convenience. "It was crazy: If it was in the Recovery Act, they had to fight it," Furman recalls. Republicans flatly refused to continue the wildly popular Build America Bonds, which had begun as a bipartisan proposal, and had expanded to one fifth of the municipal bond market in two years. They also refused to extend the advanced manufacturing tax credit, which had helped finance 183 factories producing clean-energy components, as well as the cash-in-lieu-of-tax-credits for clean-energy projects, which had kept the wind and solar industries afloat after the financial crisis. Gene Sperling, who would soon replace Summers at the National Economic Council, half jokingly asked if they would also oppose the annual relief from the Alternative Minimum Tax, since it was now tainted by the stimulus.

The White House did take advantage of the Republican jihad against Recovery Act provisions to swap the Making Work Pay tax cuts for a one-year payroll tax cut, the policy it had kept in its back pocket since the summer. The substitution let Republicans claim the scalp of a signature Obama initiative, but the alternative was quite similar to Making Work Pay, and the White House preferred it. It would inject more stimulus in a form the public would be more likely to notice. And Republicans would probably agree to extend it in 2011 to avoid a tax hike, so it could inject even more stimulus down the road.

The initial media coverage focused on Obama's policy retreat, but the deal provided over $300 billion in new stimulus, while preventing the anti-stimulus of tax hikes. After the Recovery Act, $300 billion sounded a bit piddly, but it was bigger in real dollars or as a slice of GDP than any New Deal initiative.

"There was nothing accidental about that," Biden boasted to me later. "We needed another stimulus!"

The deal gave high earners another windfall, but over two thirds of its benefits went to ordinary families and small businesses. And most of those benefits came from Recovery Act extensions that the Republicans eventually agreed to swallow. In addition to the payroll tax cut and unemployment benefits, the deal extended the Recovery Act's expansions of tax credits for children, college tuition, and the working poor through 2012. It also extended incentives for firms to buy equipment, along with another year of alternative minimum relief. And at the last minute, Reid told McConnell the deal wouldn't fly without the renewable-energy cash grants, so those got a one-year extension as well.

What's more, the deal kept the Senate open for business, allowing the Democratic Congress to repeal Don't Ask Don't Tell, one of the most significant civil rights advances since the civil rights era. The Senate also ratified Obama's nuclear treaty, which never would have happened in 2011. The DREAM immigration bill fell short of sixty votes, but the lame-duck session was far more productive than anyone except Obama expected.

As usual, most progressive activists greeted this historic string of progressive achievements with contempt. Obama had caved to Republicans, breaking his promises and betraying his supporters. He had made the Bush tax cuts his own, and approved an estate tax giveaway that Bush couldn't even get when Republicans ran Washington. And he had rewarded hostage takers, which would only invite more hostage taking. At a private post-election meeting of top Democratic funders and activists, the billionaire George Soros said it was time for the left to start recruiting a new presidential candidate for 2012, someone who wouldn't take liberals for granted and suck up to conservatives.

"We've been given the opportunity to govern, and we're failing," Soros said.

Seriously? Even the conservative pundit Charles Krauthammer credited Obama with pulling off "the swindle of the year." Obama had come to view liberal activists as the kind of people who would yell at Lassie for tracking mud on the carpet after saving the kid from the well. They wanted a fight? They just had a fight, and Democrats had gotten crushed.

Around this time, Obama met with some of his left-leaning economic critics, including Robert Reich, Joseph Stiglitz, and Paul Krugman. "You guys are the last Keynesians left," he cracked. Everyone laughed uncomfortably. Obama had just gotten a dozen stitches in his lip after getting elbowed playing hoops, and he quipped that he didn't feel nearly as wounded as he felt when he read Krugman. The columnist seemed genuinely pleased to hear he had irritated the president. For the most part, the meeting felt like a waste of time. The liberals all wanted new stimulus, but they were horrified by this particular new stimulus. They also wanted Obama to stop talking about deficit reduction and fiscal restraint, which would have been an odd political response to the Republican triumphs of November. "Within the political constraints,"

Obama asked, "what do you think I can do?" Yes, he had ransomed another hostage, because the hostage was the American people. He understood the value of a good fight, but he wasn't interested in letting utopian fantasies become the enemy of good policy.

"If that's the standard by which we're measuring success, let's face it, we'll never get anything done," Obama said at a news conference the next day. "People will have the satisfaction of having a purist position and no victories for the American people. And we'll be able to feel good about ourselves and sanctimonious about how pure our intentions are and how tough we are."

The End of the Line?

After the shellacking, the Obama administration didn't even wait for Scott Walker and John Kasich to take office in Wisconsin and Ohio before taking away their high-speed rail money. The two newly elected Republican governors had made it perfectly clear they planned to shut down their projects, so Secretary LaHood beat them to the punch, redirecting $1.2 billion to the other first-round winners. That meant another cash infusion for Florida, where Governor-elect Rick Scott had been less than perfectly clear about his plans for the Tampa–Orlando bullet train, and California, where Governor Schwarzenegger wrote a teasing thank-you note to his friend Kasich.

"I told John: Thanks for your fiscal responsibility!" Schwarzenegger recalls.

For the White House, it was an annoying episode. Granted, the 3-C plan to start rail service from scratch in Ohio had been a stretch, but the Milwaukee–Madison line had real promise, as a stand-alone route and as a link toward Chicago–Minneapolis. The good news was that the reshuffling seemed likely to salvage Obama's showcase project in Florida, since Scott had said his main concern was the potential drain on state finances. Now the feds were covering 90 percent of the cost of the Tampa–Orlando line, and several multinational firms hoping to build and run it indicated that they'd be willing to cover the rest—and would even absorb any risk of operating losses. Ron Klain told me in late 2010 that he expected high-speed rail to work politically for Obama in 2012, when thousands of workers would be laying tracks for the Sunshine State bullet train.

"Can you imagine in two years, when that high-speed rail money from Wisconsin is actually creating jobs in Florida, and somebody runs a campaign ad with a guy in a hard hat saying: 'Hey, I've got a great job. Thanks, Wisconsin!'" Klain said. "I think people in Wisconsin would say: *What?* That's not a hypothetical job. It's a real job."

Victorious Republicans were vowing to cancel unspent stimulus funds, and Klain almost hoped they would try. The Recovery Act still had a counterfactual problem, with Americans refusing to believe it had averted worse outcomes, but they'd get to see those outcomes if stimulus projects were scrapped. "Republicans keep talking about rescissions. Okay, what do you want to rescind?" he said. "We can shut down a hundred road projects, and lay people off right now. That would be the best communications strategy for the Recovery Act." The Spanish train manufacturer Talgo had already announced plans to shut down its Milwaukee factory, because Wisconsin no longer had a high-speed future. Walker couldn't blame those job losses on Obama.

"It's going to be a lot easier for us on defense than it was on offense," Klain said.

But Scott, whose first foray into politics had been his ads attacking Obama's health policies, began to signal he might kill the president's signature project even if it wasn't going to cost Florida a cent. At a Tea Party rally, he pointedly asked whether anyone planned to ride the train. Of course, no hands were raised. In a Washington meeting, he suggested he'd only let the project go forward if LaHood agreed to dredge the port of Miami, as if Florida would be doing Obama a favor by accepting his money. LaHood patiently explained that the Transportation Department doesn't dredge ports. Congressman Mica of Orlando, who had been publicly critical of the train in his backyard, did not want Scott to kill it; Mica was about to take over the House Transportation and Infrastructure Committee, and he assured me at the time that his new governor was just trying to drive a better bargain for his state. But Scott was starting to sound like a passive-aggressive fiancé who didn't want to get married but didn't want to be the one to break the engagement. "If I do this, it's going to be grudgingly," he told federal officials. "It's not my priority."

Scott had run on a jobs-jobs-jobs platform, and the U.S. Conference of Mayors estimated the Tampa–Orlando line would create 27,000 jobs. Two private reports commissioned by the state concluded that it would be highly profitable, and Orlando–Miami even more profitable. And LaHood offered unprecedented assurances that Florida would bear no risk for overruns or losses. "This was going to be the greatest deal on the planet," one LaHood aide says. "If other states had heard about the guarantees Florida was getting, all hell would have broken loose."

Scott decided to cancel the project anyway, claiming Florida could have been on the hook for overruns if the project failed, citing research by a libertarian think tank that had never met a train it didn't hate. Scott's slogan was "Let's Get to Work," but his base wasn't interested in work funded by the government—especially Obama's government. Scott instantly became a national hero in the twilight struggle against Obamaism.

LaHood had trouble comprehending how his party's version of political correctness now required governors to reject transportation projects they didn't even have to pay for. What had happened to the party of Lincoln, father of the transcontinental railroad, and Eisenhower, father of the interstate highways? "Now people listen to Beck and Hannity and Rush all day long," LaHood says. "Trash talk, 24-7." But so be it. If Florida didn't want $2.4 billion, other states would gladly take it. And even Governor Scott, who had threatened to kill the Orlando commuter rail line as well—the project that LaHood had persuaded Florida to pursue in order to qualify for the high-speed rail money—agreed to let the project go forward after Chairman Mica went ballistic.

"We still know how to do big things in this country," LaHood told me.

• • •

There is no bigger thing being done in this country than the California high-speed rail project, a shoot-the-moon effort to connect San Francisco to Los Angeles in less than three hours. It will have to overcome seismic faults, rugged mountain passes, and ferocious opposition from deep-pocketed homeowners and farmers who don't want trains whipping through their communities. Ultimately, it could take more than twenty years and cost as much as $100 billion to complete. It's often described as a political football, which seems wrong. Footballs get tossed and carried and fumbled, while the rail project just seems to get kicked—and not only by Republicans eager to embarrass Obama. California Democrats have also churned out reports questioning its route, costs, and sketchy ridership projections. But thanks to Governor Scott, it's Obama's only bullet train that still has a chance to be built. And thanks to the money diverted from Wisconsin, Ohio, and Florida, its first phase of construction will no longer be a train from nowhere to nowhere in the Central Valley. It now has enough cash to get from Fresno to Bakersfield—not exactly Paris–Lyon, but at least recognizable names on a map.

"You've got to start somewhere," explains Fresno mayor Ashley Swearengin, a Republican who has bucked her party to support the project.

Yes, but in *Fresno*? The city began as a depot on the Central Pacific railroad, and as high-speed rail officials point out, it's about the size of Lyon. But its downtown is now a dismal collection of boarded-up buildings, pawn shops, *botanicas* selling cheap statuary, check cashers, and, incongruously, a bronze Renoir sculpture of a washerwoman next to a Payless shoe store. And Bakersfield will never be confused for Paris. It's got the nation's least educated population, according to Brookings, and worst air quality, according to the American Lung Association. In 2010, Fresno and Bakersfield had the nation's third- and fifth-highest Latino unemployment rates.

Swearingen envisions high-speed rail as an economic redevelopment engine that could help revive both cities, and help connect the fast-growing Central Valley to the rest of California. But that's not the real reason the project is starting in the middle, hundreds of miles from its target markets in L.A. and the Bay Area. The Central Valley, with its flat terrain and sparse population, is the easiest and cheapest place to get started, and the project's boosters are desperate to get it started before critics can stop it. As New York's master builder Robert Moses used to say about public works, once you sink that first stake, they'll never make you pull it up. Fresno–Bakersfield would be ludicrous as a stand-alone, but it's a nice foot in the door. By contrast, building tracks in congested urban areas would be much more disruptive and expensive, and the trains would have to travel much slower; the wide-open Central Valley is where they can hit 220 mph.

"It makes no sense to start in the Central Valley if we're not serious about finishing. It's like designing a moon mission to go a quarter of the way there," says Roelof van Ark, the former head of California's high-speed rail agency. "But if we're serious, that's the place to start. If we start at the ends, we'll never do the middle."

Even in the Central Valley, it won't be easy to sink that first stake. I went to a public meeting in the small farm town of Hanford, where high-speed rail was seen as a federal assault on rural culture. The proposed route sliced through high-value crops—almonds, walnuts, grapefruits, a cherry orchard—as well as a local subdivision, and the residents didn't want compensation. They wanted blood. John Tos, a fruit and nut farmer with six properties in the path of the train, warned the project's officials that they would take his land over his dead body. "You know what it's called when you take something without permission?" asked Tos, a fourth-generation farmer with fiery blue eyes and a gray Abe Lincoln beard. "RAPE!" The consensus in the room was that high-speed rail was a snobby metropolitan plot, designed to boost urban hellholes like Fresno at the expense of communities with bedrock values, financed by a liberal president on a borrowing binge. "The federal government is nothing but a Ponzi scheme!" shouted Tos, pronouncing "Ponzi" to rhyme with "bonsai."

The Central Valley route should only affect about three thousand acres of farmland, a pittance compared to the thirty thousand acres the area already loses to sprawl every year. Passing trains aren't the main threat to Hanford's rural character. But they do represent change. California expects to add twenty million residents over the next few decades, and there are only so many freeways and airports it can build. Schwarzenegger and his Democratic successor, Jerry Brown, both see high-speed rail as a big bet on a new era of American mobility, with California leading the way for trains just as it did for cars. "You've got to imagine the possibilities," Schwarzenegger says. Valuable runway slots currently used to shuttle travelers between Northern and Southern California could be opened up for flights to Shanghai and Seoul. Intrastate trips would be comfortable, and the hours billable.

The problem is funding—or, more precisely, uncertainty about future funding. The feds have provided $3.6 billion in cash, and California voters have approved nearly $10 billion in bonds, more than enough to complete the Central Valley leg. But private firms, which see L.A.–San Francisco as a gold mine, are unwilling to provide financing without assurances the entire line will be built. And the California legislature is reluctant to start spending without assurances of continued federal support. When Obama unveiled a six-year, $53 billion plan to expand high-speed rail, Washington Republicans proclaimed it dead on arrival.

"The big challenge is convincing people this is a long-term project," says van Ark, a former executive with several European train manufacturers. "This can't be built in one election cycle. We need long-term vision." Unfortunately, van Ark told me, the U.S. political system doesn't work that way: "Asia has a long-term mentality. Europeans have a medium-term mentality. Americans are now, now, now."

The state plan still calls for construction to begin in late 2012, Fresno–Bakersfield to be done by 2017, and the whole line to be running around 2030. Its fate may depend on the November election. No one wants to go a quarter of the way to the moon.

In California, high-speed rail is still a debating point, a futuristic vision of a new way to travel. In Illinois, the TRT-909—or Track Renewal

Train, affectionately known as the "yellow beast"—is already laying the groundwork for higher-speed rail. The TRT is a noisy mobile factory that replaces tracks as it trudges along them, pulling up old wooden ties and rails, putting down concrete ties and sturdier new rails. I watched the TRT clattering along the St. Louis–Chicago line near Normal, Illinois, and it was mesmerizing. Thanks to the yellow beast, an initial section will be upgraded from 79 mph to 110 mph this year, and travelers will save an hour when the project is done in 2014.

"It's going to be an unbelievable boon for us," says Normal mayor Chris Koos.

Trains are already so vital to Normal that its dumpy little yellow-brick Amtrak station—unaffectionately known as the "Amtrak shack"—is the fourth-busiest in the Midwest, behind only Chicago, Milwaukee, and St. Louis. And the town won a $22 million TIGER grant to replace it with an eco-friendly multi-modal station that will anchor its New Urbanist downtown revitalization. The station is rising next door to a children's museum, a stone's throw from a new nine-story Marriott with a conference center. Koos says the new downtown has attracted over $200 million in private investment, including an upscale restaurant founded by a Chicago chef, a gourmet coffee shop selling $5 caramel-vanilla lattes, and other telltale signs of revival. Normal is the home of Illinois State University—originally a "normal school" for teachers, which is how the town got its name—and the promise of fast access to Chicago is already helping with faculty and student recruitment as well. As we watched workers pour concrete for the station's ticketing area, Koos told me the Recovery Act was transforming his town.

"People will start appreciating the stimulus when things start coming out of the ground," he said.

Whether or not people appreciate it, the Recovery Act is already renovating train stations in cities like Portland, San Jose, St. Paul, and yes, Wilmington, where the newly improved Victorian station has already been renamed for Amtrak Joe Biden. Amtrak's high-speed rail projects are under way in states like Missouri, Michigan, and Maine, where the Downeaster service is being extended twenty-six miles to Brunswick; like Normal, the town is enjoying a train-related boom, with $100 million worth of investments in retail, office, condominiums, and a hotel near the station. Thanks in large part to funds diverted from Florida, the Recovery Act is also financing improvements to the Northeast Corridor, including a new electrical system that will increase speeds in New Jersey, a new bypass that will unclog a choke point in Manhattan, and extra tracks that will allow faster trains to pass in Delaware and Rhode Island.

These projects aren't game-changers. They're game-adjusters, baby steps toward better service. And they aren't happening on a stimulus timetable. As they start producing results, shaving minutes off trips, travelers won't associate them with the Recovery Act. But over time, LaHood says, passenger trains will become a more attractive option.

"I've got nine grandchildren," he says. "High-speed rail is for them, not for me."

"No Es Bueno."

No matter how badly a day was going at the White House, there was always one word that could make it go worse: Solyndra. The day after the election, the company announced it was shutting down a factory and laying off two hundred employees. Wait: Wasn't the stimulus supposed to *create* jobs?

Solyndra tried to spin the moves as good news, and in a way they were. The company still had a thousand employees, and was executing new CEO Brian Harrison's plan to shrink its bloated research division. Shutting down its old factory made sense, too, since its more efficient new stimulus-funded factory was scheduled to come online soon. But White House energy adviser Heather Zichal had a more realistic assessment of the news in an internal email: "No es bueno." And there was more bad news that Solyndra chose not to announce. It was running out of cash again. Solar prices were still plummeting, and the European crisis was killing its best market.

Before the year's end, Solyndra's investors agreed to one last $75 million loan to stave off bankruptcy, but this time they insisted they had to be first in line for repayment if the company failed anyway. So the Energy Department had a tough decision to make; as Jonathan Silver wrote in an internal document, the loan office first had to "determine if the company still had a viable business." One OMB official noted in an email that politically, it would probably make sense to let Solyndra fail now, rather than risk a bankruptcy during the president's reelection campaign. "The optics will arguably be worse later than they would be today," the official wrote. Nevertheless, in January, the department agreed to restructure its original loan to give Solyndra a chance to finish its new factory, execute its new sales strategy, and try to raise new private capital. Even if the company still went under, it would be more valuable in bankruptcy if it had a completed plant.

"Our goal was taxpayer safety," Silver told me. "We decided to give Solyndra a fighting chance to succeed."

It was a risky move, but it looked like a smart one at first. The factory was completed on time and on budget. Sales steadily increased. Costs steadily decreased.

"We were executing our plan," says David Miller, Solyndra's corporate communications director. "We were so damn sure we were out of the woods."

There was even low-level White House discussion about inviting Solyndra's executives to sit in the First Lady's box during the State of the Union, to illustrate the president's theme of "winning the future." Obama's events director shot down that idea: "Can't do Solyndra . . . they've run into some issues recently. :("

That particular emoticon was probably appropriate.

"The stimulus worked!"

Ed Rendell—two-term Pennsylvania governor, two-term Philadelphia mayor, two-term district attorney, lifelong pol—had five days left in public office. A Tea Party governor was about to take over, and his activist legacy was at risk. At the final meeting of his Stimulus Oversight Commission, he wanted to set the record straight.

"I know it's not popular to say it," Rendell said. He had just been to the dentist, and he couldn't feel the left side of his face, so he was slurring his words a bit. "I know our citizens think the stimulus failed. But it's not true! These investments helped us weather the storm. And they are changing the face of Pennsylvania."

Rendell's stimulus commission chairman, a Republican businessman named Ron Naples, had insisted on measurable outcomes; early on, he had bewildered staffers of a stimulus-funded domestic violence program by asking how they calculated their return on investment. So now the governor had numbers to back up his words. The Recovery Act had resurfaced 940 miles of Pennsylvania roads. Its clean-energy projects would power 36,000 Pennsylvania homes, and its efficiency investments would save enough to power another 16,000. It was bringing broadband to 255 health providers, 142 libraries, and 939 schools. It had filled a $2.6 billion gap in a $28 billion state budget, avoiding a fiscal blood bath. The Keystone Research Center, a Harrisburg think tank, estimated the state's unemployment rate would have reached 14 percent without the stimulus; it was now 8 percent.

Yawn. Most reporters hate numbers. When Rendell finished his blizzard of triumphant data, the media didn't ask a single question about the stimulus. The event barely registered in the statewide press. *Philadelphia* magazine's political blogger did file a bit of snark, titled: "Rendell Declares Stimulus a Success. Don't You Feel Better?"

Afterward, Rendell invited me into his office, which was lined with portraits of past Pennsylvania governors. He pointed out Ben Franklin, who had held the job in his eighties, but had somehow persuaded the artist to make him look much younger. "Politicians never change," Rendell mused. His point was that image matters. Politics matters. In a democracy, good works are never their own reward. Rendell showed me the portrait of William Penn, who served thirty-seven years as royal governor; okay, that guy didn't have to worry about public opinion. But elected politicians do, and Rendell wondered whether Obama thought his policies were so brilliant they would sell themselves.

"We have a great communicator in the White House, but he failed to communicate," Rendell said. "I'm not Barack Obama, but if you gave me an hour to explain the Recovery Act to the country, I could've made the case!" I suggested that Obama was in a tough spot from the start, because no matter how he had handled the stimulus, jobs would have continued to disappear for months after it passed.

"Yeah, well, he should've explained that, too," Rendell said. "The White House gets very defensive about this. They're frustrated they're not getting the credit they deserve. Okay, but whose fault is that?"

From the start, he said, Obama overpromised on the Recovery Act's short-term benefits, and failed to sell its visionary long-term investments. "Even people who keep up with this stuff don't understand how this is laying a foundation," Rendell said. "The only time you hear about infrastructure or clean energy, someone's saying it's too slow, it's not stimulus." I agreed about the overpromises, but didn't Obama talk about investing in the future all the time? What about his New Foundation speech in April 2009?

"Too late," Rendell said. "By that time, the Republicans had already spun the stimulus into the graveyard."

We'll never know how much better messaging would have improved the Recovery Act's reputation. It's another unanswerable counterfactual. For what it's worth, I suspect it wouldn't have made that much of a difference. It was always going to be hard to sell a recovery package during a tepid recovery. And it's incredibly hard to recover from financial cataclysms. It's preferable not to have them in the first place, which, of course, was why Obama had enacted financial reform.

Anyway, change is always a tough sell. And Washington isn't the only city with a status quo bias. The day before I saw Rendell, one of his former aides, Philadelphia deputy mayor Rina Cutler, told me about BigBellies, the stimulus-funded, solar-powered compactors that were replacing traditional trash cans in downtown Philly. BigBellies had reduced trash pickups from three times a day to five times a week, saving the city big bucks. And they were cute, painted bright colors to look like garbage-eating monsters. But some residents were outraged. I asked Cutler why.

"Oh, people love change," Cutler said. "As long as it looks exactly the same."

— NINETEEN —

The Legacy

A Year of Sound and Fury

The first two years of the Obama presidency were two of the most productive years in modern political history. Then in 2011, nothing happened.

Okay, that's an exaggeration. The president did order the raid that killed Osama bin Laden. He brought the last combat troops home from Iraq, as promised. And he helped lead a NATO intervention against Libyan dictator Muammar Gaddafi, which critics predicted would become a quagmire. It didn't. It didn't end well for Gaddafi, either.

On the domestic front, though, it was a year of sound and fury, signifying very little. Politically, divided government produced constant drama, as House Republicans engineered a series of new hostage negotiations that made Washington look nuttier than ever. At times, there seemed to be an imminent danger of a chaotic government shutdown, or even a catastrophic government default. At other times, there seemed to be real hope for a bipartisan deal to rein in long-term deficits. The GOP rallied around a radical plan to reinvent Medicare and shrink spending, and Obama floated a new stimulus plan to inject $450 billion into the economy. But none of those things came to pass. Substantively, the clashes of 2011 produced a stalemate.

The first showdown dominated the spring, as House Republicans refused to pass a routine bill to keep the government running unless Obama accepted severe spending cuts, plus restrictions on Planned Parenthood and other right-wing demands. Minutes before the deadline, Boehner and Obama cut a deal to slice $38 billion out of the budget, which both described as "the largest spending cuts in history." The left erupted, accusing Obama of repeating FDR's slam-on-the-brakes mistakes of 1937, capitulating to hostage takers and validating their antigovernment worldview. At the progressive Netroots Nation conference, there was a panel discussion on "What to Do When the President Is Just Not That into You."

But the fine print revealed that Obama paid a paltry ransom to rescue the hostage. Republicans wanted to whack Democratic priorities like Head Start and Pell grants, but the deal only trimmed $352 million-with-an-m in 2011, mostly smoke-and-mirrors cuts of money that never would have been spent. It didn't rescind one cent of stimulus funds, and expanded stimulus programs like Race to the Top, TIGER, and ARPA-E. Republicans did block Obama's push for new investments in clean energy, science, and high-speed rail, but they didn't dismantle his earlier investments, or Planned Parenthood for that matter. Basically, the deal extended the status quo, neither advancing Obama's agenda nor rolling it back. And that posed a problem for Boehner, whose Tea Party freshmen thought they had a mandate to repeal the Obama presidency. The speaker was reduced to bragging about eliminating four "czars," Fox News shorthand for Obama policy aides, and even those four aides had already left government.

The next showdown dominated the summer, after House Republicans threatened to force the Treasury into default unless Obama agreed to more cuts. The insane spectacle of a superpower debating whether to pay its bills led to an unprecedented downgrade of the U.S. credit rating. And the bipartisan negotiations over a $4 trillion "Grand Bargain," which would have attacked long-term deficits with tax hikes and entitlement reforms as well as spending cuts, inspired endless what-if rehash. But after all the melodrama—Cantor blowing off Biden, Obama walking out on Cantor, Boehner refusing to return Obama's calls,

Boehner quelling Tea Party rebellions—there was no default, no grand bargain, and no overthrow of the speaker. Republicans refused to accept any tax hikes, and Obama resisted short-term cuts that could tank the economy. The result was a last-minute mini-bargain that stretched $2 trillion worth of paper cuts over a decade.

Again, liberals were enraged, denouncing Obama's focus on deficits during a jobs crisis, his acceptance of spending cuts without new taxes, and his willingness to consider squeezing Social Security and Medicare. While Summers, Romer, Bernstein, and even Orszag were all calling for short-term stimulus now that they had left the White House, the deficit-minded Geithner, the only survivor from Obama's original economic team, was now his dominant adviser. In a hostage crisis where Tea Party Republicans seemed downright eager to shoot the hostage, and the global economy depended on the survival of the hostage, Obama didn't think this was the time to make a public stand for Keynesian principles. And after a conservative wave election, his political advisers hoped a big bipartisan deal would reassure independent voters about his fiscal responsibility.

But again, the deal Obama actually struck was quite modest, delaying the vast majority of the cuts until 2013 or later. So they'll depend on the 2012 election.

Which was what 2011 was really about.

The recovery stalled again while Washington was obsessing over spending and debt. Economists cited supply chain glitches created by the Japanese nuclear disaster, high fuel prices spurred by Middle East instability, and European austerity measures in response to the Greek crisis. The U.S. debt limit circus didn't help, either, and the new stimulus from the lame-duck tax cut deal did not quite offset the loss of stimulus from the Recovery Act winding down. Meanwhile, states and cities kept slashing services and employees, creating more fiscal drag on the recovery.

In the fall, once Obama no longer needed Republican permission to keep the government from shutting down or stiffing creditors, he pivoted back to jobs, unveiling an American Jobs Act to give the economy more gas. Republicans called it "son of stimulus," and it did feature more payroll tax cuts, unemployment benefits, public works, and state aid, plus the school construction binge that Senator Collins stripped out of the Recovery Act. Once again, Obama was betting his presidency on the unspoken S-word.

Even the political theater critics who usually panned Obama for failing to market his policies clearly and repetitively had to admit he followed their advice on his jobs bill. He proposed it in a prime-time speech to Congress, then led raucous rallies for it around the country, including an in-your-face event at the creaky bridge connecting McConnell's state of Kentucky to Boehner's state of Ohio. At every stop, he led chants of: "Pass this bill!" But Congress didn't pass the bill. Reid broke it into individual components, but those didn't pass, either. They were dead on arrival in the Republican House, and some Democratic senators were distancing themselves from the Obama agenda, too.

Whatever muddled-message or *mythos-logos* problems Obama had, his real problem was 9 percent unemployment. He had said that if he couldn't fix the economy in three years, he was looking at a one-term proposition. Time was almost up. Republicans mocked him as Herbert Hoover 2, Jimmy Carter Jr., and after an August jobs report with no jobs, President Zero. (The report was later revised to 100,000 jobs. Nobody revised the nickname.) The people had spoken, and Republicans were flexing their muscles. When independent economists warned that the GOP plans for sharp short-term spending cuts would kill hundreds of thousands more jobs, Boehner blithely responded: "So be it."

But now that he had no chance to pass legislation, Obama was happy to "get caught trying," fighting losing battles that would highlight his differences with the GOP and start framing the 2012 campaign. He was positioning himself as a Reasonable Man with a Balanced Approach, supporting investments in education, innovation, and other popular things, paid for by modest tax hikes on oil profits and million-dollar incomes. He contrasted that with the extremism of so-be-it Republicans, who wouldn't even close a tax loophole for corporate jet owners. They had closed ranks around House Budget chairman Paul

Ryan's plan to replace Medicare's health care guarantee for the elderly with private vouchers and shred nonmilitary spending; after Gingrich called the plan "right-wing social engineering," he took so much heat from the Limbaugh wing of the party he had to call Ryan to apologize. At one Republican debate, the candidates vying to replace Obama were asked if they would reject a deficit reduction deal that included $10 in spending cuts for every $1 in tax hikes, and all eight raised their hands.

Reasonable and balanced were not selling points in the Republican primary. For a few weeks, the front-runner was the megalomaniac reality TV star Donald Trump, who built his groundswell by questioning Obama's citizenship. (The president finally released his birth certificate to prove he was native-born. Fewer than half of GOP primary voters were convinced.) Tea Party congresswoman Michele Bachmann, who claimed the 2011 East Coast earthquake was God's way of demanding spending cuts, also took a turn on top of the polls. So did an obscure right-wing businessman named Herman Cain, who suggested the unemployed should blame themselves instead of Wall Street; Texas governor Perry, who dismissed Social Security as a Ponzi scheme; former speaker Gingrich, who proposed putting poor kids to work as janitors; and former Pennsylvania senator Rick Santorum, who called Obama a snob for urging young people to go to college.

There was one Republican candidate who terrified the White House: former Utah governor Jon Huntsman, the reality-based conservative who had slammed his own "very narrow party of angry people" before serving as Obama's ambassador to China. But trashing the GOP and working for Obama was not a winning primary strategy, especially after his virtually disqualifying admission via Twitter that "I believe in evolution and trust scientists on global warming. Call me crazy." Former Massachusetts governor Mitt Romney, widely considered the Republican favorite, also had a history of reality-based behavior, including the health reforms that inspired Obamacare. But he was furiously backpedaling from his sensible-moderate past for the primary, vowing to repeal Obamacare, questioning climate science, embracing the Ryan plan to privatize Medicare. He accused Perry of insufficient hostility to illegal immigration, Gingrich of insufficient fervor for the free market, Santorum of sympathy for Big Labor and Big Government.

"It's been a lot of fun watching Mitt bash these right-wingers from the right," says one Obama aide.

By the end of 2011, Obama's approval ratings were starting to rebound, thanks in part to the Republican presidential freak show. He began quoting a line from Biden, who had cribbed it from an old Boston pol: "Don't compare me to the Almighty. Compare me to the alternative." In December, overconfident House Republicans made Obama look even better when they tried to seize one hostage too many, threatening to let the lame-duck payroll tax cuts and jobless benefits expire if the president didn't agree to deep cuts in Obamacare and other concessions on the Tea Party wish list. This time, Obama called their bluff, daring Boehner to raise taxes on 160 million Americans. Eventually, Boehner caved. So the economy got an extra year of stimulus, just as the White House had planned, and Obama got another opportunity to highlight Republican intransigence.

But the main reason Obama's approval ratings started inching up was that the jobless rate started inching down. As I write this in March 2012, unemployment has dropped to 8.3 percent, still terribly high—and yes, still higher than the Romer-Bernstein 8 percent prediction—but heading in the right direction. Even Romney is no longer saying the economy is weak because of Obama. He's saying the economy would have been even stronger without Obama. For a change, the counterfactual shoe is on the other foot.

Still, Obama is the ultimate counterfactual president. "That's us: avoiding even bigger messes since 2009," one aide quips. He helped reduce our dependence on foreign oil, but we're still dependent. He helped prevent atrocities in Libya, but he didn't get credit, because the atrocities were prevented. His financial reforms could avert another disaster, but presidents rarely earn points for averting disaster. One exception was George W. Bush, who got huge mileage out of "keeping us safe" after September 11. Obama has kept us safer, and wiped out most of al Qaeda's leaders, but apparently there needs to be a spectacular terrorist attack on U.S. soil during your presidency before you can get credit for avoiding another one.

The Recovery Act is the ultimate counterfactual policy. It's impossible to know precisely what the economy would look like without stimulus, because there's no way to run a double-blind study of an alternative U.S. economy. Nevertheless, it's possible to start drawing conclusions about the Recovery Act's impact.

Easing the Pain

The Great Recession will be remembered for rampant unemployment and rampant foreclosures. It won't be remembered for rampant homelessness. There was no epidemic of foreclosed families on the streets, no Obama-era version of the Hooverville tent cities. The number of Americans without shelter actually declined one percent from 2009 to 2011.

That wasn't happenstance. That was the Recovery Act.

Remember that $1.5 billion homelessness prevention experiment with the sixty-fold funding increase? Early data suggest it's been shockingly effective in keeping roofs over the heads of at-risk families. In the Miami area, it's helped over 7,500 people with rent, utilities, and emergency rehousing, and only 103 have shown up in the shelter system. Nationwide, it's helped house over 1.2 million Americans in crisis; if half of them had ended up on the streets instead, the homeless population would have doubled. Shelters would have been overwhelmed, along with emergency rooms and local jails.

"It works," says Ron Book, a Florida Republican lobbyist who chairs the Miami-Dade County Homeless Trust. "It keeps people off the streets and saves an astronomical amount of money. I'm not a fan of the stimulus, but this is a huge bright spot."

Whatever one thinks of using tax dollars to help people in precarious economic situations, the Recovery Act did help make their situations less precarious. It made food stamps more generous, transferring $20 billion to low-income families. It sent $250 checks to 55 million elderly and disabled Americans, helping them make rent, buy groceries, and keep their lights on. It boosted unemployment benefits $25 a week, extended their duration to almost two years, and helped laid-off workers keep their health insurance by subsidizing most of their premiums. It gave states about $100 billion to prevent massive cuts in Medicaid funding, and instead cover nine million additional low-income patients. Its refundable tax cuts redistributed billions more to the working poor.

The Great Recession did slightly increase the U.S. poverty rate, from 14.9 percent to 15.5 percent, but experts had expected a dramatic spike. An analysis by the Center for Budget and Policy Priorities found the Recovery Act's transfer payments directly lifted at least seven million Americans above the poverty line of $22,000 for a family of four. They also made 32 million poor Americans less poor.

When Romney infamously said he's "not concerned about the very poor," he was actually making a legitimate point: The safety net was covering their basic needs. But that had a lot to do with the Recovery Act that Romney and his party consider such an unmitigated disaster. Killing the stimulus would have killed funding for Meals on Wheels for poor seniors, subsidized lunches for poor children, subsidized child care for poor families, and other safety net programs. The center calculated that without the Recovery Act's aid to the vulnerable, the poverty rate would have increased at least five times more than it did. And that didn't take into account the stimulus produced by that aid, which went to families with the highest propensities to spend it.

This is where evaluating the Recovery Act gets a bit trickier. The stimulus definitely helped tens of millions of people in need. But it didn't produce full employment, which would have reduced the number of people in need. Republicans often claim the stimulus hurt the economy by growing the public sector, crowding out private investments, and using borrowed money that will have to be paid back with interest. Sometimes they merely dismiss the stimulus as an illusory "sugar rush." Even Keynesian true believers often criticize the way the Recovery Act was put together.

Economists will study the stimulus for decades to come. But so far, the evidence suggests that in the short term it basically did what it was supposed to do.

No, it didn't keep unemployment below 8 percent.

This is the most common partisan indictment of the Recovery Act: Obama broke his 8 percent promise. But unemployment passed 8 percent the same month Obama signed the stimulus into law. It shouldn't be blamed for failing to prevent an outcome that preceded its existence. And with the economy losing over 700,000 jobs that month, the jobless rate was clearly heading up no matter what Obama did. As impolitic as it was, the Romer-Bernstein report's poor guess about the pre–Recovery Act baseline implied nothing about its forecasts of the Recovery Act's impact.

In fact, the major private forecasting firms have mostly validated the White House forecasts of the Recovery Act's impact. They estimate it increased GDP 2.1 percent to 3.8 percent at its peak, in line with Romer-Bernstein, and created or saved about 2.5 million jobs, slightly fewer than Romer-Bernstein. They've suggested that without the Recovery Act, unemployment would have hit 12 percent or higher, and would have remained in double digits through 2012. Their estimates largely depend on models of the economy rather than the actual economy, but it's still notable that the leading forecasters all seem to agree.

Most economists do. Before it got caught up in Obama-era politics, Keynesian stimulus was the textbook response to a sharp downturn; as Romer said, it was about as controversial in the economics profession as antibiotics in the medical profession. Even now, 80 percent of the economists in a University of Chicago survey agreed the Recovery Act lowered unemployment, while only 4 percent disagreed. A *Washington Post* review of early stimulus studies identified six that demonstrated a positive effect on growth and jobs, versus only one useful study (by prominent Republican economist John Taylor) that found the stimulus failed—and critics noted that Taylor's data just as easily support the conclusion that the stimulus was too small. Even most Republican politicians stopped arguing that the stimulus failed to produce any jobs, instead claiming it cost too much per job. After all, the recipient reports alone documented 750,000 direct stimulus-funded jobs, and they only applied to one third of the Recovery Act.

If there's no smoking gun to prove the stimulus helped stop the free-fall, the ballistics certainly match. Job losses peaked in January 2009, just before it passed. Output began improving that spring, just as it ramped up. The recession technically ended in June, just as it hit its stride. In pure macroeconomic terms, the Recovery Act seems to have outperformed the New Deal, because it injected more fiscal stimulus than the New Deal. "The evidence is so clear," Mark Zandi says. "If it hadn't become so politicized, every economist would agree." Europe's struggles after austerity have provided equally strong circumstantial evidence that anti-stimulus deepens slumps; similarly, the U.S. states that cut the most spending tended to lose the most jobs.

The obvious question is why, if the stimulus worked as planned, unemployment has remained so high for so long. Obama's shadow transition team gave away part of the answer before he was even elected: Historically, recoveries from financial shocks are always slow and tough. And by some measures, the shocks of 2008 were nastier than the crash of 1929. Eight trillion dollars in housing wealth vanished almost overnight. The construction industry that created the bubble shut down, and millions of Americans could no longer use their homes as ATMs to finance the consumption that inflated the bubble. Families, businesses, and governments were all saddled with debt, leaving virtually no demand in the economy. Deleveraging takes time. So does restoring confidence.

The rest of the answer is that the Recovery Act wasn't big enough to fill that giant hole in demand. As Biden says, it was never supposed to carry the whole sleigh. The December 2008 memo from Obama's economic team acknowledged that it would plug less than half the output gap, and the team seriously underestimated that gap. Ultimately, the Recovery Act's fiscal expansion didn't even offset the contraction by state and local governments, and getting Congress to approve more stimulus turned out to be much harder than the team expected. For all the vitriol about Obama's new era of big government, the United States has shed over half a million public sector jobs during his presidency, or about two thirds of the government jobs added during the Bush era. This has prompted some liberals to complain that Keynesian stimulus was never tried; a more charitable reading is that Keynesian stimulus prevented even harsher anti-Keynesian cuts in the public sector. Meanwhile, the economy has added private sector jobs every month for two years, corporate America has enjoyed record profits, and the stock market has recovered its losses. It's an odd brand of socialism.

The Republican counterargument is simple: Unemployment is too high and the deficit is too big, so Keynes was wrong and the stimulus failed. Of course, Republicans supported Bush's stimulus in 2008 when unemployment was only 5 percent; most of them supported the concept of a stimulus in 2009; and Obama inherited a $1.2 trillion deficit that has not increased on his watch. So the partisan critiques seem awfully convenient. Republicans say they're worried about borrowing, but borrowing costs are historically low. They never seemed to worry about borrowing during the Bush era, and they're still happy to borrow to finance high-end tax cuts. The Recovery Act's impact on the national debt was negligible compared to the impact of the Bush tax cuts or the Great Recession. Yet the GOP, after frittering away the Clinton surplus and leaving the economy in a ditch, has trashed Obama for putting the emergency tow on the Treasury's credit card.

The sudden Republican horror that federal spending is "crowding out" private investments also seems curiously timed. For example, Romney, who launched a Green Energy Fund to seed start-ups in Massachusetts, has accused Obama of "killing solar energy by having the government play the role of venture capitalist." That's precisely backward; the U.S. solar industry was on the brink of death before the Recovery Act, but it has expanded sixfold over the last three years. While crowding out is a legitimate concern, there was probably less danger of it during the capital strike of early 2009 than at any time since the Depression. The Recovery Act actually "crowded in" private investments through matching requirements, which drew more than $100 billion in clean-energy funding off the sidelines at a time when hardly anyone was investing in anything.

The bottom line is that the Keynesian story line fits the facts of the last few years. With the economy in a death spiral, the federal government stepped in as the spender of last resort, providing enough fiscal impulse to reverse the slide but not enough to revive a shattered labor market in a hurry. By contrast, the Republican "cut-and-grow" story line makes little sense. In an economy without demand, spending cuts kill jobs and growth. As Romney explained in one of his off-message campaign moments: "If all you're thinking about doing is cutting spending, as you cut spending you'll slow down the economy." Governor Sanford at least made an honest case for short-term austerity, arguing that the immediate pain would produce long-term gain. But when demand is slack, more pain means fewer jobs, less revenue, and bigger deficits. And pain hurts.

The Recovery Act helped ease a lot of pain, and helped avert a depression that would have caused immeasurable pain. Remember, in the fourth quarter of 2008, the economy withered at an 8.9 percent annual rate. At that pace we would have shed an entire Canada's worth of output in 2009. Modest growth, while frustrating, has been infinitely preferable to hellacious contraction. Like Romer said: Depressions really, really suck.

The Obama economy hasn't been fun, either. You don't have to believe in austerity fantasies or supply side fairy tales to wonder what the president could have done to make the last three years suck less, or how the Recovery Act could have been improved. But even nonpartisan critiques have often ignored the political and economic constraints that Obama has faced. He's not the king—or the Almighty.

Progressives still complain that Obama's stimulus should have been bigger. Just about every economist who ever worked for Obama agrees. But Congress wasn't going to give him a bigger stimulus after the backlash over the financial bailout. The absolute maximum for the three Republican defectors and at least half a dozen Senate Democrats was

$800 billion. Similarly, it's true the Alternative Minimum Tax fix didn't belong in the stimulus. Obama's economists always said it wasn't stimulus, and shifting that $75 billion to state aid or construction projects might have sliced a half point off the jobless rate. But Senator Snowe insisted on including it, and key Democrats wanted it, too. Obama correctly calculated that a $787 billion stimulus diluted by the AMT fix would provide a greater economic jolt than a filibustered stimulus that died in the Senate.

The most glaring example of magical thinking is the conventional wisdom that Obama should have split the Recovery Act into a short-term save-the-economy stimulus bill and a long-term change-the-economy investment bill. Surely that would have united Washington! Uh, no. The short-term bill might have passed, although the assumption that Republicans would have embraced it deeply misreads Republicans, and the assumption that Democrats would have agreed to start the Obama era with more tax cuts rather than clean energy, health care, education, or infrastructure is a stretch as well. In any case, unemployment would have kept rising, an outcome already baked into the economic cake, and the long-term bill stuffed with Obama's campaign priorities would have gone nowhere. Every Republican would have opposed it, and quite a few centrist Democrats also would have refused to support another spending bill, especially another spending bill that wasn't even designed to address the short-term jobs crisis. The result would have been much less overall stimulus, a possible double-dip recession, none of the Recovery Act's Change We Can Believe In, and, since Senator Specter presumably would have remained a Republican, no Obamacare.

While complaints about the Recovery Act's size tend to ignore political realities, complaints about its contents often gloss over economic realities, exaggerating the impact that modest tweaks or even major rewrites could have had on jobs and growth. There were legitimate arguments for including more of this and less of that, but there was only so much stimulus Obama could have produced with a $787 billion package.

For instance, some critics wanted more support for the economy in 2009. That would have required more tax cuts, which would have weakened the overall stimulus and infuriated many Democrats, or more state aid, which wouldn't have made it through Congress. Other critics wanted more infrastructure projects, which have high bang for the buck, and might have attracted a few votes from House Republican concrete lovers, but weren't shovel-ready enough to produce many jobs in 2009. Some argued that longer-term investments like high-speed rail and health IT didn't belong in the stimulus, since they barely got started before 2011, but as it turned out the economy still needed stimulus in 2011. Others questioned whether random spending on crime victims, wildfire management, and floodplain easements really produced stimulus; the answer is yes, although somewhat less than more targeted spending. Anyway, those programs comprised less than 0.1 percent of the bill.

The larger point is that reshuffling the Recovery Act might have helped at the macroeconomic margins, but it wouldn't have changed the narrative. Personally, I would have liked to see aid to help transit agencies avoid fare hikes and service cuts, and more tax incentives for energy efficiency improvements; I'm less enthusiastic about the Recovery Act's "unparalleled investments" in rural housing, rural broadband, and other sprawl-inducing goodies for rural communities. But I'm under no illusion that my ideal $787 billion package would have produced a much better economy than the actual $787 billion package.

A more compelling critique of the Recovery Act is that it was a hodgepodge. It did throw cash at just about every problem imaginable, from lead paint to invasive carp to leaking underground storage tanks. It was like the Blob, seeping into every sector of society. Even I didn't realize until recently that it's funding a $49 million rail tunnel to the Port of Miami, about a mile from my home. It was mostly big-ticket items, but it included enough cats and dogs—$50 million for the National Cemetery Administration, $20 million for radios for immigration officers, $10 million for urban canals—to make messaging a real challenge. Distributing the cash through fewer channels and a handful of marquee initiatives might have been better politics.

It wouldn't have been better stimulus, though. Diminishing returns are a real problem; the more money a program has, the longer it takes to spend. Congress could have shifted that $50 million for repairing monuments at national cemeteries into larger pots for repairing roads or federal buildings, but the top project on the cemetery list was a lot more likely to be shovel-ready and shovel-worthy than the 14,001st road project or the 301st federal building project. So spreading the spending around made sense. Inevitably, there were still dubious expenditures—new runways at little used airports, costly broadband connections in the Alaskan tundra, $10,000 for the Colorado Dragon Boat Festival. The incorrigible Army Corps of Engineers is spending $50 million to build wing dikes and weirs along the Mississippi River, despite mounting evidence that these "river improvements" make floods worse. But even dumb projects provide stimulus.

The bottom line is that the tepid growth of 2010 and 2011 was not the Recovery Act's fault.

Was it Obama's fault? You'd never know it from the cult-of-the-presidency media, but he doesn't control every bob and weave of the economy. Obama couldn't stop the Japanese tsunami or Arab Spring or Greek crisis from dragging down U.S. growth any more than he could plug that hole in the Gulf. The Fed has more power to manipulate the economy in the short term through monetary policy, but it's independent of the White House.

The leader of the free world does help set fiscal policy, in conjunction with 535 difficult congressional partners, not to mention the modern-day Hoovers who inhabit so many statehouses. Some liberal economists will never forgive Obama for pivoting from gas to brakes instead of following up the Recovery Act with more stimulus. But he did follow up the Recovery Act with nearly $700 billion more stimulus: tax cuts for families and businesses, state aid to prevent teacher layoffs and Medicaid cuts, unemployment benefits, and much more. Not all of it was ideal stimulus; he would have preferred not to extend the Bush tax cuts for the rich in the lame-duck deal. But it all helped prevent economic backsliding. The notion that he gave up on gas ignores a dozen fiscally expansive bills he extracted from a reluctant Congress. And the deals he cut with austerity-mad Republicans in 2011 to avoid closing the government or welshing on national debts were remarkably free of short-term anti-stimulus. The left still accuses him of caving to the Tea Party, but it's hard to win a game of chicken outright when your opponents don't fear a crash.

It's true that even more stimulus would have been even more helpful. Obama tried to get more, but there weren't sixty votes for more state aid or a bigger hiring tax credit, much less a new stimulus bill like the American Jobs Act. The Senate wouldn't even extend unemployment benefits after Robert Byrd died. This was often portrayed as a failure of leadership, as if a more forceful commander in chief would have gotten his way, as if members of Congress are powerless bystanders in a presidential psychodrama. Obama did shift focus from jobs to health care in spring 2009, and the gas-versus-brakes bickering among his economists probably did prevent a more coherent jobs message in fall 2009. But it's not clear how a more intense focus or a more coherent message would have changed the political calculus for stimulus. Generally, the more Obama talks about things he wants—from the American Jobs Act to the Chevy Volt—the more politically toxic they become. And if he hadn't prioritized health care, he wouldn't have passed his historic reforms.

Obama certainly made mistakes. Scuttling the transportation bill in 2009 was a blunder, a missed opportunity to create jobs, fix infrastructure, and ensure the survival of high-speed rail, quite possibly with bipartisan support. I'm more sympathetic to Obama's much maligned decision to reappoint Bernanke—the guy had just saved global finance—but the White House did drop the ball by leaving two vacancies on the fractious Fed board at a time when the economy was crying out for monetary stimulus. (Then again, when Obama finally tried to fill a vacancy with Nobel laureate economist Peter Diamond, Republicans blocked him, at one point deeming him "unqualified.") And even Obama thinks his housing policies have been too timid. More aggressive action to prevent foreclosures and revive the real estate market would have been economically and politically risky, but as it turned out, so was doing too little.

There are reasonable explanations for most of Obama's economic policies. He didn't do more stimulus because he didn't have the votes for more stimulus. He didn't do more to help foreclosed homeowners because a bailout would have been wildly expensive and unpopular, and could have made the problem worse by encouraging more homeowners to stop paying their mortgages. But it's fair to say that somehow, he should have figured out a way to do more to relieve the pain of persistent unemployment.

Then again, one could say the same about FDR and the New Deal before the bombing of Pearl Harbor. Context really matters. While it's boring to keep repeating that Obama inherited an economy in shambles, he did inherit an economy in shambles, along with implacable Republican opponents and unreliable Democratic allies. Obama aide Gene Sperling explained the predicament to me one day in 2010, waxing metaphorical about his love for the Detroit Lions.

"We were 0-16 in 2008. Then we went 2-14. If we go 8-8 this year, some fans still won't be happy, and it's still not good enough," said Sperling, a Michigan native who kept a Lions helmet in his office. "But objectively, it's *way* better than 0-16!"

For the record, the Lions went 6-10 that year, but improved to 10-6 the next year. The economy's trajectory has been similarly encouraging. There are no more pathetic words in politics than "it could've been worse," but seriously, it could've been worse.

Beyond the *#~@ Show

From the start, Obama insisted that his new New Deal should be about reshaping the economy as well as juicing the economy. His critics on the left and the right say he was insufficiently "focused" on the economy's short-term needs. But those needs were pretty simple—more demand—and Obama believed the economy would never produce sustainable long-term growth until its long-term needs were addressed. As Obama often said, a president needs to be able to walk and chew gum at the same time, and after campaigning for change, he managed to slip a lot of it into the Recovery Act.

For example, the Recovery Act didn't just provide unemployment benefits to millions of Americans in need. It also pushed thirty-nine states to rewrite their eligibility rules in order to qualify for stimulus bonuses, dragging the New Deal–era unemployment system into the computer age, permanently extending the countercyclical safety net to part-time workers and domestic abuse victims. Similarly, HUD has incorporated the Recovery Act's homelessness prevention strategy into its emergency shelter program on a permanent basis, and the VA has launched a similar program for veterans.

The most ambitious stimulus investments focused on clean energy, and they're already generating long-term returns. So far, the Recovery Act has financed the weatherization of 680,000 low-income homes, energy efficiency retrofits of 120,000 buildings, and the installation of ten million smart meters. The energy savings from these projects will recur automatically every year; they're not like new coal plants, which have to burn more coal to produce more energy. Meanwhile, as promised, renewable electricity doubled during Obama's first three years, while the number of wind, solar, and geothermal projects approved on federal land increased from zero to twenty-nine. Those projects alone will have the capacity of a dozen coal plants, and another seventeen projects that could displace another dozen coal plants are in the pipeline. Even without cap-and-trade or a price on emissions, the United States has begun a transition toward a low-carbon economy.

"Right now, we're being judged on jobs," the Energy Department's Matt Rogers once told me. "In a decade, we'll be judged on whether we transformed the economy."

First, though, they would be judged on a single failed solar investment.

Solyndra's new glass-and-steel plant had five times the floor space of the White House. When I visited in June 2011, robots were cranking out tubular solar cells and mounting them on rectangular racks through an impossibly complex nineteen-step process—casting, coating, "sputtering," and so forth. Driverless dollies were whipping materials around the factory floor, playing peppy music to alert human beings to stay away. My hosts boasted that almost every machine was custom-made. I told them the factory felt a bit *too* awesome; solar panels didn't usually require such an elaborate production. In retrospect, it was also an odd use of prime Silicon Valley real estate.

At the time, though, the company seemed to have its groove back. "The reports of Solyndra's death have been greatly exaggerated," I wrote in an idiotic blog post. (In my quasi-defense, I did add: "Of course, Solyndra could still fail. Energy is a ruthlessly competitive market, and solar is getting particularly Darwinian.") It was having its best quarter ever, and was on track for over $200 million in revenues for 2011, up from $6 million in 2008. After the hubbub over its R&D layoffs, it had quietly doubled its sales and marketing staff, and it was still hiring. It had completed projects for Coca-Cola, Frito-Lay, and Costco, and had just signed a huge deal to supply panels to a California utility. It had cut its costs in half, and expected further reductions as it ramped up production. "You can see that we've changed," CEO Brian Harrison said. He told me Solyndra would be profitable by 2012, and that summer he told Congress the same thing.

Solyndra never made it to 2012. After a private financing deal collapsed in August, the company had to beg the Energy Department for another lifeline. At the White House, energy adviser Heather Zichal again pithily summarized the situation: "*#~@ show." This time, the administration refused to throw good money after bad. Solyndra declared bankruptcy and laid off its nearly 1,200 employees. The FBI raided the firm, and Harrison and other executives took the Fifth at congressional hearings. The *#~@ show was just starting.

Republicans hyped Solyndra into a classic Washington scandal, with a "gate" suffix, drip-drip-drip document leaks, and endless, breathless who-knew-what-when media speculation. Michelle Bachmann said it "makes Watergate look like child's play." The Republican National Committee declared it proof of the "Corruption at the Heart of the Obama

Economic Strategy." Anti-Obama groups bankrolled millions of dollars' worth of crony capitalism ads. One deceptively edited spot featured Obama saying he didn't regret his kind words for Solyndra: "No, I don't . . . overall, it's doing well." The unedited quote was: "No, I don't. If you look at the overall portfolio of loan guarantees that have been provided, overall, it's doing well." The same Republicans who had bashed Obama for spending too slowly began bashing him for rushing money out the door on sweetheart deals.

Most of the Solyndra inquisitors in the House had pushed clean-energy loans for their own constituents before discovering their inner Torquemadas. Energy and Commerce chairman Fred Upton—a long-time moderate who considered voting for the stimulus in 2009, but had to pledge allegiance to the Tea Party to secure his chairmanship in 2011—had supported a loan for a Michigan solar company that later failed. House Government Oversight chairman Darrell Issa—who called Obama "one of the most corrupt presidents in modern times"—had written Chu on behalf of an electric vehicle start-up. But once the witch hunt began, the past didn't matter, and neither did the facts.

So far, after holding a dozen hearings, subpoenaing hundreds of thousands of pages of documents, and threatening numerous White House officials with contempt, Republicans have drawn a blank. Their efforts to prove that the administration was reckless or corrupt have done nothing of the sort. They have exposed plenty of internal debate, but no evidence of anyone doing anything wrong. "Is there criminal activity? Perhaps not," Issa admitted after a year of relentless investigations. "Is there a political influence and connections? Perhaps not." Still, Issa insisted the administration "bent the rules for an agenda," the agenda being energy that doesn't endanger our security or the planet. Is it possible that a government official urged Solyndra to delay a layoff announcement for a week until after the midterm? Perhaps. That's not quite Watergate.

It's no fun to watch a half-billion-dollar loan go bad, but loans go bad all the time, because businesses fail all the time, especially in cutting-edge industries. Republicans suggested the Recovery Act's loans ought to be safer than the private sector's, but in fact they were supposed to be riskier, carrying clean-energy technologies across the Valleys of Death that scared off private lenders. Congress had set aside $2.5 billion for busted loans, and an independent review of the administration's portfolio (led by the former finance chairman of John McCain's presidential campaign) found no danger of exceeding those losses. Most of the loans went to lower-risk generation projects with contracts in place to sell clean electricity, and a Bloomberg Government analysis found the program has more than enough reserves to absorb the failure of every one of its higher-risk manufacturing projects.

Solyndra and its ingenious technology attracted some of the smartest money on the planet, but its business plan didn't account for solar prices plunging 60 percent in three years. It just couldn't compete on costs, especially after the Chinese government poured $30 billion into solar manufacturers in 2010. Solyndra did make strategic mistakes, and burned through cash as if it was a billion-dollar company before it ever turned a profit—although, in fairness, it was a billion-dollar company. But nothing about one solar firm flying too close to the sun justified the Republican obituaries for the solar industry.

On the contrary, the collapsing prices that doomed Solyndra reflected an industry on a roll, building the scale it needed to cut costs. The *#~@ show was a sideshow. Solar is now cheaper than new nuclear, and in sunny states with incentives for renewables, it's becoming competitive with fossil fuels for long-term contracts, even though natural gas prices have plunged. U.S. solar installations increased from just 290 megawatts in 2008 to 1,855 megawatts in 2011, and an astonishing 7,000 megawatts worth of new projects were proposed in the two months before Solyndra went belly up. That's the equivalent of seven nuclear reactors, seven more than the United States has built in the last three decades. And that doesn't even include residential solar, which is also booming. The ruckus over Solyndra helped scuttle a loan guarantee for Solar Strong, a $1 billion effort to install solar panels on 160,000 rooftops' worth of military housing across thirty-three states. But the project is still going forward with financing from Bank of America, and could singlehandedly double America's residential solar generation.

"The common mind-set doesn't understand what's happening," says Lyndon Rive of SolarCity, which will install the panels for Solar Strong, and is now preparing for an IPO. "Yeah, a big solar manufacturer went out of business. It went out of business because of the success of the solar industry! We're hiring like crazy."

Innovation doesn't move in a straight line. Disruptive technologies can putter around the margins of the economy for years, failing to disrupt much of anything. But if they get better or cheaper, at some point they can suddenly take off, challenging the status quo. And as they scale up, they get even cheaper. That's what's happening as solar power travels down the cost curve. It's also starting to happen for energy-saving LED lighting, which could replace traditional incandescent bulbs and even advanced compact fluorescents within a decade. LED prices have dropped by half since 2009, upending the outdoor lighting market, and they're still dropping, threatening to invade the indoor market next. While Congress has squabbled over Obama's supposed ban on incandescents—actually just a requirement for more efficient bulbs, originally promoted by Upton before his rush to the right—the march of innovation could render the entire debate irrelevant.

The Recovery Act's state and local energy grants have financed nearly 400,000 LED streetlights and traffic signals, helping to scale up the technology. LEDs are now 2 percent of the overall lighting market, but Rogers says that could grow to 80 percent by 2020, which could lower U.S. electricity demand by the equivalent of over thirty power plants.

"LEDs are approaching the tipping point where everything changes," he says.

The Recovery Act has also helped cut the cost of electric vehicle batteries in half. It will need to be halved again before plug-ins can be truly competitive with gasoline, but that could happen in the next five years, thanks to innovators like Envia and the stimulus-funded battery factories. Sales of the Volt and the Leaf have been a bit disappointing, and America might not meet Obama's goal of one million electric vehicles on the road by 2015. But there will be far more than there would have been without Obama or the stimulus.

Obama probably won't be able to keep some of his aggressive green promises; for example, the economics of clean coal remain bleak without a price on carbon. But he has made a huge down payment on a greener economy. Just a decade after Clinton proposed a five-year, $6.3 billion clean-energy initiative that was considered hopelessly unrealistic, Obama pushed $90 billion into the sector with one signature, leveraging over $100 billion in additional private capital. Gingrich has mocked Obama for promoting algae instead of oil, and Republicans have blistered the Navy for buying a batch of renewable biofuel from Solazyme at four times the usual price. But as Solazyme scales up, its costs will come down. Before the Recovery Act rescued the advanced biofuels industry and dragged it out of the lab, no one would have imagined that U.S. destroyers and jets would be running on U.S. algae in 2011. That's what change looks like.

Of course, down payments disappear if they're not followed up with regular payments. The Energy Department followed up the Recovery Act's solar investments with SunShot, an initiative to make solar energy cost-competitive without subsidies by 2020, incubating more innovative firms and launching a nationwide effort to reduce "soft costs" like permitting. Obama also followed up the Recovery Act's efficiency push with Better Buildings, an effort to reduce energy consumption 20 percent by 2020. The federal government will do $2 billion worth of retrofits through contracts financed by electricity savings, so they won't cost taxpayers a dime; private companies have also committed $2 billion to retrofit 1.6 billion square feet of commercial and industrial space.

Meanwhile, ARPA-E is exploring the next green revolutions. For example, after inventing the concept of electrofuels that don't rely on photosynthesis, the agency has launched a new program to improve photosynthesis, by manipulating crops like sugarcane and sorghum to grow fuel. Not cellulosic material that can be converted into fuel, but actual fuel that can be dropped into a tank. PETRO (Plants Engineered to Replace Oil, a rare acronym that works) aims to eliminate the inefficiencies of converting carbohydrates into hydrocarbons by growing the hydrocarbons directly; one national lab's project is modifying tobacco plants, America's original cash crop, to produce gasoline or diesel that would leak out when you squeeze the leaves. It sounds crazy, but soybeans can produce about 50 gallons of biofuel per acre, while petroleum crops could conceivably produce 5,000.

"All this stuff sounds crazy, until it changes the world," Majumdar says.

Solyndra was just a bump on the road to a clean-energy future, and we're further down the road than people realize. But Republicans are pushing to close the road. They've blocked Obama's "Cash for Caulkers" proposal to expand energy efficiency tax credits, as well as extensions of the Recovery Act's renewable energy tax credits, while defending tax breaks for oil giants that vacuumed up $140 billion in profits in 2011. They no longer support formerly bipartisan initiatives like the smart grid, wind power, or electric vehicles now that they're identified with Obama's green agenda.

So the 2012 election will be a fork in that road to clean energy.

Change Is Here

Change isn't always obvious.

The Making Work Pay tax cuts affected almost all of us, but few of us noticed the extra $8 slipped into our weekly paychecks. The Recovery Act funded the world's largest dam removal project on the Elwha River, but how many of us pay attention to salmon runs in the Olympic peninsula? The stimulus has upgraded 236 miles of flood control levees, 350 military bases, 850 wastewater systems, and over 400,000 public housing apartments, but you probably haven't noticed unless they were in your area. My last book was about the Florida Everglades, and I still haven't checked out $100 million worth of stimulus-funded projects to help restore the River of Grass. And so far, it's hard to tell whether nationwide gains in high-speed Internet access have anything to do with the Recovery Act's $7.2 billion worth of broadband grants to underserved communities.

But the stimulus-funded revolution in health IT is hard to miss. We all go to the doctor, and soon just about all our doctors will use electronic health records. The statistics are already striking. In 2008, just 17 percent of physicians and 12 percent of hospitals used digital records; it's now 34 percent of physicians and 40 percent of hospitals, and the Recovery Act's $27 billion in health IT money just started going out the door last year. In 2008, only one in twenty doctors dispensed prescriptions electronically; now nearly half of them e-prescribe. The era of illegible scribbles and telephone tag causing deadly overdoses is coming to an end, as is the era of misplaced results and inaccessible files causing redundant tests. And according to the Bureau of Labor Statistics, health IT is becoming America's fastest-growing occupation. Health and Human Services Secretary Kathleen Sebelius says more than fifty thousand jobs have been created in the health IT industry since the stimulus passed.

Electronic medicine will do more than replace your doctor's clipboard with an iPad, help you make appointments online, and eliminate all that time you waste filling out forms in waiting rooms. It's also the foundation for health reform, what Sebelius calls "the single biggest component in improving quality and lowering costs." As Zeke Emanuel points out, health IT firms that used to spend their time devising new ways to bill insurers and Medicare are now developing new ways to improve care and coordination, bringing hundreds of new products to market, attracting a wave of new venture capital. They will help doctors monitor the blood sugar levels of diabetic patients remotely, share MRI results with specialists on the other side of the country instantly, and change medical care in countless ways no one has thought of yet. Like the smart grid, health IT is a software play: Its killer apps are still waiting to be invented.

The computerization of medicine will also promote evidence-based care, by helping researchers collect data and helping providers use the results. The insurer WellPoint has announced plans to use Watson, the IBM computer best known as a *Jeopardy!* champion, to comb through data to suggest treatment options to doctors. And the Recovery Act's investments in comparative effectiveness are already producing news doctors and patients can use. One stimulus-funded study found that a $50-per-dose drug is just as effective as a $2,000-per-dose drug in treating macular degeneration. Another suggested bypass surgery might be more effective than stents at treating heart blockages.

Some doctors who consider medicine more art than science have bristled at the idea of computers suggesting evidence-based protocols. And during the Obamacare debate, well-funded critics denounced comparative effectiveness as vicious rationing; the drumbeat got so loud that Rahm argued for abandoning the White House's efforts to expand and institutionalize the research, prompting a predictably indecorous response from his brother Zeke. In the final compromise, Congress refused to allow the new board overseeing comparative effectiveness to consider costs. Still, the trend is toward more data in more accessible forms, which should make the system more logical over time.

"We're not naive. We know some of these studies may lead to challenging policy decisions," says immunologist Richard Hodes, cochair of NIH's comparative effectiveness council. "But our feeling is: First, let's get the facts."

Even before Obamacare, the Recovery Act started pushing the medical system in the directions Obama wanted it to go. States had been limiting access to Medicaid; the stimulus expanded access. It also expanded preventive care, built or upgraded more than one thousand community health clinics, and started addressing the shortage of primary care doctors and nurses. And it's the reason our health care system no longer manages patient data with the same technologies Hippocrates used. It's unlikely that all Americans will have an electronic record by 2014, Obama's goal, but the vast majority should.

Before the stimulus, 91 percent of Tennessee's students were reported to be proficient in math. In 2011, thanks to the state's Race to the Top grant, that figure was down to 34 percent. And the minority achievement gap had doubled. Yet Secretary Duncan was delighted.

That's because the statistical nosedive was purely the result of much stricter standards—and as they say in recovery, the first step is admitting you've got a problem.

"They stopped dumbing down their standards and lying to their kids," Duncan told me. "Now they know the truth, which is a very liberating and motivating thing."

Some of the Recovery Act's impact on schools is obvious. Its fiscal relief saved at least 350,000 education jobs. It extended Pell Grants so that three million more low-income students could attend college, and more than doubled overall tuition aid. But it's too early to know how the long-range school reforms slipped into the stimulus will change education. So far, the winning Race to the Top states have been setting up new training and evaluation programs for teachers and principals, while starting to implement the new Common Core standards for kids. Other than a few hiccups—labor disputes in New York, foot-dragging in Hawaii—things seem to be going as planned. The Race will drive new approaches to teaching and testing, and Duncan says some of the failing schools that received turnaround grants have already reported improved test scores, attendance records, and other signs of improvement. But the evidence is not yet clear.

What's clear is that the Race and the Recovery Act's other reforms, backed by less than 0.5 percent of annual U.S. education spending, will have an outsized impact on the future of schools. Their emphasis on competition is eroding the entitlement mentality in education funding, forcing applicants to demonstrate merit instead of lining up for automatic handouts. Reform is also expanding the federal role in local schools, imposing Obama's technocratic vision through the strings attached to the cash.

But while most of the early attacks on the Race came from progressives, Washington Republicans are now attacking it as a federal assault on local prerogatives. It is, after all, an Obama initiative. So its fate might depend on 2012 as well.

Vice President Biden was having a bit of fun at my expense, thanking me for my journalistic work as a Recovery Act cheerleader. "As you might guess, I've read all your articles, because you're the only guy that wrote anything remotely positive," he needled me. I'm generally more Debbie Downer than Little Mary Sunshine, and I told Biden this was unusual for me. He grinned. "I took 'em to bed, slept on 'em . . ."

It was kind of funny because it was kind of true. At times, I did feel like I was writing about an alternative universe stimulus. But the facts were the facts. The Recovery Act was on schedule, and was so far under budget that the administration had financed an extra three thousand construction projects with the savings. As Biden liked to say, fraud was the dog that hadn't barked. Experts had predicted tens of billions of dollars in losses, but there had only been 298 convictions, for scams totaling just $7.2 million; the Recovery Act's unprecedented transparency and scrutiny made it an uninviting target for crooks. And its oversubscribed competitive grant programs—for everything from brownfields redevelopment to emissions-reducing transit projects—really did seem to promote a culture of responsibility, forcing bureaucrats to use judgment instead of just checking boxes. Even when their judgments were wrong, as with Solyndra or the busted battery manufacturer Ener1, there was no indication of corruption or cronyism.

Good government is hard to quantify. It's mostly a counterfactual achievement, measured by the lack of scandals and other flubs. But I've heard countless stories about public servants like Claire Broido Johnson whipping the weatherization turkey farm into shape, Seth Harris lying awake worrying about that 13(c) provision, ARPA-E's Eric Toone inventing electrofuels, and OMB's Danny Werfel wishing he could bottle the Recovery Act for the rest of the government. After Obama and Biden made it clear the stimulus was a top priority, the federal bureaucracy mobilized. It was still the federal bureaucracy, with all the paperwork and legalisms that implies, but the Recovery Act inspired a much more collaborative, results-oriented, businesslike approach. I wish I had a dollar for every time I heard about "returns on investment" or "value propositions," or for that matter "silos" or "stovepipes."

"This is the first time we really did go in and absolutely knocked down these goddamned stovepipes," Biden says. "We took sledgehammers like, Bah-Wham!"

The president has already signed an executive order creating a government-wide version of the Recovery Accountability and Transparency Board, to extend its oversight to all federal spending. Obama has also proposed a bunch of new races to the top, from a Race to Green competition to encourage local building codes to a Workforce Innovation Fund for job-training programs to a $5 billion competition to help schools attract and reward excellent teachers. "The Recovery Act is going to create a new template for making government function," Biden says. "Literally! Literally!"

These were worthy reforms, but after the soaring poetry of the Obama campaign, after all those lofty promises of unity and prosperity and an ennobling new politics, his supporters expected more inspirational change. They expected more Bah-Wham! When he had pledged to create a new Washington, and portrayed Hillary Clinton as old Washington, he hadn't suggested that she was insufficiently focused on data collection or overly wedded to formula programs. He had suggested that she was too enmeshed in the city's tawdry culture of partisan bickering and backroom horse-trading to change it. And by the time Obama signed the stimulus, it was clear he was unable or unwilling to change it as well.

But the question isn't whether Obama has lived up to the hype. Nothing in life except parenthood lives up to the hype. The question is whether he has produced change. Change doesn't mean perfect. Change means better. It's a direction, not a destination. And the Recovery Act was exactly the policy direction he had promised, even if it wasn't delivered through the uplifting process he had promised. He had said that America's intractable policy messes would never be fixed until Washington's intractable political messes were fixed, but he quickly proved himself wrong.

Before Obama had completed his first month in office, the stimulus started building all four pillars of his New Foundation. It took a giant leap toward cleaner energy, including a smarter grid, greener buildings, and low-carbon fuel and electricity. It dragged health care into the digital era, toward a less expensive and more rational system. It laid the groundwork for data-driven education reforms that Democrats had always resisted. And it began to advance his long-term vision for the economy, with a more progressive tax code, a more expansive safety net, and more aggressive investments in research and infrastructure. Meanwhile, the Recovery Act was saving the economy from sinking into a depression. It didn't produce robust growth, but it made a nightmarish situation better. And better is better than worse.

The new New Deal has not left an indelible mark on the national psyche the way the New Deal did. It didn't have a Hoover Dam, or a CCC, or a visible public works campaign. Its iconic solar arrays and wind farms are in remote areas; its bullet trains are still question marks; its smarter grid and refundable tax cuts have mostly gone unnoticed. Its innovations like electronic medical records and homelessness prevention aren't associated with the stimulus in the public mind. Most governors wouldn't even put Recovery Act signs alongside Recovery Act construction projects. And the relentless Republican campaign to brand the stimulus as a big-government failure has been an overwhelming success.

The Recovery Act has already launched America on an inexorable course toward digital medicine and a digital grid, and helping to rescue the country from a second depression will always be part of its legacy as well. But much of its legacy is still up for grabs. Obama wants renewable energy, electric vehicles, and energy efficiency retrofits to reach critical mass; Republicans want to end their subsidies and scuttle his green agenda. Obama wants to make "refundable" credits for the working poor a permanent feature of a progressive tax code; Republicans talk about "broadening the base" to stop coddling Americans who don't pay income taxes. At this point, just about everything in the Obama stimulus is toxic to the GOP, by virtue of being in the Obama stimulus; the president has joked that he ought to say he's adamantly opposed to investments in education and infrastructure, just so Republicans will support them.

Politically, the most obvious legacy of the stimulus is that politicians want nothing to do with "stimulus." It's become a four-letter word, shorthand for reckless spending and wasteful pork and political shenanigans. That doesn't describe the Recovery Act at all, but Obama still won't say the S-word, and the bipartisan consensus for fiscal expansion during recessions has completely unraveled.

"This is going to be the last stimulus we see for a long time," says former Democratic senator Evan Bayh. "That can be the last sentence of your book."

Well, not quite. The ultimate legacy of the stimulus will be decided in 2012.

The Choice

Back in January 2008, as the economy softened, Mitt Romney was all about stimulus. When his Republican rival John McCain said spending cuts were the path to prosperity, Romney scoffed: "That's not stimulative." When deficit hawks said his $250 billion plan for permanent high-end tax cuts would create too much red ink, he argued that a recession would create even more. When the *Washington Post*'s Ruth Marcus wrote her column grading stimulus proposals—the report card that gave Barack Obama an A-minus for focusing on timely, targeted, and temporary—she gave Romney a D, not only because his plan flunked the three-T test, but because it was "too big."

A year later, as the economy cratered, Romney still sounded like a Keynesian. "A stimulus plan is needed without further delay," he wrote. Consumers and businesses were reeling, so "what's left is the government sector," he told a panel of House Republicans. He was still pushing permanent tax relief for the rich—eliminating taxes on dividends and capital gains, slashing corporate rates, making the Bush tax cuts permanent—but he also called for some spending. Infrastructure projects were slow, but "should be part of the picture." Romney had mixed feelings about state aid, but said he "won't prescribe zero help for the states." He also said the package should include "spending for energy research and energy infrastructure"—and no earmarks.

The Recovery Act followed those suggestions—except for the budget-busting permanent tax cuts—and in his 2010 book *No Apologies*, Romney acknowledged that it would "accelerate the timing of the start of the recovery." But for the paperback edition in 2011, Romney airbrushed out those tempered words, and any suggestion that he might have favored stimulus in the past. "The Obama stimulus, funded with a mountain of debt, was a bust," he wrote. The politics of stimulus had shifted, and so had Mitt Romney.

Romney will probably be Obama's opponent in the fall, and consistency is not his particular hobgoblin. As the governor of Massachusetts, he not only enacted the health reforms that inspired Obamacare—which he now vows to repeal—he supported many of the transformative policies in the Obama stimulus, including electronic health records, tax credits for energy efficiency, and investments in renewables. One of the firms backed by his green-energy government venture fund developed those BigBelly solar trash compactors that the stimulus financed in Philadelphia. But as a presidential candidate, Romney was determined to avoid the fate of Arlen Specter, Charlie Crist, and other moderates scozzafavaed by Tea Party conservatives in Republican primaries.

The new Romney has mocked the Chevy Volt, tweaked Obama's "unhealthy obsession with green jobs," and seized on Solyndra as a symbol of the Obama economy. And he has based his candidacy around the Tea Party creed that the U.S. government is an enemy of liberty, redistributing your money to someone less deserving, hindering the job creators who make the economy go. He is framing the 2012 election as a choice between Big Government and Free Enterprise, between a failed president who thinks the economy needs the government to provide stimulus and a successful businessman who knows the economy needs the government to get out of its way.

Meanwhile, Obama is framing 2012 as a choice between We're In This Together and You're On Your Own, between bottom-up growth and trickle-down growth, between the president who got the economy out of the ditch and the party that drove it into the ditch—the party whose standard-bearer wants to go back to driving the same way.

• • •

In 2008, Obama was like a blank slate onto which voters could project their Yes We Can fantasies of change. Now the slate is no longer blank, and voters won't have to imagine what kind of president Obama would be or what he meant by change. Starting with the Recovery Act, he's been pretty much the president he said he'd be, even if the immediate results haven't been what he hoped they'd be.

Ideologically, he's been a consistent left-of-center Democrat. He's pursued big reforms rather than school uniforms, and he's kept pushing for investments in clean energy, medical research, better schools, better infrastructure, and the rest of his New Foundation. But he's been willing to take the ham sandwich when he couldn't get the whole hog, and he's been less liberal than advertised. He chose aides from the corporate-friendly Rubin wing of his party, abandoned "card check" for unions when the business lobby objected, grudgingly extended the Bush tax cuts for the rich, and cut taxes for everyone else. Race to the Top was a real departure from Democratic education traditions, and even when he was adding $800 billion to the national debt through the stimulus, he was always trying to minimize the fiscal fallout. The Recovery Act did end up with a few "tails"—like increases in Pell Grants for low-income students and a more generous Earned Income Tax Credit for low-income workers—but otherwise it has virtually no impact on current deficits. And it did not grow government; public-sector employment has steadily declined.

The rap on Obama in 2008 was that he was a words guy, not a deeds guy, a great communicator but an unaccomplished legislator. It turned out that he was more of a deeds guy. The professor-in-chief has utterly failed to educate Americans about Keynesian stimulus or global warming. He's also succeeded in injecting record amounts of stimulus and making unprecedented inroads against global warming. Even his partisan critics now admit, to their regret, that he's gotten a lot done. They portray his stimulus, auto bailout, health reforms, financial reforms, and other achievements as a giant leap toward the Europeanization of America. And even his allies complain that he's failed to communicate what he's done, that he's let Republicans define him, that his immersion in legislative sausage-making has undermined his narrative of change.

Obama did have two obvious failures that have muddled his message and cast a shadow over his presidency. He failed to change the tone of Washington politics, which remains as rancid as ever. It wasn't his fault that Republicans settled on a strategy of *Horse Feathers* obstructionism before he even took office, and gleefully compared their stand against the stimulus to Patton's stand against the Nazis. But Obama was the one who made post-partisan promises he couldn't keep. Obama also failed to produce a strong enough recovery to return unemployment to normal levels, which meant that everything else he's done has been couched in caveats. Again, it wasn't his fault that he inherited an obliterated economy, or that recoveries are always slow after financial cataclysms, or that Republicans blocked more aggressive responses to create jobs. But Obama was the one who promised a stronger middle class and a return to prosperity.

For a long time, Obama's political advisers didn't even want him bragging about the accomplishment side of his ledger, fearing that self-congratulation at a time of brutal unemployment would evoke Bush's premature "Mission Accomplished" banner. But in 2012, Obama has started talking about change again, including the change produced by the Recovery Act. His campaign film, "The Road We've Traveled," included shout-outs to its middle-class tax cuts, infrastructure projects, Race to the Top, and state aid to "keep teachers in the classroom, cops on the street, and first responders ready," as well as its impact on the free-falling economy that greeted Obama at the start of 2009. The White House has started talking a lot about promises kept, and the stimulus kept a lot of promises—about energy efficiency, renewable electricity, middle-class tax cuts, electronic medicine, early childhood education, scientific research, and more. Some of those investments will start producing more visible change over the next four years, and Obama would like to be celebrating them in the White House.

Obama still avoids the word "stimulus," but the Recovery Act is at the heart of his case for reelection. It's central to his explanation of why Americans actually are better off than they were four years ago, even if they don't feel so great. It started his New Foundation, and it's the template for the follow-up investments he hopes to make if he's reelected. It's also a handy way to illustrate his differences with Republicans, who marched in lockstep against his recovery plan, and have proposed to tear down his New Foundation in favor of the policies that preceded his arrival in the White House.

Obama hopes to use a second term to consolidate and expand his new New Deal, continuing support for clean energy, implementing electronic health records and Race to the Top, making high-speed rail a reality, shifting the tax code in more progressive directions. Republicans have taken the other side of all those issues, and they are sure to resurrect their failed-stimulus attacks during the campaign, especially if Solyndra returns to the news, or a stimulus-funded company like A123 flounders in the fall. To Obama, the new New Deal is about "winning the future," rising to our new Sputnik moment, "out-building, out-educating, and out-competing" our economic rivals. To Romney, it's about "industrial policy," "crony capitalism," and government picking winners and losers.

It's a philosophical and factual debate worth having. But 2012 won't just be about litigating the new New Deal. It will also be about relitigating the old New Deal.

Romney's history of flip-floppery has spurred a lot of speculation about the "real Romney." Is he a true conservative who was just pandering to liberal Massachusetts when he passed universal health care with an individual mandate? Is he a true moderate who was just pandering to Tea Party primary voters when he raised doubts about climate science? Is he somewhere in between? They're fun questions, but the answers probably don't matter much. What matters are the policies that Romney has vowed to pursue on the campaign trail, because presidents usually try to keep their promises. The single best predictor of President Obama's policies has been his 2008 campaign agenda.

Romney basically wants to undo everything Obama has done—from health reform to Wall Street reform to clean-energy subsidies—and return to a pre-Change America. He's been a bit vague about his other plans, but his general policies are mostly indistinguishable from Bush's, except that he wants even deeper high-end tax cuts, and says he wants deep but unspecified cuts in government spending. He's embraced House budget chairman Paul Ryan's plan to squeeze Medicare and roll back non-military spending, a Tea Party blueprint that would leave virtually no room in the federal budget for anything but Social Security, health care, and defense within a few decades.

Romney doesn't have the personality of an angry ideologue, and it's possible that he does see the Tea Party as a ferret biting the hand that wants to save it from the dishwasher. But a President Romney would still preside over a party fueled by the resentments of its uncompromising Tea Party base. The New Deal notion that the government can help solve national problems or improve people's lives is anathema to modern Republican dogma. As Obama discovered on his first presidential visit to Congress, Washington Republicans don't think the New Deal worked. There were hints during the Supreme Court arguments on Obamacare that some conservative justices don't even think the New Deal was constitutional. U.S. politics has always featured a healthy skepticism of the federal leviathan, but the GOP has defined government spending (except military spending) as an assault on freedom, essentially state-sanctioned theft.

The rising fury about government is curiously disconnected from the facts. Our federal tax burden is the lowest it's been in decades; Obama made it even lower. The federal deficit is high, but it hasn't increased under Obama, and it's got almost nothing to do with the Recovery Act or the bank bailouts that came before it. The Republican rap on the Recovery Act—$1 trillion worth of wasteful earmarks, rampant fraud, political shenanigans, and wackadoodle liberalism—flies in the face of the evidence. But the fury is real. As Rick Santelli wrote after his rant, it's driven by the suspicion that government is giving your hard-earned money to freeloaders, that Obama's bureaucrats are picking winners who aren't you, that Washington is out of control.

Clearly, Romney plans to run against a crippled economy that's been slow to heal, while Obama will try to remind Americans which party and which policies crippled it. At a deeper level, though, the 2012 election will be about values, about the purpose of the federal government, about our obligations to each other as Americans. The former community organizer whose rise was assisted by food stamps and student loans will argue that government can be a force for positive change, reining in the excesses of the free market, making strategic investments to help the nation and its people compete. The private equity titan from a wealthy family will make the case that government is the problem, constraining the genius of the free market, interfering with the decisions of "job creators." Is Uncle Sam supposed to promote great national missions and a spirit of common purpose? Or is he just supposed to keep us safe and protect our rights?

These questions once seemed settled. The federal government gave us land-grant universities and the transcontinental railroad, the interstates and the Internet, the space program and semiconductors. The New Deal established the principle that Americans ought to take care of each other in hard times. Yet here we are, four years after the genius of an unconstrained free market brought the global economy to its knees, still unsure whether government ought to try to reshape our direction or just get out of the way.

It's a legitimate question. The Founding Fathers would be amazed by the size and scope of today's federal government. And it's easy to imagine a pair of data-loving technocrats like Mitt Romney and Barack Obama having a wonky debate about how to make it work better. But the 2012 election will be about whether it can work at all. To Obama, the Recovery Act is proof that the federal government really can work, that it can create jobs and produce change. To Republicans, it's proof of the exact opposite.

Obama has the facts on his side, but so far, he doesn't have the public on his side. The stimulus has changed millions of lives, and it's changing dozens of industries. But politically, what the ARPA-E chemist Eric Toone said about electrofuels applies to the Recovery Act as well: We know it worked. We just don't know if it matters.

Change Is Possible

President Obama's second inauguration felt a bit anticlimactic. We already had a black president, so the moment didn't seem as historic as the one four years earlier. The economy wasn't plunging toward depression, just sputtering along, so there wasn't an atmosphere of crisis, just unease. The crowd was less gigantic, less enthusiastic. Chief Justice Roberts didn't flub the oath. And while the media hyped the president's second inaugural address as Obama Unleashed, a new case for unshackled liberalism, his themes were his usual themes: equal opportunity for all, better but not bigger government, winning the future. His main theme was his campaign's main theme: We're-In-This-Together beats You're-On-Your-Own.

"No single person can train all the math and science teachers we'll need to equip our children for the future, or build the roads and networks and research labs that will bring new jobs and businesses to our shores," Obama said. "Now more than ever, we must do these things together, as one nation." He once again vowed to end "outworn" government programs but defended aid to the disabled, the poor, the sick, the old: "These commitments we make to each other . . . do not make us a nation of takers. They free us to take the risks that make this country great."

The "takers" line, of course, was a swipe at Mitt Romney's infamous whine to his donors that the 47 percent of Americans who don't pay income taxes (but do pay payroll taxes, gas taxes, and other taxes) are government-dependent moochers, a whine that indelibly branded him a You're-On-Your-Own guy after the video leaked. Romney's running mate, Paul Ryan, had expressed similar makers-versus-takers sentiments in the past. This was the modern Republican worldview; Eric Cantor had told Obama, during their first meeting about the Recovery Act in January 2009, that the GOP didn't consider "refundable" tax cuts for the 47 percent to be real tax cuts.

Now Obama was declaring publicly to the country what he had declared privately to Cantor four years earlier: Elections have consequences, and I won.

The Recovery Act was the ultimate expression of Obama's We're-In-This-Together philosophy, but he hadn't tried to rehabilitate its toxic reputation during his campaign. He never even mentioned the stimulus on the stump, although in August, after reading a stimulus defense I had written in the *Washington Post,* he mock-threatened his campaign aides on an Air Force One flight to Iowa: "I'm going to start talking about the stimulus in every speech!" They responded: "Noooo!" In the first presidential debate, Obama's listless debacle in Denver, Romney claimed that half the firms receiving clean-energy stimulus funds had failed, when in fact hardly any had failed; the president didn't even bother to correct the record.

In many ways, though, the stimulus was at the heart of the race. Romney's basic case for his candidacy was the Ronald Reagan question: Are you better off than you were four years ago? The majority answer was yes. Four years earlier, the economy had been imploding and hemorrhaging jobs, before the stimulus stopped the bleeding. Now the economy was growing and adding jobs. It was still weak, and unemployment was still high; Romney would have been smarter to ask "How ya doin'?" But by reminding Americans how horrible things had been in 2008—after eight years of Republican rule—the GOP helped make Obama's case for recovery.

One example was a Republican ad called "Actually Happened," savaging Obama for his "promise" that the stimulus would keep unemployment below 8 percent. (He made no such promise, but never mind.) The ad showed a graph with a blue line, the January 2009 Romer-Bernstein report's rosy forecast, then overlaid an orange line demonstrating what Actually Happened. As a narrator pointed out, the blue line was lower than the orange line; remember, the economy before the stimulus was far worse than Romer and Bernstein had realized. But both lines sloped downwards, because what Actually Happened was exactly what Romer and Bernstein had predicted: a steady reduction in unemployment after the stimulus. In other words, the Republicans poured $11 million into graphic evidence that the stimulus worked.

Romney and Ryan relentlessly bashed the stimulus as the essence of Obamanomics, a pork barrel exercise in crony capitalism. But their dishonest attacks often backfired. In the vice presidential debate, Ryan mocked Joe Biden's stimulus oversight, asking why he had allowed taxpayer dollars to build wind turbines in China. In fact, the stimulus built no wind turbines in China, and not only did it double the turbines in America, it doubled the American manufacturing content of those turbines. Biden laughed off Ryan's smears—"All this talk about cronyism, they investigated and investigated and did not find one single piece of evidence"—and pointed out that Ryan, like so many cash-and-trash Republicans, had written to the administration begging for stimulus funds that would create "growth and jobs" in his district. Biden also did what his boss would not. He defended the entire stimulus, noting that most economists agreed "that this was exactly what we needed that stopped us from going off the cliff. It set the conditions to be able to grow again."

Even Obama, while avoiding the S-word, bragged about its contents on the trail: Pell Grants for students, middle-class tax cuts, unemployment benefits, medical research, renewable energy. While Romney ran on the idea that government was the problem, Obama ran on the idea that government could be part of the solution. And even though the jobless rate stubbornly hovered around 8 percent, voters agreed with Obama. He won every state he had won in 2008 except Indiana and

North Carolina, thrashing Romney by five million votes. He became the first president since Eisenhower to reach 51 percent twice, while Romney, fittingly, finished with 47 percent.

Congressional Republicans took a beating, too. The GOP had been favored to take back the closely divided Senate, since Democrats had twice as many seats at risk. But Democrats gained seats, crushing Scott Brown in Massachusetts, replacing his fellow moderate Olympia Snowe after she retired in Maine, and defeating a Tea Party right-winger who had scozzafavaed the conservative-but-not-combative Richard Lugar in a primary in Indiana. (Republicans did reclaim Ben Nelson's seat in Nebraska after he retired, so Susan Collins is now the only member of the Gang of Four stimulus centrists who's still in the Senate.) Democrats also gained eight seats in the House, but Republicans kept control, thanks to the shrewd redistricting work after their 2010 landslide that helped them choose their own voters.

The 2012 election was as clear-cut a victory for Democrats as 2010 had been for Republicans, a solid endorsement of Obama's vision of change. He suggested the shock of his reelection might "break the fever" of Republican obstructionism, forcing GOP elites to wake up and see they were demographically and ideologically out of step with America. But they still held the House. They could still block legislation in the Senate. There were almost no moderate Republicans left on Capitol Hill, and even conservative Republicans had to worry about getting scozzafavaed if they drifted toward the middle. Obama could claim whatever mandate he wanted, but congressional elections have consequences, too.

So the fever has not broken.

Shortly after Obama's victory, Republican senators scuttled his top choice for secretary of state, Susan Rice, and nearly blocked his nominee for secretary of defense, Chuck Hagel, even though Hagel is a former Republican senator. When Obama invited five GOP senators to a post-election White House screening of *Lincoln,* a film about Honest Abe's backroom dealings with ideological opponents, all five declined.

House Republicans have been even more defiant, from backbenchers attacking Obama for playing too much golf and letting his daughters vacation in the Bahamas to Speaker Boehner insisting the public has somehow rejected Obama's ideas about taxes and spending. The Republican National Committee did publish a self-critical 2012 campaign "autopsy" calling for better technology, better messaging, and better minority outreach, even suggesting the party might be doomed with Latino voters if it doesn't embrace immigration reform. Otherwise, though, Republican leaders seem to think that their policies are just fine, that they just need more attractive candidates who can do a better job of selling the same product.

The clearest evidence Republicans hadn't changed was the House passing a new Ryan budget. It looked a lot like the old Ryan budget: deep cuts in Medicaid and other nonmilitary spending, repealing Obamacare and transforming Medicare into a voucher program, massive tax cuts for rich families and corporations supposedly paid for by closing unspecified tax loopholes. The budget was unveiled with a flurry of rhetoric about out-of-control deficits caused by out-of-control spending, even though Ryan's own graphs showed the deficit, estimated at over $1.2 trillion when Obama took office, was down to $850 billion, and was on track to fall to $400 billion by the end of his presidency. Another chart titled "Spending Is the Problem" showed spending had declined as a percentage of GDP since 2009, and was on track to continue declining in Obama's second term.

Obama's victory ensured the Ryan budget wouldn't happen. But something had to happen before the "fiscal cliff" of January 1, 2013, when the Bush tax cuts (extended by the 2010 Biden-McConnell deal) would expire and the harsh spending cuts known as the "sequester" (created by the 2011 Obama-Boehner budget fight) would take effect. Going over the cliff would have created a tremendous anti-stimulus, driving the economy back into recession. So Obama proposed to preserve the Bush tax cuts on income below $250,000 and postpone any spending cuts, while adding $200 billion worth of infrastructure projects and other new stimulus. Republicans wanted to make all the

Bush tax cuts permanent, cancel any defense spending cuts—which, in true military-Keynesian form, they said would destroy jobs—while slashing entitlements like Medicare. The Republicans had just spent the campaign blasting Obama for slashing Medicare, but now they were back in austerity mode, mocking Obama for even considering new stimulus.

At the last minute, the two sides agreed to make the Bush tax cuts permanent on income below $450,000 while restoring Clinton-era rates above it—a higher threshold than Obama wanted, but a step toward his long-term goal of a more progressive tax code. The deal also extended the Recovery Act's refundable tax credits for low-income workers and students, as well as unemployment benefits and a tax credit for the resurgent wind industry, while enacting a permanent fix for the Alternative Minimum Tax mess that had caused such angst during the stimulus debate. It did not extend the temporary payroll tax cuts that had originated with Making Work Pay, a step backward for Obama's tax goals, and it only postponed the sequester for two months. But such is life in a divided government. Magic-wand liberals accused Obama of making too many concessions, but he was lucky to get what he got from the GOP; Boehner had to ram the deal through the House without a majority of his own members, and later had to promise his caucus he would never again negotiate one-on-one with Obama.

That basically ensured that the sequester would begin in March, even though its haphazard spending cuts were designed to be so unpalatable that the two parties would be forced to cut a deal to replace them. They didn't, and as I write these words in April, they still haven't. The sequester has begun to slash popular services like Head Start and cancer clinics, but Republicans have refused to even discuss replacing it. At the same time, they've dubbed it the "Obamaquester," like kidnappers claiming their ransom was their victim's idea because he devised the method of payment. (The White House did propose the sequester in 2011, but only as a last-ditch alternative to GOP threats to force the government into default.) If the sequester isn't canceled, it will suck $85 billion out of the economy this year—probably not enough to trigger a recession, but enough to continue the Obama-era trend of decent private-sector performance (6.5 million jobs added since 2009) dragged down by public-sector shrinkage (600,000 jobs lost). One frustrating example is Build America Bonds, the stimulus-within-the-stimulus that's funding thousands of state and local infrastructure projects. It's beloved by governors and mayors, but the sequester will cut its subsidies by 7.6 percent, which will make its bonds less attractive to investors, and will end up scuttling desperately needed projects. Even innovative Recovery Act programs with some Republican support, like ARPA-E for energy and TIGER for transportation, are taking sequester haircuts.

More than $800 billion of the Recovery Act has been spent, and unless Democrats somehow take back the House in 2014, there won't be much more short-term stimulus in the Obama era. But the Recovery Act's long-term investments continue to bear fruit. The battle over their legacy continues, too.

Predictably, the Ryan budget trashed Obama's green energy subsidies, especially the Recovery Act's "failed" loan projects: "Beyond Solyndra, the latest ill-fated ventures include a $737 million loan guarantee for SolarReserve for a 110-megawatt solar tower on Federal land in Nevada. . . ."

Uh, stop right there. There's nothing "ill-fated" about SolarReserve. Not only is its plant under budget and ahead of schedule, it already has a twenty-five-year contract to sell its power, which dramatically reduces its risk of default. And this is no ordinary plant. When it comes online in 2014, it will be the world's first solar plant that stores electricity for use when the sun isn't shining. That may not sound like rocket science, but it is; a NASA supplier developed the molten salt technology that will help electrify Las Vegas at night. "If you Google 'solar energy storage,' half the articles call it the Holy Grail," says SolarReserve CEO Kevin Smith. "We're making it happen. And we couldn't have done it without the loan program." The plant will create more than four thousand construction jobs, and it could create a global model for an emissions-free technology—as well as a global market for a U.S.

company. Observers from twenty countries have descended on Nevada to see it; SolarReserve is now planning projects in South Africa, Saudi Arabia, and Chile. "The world is desperate for energy storage," Smith says. "We can run just like a conventional power plant, except we don't have to worry about the price of fuel. This technology is going to change the world."

That was the point of the loan program. It was always understood that some loans would go bad, and some have. The spectacular plunge in solar prices that doomed Solyndra also bankrupted the Colorado manufacturer Abound Solar; Ryan's budget griped that it "received $400 million in loan guarantees," but it actually collected only $70 million before failing. Electric automaker Fisker Automotive, which Romney famously called a "loser," is also going under after receiving $193 million (not the $527 million Republicans have claimed) from the feds. But its rival Tesla Motors, also dubbed a "loser" by Romney, just turned its first profit, and is paying back its government loan nine years early; its Model S swept just about every Car of the Year award and received one of the best *Consumer Reports* ratings ever. So far, only 3 percent of the Energy Deparment's loans have gone bad; overall, the portfolio is doing fine. And its projects are transforming the energy landscape. America's largest wind farm (in Oregon) is now online. The world's largest photovoltaic solar plant (in Arizona) and solar thermal plant (in California) are coming online soon. So who's the loser?

The big loan projects are just the vanguard of the clean-energy revolution launched by the Recovery Act. In 2008, the United States installed less than 300 megawatts of solar power; in 2012, it installed more than 3,300 megawatts. The price of panels has plummeted by 80 percent, a nightmare for manufacturers like Solyndra and Abound Solar but a boon for consumers, as well as rooftop installers like SolarCity, which had a successful IPO, and SunRun Homes, which grew from less than 500 customers in 2009 to more than 35,000 today. "It's like the transition from landlines to cell phones, or mainframes to PCs," says SunRun's Ed Fenster. "We're blowing up the business model." While the media have focused on the natural gas boom, wind was the leading source of new U.S. power generation in 2012. In January and March 2013, 100 percent of new capacity added to the grid was renewable. Obama has approved 37 renewable-energy projects on federal land; previous presidents approved zero.

Another book could be written about this revolution. The point here is that the Recovery Act gave clean energy the push it needed to travel from fringe to mainstream. Home Depot now sells $10 LED bulbs (manufactured by stimulus recipient Cree, Inc.) that use 84 percent less energy and last 25 times longer than traditional bulbs. Lithium-ion battery costs have fallen by more than half since 2009, and with $4 gasoline becoming the new normal, eight automakers are debuting electric vehicles in the United States this year. The smart grid is becoming a reality, with half of U.S. homes expected to have smart meters by 2015. After Superstorm Sandy battered the East Coast, meters helped Washington, D.C.'s, utility pinpoint outages and restore service to tens of thousands of homes within hours. As an investment space, the smart grid hasn't yet boomed the way Silver Spring Networks engineer Raj Vaswani expected when he compared it to the Internet circa 1994, but it's boomed enough for Silver Spring to hold its own IPO in March.

The media have not demonstrated much interest in these stories. On electric vehicles, for example, the big news (before the failure of Fisker) was the failure of Fisker's batterymaker, A123 Systems, which had drawn down about half of its $249 million federal grant. The main theme of industry coverage is that Obama will probably fall short of his goal of one million plug-ins on U.S. roads by 2015; so far, there are only about 100,000. But that's about 100,000 more than there were when Obama set the goal during his first campaign. That's an amazing growth rate, better than hybrids at a similar stage of development. As costs keep dropping and range keeps growing, the trend should continue. And thanks to the Recovery Act, the U.S. can supply the batteries domestically; Republicans had a field day with a Chinese firm's plans to take over A123's plant, but the jobs will still be in Michigan.

In 2008, Obama made a lot of hopey-changey promises to slash oil imports and carbon emissions. Well, in 2012, U.S. oil imports and carbon emissions dipped to their lowest levels in two decades. Energy consumption dropped to 1999 levels, even though GDP was $6 trillion higher and the population was 40 million larger. Change is here.

The change is not just limited to energy. A few more examples:

• By the end of 2012, nearly three fourths of America's doctors used electronic medical records. "E-prescribing" more than doubled in the first two years the stimulus incentives were available. The press has focused on the grumbling of doctors—although 85 percent surveyed say they're satisfied—and the possibility that health IT will make it easier to commit fraud. That may be true, because health IT will make it easier to do everything. It's more efficient. That's the point.

• California's high-speed rail project survived a series of legal and legislative challenges, so construction should begin in the Central Valley this year. Meanwhile, routes like Chicago–St. Louis, Chicago–Detroit, Portland–Seattle, and even the Northeast Corridor are running at higher speeds with better on-time performance. Republicans have blocked any additional funding, and media outlets like CNN have ridiculed the program for failing to produce bullet trains, but as a recent Brookings report concluded, "American passenger rail is in the midst of a renaissance."

• The Recovery Accountability and Transparency Board, the independent watchdog for the stimulus, was supposed to shut its doors in September 2013. But even though it has documented virtually no fraud—still less than 0.01 percent of all stimulus spending—it's been a rare Recovery Act product with bipartisan support. Congress extended the agency's charter so that it could monitor the $60 billion in federal Sandy relief. And the Republican-controlled House has passed a bill that would extend the RAT Board's data-driven oversight model to all federal spending.

• It's too early to tell whether Race to the Top and President Obama's other education reform efforts are working, but they're definitely happening. Thirty-six states have adopted new teacher evaluation policies, most tied to test scores or other forms of student performance. And as districts have begun to use the evaluations in hiring and promotion decisions, unions have begun to fight back. The nastiest clash was in Chicago, where teachers walked off the job for a week to protest the get-tough policies of Mayor Rahm Emanuel, who had helped ensure that Race to the Top stayed in the Recovery Act when he was Obama's chief of staff.

Of course, the most important legacy of the Recovery Act was the survival of the economy. A recent issue of the *American Economic Journal* had six more studies of the Recovery Act, all concluding it helped create jobs and growth. Today, the jobless rate is still an awful 7.6 percent, and growth remains mediocre. But the stock market is near its all-time high, real estate is rebounding, and manufacturing is stronger than before the crash. Maybe 200,000 new jobs a month isn't much, but it's a lot better than the 800,000 jobs we were losing every month at the start of 2009. What many economists believe is needed is more stimulus, to offset state and local government retrenchment and the end of the payroll tax cuts, or at least less anti-stimulus like the sequester. But even though the deficit is shrinking, even though federal spending is growing at the lowest rate since the Eisenhower years, even though everyone in Washington seems to call for more investment in infrastructure, Republicans are threatening to force another showdown over the debt ceiling, putting the U.S. credit rating at risk again to try to cut more spending.

That's just the reality of politics in the Obama era. He managed to put off any significant anti-stimulus until his second term, which is why the United States performed so much better than austerity-battered nations like Great Britain. But now we seem to be entering our own era of austerity. Obama has proposed all kinds of initiatives that would essentially double-down on the Recovery Act: a $50 billion fix-it-first effort on infrastructure, new "Races to the Top" that would let states compete for energy efficiency and grid modernization money, new investments in advanced manufacturing, renewable energy, and high-speed rail. But Republicans are not eager to help him preside over an economic boom in the short term or shore up his New Foundation for the long term. Republicans are not eager to help him, period.

So the gridlock of 2011 and 2012 seems likely to continue. Even after a massacre of first graders in Newtown, Connecticut, modest gun restrictions stalled in the Democratic Senate; if they hadn't, they would have been crushed in the Republican House. With both parties eager to woo Latinos, there has been some bipartisan momentum for immigration reform. But it's not at all clear whether legislation will get through Congress, and otherwise, there doesn't seem to be much appetite for cooperation. Obama has vowed to push for new climate legislation, but Republicans don't want it. The president would love a long-term fiscal deal, too, but he insists it must include new taxes. Republicans insist it can't include new taxes, and never the twain shall meet.

Let's face it: Obama didn't run on much of an agenda in 2012. He mostly rehashed his 2008 agenda and warned that Romney would bring back the Bush agenda. So Obama's biggest second-term achievements may depend on using the power of his office to consolidate his first-term achievements, by implementing health reform, education reform, and financial reform, while fueling the revolution in clean energy with new regulations cracking down on dirty energy.

The thing is, even without new legislation, those accomplishments would add up to a hugely consequential presidency.

So what are the lessons of all that change?

The first lesson is that change can be extremely unpopular. The stimulus is still a political albatross, and it's possible that the next time the economy free-falls, politicians will hesitate to open the Keynesian handbook. The Republican strategy of bashing the stimulus (and government spending in general) paid real dividends in 2010. The GOP has stuck with the rhetoric of austerity, and even though there's still slack in the economy, Democrats remain terrified of looking like big spenders.

But there's another way to look at Obama's first term. He began with the hideously unpopular stimulus. Then he engineered the equally unpopular auto bailout. He then spent a year pushing politically suicidal health reforms, even after his top aides advised him to drop the issue. His approval ratings drooped, and as he kept doing controversial things—pulling out of Iraq, pushing cap-and-trade, endorsing gay marriage—pundits kept accusing him of political malpractice.

Yet he got reelected anyway.

So the second lesson of the Obama era is: Do stuff! Politicians in both parties spend an extraordinary amount of time and energy fretting about the political consequences of their policies, which is understandable, because politicians who don't get reelected become ex-politicians. But in the end, your reelection might come down to a bartender with an iPhone at a Boca Raton fund-raiser, so you might as well do what you think is right while you've got the power to do it.

Obama is a politician, and he didn't become the first black president by being a bad politician. But he made it a point of pride that his administration would focus on getting the policy right and let the political chips fall where they may. Sometimes that was a mistake; it's amazing that the Recovery Act cut taxes for 95 percent of Americans and less than 10 percent of them noticed. For the most part, though, Obama's focus on policy goals over political strategy led to a lot of policy change. In a 50-50 nation, it's hard to imagine that he would have been any more popular if he had punted on health reform, or the auto rescue, or even the Recovery Act.

There's no way to know for sure. But this much is sure: If he had punted on the Recovery Act, millions of vulnerable Americans wouldn't have gotten help from their government when they needed it. States and cities would have been forced to eliminate far more employees and services. Oahu wouldn't have increased its solar installations 3,300 percent. The American Society of Civil Engineers wouldn't have improved its overall grade for America's infrastructure (from a D to a D-plus, but still) for the first time ever. The largest U.S. steel plant wouldn't be re-cycling waste heat into electricity, saving $20 million a year and enough energy to power thirty thousand homes. Our medical system would still be stuck in the analog age, our schools still making decisions without data, our economy still almost entirely fossil-fueled.

Instead, Obama did stuff. Whether or not you like what he did, he proved that making change in Washington, though difficult, is not impossible. Now he'll have a chance to do more stuff, and make more change.

Michael Grunwald
April 2013

— ACKNOWLEDGMENTS —

This book exists because of Walter Alarkon, a wonderful journalist and a spectacular research assistant. Walter was a star reporter at *The Hill* before I lucked into hiring him, and he's been getting a law degree at Georgetown University while making this book happen. I'm not sure when the dude sleeps, but I can't thank him enough for all his terrific work. Walter tracked down countless facts, saved me from countless mistakes, and gave me perceptive advice every day. He gave the first edit of every word in this book. He also did some of the most important reporting in this book, working his congressional sources to help tell the Capitol Hill side of the stimulus story. The roots of the Republican strategy of obstructionism—the bulk of Chapter Seven—grew out of his reporting. The entire book was a partnership, and Walter was the perfect partner—smart, funny, supportive, unbelievably hardworking, and infinitely patient, a self-overrated tennis player but a great guy. I'm glad to be his friend, and I look forward to working for him someday.

I was also fortunate to work again with Simon & Schuster, especially my legendary editor Alice Mayhew, who dispensed typically wise advice and typically hilarious rants about the incompetence of the Obama message machine. Thanks also to publisher Jonathan Karp for his faith in this book, to Julia Prosser, Maureen Cole, and Rachelle Andujar for helping to sell it, and to copy editor Fred Chase, Jonathan Cox, Mara Lurie, and the rest of the S&S crew. My agent, Andrew Wylie, is the best in the business; Scott Moyers was also a delight to work with before he went back to the editing world. And my pal Ashleigh Lindenauer did a beautiful job with the graphics.

I am especially grateful to my indulgent editors at *Time* magazine and Time.com, who have allowed me to pursue my dorky interests while living in the policy mecca that is South Beach. Michael Duffy, who first assigned me to write about the stimulus, is a fantastic boss and a good friend. As he will surely remind me, I owe him big-time. I am also grateful to Rick Stengel, who let me write about this stuff in the magazine and then granted me a leave of absence to finish the book. John Huey and Nancy Gibbs has also supported me at *Time*, as have Jim Frederick, Daniel Eisenberg, Mike Crowley, Adam Sorenson, and the dearly departed (from *Time*, not life) Josh Tyrangiel. Thanks to Jay Newton-Small for her gracious help, and to David Von Drehle for being David Von Drehle.

It helps to have friends who really know how to read. Peter Canellos and Manuel Roig-Franzia were awesome pro bono editors. They really saved me. Phil Arlen, Gary Bass, Jon Cohn, Alan Farago, Jed Kolko, Indira Lakshmanan, and Mark Wiedman also read chapters and provided valuable feedback. So did a few sources who will have to go unnamed but not unappreciated. And Cristina Dominguez, whose interest in the stimulus did not extend too far beyond the high-speed trains we had hoped to ride to visit her parents in Orlando, slogged through my drafts anyway, surely the ultimate marital sacrifice. Peter Baker, the best White House reporter, and Susan Glasser, the smartest Washington journalist, helped me figure out what I wanted to say during one of my frequent visits to their home.

I have a separate note on sources, but I did want to single out my two patient guides to the Energy Department, Sanjay Wagle and Matt Rogers. I've been pals with Sanjay since he was breaking sleep records in college; Matt is a new friend. I was lucky to be able to pick their brains about clean energy, and all of us who pay taxes in the United States were lucky to have them working for us. I also want to thank my official sherpas, Liz Oxhorn and Jamie Smith, for helping me navigate the White House from a thousand miles away. My unofficial sherpas have my gratitude as well.

Finally, I want to thank my family for tolerating me and my disappearances during this project. Judy, Steve, Zach, Allie, Jake, Dave, Ruchi, Maylen, Phil, Sofia, Carmen, Jim, and Humberto, I'm looking forward to catching up. I also need to spend some quality time with my parents, Doris and Hans Grunwald, who are still an inspiration. I can't thank them enough for their love, support, and babysitting. Speaking of which, *muchas gracias a* Gloria Herrera, my semi-replacement over the last year while I've been a presentee dad. I'm tired of telling Max that I can't play right now, and seeing Lina's sad little face before I close my office door. They're such amazing kids, and they've been so patient and loving. They make me so proud. They're about to get some serious Daddy time, and I can't wait.

Finally, this book is dedicated to Cristina, who really is my stimulus, my teammate, my partner, the love of my life. She picked up the slack while I was in my hidey-hole, and she got me through this with my sanity intact. I can't express how lucky I am to be a part of her life. She's going to get some serious Daddy time, too.

I don't want to be ungrateful, but since this is a note on sources, I do want to be honest: Sources lie. They embellish. They omit. They have agendas, hidden and not. They exaggerate their own prescience and the folly of their rivals. And sometimes their memories honestly fail them. Phil Schiliro, President Obama's legislative director, warned me about this when I interviewed him in the West Wing: "Everybody has a different recollection, sometimes of the same facts." I told him that's why I beg my sources for documents. "Documents are sometimes misleading, too," he said.

This is a long-winded way of admitting the inherent weaknesses of books like this. *The New New Deal* is a work of nonfiction, based on interviews with more than four hundred sources—I do appreciate their help!—as well as hundreds of pages of administration documents. It's written in that omniscient tone that has become standard for reported narratives. But I'm not omniscient. I've tried to confirm every scene with multiple sources, and when sources have disagreed about what happened I've erred on the side of omitting the scene. I've tried to put as many quotes as possible on the record, although quite a few White House officials, members of Congress, and staffers spoke to me and my amazing research assistant, Walter Alarkon, on a not-for-attribution basis. And I'll post some of the documents on my website, www.michaelgrunwald.com. Still, I'm painfully aware of the shortcomings of this genre. This won't be the last draft of history.

One specific shortcoming of this book is that President Obama did not grant me an interview. I've only met him once, at the White House holiday party. When I told him I was writing a book about the Recovery Act, he said: "You've gotta talk to Biden." The vice president did graciously grant me two on-the-record interviews, in April 2010 and March 2011, and it probably goes without saying that they were lengthy. He and his staff were also kind enough to let me sit in on Recovery Act cabinet meetings he led in April 2010 and September 2010. I also spoke to half a dozen cabinet secretaries, and most of the major economic players from the Obama White House. And I traveled to stimulus projects around the country.

Now that I've dissed the genre, I should acknowledge that I've benefited from several earlier books about Obama and his administration, which are all included in the source notes. The president's own books, *Dreams from My Father* and *The Audacity of Hope*, provide a valuable introduction to his life and his mind. And Vice President Biden's stream-of-consciousness autobiography *Promises to Keep* is a trip. Otherwise, I'm particularly indebted to David Mendell and David Remnick for their insightful Obama biographies; John Heilemann and Mark Halperin, Obama campaign manager David Plouffe, and Richard Wolffe for their accounts of the Obama campaign; Bush treasury secretary Hank Paulson, Andrew Ross Sorkin, and David Wessel for their accounts of the financial crisis; Steven Brill for his look at Race to the Top; Eric Pooley for his investigation of the political wars over climate change; and Jonathan Alter, former White House official Steve Rattner, Ron Suskind, and Wolffe for their accounts of the Obama White House. There is valuable stuff in every one of those books. (Alter gets extra credit for writing a terrific book about the old New Deal as well.) Finally, I want to acknowledge three authors who scooped me by publishing books while I was finishing mine: David Corn, Noam Scheiber, and Michael Grabell, who wrote an alternative take on the Recovery Act.

I've been harsh on the media coverage of the stimulus, but I still relied heavily on the reporting of great national newspapers like the *New York Times*, the *Washington Post*, and the *Wall Street Journal*, as well as Washington watchdogs like *Politico*, Roll Call, ProPublica, and Congressional Quarterly. I also consulted *The New Yorker, The New Republic, The Atlantic, The Economist, Slate*, and of course the work of my colleagues at *Time*. I often learned a lot from websites like Talking Points Memo, Daily Kos, the Huffington Post, ThinkProgress and ClimateProgress on the left, or *National Review*'s The Corner and RedState on the right; even for source materials that aren't solely on the Internet, I've tried to include links whenever possible. For what it's worth, I particularly admired the work of Ezra Klein and Alec McGillis of the *Washington Post*, David Leonhardt of the *Times*, Ryan Lizza of *The New Yorker*, Jonathan Chait of *The New Republic*, Joshua Green at *The Atlantic*, Matthew Yglesias of *Slate*, and David Roberts of Grist. My former boss at the *Washington Post*, Steve Coll, blogged the text of the Recovery Act with his usual brilliance. And like everyone else who wants to know what's going on in D.C., I read my friend Mike Allen's Playbook every morning.

Thanks to my indulgent bosses, some of the reporting in this book first appeared in *Time* and Time.com. My first Recovery Act article, "How to Spend a Trillion Dollars," ran in January 2009; my story in May 2010, "How the Stimulus Is Changing America," gave me the idea for this book. I've also cannibalized my *Time* articles on topics like energy efficiency, biofuels, green infrastructure, high-speed rail, health care costs, Steven Chu, Ben Bernanke, John Boehner, President Obama, California, and the Republican Party, as well as my blog posts about politics at Swampland.

I also spent an inordinate amount of time reading government websites and reports. The White House Council of Economic Advisers (www.whitehouse.gov), the Government Accountability Office (www.gao.gov), and the Congressional Budget Office (www.cbo.gov) all issued regular reports on the Recovery Act. Biden's office and the Department of Energy (www.energy.gov) also produced helpful reports, as did inspector generals across the government. The official Recovery Act website, www.recovery.gov, is also an excellent source of information, notwithstanding the occasional brouhahas over phantom congressional districts and what-not. The American Presidency Project at the University of California-Santa Barbara has compiled Obama's public remarks at http://www.presidency.ucsb.edu/index.php. The Bureau of Labor Statistics (www.bls.gov) and Bureau of Economic Analysis (www .bea.gov) were my sources for data on employment and the economy, while I relied on the Energy Information Administration (www.eia.gov) for energy data. The House and Senate debates on the Recovery Act are all in the Congressional Record.

In these endnotes, I've tried to identify sources of information that weren't readily available elsewhere. I also occasionally used the notes to provide information—usually scintillating factoids like the difference between the 1703 and 1705 loan guarantee programs—that didn't fit into the text of the book. I didn't put interviews in the endnotes. When I quoted someone talking to me directly, I tried to use signals like "says" or "recalls" or "told me." I tried hard to confirm that what they said and recalled and told me was correct; I'm confident that this book is the truth. But again, I realize it's not the whole truth.

Introduction: Things That Never Were

1 *usher in a new birth of freedom:* Obama announcement speech, February 10, 2007, http://www.presidency.ucsb.edu/ws/index.php?pid=76999#axzzlpxkCjpbY.

2 *"reinvent the economy to seize the future":* Barack Obama, *Change We Can Believe In: Barack Obama's Plan to Renew America's Promise* (New York: Three Rivers Press, 2008), p. 246.

3 *Steven Chu, a quantum physicist:* Michael Grunwald, "Can Steven Chu Win the Fight over Global Warming?," *Time*, August 23, 2009, http://www.time.com/time/magazine/article/0,9171,1916282,00.html. I first heard Chu complain about photosynthesis when I traveled with him to China in the spring of 2009 for this profile.

3 *using an atom interferometer:* Holger Müller, Achim Peters, and Steven Chu, "A Precision Measurement of the Gravitational Redshift by the Interference of Matter Waves," *Nature*, February 18, 2010.

4 *Chu was ARPA-E's intellectual godfather:* Steven Chu testimony, House Committee on Science, March 9, 2006, http://www7.nationalacademies.org/ocga/testimony/Should_Congress_Est_ARPA_E_Rising_Above_the_Gathering_Storm.asp.

6 *a cabinet meeting led by Vice President Joe Biden:* I attended the meeting in the Eisenhower Executive Office Building on April 29, 2010.

7 *Obama's approval ratings were around 70 percent:* Gallup has tracked Obama's approval ratings throughout his presidency at http://www.gallup.com/poll/113980/gallup-daily-obama-job-approval.aspx.

7 *Within a year, the percentage of Americans:* According to a CBS News/*New York Times* poll on February 11, 2010, just 6 percent of the public thought the stimulus had created any jobs. According to a CBS News poll from 2002, 7 percent of Americans believe Elvis is alive.

8 *"avoid the word 'stimulus' like the plague":* Obama press conference, September 10, 2010.

8 *A politically disastrous January 2009 report:* Christina Romer and Jared Bernstein, "The Job Impact of the American Recovery and Reinvestment Plan," January 10, 2009, http://otrans.3cdn.net/ee40602f9a7d8172b8_ozm6bt5oi.pdf.

10 *the official price tag would eventually climb to $831 billion:* "Estimated Impact of the American Recovery and Reinvestment Act on Employment and Economic Output

from July 2011 Through December 2011," Congressional Budget Office, February 2012, http://www.cbo.gov/publication/43014.

12 *the stimulus helped stop the bleeding:* CBO report on ARRA, February 2012; Alan S. Blinder and Mark Zandi, "How the Great Recession Was Brought to an End," July 27, 2010, http://www.economy.com/mark-zandi/documents/End-of-Great-Recession.pdf; "MA on Fiscal Stimulus, the Definitive Answer: It Works. MA Refutes the Demagoguery," Macroadvisers: The Blog of Macroeconomic Advisers LLC, February 19, 2010, http://macroadvisers.blogspot.com/2010/02/ma-on-fiscal-stimulus-definitive-answer .html; "Fiscal Stimulus: A Little Less in Q2, A Little More Later," Goldman Sachs, August 4, 2009; Jackie Calmes and Michael Cooper, "New Consensus Sees Stimulus Package as Worthy Step," *New York Times*, November 20, 2009.

12 *the low point came right before:* The biggest monthly job loss during the recession was in January 2009, when the economy shed 818,000 jobs.

13 *The economy was shrinking at an unheard-of 8.9 percent rate:* "Results of the 2011 Flexible Annual Revision of the National Income and Product Account," Bureau of Economic Analysis, July 29, 2011, http://www.bea.gov/national/pdf/NIPAbriefing _AR2011.pdf. The BEA is my source for all data on economic output.

13 *Today, those independent analysts:* The various estimates are listed in "The Economic Impact of the American Recovery and Reinvestment Act of 2009: Eighth Quarterly Report," White House Council of Economic Advisers, December 9, 2011, http://www.whitehouse.gov/sites/default/files/cea_8th_arra_report_final_draft.pdf.

14 *the Recovery Act increased output over 2 percent:* A February 2012 CBO report found that the stimulus boosted quarterly economic growth by as much as 4.6 percent, http://www.cbo.gov/sites/default/files/cbofiles/attachments/02-22-ARRA.pdf. Private forecasters have estimated that the maximum effect was as little as 2.1 percent and as much as 3.8 percent. White House CEA report, December 2011.

18 *"Oprah, I've got to tell you":* Obama interview, *The Oprah Winfrey Show,* May 2, 2011.

19 *this was the moment:* Obama speech following Iowa caucuses, January 3, 2008, http://www.presidency.ucsb.edu/ws/index.php?pid=76232.

1. A Man With a Plan

25 *Obama's speech was memorable:* Obama inauguration speech, January 20, 2009, http://www.presidency.ucsb.edu/ws/index.php?pid=44&st=&st1=#axzzlmfRjZahX

26 *The Recovery Act checked off:* The text of the Recovery Act can be found at http:// www.gpo.gov/fdsys/pkg/BILLS-111hr1enr/pdf/BILLS-111hr1enr.pdf.

27 *"a president we know less about":* The quote is from former Mississippi governor Haley Barbour at a Washington round table on September 7, 2010.

27 *We know plenty about Barack Obama:* Obama's own books, *Dreams from My Father: A Story of Race and Inheritance* (New York: Three Rivers Press; 2004 edition) and *The Audacity of Hope: Thoughts on Reclaiming the American Dream* (New York: Three Rivers Press, 2006), are the best introduction to his life and his mind. The best Obama biographies so far are David Remnick, *The Bridge: The Life and Rise of Barack Obama* (New York: Knopf, 2010) and David Mendell, *Obama: From Promise to Power* (New York: HarperCollins, 2007). (I reserve the right to revise and extend those remarks after David Maraniss weighs in.) David Freddoso's *The Case Against Barack Obama* (Washington, D.C.: Regnery, 2008) looks at Obama without sympathy but with facts from a conservative perspective. James T. Kloppenberg's *Reading*

Obama: Dreams, Hope, and the American Political Tradition (Princeton: Princeton University Press, 2009) is an interesting intellectual biography.

28 *"could probably do every job":* David Plouffe, *The Audacity to Win* (New York: Viking, 2009), p. 8.

28 *"white folks this and white folks that":* Obama, *Dreams from My Father*, p. 81.

28 *"We should be guided by what works":* Obama, *The Audacity of Hope*, p. 159.

28 *Aside from the wingnut screeds:* Jack Cashill, *Deconstructing Obama: The Life, Loves and Letters of America's First Postmodern President* (New York: Threshold Editions, 2011); Dinesh D'Souza, *The Roots of Obama's Rage* (Washington, D.C.: Regnery, 2010).

30 *Obama's mother, Ann Dunham:* Obama, *The Audacity of Hope*, pp. 45, 59; Obama, *Dreams from My Father*, p. 72.

30 *As he explained to the uninitiated:* Obama, *The Audacity of Hope*, pp. 156–57.

32 *the launch of the Hamilton Project:* Video of Obama speech, April, 5, 2006, http://www.youtube.com/watch?v=P-5Y74FrDCc.

32 *"the draft letter saga":* Obama, *The Audacity of Hope*, p. 35.

33 *"We Are One People" speech:* Video of Obama speech, July 27, 2004, http://www.youtube.com/watch?v=eWynt87PaJ0.

34 *"Maybe there's no escaping":* Obama, *The Audacity of Hope*, p. 41.

35 *Obama announced his candidacy:* Obama announcement speech, February 10, 2007, http://www.presidency.ucsb.edu/ws/index.php?pid=76999.

2. The Four Pillars

37 *In his first policy speech of the campaign:* Obama speech, Detroit, May 7, 2007, http://www.presidency.ucsb.edu/ws/index.php?pid=77000. Obama's campaign book: *Change We Can Believe In: Barack Obama's Plan to Renew America's Promise* outlines his specific policy agenda. The transition then posted much of it at http://change.gov/agenda.

37 *Those last five words:* Franklin Delano Roosevelt inauguration speech, March 4, 1933, http://www.presidency.ucsb.edu/ws/index.php?pid=14473.

38 *Oil imports had more than doubled since 1973:* 1.4 billion barrels of oil were imported in 1973; 3.7 billion were imported in 2007: U.S. imports of crude oil, 1973 to January 2012, U.S. Census Bureau, Foreign Trade Division, http://www.census.gov/foreign-trade/statistics/historical/petr.pdf. "World Proved Reserves of Oil and Natural Gas, Most Recent Estimates," U.S. Energy Information Administration, March 3, 2009, http://www.eia.gov/international/reserves.html.

38 *The ten hottest years on record:* Currently, the ten hottest years by temperature, according to the NASA Global Land Temperature Index, are: 2010, 2005, 2007, 1998, 2009, 2002, 2003, 2006, 2011, and 2004. So far, 2012 is looking like another hot one.

39 *In an October speech in Portsmouth, New Hampshire:* Obama speech, October 8, 2007, http://www.presidency.ucsb.edu/ws/index.php?pid=93305&st=portsmouth&st1=obama#axzz11AFdDYKd.

39 *"standard goody-bag politics":* Robert Samuelson, "The Obama Delusion," *Washington Post*, February 20, 2008.

39 *a renewable energy resource that's perfectly clean:* Michael Grunwald, "America's Untapped Resource," *Time*, December 31, 2008, www.time.com/time/magazine/article/0,9171,1869224,00.html.

40 *A McKinsey & Co. study found that efficiency:* "Unlocking Energy Efficiency in the

US Economy," July 2009, http://www.mckinsey.com/Client_Service/Electric_Power
_and_Natural_Gas/Latest_thinking/Unlocking_energy_efficiency_in_the_US_economy.

41 *It was analog in a digital world:* I learned a lot about the smart grid from Peter Fox-
    Penner and his book *Smart Power: Climate Change, the Smart Grid, and the Future
    of Electric Utilities* (Washington, D.C.: Island Press, 2010). I wrote about it in *Time*:
    Michael Grunwald, "Street Smarts," September 30, 2011, http://www.time.com/
    time/magazine/article/0,9171,2094362,00.html.

42 *"It's safe to say":* David Roberts, "Obama Talks Up Electrical Grid Improvements on
    Cable TV—Seriously, I Have Video Evidence," Grist, October 31, 2008, http://grist
    .org/politics/grid-me-barry-one-more-time/.

42 *The ethanol boom:* Grunwald, "The Clean Energy Scam," *Time*, March 27, 2008,
    www.time.com/time/magazine/article/0.9171.1725975,00.html.

43 *our share of the market had plummeted from 40 percent to 8 percent in a decade:*
    "Trends in Photovoltaic Applications," International Energy Agency, Photovoltaic
    Power Systems Programme, August 2011.

43 *the Energy Department's research budget had plunged 85 percent:* Daniel M. Kammen
    and Gregory F. Nemet, "Reversing the Incredible Shrinking Energy R&D Budget,"
    University of California, Berkeley, Issues in Science and Technology, Fall 2005, http://
    rael.berkeley.edu/sites/default/files/old-site-files/2005/Kammen-Nemet-Shrinking
    RD-2005.pdf.

44 *U.S. health spending had quadrupled in two decades:* For more on U.S. health
    spending, see the National Health Expenditure database at the Center for Medicare
    and Medicaid Services website: http://www.cms.gov/NationalHealthExpendData/02
    _NationalHealthAccountsHistorical.asp#TopOfPage.

45 *The Congressional Budget Office warned:* "The Long-Term Outlook for Health Care
    Spending," CBO, November 2007, http://www.cbo.gov/sites/default/files/cbofiles/
    ftpdocs/87xx/docs8758/11-13-lt-health.pdf.

45 *One study of preventable deaths:* "Measuring the Health of Nations: Updating an
    Earlier Analysis," *Health Affairs*, January 2008.

47 *Less than half of U.S. medical treatment:* "Learning What Works Best: The Nation's
    Need for Evidence on Comparative Effectiveness in Health Care," Institute of Medi-
    cine of the National Academies, September 2007, http://www.iom.edu/~/media/
    Files/Activity%20Files/Quality/VSRT/ComparativeEffectivenessWhitePaperF.ashx.

47 *Studies by Dartmouth researchers:* Jonathan Skinner and Elliot S. Fisher, "Reflec-
    tions on Geographic Variations in U.S. Health Care," Dartmouth Institute for Health
    Policy and Clinical Practice, March 31, 2010, http://www.dartmouthatlas.org/down
    loads/press/Skinner_Fisher_DA_05_10.pdf.

47 Consumer Reports *had compiled evidence:* Consumer Reports Best Buy Drugs stud-
    ies, February 2011, http://www.consumerreports.org/health/best-buy-drugs/best
    -buy-drugs/generic-and-brand-drugs/index.htm.

47 *Gingrich coauthored an op-ed:* Billy Beane, Newt Gingrich, and John Kerry, "How
    to Take American Health Care from Worst to First," *New York Times*, October 24,
    2008.

47 *"It's an attempt to say to patients":* David Leonhardt, "After the Great Recession,"
    New York Times, April 28, 2009.

49 *"They wanted more school":* Obama, *The Audacity of Hope*, p. 250.

49 *"Few of these educators":* Obama, *Dreams from My Father*, p. 386.

50 *"labeling a school and its students as failures":* Obama speech to the American Fed-
    eration of Teachers convention, July 2, 2008, http://www.presidency.ucsb.edu/ws/
    index.php?pid=77653.

50 *"I'm running for president":* Obama speech, Dayton, Ohio, September 9, 2008, http://www.presidency.ucsb.edu/ws/index.php?pid=78610.

51 *"will help determine not only whether our children":* Obama speech, Indianapolis, Indiana, May 3, 2008, http://www.presidency.ucsb.edu/ws/index.php?pid=77203.

51 *his first major economic speech:* Obama speech, Nasdaq headquarters, September 17, 2007, http://www.presidency.ucsb.edu/ws/index.php?pid=77012.

51 *wages had been flat:* "Income, Poverty, and Health Insurance Coverage in the United States: 2008," U.S. Census Bureau, September 2009, http://www.census.gov/prod/2009pubs/p60-236.pdf.

53 *Bush returned more cash to the top 1 percent of taxpayers:* "Tenth Anniversary of the Bush Tax Cuts," Economic Policy Institute, June 1, 2011, http://www.epi.org/publication/tenth_anniversary_of_the_bush-era_tax_cuts/.

53 *In a speech at Brookings:* Obama speech, September 18, 2007, http://www.presidency.ucsb.edu/ws/index.php?pid=93293.

53 *when your drapes cost more than an average worker's yearly salary:* Obama, *The Audacity of Hope,* p. 193.

54 *"more of the same old Democratic campaign playbook":* Ruth Marcus, "The Two Obamas," *Washington Post,* September 26, 2007.

54 *A magazine profile about "Larry Summer's Evolution":* David Leonhardt, *New York Times Sunday Magazine,* June 6, 2007.

3. The Collapse

57 *"the Bush boom is alive and well":* Larry Kudlow, "Bush Boom Continues," the Corner blog, *National Review,* December 7, 2007, http://www.nationalreview.com/corner/153626/bush-boom-continues/larry-kudlow.

57 *"History has cautioned":* Speech by Larry Summers, Brookings Institution, Washington, D.C., December 19, 2007, http://www.brookings.edu/~/media/Files/events/2007/1219_economy/20071219_summers.pdf.

58 *Republican Mitt Romney proposed the most aggressive plan:* John Harwood, "Romney Offers an Economic Stimulus Plan," *New York Times,* January 19, 2008.

58 *Keynes wrote his masterpiece:* John Maynard Keynes, *The General Theory of Employment, Interest and Money* (New York: Classic Books America, 2009; first published, 1936).

58 *Summers thought it should have been titled:* Ezra Klein, "Larry Summers: 'I Think Keynes Mistitled His Book,'" *Washington Post,* July 11, 2011.

61 *"Poorly designed fiscal stimulus":* Larry Summers, "Why America Must Have a Fiscal Stimulus," *Financial Times,* January 6, 2008.

62 *A new Brookings analysis . . . :* Douglas W. Elmendorf and Jason Furman, "If, When, How: A Primer on Fiscal Stimulus," Brookings Institution, January 10, 2008, http://www.brookings.edu/papers/2008/0110_fiscal_stimulus_elmendorf_furman.aspx; Mark M. Zandi, "Assessing the Macro Economic Impact of Fiscal Stimulus 2008," Moody's Economy.com, January 2008, http://www.economy.com/mark-zandi/documents/Stimulus-Impact-2008.pdf; "Options for Responding to Short-Term Economic Weakness," Congressional Budget Office, January 2008, http://www.cbo.gov/ftpdocs/89xx/doc8916/01-15-Econ_Stimulus.pdf.

63 *their plan included state aid and unemployment benefits:* "Barack Obama's Plan to Stimulate the Economy," Obama campaign fact sheet, http://obama.3cdn.net/8335008b3be0e6391e_foi8mve29.pdf.

64 *"I know that Mr. Obama's supporters hate to hear this"*: Paul Krugman, "Responding to Recession," *New York Times,* January 14, 2008.

64 *Obama won easily with an A-minus:* Ruth Marcus, "Whose Stimulus Makes the Grade?," *Washington Post,* January 23, 2008.

66 *Boehner was a conservative K Street Republican:* Michael Grunwald and Jay Newton-Small, "Mr. Speaker," *Time,* November 5, 2010, http://www.time.com/time/magazine/article/0,9171,2029476,00.html.

68 *The rest of 2008:* I consulted several books about the financial crisis. David Wessel's *In Fed We Trust: Ben Bernanke's War on the Great Panic* (New York: Crown, 2009) is an excellent account of the Federal Reserve's role. Andrew Ross Sorkin's *Too Big to Fail* (New York: Viking, 2009) is a gripping yarn from the Wall Street perspective. Henry Paulson Jr.'s *On the Brink: Inside the Race to Stop the Collapse of the Global Financial System* (New York: Business Plus, 2010) tells the treasury secretary's story. And Carmen M. Reinhart and Kenneth S. Rogoff basically foretold the last few years in *This Time Is Different: Eight Centuries of Financial Folly* (Princeton: Princeton University Press, 2009).

68 *the first in a series of unprecedented interventions:* Michael Grunwald, "Ben Bernanke: Person of the Year," *Time,* December 16, 2009, www.time.com/time/specials/packages/article/0,28804,1946375_1947251_1947520,00.html.

68 *By the time Obama clinched:* I relied on three fun books about the 2008 campaign in addition to my own reporting: Obama campaign manager David Plouffe's *The Audacity to Win* (New York: Viking, 2009), John Heilemann and Mark Halperin's *Game Change* (New York: Harper, 2010), and Richard Wolffe's *Renegade* (New York: Random House, 2009).

71 *"Nancy, we're racing to prevent a collapse"*: Paulson, *On the Brink,* p. 255.

4. "We Were Staring into the Abyss."

74 *his run-in with a bald, strapping, tax-averse plumber:* Obama-Wurzelbacher exchange, October 12, 2008, http://www.youtube.com/watch?v=BRPbCSSXyp0&feature=related.

75 *he unveiled his "Rescue Plan for the Middle Class"*: Obama campaign speech, Toledo, Ohio, October 13, 2008, http://www.presidency.ucsb.edu/ws/index.php?pid=84562.

75 *Reporters described it as a $60 billion proposal:* Jackie Calmes, "From 2 Rivals, 2 Prescriptions," *New York Times,* October 14, 2008; Don Gonyea, "Obama Proposes $60 Billion in Tax Breaks," NPR *Morning Edition,* October 14, 2008.

76 *"stimulus proposals are proliferating like Halloween pumpkins"*: Lori Montgomery and Dan Eggen, "Spending Surge Pushing Deficit Toward $1 Trillion," *Washington Post,* October 18, 2008.

76 *"open its wallet, not tighten its belt"*: David R. Sands, "Economists Prescribe Deeper Deficit," *Washington Times,* October 17, 2008.

77 *a fifty-six-chapter blueprint:* Mark Green and Michele Jolin, eds., *Change for America: A Progressive Blueprint for the 44th President* (New York: Basic Books, 2009).

77 *His own book:* John Podesta, *The Power of Progress: How America's Progressives Can (Once Again) Save Our Economy, Our Climate, and Our Country* (New York: Crown, 2008).

80 *a Goldman Sachs report:* Jan Hatzius et al., "US Economics Analyst," Goldman Sachs, October 24, 2008.

80 *conservative Harvard economist Martin Feldstein:* Martin Feldstein, "The Stimulus Plan We Need Now," *Washington Post,* October 30, 2008.

81 *Lew's final stimulus presentation:* "Economic Team: Fiscal Stimulus," November 2, 2008, discussion document provided to the author.

84 *Soon the president-elect came on the screen:* Obama victory speech, November 4, 2008, http://www.presidency.ucsb.edu/ws/index.php?pid=84750.

5. Ready Before Day One

89 *Obama's first post-election move:* Several authors have written with insight about the Obama transition and White House. The best account of his first year is Jonathan Alter's *The Promise: President Obama, Year One* (New York: Simon & Schuster, 2010). Other books covering this period include Ron Suskind's *Confidence Men* (New York: Harper, 2011), Noam Scheiber's *Escape Artists: How Obama's Team Fumbled the Recovery* (New York: Simon & Schuster, 2011), and Richard Wolffe's *Revival: The Struggle for Survival Inside the Obama White House* (New York: Crown, 2010).

90 *The* New York Times *noted with dry understatement:* Peter Baker and Jeff Zeleny, "For Obama, No Day to Bask as He Starts to Build a Team," *New York Times,* November 6, 2008.

91 *"These reports don't get much worse than a loss of 240,000 jobs in a single month":* "Waiting for Obama," *Wall Street Journal,* editorial, November 8, 2008.

91 *Obama held his first news conference as president-elect:* Obama transition press conference, Chicago, Illinois, November 7, 2008, http://www.presidency.ucsb.edu/ws/index.php?pid=84773.

91 *As Jonathan Alter chronicled in* The Defining Moment: Jonathan Alter, *The Defining Moment* (New York: Simon & Schuster, 2006). Rahm Emanuel was reading *The Defining Moment* during the transition, too, and Rob Nabors was listening to it on his iPod.

94 *Nobel laureate Joseph Stiglitz:* Joseph Stiglitz, "A $1 Trillion Answer," *New York Times,* November 29, 2008.

94 *"You really, really don't want to lowball this":* Paul Krugman, "Stimulus Math (Wonkish)," The Conscience of a Liberal blog, *New York Times,* November 10, 2008, http://krugman.blogs.nytimes.com/2008/11/10/stimulus-math-wonkish/.

94 *Furman's eleven-page Confidential Discussion Draft:* "Economic Team: Fiscal Stimulus," November 12, 2008; document provided to the author.

94 *At the time, 387 predominantly liberal economists:* Economists' letter to Harry Reid, Mitch McConnell, Nancy Pelosi, and John Boehner, November 19, 2008, http://www.cepr.net/documents/publications/Economists_letter_2008_11_19.pdf.

95 *a "Green Stimulus" memo:* "Memorandum for the Economic Team," November 11, 2008; memo provided to the author. The proposals included $11 billion to install smart meters in 110 million U.S. homes, $4 billion for solar roofs on federal buildings, $20 billion for renewable energy tax credits, $30 billion for mass transit, and $7.25 billion for green schools. The transit estimates, cribbed from Transportation 4 America, turned out to be way more than agencies could spend, so the team reduced them.

96 *Bob Greenstein came bearing especially bad news:* Greenstein's eighteen-page presentation was provided to the author: "Economic Team: Federal Budget Baseline and Selected Policy Issues," November 11, 2008. Greenstein's think tank, the Center for Budget and Policy Priorities, produced a number of reports about state fiscal gaps.

98 *The council's number-one priority:* David Wessel, "Shaping the New Agenda (A Special Report)—Finance and the U.S. Economy," *Wall Street Journal,* November 24, 2008; Jon Hilsenrath, "CEOs Say Stimulus Top Priority," *Wall Street Journal,* No-

vember 19, 2008; Jon Hilsenrath, "Obama Aides Say Economy Needs Big Lift," *Wall Street Journal*, November 18, 2008.

100 *GOP leaders and conservative pundits were laying down markers:* For example, Senate Republican whip Jon Kyl of Arizona warned: "If they go after things like card check and the Fairness Doctrine, or some big tax increase or get-out-of-Iraq-immediately, that is likely to unify Republicans." Obama didn't go after any of those things, but Republicans managed to remain unified anyway. Kirk Victor, "Q&A: Kyl Talks About Playing Defense," *National Journal*, November 17, 2008, http://lostintransition.nationaljournal.com/2008/11/kyl-talks-about-playing-defense.php. Also: Amy Schatz, "Fairness Doctrine Stirs Angst Among the Right," *Wall Street Journal*, November 3, 2008; "Do Gun Owners Fear an Obama Presidency?," America's Election HQ, Fox News, October 31, 2008, http://www.foxnews.com/story/0,2933,445627,00.html; David Ignatius, "Mr. Cool's Centrist Gamble," *Washington Post*, January 9, 2009; Karl Rove, "Thanksgiving Cheer from Obama," *Wall Street Journal*, November 28, 2008.

101 *"a virtual Rubin constellation":* Jackie Calmes, "Rubin Protégés Change Their Tune as They Join Obama's Team," *New York Times*, November 24, 2008.

102 *"I don't know what the exact number is":* Austan Goolsbee on *Face the Nation*, CBS, November 23, 2008.

103 *"before exchanging hellos or even shaking hands":* Suskind, *Confidence Men*, p. 150. To his credit, Suskind says he plans to correct this scene in his paperback edition.

104 *Obama pitched his new New Deal:* Obama press conference, November 24, 2011, http://blogs.suntimes.com/sweet/2008/11/presidentelect_obama_second_pr.html.

105 *"It's as if the news is full of floods":* Peggy Noonan, "Turbulence Ahead," *Wall Street Journal*, November 28, 2008.

106 *"The economy is unraveling so fast":* Neil Irwin and Steven Mufson, "Economic Indicators Continue Nose Dive; Half-Million Jobs Cut: Worst Month Since 1974," *Washington Post*, December 6, 2008.

106 *As Romer later pointed out:* Christina Romer, "So Is It Working? An Assessment of the American Recovery and Reinvestment Act at the Five-Month Mark," Speech at the Economic Club of Washington, D.C., August 6, 2009, http://elsa.berkeley.edu/~cromer/DCEconClub.pdf.

107 *about as much as the United States spent on Medicare and Medicaid:* In 2008, net mandatory Medicare spending was $386 billion, while federal spending on Medicaid was $201 billion. "The Long-Term Outlook for Medicare, Medicaid, and Total Health Care Spending," Congressional Budget Office, June 2009, http://www.cbo.gov/ftpdocs/102xx/doc10297/chapter2.5.1.shtml.

107 *In a four-page summary distributed in early December:* "The American Economic Recovery Plan," undated discussion draft provided to the author. It proposed $70 billion for building a clean energy economy, $80 billion for strengthening American infrastructure, $125 billion for health IT and state Medicaid relief, $25 billion for education, and $280 billion for tax cuts and protecting the vulnerable.

108 *Geithner had told Obama that no matter what happened:* Scheiber, *Escape Artists*, pp. 15–16.

108 *In his radio address:* Obama radio address, December 6, 2009, http://www.presidency.ucsb.edu/ws/index.php?pid=84776#axzz1mIf49S9E.

108 *Obama chose his cabinet faster:* White House Transition Project, http://uncnews.unc.edu/content/view/1971/70/.

110 *even two centrist Democrats had voted no:* Democratic senators Evan Bayh (Indiana)

and Claire McCaskill (Missouri) joined forty Republicans in voting against the $56 billion stimulus. The vote was 52–42 in favor, but the bill died because sixty was needed to overcome a Republican filibuster.

111 *That was even bigger than TARP:* The cost of Afghanistan and Iraq through 2008 was $795 billion. Amy Belasco, "The Cost of Iraq, Afghanistan, and Other Global War on Terror Operations Since 9/11," Congressional Research Service, March 29, 2011.

111 *a fifty-seven page "Executive Summary of Economic Policy Work":* The New Yorker's excellent Ryan Lizza was the first reporter to report on this memo, in "Inside the Crisis," October 12, 2009, and then to obtain the memo, in "The Obama Memos," January 30, 2012. He posted it at http://www.newyorker.com/online/blogs/news desk/2012/01/the-summers-memo.html.

6. The Moment

113 *The stories Obamaworld tells about itself:* The best narrative journalism about the Obama administration and the stimulus always seems to home in on December 16. For example: Scott Wilson, "Bruised by Stimulus Battle, Obama Changed His Approach to Washington," *Washington Post,* April 29, 2009; Ryan Lizza, "Inside the Crisis," *The New Yorker,* October 12, 2009; Peter Baker, "Education of a President," *New York Times,* October 12, 2010; Ezra Klein, "Financial Crisis and Stimulus: Could This Time Be Different?," *Washington Post,* October 8, 2011. The "holy-shit moment" also appears in several books about the administration.

114 *Romer had searing memories:* Christina D. Romer, "Not My Father's Recession: The Extraordinary Challenges and Policy Responses of the First Twenty Months of the Obama Administration," Speech at the National Press Club, September 1, 2010, http://www.whitehouse.gov/sites/default/files/microsites/100901-National-Press-Club.pdf.

115 *In FDR's most aggressive year:* Romer, citing Bureau of Economic Analysis and Census data, said the largest fiscal impact took place in 1936. Romer, "Back from the Brink," Speech to the Federal Reserve Bank of Chicago, September 24, 2009, http://www.whitehouse.gov/assets/documents/Back_from_the_Brink2.pdf.

115 *the biggest deficit in history:* The Congressional Budget Office projected the 2009 deficit to hit $1.2 trillion. The actual deficit that year was $1.4 trillion. The previous largest deficit was $459 billion in 2008. "The Budget and Economic Outlook: 2009 to 2019," Congressional Budget Office, January 2009, http://www.cbo.gov/ftpdocs/99xx/doc9957/01-07-Outlook.pdf.

116 *Summers hadn't mentioned Romer's $1.2 trillion figure:* Lizza, "Inside the Crisis," *The New Yorker.* I don't entirely agree with Lizza's take on this memo, but he was the first reporter to write about it and then the first reporter to publish it. Felix Salmon's criticism was typical. "How Larry Summers Hobbled Obama's Economic Policy," Reuters, January 19, 2011, http://blogs.reuters.com/felix-salmon/2011/01/19/how -larry-summers-hobbled-obamas-economic-policy/.

116 *Romer had suggested in one draft:* Scheiber, *The Escape Artists,* p. 27. I think Scheiber makes way too much out of this tidbit, but he deserves credit for breaking the news and publishing the draft on his website (www.noamscheiber.com). Incidentally, by December 16, the situation had deteriorated to the point where Romer believed that even $1.8 billion would have been insufficient to fill the hole in demand.

117 *Pelosi didn't even want to go past $600 billion:* Her staff told the Obama transition team, "The Speaker at this stage is at $600 billion and is extremely nervous about going above that." She was also pushing to reduce the size of the package by using it

to repeal the Bush tax cuts for the wealthy. "Issues in Congressional Discussions on Economic Recovery," December 20, 2008, four-page transition memo provided to the author.

118 *"It is easier to add down the road":* "Executive Summary of Economic Policy Work," p. 57, http://s3.documentcloud.org/documents/285065/summers-12-15-08-memo .pdf.

118 *Paul Krugman also predicted:* "Behind the Curve," *New York Times,* March 9, 2009.

119 *I made the same assumption:* Michael Grunwald, "How to Spend a Trillion Dollars," *Time,* January 15, 2009, http://www.time.com/time/magazine/article/0,9171, 1871915,00.html. Otherwise, the article holds up pretty well. I didn't grasp the macroeconomic importance of bailing out even irresponsible states, but I still think my idea of attaching more strings to state aid made sense. The stimulus did attach more strings than I realized, although most of them were "maintenance of effort" requirements to make sure governors didn't just use the money as an excuse to make even deeper cuts to Medicaid and education.

121 *he called it "unforgettable":* Obama speech at Brookings Institution, December 8, 2009, http://www.presidency.ucsb.edu/ws/index.php?pid=86975.

122 *Advocates had identified $10 billion in shovel-ready water and sewer projects:* Letter to Democratic senators, American Water Works Association, January 26, 2009, http://www.awwa.org/files/GovtPublicAffairs/PDF/SenateStimulus.pdf.easier

122 *the National Park Service had less than $1 billion in ready-to-go projects:* The "Green Stimulus" memo said the NPS had identified $440 million worth of projects that could be contracted out in less than six months. "By focusing on NPS infrastructure investment, this effort could generate jobs and follow in spirit with the WPA and CCC," the memo said. The National Parks Conservation Association later said there were $2.5 billion in ready-to-go projects.

123 *History has bathed the CCC in a romantic glow:* I consulted several books on the original New Deal including Alter's *The Defining Moment,* Alan Brinkley's *The End of Reform: New Deal Liberalism in Recession and War* (New York: Random House, 1996), Anthony J. Badger's *The New Deal: The Depression Years, 1933–1940* (New York: Hill & Wang, 1989), and William E. Leuchtenburg's *Franklin D. Roosevelt and the New Deal* (New York: Harper Perennial, 2009; first published, 1963).

124 *He didn't have another cake:* Jonathan Alter first wrote about the smart grid discussion in "The PDQ Presidency," *Newsweek,* October 23, 2009, and *The Promise.* I also wrote about it in "How the Stimulus Is Changing America," *Time,* September 6, 2010. Suskind and others who wrote about Obama's obsession with the grid tend to portray it as a sign of his misplaced priorities. Even Alter portrays the episode as a failure, but the Recovery Act would end up jump-starting the smart grid.

126 *Bob Greenstein would soon ratchet up:* "State Budget Troubles Worsen," the Center on Budget and Policy Priorities, December 23, 2008.

126 *polls would find that fewer than 10 percent of them were aware:* For example, Michael Cooper, "From Obama, the Tax Cut Nobody Heard Of," *New York Times,* October 18, 2010.

126 *Behavioral economics had become trendy:* Steven D. Levitt and Stephen J. Dubner, *Freakonomics: A Rogue Economist Explores the Hidden Side of Everything* (New York: William Morrow, 2005); George A. Akerlof and Robert J. Shiller, *Animal Spirits: How Human Psychology Drives the Economy, and Why It Matters for Global Capitalism* (Princeton: Princeton University Press, 2009); Richard H. Thaler and Cass R. Sunstein, *Nudge* (New Haven: Yale University Press, 2008). I wrote the first journalistic piece about the influence of behavioral economics in Obamaworld:

Michael Grunwald, "How Obama Is Using the Science of Change," *Time*, April 2, 2009, www.time.com/time/magazine/article/0,9171,1889153,00.html. My former colleague Justin Fox has written a smart book about the follies of neoclassical thinking, *The Myth of the Rational Market* (New York: HarperBusiness, 2009).

127 *Democrats had criticized Bush:* Devlin Barrett, "Dear Taxpayer: This Letter Cost You $42 million," Associated Press, March 7, 2008.

133 *As the team reported in a four-page memo:* "Issues in Congressional Discussions on Economic Recovery," December 20, 2008, memo provided to the author. David Obey was the only member of Congress the team met; otherwise, its meetings were all with Democratic staffers. There were a few discordant notes, like "skepticism about the magnitude of our smart grid numbers," "somewhat more distance" on education, and "strong desire" to include a patch to the Alternative Minimum Tax.

134 *"We have communicated our willingness":* This memo from Gary Myrick was reported at the time. Jackie Calmes, "As Outlook Dims, Obama Expands Recovery Plans," *New York Times*, December 20, 2008.

135 *The seventy-four-year-old chairman of the House Transportation and Infrastructure Committee:* Michael Grunwald, "Bridges to Nowhere," *Time*, August 6, 2007, http://www.time.com/time/nation/article/0,8599,1650149,00.html.

135 *"The biggest issue is less the reaction to our topline numbers":* "Issues in Congressional Discussions on Economic Recovery," December 20, 2008.

137 *The U.S. Conference of Mayors identified $180 billion:* "Main Street Economic Recovery," U.S. Conference of Mayors, December 2, 2008, http://www.uptown-indy.com/pdf/Main_Street_Economic_Recovery%20_Plan_120308.pdf.

137 *he went on Fox to warn:* Neil Cavuto interview with Evan Bayh, February 3, 2009.

139 *Schiliro was spreading the word:* Mike Allen, "Big Tax Cuts in the Works," *Politico*, January 5, 2009, http://www.politico.com/news/stories/0109/17039.html.

7. The Party of No

140 *Just a few years earlier:* Tom Hamburger and Peter Wallsten, *One Party Country* (Hoboken, N.J.: Wiley, 2006); Thomas Byrne Edsall, *Building Red America* (New York: Basic Books, 2007).

140 *Now publishers were rushing out titles:* Sidney Blumenthal, *The Strange Death of Republican America* (New York: Union Square Press, 2007); James Carville, *40 More Years: How Democrats Will Rule the Next Generation* (New York: Simon & Schuster, 2009).

142 *"If the Purpose of the Majority":* Pete Sessions, "Who Wants to Be in the Majority?: A Blueprint for Victory," January 2009; copy of this PowerPoint provided to the author. The *New York Times* first reported on it: Jim Rutenberg and Jeff Zeleny, "Democrats Outrun by a 2-Year G.O.P. Comeback Plan," *New York Times*, November 3, 2010.

144 *Cole had been a political consultant:* Juliet Eilperin and Michael Grunwald, "A New Pitchman—And a New Pitch," *Washington Post*, May 9, 2007.

147 *Five of the forty-one surviving Republican senators:* Christopher (Kit) Bond of Missouri, Sam Brownback of Kansas, George Voinovich of Ohio, Mel Martinez of Florida, and Judd Gregg of New Hampshire (after some drama) would all announce their retirements soon.

147 *He had dubbed himself the Abominable No-Man:* Edwin Chen, "Free Speech Will Pay Heavy Price Under Campaign Finance Reform, Key Foe Says," *Los Angeles Times*, March 15, 1997.

147 *he stuck to his talking points:* A copy of the talking points was provided to the author.

148 *the CBO had just* tripled *its deficit projection:* "The Budget and Economic Outlook: 2009 to 2019," Congressional Budget Office, January 2009, http://www.cbo.gov/ftpdocs/99xx/doc9957/01-07-Outlook.pdf.

149 *"We thought—correctly, I think":* Joshua Green, "Strict Obstructionist," *The Atlantic,* January 2011, http://www.theatlantic.com/magazine/archive/2011/01/strict-obstructionist/8344/.

149 *McConnell slyly questioned why America needed 600,000 new government jobs:* McConnell interview, *This Week,* ABC, January 4, 2009, http://abcnews.go.com/ThisWeek/story?id=6573506.

150 *Gregg himself had just published an op-ed:* Judd Gregg, "How to Make Sure the Stimulus Works," *Wall Street Journal,* January 5, 2009.

152 *"I do not work for Barack Obama":* Bob Cusack, J. Taylor Rushing, and Hugo Gurdon, "Reid: 'I Don't Work for Obama,'" *The Hill,* January 6, 2009.

152 *"May be hard to enact without significant consensus":* Memo to Rahm Emanuel, "State Fiscal Relief Plans," December 27, 2008, draft provided to the author.

154 *"We cannot depend on government alone":* Obama speech, January 8, 2009, George Mason University, Fairfax, Virginia, http://www.presidency.ucsb.edu/ws/index.php?pid=85361.

155 *"To me it looks a little bit like trickle-down":* Elana Schor, "Harkin Fears 'Trickle-Down' Stimulus," Talking Points Memo, January 8, 2009, http://tpmelectioncentral.talkingpointsmemo.com/2009/01/harkin_fears_trickle-down_stimulus.php.

155 *the headlines were all about friendly fire:* Peter Baker and David M. Herszenhorn, "Senate Allies Fault Obama on Stimulus," *New York Times,* January 8, 2009; Steve Holland, "Democrats Make Clear They Will Guard Turf," Reuters, January 10, 2009; Shailagh Murray and Paul Kane, "Democratic Congress Shows Signs It Will Not Bow to Obama," *Washington Post,* January 11, 2009.

156 *Oberstar upped his request to $85 billion:* "A Proposal to Rebuild America by Investing in Transportation and Environmental Infrastructure," December 12, 2008, http://www.dot.ca.gov/fedliaison/documents/Rebuild_America_proposal.pdf.

157 *Mark Zandi warned that the economy was "shutting down":* Democratic Steering and Policy Committee hearing on the economy, January 7, 2007.

157 *the Romer-Bernstein report:* Romer and Bernstein, "The Job Impact of the American Recovery and Reinvestment Plan."

158 *Most analysts believe Romer and Bernstein came close to the delta:* Romer and Bernstein predicted the Recovery Act would boost GDP by approximately 3.6 percent and employment by 3.3 million to 4.1 million jobs compared to the no-action case. Private economic forecasting firms have said the boost has been 2.1 percent to 3.8 percent of GDP and roughly 2.5 million jobs: http://www.whitehouse.gov/sites/default/files/cea_8th_arra_report_final_draft.pdf.

158 *"We'll be lucky if the unemployment rate is below double digits":* Michael M. Grynbaum, "In String of Bad News, Omens of a Long Recession," *New York Times,* December 7, 2008.

160 *Several days after Romer-Bernstein hit the streets:* Macroeconomic Advisers changed its initial estimate of GDP growth for the first quarter of 2009 from −1.3 percent to −4.3 percent. Jon Hilsenrath and Jonathan Weisman, "As Economy Falters, Doubts on Obama Plan Mount," *Wall Street Journal,* January 28, 2009.

8. "Wow. We Can Actually Do It."

161 *The big ticket items in the Recovery Act:* The initial estimates for the Recovery Act included $141 billion for state aid, $116 billion for the Making Work Pay tax cut, and $40 billion for unemployment insurance, according to CBO and Joint Committee on Taxation estimates from February 2009. CBO cost estimate, February 13, 2009, http://www.cbo.gov/sites/default/files/cbofiles/ftpdocs/99xx/doc9989/hrlcon ference.pdf; Joint Committee on Taxation cost estimate, February 12, 2009, http://www.jct.gov/publications.html?func=startdown&id=1172.

162 *aid to poor families with high propensities to spend:* Mark Zandi testimony before the House Small Business Committee, July 24, 2008, http://www.economy.com/mark-zandi/documents/Small%20Business_7_24_08.pdf.

162 *the transition team secured hefty increases:* The line items for the safety net included $20 billion for food stamps, $2.3 billion for child care, $2 billion for rental assistance, $4.7 billion for the Earned Income Tax Credit, and $25 billion to subsidize 65 percent of the COBRA health insurance premiums for laid-off workers. Other investments in Obama priorities included $360 million for construction at the National Institute of Standards and Technology, $2 billion for community health clinics, $1.3 billion for Amtrak (not including the high-speed rail funding), $4 billion for public housing renovations, $145 million for floodplain easements, $1.1 billion for Early Head Start, $1 billion for preventive medicine, and $200 million for Americorps.

163 *stimulus would be one blade of the scissors:* Eric Pooley, *The Climate War: True Believers, Power Brokers, and the Fight to Save the Earth* (New York: Hyperion, 2010), p. 313.

164 *more than Bush had managed to spend in eight years:* The Bush administration spent $2.5 billion on clean coal programs. "Fact Sheet: DOE to Demonstrate Cutting-Edge Carbon Capture and Sequestration Technology at Multiple FutureGen Clean Coal Projects," Department of Energy, June 24, 2008, http://www.fossil.energy.gov/pro grams/powersystems/futuregen/FutureGen_Fact_Sheet_2008.06.24.pdf.

167 *the Energy Department's loan guarantee program:* The federal government has given out loan guarantees for years, but the Energy Department's program only began in 2005, and it hadn't closed a single deal before Obama took office. Normally, the government promises to repay all or most of a recipient's obligations to private investors in case of a default; after the Great Recession, though, credit was so tight that the federal government usually ended up loaning the money directly. The Energy Department's loan office oversaw three programs. The Advanced Technology Vehicles Manufacturing program, for factories making fuel-efficient cars, was separate from the Recovery Act. The 1703 program for "innovative" clean-energy technologies that had never been commercialized before received new credit subsidies under the Recovery Act. The 1705 program for more mature clean-energy technologies was created by the Recovery Act. Matt Rogers, the department's stimulus czar, oversaw all three programs until November 2009, when Jonathan Silver was hired to run the loan office.

168 *"The apparent haste in recommending the project":* Many of the Solyndra documents released by the Obama administration have been made available online by House Republicans at http://energycommerce.house.gov/hearings/hearingdetail.aspx?News ID=9090; http://energycommerce.house.gov/hearings/hearingdetail.aspx?NewsID=9000; and http://energycommerce.house.gov/hearings/hearingdetail.aspx?NewsID=8897. The White House has released more Solyndra documents that were made available only in hard copies.

168 *The Census Bureau needed to hire:* The Recovery Act provided $1 billion to the Census Bureau, $650 million for the analog-to-digital television transition, $730 million to the Small Business Administration, and $1.2 billion for the Labor Department's summer jobs program.

171 *The idea was to keep stormwater out of overwhelmed sewers:* Grunwald, "Smart Streets." Energy efficiency is attractive for similar reasons; it's cheaper and easier to reduce demand for electricity than it is to expand the supply of power with new plants. Similarly, water conservation is cheaper than new reservoirs; drug treatment programs are cheaper than new prisons; and congestion pricing, incentives for carpooling and telecommuting, and other public policies designed to reduce traffic tend to work better than building new highway lanes.

171 *he left most of the details to Congress:* The Recovery Act actually included $27 billion for health IT, but the CBO estimated that wiring medical offices would save the government $7 billion in health care costs within ten years, so it came out to $20 billion.

171 *mandating adoption of the Veterans Administration's computer system:* In *The Promise,* Jonathan Alter suggested the Recovery Act should have mandated that all health IT programs use the VA's VISTA system. But there was no need for such heavy-handed government intrusion. Instead, the Recovery Act set up a partnership with the industry to promote "interoperability," to make sure the various IT systems will be able to communicate with each other, and a process for government certification of eligible products. That way doctors and hospitals can decide if they want VISTA, and private firms can try to develop something better. The Department of Health and Human Services has already certified more than six hundred products.

172 *private disincentives to build a network:* Nobody wanted to invest in a fax machine before anyone they communicated with had a fax machine. Similarly, doctors didn't want to be early adopters of health IT if they wouldn't have colleagues to share data with. The Recovery Act helped solve this classic network problem by bringing almost the entire country on board at once.

172 *Summers had spent one of the most traumatic hours of his life:* Lawrence Summers remarks at Department of Health and Human Services event, December 8, 2010, video available at http://www.youtube.com/watch?v=NpZBF7FKk2M.

173 *Republican health care propagandist Betsy McCaughey wrote a column:* "Ruin Your Health with the Obama Stimulus Plan," Bloomberg, February 9, 2009. McCaughey wrote a famously dishonest slam of the Clinton health plan, "No Exit," that *The New Republic* later retracted.

173 *Rush Limbaugh began trashing:* "Outrage over Socialized Health Care Hidden Inside Porkulus Bill," *The Rush Limbaugh Show,* February 10, 2009, http://www.rushlimbaugh.com/daily/2009/02/10/outrage_over_socialized_health_care_hidden_inside_porkulus_bill.

174 *America's freight rail was the envy of the world:* Michael Grunwald, "Can High-Speed Rail Get on Track?" *Time,* July 19, 2010.

176 *After David Obey's tantrum:* Steven Brill has already written a compelling book about the genesis of Race to the Top and its impact on the national debate over public education: *Class Warfare: Inside the Fight to Fix America's Schools* (New York: Simon & Schuster, 2011).

177 *a short list compiled by ProPublica:* Michael Grabell and Christopher Weaver, "In the Stimulus Bill: An Earmark by Any Other Name," ProPublica, February 5, 2009, http://www.propublica.org/article/welcome-in-the-stimulus-bill-an-earmark-by-any-other-name.

179 *about $150 billion to long-term change:* That includes about $90 billion for clean energy, $30 billion for health IT and other transformative health programs, $8 billion for education reform, $8 billion for high-speed rail, $7 billion for broadband, and $7 billion for unemployment modernization. There's also TIGER, homelessness prevention, green infrastructure, and other assorted innovations scattered around the Recovery Act.

9. Shirts and Skins

180 *lists of dubious-sounding provisions:* The provisions were part of a "Wasteful Spending Resource" maintained by GOP Senate aides, including a running list of "Top Ten Stimulus Boondoggles from Congressional Democrats." Many of these showed up in a CNN.com list of Republican complaints about the Recovery Act: "What GOP Leaders Deem Wasteful in Senate Stimulus Bill," CNN.com, February 2, 2009, http://articles.cnn.com/2009-02-02/politics/gop.stimulus.worries_1_green-buildings-homeland-security-summer-job-programs?_s=PM:POLITICS.

181 *Eric Cantor claimed that it would direct $300,000 to a Miami sculpture garden:* PolitiFact rated this claim "Pants on Fire." "Does the Stimulus Package Really Include $300,000 for a Sculpture Garden?", PolitiFact, January 23, 2009. http://www.politifact.com/truth-o-meter/statements/2009/jan/26/eric-cantor/does-stimulus-package-really-include-300000-sculpt/.

181 *a previously uncontroversial disaster aid program:* Michael Hiltzik, "Republican Buzz on Stimulus Plan Has No Sting," *Los Angeles Times,* February 5, 2009.

181 *"In fact, there's no money in the bill for mice":* PolitiFact rated this claim "False." "No money in the stimulus for San Francisco mice," PolitiFact, February 13, 2009, http://www.politifact.com/truth-o-meter/statements/2009/feb/13/mike-pence/no-money-stimulus-san-francisco-mice/.

181 *Republicans kept harping on the mouse anyway:* S. A. Miller, "GOP Hits Pelosi for Mouse Funds," *Washington Times,* July 10, 2009.

182 *The CBO concluded that the family planning money:* "Estimated Effect on Direct Spending and Revenues of H.R. 3162, the Children's Health and Medicare Protection Act, for the Rules Committee," Congressional Budget Office, August 1, 2007, http://www.cbo.gov/sites/default/files/cbofiles/ftpdocs/85xx/doc8519/hr3162.pdf.

182 *It sounded like a crass giveaway to the Hollywood elite:* The movie industry was excluded from the bonus depreciation tax break when it was first created in 2004 at the insistence of Bill Thomas, the Republican House Ways and Means chairman at the time. Thomas objected to the Motion Picture Association of America's hiring of Dan Glickman, a former Clinton cabinet secretary. "Senate Votes Down Repatriation, Hollywood Provisions," CongressDaily, February 4, 2009.

183 *The conservative* Washington Times *even trumpeted:* Stephen Dinan and S. A. Miller, "EXCLUSIVE: Stimulus Has Plum for Lawmaker's Son," *Washington Times,* February 29, 2009.

183 *GOP leaders cherry-picked a preliminary Congressional Budget Office analysis:* "Estimated Cost of the American Recovery and Reinvestment Act of 2009 as Provided on the Appropriation Committee Website on January 15, 2009," http://www.tampabay.com/universal/politifact/files/recoveryactsummary.pdf; "REPORT: TV Media Cited Disputed CBO 'Report' at Least 81 Times in Past Six Days," ThinkProgress, January 26, 2009, http://thinkprogress.org/media/2009/01/26/35288/report-cbo-tv/.

183 *the CBO confirmed that in an actual report:* CBO cost estimate for ARRA confer-
     ence report, February 13, 2009, http://www.cbo.gov/publication/41762.
184 *The Associated Press ran an "analysis":* "Analysis: Stimulus Bill That's Not All
     Stimulating," Associated Press, January 31, 2009.
184 *cable networks interviewed Republican lawmakers:* "REPORT: GOP Lawmakers Out-
     number Democratic Lawmakers 2 to 1 in Stimulus Debate on Cable News," Think-
     Progress, January 28, 2009, http://thinkprogress.org/media/2009/01/28/35450/
     cable-news-stimulus/. Despite the report being done by liberal blog ThinkProgress,
     Senate Republican staffers touted the results in a February 5, 2009, email to report-
     ers with the headline: "GOP Message Resonates with America."
184 *environmentalists attacked a provision:* "Stop Senate's $50 Billion Bailout to the
     Nuclear Industry," Friends of the Earth press release, http://action.foe.org/campaign
     .jsp?campaign_KEY=26528. I often bang my spoon on my high chair about the
     impossible economics of new nuclear power. Michael Grunwald, "Nuclear's Come-
     back: Still No Energy Panacea," *Time,* December 31, 2008; Michael Grunwald, "The
     Real Cost of U.S. Nuclear Power," *Time,* March 25, 2011.
184 *White House officials had encouraged him to add to the drumbeat:* "Cooper: Obama
     Staff Encouraged Defiance of Pelosi," *Politico,* February 3, 2009, http://www.politico
     .com/blogs/glennthrush/0209/Cooper_Obama_staff_encouraged_defiance_of_Pelosi
     .html.
186 *a poll he had commissioned:* McLaughlin & Associates, "National Survey Presented
     to Congressman Eric Cantor, Republican House Whip Team," January 21, 2009, copy
     provided to the author. The results were reported by ABC News: Jonathan Karl and
     Rick Klein, "GOP Strategy: Oppose Pelosi, Not Obama," ABC News, January 29,
     2009, http://abcnews.go.com/blogs/politics/2009/01/gop-strategy-op/.
187 *"It's my way or the highway":* Paul Ryan, Eric Cantor, and Kevin McCarthy, *Young
     Guns: A New Generation of Conservative Leaders* (New York: Threshold, 2010),
     p. 52.
188 *One Republican congressman who said Limbaugh should "back off":* That was Phil
     Gingrey of Georgia.
188 *The Energy and Commerce Committee did approve six minor GOP amendments:*
     Amendment list available here: http://democrats.energycommerce.house.gov/
     Press_111/20090122/markupaction.pdf. The three Republican amendments that
     weren't included in the final House bill were offered by Cliff Stearns (to exclude mil-
     lionaires from receiving COBRA health care subsidies), Tim Murphy (to require that
     health IT grant recipients purchase American-made equipment), and Roy Blunt (to
     allow pharmacists the same level of access as doctors to electronic health records).
189 *"We're looking forward to the the President's visit":* John Boehner's talking points for
     the House GOP Conference meeting on January 27 were provided to the author.
189 *the $815 billion stimulus bill:* CBO cost estimate of the House bill, January 26, 2009,
     http://www.cbo.gov/sites/default/files/cbofiles/ftpdocs/99xx/doc9968/hrl.pdf.
190 *Shortly before 11 A.M., the AP reported:* David Espo, "House Republicans Urged to
     Oppose Stimulus Bill," Associated Press, January 27, 2009.
191 *the must-read book in Republican circles:* Amity Shlaes, *The Forgotten Man: A New
     History of the Great Depression* (New York: Harper, 2007). Jonathan Chait eviscer-
     ated Shlaes in a review, "Wasting Away in Hooverville," *The New Republic,* January
     28, 2009, http://www.tnr.com/article/books/wasting-away-hooverville.
195 *mostly they supplied information, sending out memos:* Cantor's whip team listed the
     money for artists and STDs in memos tailored to each Republican House member

under the headline, "What Competing Stimulus Plans Mean for Your District," designed to produce talking points that Republicans could use to attack the Democratic bill at home.

198 *The official $478 billion Republican alternative:* "US House Republican Alternative Stimulus Proposal," Reuters, January 28, 2008, http://www.reuters.com/article/2009/01/28/usa-stimulus-republicans-idUSN285350202009012_8.

198 *the GOP also crafted a second $715 billion substitute:* A summary of the substitute is here: http://rsc.jordan.house.gov/News/DocumentSingle.aspx?DocumentID=109730.

199 *claiming it would create twice as many jobs at half the cost:* This claim was utterly bogus. Republicans also had the audacity to say they derived it using Romer's model, which was absurd; Romer's model gave spending a higher multiplier than tax cuts. Factcheck.org politely noted that the Republican claims were "not backed up by independent economists": www.factcheck.org/2009/02/stimulus-bill-bravado/.

199 *the House rejected the $478 billion alternative:* The roll call is here: http://clerk.house.gov/evs/2009/roll044.xml. The vote on the $715 billion alternative is here: http://clerk.house.gov/evs/2009/roll045.xml. The vote on the Democratic bill is here: http://clerk.house.gov/evs/2009/roll046.xml.

201 *"Washington insiders and media pundits":* Ryan, Cantor, and McCarthy, *Young Guns,* p. 53.

201 *"The Republican Problem":* Memo from Pelosi communications director Brendan Daly, January 28, 2009.

201 *Gingrich addressed a House Republican retreat:* Patrick O'Connor, "Members Cheer at GOP Retreat," January 30, 2009, *Politico,* http://www.politico.com/news/stories/0109/18204.html.

202 *"I know all of you are pumped":* Patrick O'Connor, "At Retreat, Upbeat GOP Looks to 2010," *Politico,* January 31, 2009, http://www.politico.com/news/stories/0109/18238.html.

202 *In a later roundtable discussion:* Ryan, Cantor, and McCarthy, *Young Guns,* p. 8.

203 *"Republicans—short on new ideas":* E. J. Dionne, "Obama Losing Stimulus Fight to Defeated GOP," *Washington Post,* February 5, 2009, http://www.realclearpolitics.com/articles/2009/02/obama_losing_stimulus_fight_to.html; Jeanne Cummings, "Obama Losing the Stimulus Message War," *Politico,* February 5, 2009, http://www.politico.com/news/stories/0209/18444.html.

203 *support for the stimulus sank from 52 percent to 38 percent:* CBS News poll, February 5, 2009, http://www.cbsnews.com/htdocs/pdf/poll_020509.pdf.

10. From Zero to Sixty

206 *the Senate approved the new S-CHIP:* The final vote was 66–32, with nine Republicans joining all the Democrats in voting for the bill.

209 *He tracked Collins down over the holidays:* Manuel Roig-Franzia and Paul Kane, "Two Moderate GOP Senators Give Big Voice to Little Maine," *Washington Post,* February 16, 2009.

210 *There was a long history of senators "pairing votes":* Reid's staff pointed out that two Republicans, John Warner of Virginia and Pete Domenici of New Mexico, paired votes with Ted Kennedy and Robert Byrd, both ill, on a June 2008 vote on a Democratic budget plan. Warner and Domenici retired later that year. *Congressional Record,* June 4, 2008. In 2001, Biden offered to pair his vote with ninety-eight-year-old

Senator Strom Thurmond on George W. Bush's tax cut bill so that Thurmond could go home and rest. Thurmond declined the offer. "Attempt Nixed to Let Senator Miss Late-Night Votes," Associated Press, May 22, 2001.

210 *The only Republican to defeat an incumbent senator that year:* In 1984, eleven Democrats ran for reelection. They all won except for Walter Huddleston of Kentucky. More Republican senators (two) lost that year than Democrats, despite President Reagan's forty-nine-state victory.

211 *a procedural trick called a "clay pigeon":* A senator uses the clay pigeon by calling up an amendment and later splitting it into dozens of pieces, each of which must be voted on. The technique gets its name from the skeet shooting target that explodes into bits.

211 *In fact, he was the senator most responsible:* The use of the filibuster roughly doubled when McConnell took over as minority leader in the Senate in 2007. Cloture motions—the procedure necessary to overcome a filibuster—averaged sixty-nine a year from 2007 to 2010. In the previous decade, the average number of cloture motions per year was just thirty-four. Records are available here: http://www.senate .gov/pagelayout/reference/cloture_motions/clotureCounts.htm.

212 *Kan read everything:* The CBO cost estimate of the Senate bill said that 78 percent of the stimulus money would be spent in 2009 and 2010. CBO cost estimate, February 10, 2009, http://www.cbo.gov/publication/20471, staff summary of Senate Democratic bill for Senate GOP leadership staff, February 7, 2009, document provided to the author. Senate Appropriations Committee report, January 27, 2009, http://www .gpo.gov/fdsys/pkg/CRPT-111srpt3/pdf/CRPT-111srpt3.pdf. Senate GOP spreadsheet on cost-per-job of Recovery Act spending programs, January 30, 2009, document provided to the author.

215 *a perfect image of bipartisan cooperation:* The White House photo of President Obama and Governor Douglas moving the couch, February 2, 2009, can be viewed at http://www.flickr.com/photos/whitehouse/4291167739/.

215 *"an extraordinarily bold and aggressive, effective and comprehensive plan":* Obama announcement of Gregg as commerce secretary nominee, February 3, 2009, http:// www.presidency.ucsb.edu/ws/index.php?pid=85721.

216 *"make it harder for his fellow Republicans to demonize Obama":* David Rogers, "Reid, Emanuel Pushed for Gregg," *Politico,* February 9, 2009, http://www.politico.com/ news/stories/0209/18385.html.

217 *he temporarily shed his Mr. Nice Guy persona:* Obama speech at House Democratic retreat, February 5, 2009, http://www.presidency.ucsb.edu/ws/index.php?pid =85739.

217 *He marveled at the gall of Republicans:* The national debt was at $5.7 trillion and falling when George W. Bush entered office in January 2001. When Bush left office eight years later, the national debt was at $10.6 trillion and soaring, an increase of $4.9 trillion. The Congressional Budget Office two weeks before Obama became president had already projected that the debt would grow by $1.2 trillion in 2009 without factoring in Obama's policies. Official debt figures are posted by the Treasury Department at http://www.treasurydirect.gov/govt/reports/pd/pd.htm. The CBO's early January 2009 projection of that year's deficit is available at http://www .cbo.gov/publication/41753.

218 *"The American Option":* A summary of Senator DeMint's stimulus plan is here: http://www.demint.senate.gov/public/_files/2009-02-02_DeMint_Jobs_Plan_Sum mary.pdf.

219 *at least a dozen Democrats and half a dozen Republicans:* Jay Newton-Small, "Can

Ben Nelson Get a Bipartisan Stimulus Win?," Time.com, February 6, 2009, http://www.time.com/time/politics/article/0,8599,1877535,00.html.

221 *The Washington press corps showered the gang members:* Dana Milbank, "A Horse and Pony Show," *Washington Post,* February 6, 2009; David Brooks, "The Gang System," *New York Times,* February 6, 2009.

224 *unless somebody could figure out how to get Al Franken seated:* Emanuel made the same complaint in an early profile by Ryan Lizza, when he unloaded on Paul Krugman's criticism of the White House legislative strategy. "Write a fucking column on how to seat the son of a bitch," Emanuel said. Lizza, "The Gatekeeper," *The New Yorker,* March 2, 2009, http://www.newyorker.com/reporting/2009/03/02/090302fa_fact_lizza#ixzzlrTVWPrzL.

225 *The Senate passed the slimmed-down bill:* The roll call is here: http://www.senate.gov/legislative/LIS/roll_call_lists/roll_call_vote_cfm.cfm?congress=111&session=1&vote=00061.

226 *McCain scoffed that Obama would need more than three Republicans:* John McCain on *Face the Nation,* CBS, February 8, 2009.

226 *"I am so happy bipartisanship is important":* Saturday Night Live, NBC, February 7, 2009, http://www.hulu.com/watch/56638/saturday-night-live-pelosireid-open.

226 *Obama had written about the pathologies of modern Washington:* Obama, *The Audacity of Hope,* p. 64.

227 *Obama mused that he probably should have pretended:* Obama press conference, February 9, 2009, http://www.presidency.ucsb.edu/ws/index.php?pid=85728.

11. Done Deal

228 *Rahm delivered a White House list:* A ten-page "Detail Table—Spending Components," dated February 10, 2009, provided to the author. It adds up to $512.53 billion, not including tax cuts.

229 *The Congressional Budget Office had priced:* CBO cost estimate, February 7, 2009, http://www.cbo.gov/publication/20468; CBO cost estimate for House-passed bill, January 30, 2009, http://www.cbo.gov/publication/41758.

229 *Obama's economists were clamoring:* The December 20 transition memo on the meetings with Democratic staffers had flagged the AMT as a potential problem, noting their "strong desire" to include it. "Unless the Recovery bill's topline total was adjusted to reflect the inclusion of AMT it would effectively shrink the stimulus resulting from the bill," the memo warned. That's exactly what happened.

231 *an independent watchdog had concluded:* "Audit Report: Rural Utilities Service Broadband Grant and Loan Programs," USDA Office of Inspector General, September 2005, http://www.usda.gov/oig/webdocs/09601-04-TE.pdf.

233 *The final spat on the Senate side:* Lizza was the first to write about this encounter in his Rahm profile: "The Gatekeeper," *The New Yorker,* March 2, 2009, http://www.newyorker.com/reporting/2009/03/02/090302fa_fact_lizza.

234 *"They give me three aces":* David Rogers, "Senate Passes $787 Billion Stimulus Bill," *Politico,* February 13, 2009, http://www.politico.com/news/stories/0209/18837.html.

234 *The president visited a Caterpillar plant:* Obama speech, East Peoria, Illinois, February 12, 2009, http://www.presidency.ucsb.edu/ws/index.php?pid=85762.

235 *the company's CEO told reporters:* Jake Tapper, "D'oh! Caterpillar CEO Contradicts President on Whether Stimulus Will Allow Him to Re-Hire Laid Off Workers,"

ABC News, February 12, 2009, http://abcnews.go.com/blogs/politics/2009/02/doh-caterpillar/.

235 *In fact, Gregg's* Wall Street Journal *op-ed in January:* Judd Gregg, "How to Make Sure the Stimulus Works," *Wall Street Journal,* January 5, 2009.

236 *"Mr. Obama's victory feels more than a bit like defeat":* Paul Krugman, "Failure to Rise," *New York Times,* February 13, 2009.

237 *It was about the size:* Florida's output in 2009 was $737 billion, according to the Bureau of Economic Analysis. The Netherlands' 2009 GDP was $683 billion, according to the CIA *World Factbook.* The Pentagon's 2009 budget was $513 billion, and nondefense discretionary spending in 2009 was $586 billion.

237 *far more aggressive as a percentage of GDP:* The Recovery Act's cost peaked in 2010 at 2.8 percent of GDP. (It added $405 billion to the deficit, when GDP was $14.65 trillion.) The New Deal's largest one-year cost was 1.5 percent of GDP in 1936, according to Romer's analysis of Bureau of Economic Analysis data. Romer, "Back from the Brink," http://www.whitehouse.gov/assets/documents/Back_from_the_Brink2.pdf. The Recovery Act's cost was equal to 1.3 percent of GDP in 2009 and one percent of GDP in 2011, according to annual CBO budget outlook reports.

237 *It dwarfed the stimulus packages:* "Navigating the Fiscal Challenges Ahead," International Monetary Fund, May 14, 2010, http://www.imf.org/external/pubs/ft/fm/2010/fm1001.pdf. Eswar Prasad and Isaac Sorkin, "Assessing the G-20 Economic Stimulus Plans: A Deeper Look," Brookings Institution, April 2009, http://www.brookings.edu/~/media/Files/rc/articles/2009/03_g20_stimulus_prasad/03_g20_stimulus_prasad.pdf.

239 *"Stimulus for Planes, Trains, but Mostly Automobiles":* iWatchNews, January 15, 2009, http://www.iwatchnews.org/2009/01/15/2973/stimulus-planes-trains-mostly-automobiles.

240 *"We'll put people to work building wind turbines":* Obama speech, East Peoria, Illinois, February 12, 2009, http://www.presidency.ucsb.edu/ws/index.php?pid=85762.

241 *The White House also helped Cantor out:* The White House projected that Cao's district would see a boost of 4,800 jobs, far less than the 7,000 to 8,000 jobs that other districts would get. The White House said its jobs estimates were based largely on population, and that the number for New Orleans reflected the loss in population due to Hurricane Katrina. Bruce Alpert, "Job Creation, Retention Benefit from Stimulus Bill Expected to Be Lowest in 2nd District," *New Orleans Times-Picayune,* February 18, 2009.

241 *the Republicans were joined in opposition:* The House vote on the conference report is here: http://clerk.house.gov/evs/2009/roll070.xml. The Senate vote is here: http://www.senate.gov/legislative/LIS/roll_call_lists/roll_call_vote_cfm.cfm?congress=111&session=1&vote=00064.

241 *"They are in essence betting against the president":* Adam Nagourney, "A Leader in the Senate Sees Sunny Skies for Democrats," *New York Times,* February 17, 2009.

242 *Obama was about to sign the Recovery Act into law:* Obama remarks, Denver, Colorado, February 17, 2009, http://www.presidency.ucsb.edu/ws/index.php?pid=85781.

247 *"My gut tells me it's too soon":* Saturday Night Live, NBC, February 14, 2009, http://www.hulu.com/watch.

12. Ready or Not

253 *Vice President Biden also took a road trip:* "Vice President Joe Biden Visits Cumberland County," *The Patriot-News,* February 11, 2009; Michael Phillips, "Shovels Are There, but the Readiness May Not Be," *Wall Street Journal,* March 17, 2009.

257 *"The first principle of politics":* Joe Biden, *Promises to Keep: On Life and Politics* (New York: Random House, 2007) pp. xi–xxiii.

258 *"If we do everything right":* Jake Tapper, "Oh, That Joe! (No. 47 in a Series)—The Veep Lays Out the Odds," ABC News, February 10, 2009, http://abcnews.go.com/blogs/politics/2009/02/oh-that-joe-no-7/.

258 *priceless portraits of former vice presidents:* They happen to be the portraits on the covers of David McCullough's Adams biography and Joseph Ellis's Jefferson biography. It's a nice office.

259 *He'd also block 260 Recovery Act projects:* Michael Grunwald, "It's Official: The Stimulus Isn't a Waste of Money," *Time,* October 1, 2010, http://www.time.com/time/nation/article/0,8599,2022781,00.html.

260 *"All of you are on the front lines":* Obama remarks at Recovery Act implementation conference, March 13, 2009, http://www.presidency.ucsb.edu/ws/index.php?pid=85855.

262 *Outside experts had warned that 5 percent of the stimulus:* The Association of Certified Fraud Examiners estimates that U.S. organizations lose 5 percent to 7 percent of their revenues to fraud. Michael Cooper, "On the Lookout for Stimulus Fraud," *New York Times,* September 17, 2009.

262 *only $7.2 million in losses:* "2010 Fiscal Year End Report to the President on Progress Implementing the American Recovery and Reinvestment Act of 2009," the White House, September 2010, http://www.whitehouse.gov/sites/default/files/recovery_act_report_9-30-2010.PDF.

263 *An obscure Commerce Department agency:* That was the National Telecommunications and Information Administration. The Federal Railroad Administration ran high-speed rail.

264 *Only two of his fifteen cabinet departments:* Peter Baker, "Obama Team Has Billions to Spend, but Few Ready to Do It," *New York Times,* February 17, 2009.

264 *Peter Orszag's sixty-two-page single-spaced implementation memo:* Peter Orszag, "Initial Implementing Guidance for the American Recovery and Reinvestment Act of 2009," Office of Management and Budget, February 19, 2009, http://www.whitehouse.gov/sites/default/files/omb/assets/memoranda_fy2009/m09-10.pdf.

267 *he read a report chronicling the department's history of dysfunction:* "Management Challenges at the Department of Energy," DOE Office of Inspector General, December 2008, http://energy.gov/sites/prod/files/igprod/documents/IG-0808_%282%29.pdf.

272 *$1 billion from elite investors:* Michael Grunwald, "Big Name Investors Behind Obama's Failed Green Tech Bet First in Line to Recoup Losses," Swampland blog, *Time,* September 3, 2011, http://swampland.time.com/2011/09/03/big-name-investors-to-recoup-losses-before-taxpayers-in-obamas-failed-green-tech-bet/. A list of Solyndra's investors was provided to the author.

272 *The Bush administration had embraced Solyndra:* Michael Grunwald, "Solyndra Hypocrisy: David Vitter Sought Energy Loans He Now Seeks to Scrutinize," Swampland blog, *Time,* September 19, 2011, http://swampland.time.com/2011/09/19/solyndra-hypocrisy-david-vitter-sought-energy-loans-he-now-seeks-to-scrutinize/.

275 *Obama invited stimulus skeptics to visit Ohio:* Obama speech, Columbus, Ohio, March 6, 2009, http://www.presidency.ucsb.edu/ws/index.php?pid=85826.

276 *"It certainly doesn't feel like we've accomplished anything, but we have":* Christina D. Romer, "The Case for Fiscal Stimulus: The Likely Effects of the American Recovery and Reinvestment Act," Speech to the U.S. Monetary Policy Forum, February 27, 2009, http://elsa.berkeley.edu/~cromer/The_likely_effects_of_the_American_Recovery_and _Reinvestment_act.pdf.

13. Tea Leaves

278 *Louisiana governor Bobby Jindal's response:* Jindal's response to Obama's address to Congress, February 24, 2009, http://articles.cnn.com/2009-02-24/politics/sotn .jindal.transcript_1_gop-response-bobby-jindal-americans?_s=PM:POLITICS.

279 *"We can't be the antigovernment party":* Michael Grunwald, "The Republicans in Distress," *Time,* May 7, 2009, http://www.time.com/time/magazine/article/0,9171, 1896736,00.html.

279 *"a very narrow party of angry people":* Zvika Krieger, "Huntsman, Interrupted," *The New Republic,* May 20, 2009.

280 *a CNBC commentator named Rick Santelli:* "Rick Santelli's Shout Heard 'Round the World," CNBC, February 22, 2009, http://www.cnbc.com/id/29283701/Rick _Santelli_s_Shout_Heard_Round_the_World.

280 *"The real nerve struck":* "Rick Santelli: I Want to Set the Record Straight," CNBC, March 2, 2009, http://www.cnbc.com/id/29471026/Rick_Santelli_I_Want_to_Set _the_Record_Straight.

282 *scores of Republicans who had opposed and denounced the stimulus:* Gotcha journalism isn't necessarily partisan; reporters liked going after Republican hypocrites. John Solomon and Aaron Mehta, "Legislators Who Criticized Stimulus Sought Its Funding," *Washington Post,* October 18, 2010; Louise Radnofsky, "Democrats Target Stimulus Critics Who Sought Funds," *Wall Street Journal,* February 16, 2010; Jim McElhatton, "Stimulus Foes See Value in Seeking Cash," *Washington Times,* February 9, 2010; Tyler Whitley, "Cantor Criticizes Stimulus Package, Suggests Alterations," *Richmond Times-Dispatch,* July 7, 2009. The author has copies of scores of congressional letters seeking energy and transportation funds.

283 *"We lost that legislative battle, but we won the argument":* Andy Barr, "Pence: GOP Won Stimulus Argument," *Politico,* February 27, 2009, http://www.politico.com/ news/stories/0209/19375.html.

283 *"Asked About Stimulus, Tedisco Talks a Lot":* Jimmy Vielkind, *New York Observer,* February 16, 2009.

283 *Washington Republicans suggested they would stop bankrolling his campaign:* Bazile wrote an odd book about the Murphy-Tedisco race: Dan Bazile, *Too Close to Call* (Albany: ZLS, 2010).

284 *"Tedisco's victory will be a repudiation":* Michael Steele, "It's the Spending, Mr. President," *Politico,* April 1, 2009, http://www.politico.com/news/stories/0409/20764 .html.

286 *"We're essentially franchisees":* Grunwald, "Republicans in Distress," *Time.*

286 *a young conservative named Marco Rubio:* Michael Grunwald, "GOP at War with Itself in Florida Senate Race," *Time,* August 12, 2009, http://www.time.com/time/ politics/article/0,8599,1915837,00.html.

290 *love emails about "magnificent gentle kisses" and worse:* "Exclusive: Read E-mails Between Sanford, Woman," *The State,* June 25, 2009.

290 *"I think even our critics would agree that at the very least, we've been busy":* Obama
     speech at Georgetown University, Washington, D.C., April 14, 2009, http://www
     .presidency.ucsb.edu/ws/index.php?pid=86000.

291 *"The obsession with race":* Mike Allen, Jim Vandehei, and John Harris, "100 Days:
     How Obama Changed D.C.," *Politico,* April 24, 2009, http://www.politico.com/news/
     stories/0409/21546.html.

292 *the* New York Times *ran a story:* Peter Baker, "Familiar Obama Phrase Being
     Groomed as a Slogan," *New York Times,* May 15, 2009.

292 *Doris Kearns Goodwin said it sounded like a woman's girdle:* John B. Judis, "The Un-
     necessary Fall," *The New Republic,* August 12, 2010.

293 *"The recession has entered a new phase":* Neil Irwin and Annys Shin, "In Poor Jobs
     Numbers, Hints of Improvement," *Washington Post,* May 9, 2009.

293 *"She hasn't found any yet":* YouTube video of Ellie Mae available at http://www.you
     tube.com/watch?v=tl_q0afUl0E.

293 *"By any objective standard, this has been a failure":* Mitch McConnell on *Meet the
     Press,* CBS, July 19, 2009.

293 *"Fiscal stimulus is a well-tested antibiotic":* Christina D. Romer, "So, Is It Working?:
     An Assessment of the American Recovery and Reinvestment Act at the Five-Month
     Mark," Speech at the Economic Club of Washington, D.C., August 6, 2009, http://
     elsa.berkeley.edu/~cromer/DCEconClub.pdf.

294 *Jared Bernstein learned this the hard way:* White House press briefing, June 8, 2009,
     http://www.whitehouse.gov/the press office/Briefing-by-Press-Secretary-Robert
     -Gibbs-with-Jared-Bernstein-the-Vice-Presidents-Chief-Economist-6-8-09.

296 *Obama wrote "No"—and underlined it:* Ryan Lizza, "The Obama Memos," *The
     New Yorker,* January 30, 2012, http://www.newyorker.com/reporting/2012/01/30/
     120130fa_fact_lizza.

296 *Boehner scoffed on Fox News that in Ohio:* John Boehner on *Fox News Sunday,* July 5,
     2009.

296 *critics who "are already judging the effort a failure":* Obama weekly address, July 11,
     2009, http://www.presidency.ucsb.edu/ws/index.php?pid=86398.

296 *"I know voters in Ohio":* Eric Cantor on Fox News, July 9, 2009.

297 *"just when the Recovery Act was providing its maximum benefit":* Mark Zandi testi-
     mony before the Joint Economic Committee, October 29, 2009.

298 *Bernanke helped save the global economy:* Michael Grunwald, "Person of the Year
     2009: Ben Bernanke," *Time,* December 16, 2009, http://www.time.com/time/specials/
     packages/article/0,28804,1946375_1947251_1947520,00.html. When I was work-
     ing on my Bernanke profile, one White House official suggested that since fiscal
     stimulus was just as important as monetary stimulus, *Time* should expand my story
     into another "Committee to Save the World" cover like the one featuring Summers,
     Rubin, and Greenspan in February 1999. I guess I did this book instead.

298 *But the data told a powerful story:* "The Economic Impact of the American Recovery
     and Reinvestment Act of 2009: First Quarterly Report," White House Council of
     Economic Advisers, September 10, 2009, http://www.whitehouse.gov/assets/docu
     ments/CEA_ARRA_Report_Final.pdf.

298 *"What can you sell when you do not have the White House":* Ben Smith, "Exclusive:
     RNC Document Mocks Donors, Plays on 'Fear,'" *Politico,* March 3, 2010, http://
     www.politico.com/news/stories/0310/33866.html.

299 *Obama asked Grassley point-blank:* Richard Wolffe, *Revival: The Struggle for Sur-
     vival Inside the Obama White House* (New York: Crown, 2010), p. 70.

300 *Porkulus was all about dubious-sounding projects:* Scott Mayerowitz and Nathalie

Tadena, "Stimulus Waste? The $3.4 Million Turtle Crossing," ABC News, July 10, 2009, http://abcnews.go.com/Business/Economy/story?id=8045022; David Saltonstall, "Drudge Story on Pork Draws Ire from President Obama's Agriculture Chief," *New York Daily News,* July 21, 2009; Dan Eggen, "Former Hospital CEO Rick Scott Leads Opposition to Obama on Health Care," *Washington Post,* May 11, 2009.

300 *the stimulus had added at least 2 percent to GDP:* Calmes and Cooper, "New Consensus Sees Stimulus Package as Worthy Step."

300 *And the administration had fulfilled all of its pledges:* "Roadmap to Recovery: Day 200," White House report, September 2009.

301 *One poll found that 45 percent of Americans:* Rasmussen survey, June 10, 2009; Joe Biden, "What You Might Not Know About the Recovery," *New York Times,* July 26, 2009; Biden speech at Brookings Institution, September 3, 2009, http://www.brook ings.edu/events/2009/0903_recovery_biden.aspx.

301 *the event ended up in a department briefing room:* Obama remarks at Department of Transportation, April 13, 2009, http://www.presidency.ucsb.edu/ws/index .php?pid=85995.

302 *the Recovery Act logo:* Logo available at http://www.recovery.gov/News/mediakit/ Picture%20Library/circle_recovery_logo.jpg.

14. Change Is Hard

303 *In the fall of 2009:* "Funds Continue to Provide Fiscal Relief to States and Localities, While Accountability and Reporting Challenges Need to Be Fully Addressed," Government Accountability Office, September 23, 2009, http://www.gao.gov/products/ GAO-09-1016.

305 *At an event at a Home Depot in Virginia:* Obama remarks in Alexandria, Virginia, December 15, 2009, http://www.presidency.ucsb.edu/ws/index.php?pid=86995.

305 *"green the ghetto":* Van Jones, *The Green Collar Economy: How One Solution Can Fix Our Two Biggest Problems* (New York: HarperOne, 2008).

307 *The Government Accountability Office, the department's inspector general, and the media:* "Factors Affecting the Department of Energy's Program Implementation," GAO, March 4, 2010, http://www.gao.gov/products/GAO-10-497T; "Progress in Implementing the Department of Energy's Weatherization Assistance Program Under the American Recovery and Reinvestment Act," Department of Energy, Office of Inspector General, February 2010, http://energy.gov/sites/prod/files/igprod/ documents/OAS-RA-10-04.pdf.

307 *"Massive Funding: BBBBBBBBILLIONS!":* PowerPoint presentation provided to author.

310 *audits that found sporadic cases of shoddy work:* For example, "The State of Illinois Weatherization Assistance Program," DOE Office of Inspector General, October 2010, http://energy.gov/sites/prod/files/igprod/documents/OAS-RA-11-01.pdf. There were similar problems in West Virginia and several other states.

310 *The African Heritage Dancers and Drummers of Washington:* Letter from Representative Fred Upton to Energy Secretary Steven Chu, November 23, 2010, http:// upton.house.gov/UploadedFiles/Letter_to_Sec_Chu.pdf.

310 *a follow-up by the GAO found the program's start-up problems were largely solved:* "Progress and Challenges in Spending Weatherization Funds," GAO, December 2011, http://www.gao.gov/assets/590/587064.pdf.

311 *not the clean-energy economy:* "AWEA Year End 2009 Market Report," American

Wind Energy Association, January 2010; "US Solar Industry Year in Review 2009," Solar Energy Industries Association, April 15, 2010.

316 *the saga of Serious Materials: Glenn Beck,* January 20, 2010.

317 *The lead inquisitors were Senators Tom Coburn and John McCain:* Coburn and McCain issued two reports: "Stimulus Checkup: A Closer Look at 100 Projects Funded by the American Recovery and Reinvestment Act," December 2009; and "Summertime Blues: 100 Stimulus Projects That Give Taxpayers the Blues," August 2010. Coburn also issued a report by himself in June 2009: "100 Stimulus Projects: A Second Opinion." All three are available at http://www.coburn.senate.gov/public/?p=OversightAction.

319 *"Exclusive: Jobs 'Saved or Created' in Congressional Districts That Don't Exist":* Jonathan Karl, ABC News, November 16, 2009, http://abcnews.go.com/Politics/jobs-saved-created-congressional-districts-exist/story?id=9097853#.T34Fm79AZ.qs.

320 *"To read some coverage":* Earl Devaney, Chairman's Corner blog, Recovery.gov, March 22, 2010, http://www.recovery.gov/News/chairman/Pages/march222010.aspx.

320 *"Now you can go right online": Glenn Beck,* July 20, 2009.

321 *"Undercounting Concerns Stimulus Investigators":* Matt Kelley, *USA Today,* November 30, 2009.

321 *a poll during the controversy: Washington Post*/ABC News poll, November 2009.

322 *"Promises, Promises: Web Site Likely to Fall Short":* Philip Elliot, Associated Press, February 18, 2009.

322 *"the stimulus has done more to promote transparency":* Ryan Holeywell, "Did the Stimulus Do Anything for Transparency?" *Governing,* February 2012.

322 *"Traffic Set to Slow as Stimulus Gears Up":* Brad Heath, *USA Today,* May 4, 2009.

322 *"Stimulus Projects Bypass Hard-Hit States":* Heath, *USA Today,* May 27, 2009.

323 *"Pace of New Stimulus Spending Slows":* Heath, *USA Today,* September 13, 2009.

323 *"Stimulus Takes Detour Around Ailing Metropolitan Areas":* Heath, *USA Today,* September 24, 2009.

323 *"Metro Areas Get Chunk of Rural Stimulus Aid":* Heath, *USA Today,* December 27, 2009.

323 *Another example from my overflowing gotcha file:* Jennifer LaFleur, "Stimulus Weatherization Aid Favors Cold Regions," ProPublica, May 7, 2009; Michael Cooper, "Stimulus Funds Spent to Keep Sun Belt Cool," *New York Times,* June 7, 2009.

324 *the Washington Post, was a serial offender:* ClimateProgress has catalogued the *Post*'s witch hunt: http://thinkprogress.org/romm/2011/12/01/379444/washington-post-solyndra-reporting/. For example, the *Post* did forty-three articles on Solyndra in the fall of 2011, and twenty-six mentioned that one of its investors, George Kaiser, was an Obama fund-raiser. (He has testified under oath that he never discussed Solyndra with the administration. Nobody has contradicted him.) Only one story mentioned that the influential Republican Walton family also invested in Solyndra. Only one mentioned that the Bush administration had pushed the loan as well. Only one mentioned that the loan program had plenty of reserves to cover the Solyndra default. And several stories included the kind of misleading statistics and out-of-context quotes that made it clear the reporters were hunting for a scalp.

324 *One story tarred CleanTech for Obama cofounder Sanjay Wagle:* Carol D. Leonnig and Joe Stephens, "Federal Funds Flow to Clean-Energy Firms with Obama Administration Ties," *Washington Post,* February 14, 2012.

324 *when national reporters focused on "the stimulus":* I guess I should mention that I

was the main exception to all this stimulus negativity. My bosses at *Time* magazine thought I was bonkers; I spent months bugging them to let me write a story about how the stimulus is changing America, and then months bugging them to put it in the magazine. To their credit, they finally did. Michael Grunwald, "How the Stimulus Is Changing America," *Time*, August 10, 2010, http://www.time.com/time/magazine/article/0,9171,2013826,00.html.

326 *"If a school continues to fail its students year after year":* Obama speech, March 1, 2010, http://www.presidency.ucsb.edu/ws/index.php?pid=87595.

328 *That was the TIGER program:* Michael Grunwald, "Transportation Stimulus: Where Did the Federal Money Go?," Time.com, September 13, 2010, http://www.time.com/time/nation/article/0,8599,2017466,00.html.

329 *The best example was in Florida:* Michael Grunwald, "Can High-Speed Rail Get on Track?" *Time,* July 19, 2010, http://www.time.com/time/magazine/article/0,9171,2002523,00.html.

329 *"provide significant economic and environmental benefits to the state":* Letter from Alcee Hastings et al., June 19, 2009. Republicans Lincoln Diaz-Balart, Mario Diaz-Balart, and Adam Putnam were among the ten representatives who signed.

15. Gas Versus Brakes

334 *President Bush inherited a budget in the black:* The Congressional Budget Office in January 2001 projected a surplus for that year of $281 billion and surpluses for that decade that would add a total of $5 trillion to the Treasury. In January 2009, weeks before Obama became president, the CBO projected the 2009 deficit to hit $1.2 trillion and the ten-year shortfall to be $3.1 trillion. "The Budget and Economic Outlook: Fiscal Years 2002–2011," CBO, January 2001, http://cbo.gov/sites/default/files/cbofiles/ftpdocs/27xx/doc2727/entire-report.pdf; "The Budget and Economic Outlook: Fiscal Years 2009 to 2019," CBO, January 7, 2009, http://www.cbo.gov/publication/41753.

334 *a dizzying economic nosedive:* A study by Bob Greenstein's left-leaning Center on Budget and Policy Priorities estimated that the decrease in tax revenue and increase in safety net payments caused by the economic downturn were responsible for roughly 30 percent of the deficits in 2009, 2010, and 2011, while the Bush tax cuts accounted for about 26 percent of those deficits and war costs accounted for about 14 percent. Kathy Ruffing and James R. Horney, "Economic Downturn and Bush Policies Continue to Drive Large Projected Deficits," Center on Budget and Policy Priorities, May 20, 2011, http://www.cbpp.org/cms/index.cfm?fa=view&id=3490. The Recovery Act only accounted for about 13 percent of the shortfalls in those years and virtually none afterward.

336 *The actual bond market seemed perfectly calm:* Bond rating agency Fitch found "relative calm" in the corporate bond market by the second half of 2009, noting that downgrades had nearly ceased and that low-grade bonds were being issued at a far greater clip than in 2008. "U.S. Corporate Bond Market Finds Relative Calm," Fitch Ratings report, October 22, 2009.

337 *"That is oh, so wrong":* Ron Suskind was the first to report on this meeting: *Confidence Men,* p. 354.

338 *Obama had tried to explain counterintuitive Keynesian concepts:* Paul Krugman noted that one passage of Obama's inaugural address—"Our workers are no less productive . . . our goods no less needed . . . our capacity remains undiminished"—echoed the words of Keynes. "Stuck in the Muddle," *New York Times,* January 22,

2009. The George Mason speech during the transition may have been his most emphatic defense of the idea that the government needs to spend more when families and businesses are spending less.

338 *the bully pulpit doesn't come with magical powers:* Ezra Klein, "The Unpersuaded," *Washington Post,* March 19, 2012.

338 *"a consensus that the stimulus package":* Calmes and Cooper, "New Consensus Sees Stimulus Package as Worthy Step."

340 *When Summers froze Austan Goolsbee out of a key meeting on the auto bailout:* Steven Rattner, *Overhaul: An Insider's Account of the Obama Administration's Emergency Rescue of the Auto Industry* (New York: Harcourt, 2010), pp. 129–30.

341 *the White House scheduled a jobs summit:* Obama remarks at closing of jobs summit, December 3, 2009, http://www.presidency.ucsb.edu/ws/index.php?pid=86961.

341 *In a speech a few days later:* Obama speech at Brookings Institution, Washington, D.C., December 8, 2009, http://www.presidency.ucsb.edu/ws/index.php?pid=86961.

341 *Obama's political team wanted him:* Ryan Lizza, "The Obama Memos," *The New Yorker,* January 30, 2012.

342 *Obama proposed a three-year discretionary spending freeze:* State of the Union, 2010, January 27, 2009, http://www.presidency.ucsb.edu/ws/index.php?pid=87433.

343 *the president visited the Chesapeake Machine Company:* Obama remarks, Baltimore, Maryland, January 29, 2010, http://www.presidency.ucsb.edu/ws/index.php?pid=87464.

344 *breaking the Senate filibuster record:* Brian Beutler, "111th Senate Breaks a Filibuster Record," Talking Points Memo, December 23, 2011, http://tpmdc.talkingpointsmemo.com/2010/12/111th-senate-breaks-one-filibuster-record.php.

345 *about $200 billion in additional fiscal pop before the 2010 elections:* Jobs-related bills enacted after the Recovery Act and before November 2010 added up to another $212 billion in fiscal aid. They included extensions of emergency unemployment benefits and COBRA, a hiring tax credit, bond subsidies for school construction and renewable energy projects, aid to states for public sector workers and Medicaid, tax cuts for small businesses, and a new small business lending fund.

350 *"Environmentalists Need a New President":* Glenn Hurowitz, *Grist,* July 22, 2010, http://grist.org/politics/environmentalists-need-a-new-president/.

16. Green New World

352 *"Let me ask you a question":* Obama and Biden remarks in Tampa, Florida, January 28, 2010, http://www.presidency.ucsb.edu/ws/index.php?pid=87462.

353 *The Tampa–Orlando line:* Grunwald, "Will High-Speed Rail Get on Track?" *Time.*

359 *It felt like a teachable moment:* I'm afraid that I've bucked the groupthink on the spill as well; Michael Grunwald, "The BP Spill: Has the Damage Been Exaggerated?" *Time,* July 29, 2010.

360 *"Did you plug the hole yet, Daddy?":* Obama press conference, May 27, 2010, http://www.presidency.ucsb.edu/ws/index.php?pid=87963&st=&st1=#axzz1r6IS4jg6.

362 *Obama archly noted that some stimulus opponents:* Obama remarks in Holland, Michigan, July 15, 2010, http://www.presidency.ucsb.edu/ws/index.php?pid=88188.

363 *"Green jobs may be the fad of the moment":* Rattner, *Overhaul,* p. 309.

372 *It took less than two years:* Joseph Aldy, "A Preliminary Review of the Recovery Act's Clean Energy Packages," Resources for the Future, January 2012.

372 *By 2010, only 40 percent of the typical turbine was imported:* Michaela D. Platzer,

"U.S. Wind Turbine Manufacturing: Federal Support for an Emerging Industry," Congressional Research Service, September 23, 2011.

373 *the pioneering mega-state that gave us microchips:* Michael Grunwald, "Why California Is Still America's Future," *Time,* October 23, 2009.

376 *"through programs such as ARPA-E":* Jackie Kucinich, "Romney's Rhetoric Differs from Record as Governor," *USA Today,* September 7, 2011.

17. Political Recovery

380 *Bartley was introducing Biden at a Recovery Act event:* I attended the event at the UQM facility in Longmont on April 29, 2010.

381 *the White House estimated the Recovery Act:* "The Economic Impact of the American Recovery and Reinvestment Act of 2009: Third Quarterly Report," White House Council of Economic Advisers, April 14, 2010, http://www.whitehouse.gov/sites/default/files/microsites/CEA-3rd-arra-report.pdf.

383 *it nearly tripled the domestic content:* Michael Grunwald, "GOP Attacks on Stimulus Wind Power Money: Hot Air," *Time,* October 15, 2010, http://www.time.com/time/politics/article/0,8599,2025886,00.html.

384 *Obama visited a factory under construction:* Remarks at Solyndra, Fremont, California, May 26, 2010, http://www.presidency.ucsb.edu/ws/index.php?pid=87950.

387 *USEC, a former government enterprise:* The U.S. Enrichment Corporation was privatized during the Clinton administration; Larry Summers was a big advocate, while Peter Orszag argued against it.

387 *Boehner and McConnell have slammed the White House:* David Roberts, "GOP Tries to Explain Away Loan-Guarantee Hypocrisy, Fails," *Grist,* October 14, 2011, http://grist.org/politics/2011-10-13-republicans-try-to-explain-away-loan-guarantee-hypocrisy-fail/.

387 *"I hope you will realize the importance of such job creation to Kentucky":* Eric Lipton, "Republicans Sought Clean-Energy Money for Home States," *New York Times,* September 19, 2011.

390 *Obama kicked off Recovery Summer:* Obama speech in Columbus, Ohio, June 18, 2010, http://www.presidency.ucsb.edu/ws/index.php?pid=88080; Kendra Marr, "Obama's 58 Minutes in Ohio," *Politico,* June 18, 2010, http://www.politico.com/news/stories/0610/38739.html.

391 *"He created 70,000 new jobs this month":* The Tonight Show with Jay Leno, NBC, August 9, 2010.

392 *The House Republican committee borrowed Schumer's wind farm rhetoric:* Grunwald, "GOP Attacks on Stimulus Wind Power Money: Hot Air," *Time,* October 15, 2010.

392 *testy interview with the lefty comic Jon Stewart:* Obama interview on *The Daily Show with Jon Stewart,* October 27, 2010, http://www.presidency.ucsb.edu/ws/index.php?pid=97095.

393 *"You don't have to be a savvy political analyst":* Obama interview on MSNBC, July 15, 2010, http://www.presidency.ucsb.edu/ws/index.php?pid=88316.

393 *the electorate thought he had raised middle-class taxes:* Bloomberg poll, October 24–26, 2010.

393 *"I think anybody who's occupied this office":* Peter Baker, "Education of a President," *New York Times,* October 12, 2010.

394 *the White House's "unrealistic expectations":* Robert Pear, "Doctors and Hospitals Say Goals on Computerized Records Are Unrealistic," *New York Times,* June 7, 2010.

398 *Obama hit the road with a modest new jobs plan:* Obama speech in Milwaukee, Wisconsin, September 6, 2010, http://www.presidency.ucsb.edu/ws/index.php?pid=88418.

399 *"We got our mops and our brooms out":* Obama speech in New York City, May 13, 2010, http://www.presidency.ucsb.edu/ws/index.php?pid=87922.

399 *a "shellacking":* Obama press conference, November 3, 2010, http://www.presidency.ucsb.edu/ws/index.php?pid=88668.

18. Not Quite Done

403 *Before he did anything else:* David Corn has a nice recap of the lame-duck negotiations in *Showdown: The Inside Story of How Obama Fought Back Against Boehner, Cantor, and the Tea Party* (New York: William Morrow, 2012).

406 *"the swindle of the year":* Charles Krauthammer, "Swindle of the Year," *Washington Post,* December 10, 2010.

407 *"If that's the standard by which we're measuring success":* Obama news conference, December 7, 2010, http://www.presidency.ucsb.edu/ws/index.php?pid=88781.

409 *the Tampa–Orlando line would create 27,000 jobs:* "The Economic Impacts of High-Speed Rail on Cities and Their Metropolitan Areas," U.S. Conference of Mayors, June 2010, http://www.usmayors.org/highspeedrail/documents/report.pdf. The firm of Steer Davies Gleave projected a $30 million annual surplus by 2026; Wilbur Smith Associates predicted a $45 million surplus. "High-speed Rail Would Have Been Profitable, State Report says," *Tampa Tribune,* February 6, 2012. Instead, the governor relied on a policy brief by the libertarian Reason Foundation.

410 *It's got the nation's least educated population:* Alan Berube, "Degrees of Separation: Education, Employment, and the Great Recession in Metropolitan America," Brookings Institution, November 2010; "State of the Air 2011," American Lung Association, April 2011, http://www.stateoftheair.org/.

415 *"determine if the company still had a viable business":* Department of Energy loan office presentation provided to the author.

416 *the state's unemployment rate would have reached 14 percent:* Mark Price and Stephen Herzenberg, "The State of Working Pennsylvania 2010," Keystone Research Center, September 2010.

416 *"Rendell Declares Stimulus a Success. Don't You Feel Better?":* The Scoop blog, January 13, 2011, http://blogs.phillymag.com/new_philly_post/2011/01/13/rendell-declares-stimulus-a-success/.

19. The Legacy

419 *At the progressive Netroots Nation conference:* Michael Grunwald, "Earth to the Left: Obama Is into You," Swampland blog, Time.com, June 21, 2011, http://swampland.time.com/2011/06/21/earth-to-the-left-obama-is-into-you. At the conference, Dan Choi, the nation's most prominent critic of Don't Ask Don't Tell, ripped up an Obama flyer—even though Obama had just overturned Don't Ask Don't Tell.

421 *prime-time speech to Congress:* Obama speech, September 8, 2011, http://www.presidency.ucsb.edu/ws/index.php?pid=96661.

424 *The number of Americans without shelter actually declined:* Housing and Urban Development point-in-time estimates of homelessness, http://www.hudhre.info/index.cfm?do=viewResource&ResourceID=4568; "The State of Homelessness in

America 2012," National Alliance to End Homelessness, January 17, 2012, http://www.endhomelessness.org/content/article/detail/4361/.

425   *analysis by the Center for Budget and Policy Priorities:* Arloc Sherman, "Poverty and Financial Distress Would Have Been Substantially Worse in 2010 Without Government Action, New Census Data Show," Center on Budget and Policy Priorities, November 7, 2011, http://www.cbpp.org/cms/?fa=view&id=3610.

426   *major private forecasting firms:* Private forecasters' assessments were listed in the Council of Economic Advisers' eighth quarterly report on the Recovery Act's impact. "The Economic Impact of the American Recovery and Reinvestment Act of 2009 Eighth Quarterly Report," CEA, December 9, 2011.

426   *80 percent of the economists:* IGM Economic Experts Panel, University of Chicago Booth School of Business, February 12, 2012, http://www.igmchicago.org/igm-economic-experts-panel/poll-results?SurveyID=SV_cw5O9LNJL1oz4Xi.

426   *A* Washington Post *review of early stimulus studies:* Dylan Matthews, "Did the Stimulus Work? A Review of the Nine Best Studies on the Subject," Wonkblog, *Washington Post,* August 24, 2011, http://www.washingtonpost.com/blogs/ezra-klein/post/did-the-stimulus-work-a-review-of-the-nine-best-studies-on-the-subject/2011/08/16/gIQAThbibJ_blog.html. There were two other negative studies, but one had statistically insignificant results, and one didn't make empirical sense.

426   *by prominent Republican economist John Taylor:* John B. Taylor, "An Empirical Analysis of the Revival of Fiscal Activism in the 2000s," Stanford University, *Journal of Economic Literature,* September 2011, http://www.stanford.edu/~johntayl/JEL_Taylor_Final%20Pages.pdf.

428   *"killing solar energy by having the government play the role":* Charlie Rose, PBS, December 19, 2011, http://www.charlierose.com/view/interview/12045.

428   *expanded sixfold:* U.S. Solar Market Insight Reports for 2009–2011, Solar Energy Industries Association, http://www.seia.org/cs/research/solarinsight.

432   *$50 million to build wing dikes and weirs along the Mississippi River:* Michael Grunwald, "The Floods: A Man-Made Disaster?," *Time,* June 25, 2008, http://www.time.com/time/nation/article/0,8599,1818040,00.html.

435   *It also pushed thirty-nine states to rewrite their eligibility rules:* National Employment Law Project data, http://www.nelp.org/index.php/site/issues/category/modernizing_unemployment_insurance.

435   *renewable electricity doubled during Obama's first three years:* Net electricity generation for solar, wind and geothermal, Energy Information Administration, http://www.eia.gov/electricity/monthly/epm_table_grapher.cfm?t=epmt_1_1_a.

436   *"The reports of Solyndra's death have been greatly exaggerated":* Michael Grunwald, "The White House Wouldn't Answer Republicans' Questions, So I'll Try," Swampland blog, *Time,* June 24, 2011, http://swampland.time.com/2011/06/24/the-white-house-wouldnt-answer-republican-questions-so-ill-try/.

437   *"No, I don't . . . overall, it's doing well":* Jake Tapper, "Seeking to Muddy Waters on Layoffs, Conservative Group Unleashing $6 Million Ad Campaign Against President Obama and Solyndra," ABC News, January 13, 2012, http://abcnews.go.com/blogs/politics/2012/01/seeking-to-muddy-waters-on-layoffs-conservative-group-unleashing-6-million-ad-campaign-against-president-obama-and-solyndra/.

437   *"Is there criminal activity? Perhaps not":* Darren Samuelsohn, "GOP Running Out of Gas on Solyndra," *Politico,* March 27, 2012, http://www.politico.com/news/stories/0312/74564.html.

438   *the former finance chairman of John McCain's presidential campaign:* Herb Allison,

who served as McCain's national finance chairman, conducted the independent
review that found that the loan guarantee program would cost less than expected.
"Report of the Independent Consultant's Review with Respect to the Department
of Energy Loan and Loan Guarantee Portfolio," January 31, 2012, http://www.white
house.gov/sites/default/files/docs/report_on_doe_loan_and_guarantee_portfolio.pdf.
Jim Snyder and Brian Wingfield did the report for Bloomberg Government, February 11, 2012, http://www.bloomberg.com/news/2012-02-10/risk-management
-needed-for-energy-loan-guarantees-report-says.html.

439 *Innovation doesn't move in a straight line:* The Energy Department did an insightful
report on its Recovery Act work. "Making a Down Payment on the Nation's Energy
and Environmental Future," October 20, 2010.

439 *While Congress has squabbled over Obama's supposed ban on incandescents:* Michael
Grunwald, "Incandescent Light Bulb Insanity and the Groucho Marx Republicans,"
Swampland blog, *Time,* July 12, 2011, http://swampland.time.com/2011/07/12/
incandescent-light-bulb-insanity-and-the-groucho-marx-republicans/.

442 *health IT firms that used to spend their time:* Ezekiel Emanuel, "An Unsung Victory
in Health care," Reuters, March 6, 2012.

Epilogue: The Choice

449 *"A stimulus plan is needed":* Mitt Romney, A Republican Stimulus Plan, *National
Review,* December 19, 2008.

449 *"what's left is the government sector":* Mitt Romney, Testimony before House Republican Economic Stimulus Working Group, January 15, 2009.

— ILLUSTRATION CREDITS —

Time Magazine: 1
Official White House Photo by Pete Souza: 2, 3, 5, 6, 7, 9, 13, 14, 16, 23
US Department of Housing and Urban Development: 4
Ohio Department of Transportation: 11
US Department of Energy: 12, 21
House Republican Conference: 15
Steve Jurvetson: 18
National Park Service: 19
Metropolitan Transportaion Authority: 20
US Navy: 22

Pages numbers beginning with 479 refer to notes.

— ABOUT THE AUTHOR —

Michael Grunwald is a senior national correspondent at *Time* magazine. He has won the George Polk Award for national reporting and many other journalism prizes. He is the author of *The Swamp: The Everglades, Florida, and the Politics of Paradise.* He lives in Miami Beach with his wife, Cristina Dominguez, and their two children, Max and Lina. His website is www.michaelgrunwald.com.